WHOOPS

This is the back of the book!

Manga Classics™ books follow the Japanese comic (aka Manga!) reading order. Traditional manga is read in a "reversed" format starting on the right and heading towards the left. The story begins where English readers expect to find the last page because the spine of the book is on the opposite side. Flip to the other end of the book and start reading your Manga Classics!

WILLIAM SHAKESPEARE

Art by: Julien Choy

Story Adaptation by: Crystal S. Chan

Lettering: Akanovas and Jeannie Lee

STAFF:

Project Chief North America: Erik Ko
Editor: M. Chandler
VP of Sales: John Shableski
Production Manager: Janice Leung
Copy Editing: Michelle Lee

Project Chief Asia: Andy Hung
Production Manager: Yuen Him Tai
Art Assistants: Man Yiu, Peter Mak
　　　　　Shirley Yuen, Elie Li
　　　　　J.C.Chow, Vivian Huang
　　　　　Shougo, Ron, Stoon

AGE: Young Adult (12+)
BISAC: YAF010060   YAF010010   YAF009000   YAF010000
　　　　Young Adult Fiction, Comics & Graphic Novels, Manga, Classic Adaptation
DEWEY 741.5
LIBRARY SUBJECT: Romance, Manga, Shakespeare, Classic Literature

Manga Classics: Romeo and Juliet. Published by Manga Classics, Inc. 118 Tower Hill Road, C1, PO Box 20008, Richmond Hill, Ontario, L4K 0K0, Canada. Any similarities to persons living or dead are purely coincidental. No portion of this publication may be used or reproduced by any means (digital or print) without written permission from Manga Classics Inc. except for review purposes. Manga Classics name and logo is a trademark of Manga Classics, Inc. All artwork ©Manga Classics, Inc.

First Printing May 2018   Printed in Canada
HARD COVER EDITION ISBN # 978-1-947808-03-4　　　PAPERBACK EDITION ISBN # 978-1-947808-04-1

www.mangaclassics.com

Manga Classics™

Manga Classics™ proudly presents:
the finest name in adaptations of beloved classic literature!

Manga Classics, Inc. is proud to bring you this very special new line of books, adapting classic literature with the same quality and attention to detail as our fantastic graphic novels, art books, and manga releases! This Manga Classics line is the result of an ambitious international partnership with various fine artists in Japan, Korea, and Hong Kong, the aim of which is to bring the highest-quality adaptations of these works to the North American market!

The creative team has worked tirelessly to fully realize the rich worlds of these classic works of literature. Our artists have extensively researched the settings of these timeless novels in order to give the costumes and architecture a very real sense of weight and accuracy, expertly executed thanks to the studio's animation background. This high-quality work has been coupled with a generous page count of over 300 pages per book, more than double the average comics-format adaptation! This allows for more thorough, accurate, and natural adaptations of the source material, with the artists' vision given as much space as needed to be properly realized. In short, all Manga Classics adaptations look and read like great commercial manga while also being faithful adaptations of literary classics!

Intended for a young adult audience, Manga Classics are just as likely to be enjoyed in the reader's free time as in the classroom. The gripping stories and lush artwork easily place them alongside today's best-selling popular manga, with strong and accurate adaptations that are sure to please even the toughest teacher or librarian! Our books are also the perfect way for adult readers to rediscover their favorite classics - or experience them for the first time!

Now that you have read Romeo and Juliet, look for Manga Classics adaptations of other classic literature in stores!

Manga Classics™
The Adventures of
TOM SAWYER
MARK TWAIN

Manga Classics:
The Adventures of Tom Sawyer
Hard Cover $24.99
ISBN #978-1-947808-01-0
Soft Cover $17.99
ISBN #978-1-947808-02-7

Manga Classics™
Adventures of
HUCKLEBERRY
FINN
MARK TWAIN

Manga Classics:
Adventures of Huckleberry Finn
Hard Cover $24.99
ISBN #978-1-772940-16-9
Soft Cover $17.99
ISBN #978-1-772940-17-6

Manga Classics
The Stories of
EDGAR
ALLAN
POE
The Fall of the House of Usher

Manga Classics:
The Stories of Edgar Allan Poe
Hard Cover $24.99
ISBN #978-1-772940-20-6
Soft Cover $17.99
ISBN #978-1-772940-21-3

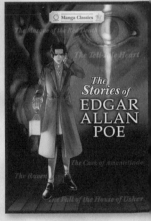

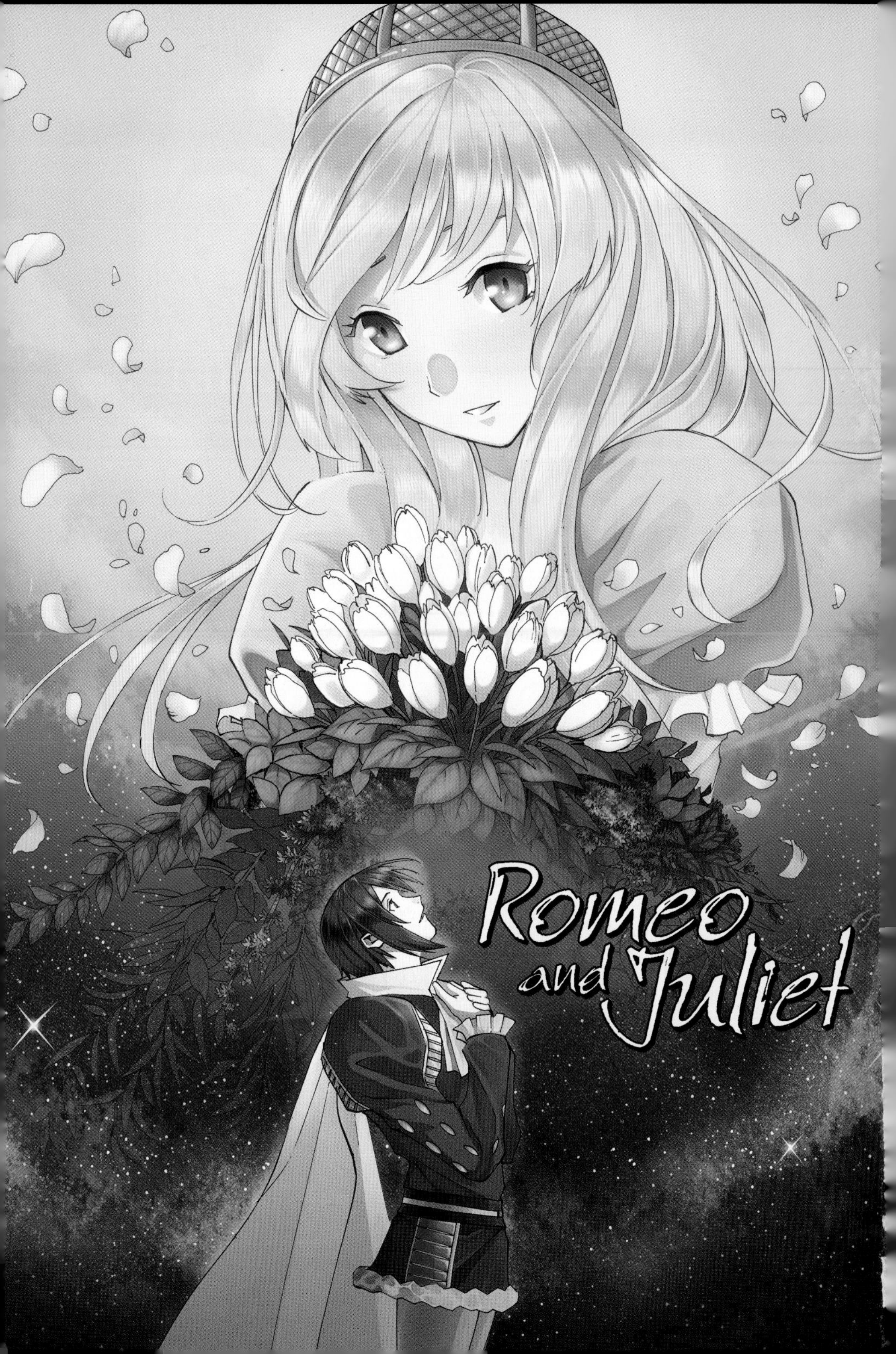
Romeo and Juliet

THE CAST

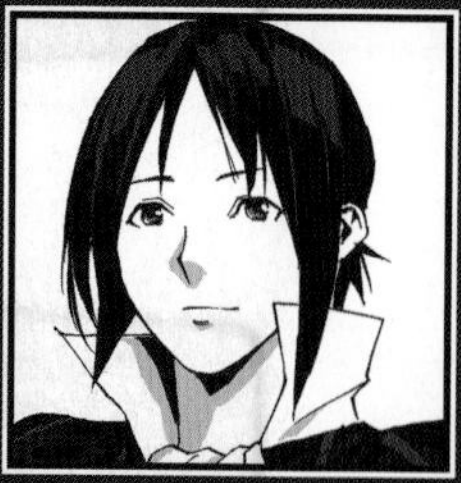
ROMEO

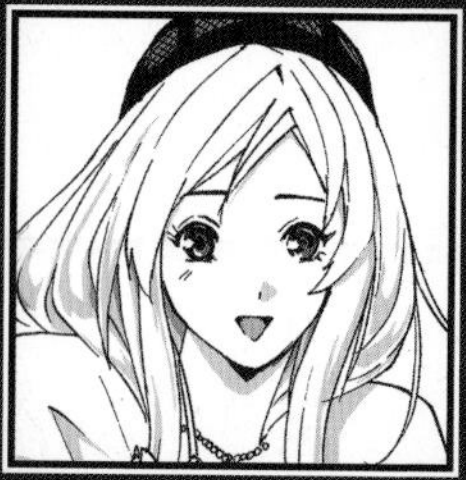
JULIET

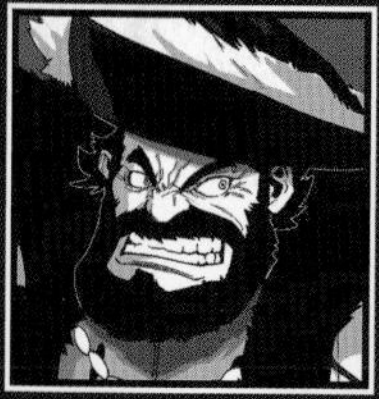
LORD MONTAGUE

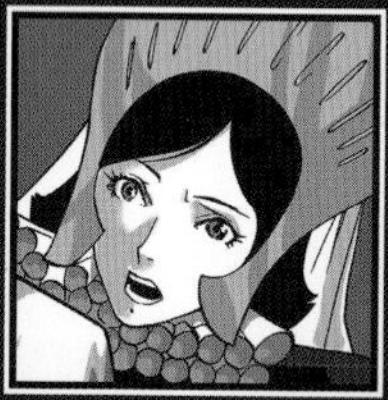
LADY MONTAGUE

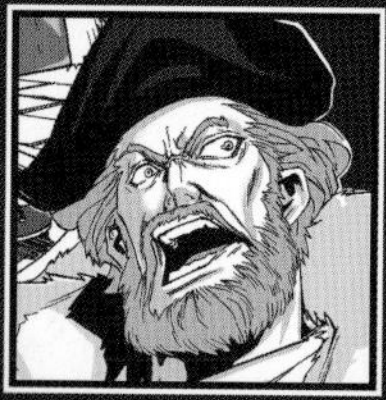
LORD CAPULET

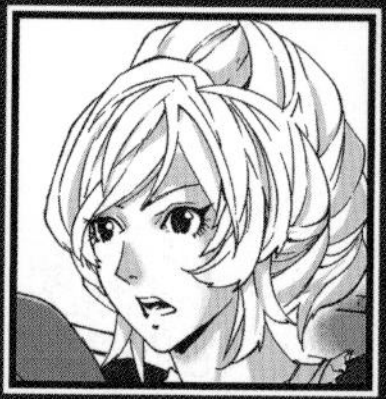
LADY CAPULET

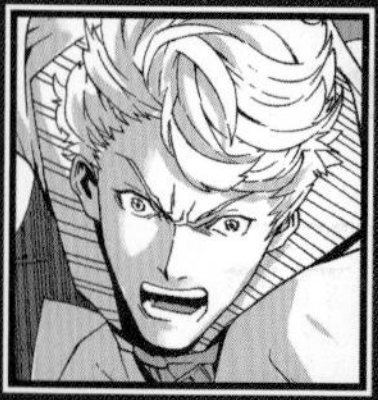
BENVOLIO

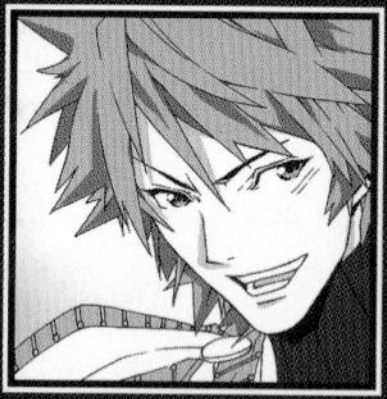
MERCUTIO

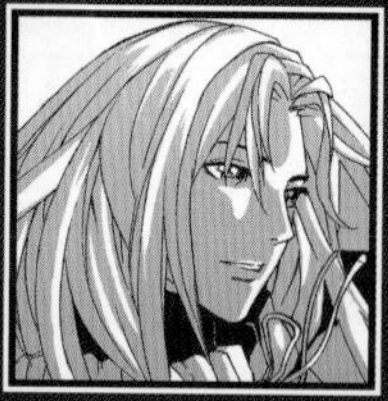
COUNT PARIS

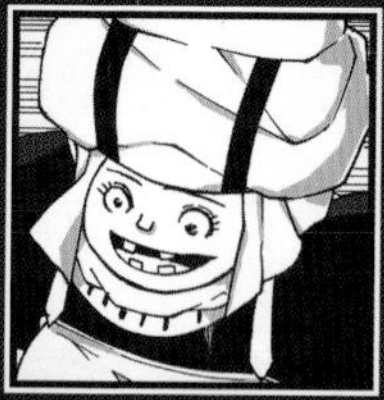
NURSE

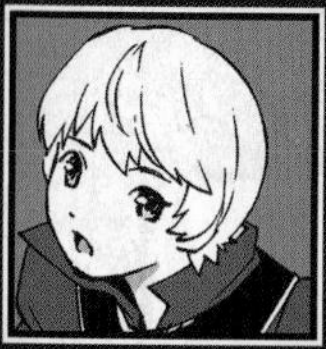
BALTHASAR

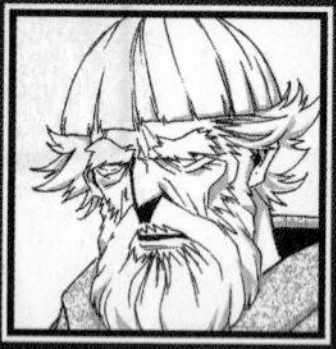
FRIAR LAURENCE

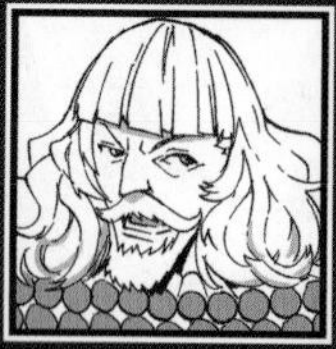
PRINCE ESCALUS

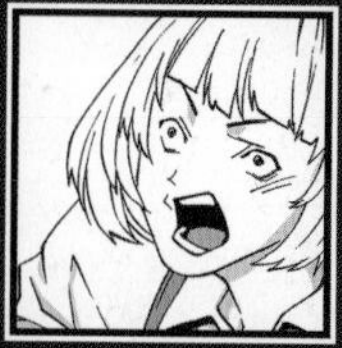
PETER

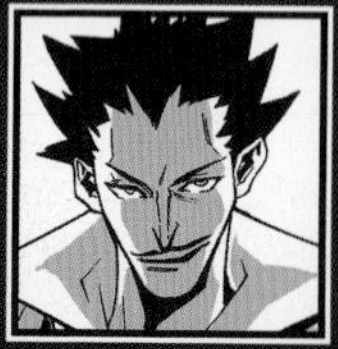
TYBALT

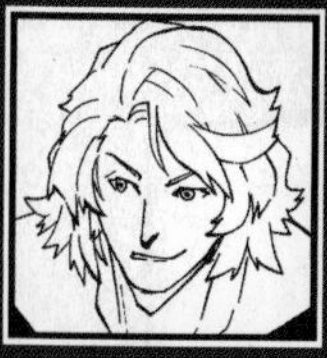
ABRAM

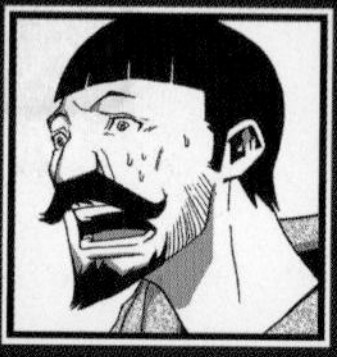
FRIAR JOHN

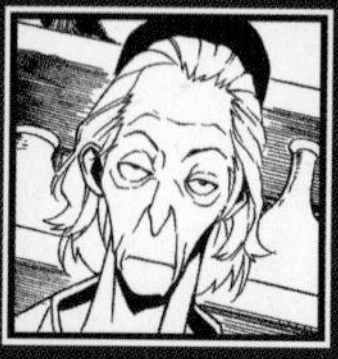
APOTHECARY

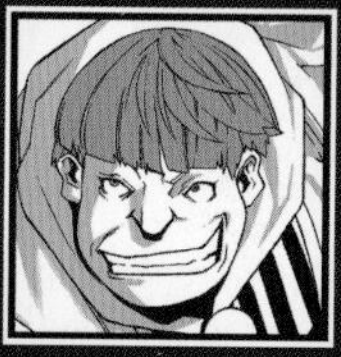
SAMPSON

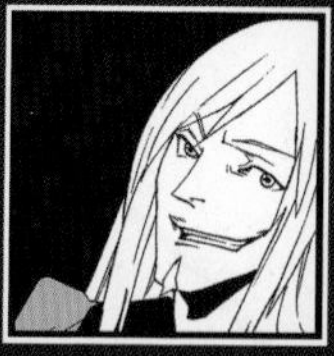
GREGORY

CONTENTS

Romeo and Juliet

WILLIAM SHAKESPEARE

HOW TO READ MANGA!

Hello there, and welcome to **Manga Classics**! "Manga" is a style of comic book originating in **Japan**.

A manga book is read from **right-to-left**, which is **backwards** from the normal books you know. This means that you will find the first page where you expect to find the last page! It also means that each page begins in the top right corner.

START HERE!

Got the hang of it? Then you're ready to start reading **Manga Classics!**

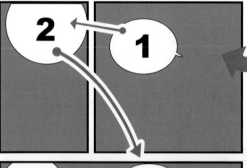

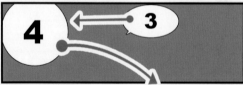

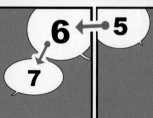

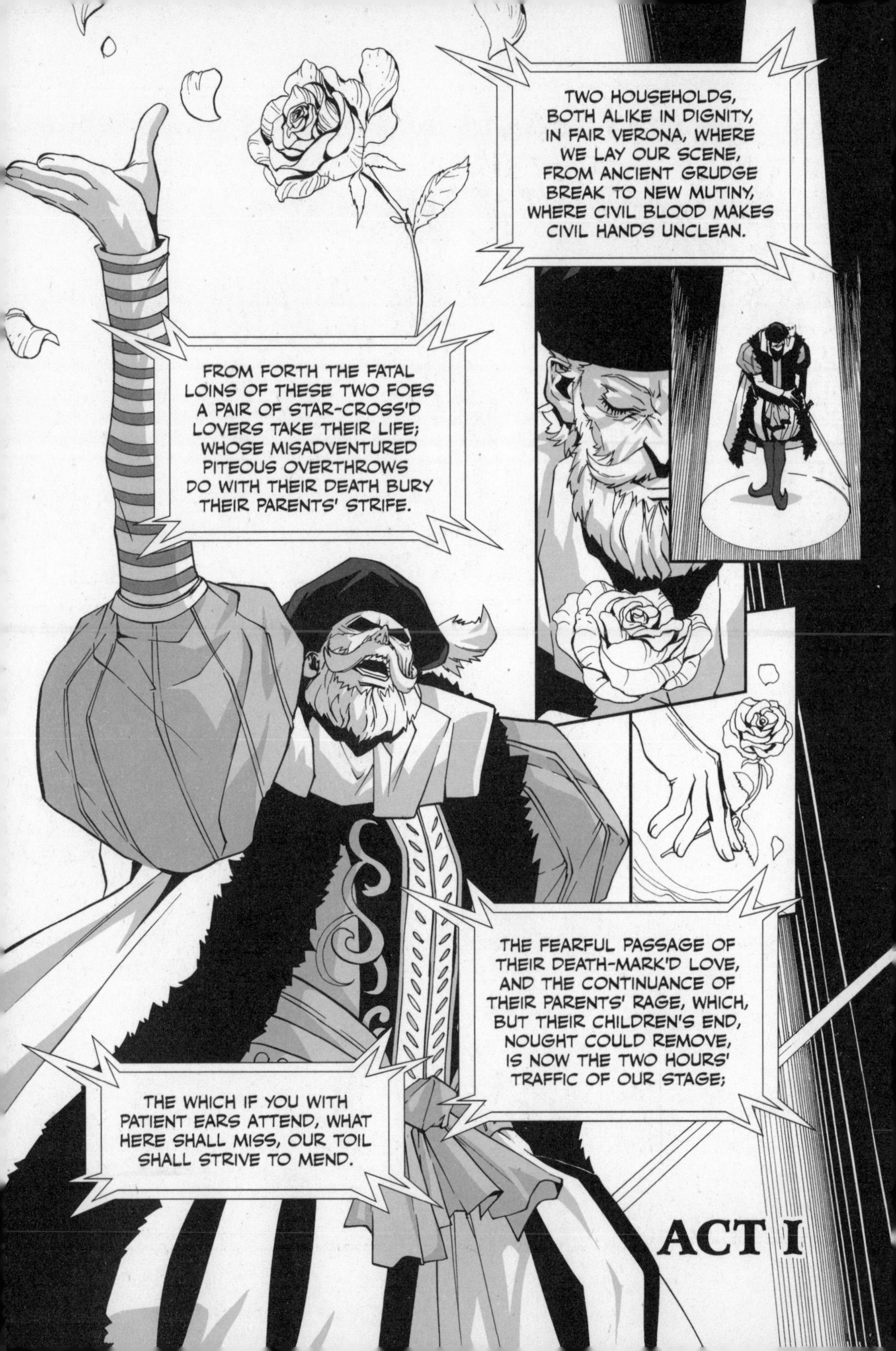
TWO HOUSEHOLDS, BOTH ALIKE IN DIGNITY, IN FAIR VERONA, WHERE WE LAY OUR SCENE, FROM ANCIENT GRUDGE BREAK TO NEW MUTINY, WHERE CIVIL BLOOD MAKES CIVIL HANDS UNCLEAN.
FROM FORTH THE FATAL LOINS OF THESE TWO FOES A PAIR OF STAR-CROSS'D LOVERS TAKE THEIR LIFE; WHOSE MISADVENTURED PITEOUS OVERTHROWS DO WITH THEIR DEATH BURY THEIR PARENTS' STRIFE.
THE FEARFUL PASSAGE OF THEIR DEATH-MARK'D LOVE, AND THE CONTINUANCE OF THEIR PARENTS' RAGE, WHICH, BUT THEIR CHILDREN'S END, NOUGHT COULD REMOVE, IS NOW THE TWO HOURS' TRAFFIC OF OUR STAGE;
THE WHICH IF YOU WITH PATIENT EARS ATTEND, WHAT HERE SHALL MISS, OUR TOIL SHALL STRIVE TO MEND.
ACT I

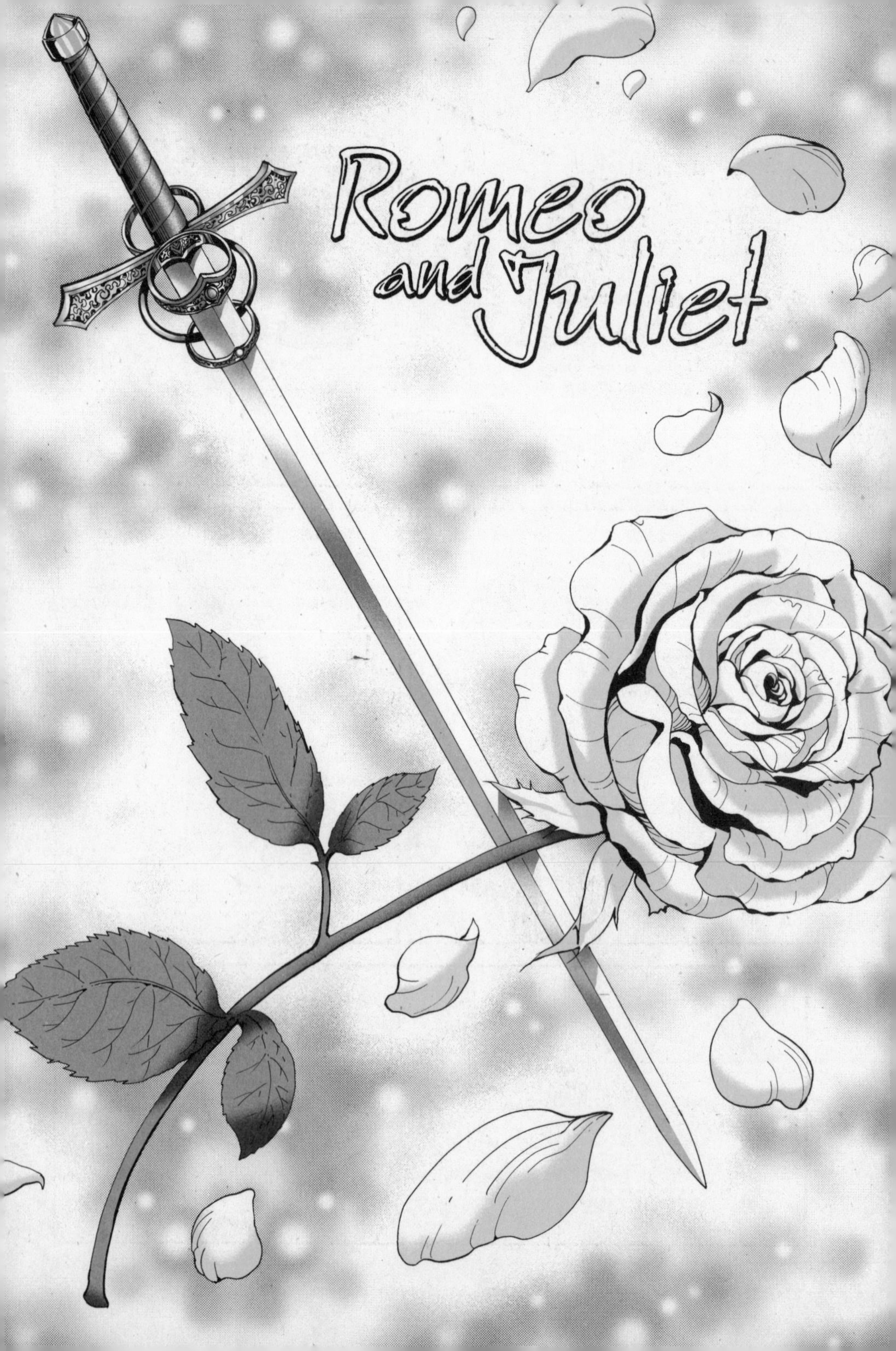
Romeo
and Juliet

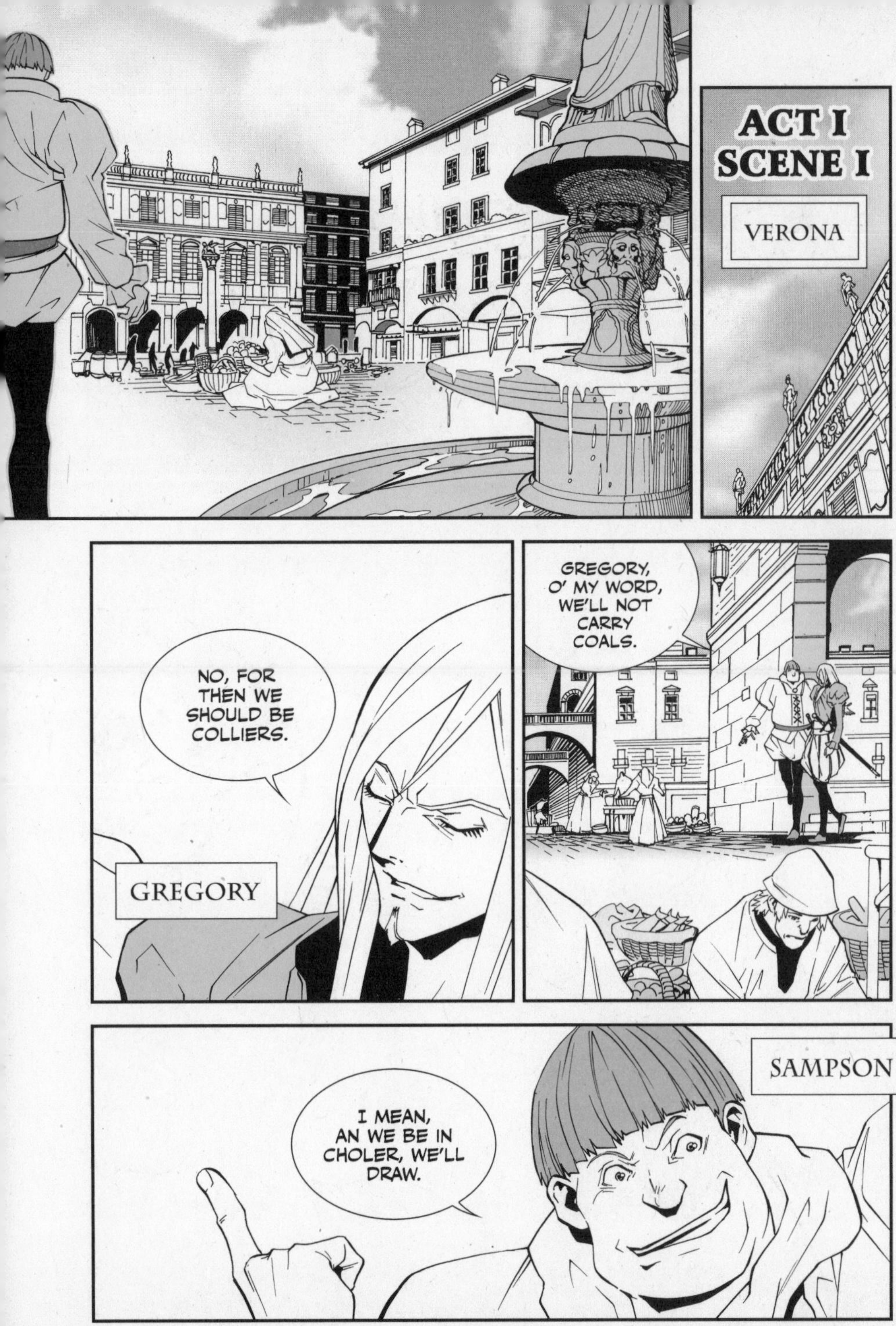
ACT I SCENE I
VERONA
GREGORY, O' MY WORD, WE'LL NOT CARRY COALS.
NO, FOR THEN WE SHOULD BE COLLIERS.
GREGORY
SAMPSON
I MEAN, AN WE BE IN CHOLER, WE'LL DRAW.

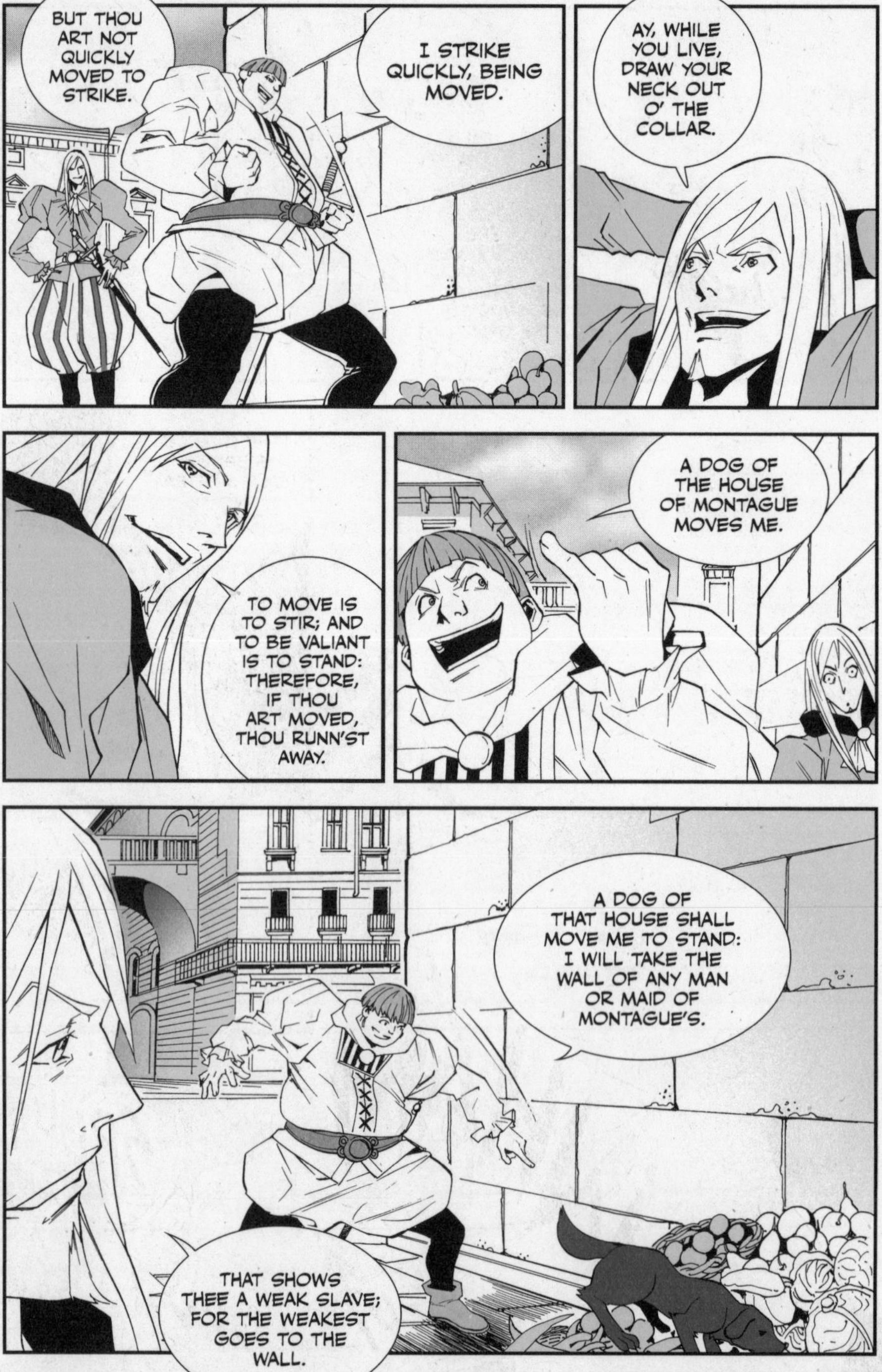
AY, WHILE YOU LIVE, DRAW YOUR NECK OUT O' THE COLLAR.
I STRIKE QUICKLY, BEING MOVED.
BUT THOU ART NOT QUICKLY MOVED TO STRIKE.
A DOG OF THE HOUSE OF MONTAGUE MOVES ME.
TO MOVE IS TO STIR; AND TO BE VALIANT IS TO STAND: THEREFORE, IF THOU ART MOVED, THOU RUNN'ST AWAY.
A DOG OF THAT HOUSE SHALL MOVE ME TO STAND: I WILL TAKE THE WALL OF ANY MAN OR MAID OF MONTAGUE'S.
THAT SHOWS THEE A WEAK SLAVE; FOR THE WEAKEST GOES TO THE WALL.

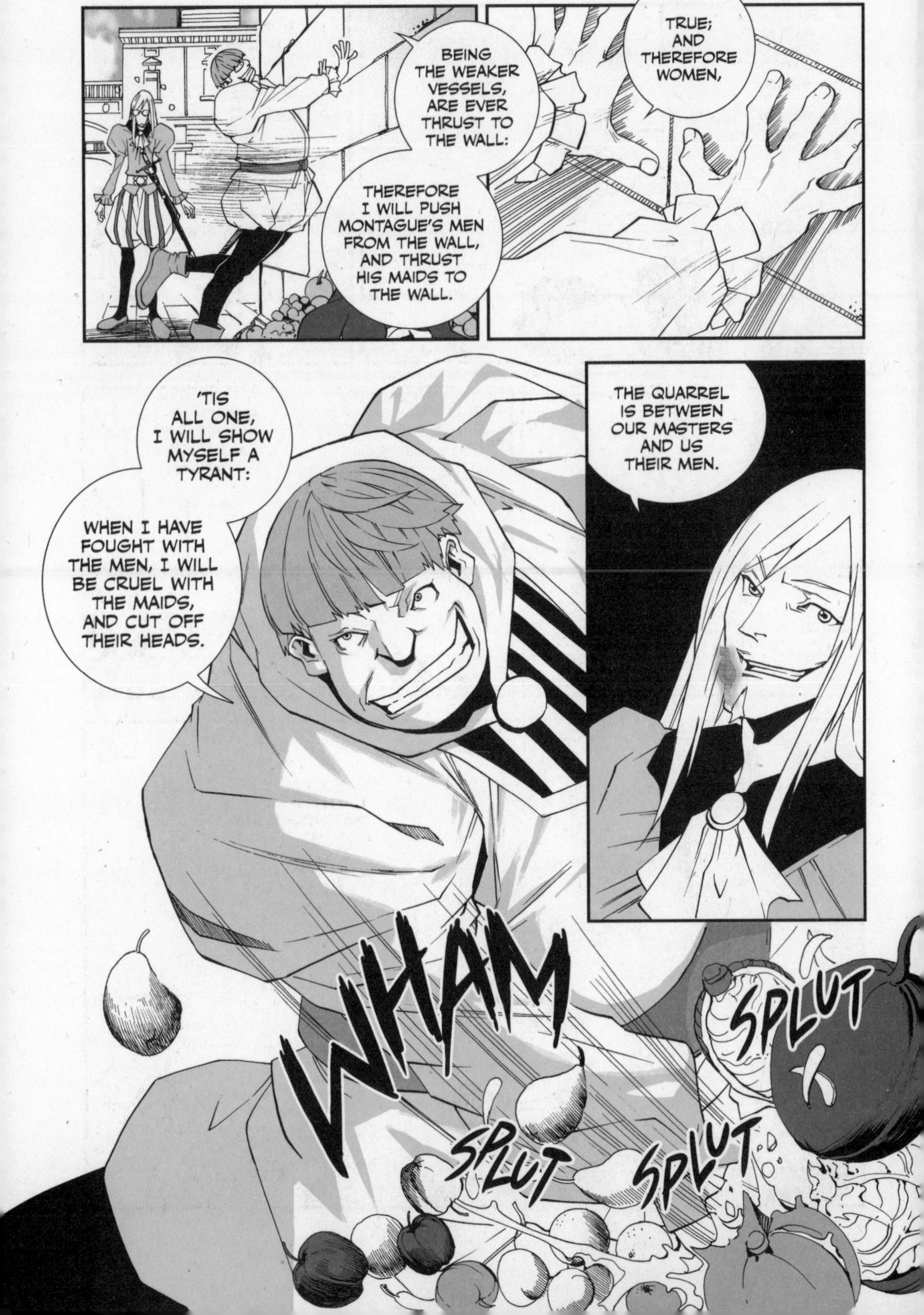
TRUE; AND THEREFORE WOMEN,
BEING THE WEAKER VESSELS, ARE EVER THRUST TO THE WALL:
THEREFORE I WILL PUSH MONTAGUE'S MEN FROM THE WALL, AND THRUST HIS MAIDS TO THE WALL.
THE QUARREL IS BETWEEN OUR MASTERS AND US THEIR MEN.
'TIS ALL ONE, I WILL SHOW MYSELF A TYRANT:
WHEN I HAVE FOUGHT WITH THE MEN, I WILL BE CRUEL WITH THE MAIDS, AND CUT OFF THEIR HEADS.
SPLUT
WHAM
SPLUT
SPLUT

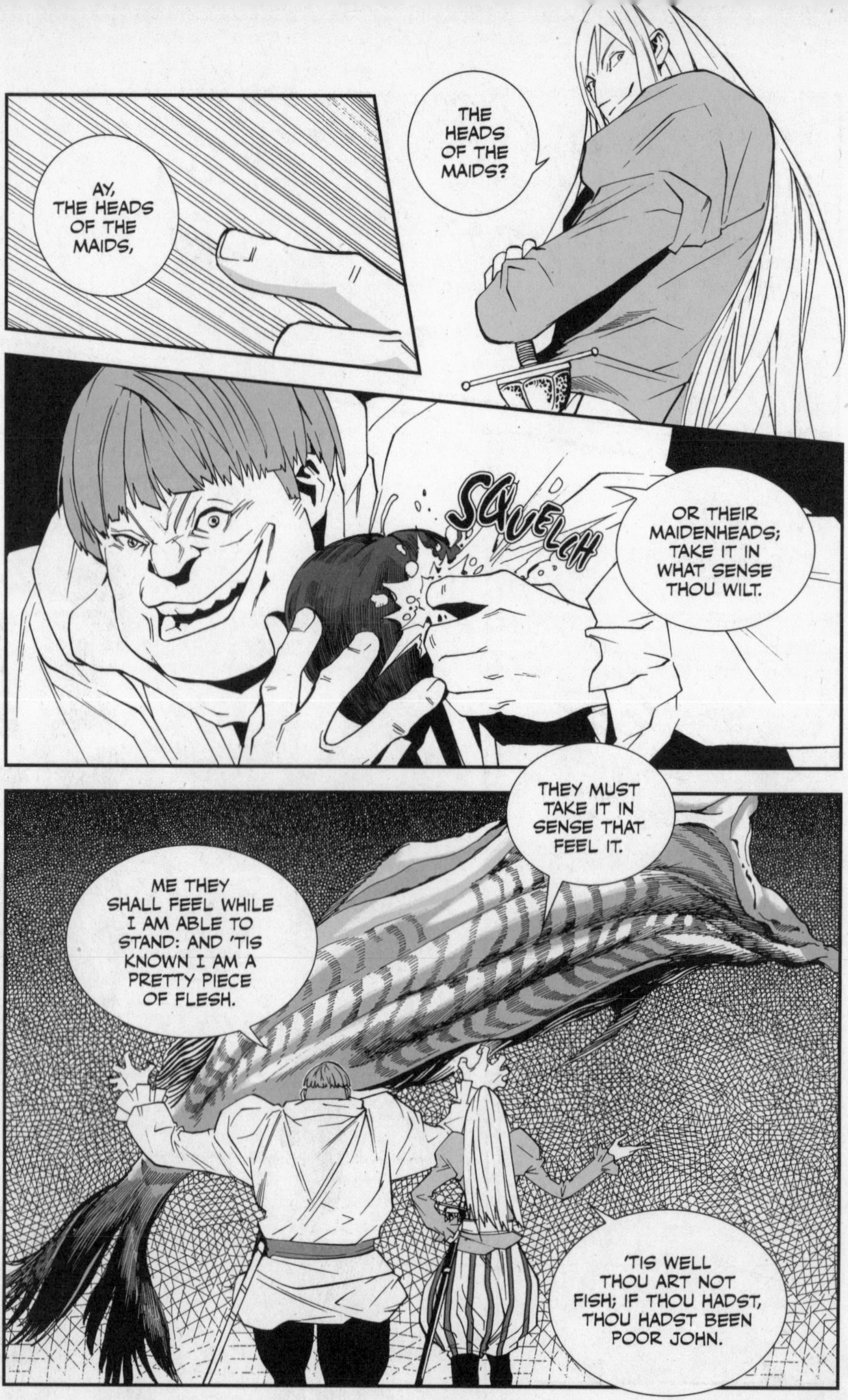
THE HEADS OF THE MAIDS?
AY, THE HEADS OF THE MAIDS,
SQUELCH
OR THEIR MAIDENHEADS; TAKE IT IN WHAT SENSE THOU WILT.
THEY MUST TAKE IT IN SENSE THAT FEEL IT.
ME THEY SHALL FEEL WHILE I AM ABLE TO STAND: AND 'TIS KNOWN I AM A PRETTY PIECE OF FLESH.
'TIS WELL THOU ART NOT FISH; IF THOU HADST, THOU HADST BEEN POOR JOHN.

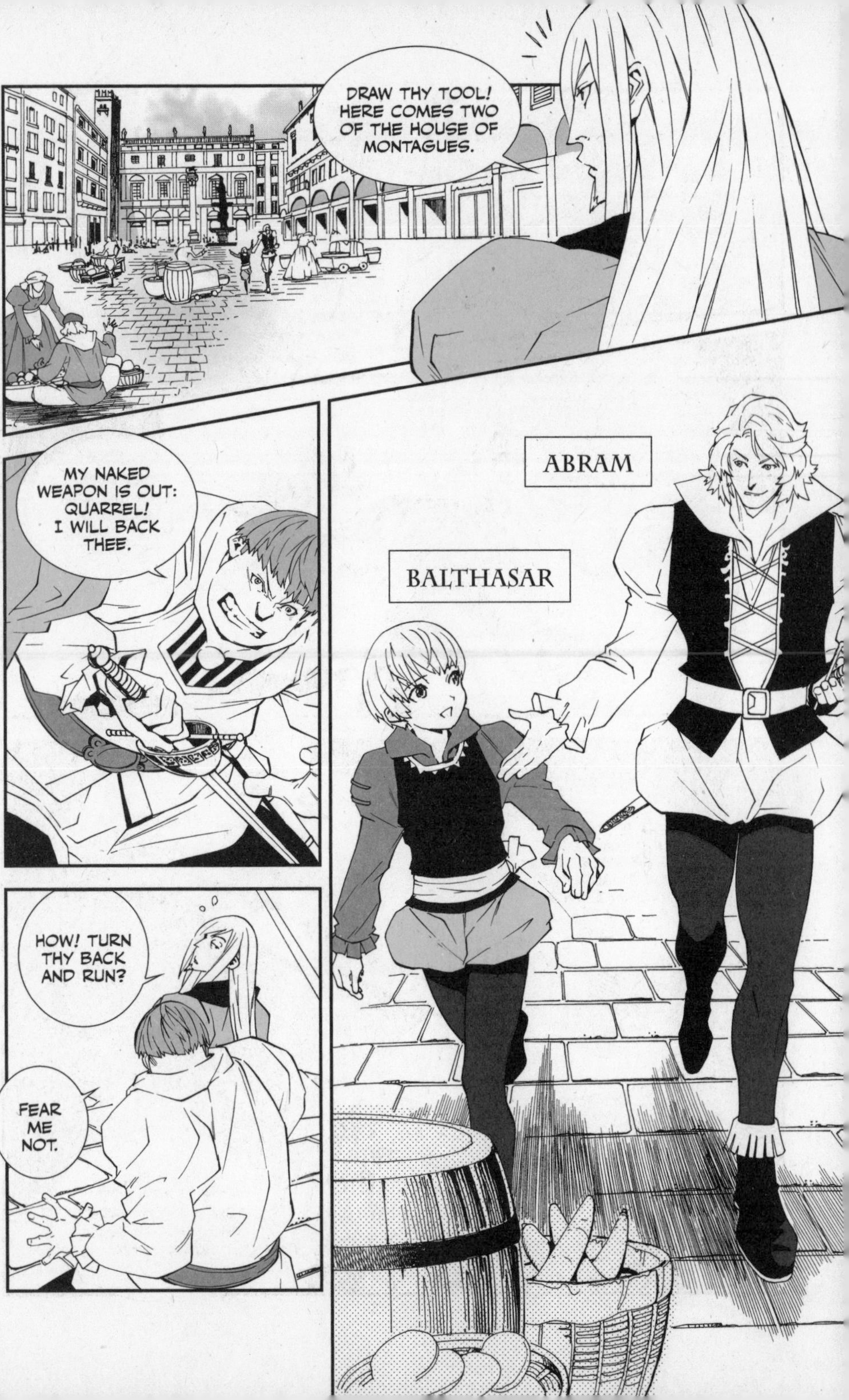
DRAW THY TOOL! HERE COMES TWO OF THE HOUSE OF MONTAGUES.
ABRAM
BALTHASAR
MY NAKED WEAPON IS OUT: QUARREL! I WILL BACK THEE.
HOW! TURN THY BACK AND RUN?
FEAR ME NOT.

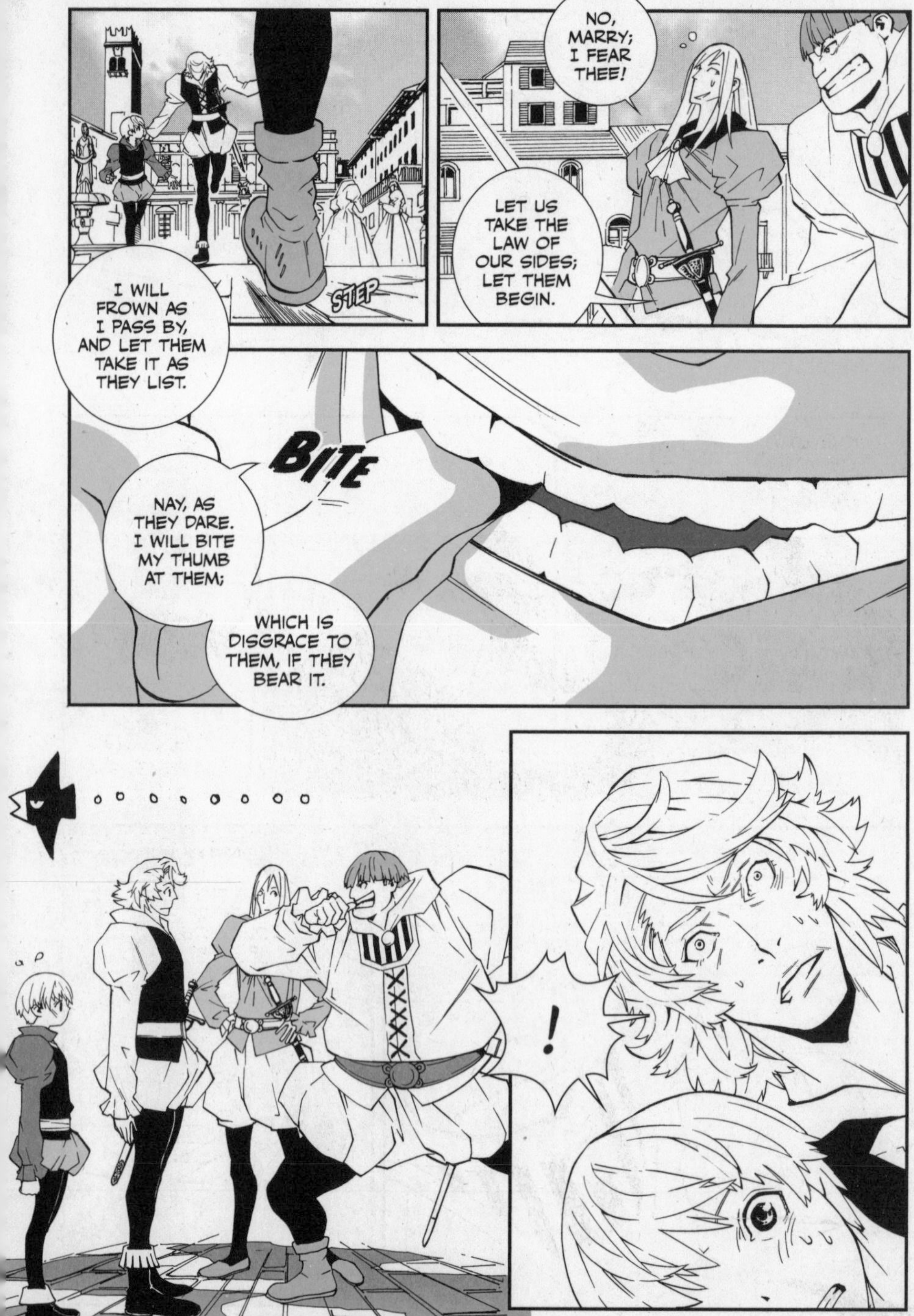
NO, MARRY; I FEAR THEE!
LET US TAKE THE LAW OF OUR SIDES; LET THEM BEGIN.
STEP
I WILL FROWN AS I PASS BY, AND LET THEM TAKE IT AS THEY LIST.
BITE
NAY, AS THEY DARE. I WILL BITE MY THUMB AT THEM;
WHICH IS DISGRACE TO THEM, IF THEY BEAR IT.
!

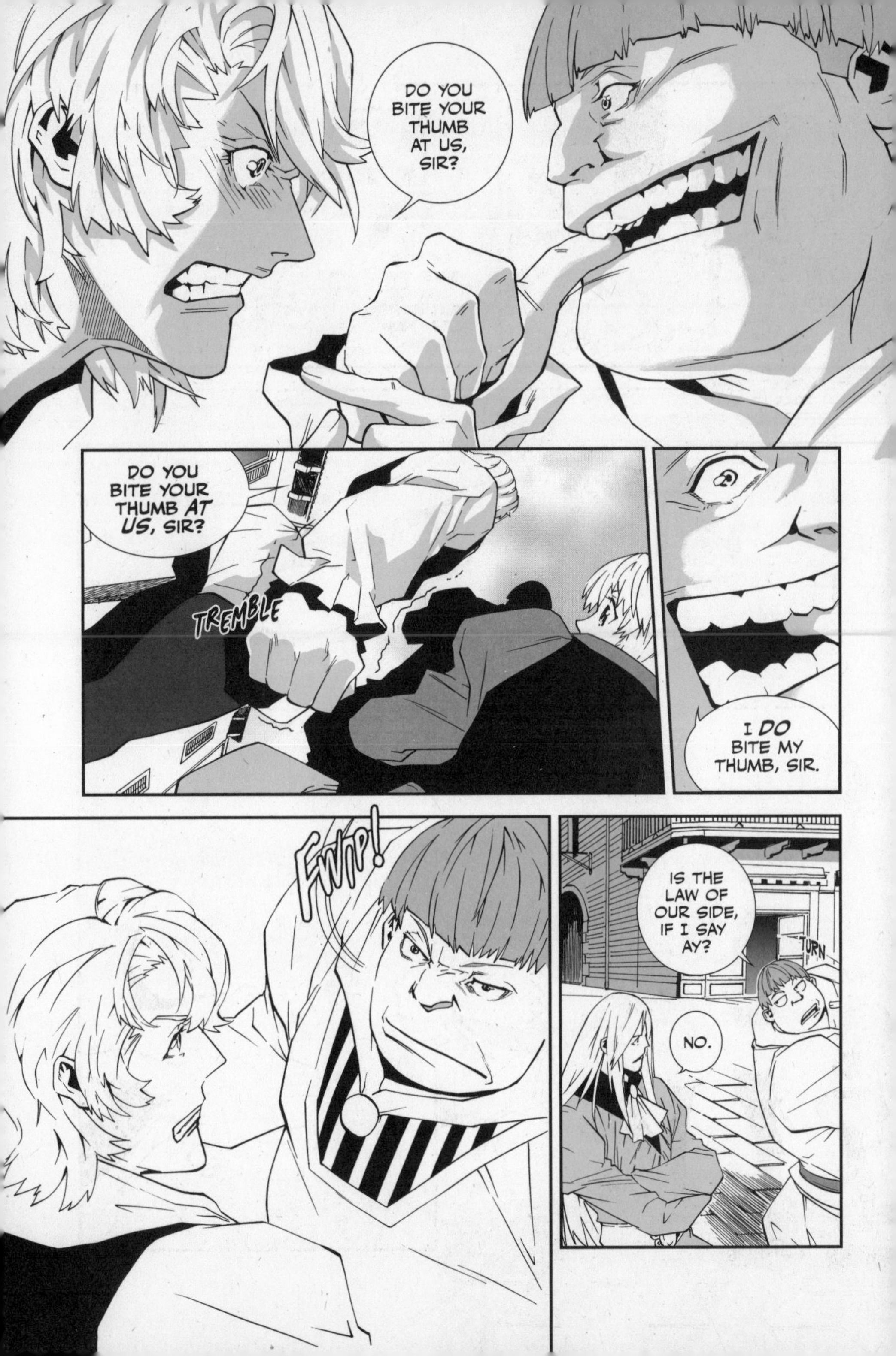
DO YOU BITE YOUR THUMB AT US, SIR?
I *DO* BITE MY THUMB, SIR.
DO YOU BITE YOUR THUMB *AT US*, SIR?
TREMBLE
IS THE LAW OF OUR SIDE, IF I SAY AY?
TURN
NO.
FWIP!

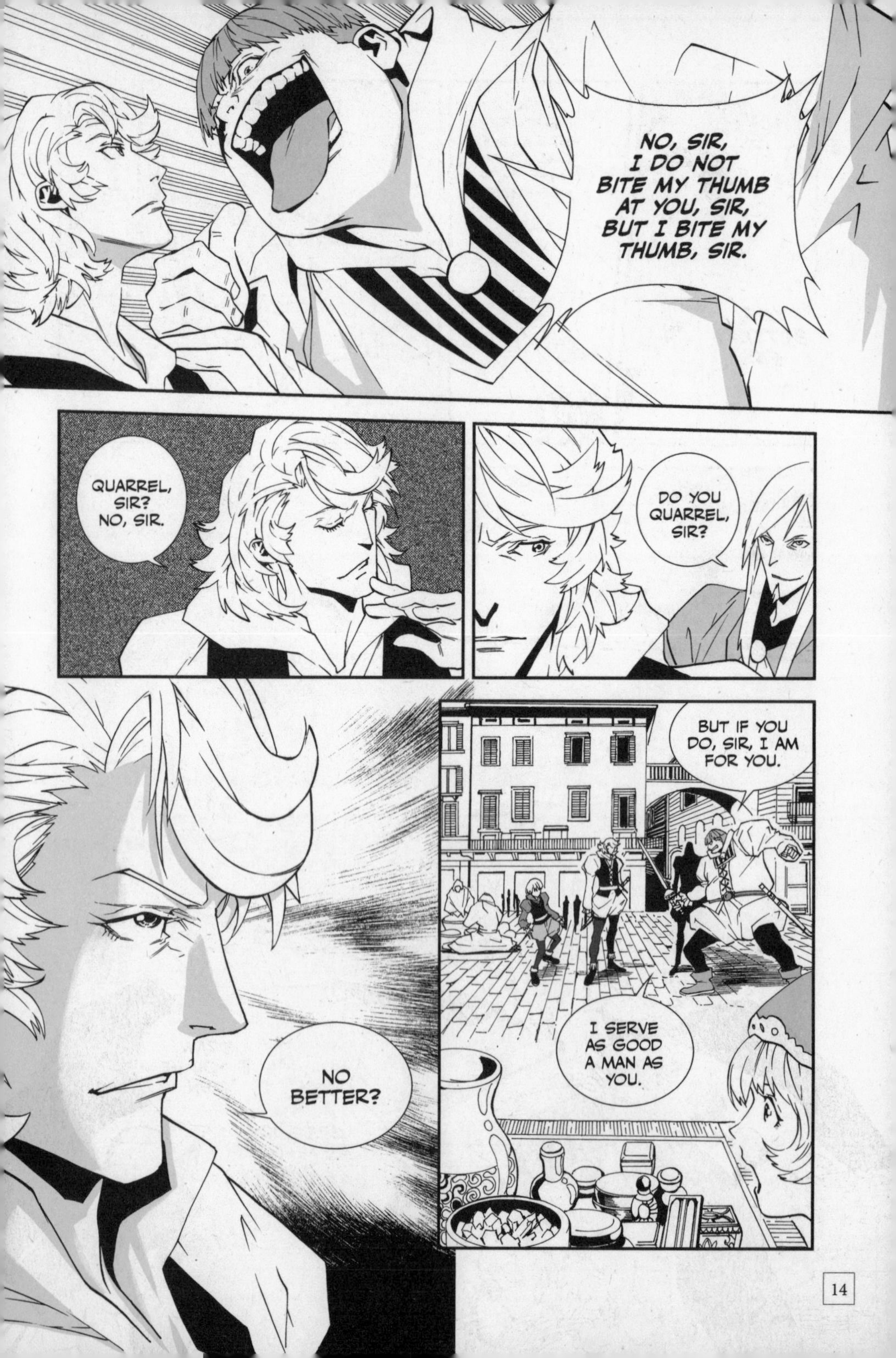
NO, SIR, I DO NOT BITE MY THUMB AT YOU, SIR, BUT I BITE MY THUMB, SIR.
DO YOU QUARREL, SIR?
QUARREL, SIR? NO, SIR.
BUT IF YOU DO, SIR, I AM FOR YOU.
I SERVE AS GOOD A MAN AS YOU.
NO BETTER?

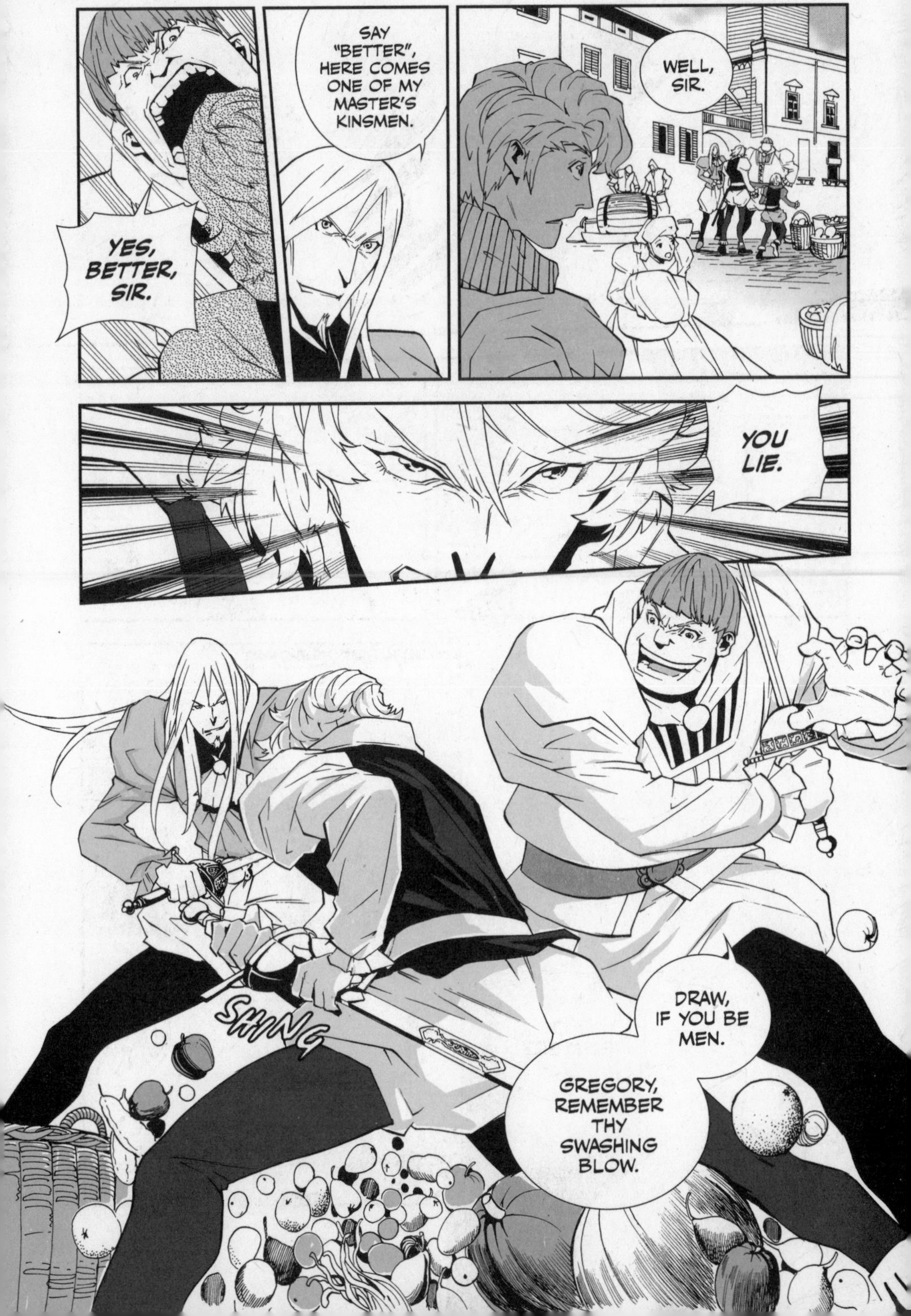
WELL, SIR.
SAY "BETTER", HERE COMES ONE OF MY MASTER'S KINSMEN.
YES, BETTER, SIR.
YOU LIE.
DRAW, IF YOU BE MEN.
GREGORY, REMEMBER THY SWASHING BLOW.
SHING

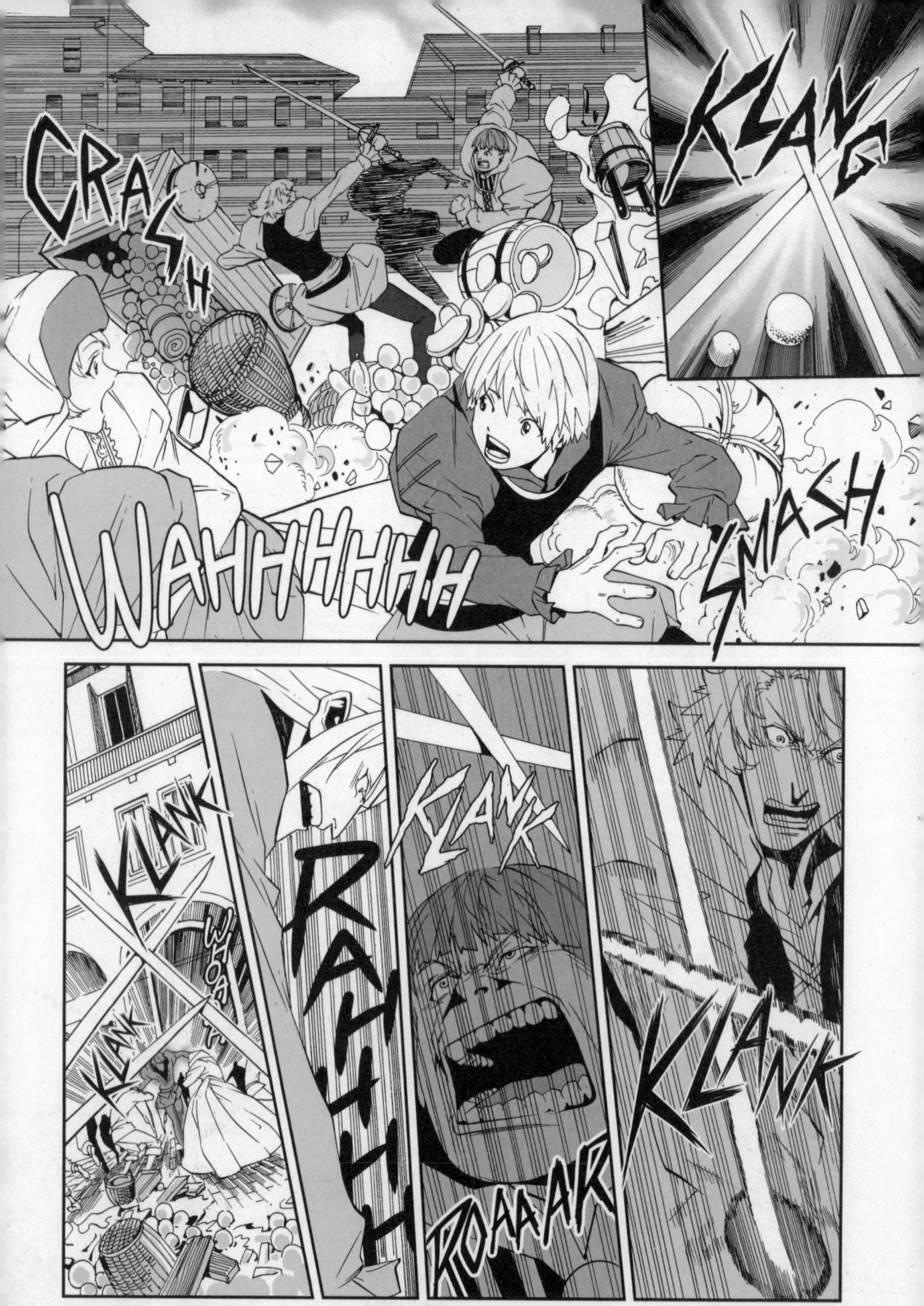

KLANG
!
CRASH
SMASH
WAHHHHHHH
KLANK
KLANK
ROAAAR
RAHHHHH
KLANK
WHOA
KLANK

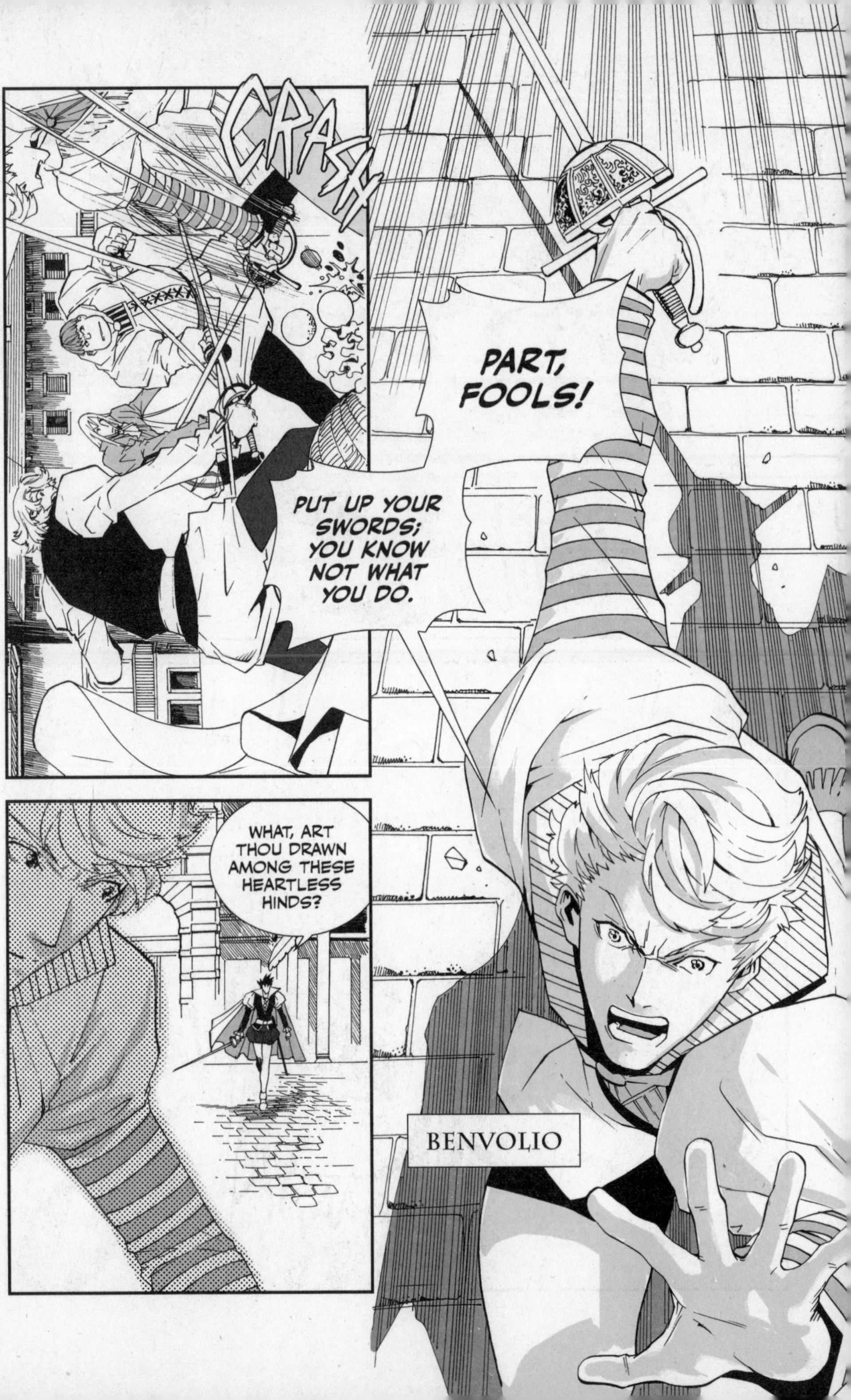
PART, FOOLS!
PUT UP YOUR SWORDS; YOU KNOW NOT WHAT YOU DO.
BENVOLIO
CRASH
WHAT, ART THOU DRAWN AMONG THESE HEARTLESS HINDS?

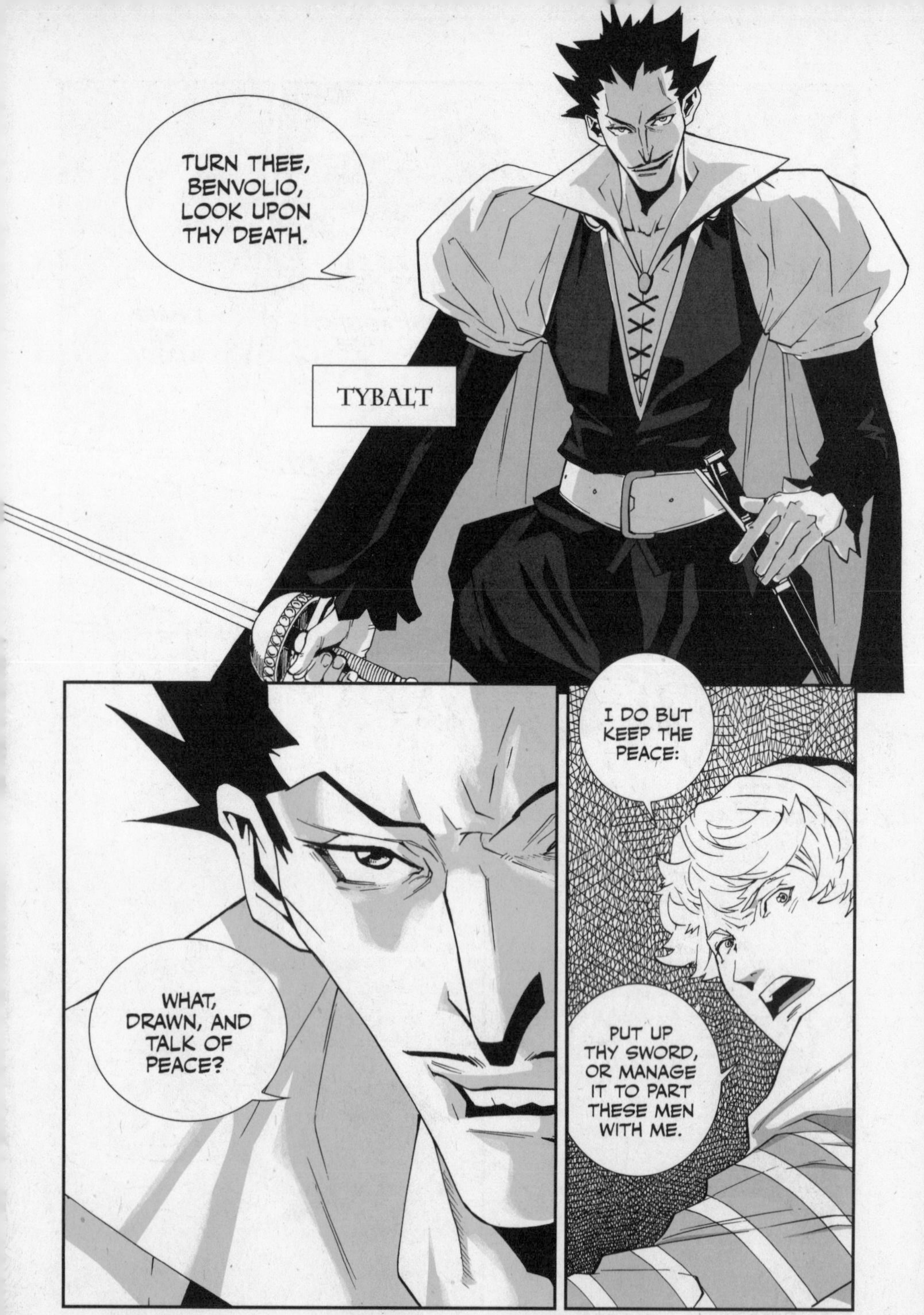
TURN THEE, BENVOLIO, LOOK UPON THY DEATH.
TYBALT
I DO BUT KEEP THE PEACE:
PUT UP THY SWORD, OR MANAGE IT TO PART THESE MEN WITH ME.
WHAT, DRAWN, AND TALK OF PEACE?

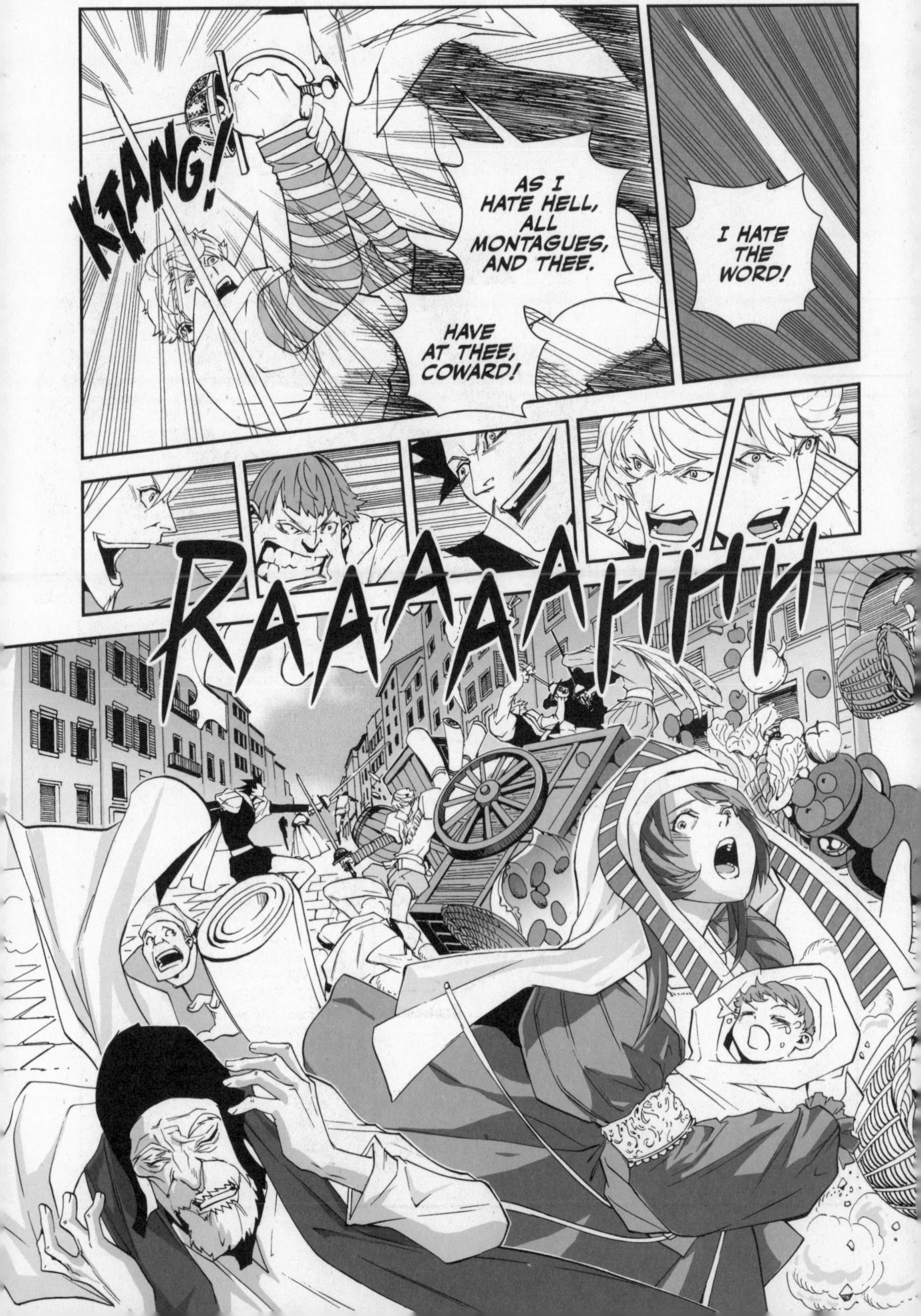
I HATE THE WORD!
AS I HATE HELL, ALL MONTAGUES, AND THEE.
KTANG!
HAVE AT THEE, COWARD!
RAAAAAHHH

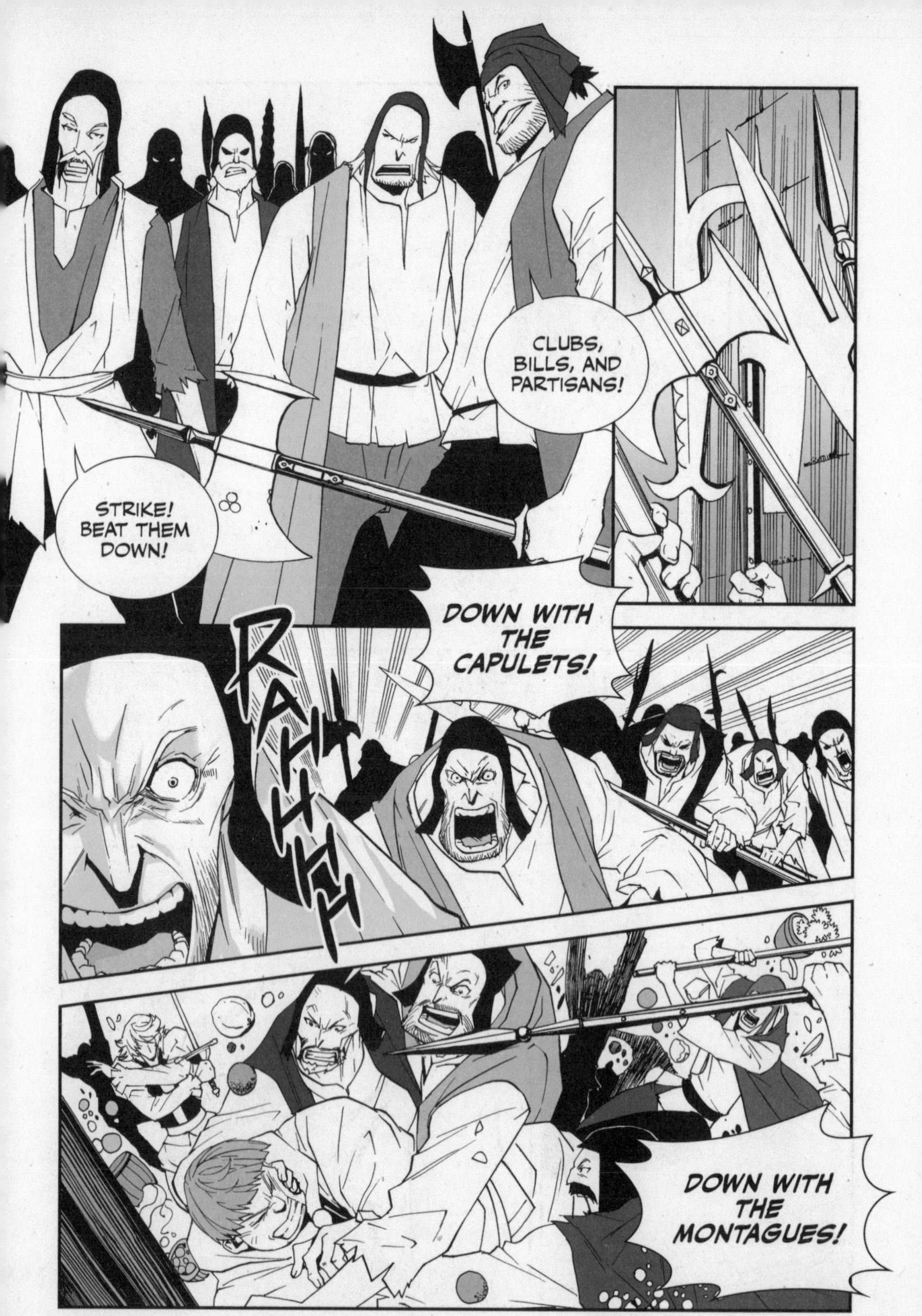
CLUBS, BILLS, AND PARTISANS!
STRIKE! BEAT THEM DOWN!
DOWN WITH THE CAPULETS!
RAHHHHH
DOWN WITH THE MONTAGUES!

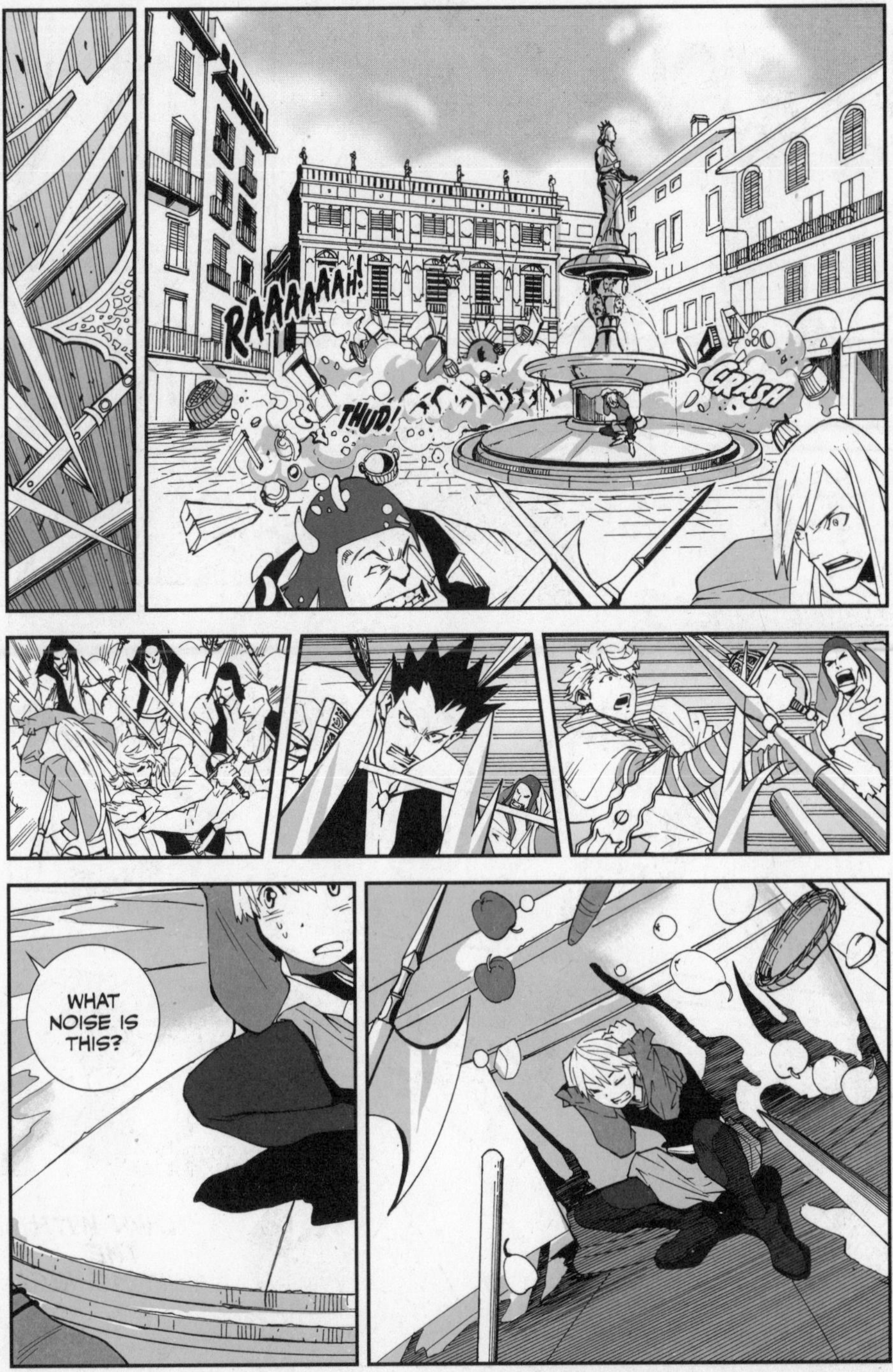
CRASH
RAAAAAAH!
THUD!
WHAT NOISE IS THIS?

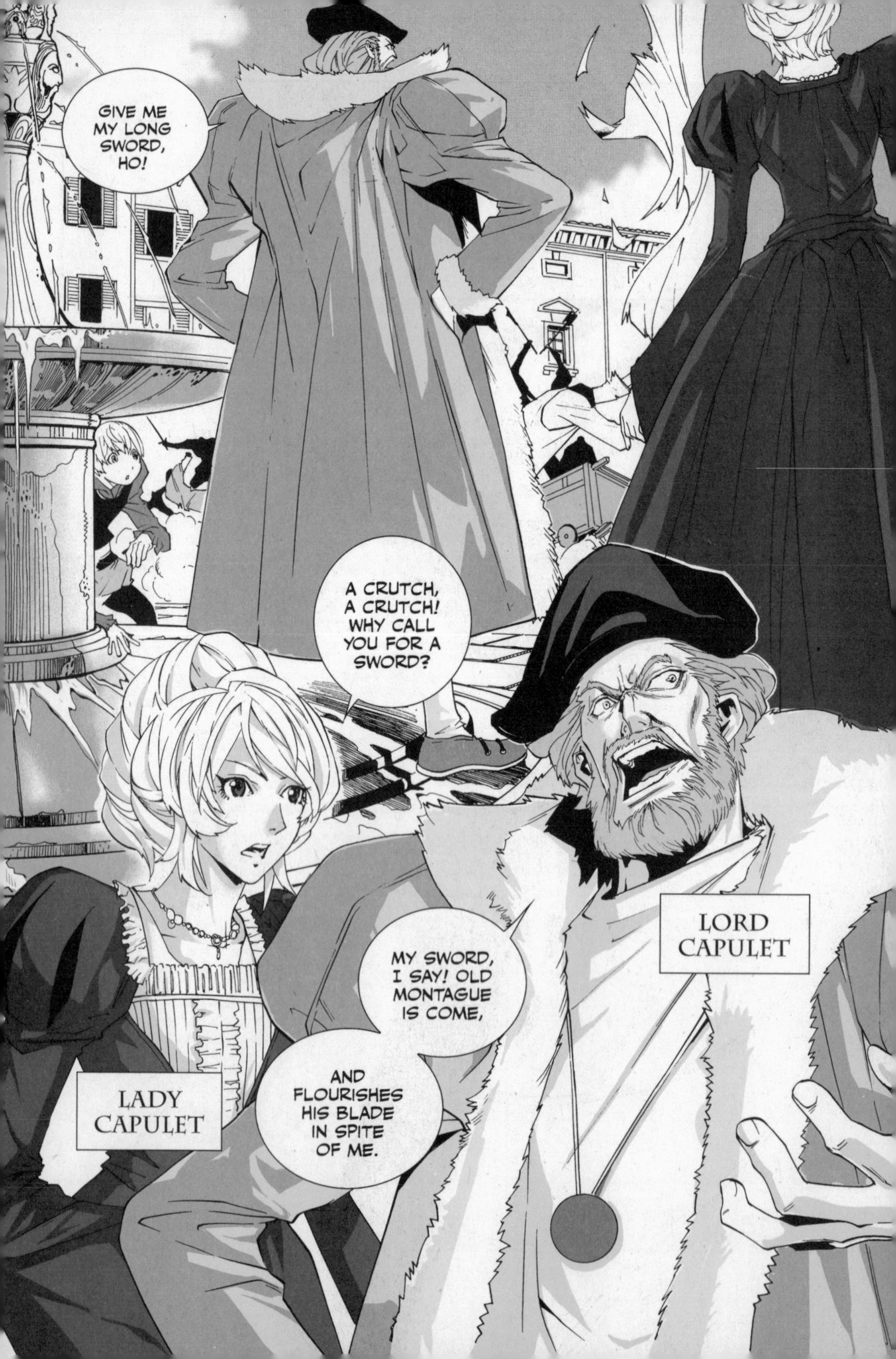
GIVE ME MY LONG SWORD, HO!
A CRUTCH, A CRUTCH! WHY CALL YOU FOR A SWORD?
LORD CAPULET
MY SWORD, I SAY! OLD MONTAGUE IS COME,
AND FLOURISHES HIS BLADE IN SPITE OF ME.
LADY CAPULET

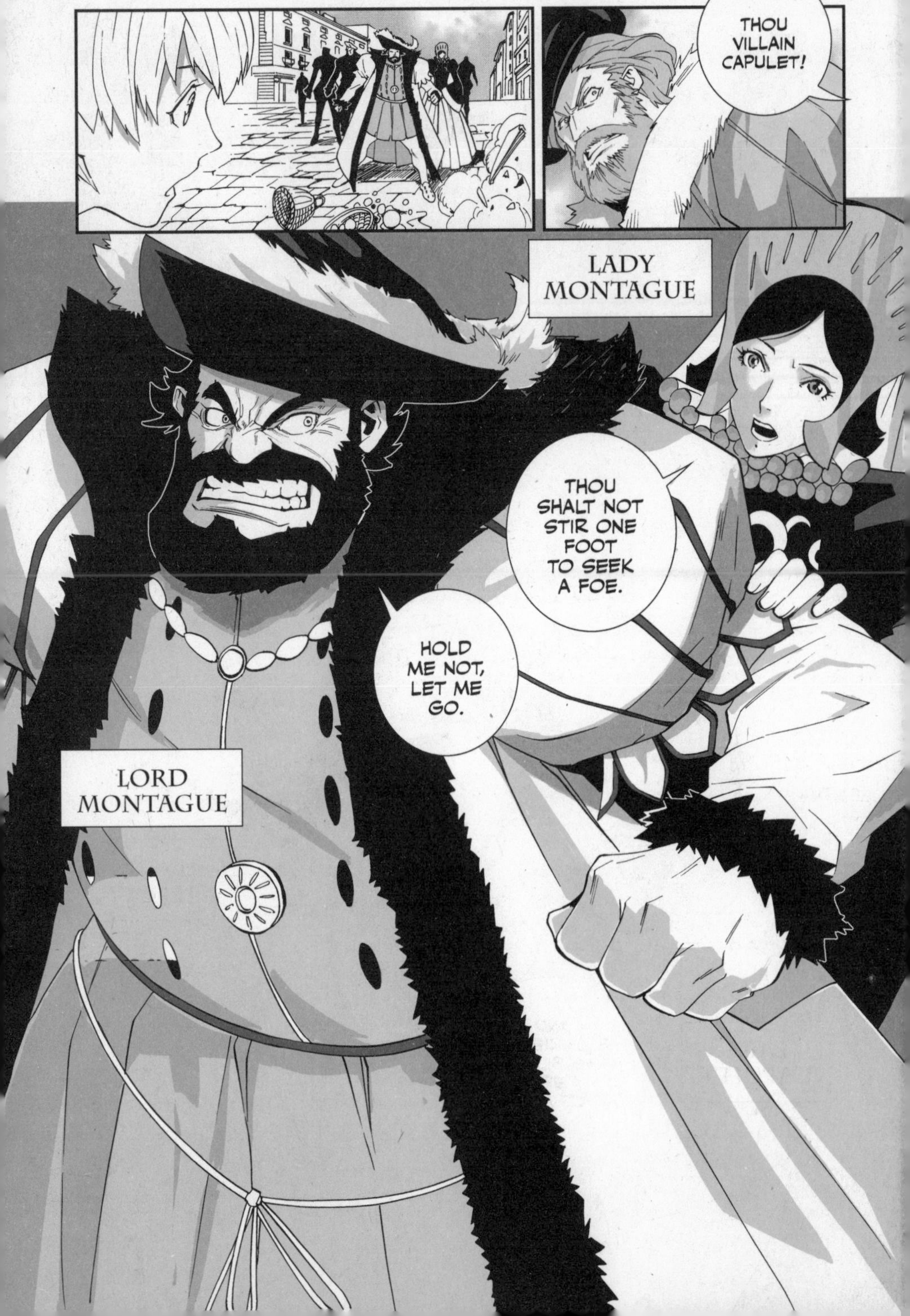
THOU VILLAIN CAPULET!
LADY MONTAGUE
THOU SHALT NOT STIR ONE FOOT TO SEEK A FOE.
HOLD ME NOT, LET ME GO.
LORD MONTAGUE

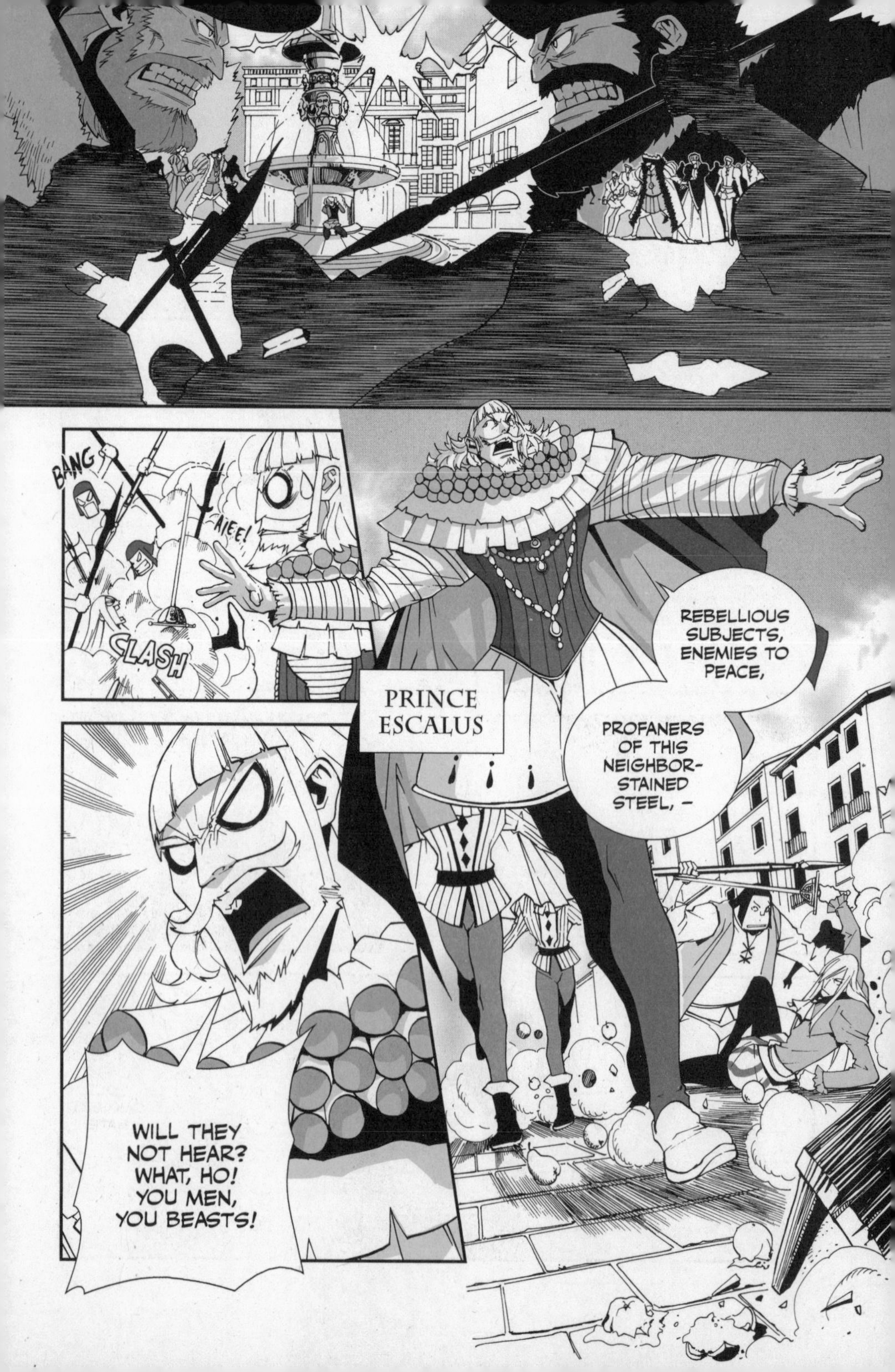
PRINCE ESCALUS
REBELLIOUS SUBJECTS, ENEMIES TO PEACE,
PROFANERS OF THIS NEIGHBOR-STAINED STEEL, –
BANG
AIEE!
CLASH
WILL THEY NOT HEAR? WHAT, HO! YOU MEN, YOU BEASTS!

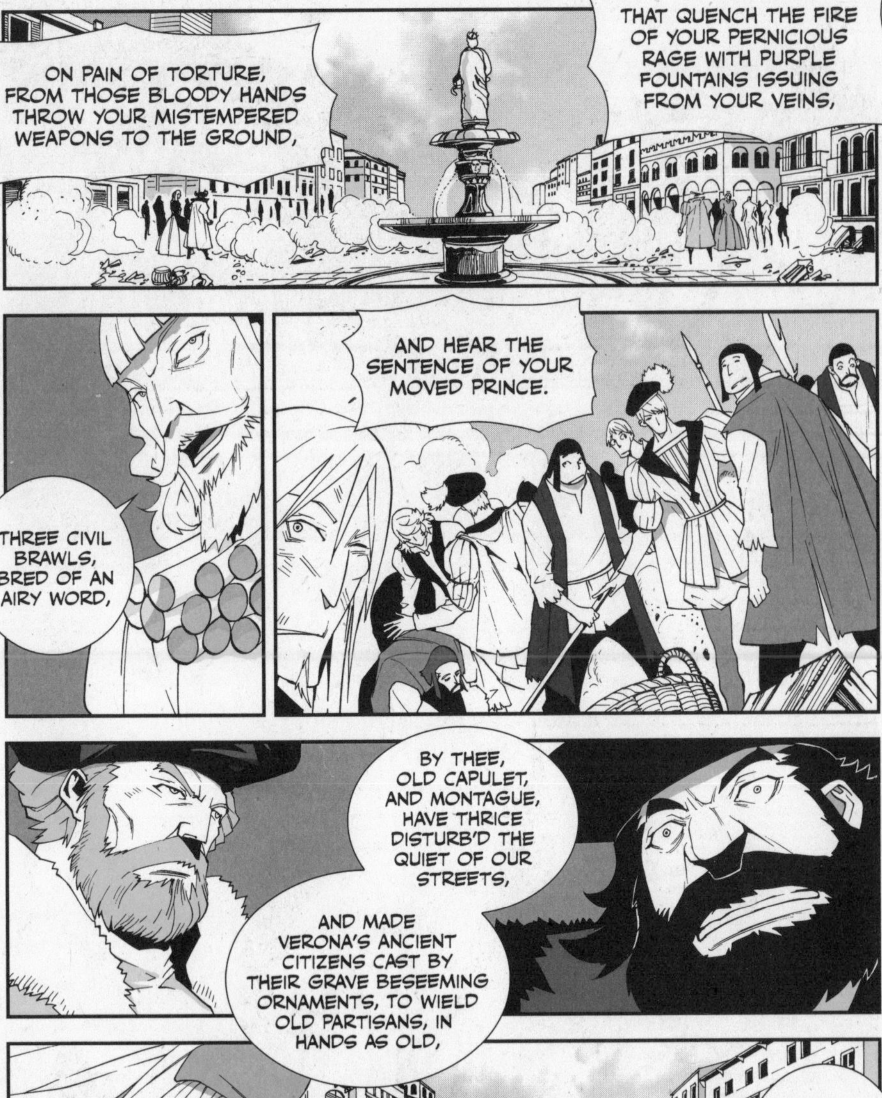
THAT QUENCH THE FIRE OF YOUR PERNICIOUS RAGE WITH PURPLE FOUNTAINS ISSUING FROM YOUR VEINS,
ON PAIN OF TORTURE, FROM THOSE BLOODY HANDS THROW YOUR MISTEMPERED WEAPONS TO THE GROUND,
AND HEAR THE SENTENCE OF YOUR MOVED PRINCE.
THREE CIVIL BRAWLS, BRED OF AN AIRY WORD,
BY THEE, OLD CAPULET, AND MONTAGUE, HAVE THRICE DISTURB'D THE QUIET OF OUR STREETS,
AND MADE VERONA'S ANCIENT CITIZENS CAST BY THEIR GRAVE BESEEMING ORNAMENTS, TO WIELD OLD PARTISANS, IN HANDS AS OLD,
CANK'RED WITH PEACE, TO PART YOUR CANKER'D HATE:

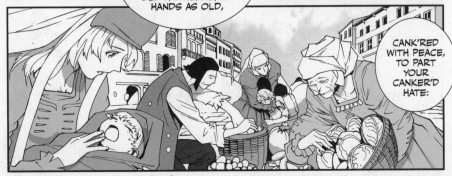

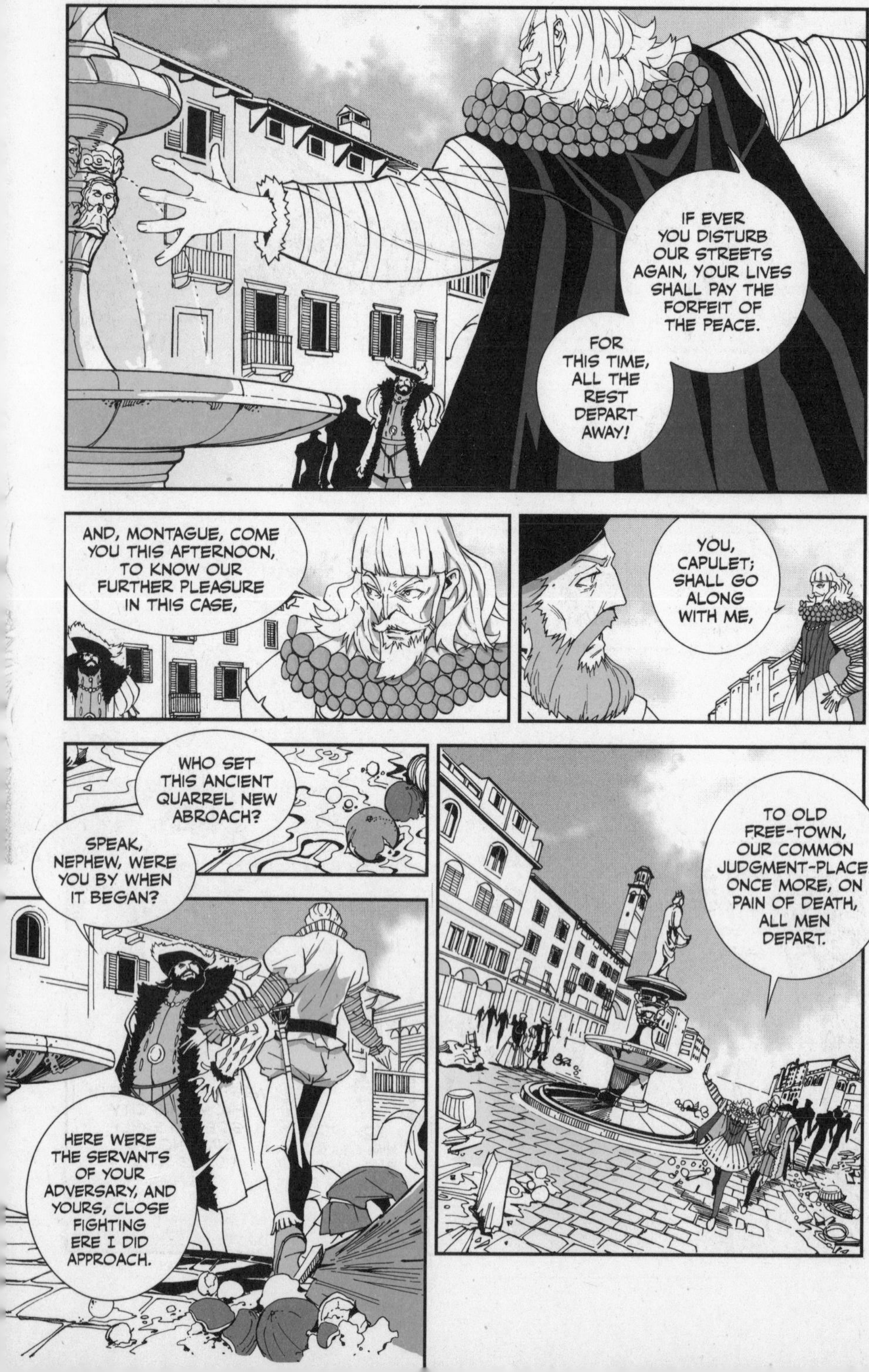
IF EVER YOU DISTURB OUR STREETS AGAIN, YOUR LIVES SHALL PAY THE FORFEIT OF THE PEACE.
FOR THIS TIME, ALL THE REST DEPART AWAY!
YOU, CAPULET; SHALL GO ALONG WITH ME,
AND, MONTAGUE, COME YOU THIS AFTERNOON, TO KNOW OUR FURTHER PLEASURE IN THIS CASE,
TO OLD FREE-TOWN, OUR COMMON JUDGMENT-PLACE. ONCE MORE, ON PAIN OF DEATH, ALL MEN DEPART.
WHO SET THIS ANCIENT QUARREL NEW ABROACH?
SPEAK, NEPHEW, WERE YOU BY WHEN IT BEGAN?
HERE WERE THE SERVANTS OF YOUR ADVERSARY, AND YOURS, CLOSE FIGHTING ERE I DID APPROACH.

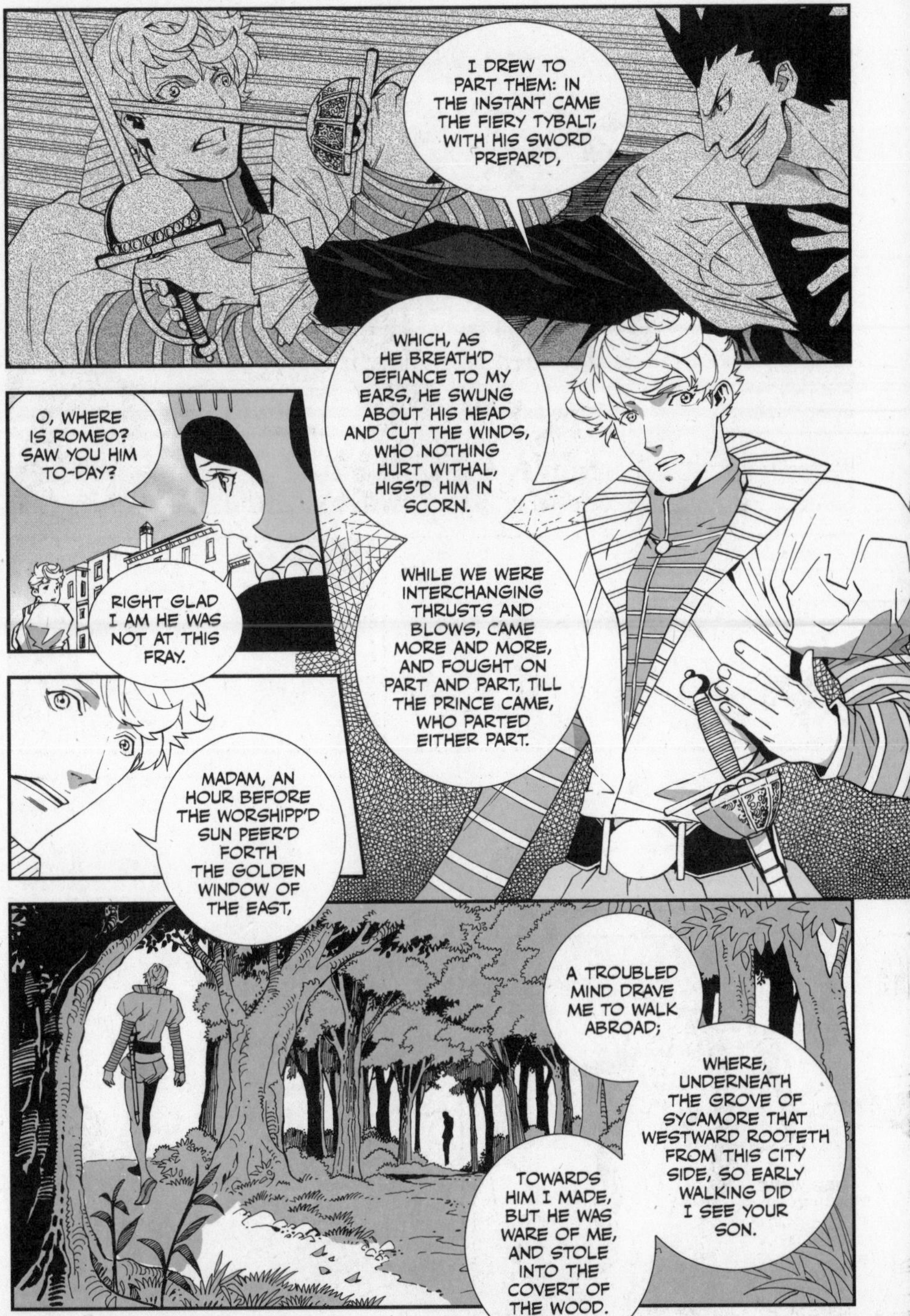
I DREW TO PART THEM: IN THE INSTANT CAME THE FIERY TYBALT, WITH HIS SWORD PREPAR'D,
WHICH, AS HE BREATH'D DEFIANCE TO MY EARS, HE SWUNG ABOUT HIS HEAD AND CUT THE WINDS, WHO NOTHING HURT WITHAL, HISS'D HIM IN SCORN.
WHILE WE WERE INTERCHANGING THRUSTS AND BLOWS, CAME MORE AND MORE, AND FOUGHT ON PART AND PART, TILL THE PRINCE CAME, WHO PARTED EITHER PART.
O, WHERE IS ROMEO? SAW YOU HIM TO-DAY?
RIGHT GLAD I AM HE WAS NOT AT THIS FRAY.
MADAM, AN HOUR BEFORE THE WORSHIPP'D SUN PEER'D FORTH THE GOLDEN WINDOW OF THE EAST,
A TROUBLED MIND DRAVE ME TO WALK ABROAD;
WHERE, UNDERNEATH THE GROVE OF SYCAMORE THAT WESTWARD ROOTETH FROM THIS CITY SIDE, SO EARLY WALKING DID I SEE YOUR SON.
TOWARDS HIM I MADE, BUT HE WAS WARE OF ME, AND STOLE INTO THE COVERT OF THE WOOD.

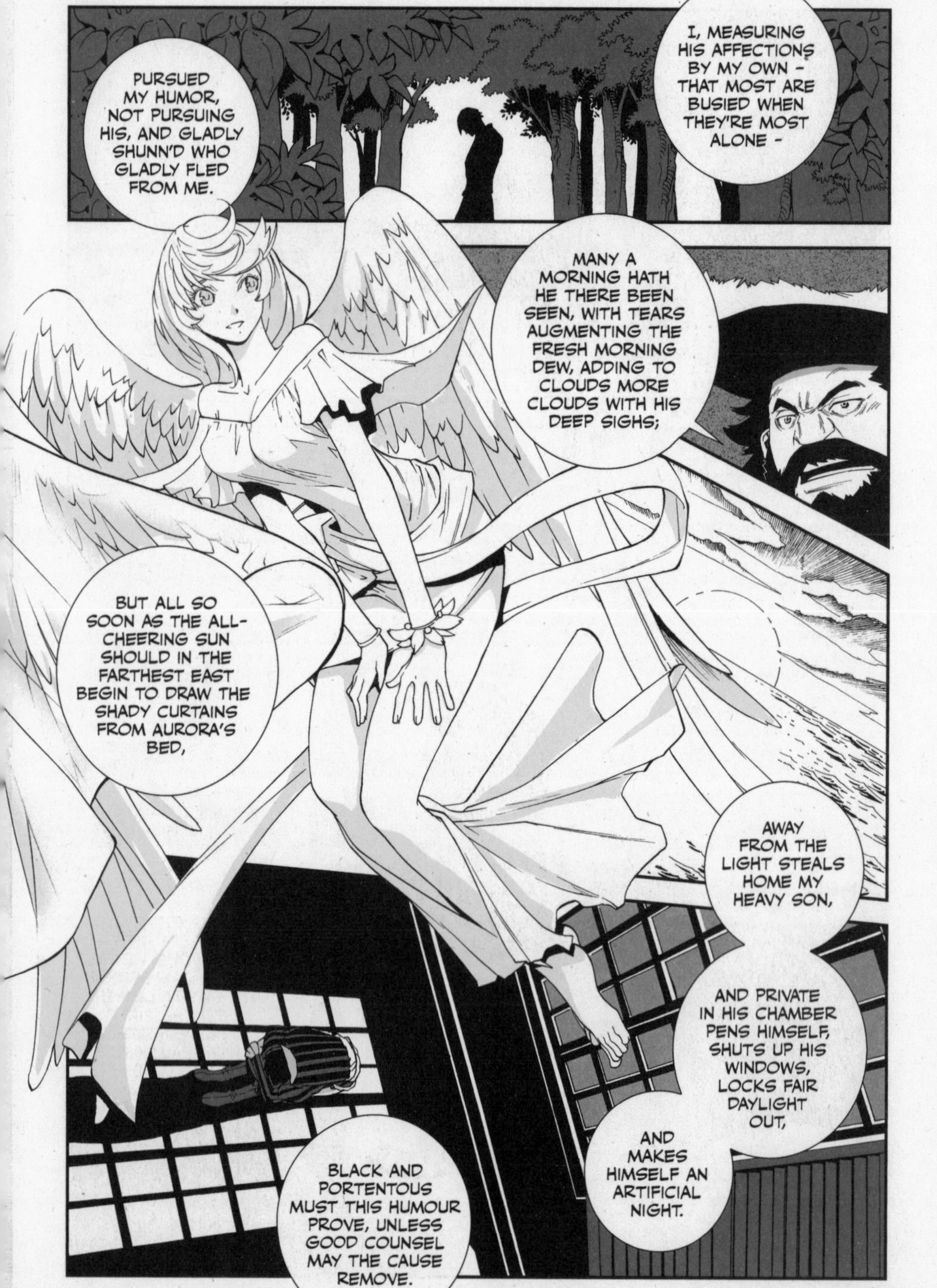
I, MEASURING HIS AFFECTIONS BY MY OWN - THAT MOST ARE BUSIED WHEN THEY'RE MOST ALONE -
PURSUED MY HUMOR, NOT PURSUING HIS, AND GLADLY SHUNN'D WHO GLADLY FLED FROM ME.
MANY A MORNING HATH HE THERE BEEN SEEN, WITH TEARS AUGMENTING THE FRESH MORNING DEW, ADDING TO CLOUDS MORE CLOUDS WITH HIS DEEP SIGHS;
BUT ALL SO SOON AS THE ALL-CHEERING SUN SHOULD IN THE FARTHEST EAST BEGIN TO DRAW THE SHADY CURTAINS FROM AURORA'S BED,
AWAY FROM THE LIGHT STEALS HOME MY HEAVY SON,
AND PRIVATE IN HIS CHAMBER PENS HIMSELF, SHUTS UP HIS WINDOWS, LOCKS FAIR DAYLIGHT OUT,
AND MAKES HIMSELF AN ARTIFICIAL NIGHT.
BLACK AND PORTENTOUS MUST THIS HUMOUR PROVE, UNLESS GOOD COUNSEL MAY THE CAUSE REMOVE.

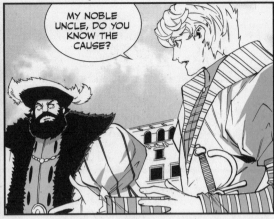

MY NOBLE UNCLE, DO YOU KNOW THE CAUSE?
I NEITHER KNOW IT NOR CAN LEARN OF HIM.
HAVE YOU IMPORTUN'D HIM BY ANY MEANS?
BOTH BY MYSELF AND MANY OTHER FRIENDS: BUT HE, HIS OWN AFFECTIONS' COUNSELLOR,
IS TO HIMSELF - I WILL NOT SAY HOW TRUE - BUT TO HIMSELF SO SECRET AND SO CLOSE,
SO FAR FROM SOUNDING AND DISCOVERY,
AS IS THE BUD BIT WITH AN ENVIOUS WORM, ERE HE CAN SPREAD HIS SWEET LEAVES TO THE AIR, OR DEDICATE HIS BEAUTY TO THE SUN.
COULD WE BUT LEARN FROM WHENCE HIS SORROWS GROW, WE WOULD AS WILLINGLY GIVE CURE AS KNOW.

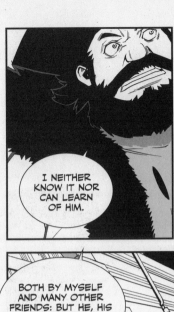

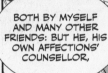

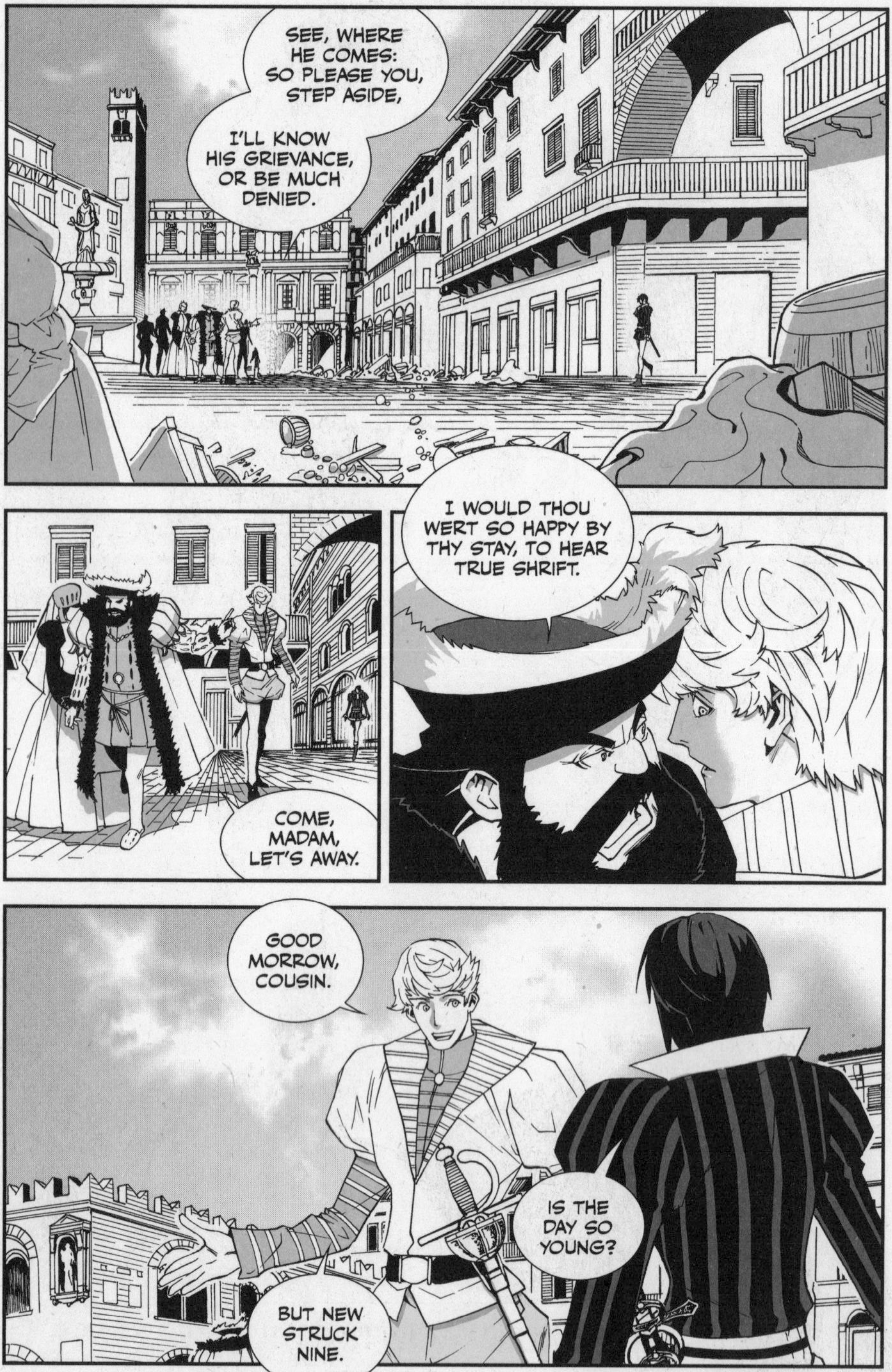
SEE, WHERE HE COMES: SO PLEASE YOU, STEP ASIDE,
I'LL KNOW HIS GRIEVANCE, OR BE MUCH DENIED.
I WOULD THOU WERT SO HAPPY BY THY STAY, TO HEAR TRUE SHRIFT.
COME, MADAM, LET'S AWAY.
GOOD MORROW, COUSIN.
IS THE DAY SO YOUNG?
BUT NEW STRUCK NINE.

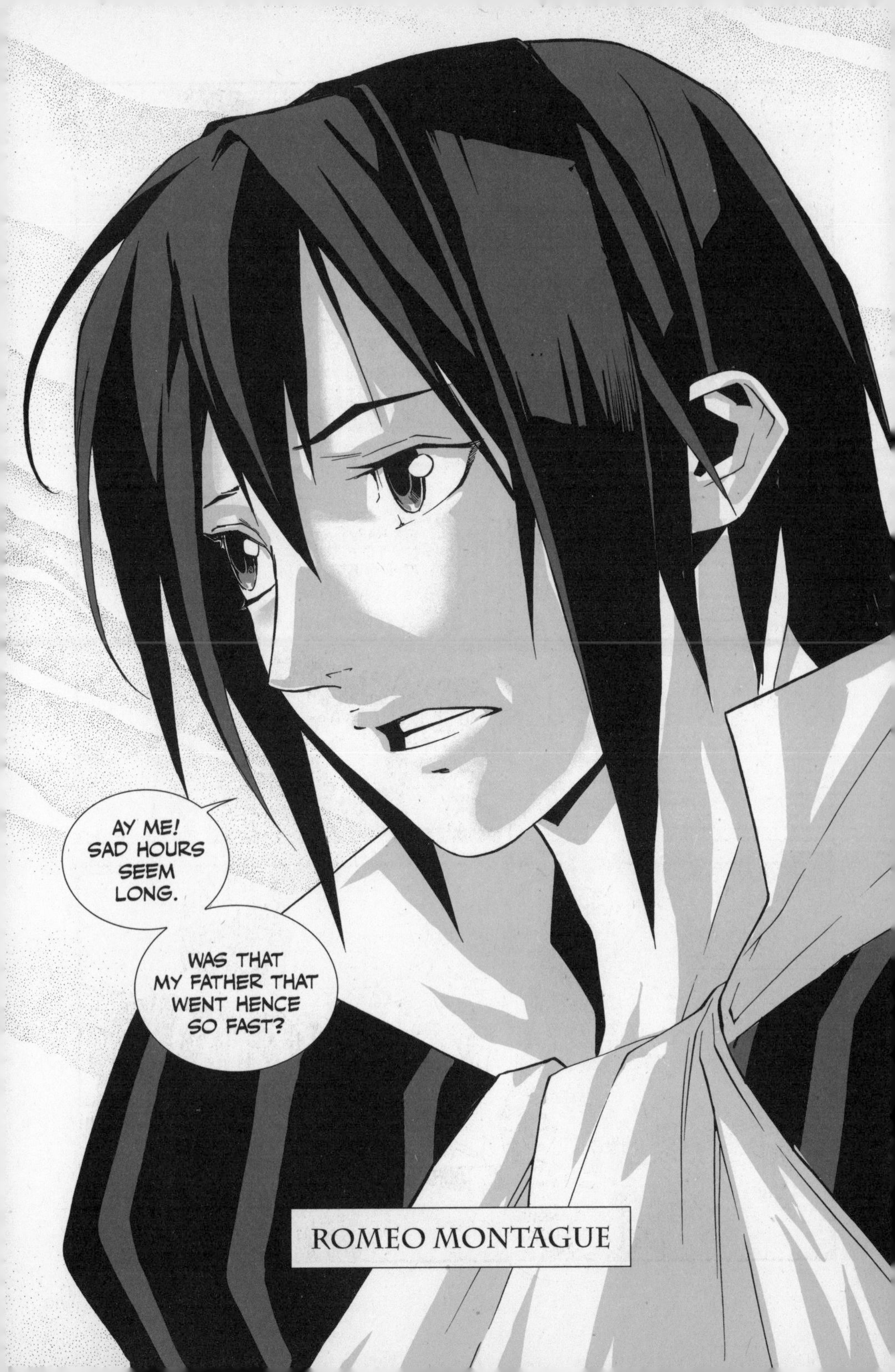
AY ME! SAD HOURS SEEM LONG.
WAS THAT MY FATHER THAT WENT HENCE SO FAST?
ROMEO MONTAGUE

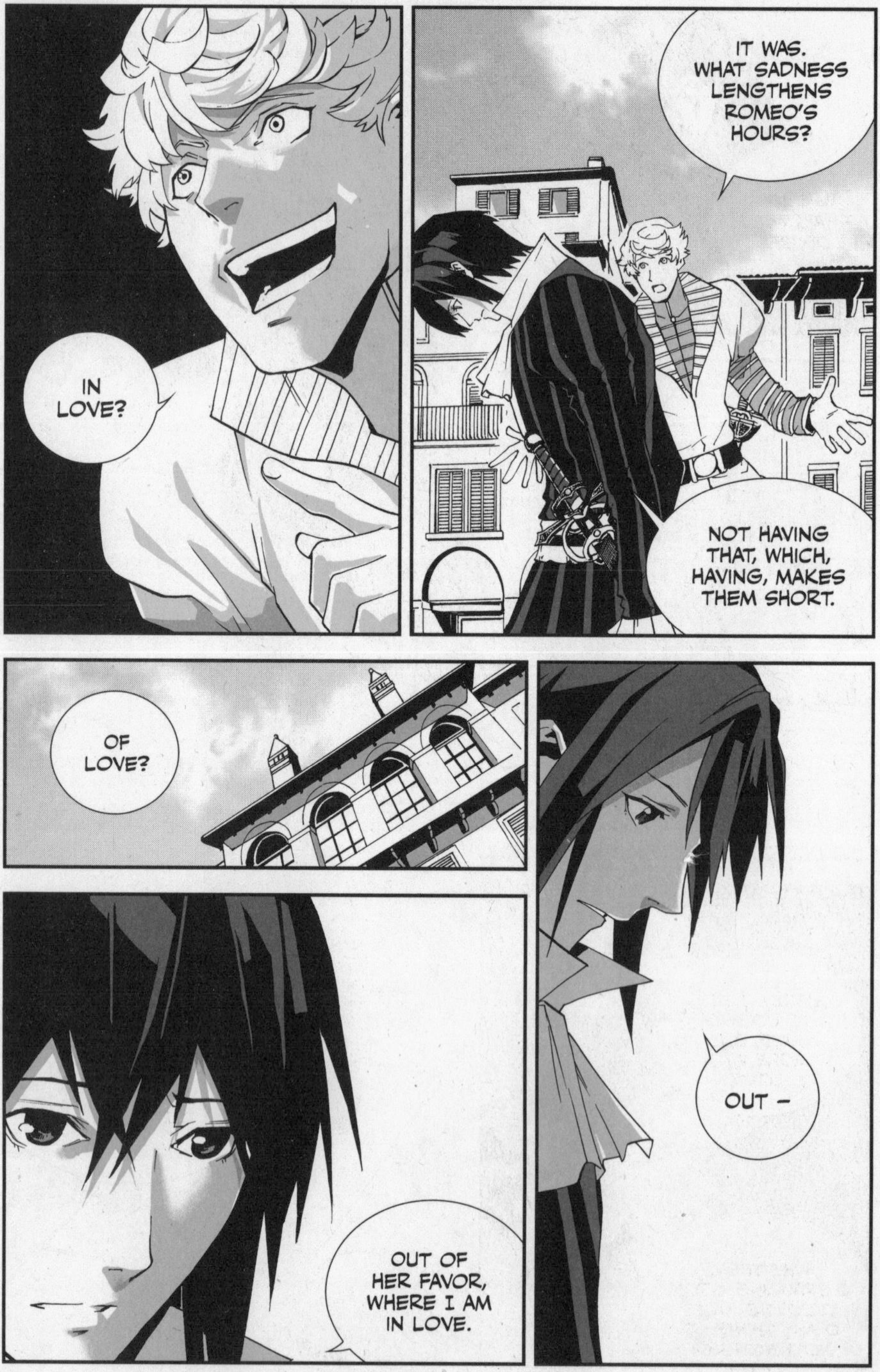
IT WAS. WHAT SADNESS LENGTHENS ROMEO'S HOURS?
NOT HAVING THAT, WHICH, HAVING, MAKES THEM SHORT.
IN LOVE?
OUT –
OF LOVE?
OUT OF HER FAVOR, WHERE I AM IN LOVE.

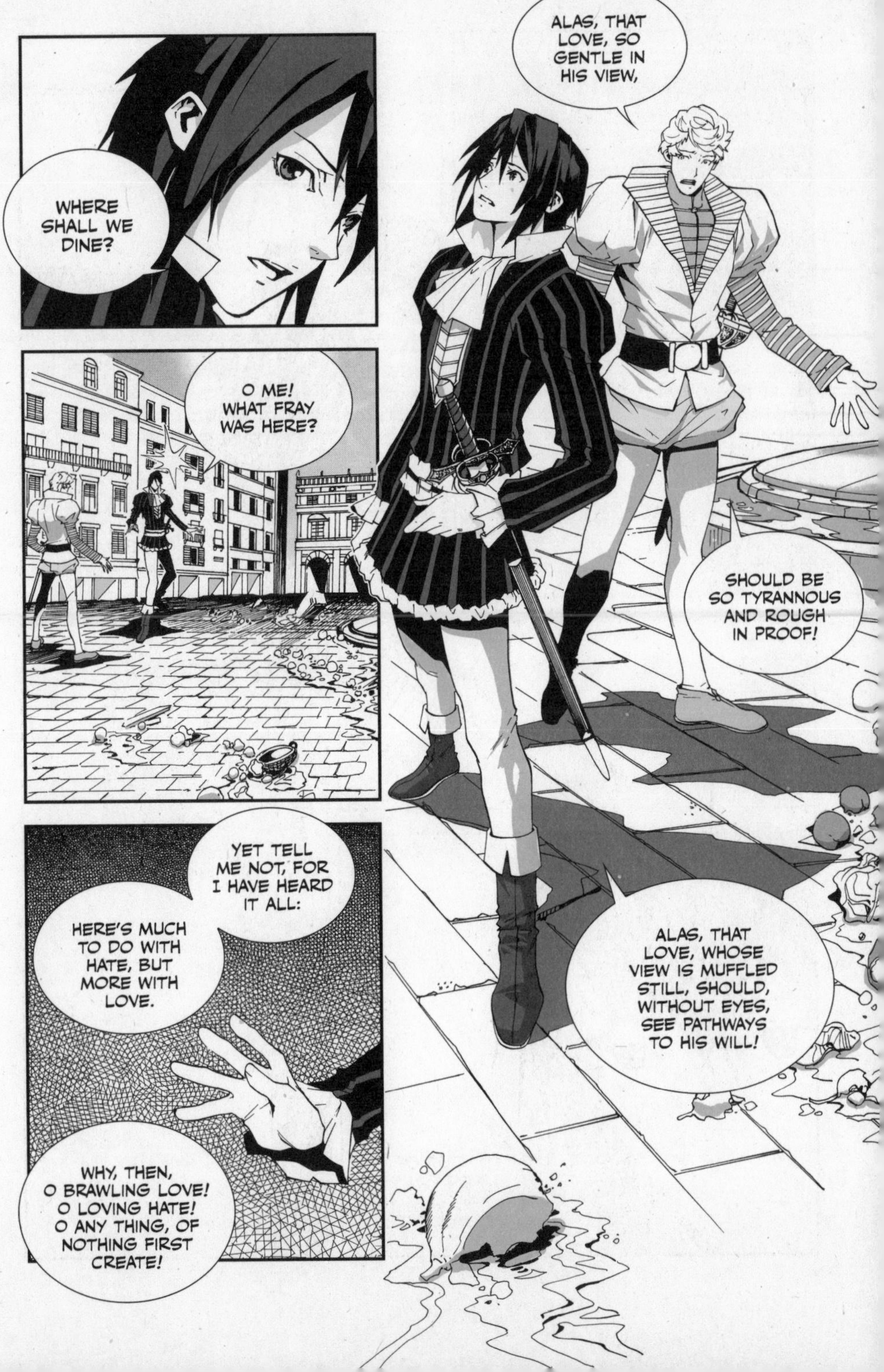
ALAS, THAT LOVE, SO GENTLE IN HIS VIEW,
SHOULD BE SO TYRANNOUS AND ROUGH IN PROOF!
ALAS, THAT LOVE, WHOSE VIEW IS MUFFLED STILL, SHOULD, WITHOUT EYES, SEE PATHWAYS TO HIS WILL!
WHERE SHALL WE DINE?
O ME! WHAT FRAY WAS HERE?
YET TELL ME NOT, FOR I HAVE HEARD IT ALL:
HERE'S MUCH TO DO WITH HATE, BUT MORE WITH LOVE.
WHY, THEN, O BRAWLING LOVE! O LOVING HATE! O ANY THING, OF NOTHING FIRST CREATE!

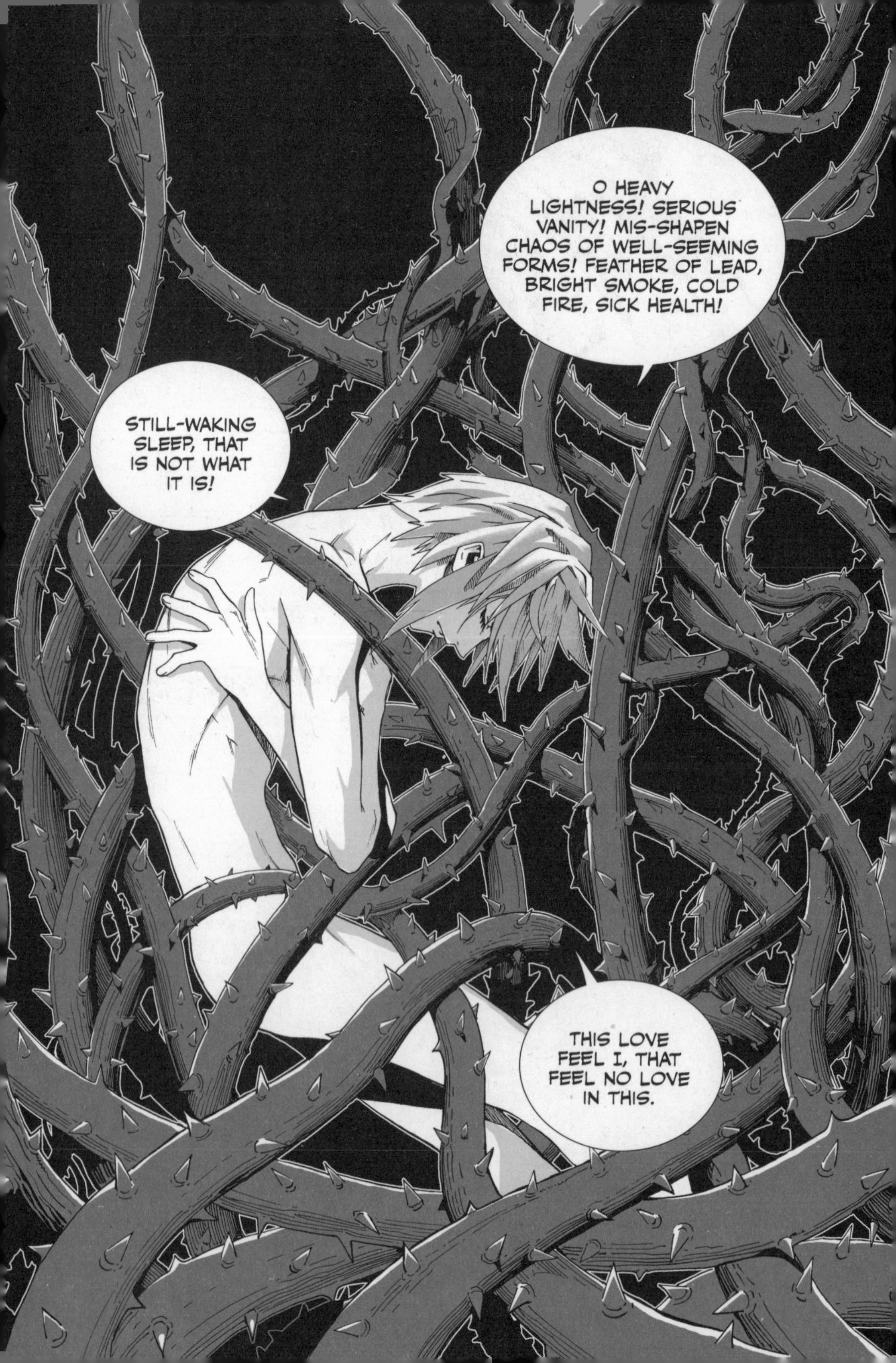
O HEAVY LIGHTNESS! SERIOUS VANITY! MIS-SHAPEN CHAOS OF WELL-SEEMING FORMS! FEATHER OF LEAD, BRIGHT SMOKE, COLD FIRE, SICK HEALTH!
STILL-WAKING SLEEP, THAT IS NOT WHAT IT IS!
THIS LOVE FEEL I, THAT FEEL NO LOVE IN THIS.

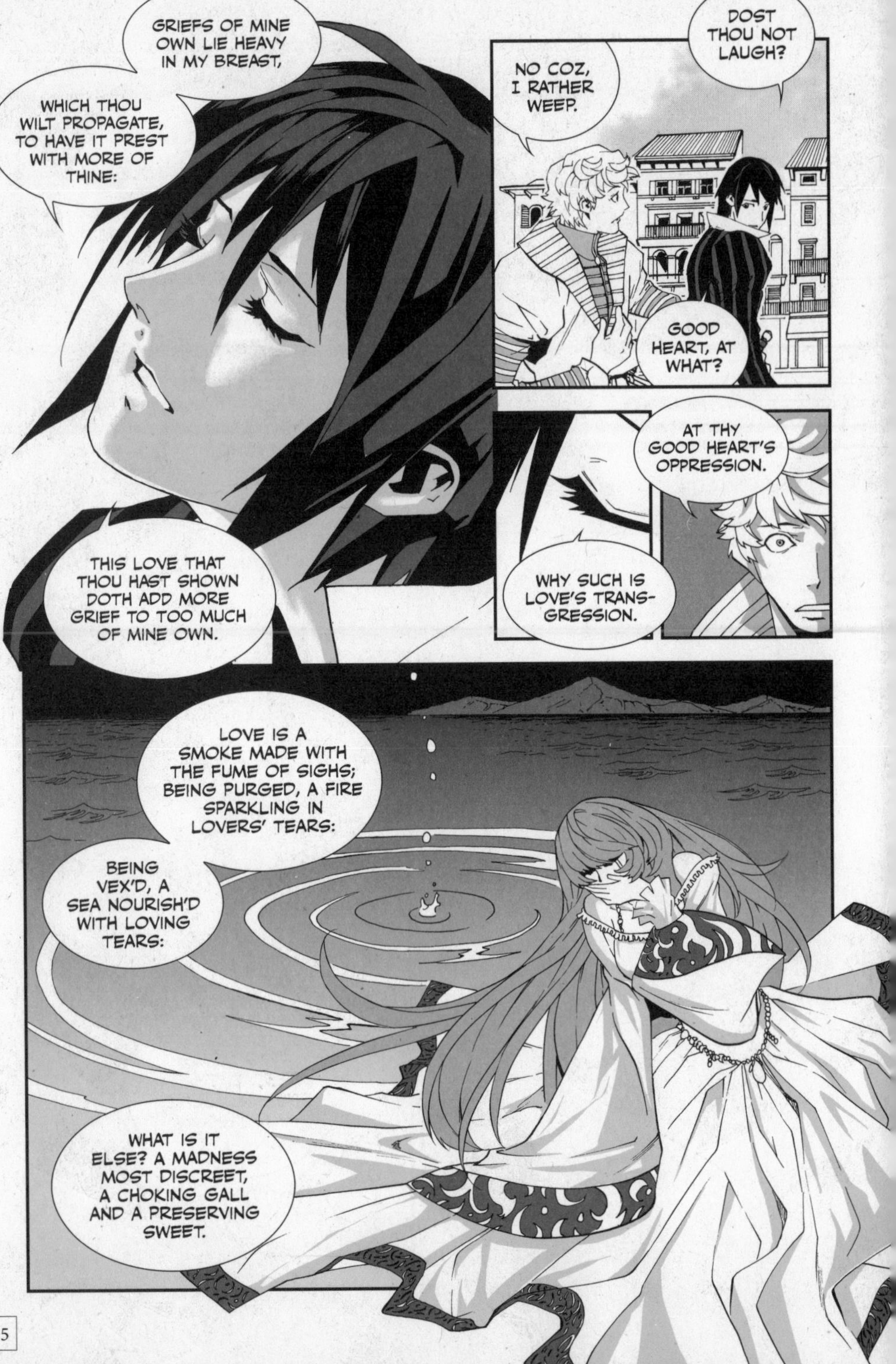
DOST THOU NOT LAUGH?
NO COZ, I RATHER WEEP.
GOOD HEART, AT WHAT?
AT THY GOOD HEART'S OPPRESSION.
WHY SUCH IS LOVE'S TRANS-GRESSION.
GRIEFS OF MINE OWN LIE HEAVY IN MY BREAST,
WHICH THOU WILT PROPAGATE, TO HAVE IT PREST WITH MORE OF THINE:
THIS LOVE THAT THOU HAST SHOWN DOTH ADD MORE GRIEF TO TOO MUCH OF MINE OWN.
LOVE IS A SMOKE MADE WITH THE FUME OF SIGHS; BEING PURGED, A FIRE SPARKLING IN LOVERS' TEARS:
BEING VEX'D, A SEA NOURISH'D WITH LOVING TEARS:
WHAT IS IT ELSE? A MADNESS MOST DISCREET, A CHOKING GALL AND A PRESERVING SWEET.

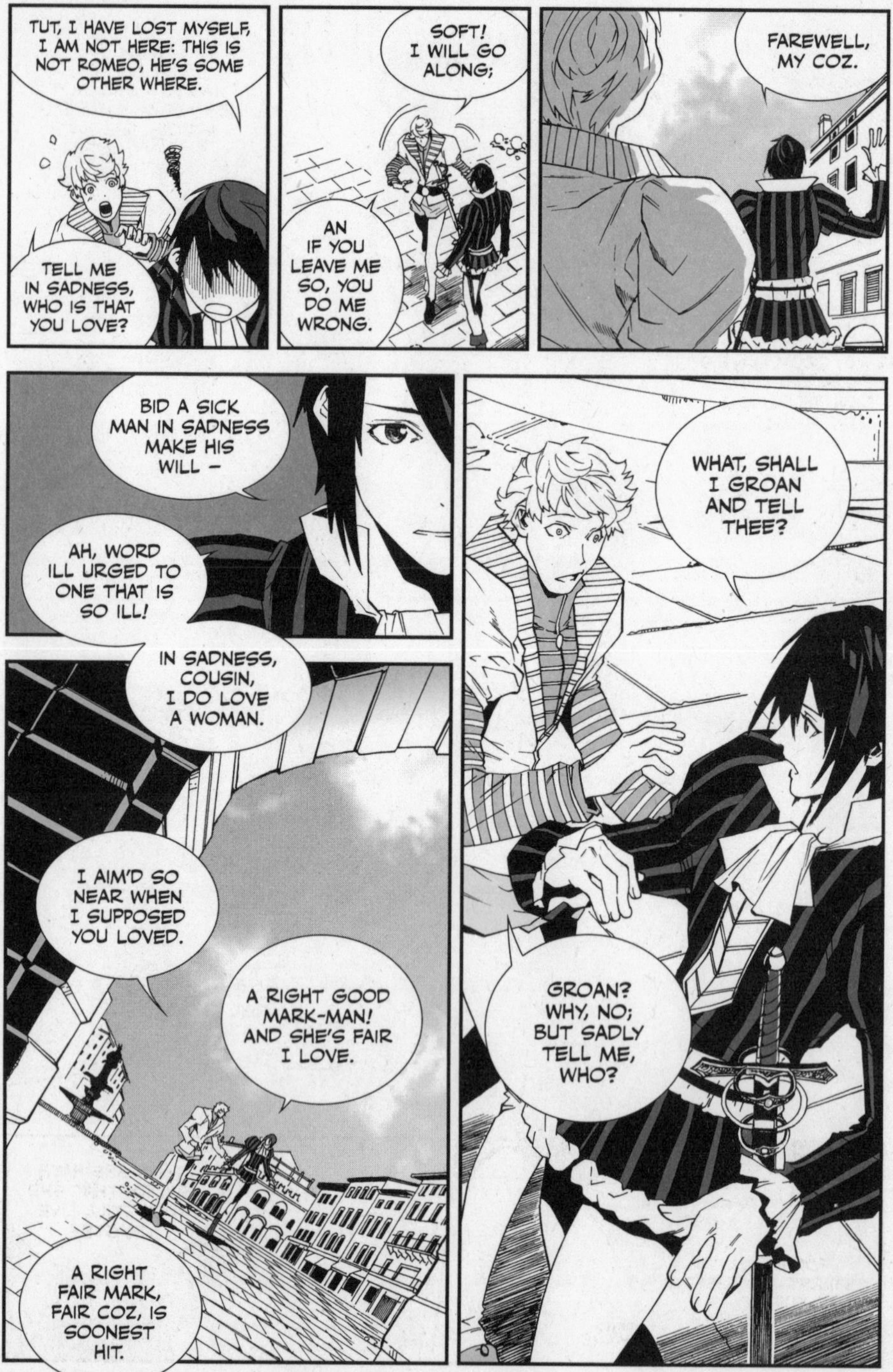

FAREWELL, MY COZ.
SOFT! I WILL GO ALONG;
AN IF YOU LEAVE ME SO, YOU DO ME WRONG.
TUT, I HAVE LOST MYSELF, I AM NOT HERE: THIS IS NOT ROMEO, HE'S SOME OTHER WHERE.
TELL ME IN SADNESS, WHO IS THAT YOU LOVE?
WHAT, SHALL I GROAN AND TELL THEE?
GROAN? WHY, NO; BUT SADLY TELL ME, WHO?
BID A SICK MAN IN SADNESS MAKE HIS WILL –
AH, WORD ILL URGED TO ONE THAT IS SO ILL!
IN SADNESS, COUSIN, I DO LOVE A WOMAN.
I AIM'D SO NEAR WHEN I SUPPOSED YOU LOVED.
A RIGHT GOOD MARK-MAN! AND SHE'S FAIR I LOVE.
A RIGHT FAIR MARK, FAIR COZ, IS SOONEST HIT.

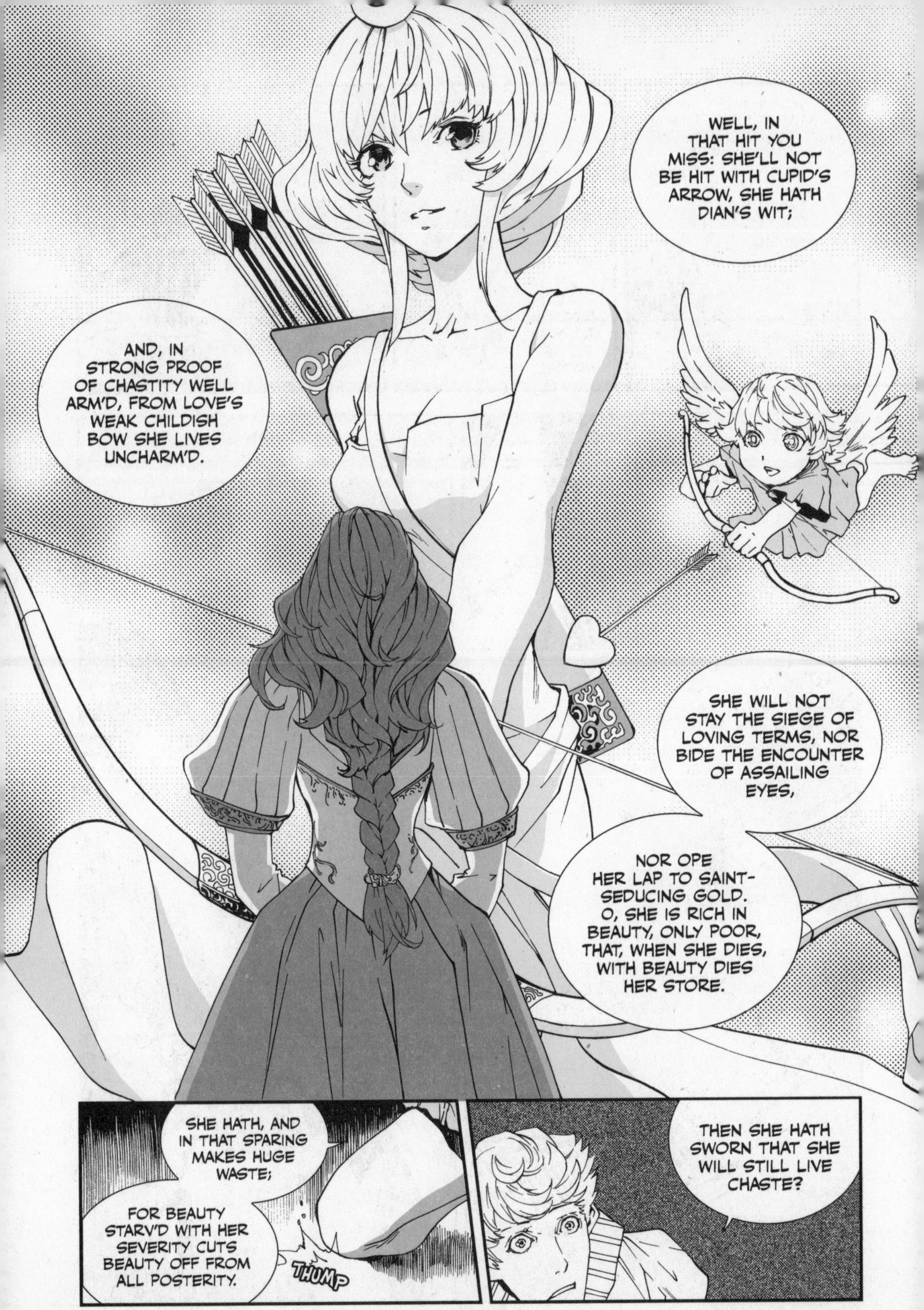
WELL, IN THAT HIT YOU MISS: SHE'LL NOT BE HIT WITH CUPID'S ARROW, SHE HATH DIAN'S WIT;
AND, IN STRONG PROOF OF CHASTITY WELL ARM'D, FROM LOVE'S WEAK CHILDISH BOW SHE LIVES UNCHARM'D.
SHE WILL NOT STAY THE SIEGE OF LOVING TERMS, NOR BIDE THE ENCOUNTER OF ASSAILING EYES,
NOR OPE HER LAP TO SAINT-SEDUCING GOLD. O, SHE IS RICH IN BEAUTY, ONLY POOR, THAT, WHEN SHE DIES, WITH BEAUTY DIES HER STORE.
THEN SHE HATH SWORN THAT SHE WILL STILL LIVE CHASTE?
SHE HATH, AND IN THAT SPARING MAKES HUGE WASTE;
FOR BEAUTY STARV'D WITH HER SEVERITY CUTS BEAUTY OFF FROM ALL POSTERITY.
THUMP

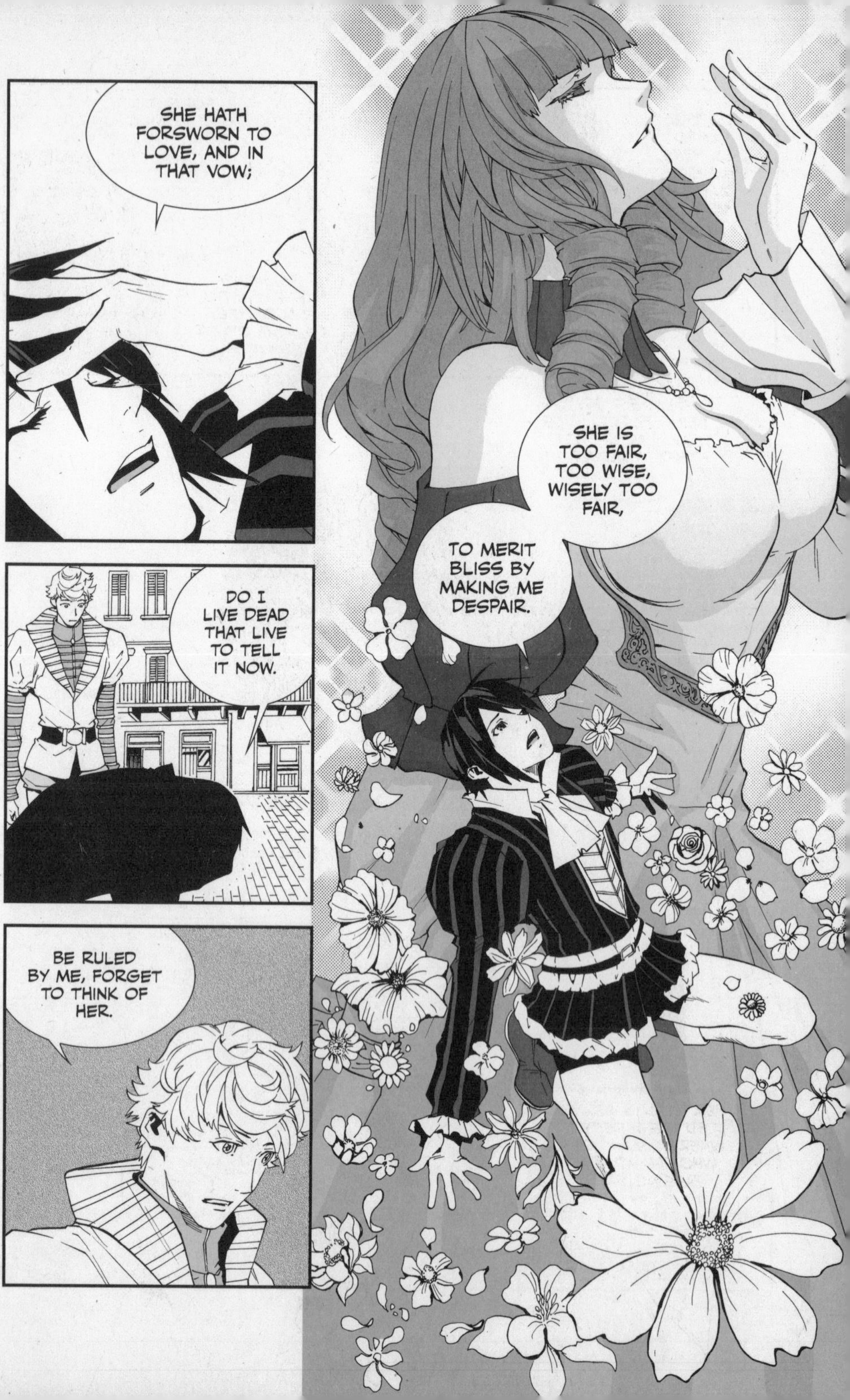
SHE IS TOO FAIR, TOO WISE, WISELY TOO FAIR,
TO MERIT BLISS BY MAKING ME DESPAIR.
SHE HATH FORSWORN TO LOVE, AND IN THAT VOW;
DO I LIVE DEAD THAT LIVE TO TELL IT NOW.
BE RULED BY ME, FORGET TO THINK OF HER.

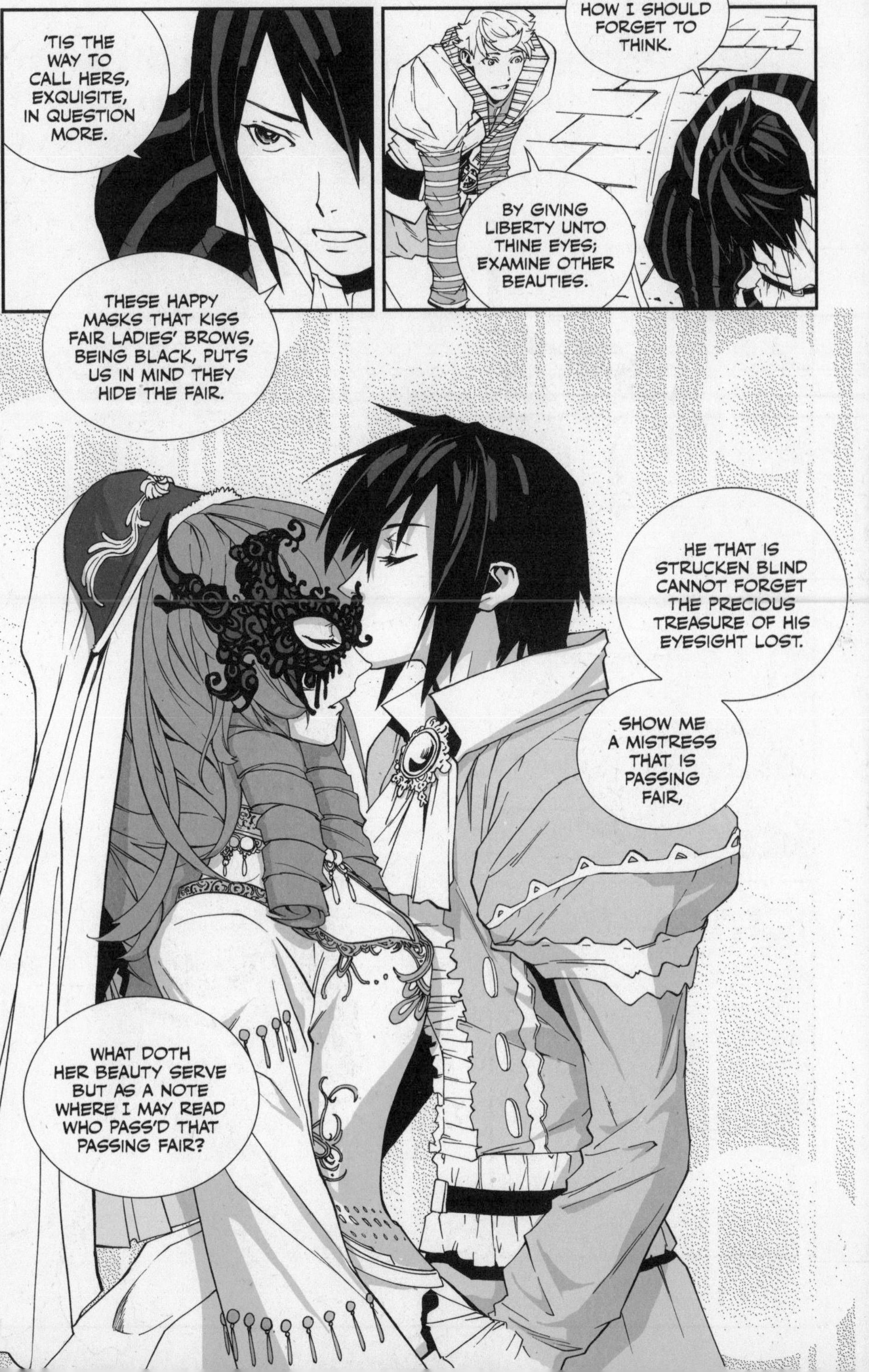
O, TEACH ME HOW I SHOULD FORGET TO THINK.
BY GIVING LIBERTY UNTO THINE EYES; EXAMINE OTHER BEAUTIES.
'TIS THE WAY TO CALL HERS, EXQUISITE, IN QUESTION MORE.
THESE HAPPY MASKS THAT KISS FAIR LADIES' BROWS, BEING BLACK, PUTS US IN MIND THEY HIDE THE FAIR.
HE THAT IS STRUCKEN BLIND CANNOT FORGET THE PRECIOUS TREASURE OF HIS EYESIGHT LOST.
SHOW ME A MISTRESS THAT IS PASSING FAIR,
WHAT DOTH HER BEAUTY SERVE BUT AS A NOTE WHERE I MAY READ WHO PASS'D THAT PASSING FAIR?

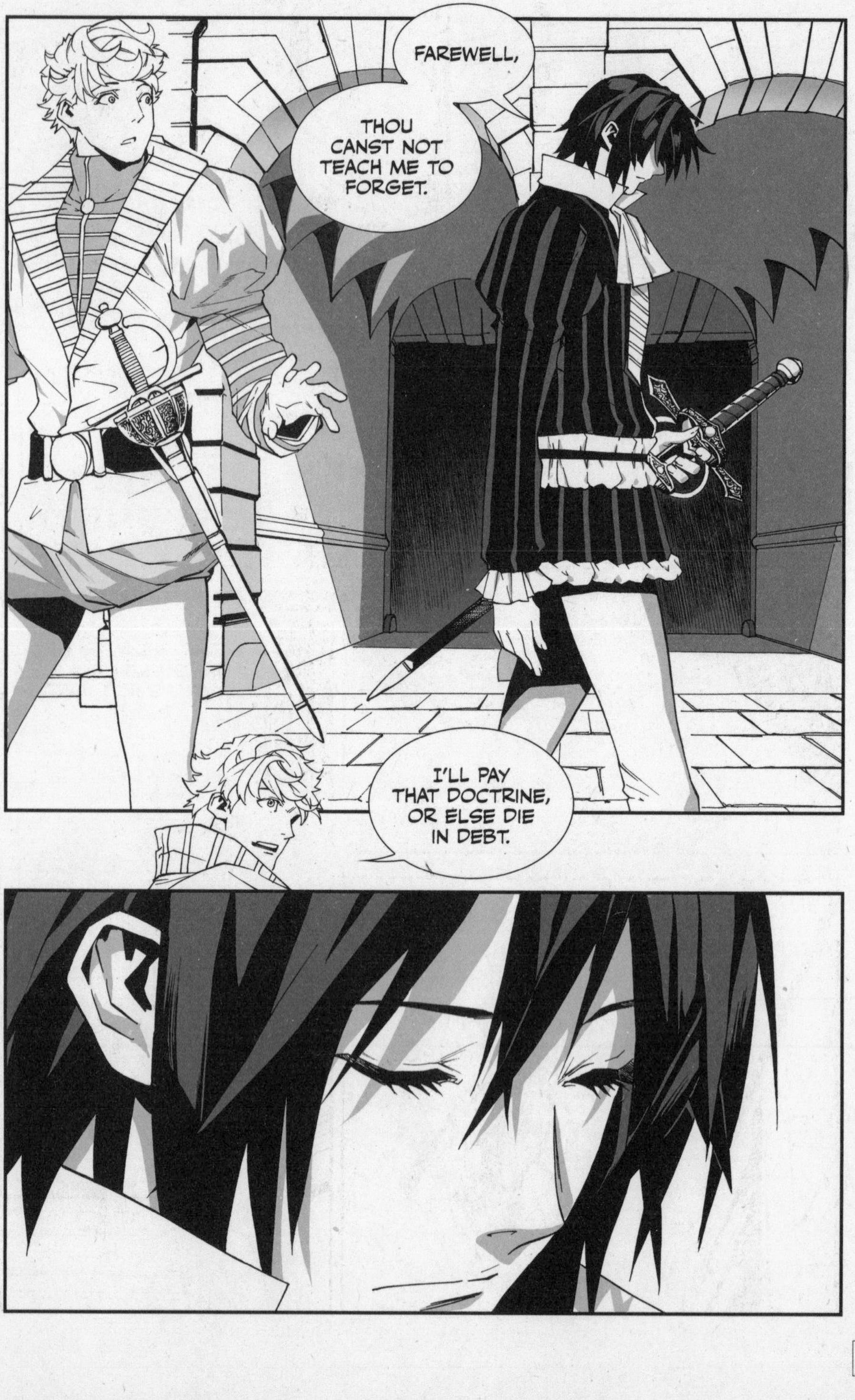
FAREWELL,
THOU CANST NOT TEACH ME TO FORGET.
I'LL PAY THAT DOCTRINE, OR ELSE DIE IN DEBT.

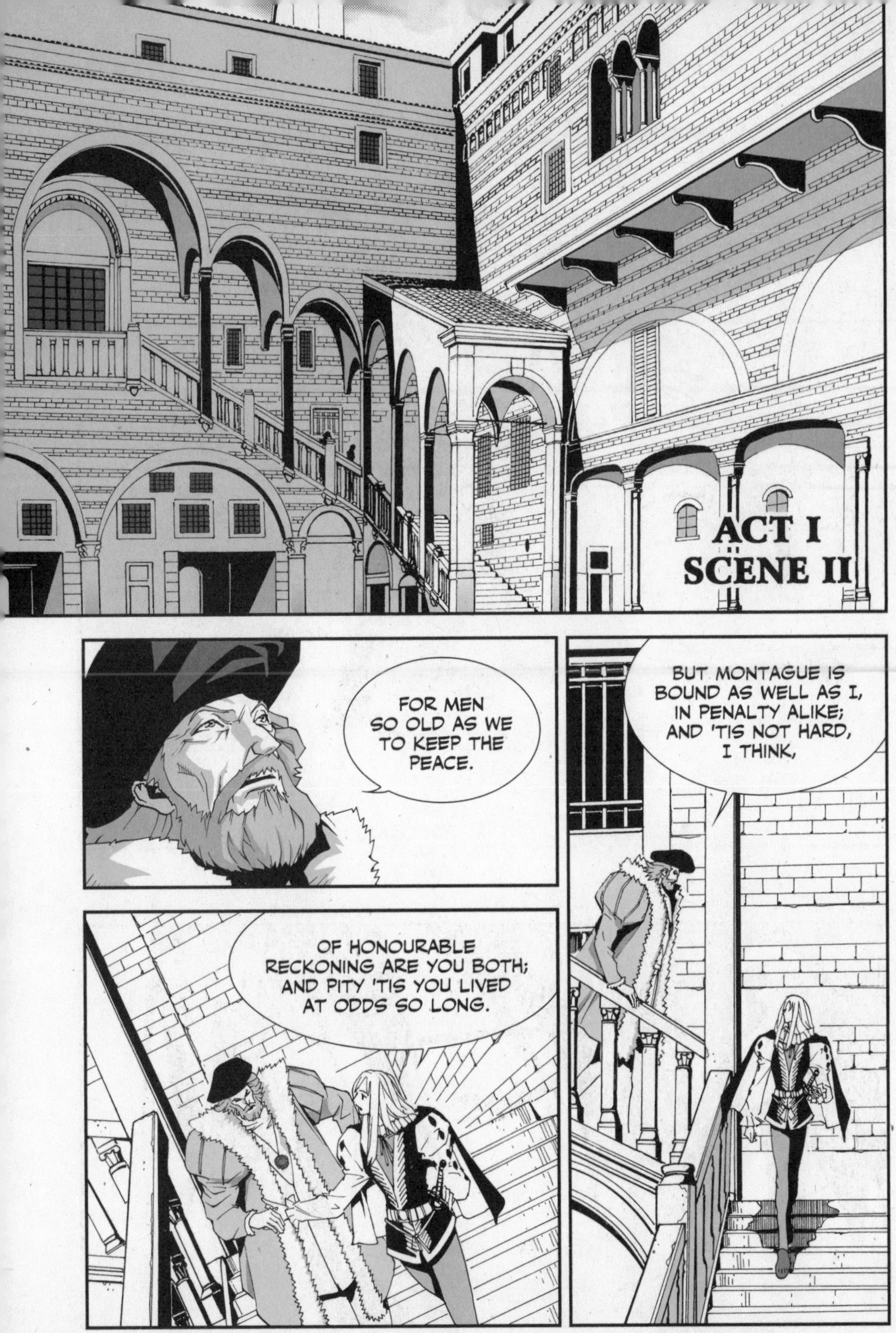
ACT I
SCENE II
BUT MONTAGUE IS BOUND AS WELL AS I, IN PENALTY ALIKE; AND 'TIS NOT HARD, I THINK,
FOR MEN SO OLD AS WE TO KEEP THE PEACE.
OF HONOURABLE RECKONING ARE YOU BOTH; AND PITY 'TIS YOU LIVED AT ODDS SO LONG.

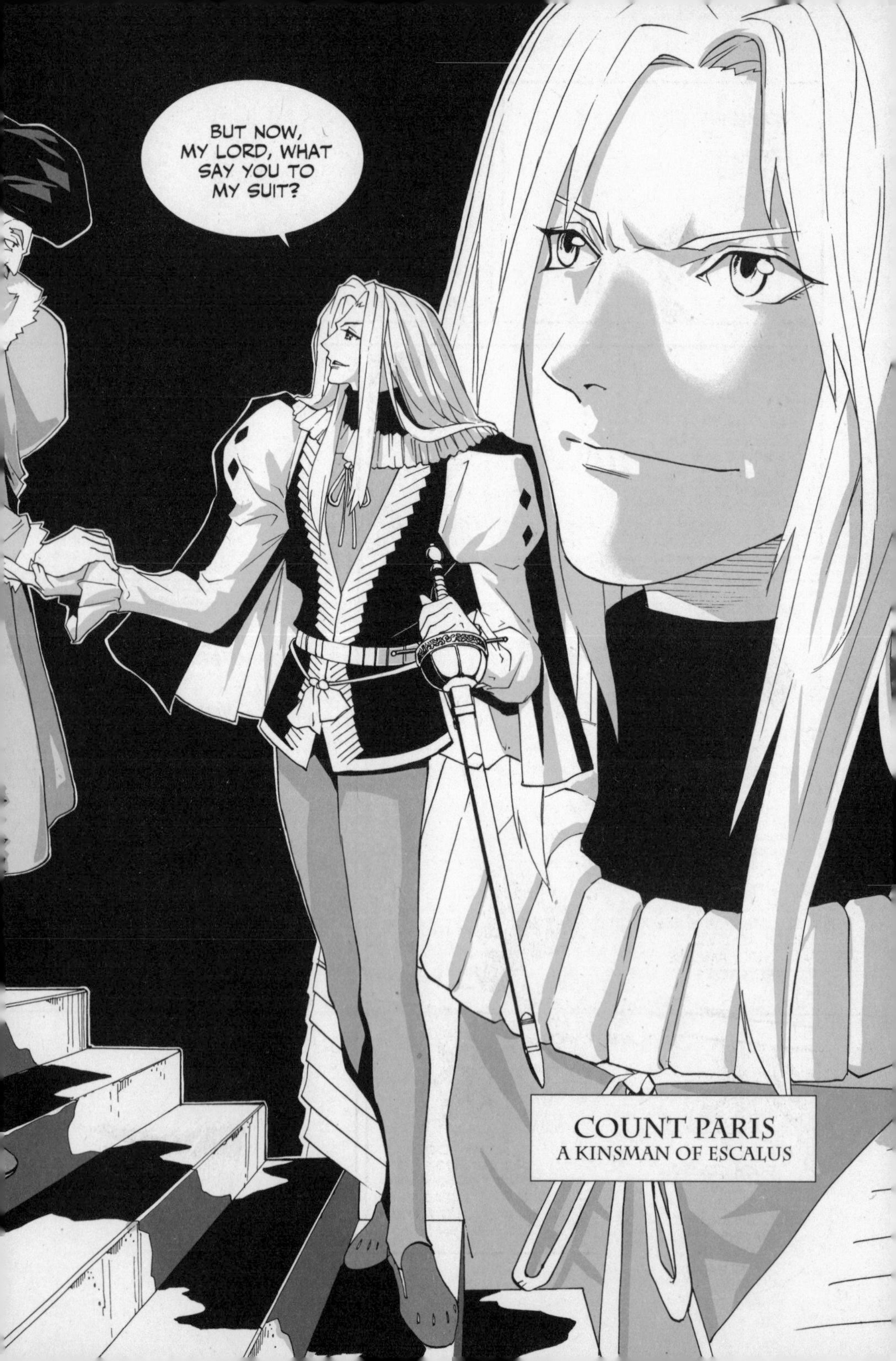
BUT NOW, MY LORD, WHAT SAY YOU TO MY SUIT?
COUNT PARIS
A KINSMAN OF ESCALUS

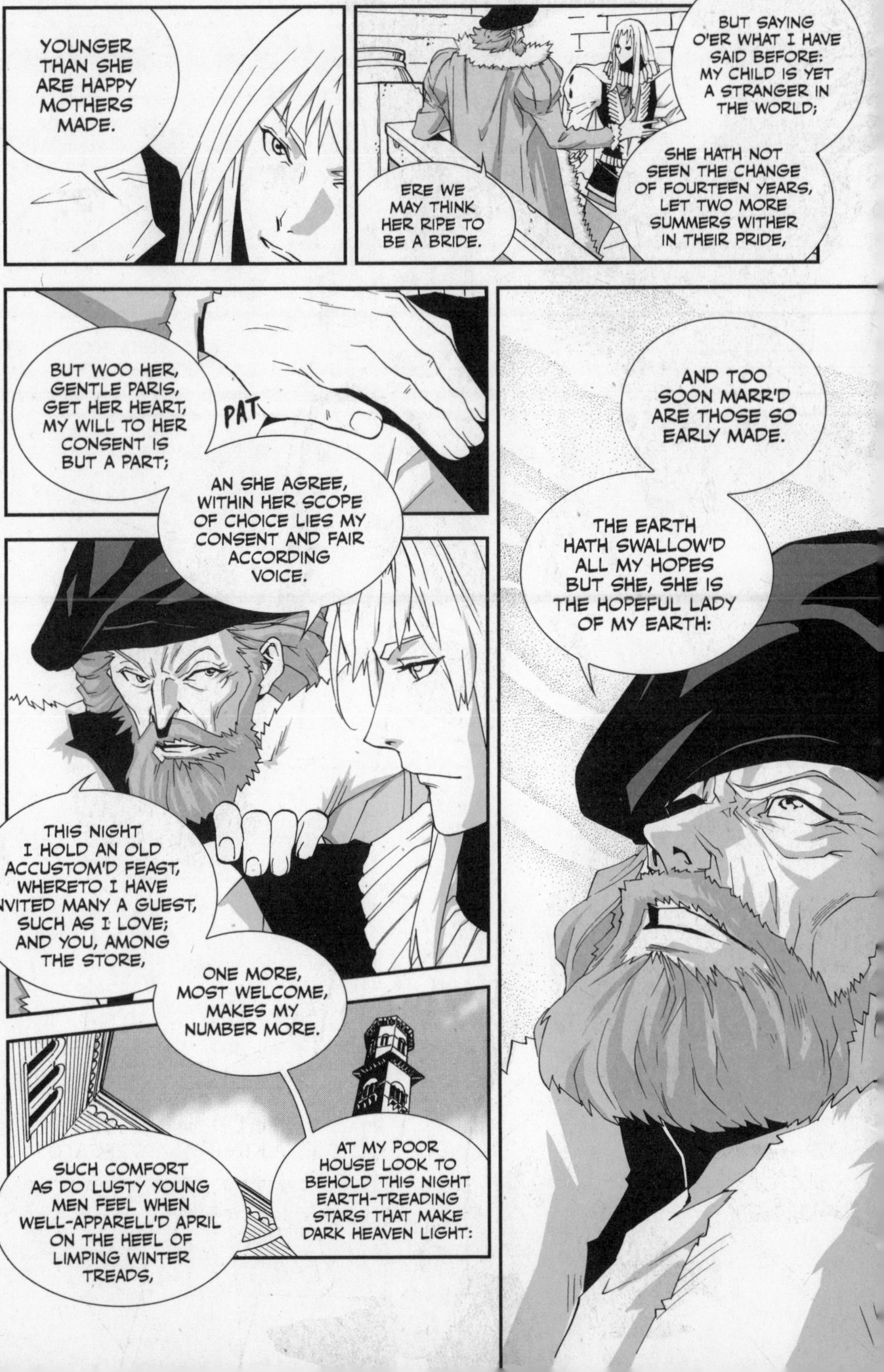

BUT SAYING O'ER WHAT I HAVE SAID BEFORE: MY CHILD IS YET A STRANGER IN THE WORLD;
SHE HATH NOT SEEN THE CHANGE OF FOURTEEN YEARS, LET TWO MORE SUMMERS WITHER IN THEIR PRIDE,
ERE WE MAY THINK HER RIPE TO BE A BRIDE.
YOUNGER THAN SHE ARE HAPPY MOTHERS MADE.
AND TOO SOON MARR'D ARE THOSE SO EARLY MADE.
THE EARTH HATH SWALLOW'D ALL MY HOPES BUT SHE, SHE IS THE HOPEFUL LADY OF MY EARTH:
BUT WOO HER, GENTLE PARIS, GET HER HEART, MY WILL TO HER CONSENT IS BUT A PART;
PAT
AN SHE AGREE, WITHIN HER SCOPE OF CHOICE LIES MY CONSENT AND FAIR ACCORDING VOICE.
THIS NIGHT I HOLD AN OLD ACCUSTOM'D FEAST, WHERETO I HAVE INVITED MANY A GUEST, SUCH AS I LOVE; AND YOU, AMONG THE STORE,
ONE MORE, MOST WELCOME, MAKES MY NUMBER MORE.
AT MY POOR HOUSE LOOK TO BEHOLD THIS NIGHT EARTH-TREADING STARS THAT MAKE DARK HEAVEN LIGHT:
SUCH COMFORT AS DO LUSTY YOUNG MEN FEEL WHEN WELL-APPARELL'D APRIL ON THE HEEL OF LIMPING WINTER TREADS,

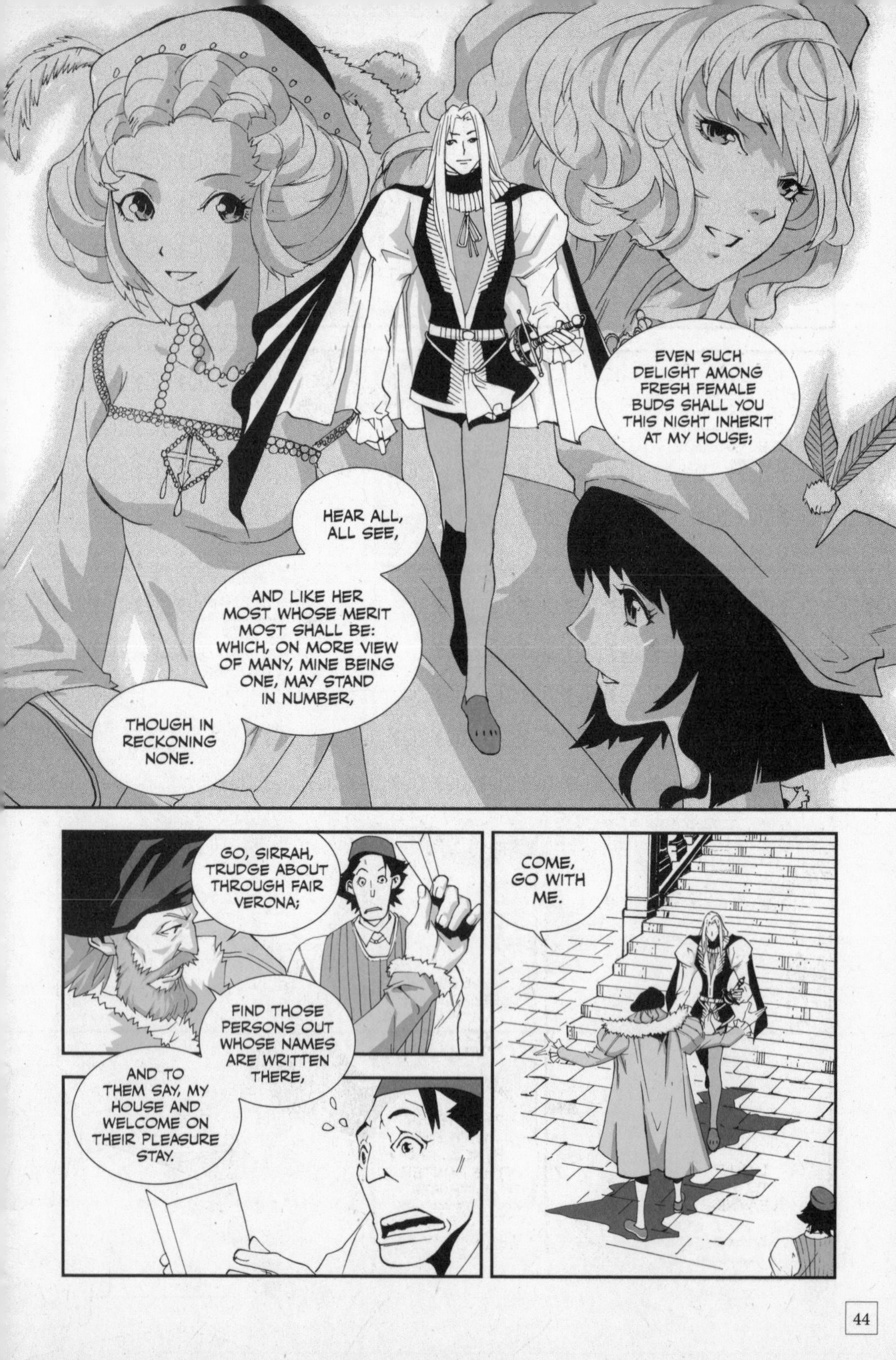
EVEN SUCH DELIGHT AMONG FRESH FEMALE BUDS SHALL YOU THIS NIGHT INHERIT AT MY HOUSE;
HEAR ALL, ALL SEE,
AND LIKE HER MOST WHOSE MERIT MOST SHALL BE: WHICH, ON MORE VIEW OF MANY, MINE BEING ONE, MAY STAND IN NUMBER,
THOUGH IN RECKONING NONE.
COME, GO WITH ME.
GO, SIRRAH, TRUDGE ABOUT THROUGH FAIR VERONA;
FIND THOSE PERSONS OUT WHOSE NAMES ARE WRITTEN THERE,
AND TO THEM SAY, MY HOUSE AND WELCOME ON THEIR PLEASURE STAY.

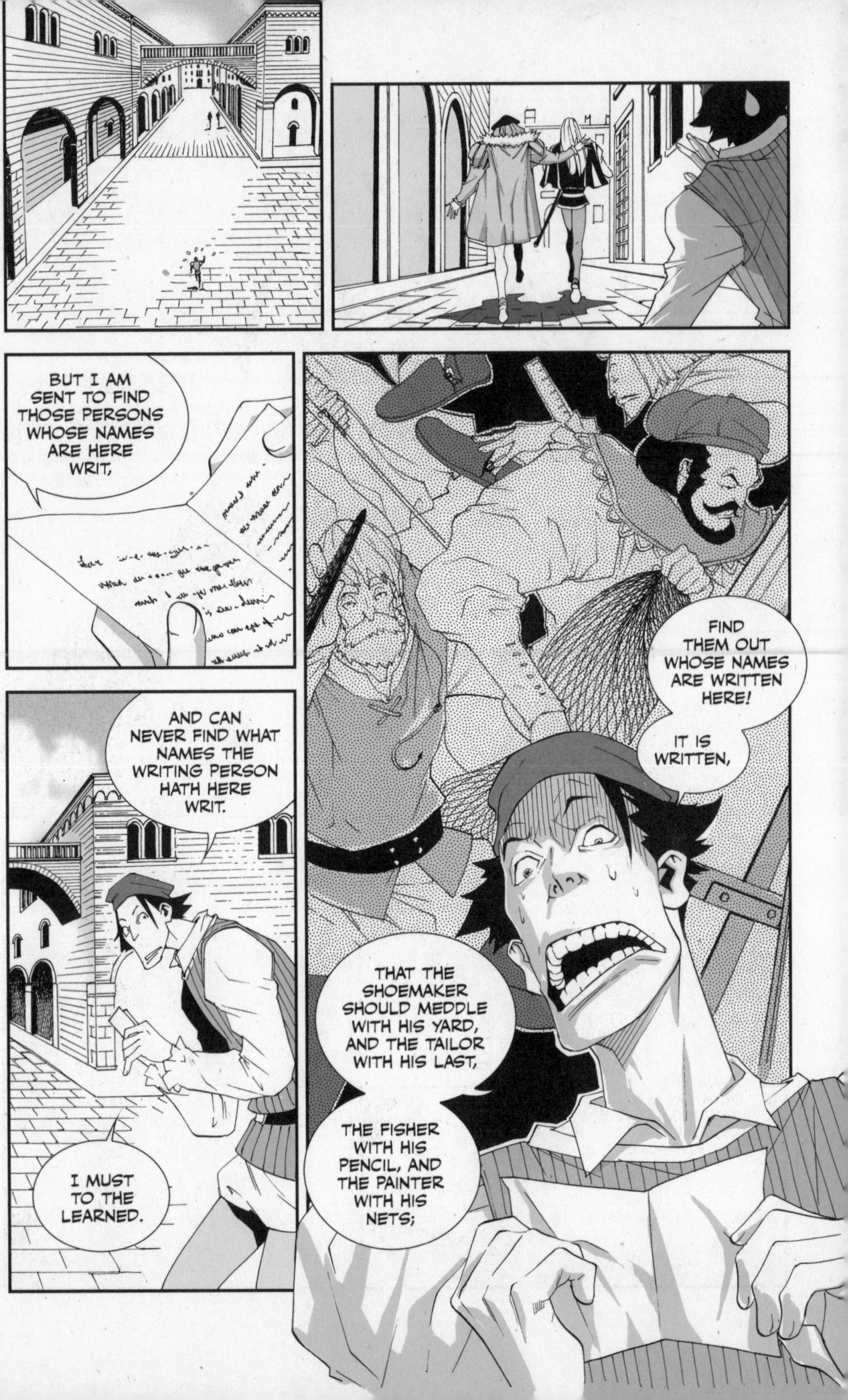
FIND THEM OUT WHOSE NAMES ARE WRITTEN HERE!
IT IS WRITTEN,
THAT THE SHOEMAKER SHOULD MEDDLE WITH HIS YARD, AND THE TAILOR WITH HIS LAST,
THE FISHER WITH HIS PENCIL, AND THE PAINTER WITH HIS NETS;
BUT I AM SENT TO FIND THOSE PERSONS WHOSE NAMES ARE HERE WRIT,
AND CAN NEVER FIND WHAT NAMES THE WRITING PERSON HATH HERE WRIT.
I MUST TO THE LEARNED.

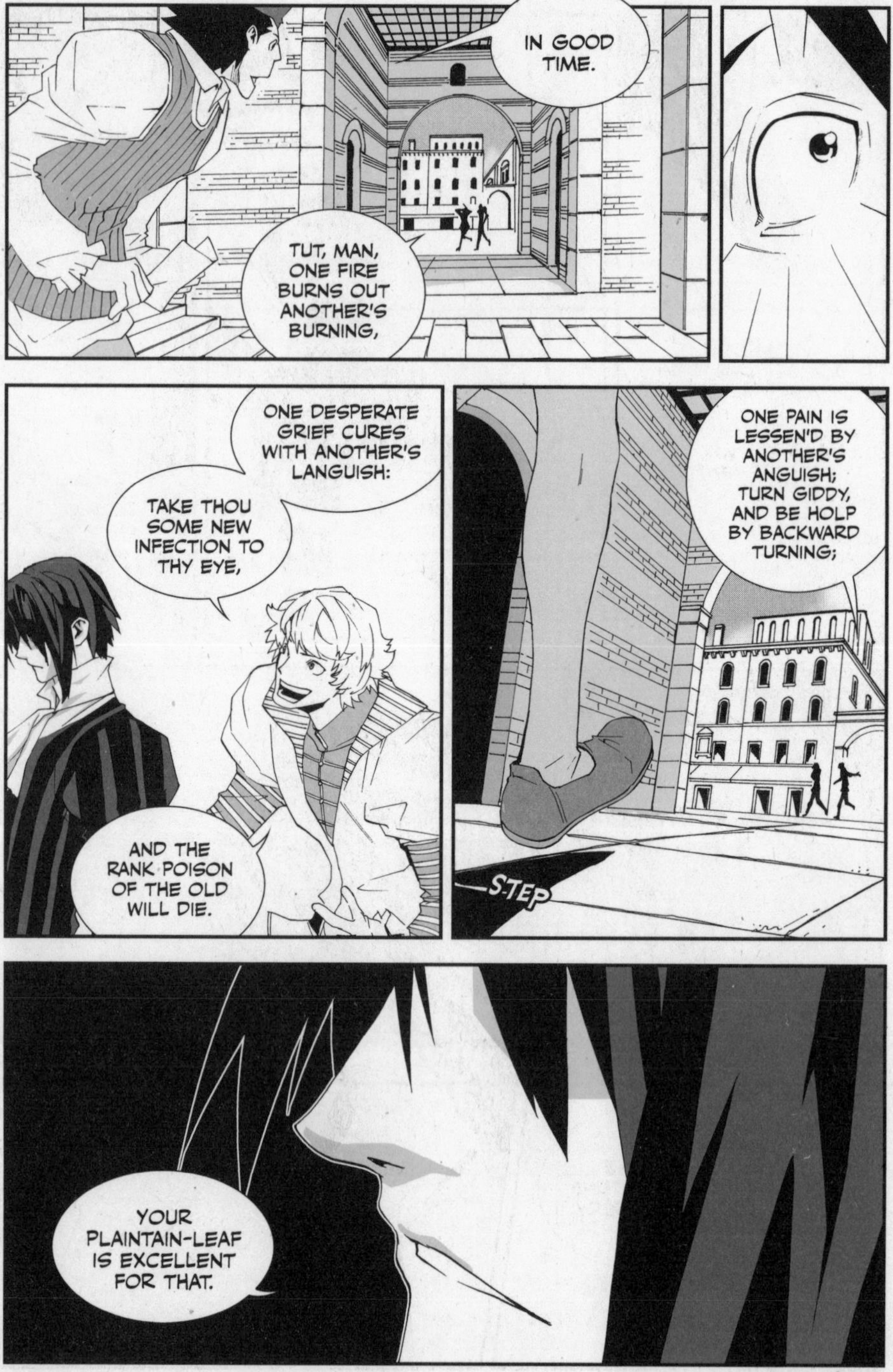
IN GOOD TIME.
TUT, MAN, ONE FIRE BURNS OUT ANOTHER'S BURNING,
ONE PAIN IS LESSEN'D BY ANOTHER'S ANGUISH; TURN GIDDY, AND BE HOLP BY BACKWARD TURNING;
S-TEP
ONE DESPERATE GRIEF CURES WITH ANOTHER'S LANGUISH:
TAKE THOU SOME NEW INFECTION TO THY EYE,
AND THE RANK POISON OF THE OLD WILL DIE.
YOUR PLAINTAIN-LEAF IS EXCELLENT FOR THAT.

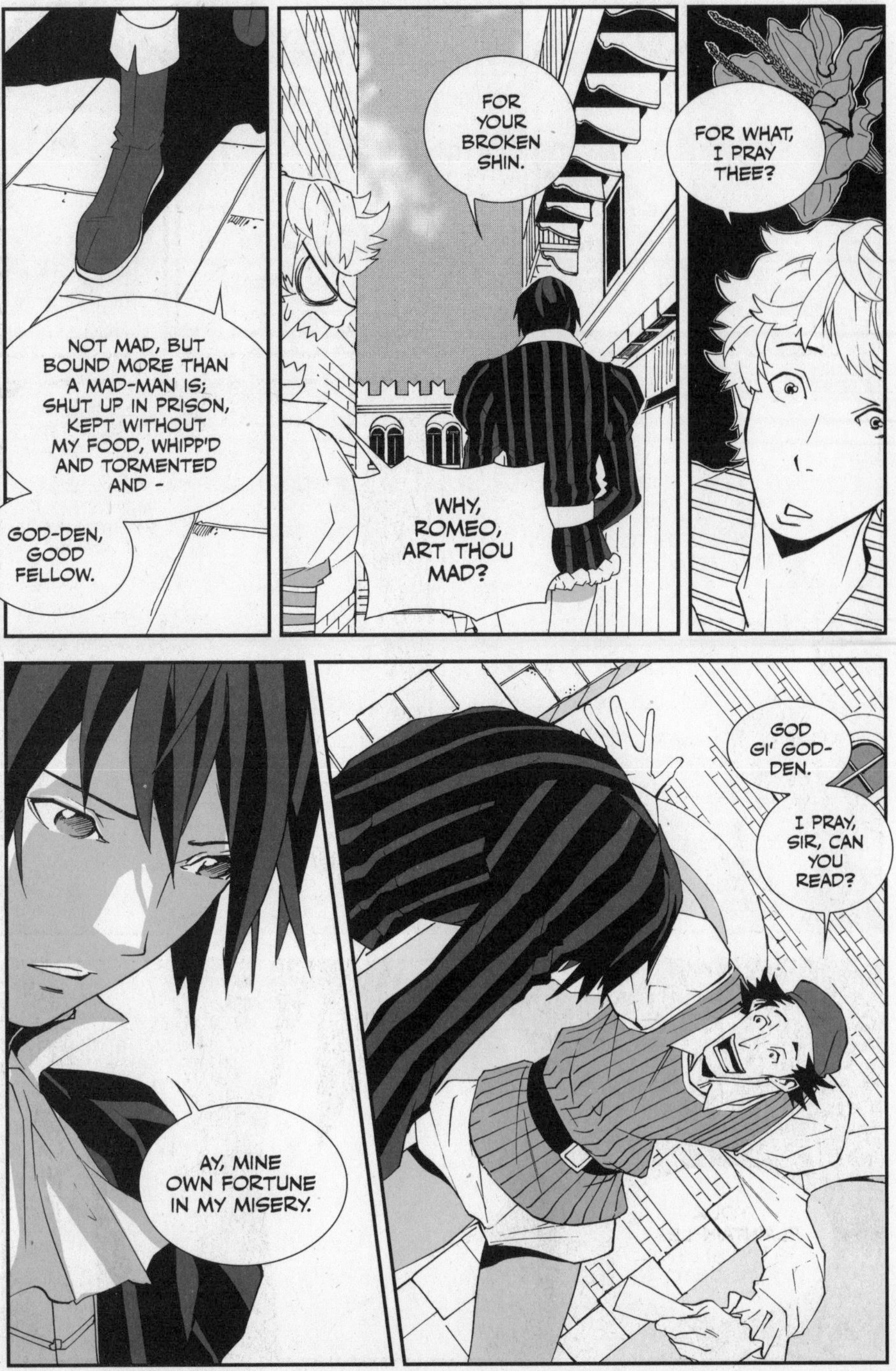
FOR WHAT, I PRAY THEE?
FOR YOUR BROKEN SHIN.
WHY, ROMEO, ART THOU MAD?
NOT MAD, BUT BOUND MORE THAN A MAD-MAN IS; SHUT UP IN PRISON, KEPT WITHOUT MY FOOD, WHIPP'D AND TORMENTED AND -
GOD-DEN, GOOD FELLOW.
GOD GI' GOD-DEN.
I PRAY, SIR, CAN YOU READ?
AY, MINE OWN FORTUNE IN MY MISERY.

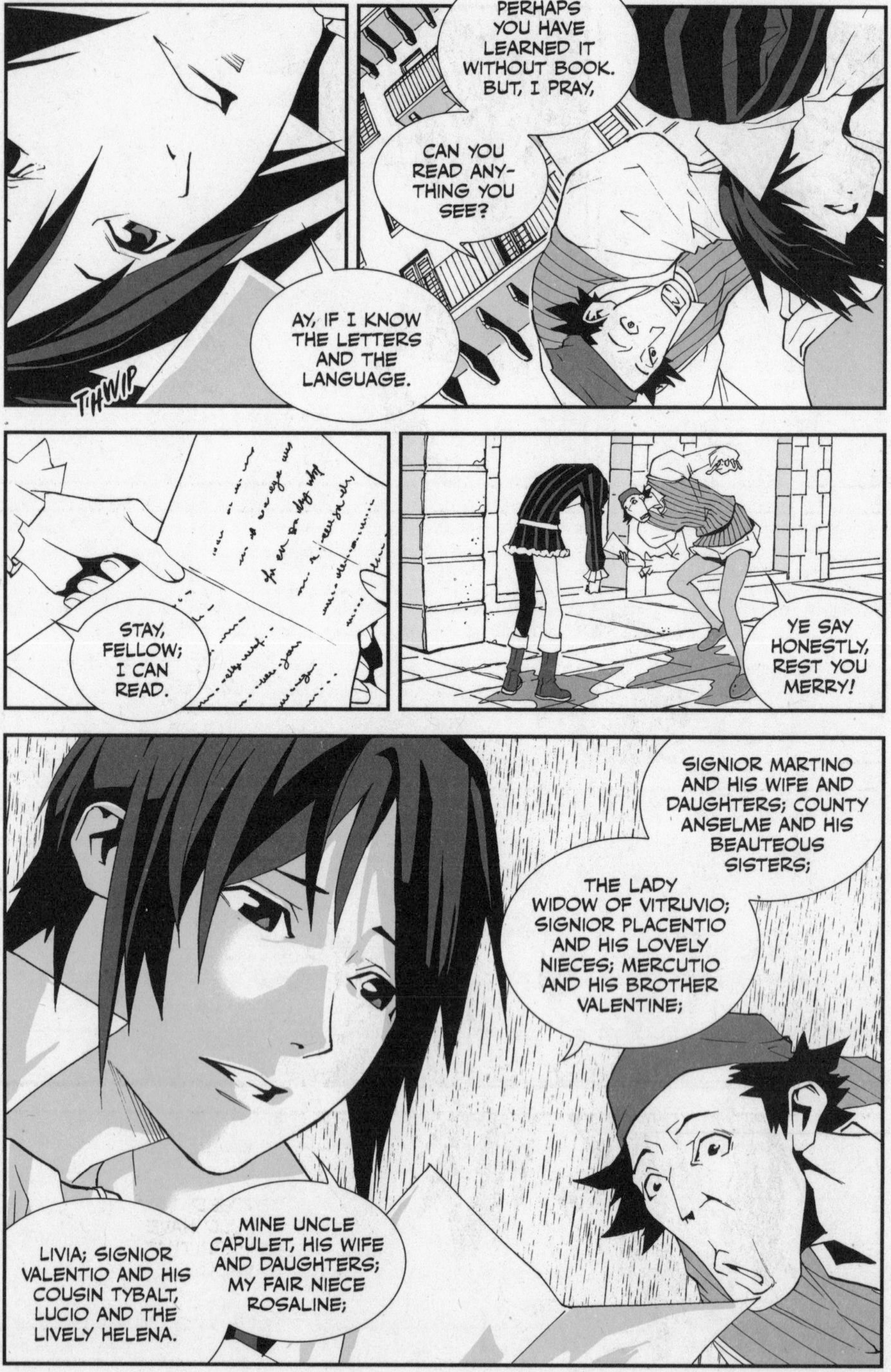
PERHAPS YOU HAVE LEARNED IT WITHOUT BOOK. BUT, I PRAY,
CAN YOU READ ANY-THING YOU SEE?
AY, IF I KNOW THE LETTERS AND THE LANGUAGE.
THWIP
YE SAY HONESTLY, REST YOU MERRY!
STAY, FELLOW; I CAN READ.
SIGNIOR MARTINO AND HIS WIFE AND DAUGHTERS; COUNTY ANSELME AND HIS BEAUTEOUS SISTERS;
THE LADY WIDOW OF VITRUVIO; SIGNIOR PLACENTIO AND HIS LOVELY NIECES; MERCUTIO AND HIS BROTHER VALENTINE;
MINE UNCLE CAPULET, HIS WIFE AND DAUGHTERS; MY FAIR NIECE ROSALINE;
LIVIA; SIGNIOR VALENTIO AND HIS COUSIN TYBALT, LUCIO AND THE LIVELY HELENA.

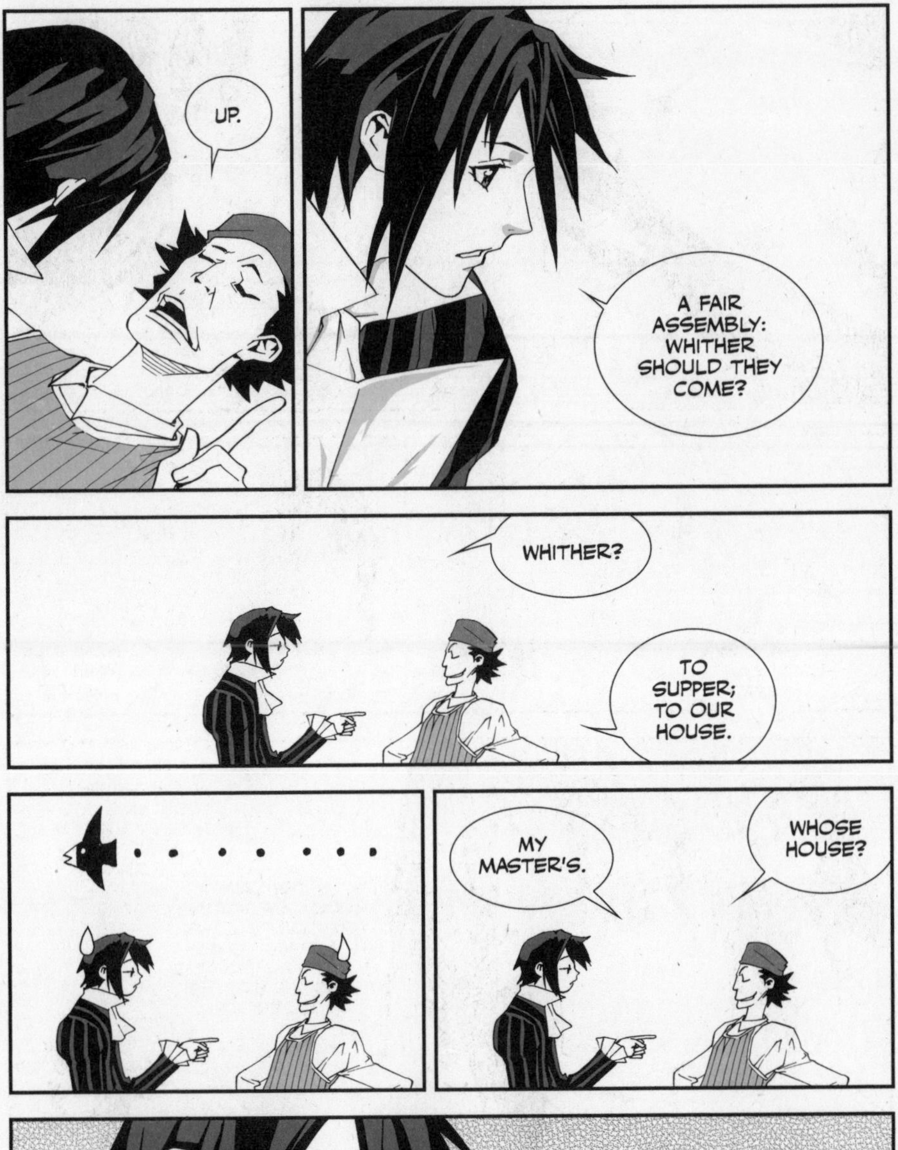
A FAIR ASSEMBLY: WHITHER SHOULD THEY COME?
UP.
WHITHER?
TO SUPPER; TO OUR HOUSE.
WHOSE HOUSE?
MY MASTER'S.
. . . .
INDEED, I SHOULD HAVE ASK'D YOU THAT BEFORE.

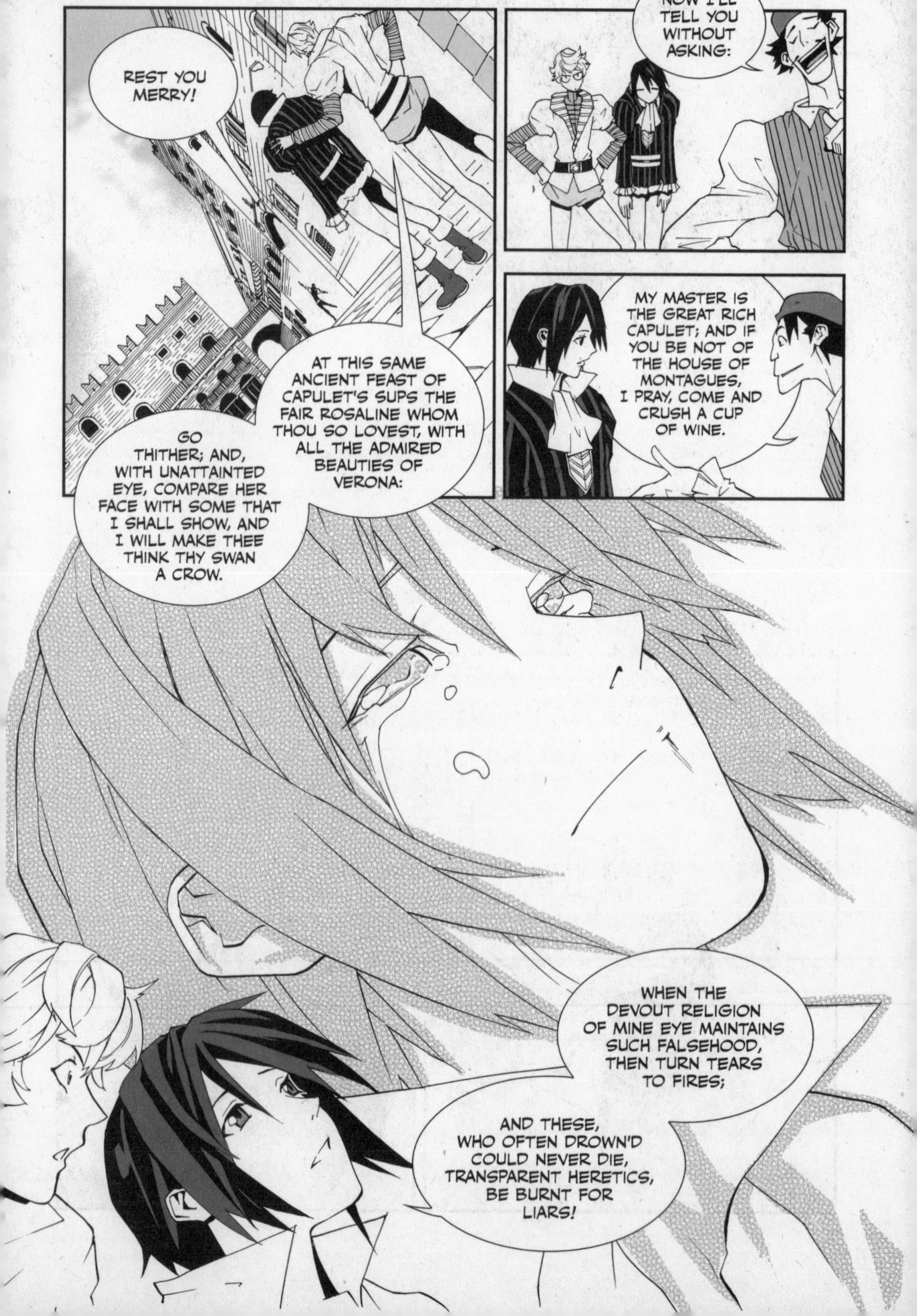
NOW I'LL TELL YOU WITHOUT ASKING:
MY MASTER IS THE GREAT RICH CAPULET; AND IF YOU BE NOT OF THE HOUSE OF MONTAGUES, I PRAY, COME AND CRUSH A CUP OF WINE.
REST YOU MERRY!
AT THIS SAME ANCIENT FEAST OF CAPULET'S SUPS THE FAIR ROSALINE WHOM THOU SO LOVEST, WITH ALL THE ADMIRED BEAUTIES OF VERONA:
GO THITHER; AND, WITH UNATTAINTED EYE, COMPARE HER FACE WITH SOME THAT I SHALL SHOW, AND I WILL MAKE THEE THINK THY SWAN A CROW.
WHEN THE DEVOUT RELIGION OF MINE EYE MAINTAINS SUCH FALSEHOOD, THEN TURN TEARS TO FIRES;
AND THESE, WHO OFTEN DROWN'D COULD NEVER DIE, TRANSPARENT HERETICS, BE BURNT FOR LIARS!

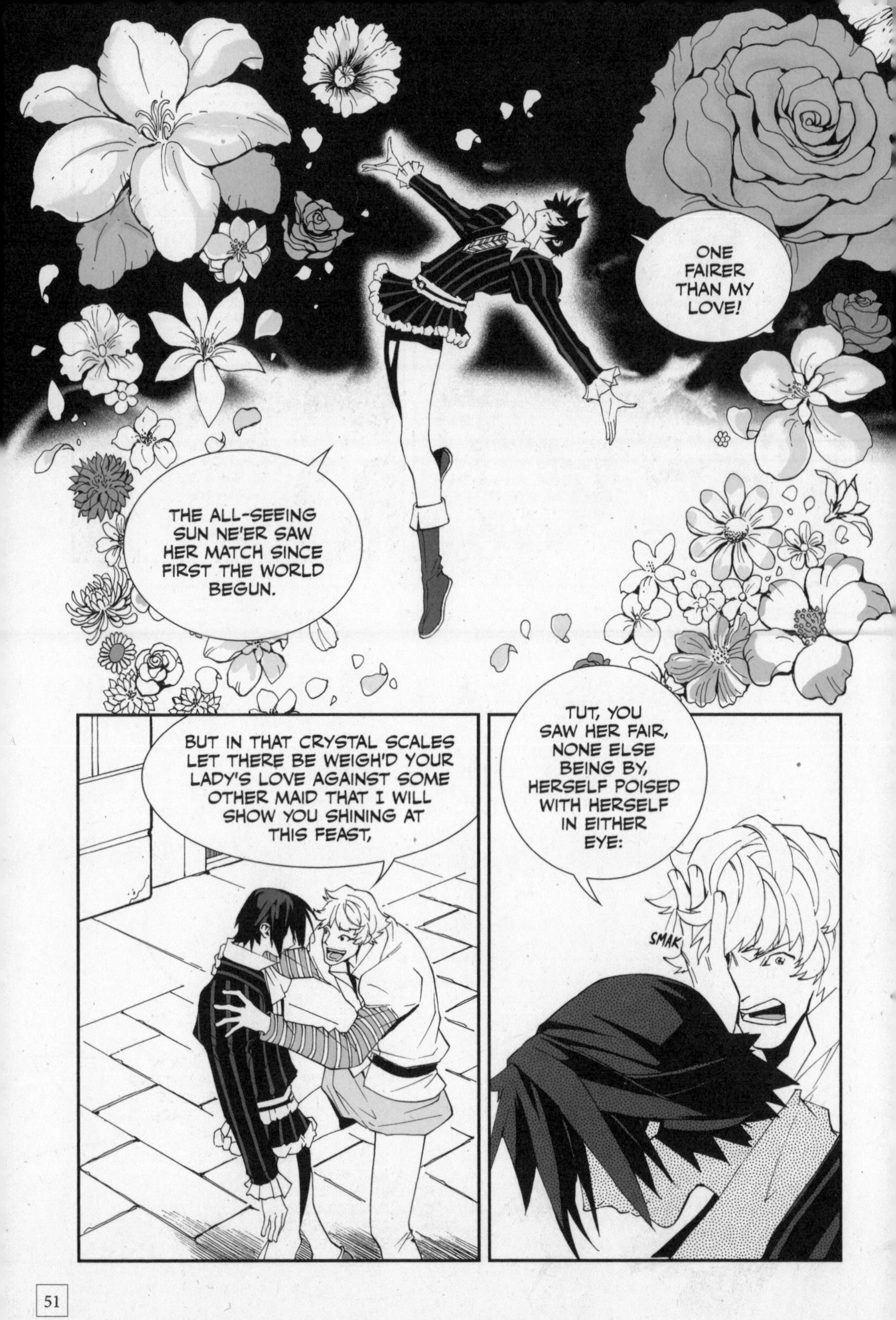
ONE FAIRER THAN MY LOVE!
THE ALL-SEEING SUN NE'ER SAW HER MATCH SINCE FIRST THE WORLD BEGUN.
TUT, YOU SAW HER FAIR, NONE ELSE BEING BY, HERSELF POISED WITH HERSELF IN EITHER EYE:
SMAK
BUT IN THAT CRYSTAL SCALES LET THERE BE WEIGH'D YOUR LADY'S LOVE AGAINST SOME OTHER MAID THAT I WILL SHOW YOU SHINING AT THIS FEAST,

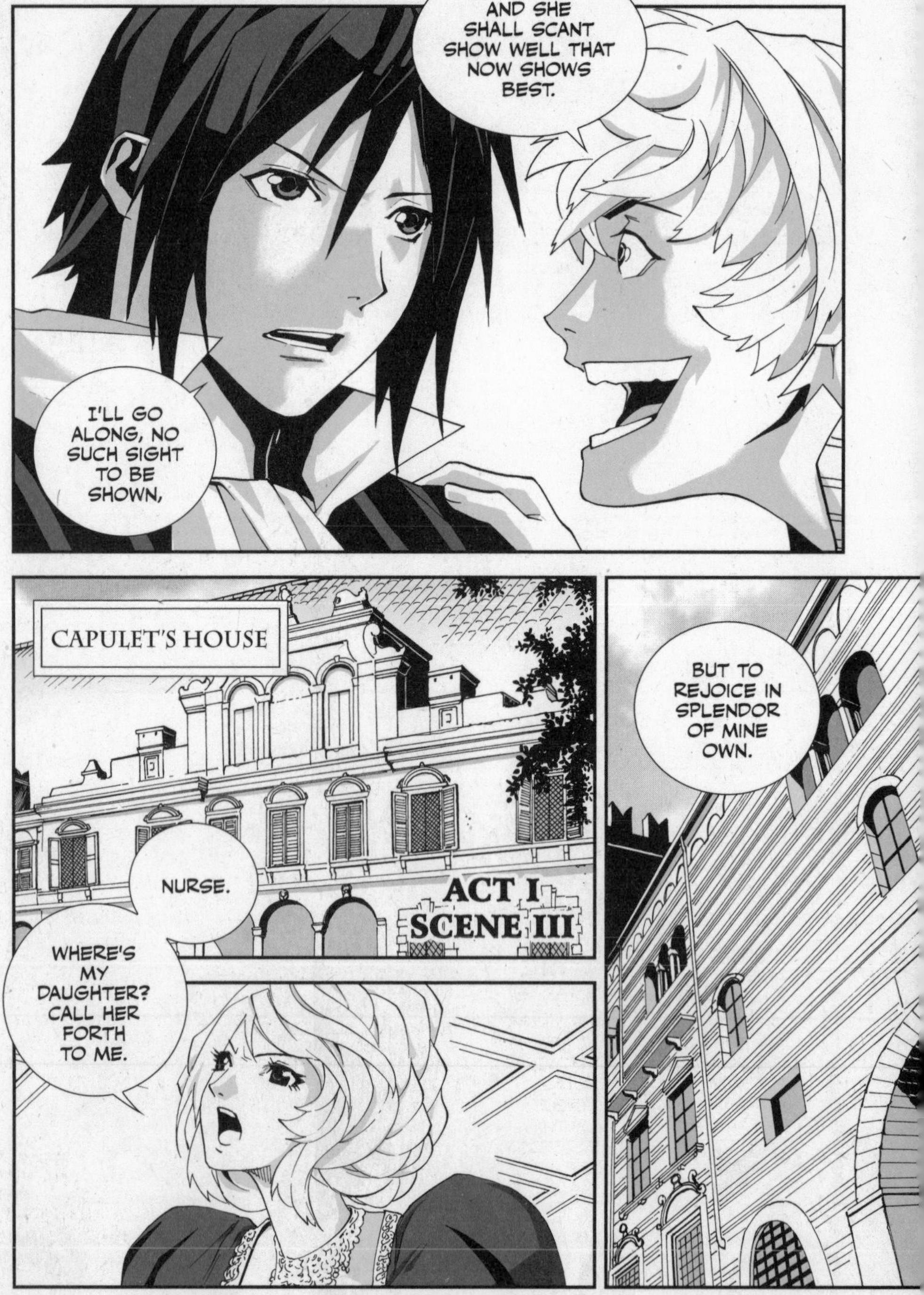
AND SHE SHALL SCANT SHOW WELL THAT NOW SHOWS BEST.
I'LL GO ALONG, NO SUCH SIGHT TO BE SHOWN,
BUT TO REJOICE IN SPLENDOR OF MINE OWN.
CAPULET'S HOUSE
ACT I SCENE III
NURSE.
WHERE'S MY DAUGHTER? CALL HER FORTH TO ME.

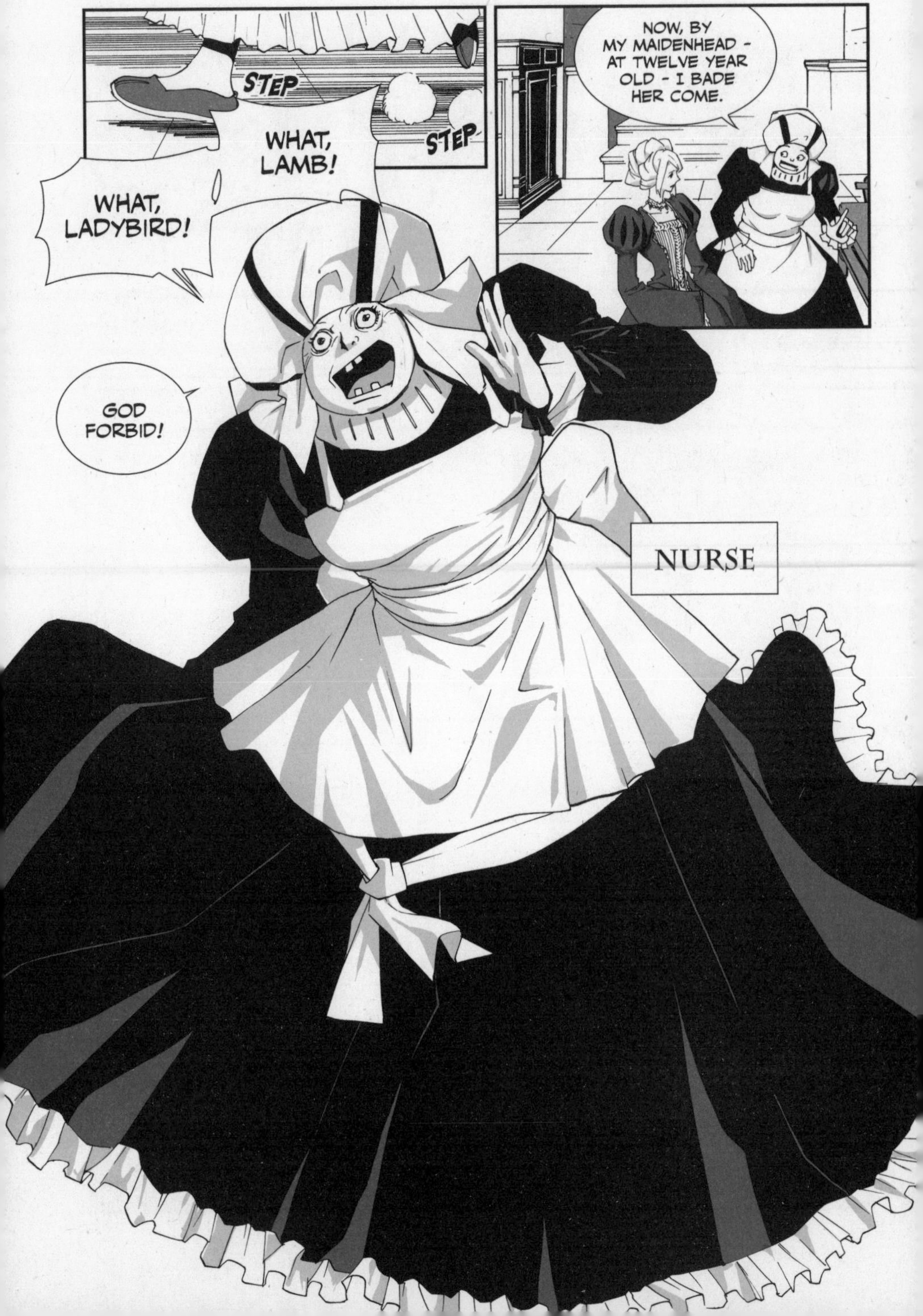
NOW, BY MY MAIDENHEAD - AT TWELVE YEAR OLD - I BADE HER COME.
STEP
STEP
WHAT, LAMB!
WHAT, LADYBIRD!
GOD FORBID!
NURSE

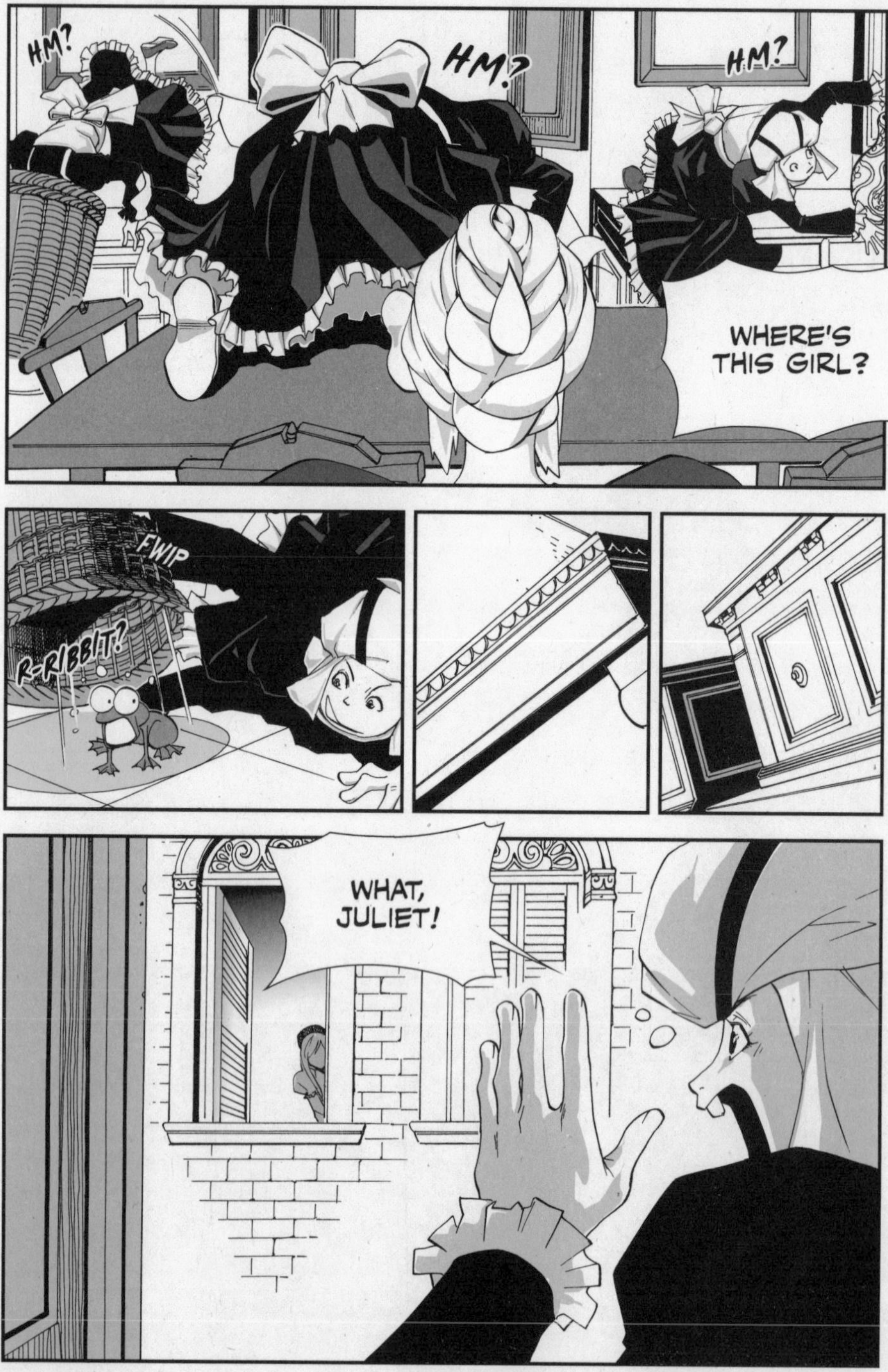
HM?
HM?
HM?
WHERE'S THIS GIRL?
FWIP
R-RIBBIT?
WHAT, JULIET!

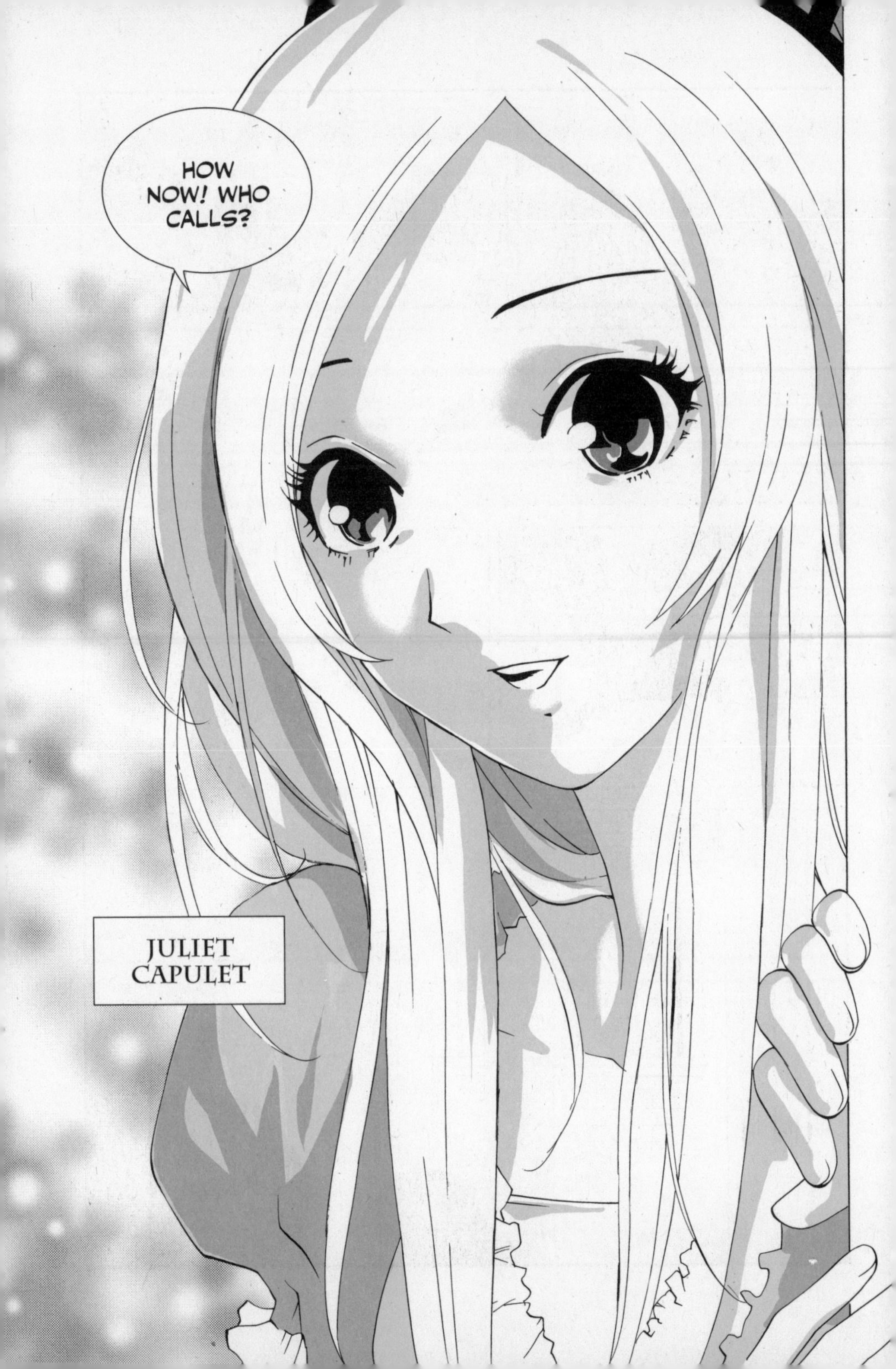
HOW NOW! WHO CALLS?
JULIET CAPULET

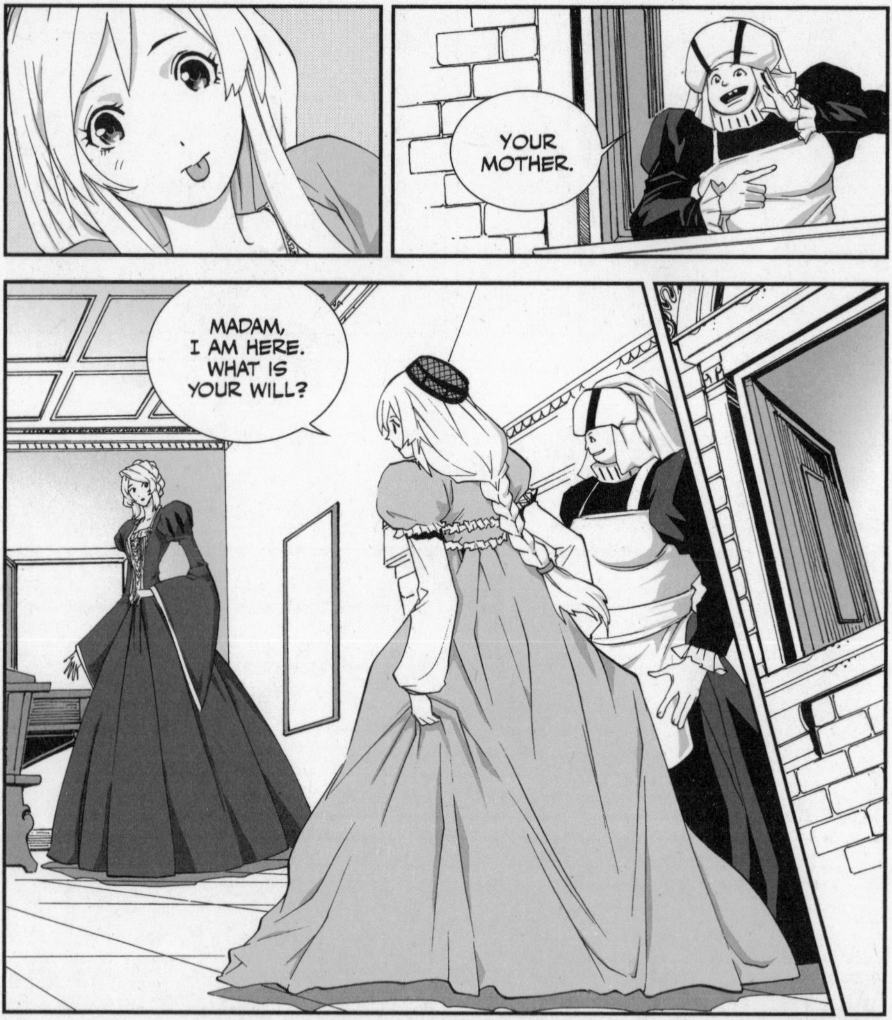
YOUR MOTHER.
MADAM, I AM HERE. WHAT IS YOUR WILL?
THIS IS THE MATTER -
NURSE, GIVE LEAVE AWHILE, WE MUST TALK IN SECRET.

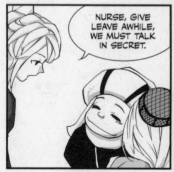

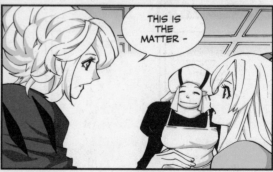

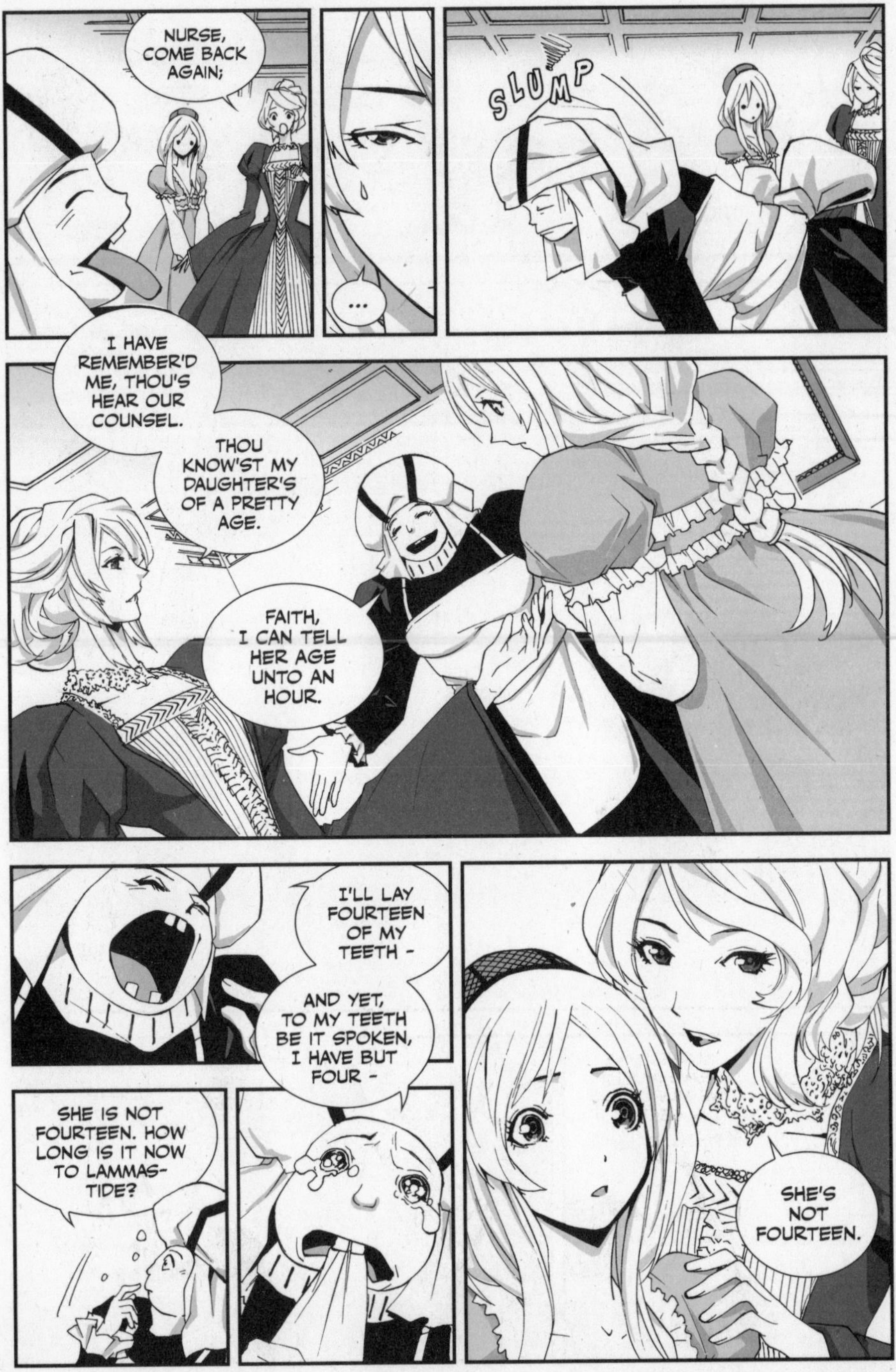
SLUMP
...
NURSE, COME BACK AGAIN;
I HAVE REMEMBER'D ME, THOU'S HEAR OUR COUNSEL.
THOU KNOW'ST MY DAUGHTER'S OF A PRETTY AGE.
FAITH, I CAN TELL HER AGE UNTO AN HOUR.
SHE'S NOT FOURTEEN.
I'LL LAY FOURTEEN OF MY TEETH -
AND YET, TO MY TEETH BE IT SPOKEN, I HAVE BUT FOUR -
SHE IS NOT FOURTEEN. HOW LONG IS IT NOW TO LAMMAS-TIDE?

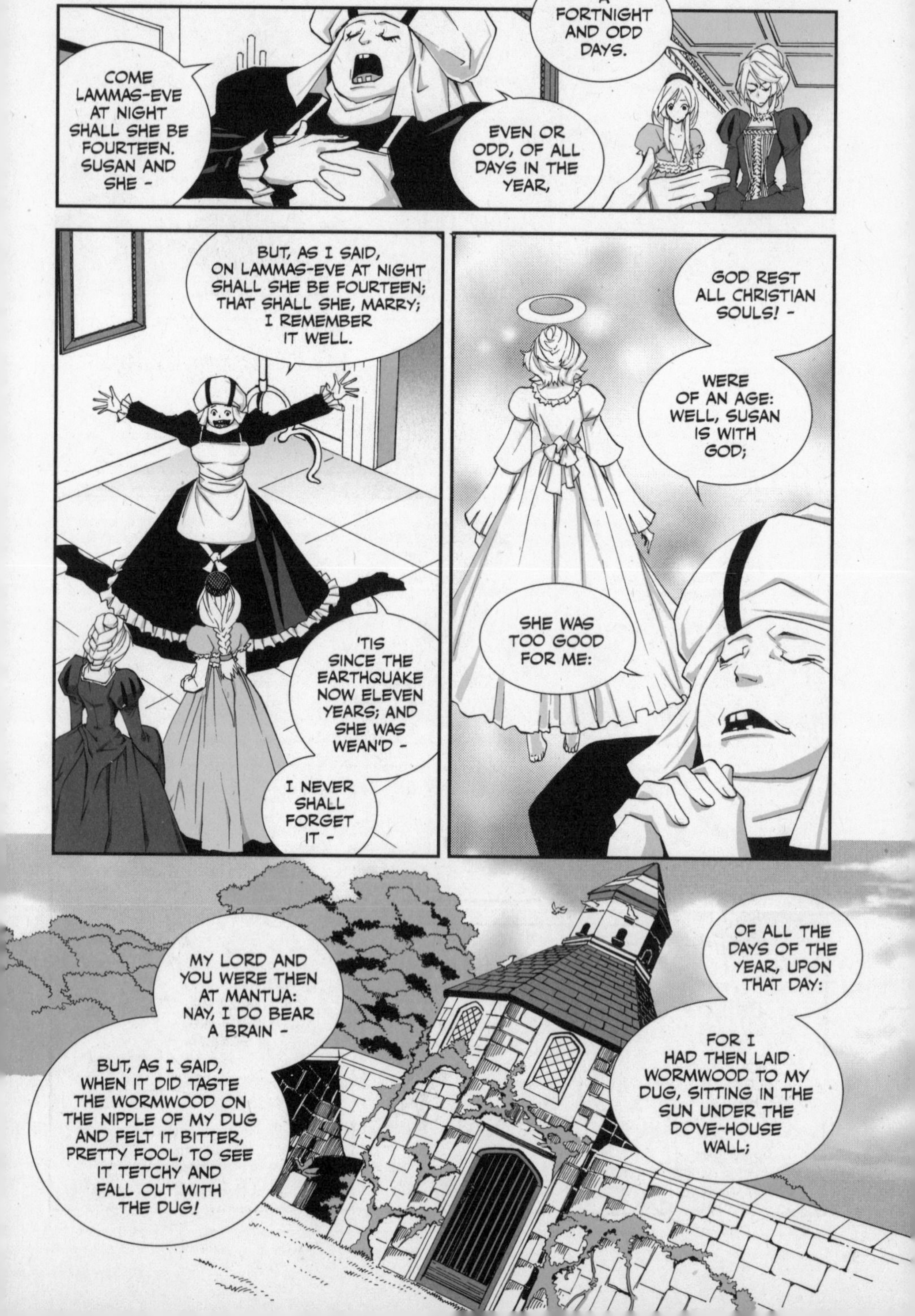
A FORTNIGHT AND ODD DAYS.
EVEN OR ODD, OF ALL DAYS IN THE YEAR,
COME LAMMAS-EVE AT NIGHT SHALL SHE BE FOURTEEN. SUSAN AND SHE -
GOD REST ALL CHRISTIAN SOULS! -
WERE OF AN AGE: WELL, SUSAN IS WITH GOD;
SHE WAS TOO GOOD FOR ME:
BUT, AS I SAID, ON LAMMAS-EVE AT NIGHT SHALL SHE BE FOURTEEN; THAT SHALL SHE, MARRY; I REMEMBER IT WELL.
'TIS SINCE THE EARTHQUAKE NOW ELEVEN YEARS; AND SHE WAS WEAN'D -
I NEVER SHALL FORGET IT -
OF ALL THE DAYS OF THE YEAR, UPON THAT DAY:
FOR I HAD THEN LAID WORMWOOD TO MY DUG, SITTING IN THE SUN UNDER THE DOVE-HOUSE WALL;
MY LORD AND YOU WERE THEN AT MANTUA: NAY, I DO BEAR A BRAIN -
BUT, AS I SAID, WHEN IT DID TASTE THE WORMWOOD ON THE NIPPLE OF MY DUG AND FELT IT BITTER, PRETTY FOOL, TO SEE IT TETCHY AND FALL OUT WITH THE DUG!

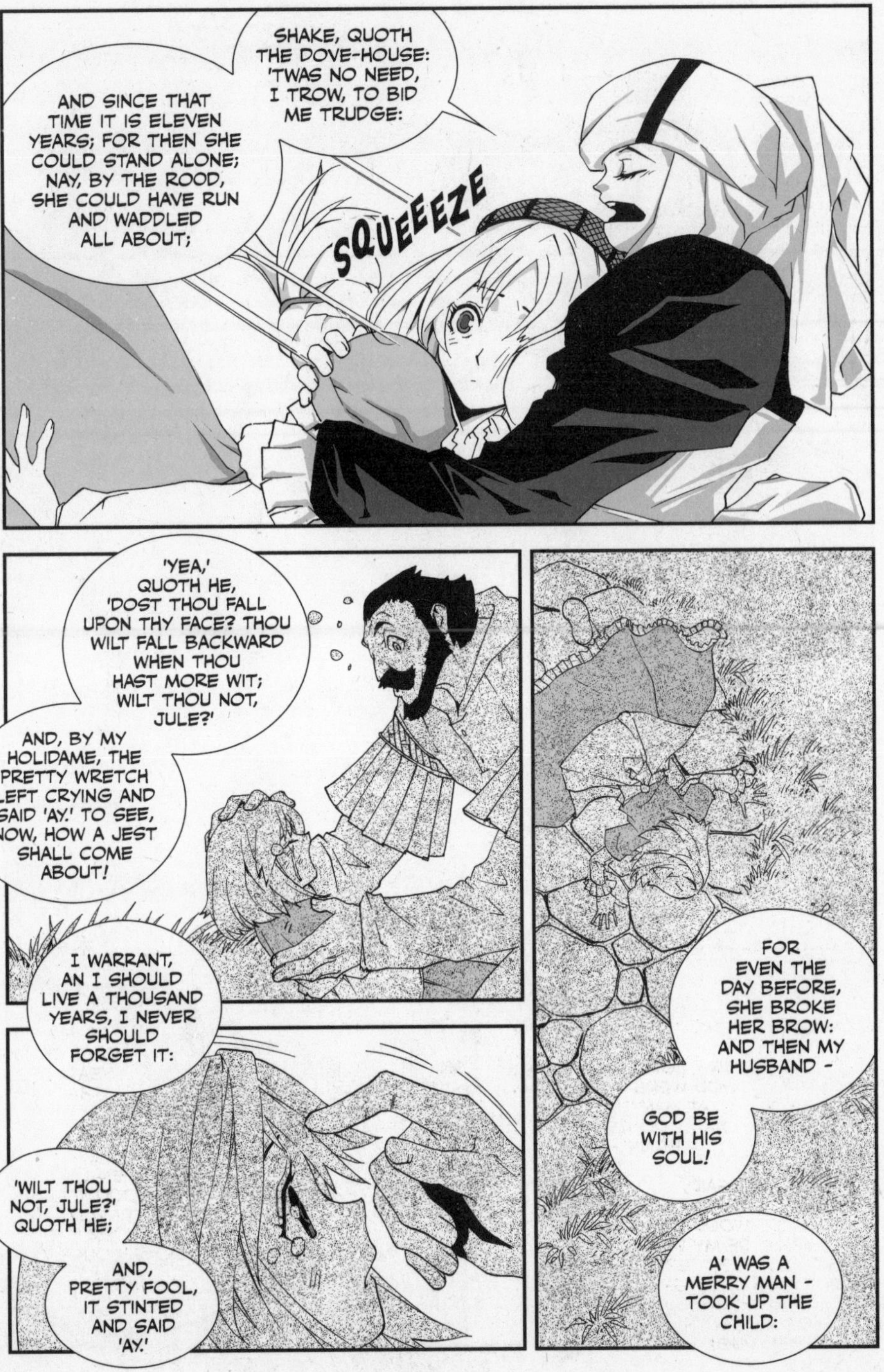
SHAKE, QUOTH THE DOVE-HOUSE: 'TWAS NO NEED, I TROW, TO BID ME TRUDGE:
AND SINCE THAT TIME IT IS ELEVEN YEARS; FOR THEN SHE COULD STAND ALONE; NAY, BY THE ROOD, SHE COULD HAVE RUN AND WADDLED ALL ABOUT;
SQUEEEZE
FOR EVEN THE DAY BEFORE, SHE BROKE HER BROW: AND THEN MY HUSBAND -
GOD BE WITH HIS SOUL!
A' WAS A MERRY MAN - TOOK UP THE CHILD:
'YEA,' QUOTH HE, 'DOST THOU FALL UPON THY FACE? THOU WILT FALL BACKWARD WHEN THOU HAST MORE WIT; WILT THOU NOT, JULE?'
AND, BY MY HOLIDAME, THE PRETTY WRETCH LEFT CRYING AND SAID 'AY.' TO SEE, NOW, HOW A JEST SHALL COME ABOUT!
I WARRANT, AN I SHOULD LIVE A THOUSAND YEARS, I NEVER SHOULD FORGET IT:
'WILT THOU NOT, JULE?' QUOTH HE;
AND, PRETTY FOOL, IT STINTED AND SAID 'AY.'

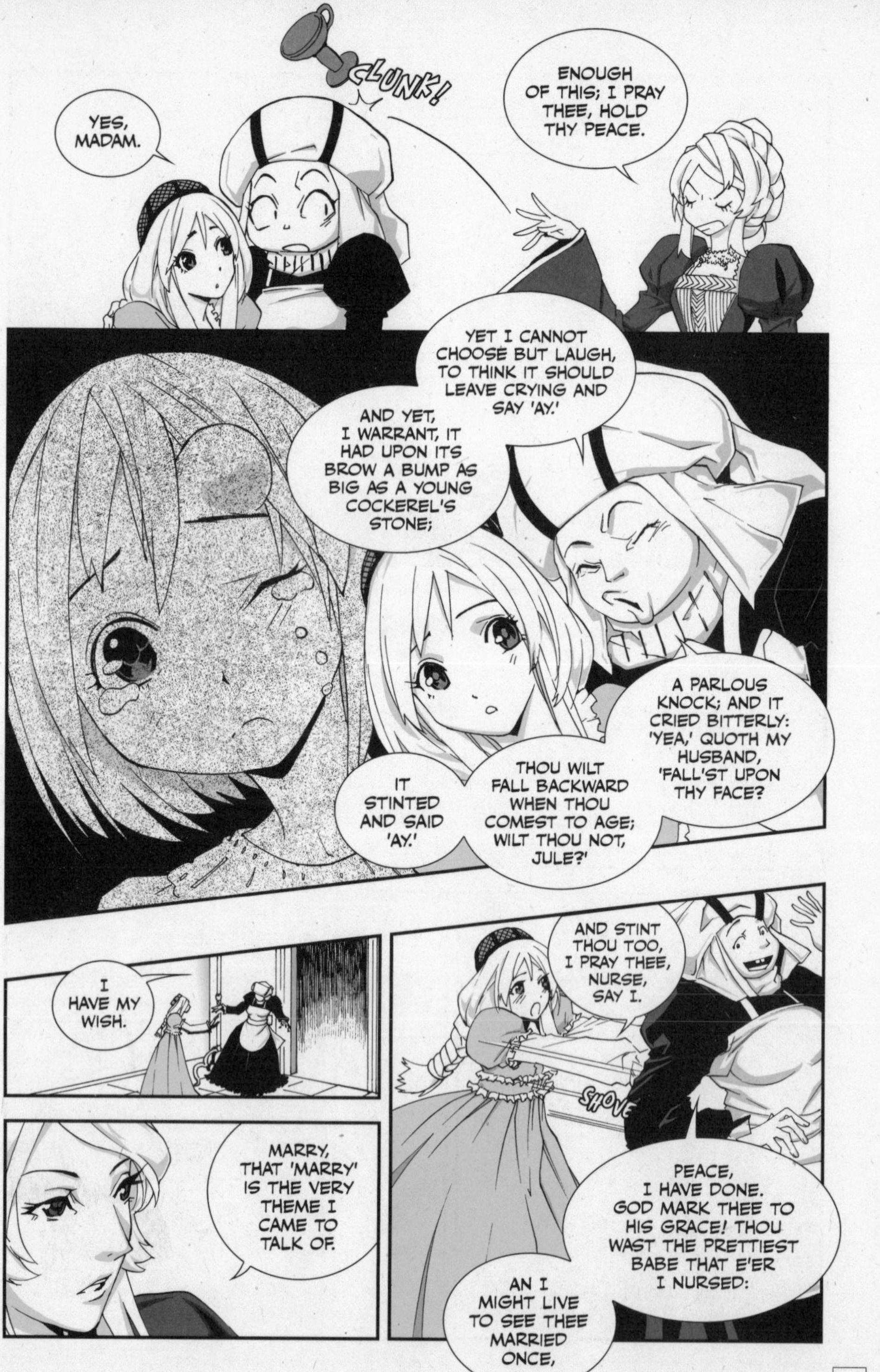
ENOUGH OF THIS; I PRAY THEE, HOLD THY PEACE.
CLUNK!
YES, MADAM.
YET I CANNOT CHOOSE BUT LAUGH, TO THINK IT SHOULD LEAVE CRYING AND SAY 'AY.'
AND YET, I WARRANT, IT HAD UPON ITS BROW A BUMP AS BIG AS A YOUNG COCKEREL'S STONE;
A PARLOUS KNOCK; AND IT CRIED BITTERLY: 'YEA,' QUOTH MY HUSBAND, 'FALL'ST UPON THY FACE?
THOU WILT FALL BACKWARD WHEN THOU COMEST TO AGE; WILT THOU NOT, JULE?'
IT STINTED AND SAID 'AY.'
AND STINT THOU TOO, I PRAY THEE, NURSE, SAY I.
SHOVE
PEACE, I HAVE DONE. GOD MARK THEE TO HIS GRACE! THOU WAST THE PRETTIEST BABE THAT E'ER I NURSED:
AN I MIGHT LIVE TO SEE THEE MARRIED ONCE,
I HAVE MY WISH.
MARRY, THAT 'MARRY' IS THE VERY THEME I CAME TO TALK OF.

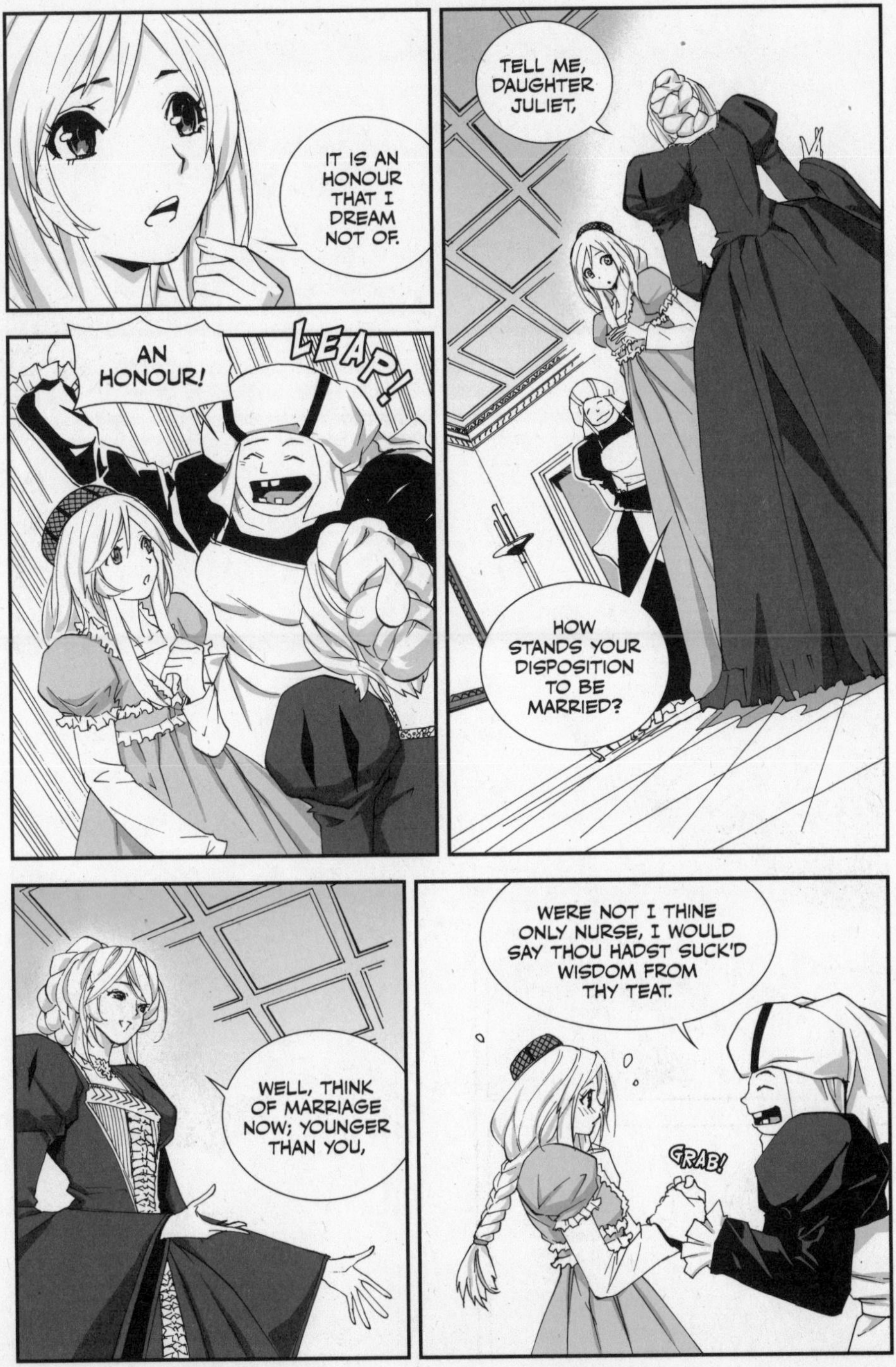
TELL ME, DAUGHTER JULIET,
HOW STANDS YOUR DISPOSITION TO BE MARRIED?
IT IS AN HONOUR THAT I DREAM NOT OF.
AN HONOUR!
LEAP!
WERE NOT I THINE ONLY NURSE, I WOULD SAY THOU HADST SUCK'D WISDOM FROM THY TEAT.
GRAB!
WELL, THINK OF MARRIAGE NOW; YOUNGER THAN YOU,

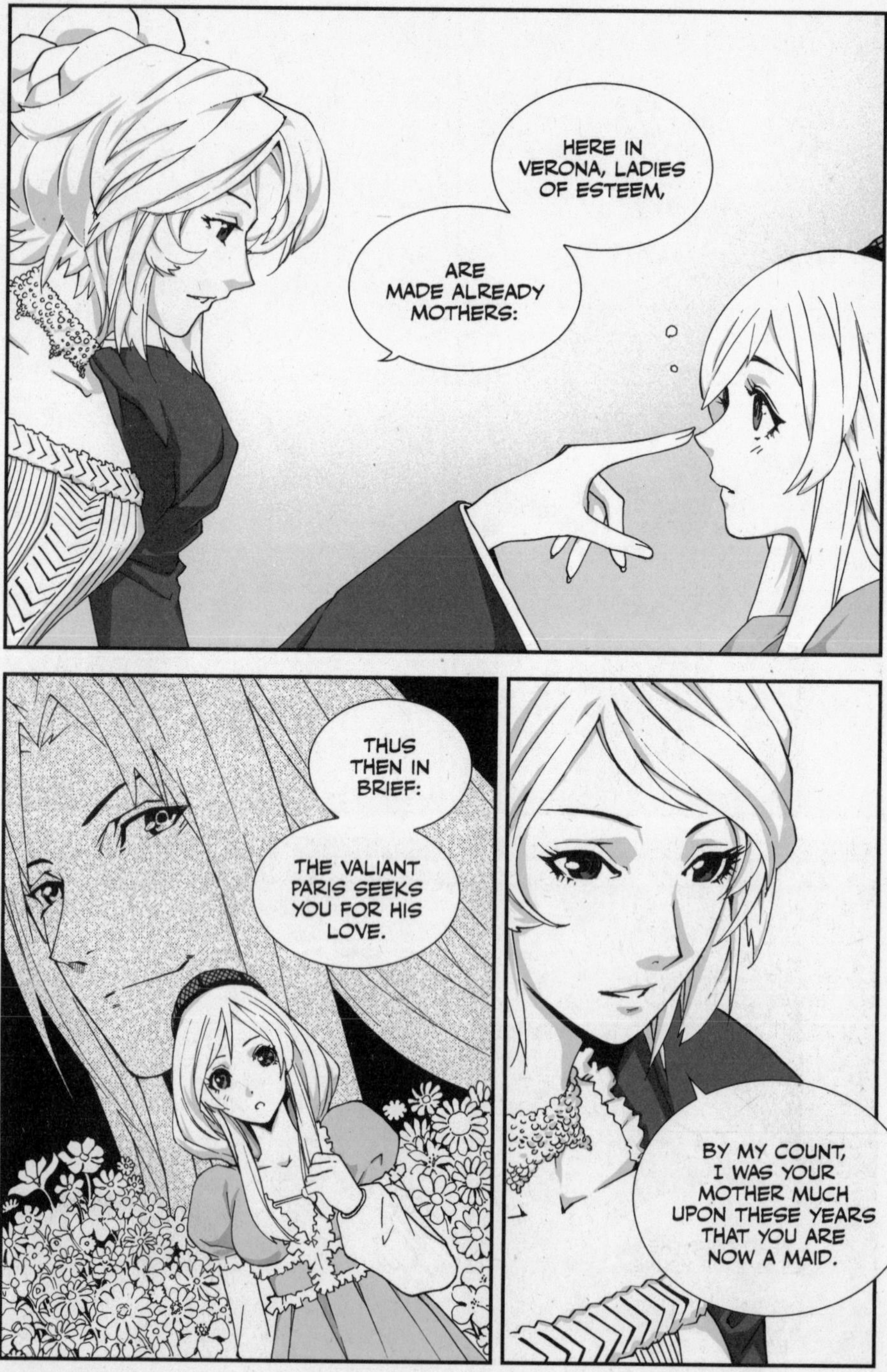
HERE IN VERONA, LADIES OF ESTEEM,
ARE MADE ALREADY MOTHERS:
BY MY COUNT, I WAS YOUR MOTHER MUCH UPON THESE YEARS THAT YOU ARE NOW A MAID.
THUS THEN IN BRIEF:
THE VALIANT PARIS SEEKS YOU FOR HIS LOVE.

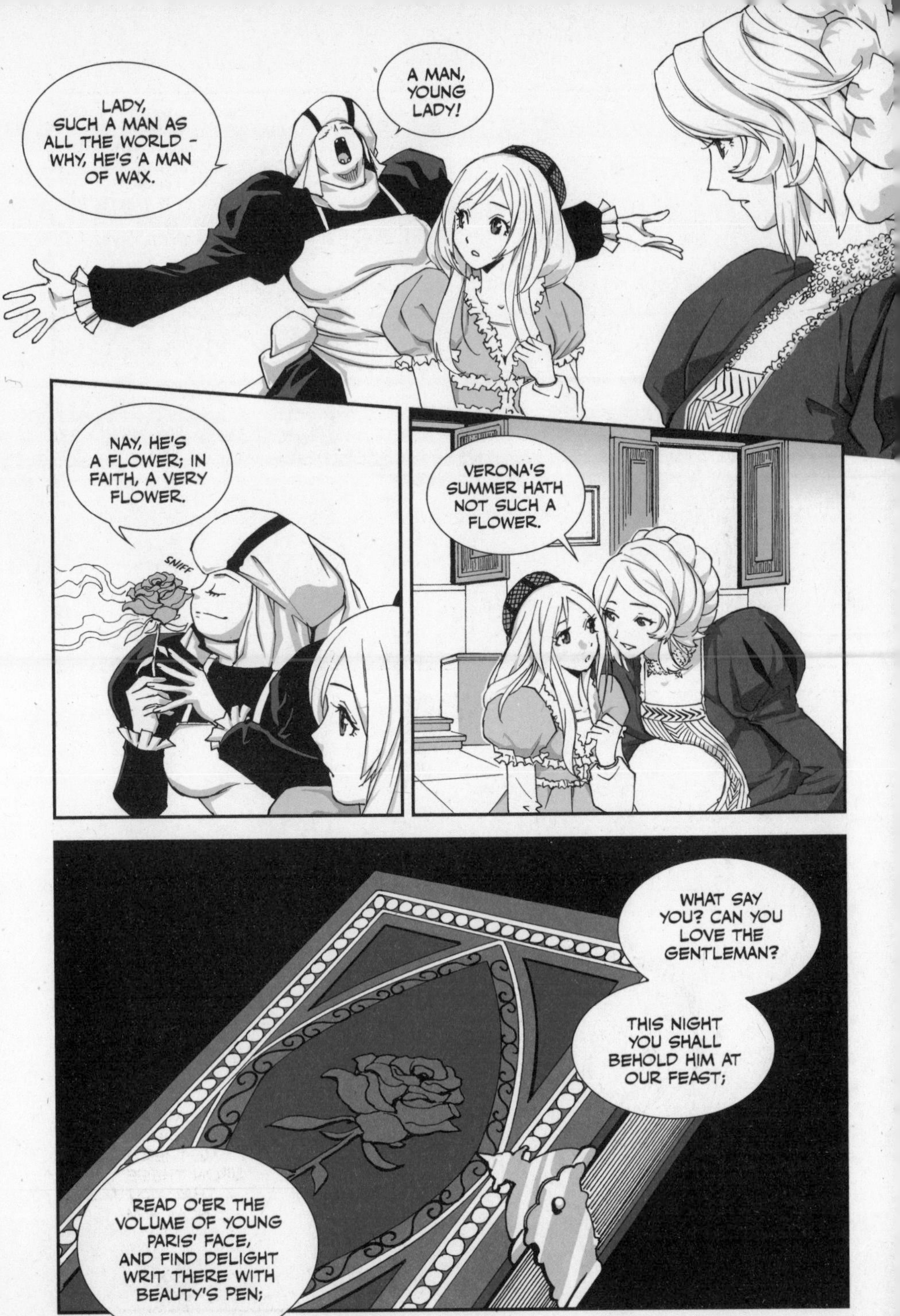
A MAN, YOUNG LADY!
LADY, SUCH A MAN AS ALL THE WORLD - WHY, HE'S A MAN OF WAX.
VERONA'S SUMMER HATH NOT SUCH A FLOWER.
NAY, HE'S A FLOWER; IN FAITH, A VERY FLOWER.
SNIFF
WHAT SAY YOU? CAN YOU LOVE THE GENTLEMAN?
THIS NIGHT YOU SHALL BEHOLD HIM AT OUR FEAST;
READ O'ER THE VOLUME OF YOUNG PARIS' FACE, AND FIND DELIGHT WRIT THERE WITH BEAUTY'S PEN;

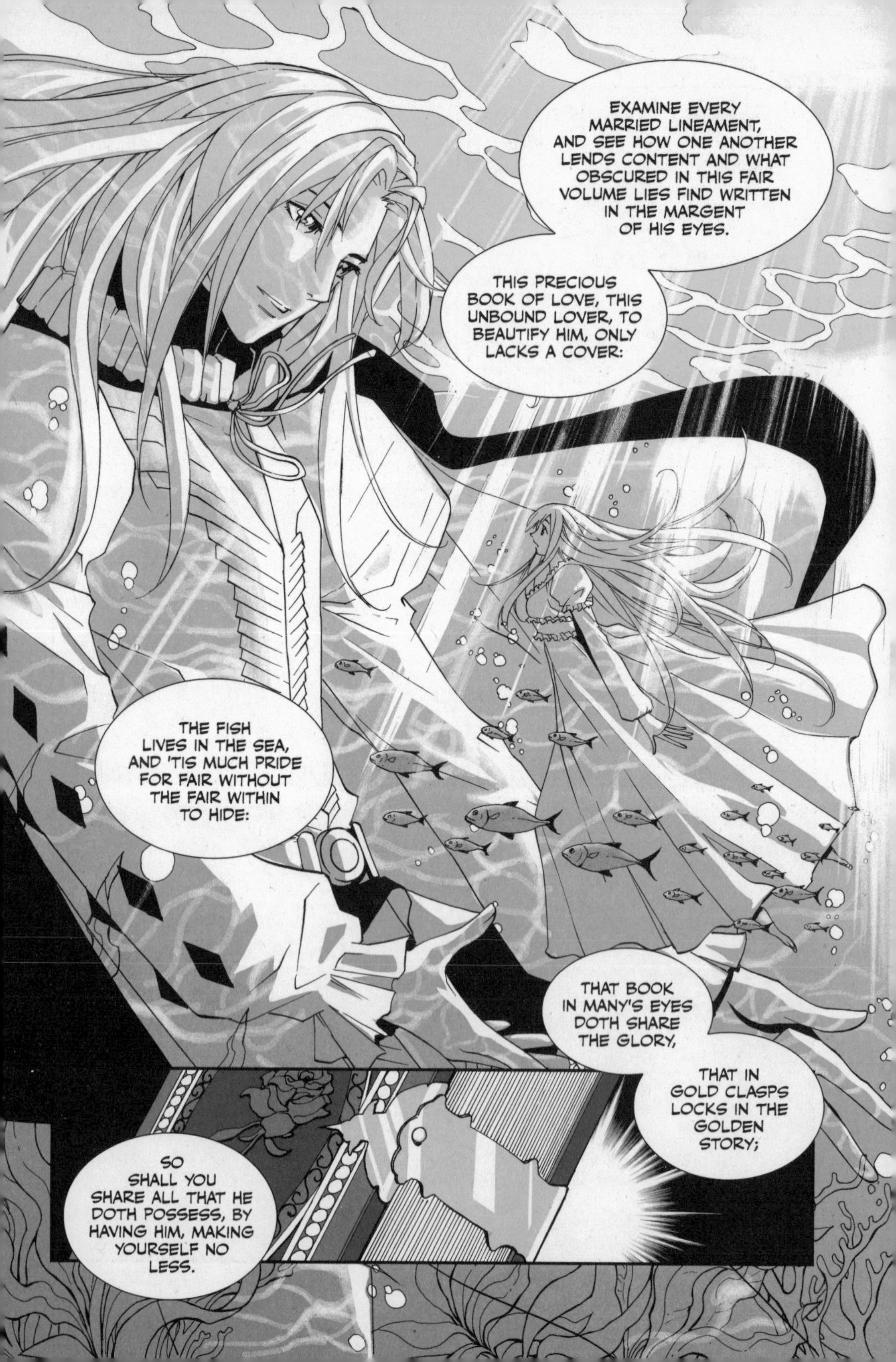
EXAMINE EVERY MARRIED LINEAMENT, AND SEE HOW ONE ANOTHER LENDS CONTENT AND WHAT OBSCURED IN THIS FAIR VOLUME LIES FIND WRITTEN IN THE MARGENT OF HIS EYES.
THIS PRECIOUS BOOK OF LOVE, THIS UNBOUND LOVER, TO BEAUTIFY HIM, ONLY LACKS A COVER:
THE FISH LIVES IN THE SEA, AND 'TIS MUCH PRIDE FOR FAIR WITHOUT THE FAIR WITHIN TO HIDE:
THAT BOOK IN MANY'S EYES DOTH SHARE THE GLORY,
THAT IN GOLD CLASPS LOCKS IN THE GOLDEN STORY;
SO SHALL YOU SHARE ALL THAT HE DOTH POSSESS, BY HAVING HIM, MAKING YOURSELF NO LESS.

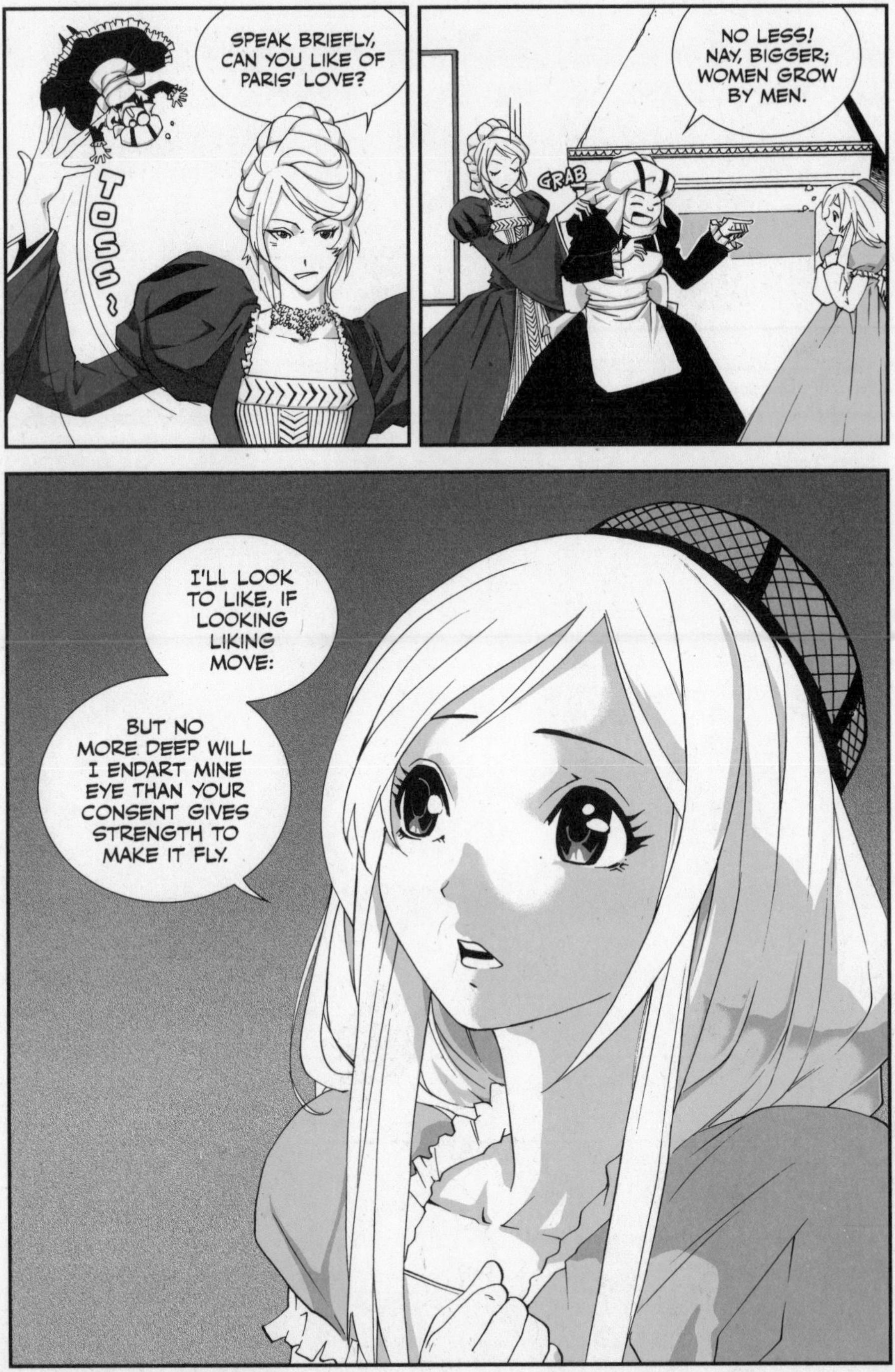
NO LESS! NAY, BIGGER; WOMEN GROW BY MEN.
GRAB
SPEAK BRIEFLY, CAN YOU LIKE OF PARIS' LOVE?
TOSS~
I'LL LOOK TO LIKE, IF LOOKING LIKING MOVE:
BUT NO MORE DEEP WILL I ENDART MINE EYE THAN YOUR CONSENT GIVES STRENGTH TO MAKE IT FLY.

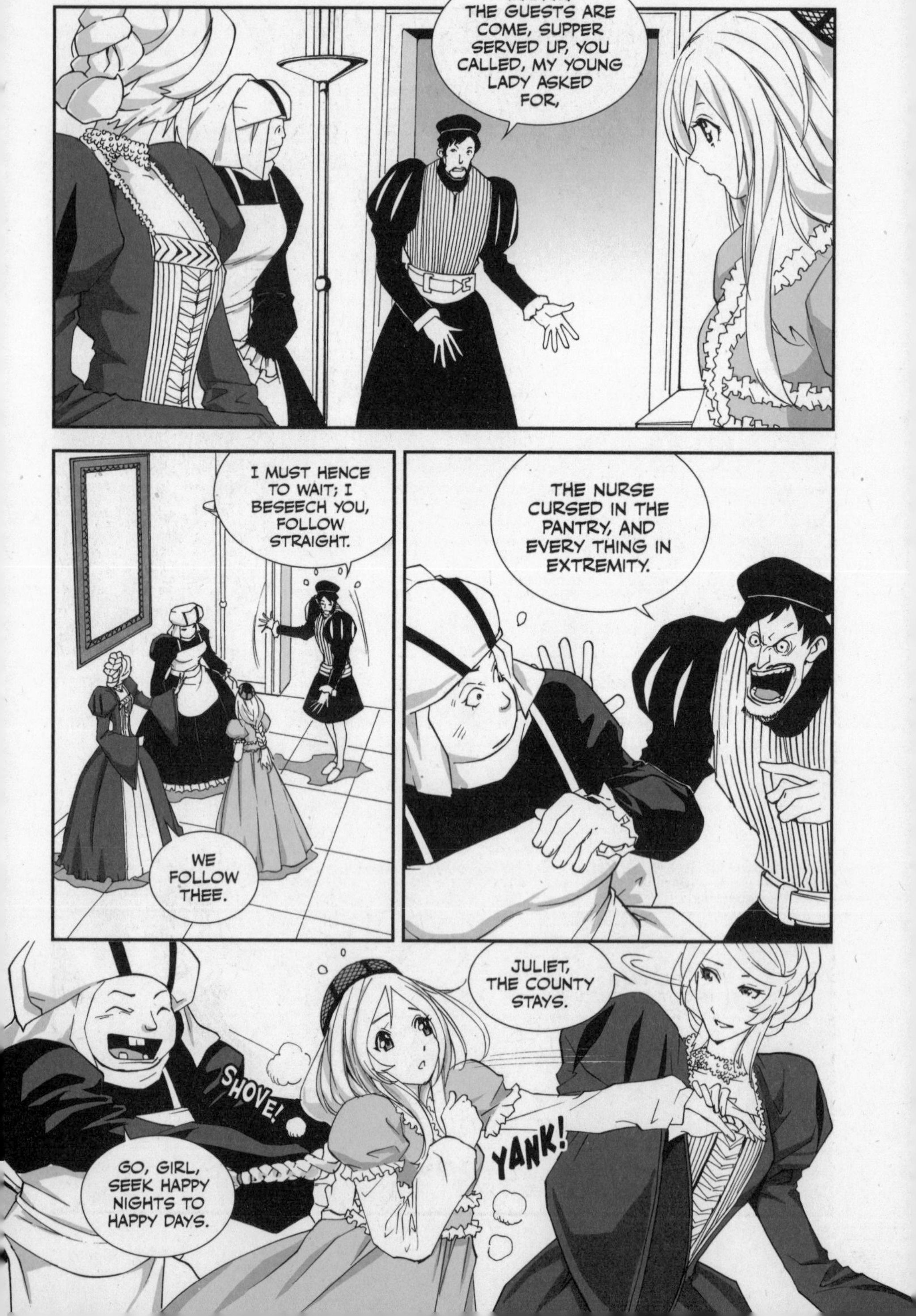
MADAM, THE GUESTS ARE COME, SUPPER SERVED UP, YOU CALLED, MY YOUNG LADY ASKED FOR,
THE NURSE CURSED IN THE PANTRY, AND EVERY THING IN EXTREMITY.
I MUST HENCE TO WAIT; I BESEECH YOU, FOLLOW STRAIGHT.
WE FOLLOW THEE.
JULIET, THE COUNTY STAYS.
YANK!
SHOVE!
GO, GIRL, SEEK HAPPY NIGHTS TO HAPPY DAYS.

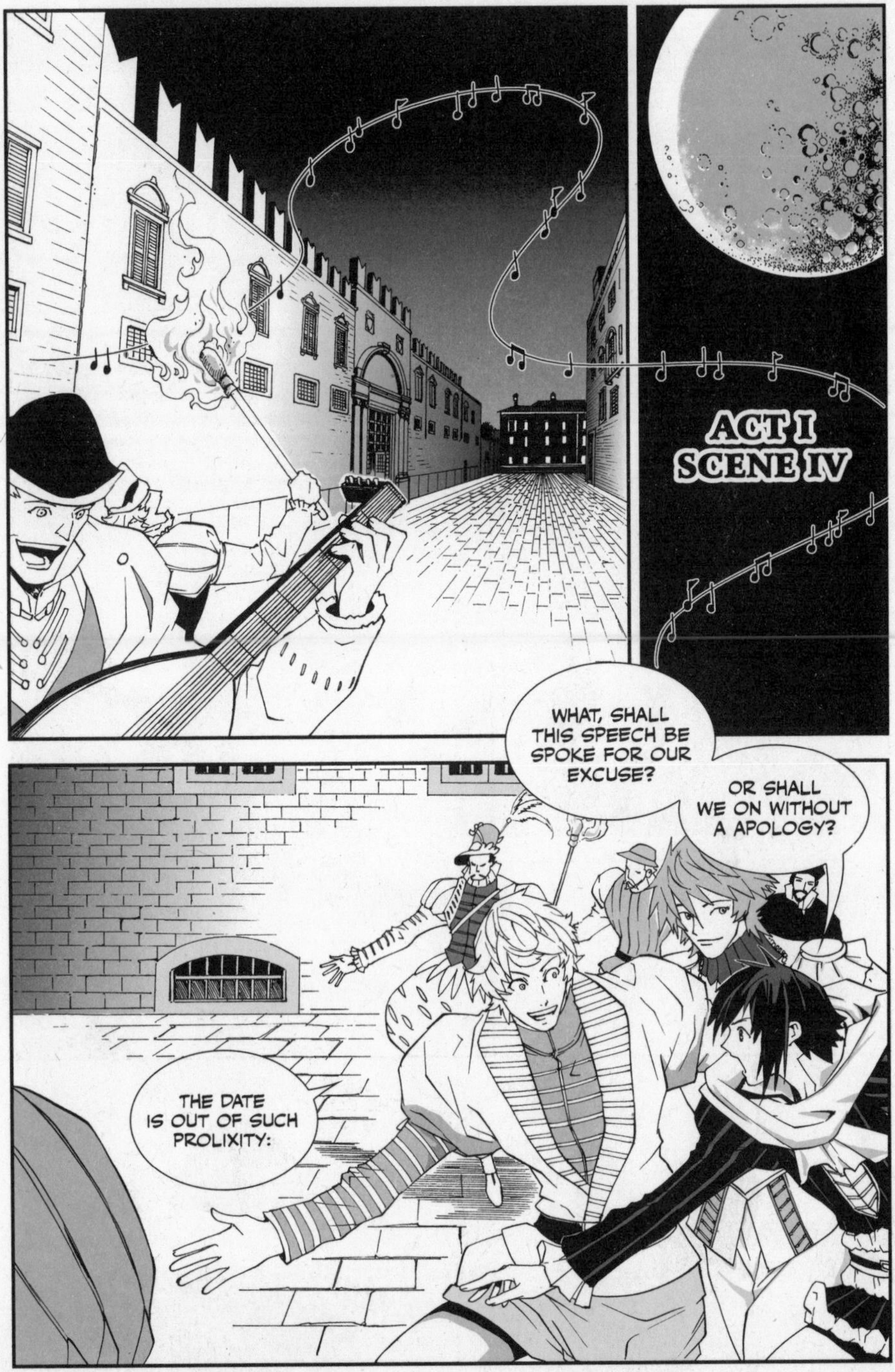
ACT I
SCENE IV
WHAT, SHALL THIS SPEECH BE SPOKE FOR OUR EXCUSE?
OR SHALL WE ON WITHOUT A APOLOGY?
THE DATE IS OUT OF SUCH PROLIXITY:

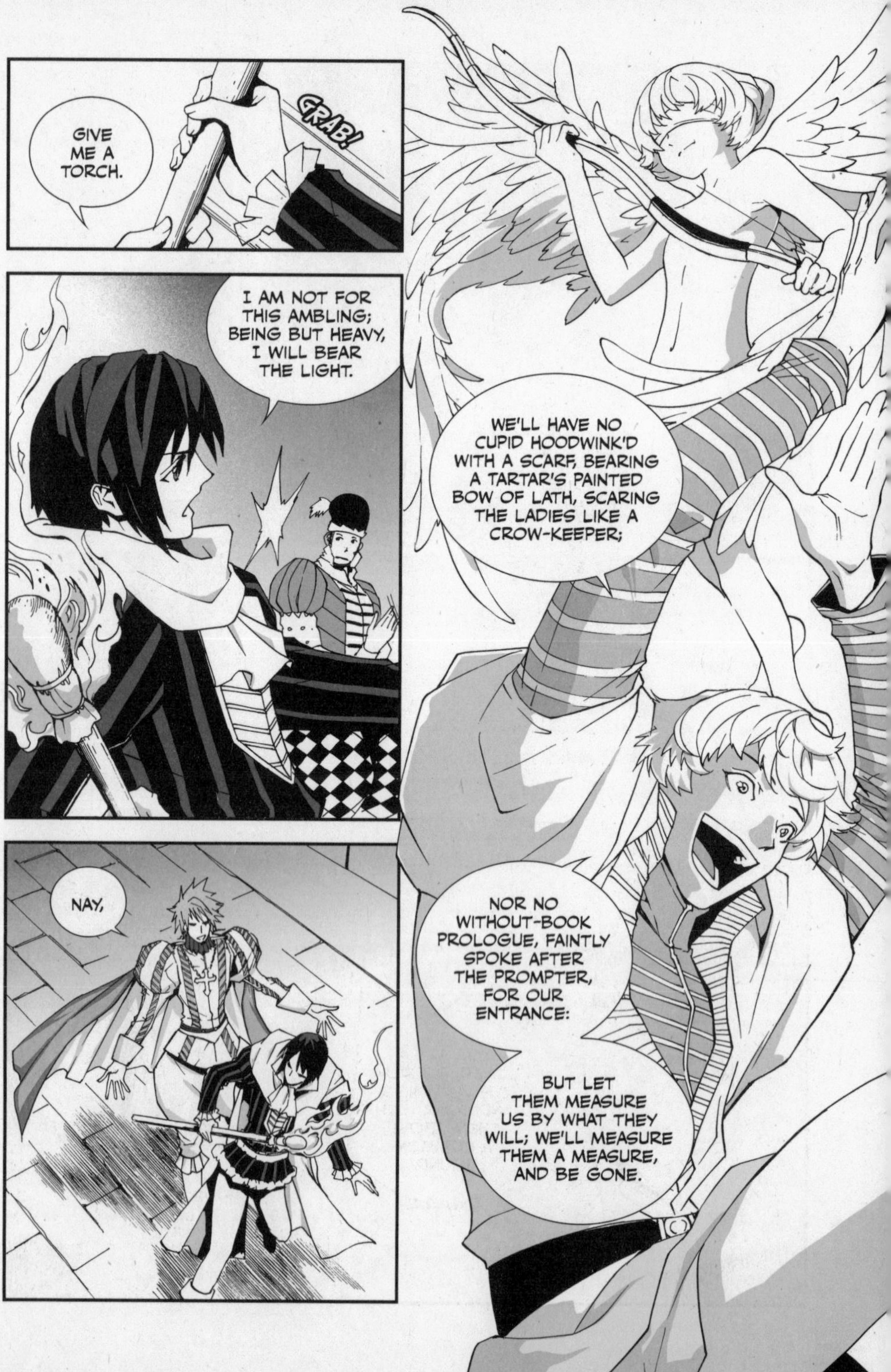

WE'LL HAVE NO CUPID HOODWINK'D WITH A SCARF, BEARING A TARTAR'S PAINTED BOW OF LATH, SCARING THE LADIES LIKE A CROW-KEEPER;
NOR NO WITHOUT-BOOK PROLOGUE, FAINTLY SPOKE AFTER THE PROMPTER, FOR OUR ENTRANCE:
BUT LET THEM MEASURE US BY WHAT THEY WILL; WE'LL MEASURE THEM A MEASURE, AND BE GONE.
GRAB!
GIVE ME A TORCH.
I AM NOT FOR THIS AMBLING; BEING BUT HEAVY, I WILL BEAR THE LIGHT.
NAY,

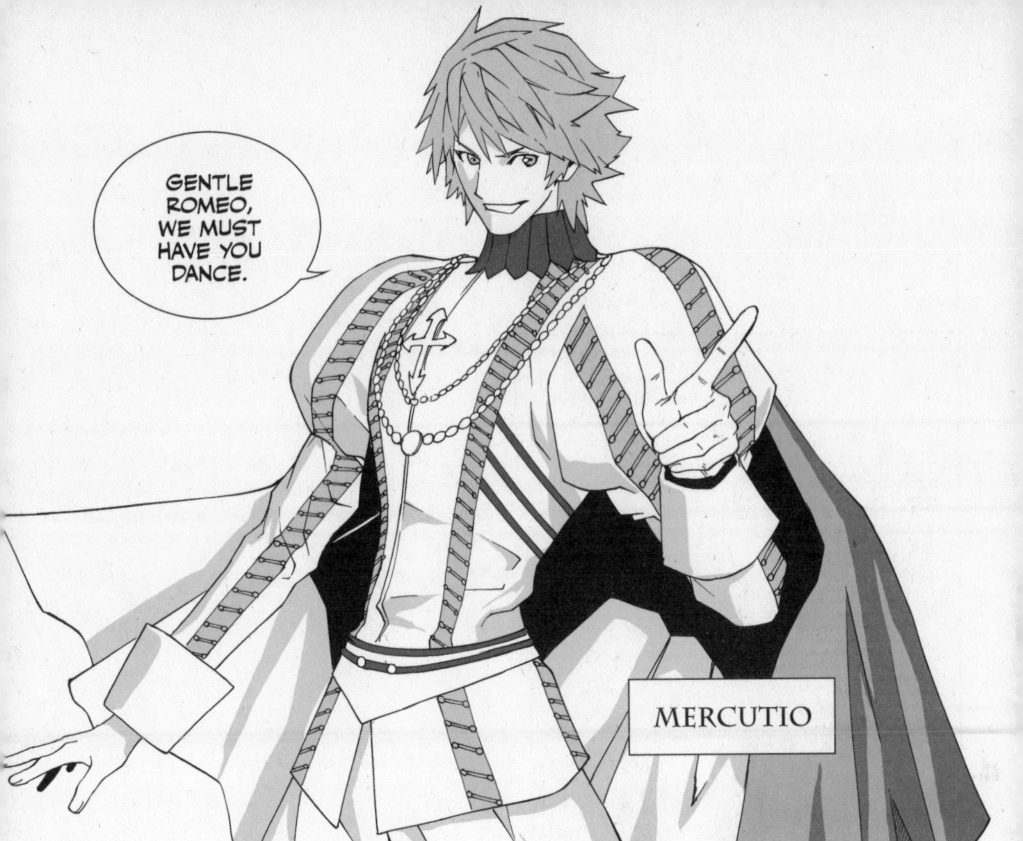
GENTLE ROMEO, WE MUST HAVE YOU DANCE.
MERCUTIO

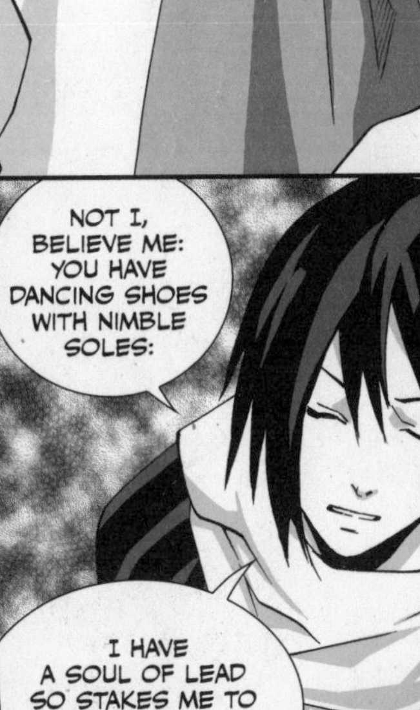
NOT I, BELIEVE ME: YOU HAVE DANCING SHOES WITH NIMBLE SOLES:
I HAVE A SOUL OF LEAD SO STAKES ME TO THE GROUND I CANNOT MOVE.

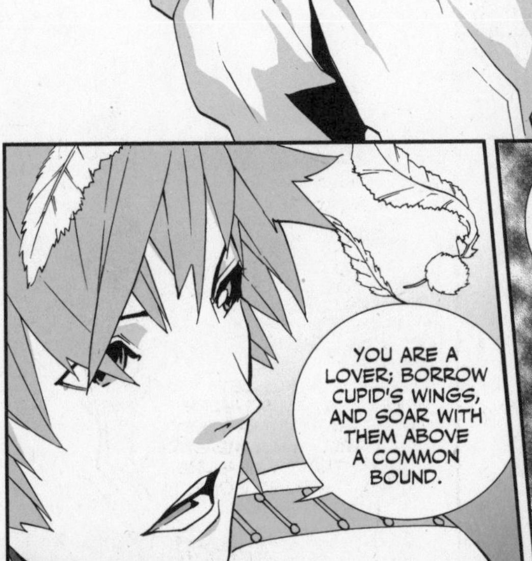
YOU ARE A LOVER; BORROW CUPID'S WINGS, AND SOAR WITH THEM ABOVE A COMMON BOUND.

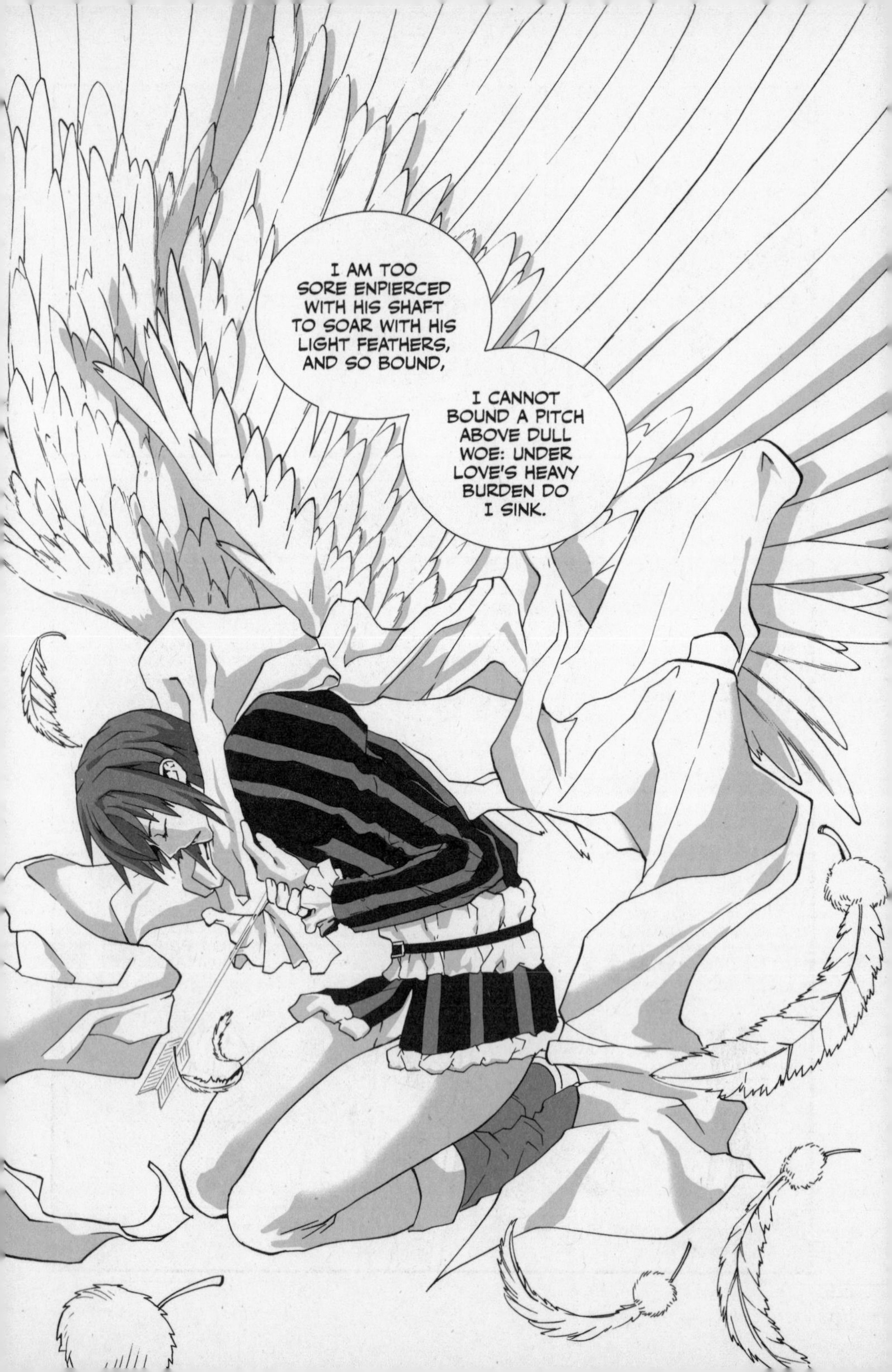
I AM TOO SORE ENPIERCED WITH HIS SHAFT TO SOAR WITH HIS LIGHT FEATHERS, AND SO BOUND,
I CANNOT BOUND A PITCH ABOVE DULL WOE: UNDER LOVE'S HEAVY BURDEN DO I SINK.

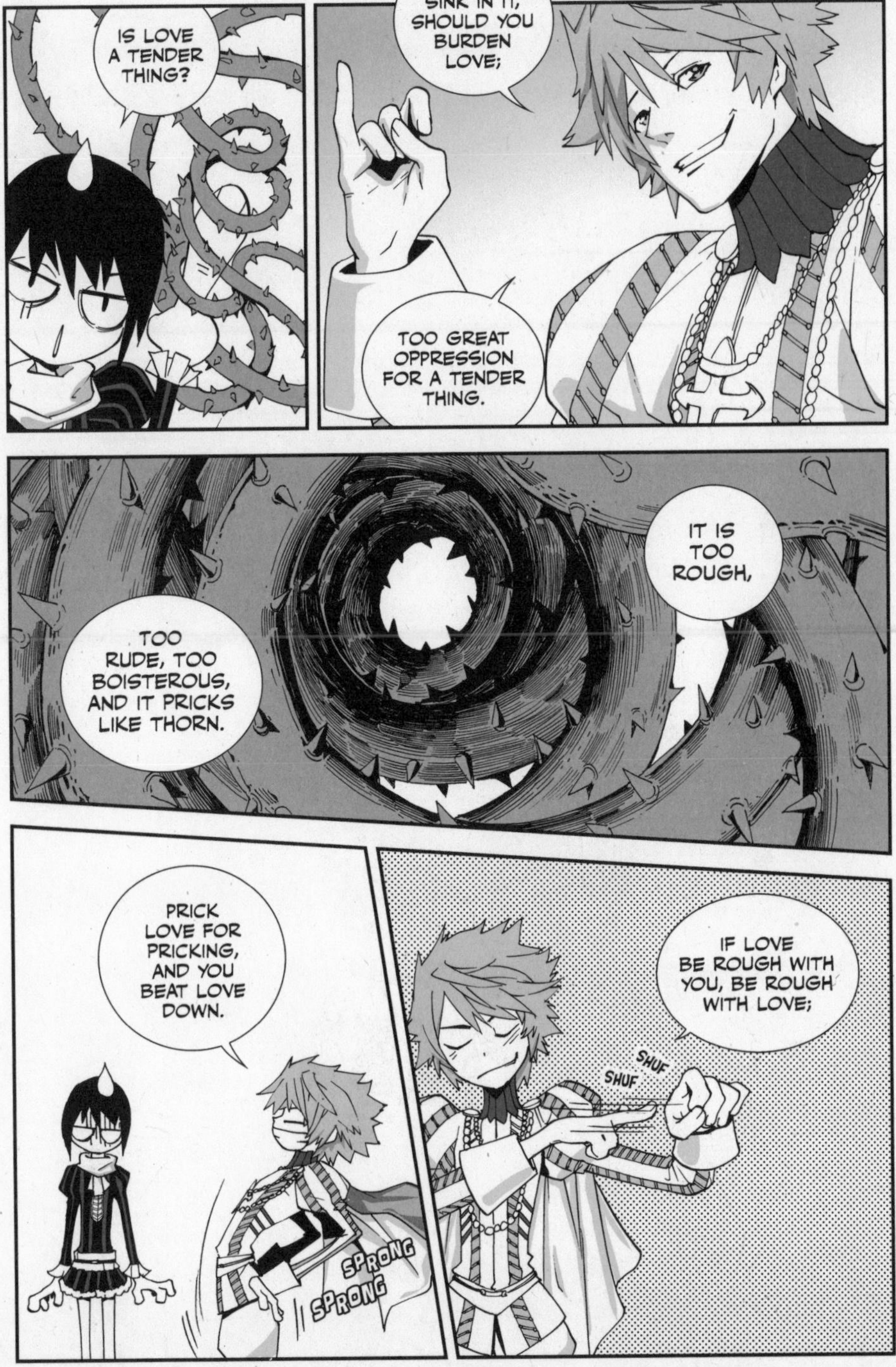

AND, TO SINK IN IT, SHOULD YOU BURDEN LOVE;
TOO GREAT OPPRESSION FOR A TENDER THING.
IS LOVE A TENDER THING?
IT IS TOO ROUGH,
TOO RUDE, TOO BOISTEROUS, AND IT PRICKS LIKE THORN.
IF LOVE BE ROUGH WITH YOU, BE ROUGH WITH LOVE;
SHUF
SHUF
PRICK LOVE FOR PRICKING, AND YOU BEAT LOVE DOWN.
SPRONG
SPRONG

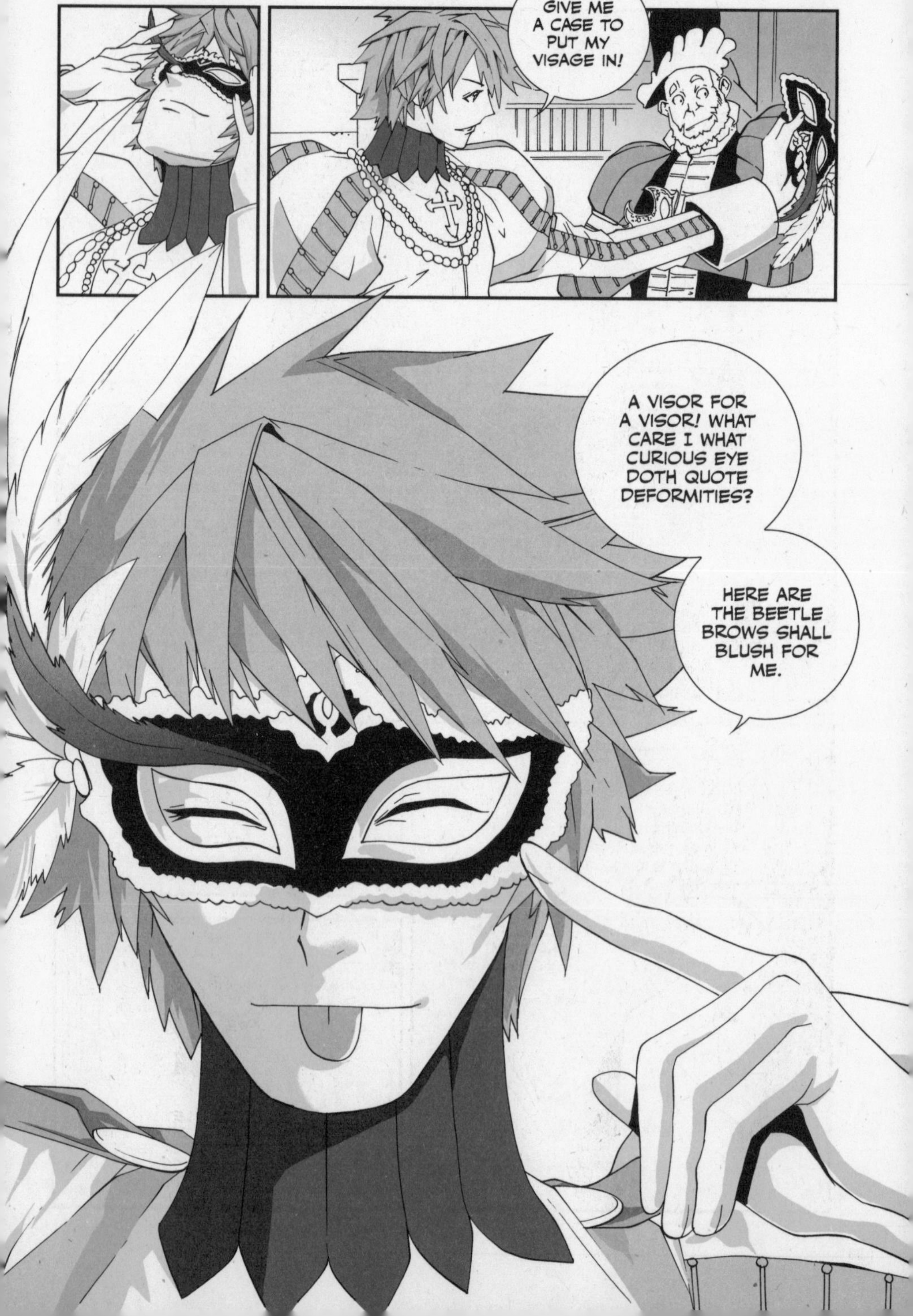
GIVE ME A CASE TO PUT MY VISAGE IN!
A VISOR FOR A VISOR! WHAT CARE I WHAT CURIOUS EYE DOTH QUOTE DEFORMITIES?
HERE ARE THE BEETLE BROWS SHALL BLUSH FOR ME.

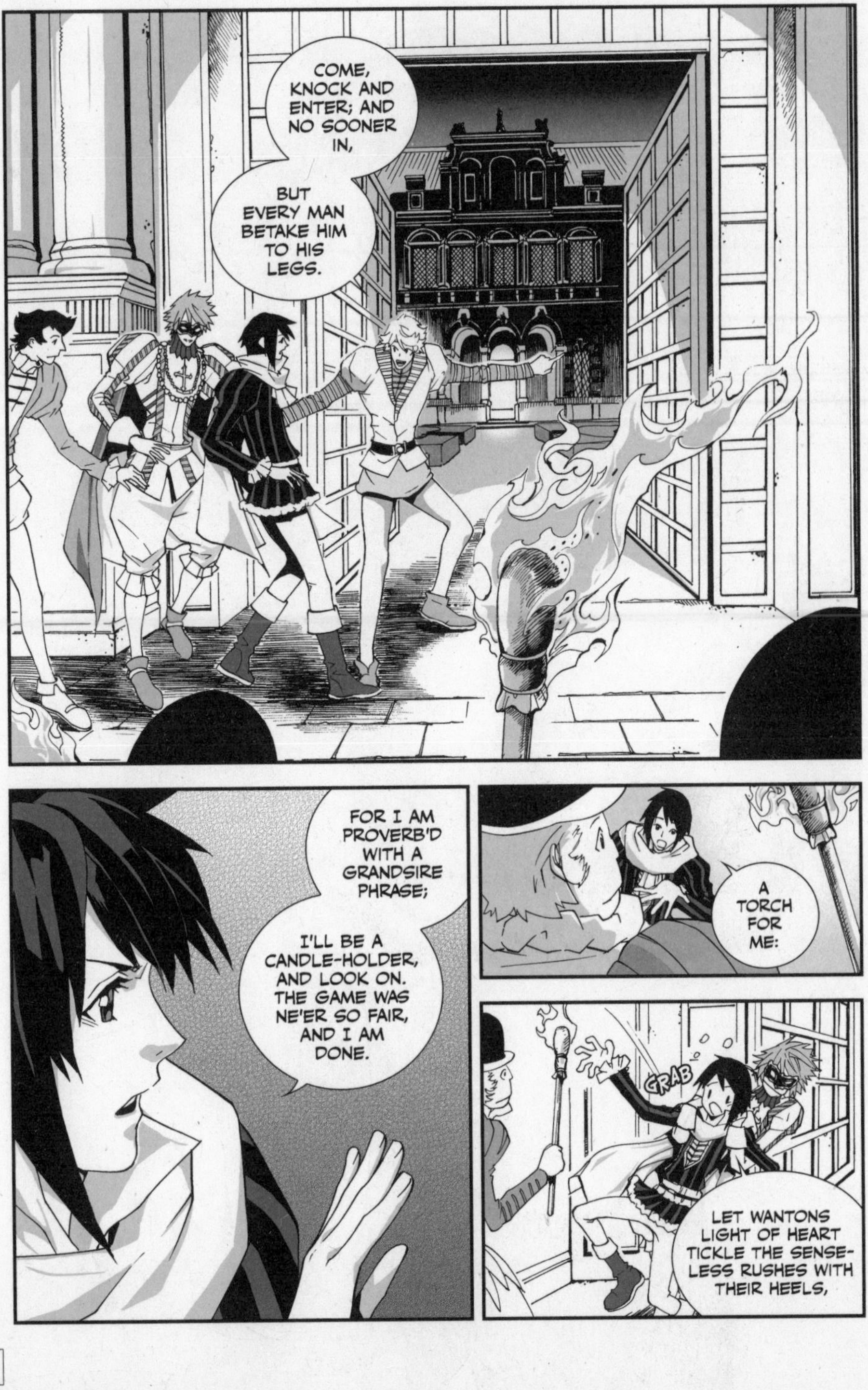
COME, KNOCK AND ENTER; AND NO SOONER IN,
BUT EVERY MAN BETAKE HIM TO HIS LEGS.
A TORCH FOR ME:
GRAB
LET WANTONS LIGHT OF HEART TICKLE THE SENSE-LESS RUSHES WITH THEIR HEELS,
FOR I AM PROVERB'D WITH A GRANDSIRE PHRASE;
I'LL BE A CANDLE-HOLDER, AND LOOK ON. THE GAME WAS NE'ER SO FAIR, AND I AM DONE.

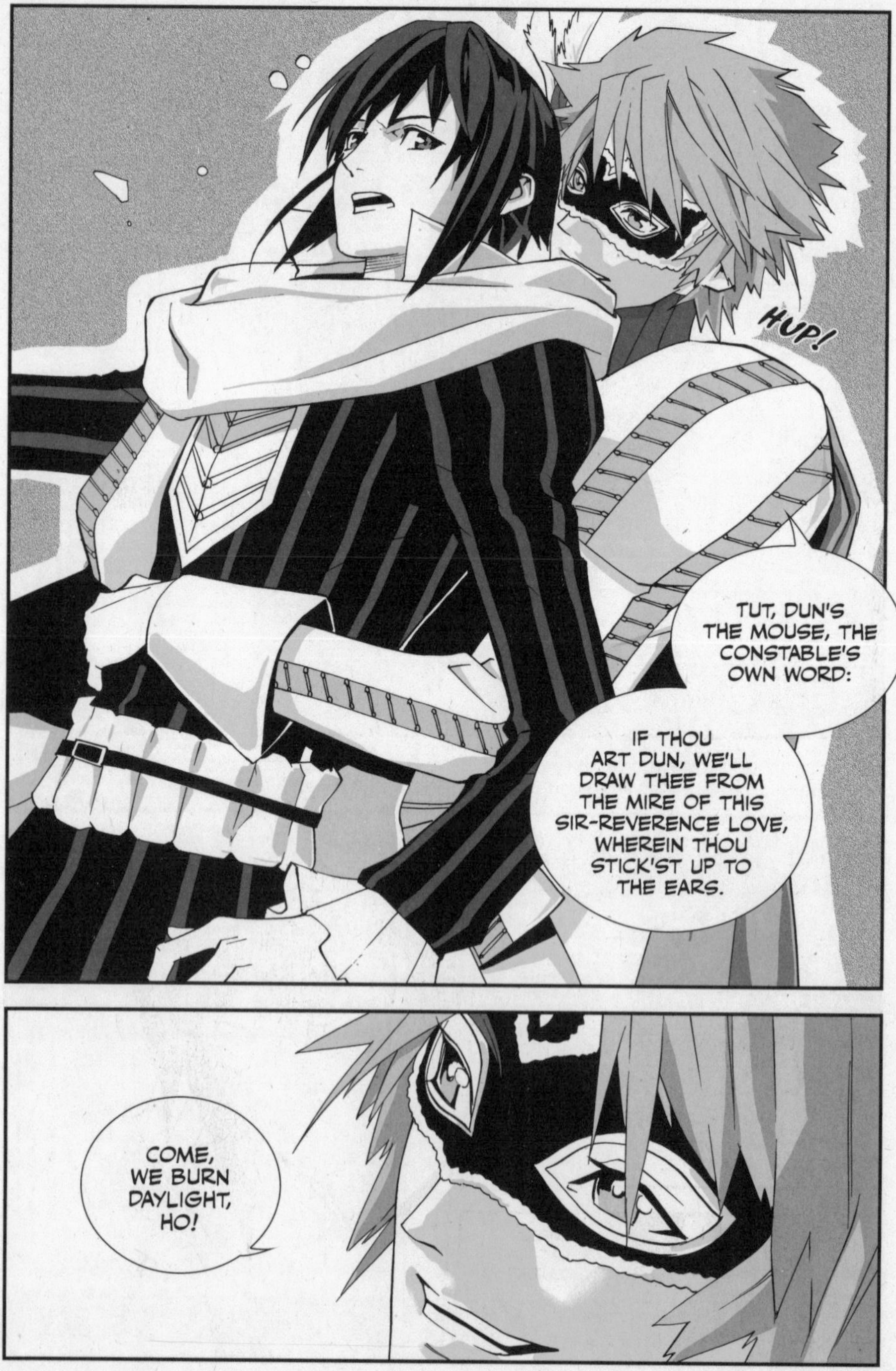
HUP!
TUT, DUN'S THE MOUSE, THE CONSTABLE'S OWN WORD:
IF THOU ART DUN, WE'LL DRAW THEE FROM THE MIRE OF THIS SIR-REVERENCE LOVE, WHEREIN THOU STICK'ST UP TO THE EARS.
COME, WE BURN DAYLIGHT, HO!

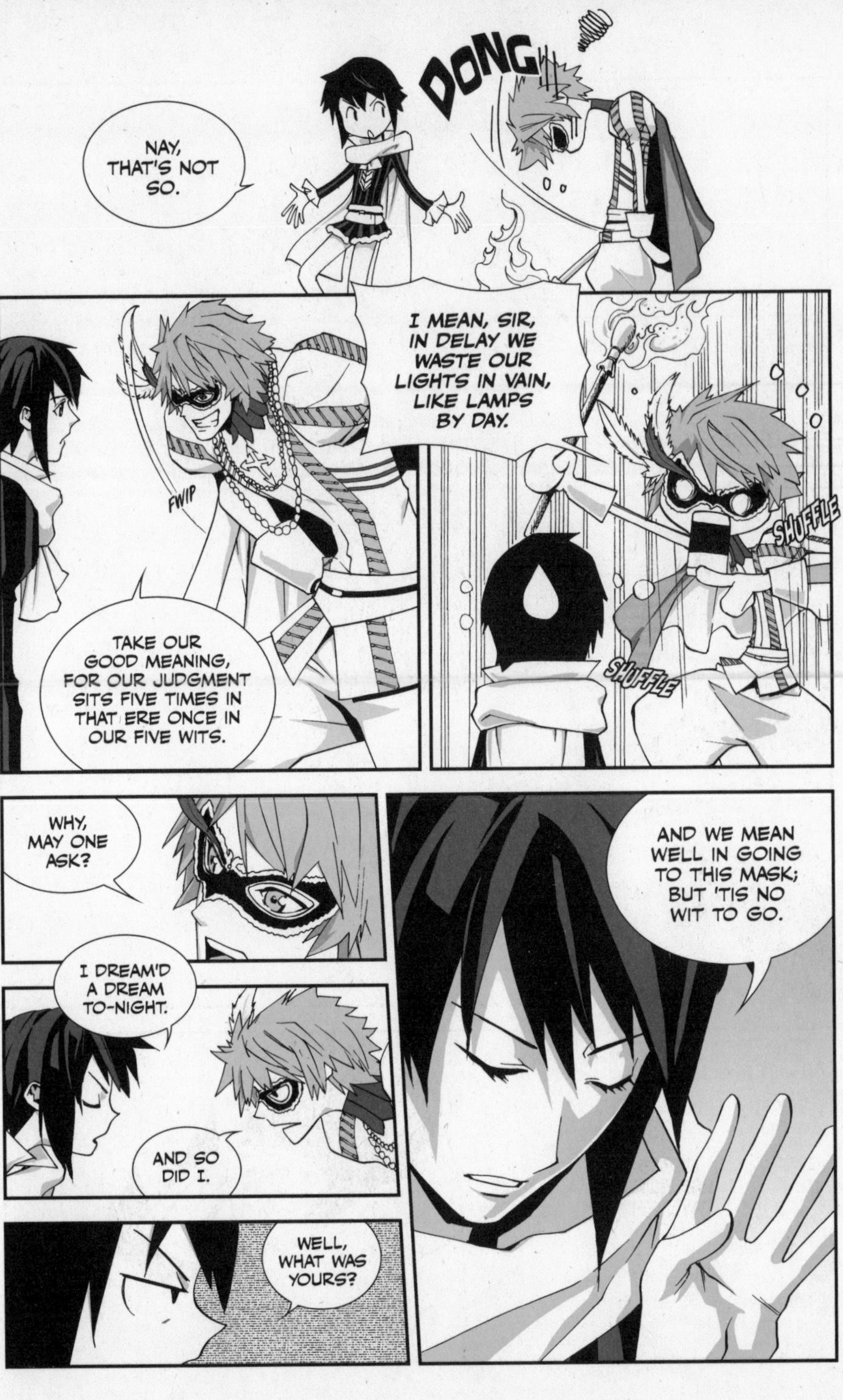
DONG
NAY, THAT'S NOT SO.
I MEAN, SIR, IN DELAY WE WASTE OUR LIGHTS IN VAIN, LIKE LAMPS BY DAY.
SHUFFLE
SHUFFLE
FWIP
TAKE OUR GOOD MEANING, FOR OUR JUDGMENT SITS FIVE TIMES IN THAT ERE ONCE IN OUR FIVE WITS.
AND WE MEAN WELL IN GOING TO THIS MASK; BUT 'TIS NO WIT TO GO.
WHY, MAY ONE ASK?
I DREAM'D A DREAM TO-NIGHT.
AND SO DID I.
WELL, WHAT WAS YOURS?

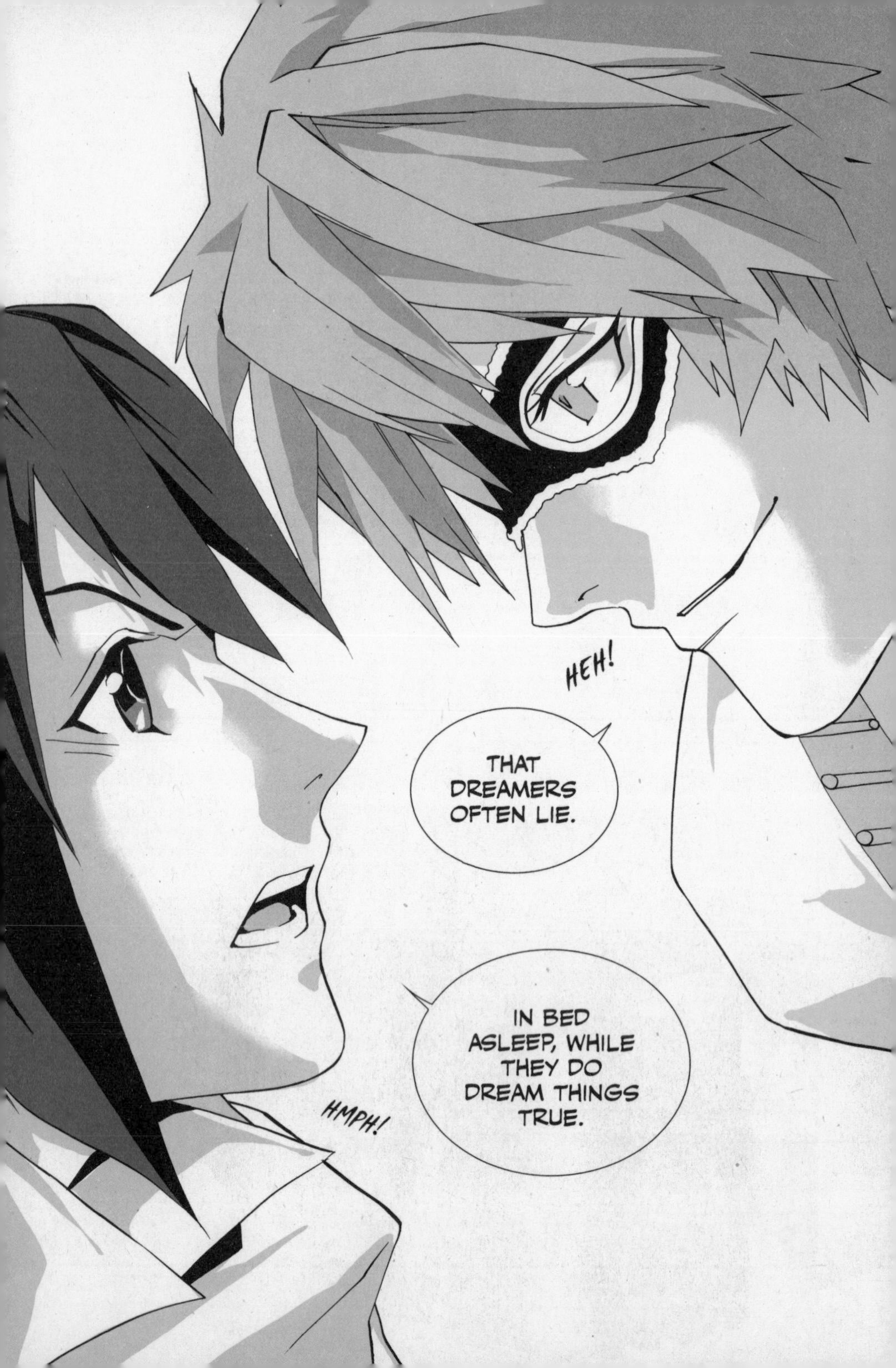
HEH!
THAT DREAMERS OFTEN LIE.
IN BED ASLEEP, WHILE THEY DO DREAM THINGS TRUE.
HMPH!

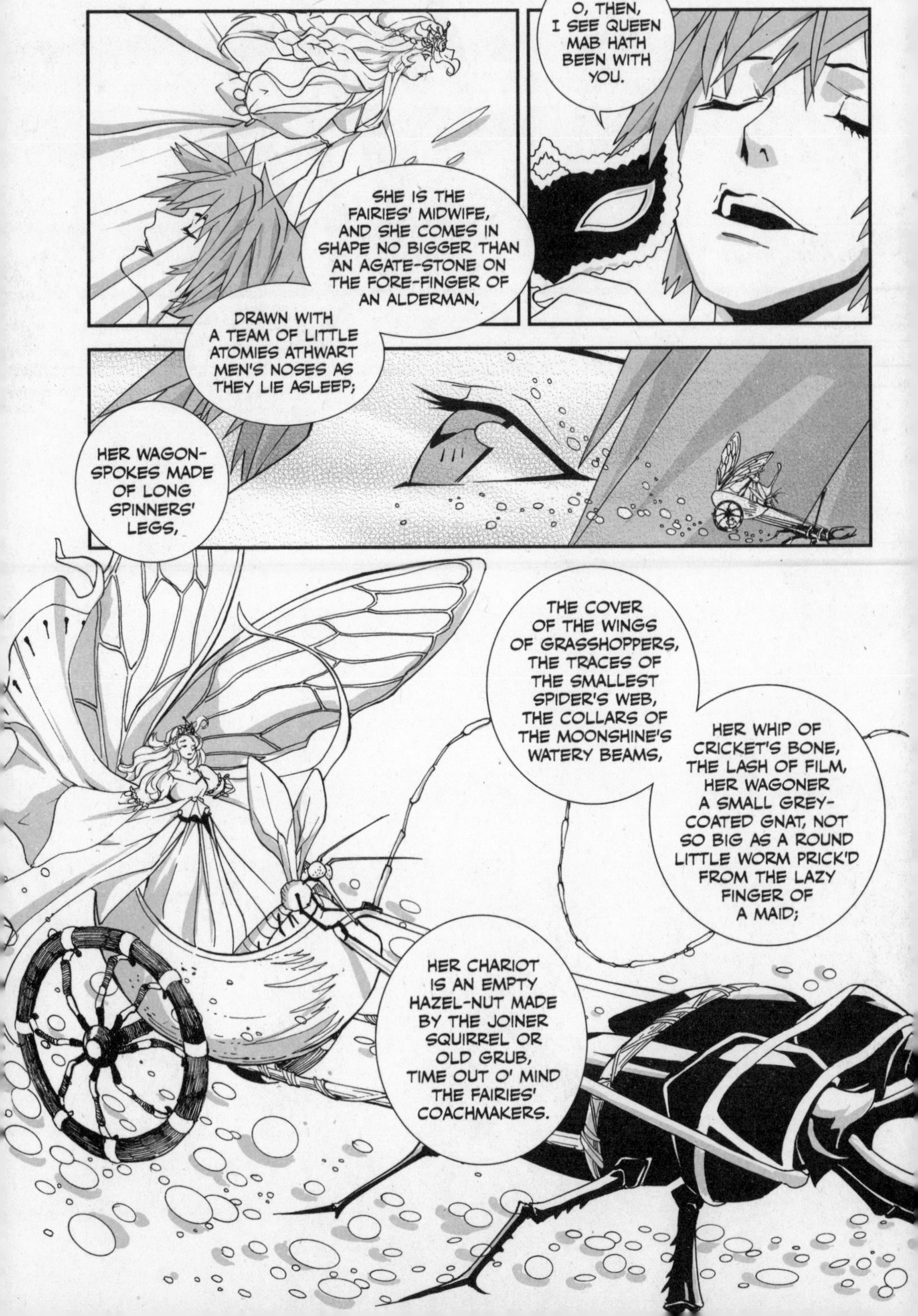
O, THEN, I SEE QUEEN MAB HATH BEEN WITH YOU.
SHE IS THE FAIRIES' MIDWIFE, AND SHE COMES IN SHAPE NO BIGGER THAN AN AGATE-STONE ON THE FORE-FINGER OF AN ALDERMAN,
DRAWN WITH A TEAM OF LITTLE ATOMIES ATHWART MEN'S NOSES AS THEY LIE ASLEEP;
HER WAGON-SPOKES MADE OF LONG SPINNERS' LEGS,
THE COVER OF THE WINGS OF GRASSHOPPERS, THE TRACES OF THE SMALLEST SPIDER'S WEB, THE COLLARS OF THE MOONSHINE'S WATERY BEAMS,
HER WHIP OF CRICKET'S BONE, THE LASH OF FILM, HER WAGONER A SMALL GREY-COATED GNAT, NOT SO BIG AS A ROUND LITTLE WORM PRICK'D FROM THE LAZY FINGER OF A MAID;
HER CHARIOT IS AN EMPTY HAZEL-NUT MADE BY THE JOINER SQUIRREL OR OLD GRUB, TIME OUT O' MIND THE FAIRIES' COACHMAKERS.

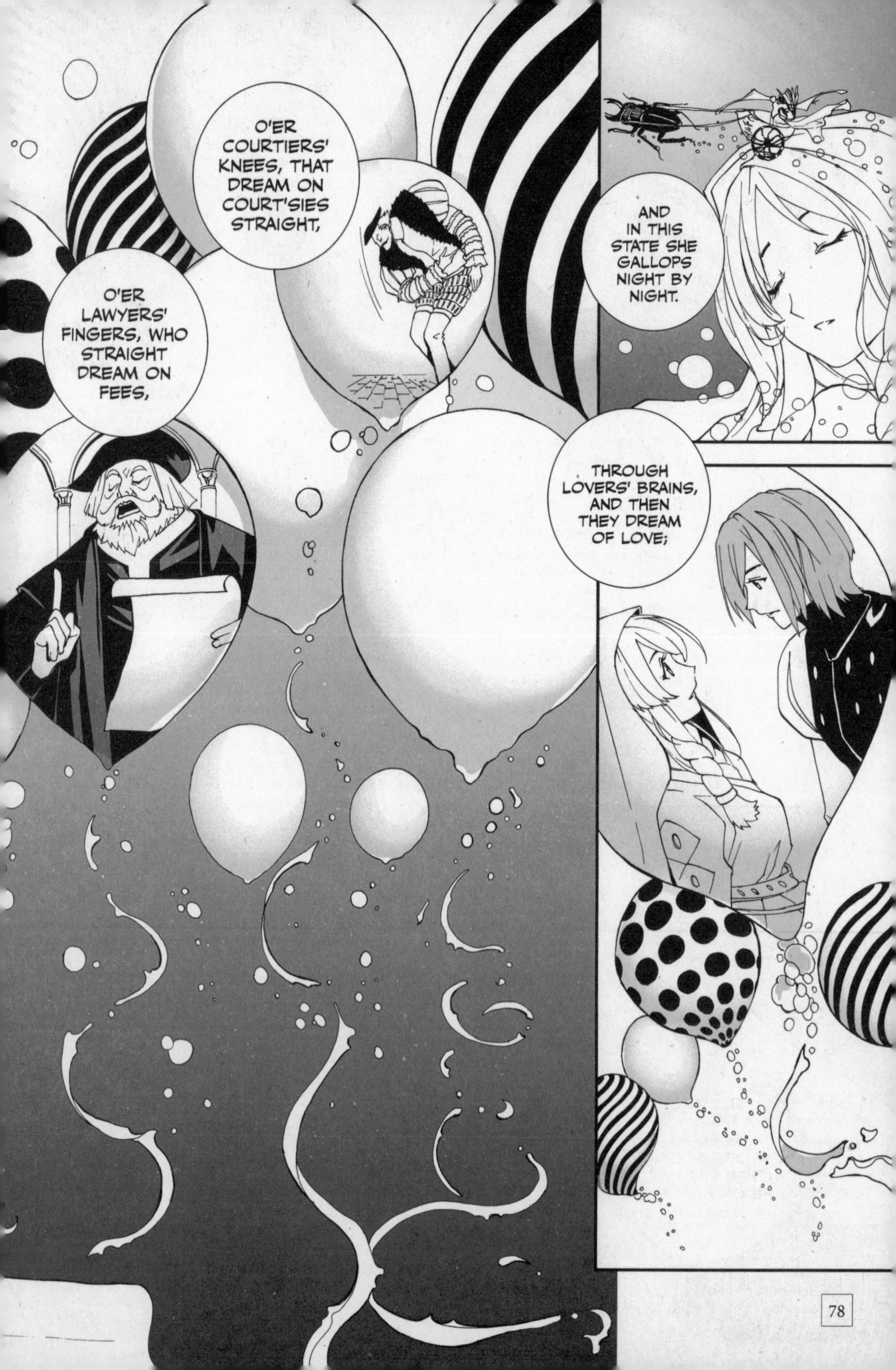
AND IN THIS STATE SHE GALLOPS NIGHT BY NIGHT.
THROUGH LOVERS' BRAINS, AND THEN THEY DREAM OF LOVE;
O'ER COURTIERS' KNEES, THAT DREAM ON COURT'SIES STRAIGHT,
O'ER LAWYERS' FINGERS, WHO STRAIGHT DREAM ON FEES,

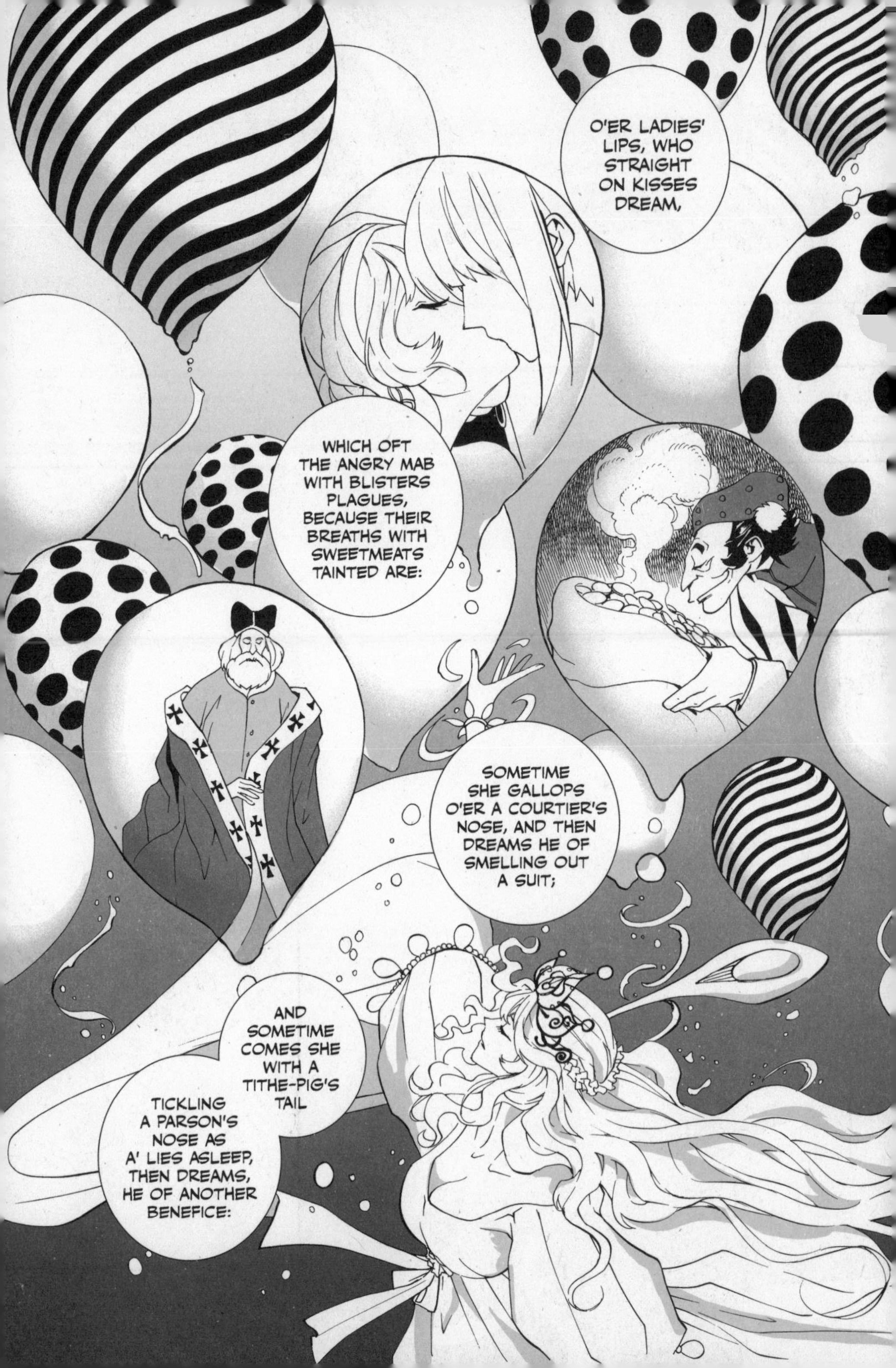
O'ER LADIES' LIPS, WHO STRAIGHT ON KISSES DREAM,
WHICH OFT THE ANGRY MAB WITH BLISTERS PLAGUES, BECAUSE THEIR BREATHS WITH SWEETMEATS TAINTED ARE:
SOMETIME SHE GALLOPS O'ER A COURTIER'S NOSE, AND THEN DREAMS HE OF SMELLING OUT A SUIT;
AND SOMETIME COMES SHE WITH A TITHE-PIG'S TAIL
TICKLING A PARSON'S NOSE AS A' LIES ASLEEP, THEN DREAMS, HE OF ANOTHER BENEFICE:

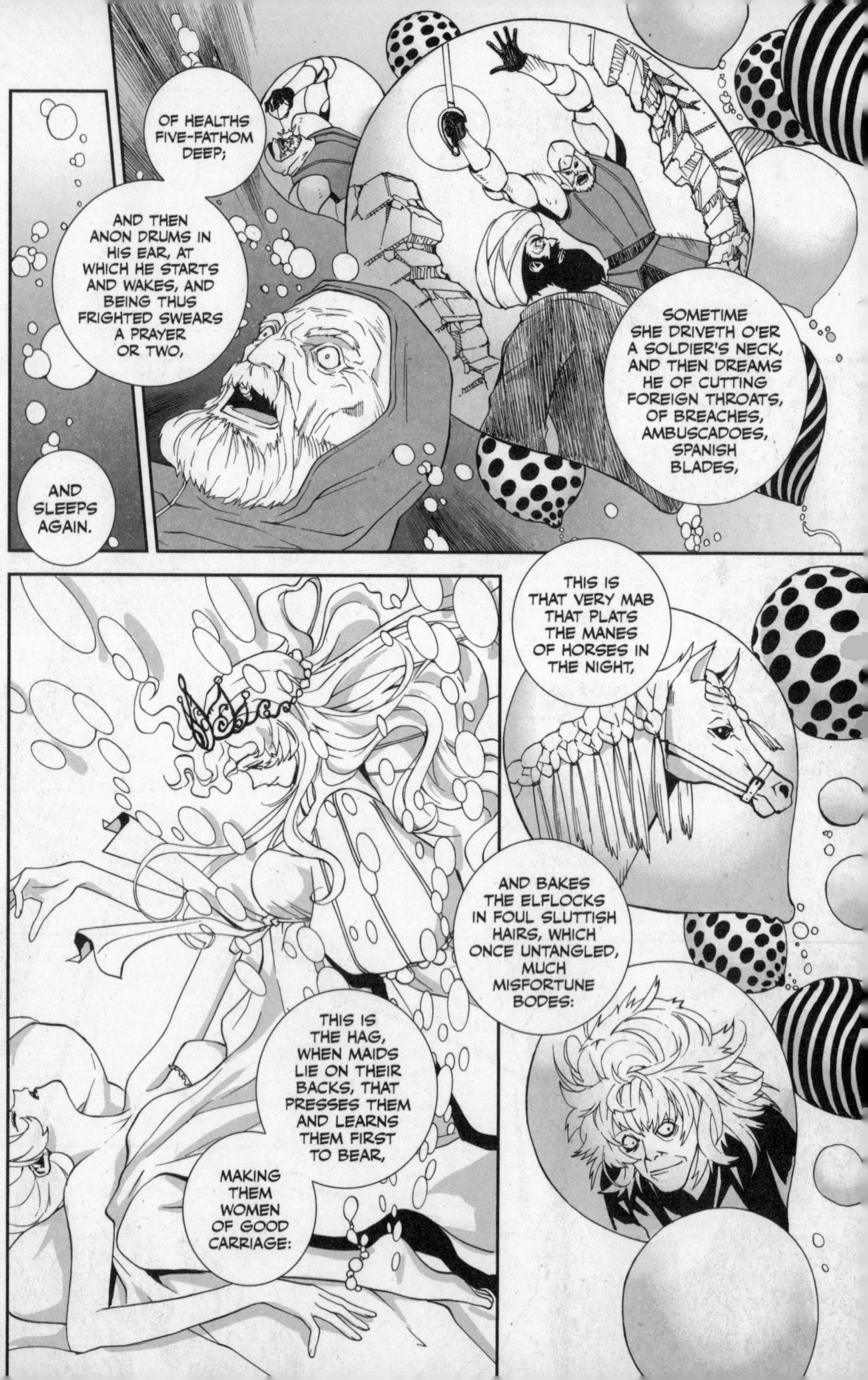
SOMETIME SHE DRIVETH O'ER A SOLDIER'S NECK, AND THEN DREAMS HE OF CUTTING FOREIGN THROATS, OF BREACHES, AMBUSCADOES, SPANISH BLADES,
OF HEALTHS FIVE-FATHOM DEEP;
AND THEN ANON DRUMS IN HIS EAR, AT WHICH HE STARTS AND WAKES, AND BEING THUS FRIGHTED SWEARS A PRAYER OR TWO,
AND SLEEPS AGAIN.
THIS IS THAT VERY MAB THAT PLATS THE MANES OF HORSES IN THE NIGHT,
AND BAKES THE ELFLOCKS IN FOUL SLUTTISH HAIRS, WHICH ONCE UNTANGLED, MUCH MISFORTUNE BODES:
THIS IS THE HAG, WHEN MAIDS LIE ON THEIR BACKS, THAT PRESSES THEM AND LEARNS THEM FIRST TO BEAR,
MAKING THEM WOMEN OF GOOD CARRIAGE:

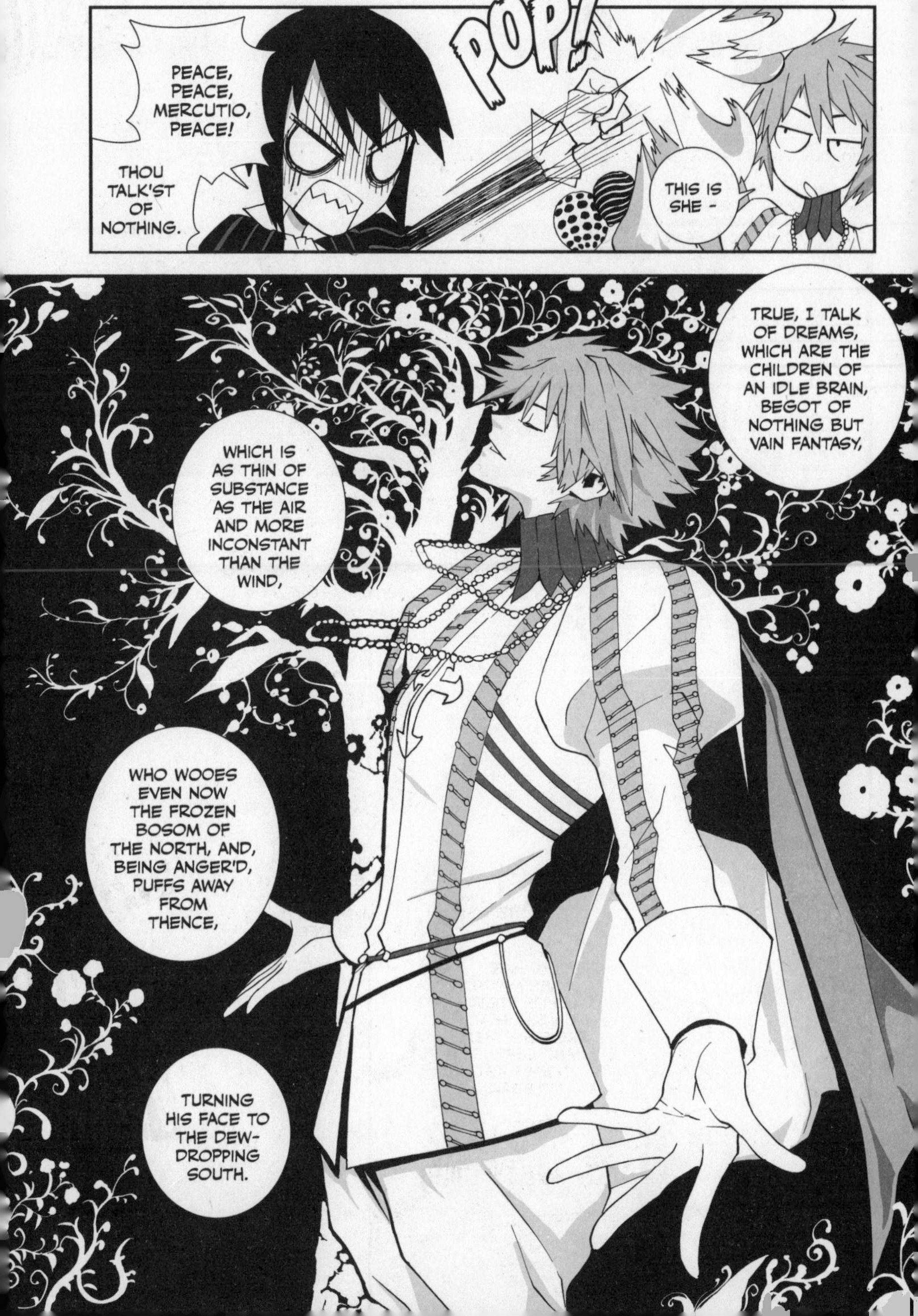
THIS IS SHE -
POP!
PEACE, PEACE, MERCUTIO, PEACE!
THOU TALK'ST OF NOTHING.
TRUE, I TALK OF DREAMS, WHICH ARE THE CHILDREN OF AN IDLE BRAIN, BEGOT OF NOTHING BUT VAIN FANTASY,
WHICH IS AS THIN OF SUBSTANCE AS THE AIR AND MORE INCONSTANT THAN THE WIND,
WHO WOOES EVEN NOW THE FROZEN BOSOM OF THE NORTH, AND, BEING ANGER'D, PUFFS AWAY FROM THENCE,
TURNING HIS FACE TO THE DEW-DROPPING SOUTH.

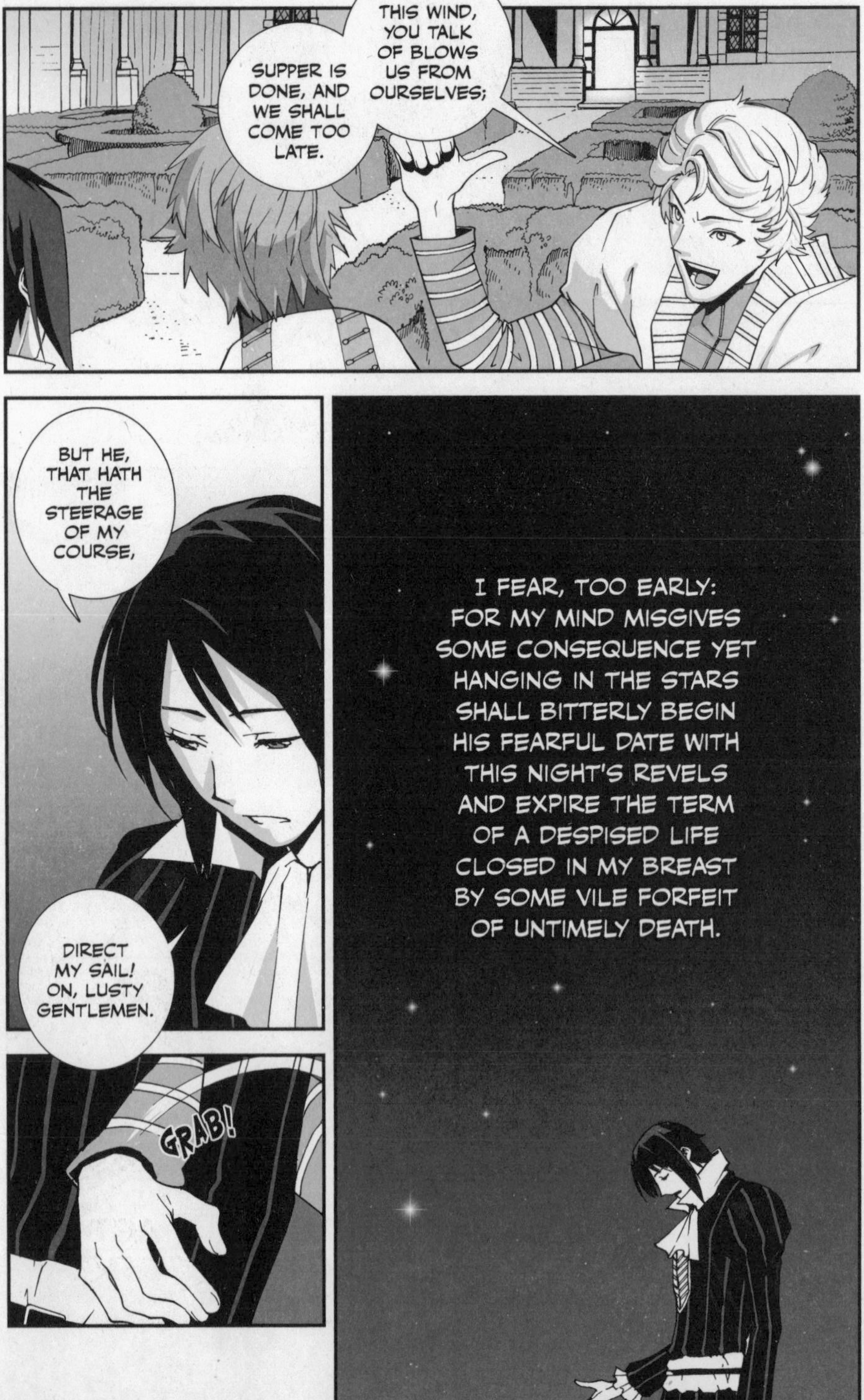
THIS WIND, YOU TALK OF BLOWS US FROM OURSELVES;
SUPPER IS DONE, AND WE SHALL COME TOO LATE.
I FEAR, TOO EARLY: FOR MY MIND MISGIVES SOME CONSEQUENCE YET HANGING IN THE STARS SHALL BITTERLY BEGIN HIS FEARFUL DATE WITH THIS NIGHT'S REVELS AND EXPIRE THE TERM OF A DESPISED LIFE CLOSED IN MY BREAST BY SOME VILE FORFEIT OF UNTIMELY DEATH.
BUT HE, THAT HATH THE STEERAGE OF MY COURSE,
DIRECT MY SAIL! ON, LUSTY GENTLEMEN.
GRAB!

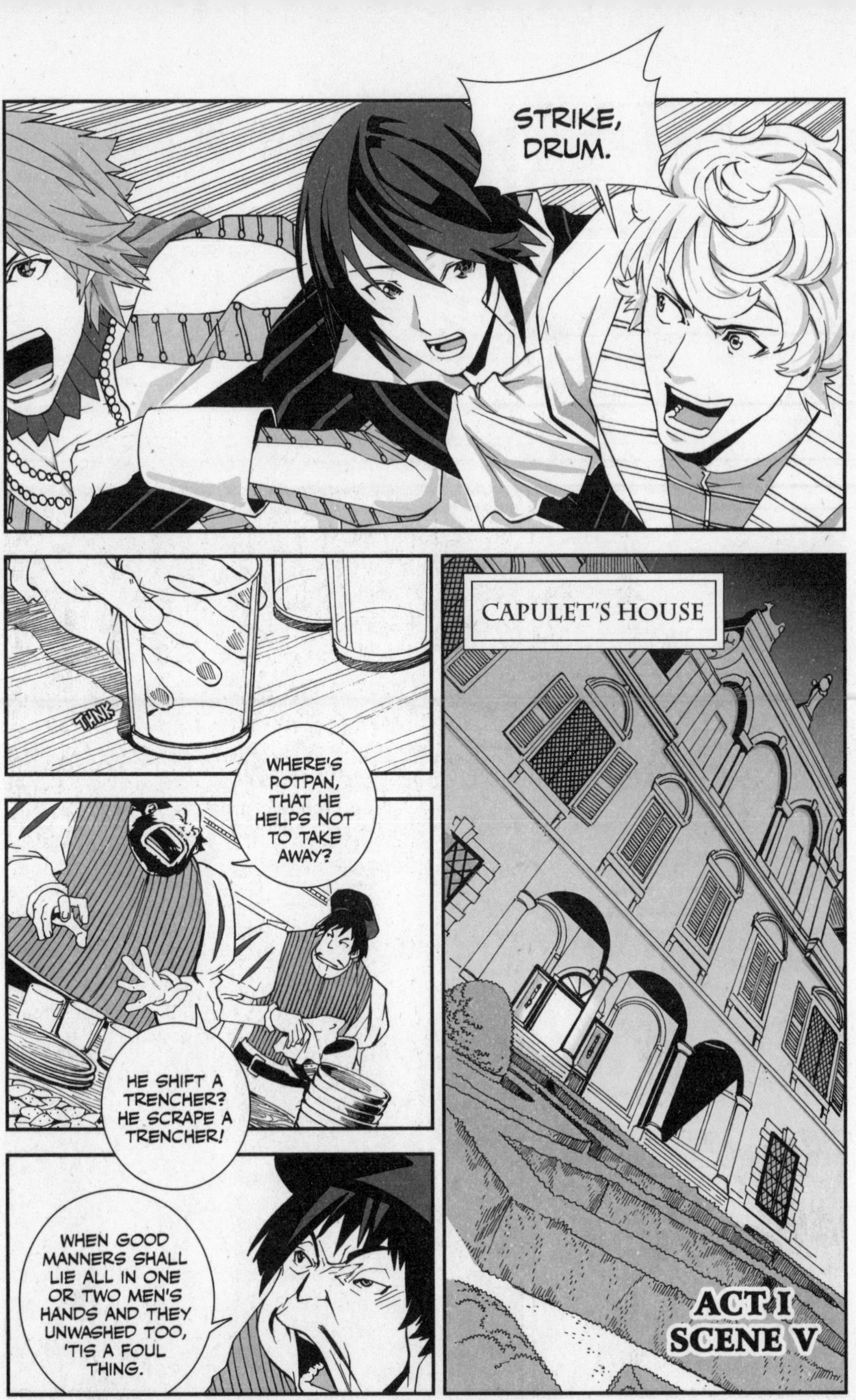
STRIKE, DRUM.
CAPULET'S HOUSE
ACT I SCENE V
THINK
WHERE'S POTPAN, THAT HE HELPS NOT TO TAKE AWAY?
HE SHIFT A TRENCHER? HE SCRAPE A TRENCHER!
WHEN GOOD MANNERS SHALL LIE ALL IN ONE OR TWO MEN'S HANDS AND THEY UNWASHED TOO, 'TIS A FOUL THING.

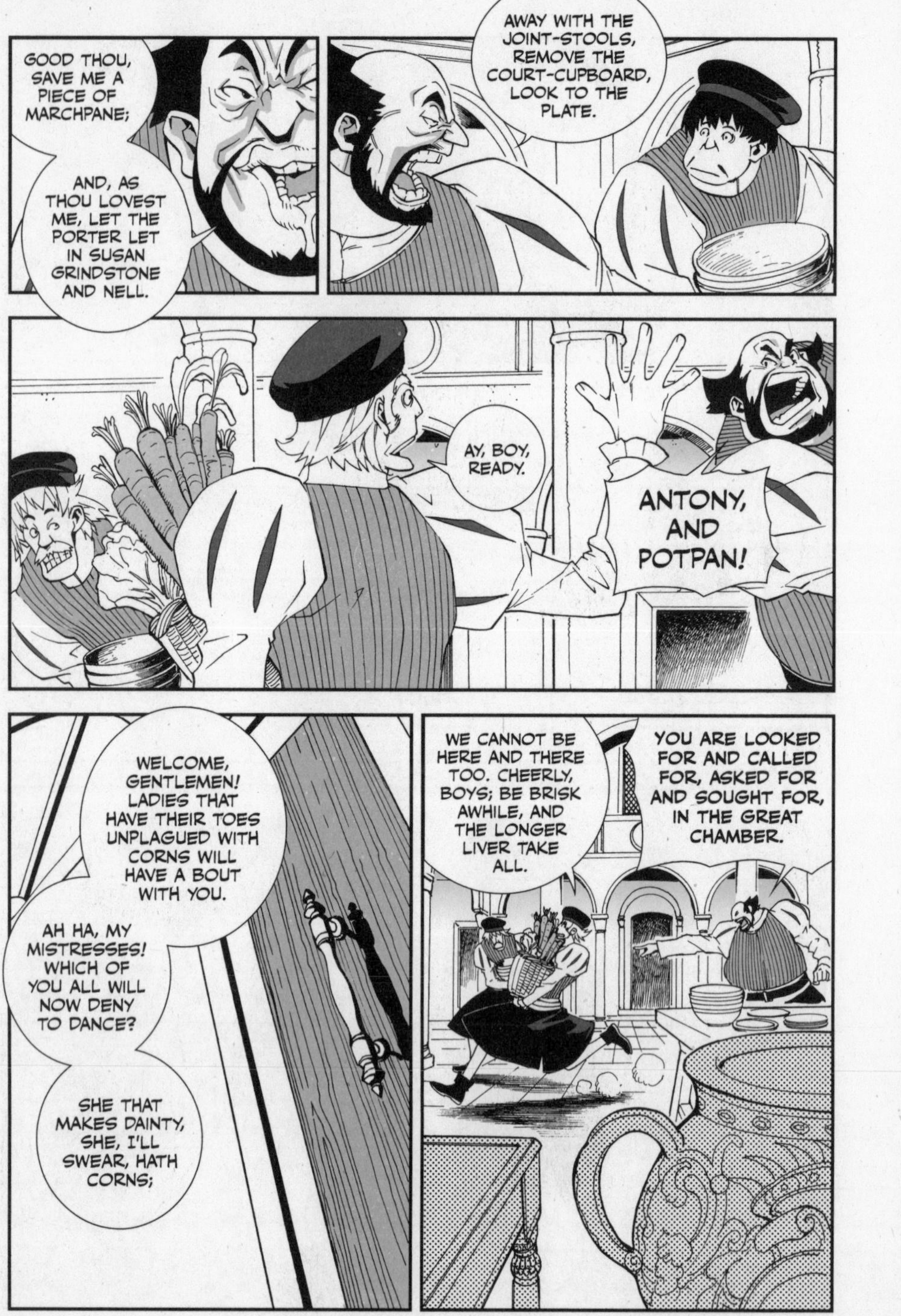
AWAY WITH THE JOINT-STOOLS, REMOVE THE COURT-CUPBOARD, LOOK TO THE PLATE.
GOOD THOU, SAVE ME A PIECE OF MARCHPANE;
AND, AS THOU LOVEST ME, LET THE PORTER LET IN SUSAN GRINDSTONE AND NELL.
ANTONY, AND POTPAN!
AY, BOY, READY.
YOU ARE LOOKED FOR AND CALLED FOR, ASKED FOR AND SOUGHT FOR, IN THE GREAT CHAMBER.
WE CANNOT BE HERE AND THERE TOO. CHEERLY, BOYS; BE BRISK AWHILE, AND THE LONGER LIVER TAKE ALL.
WELCOME, GENTLEMEN! LADIES THAT HAVE THEIR TOES UNPLAGUED WITH CORNS WILL HAVE A BOUT WITH YOU.
AH HA, MY MISTRESSES! WHICH OF YOU ALL WILL NOW DENY TO DANCE?
SHE THAT MAKES DAINTY, SHE, I'LL SWEAR, HATH CORNS;

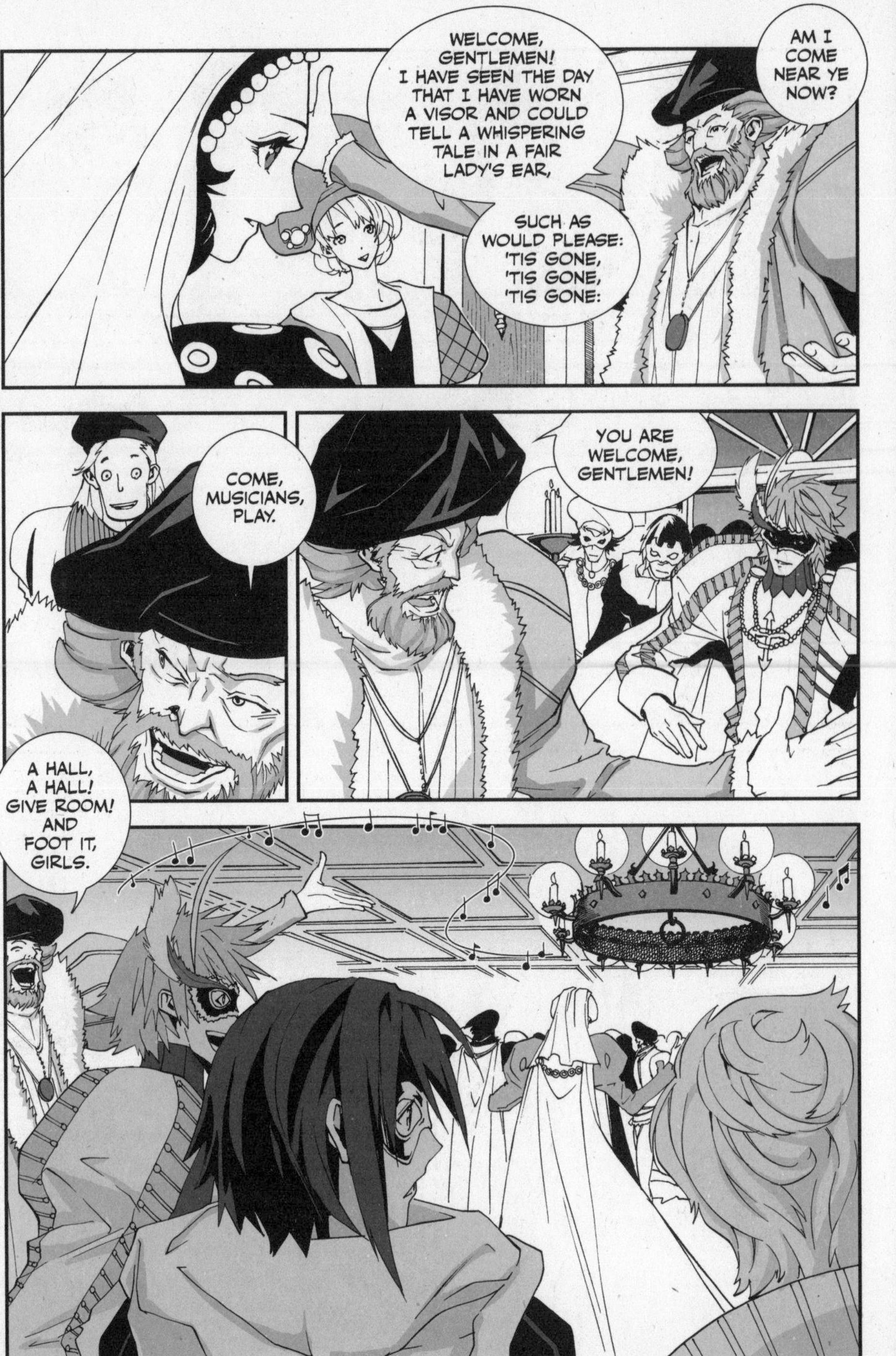
AM I COME NEAR YE NOW?
WELCOME, GENTLEMEN! I HAVE SEEN THE DAY THAT I HAVE WORN A VISOR AND COULD TELL A WHISPERING TALE IN A FAIR LADY'S EAR,
SUCH AS WOULD PLEASE: 'TIS GONE, 'TIS GONE, 'TIS GONE:
YOU ARE WELCOME, GENTLEMEN!
COME, MUSICIANS, PLAY.
A HALL, A HALL! GIVE ROOM! AND FOOT IT, GIRLS.

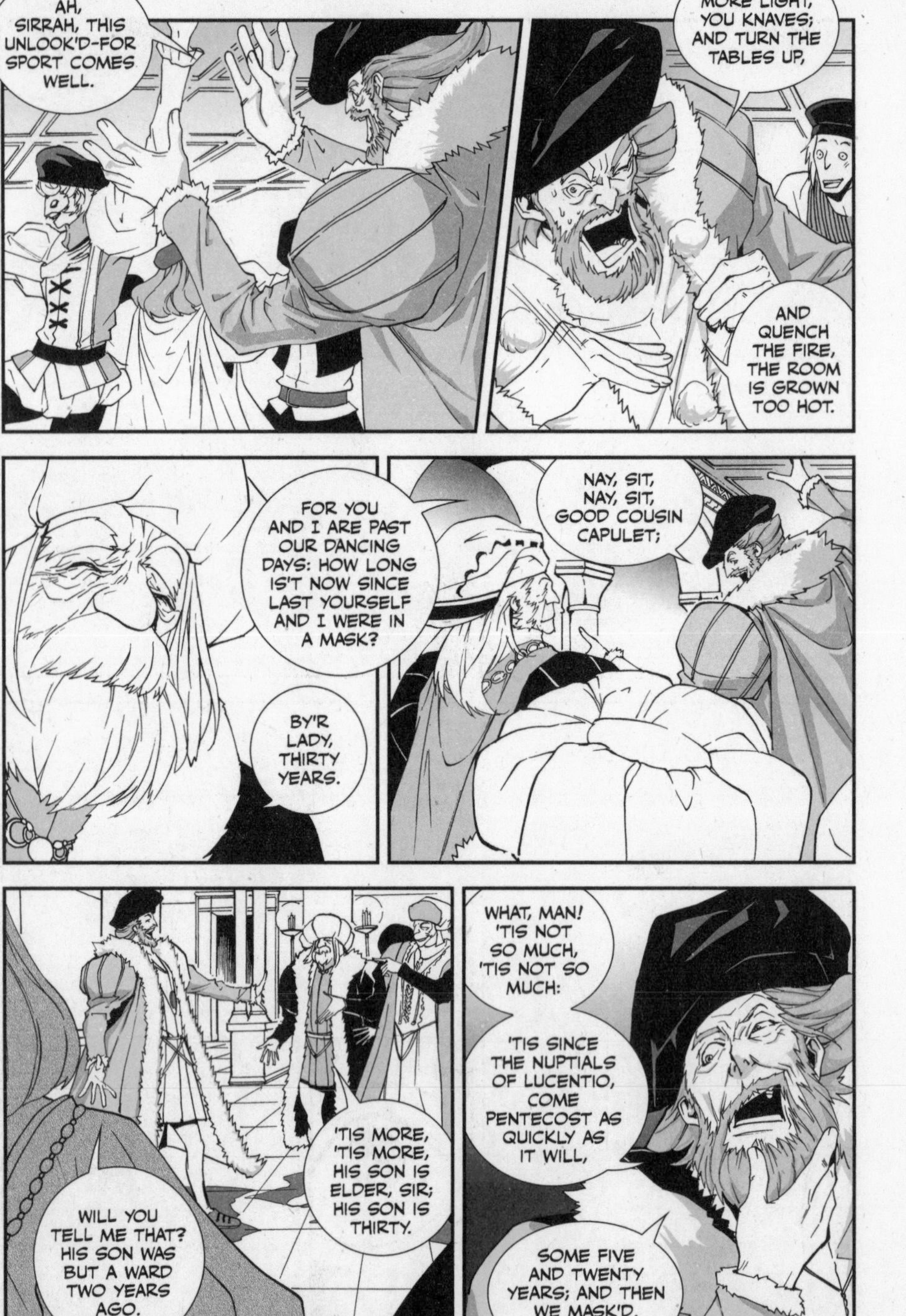

MORE LIGHT, YOU KNAVES; AND TURN THE TABLES UP,
AND QUENCH THE FIRE, THE ROOM IS GROWN TOO HOT.
AH, SIRRAH, THIS UNLOOK'D-FOR SPORT COMES WELL.
NAY, SIT, NAY, SIT, GOOD COUSIN CAPULET;
FOR YOU AND I ARE PAST OUR DANCING DAYS: HOW LONG IS'T NOW SINCE LAST YOURSELF AND I WERE IN A MASK?
BY'R LADY, THIRTY YEARS.
WHAT, MAN! 'TIS NOT SO MUCH, 'TIS NOT SO MUCH:
'TIS SINCE THE NUPTIALS OF LUCENTIO, COME PENTECOST AS QUICKLY AS IT WILL,
SOME FIVE AND TWENTY YEARS; AND THEN WE MASK'D.
'TIS MORE, 'TIS MORE, HIS SON IS ELDER, SIR; HIS SON IS THIRTY.
WILL YOU TELL ME THAT? HIS SON WAS BUT A WARD TWO YEARS AGO.

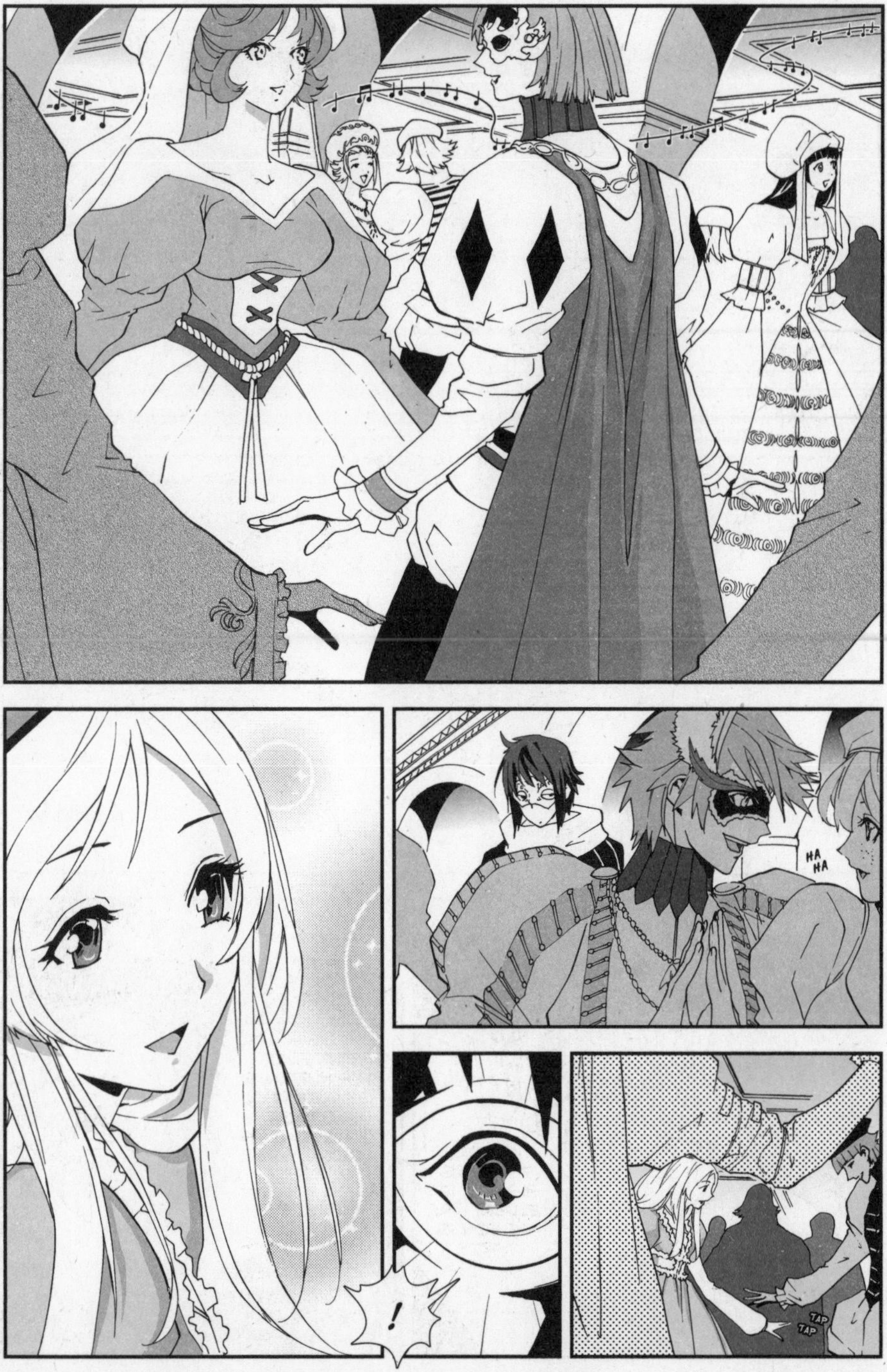
HA HA
TAP TAP
!

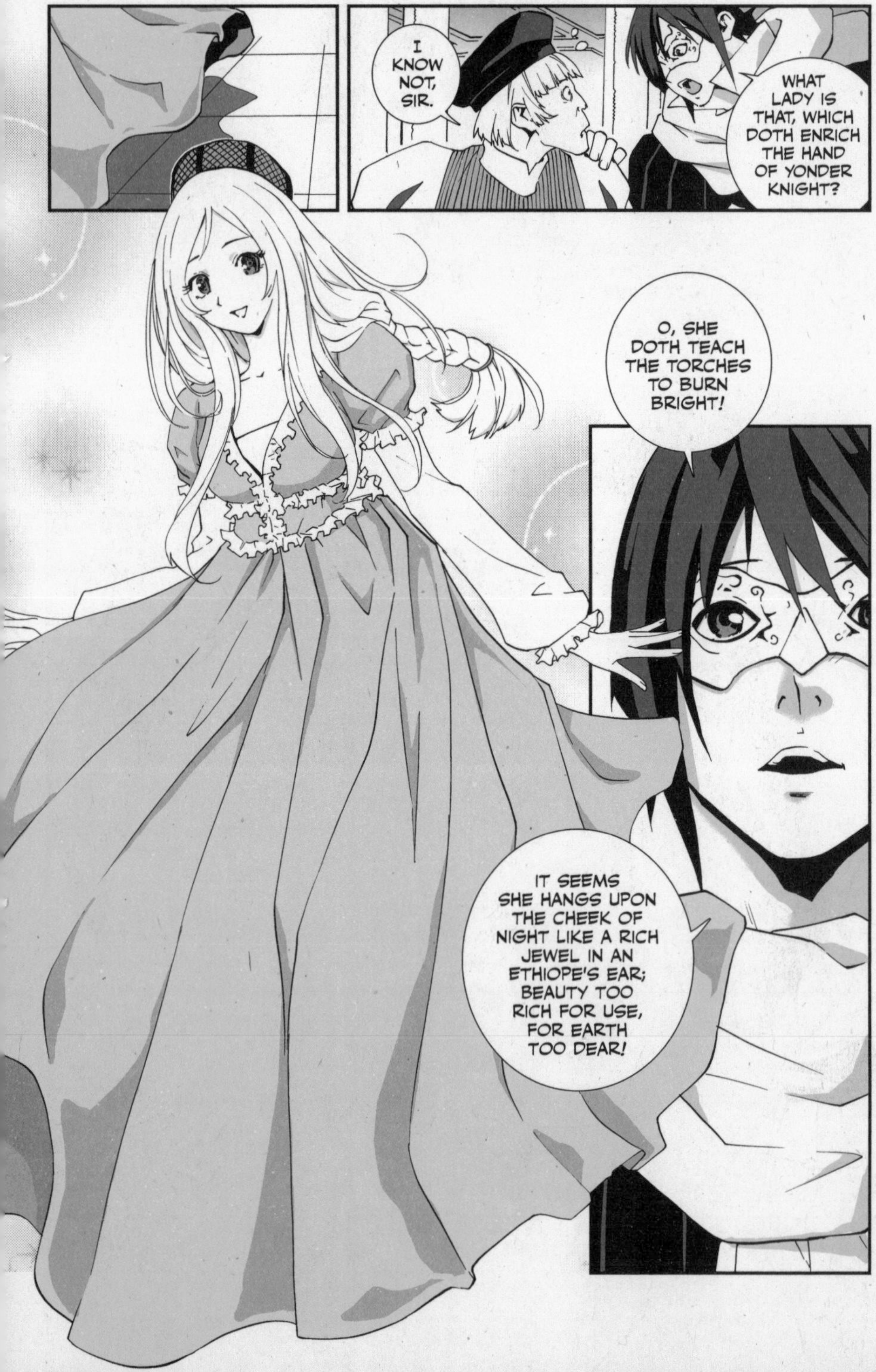
WHAT LADY IS THAT, WHICH DOTH ENRICH THE HAND OF YONDER KNIGHT?
I KNOW NOT, SIR.
O, SHE DOTH TEACH THE TORCHES TO BURN BRIGHT!
IT SEEMS SHE HANGS UPON THE CHEEK OF NIGHT LIKE A RICH JEWEL IN AN ETHIOPE'S EAR; BEAUTY TOO RICH FOR USE, FOR EARTH TOO DEAR!

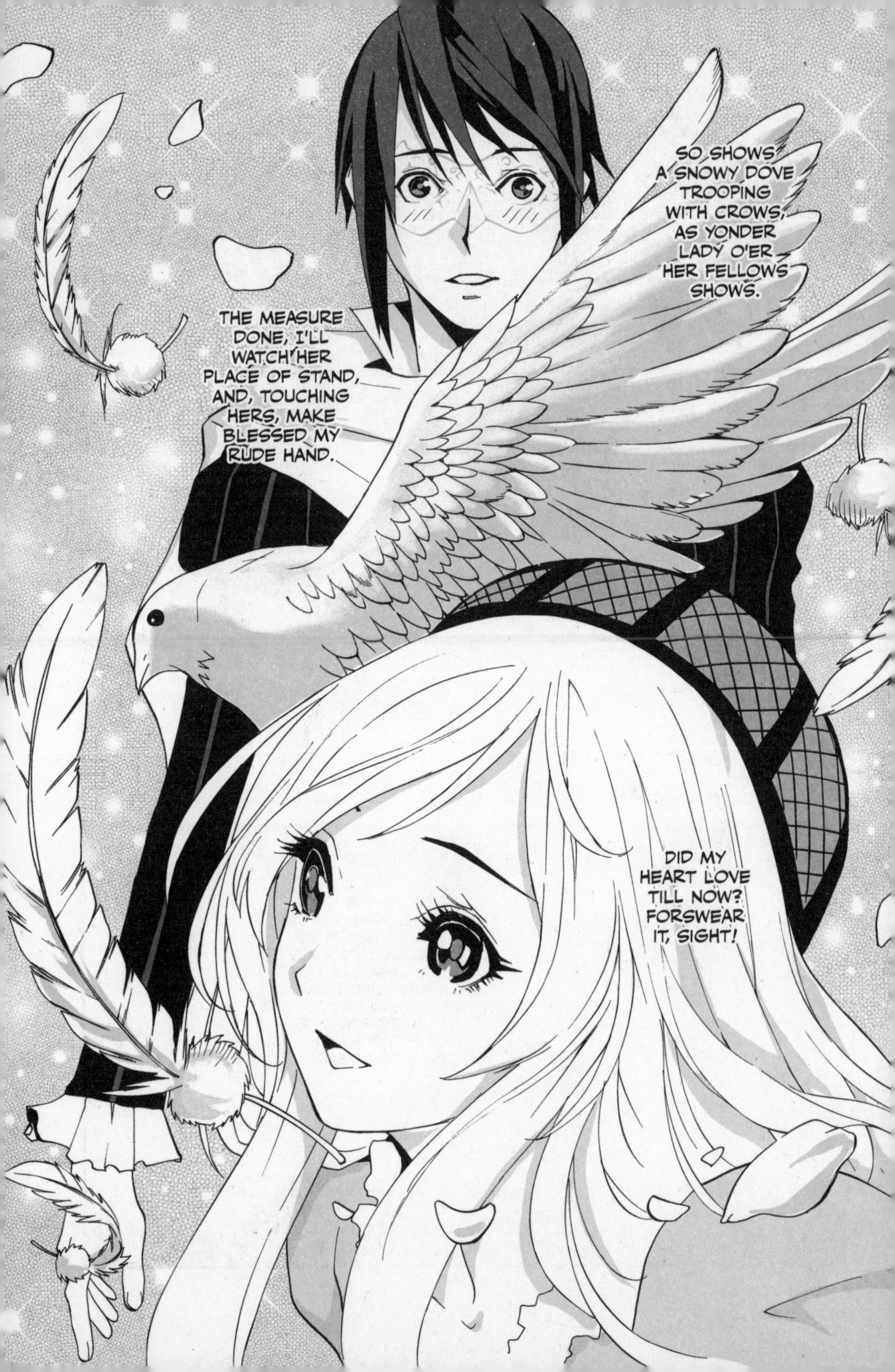
SO SHOWS A SNOWY DOVE TROOPING WITH CROWS, AS YONDER LADY O'ER HER FELLOWS SHOWS.
THE MEASURE DONE, I'LL WATCH HER PLACE OF STAND, AND, TOUCHING HERS, MAKE BLESSED MY RUDE HAND.
DID MY HEART LOVE TILL NOW? FORSWEAR IT, SIGHT!

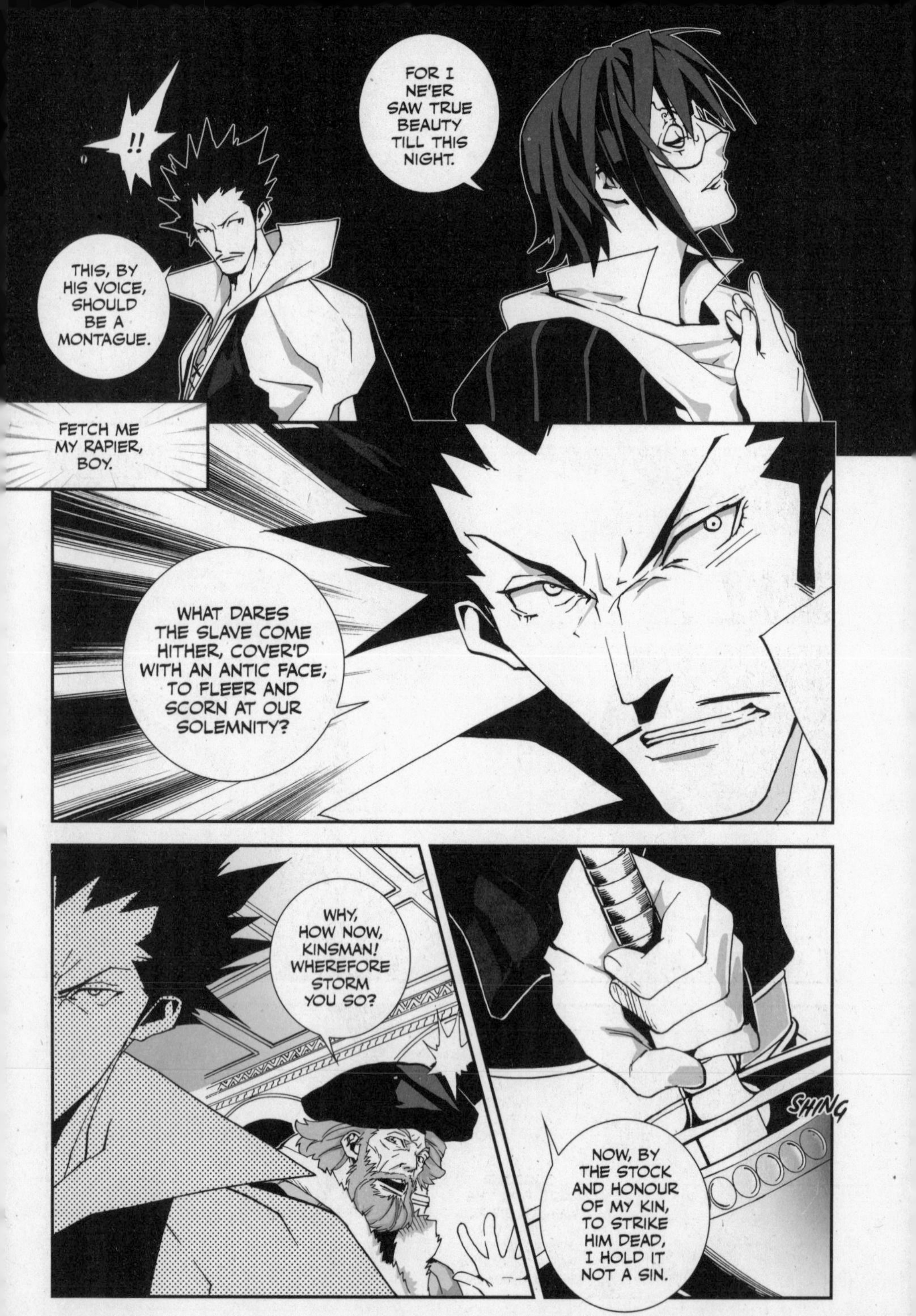
FOR I NE'ER SAW TRUE BEAUTY TILL THIS NIGHT.
!!
THIS, BY HIS VOICE, SHOULD BE A MONTAGUE.
FETCH ME MY RAPIER, BOY.
WHAT DARES THE SLAVE COME HITHER, COVER'D WITH AN ANTIC FACE, TO FLEER AND SCORN AT OUR SOLEMNITY?
SHING
NOW, BY THE STOCK AND HONOUR OF MY KIN, TO STRIKE HIM DEAD, I HOLD IT NOT A SIN.
WHY, HOW NOW, KINSMAN! WHEREFORE STORM YOU SO?

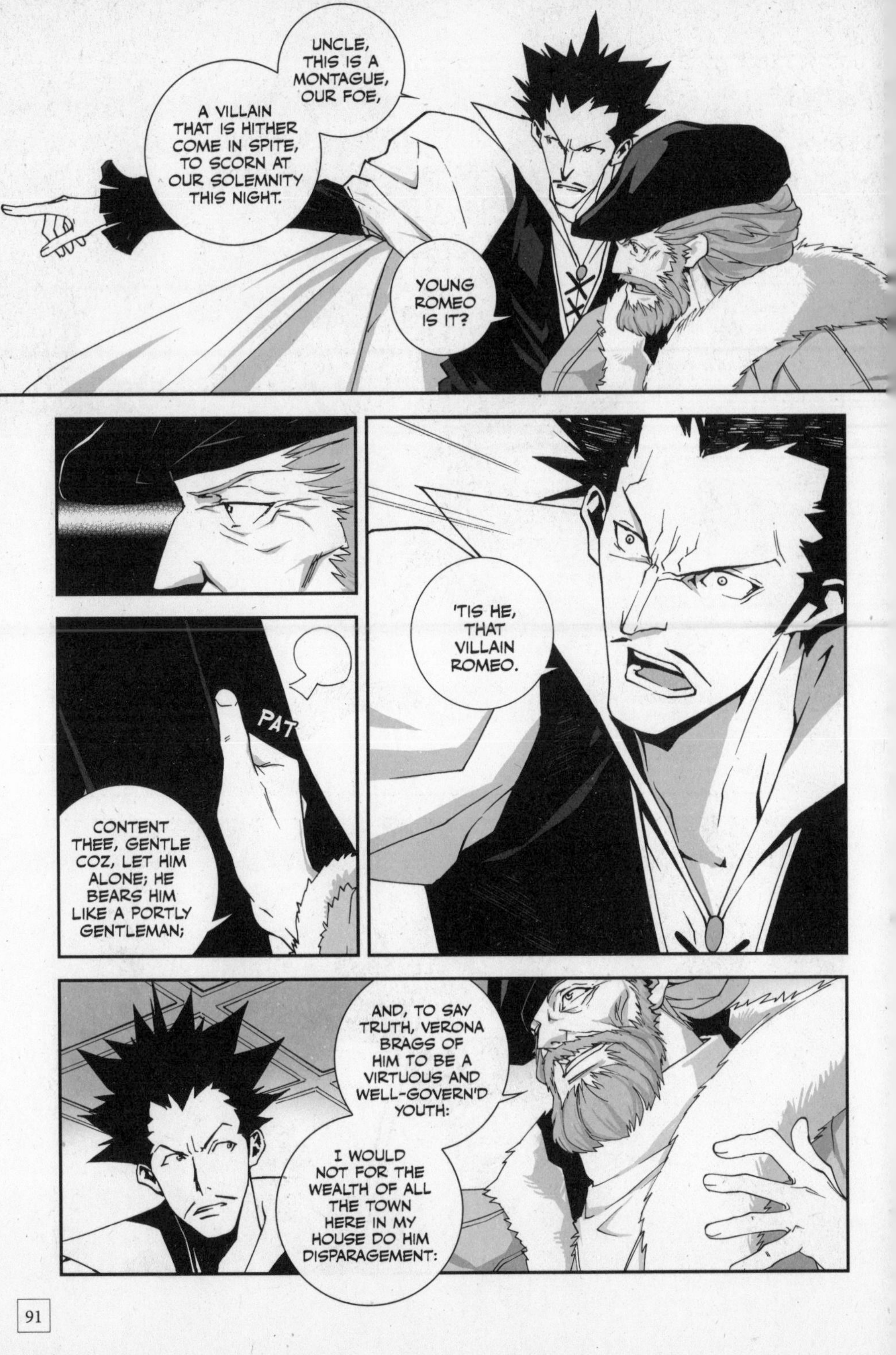
UNCLE, THIS IS A MONTAGUE, OUR FOE,
A VILLAIN THAT IS HITHER COME IN SPITE, TO SCORN AT OUR SOLEMNITY THIS NIGHT.
YOUNG ROMEO IS IT?
'TIS HE, THAT VILLAIN ROMEO.
PAT
CONTENT THEE, GENTLE COZ, LET HIM ALONE; HE BEARS HIM LIKE A PORTLY GENTLEMAN;
AND, TO SAY TRUTH, VERONA BRAGS OF HIM TO BE A VIRTUOUS AND WELL-GOVERN'D YOUTH:
I WOULD NOT FOR THE WEALTH OF ALL THE TOWN HERE IN MY HOUSE DO HIM DISPARAGEMENT:

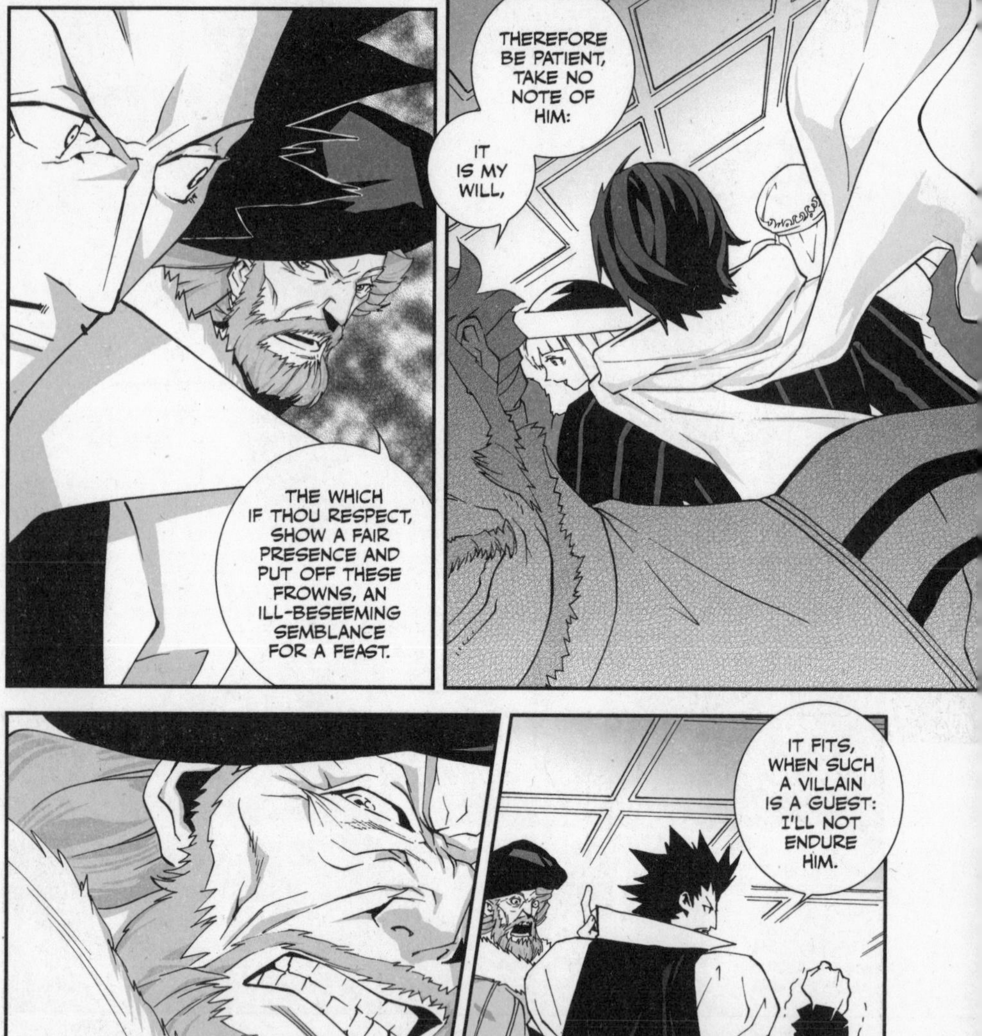
THEREFORE BE PATIENT, TAKE NO NOTE OF HIM:
IT IS MY WILL,
THE WHICH IF THOU RESPECT, SHOW A FAIR PRESENCE AND PUT OFF THESE FROWNS, AN ILL-BESEEMING SEMBLANCE FOR A FEAST.
IT FITS, WHEN SUCH A VILLAIN IS A GUEST: I'LL NOT ENDURE HIM.
TREMBLE
HE SHALL BE ENDURED:
WHAT, GOODMAN BOY! I SAY, HE SHALL: GO TO;

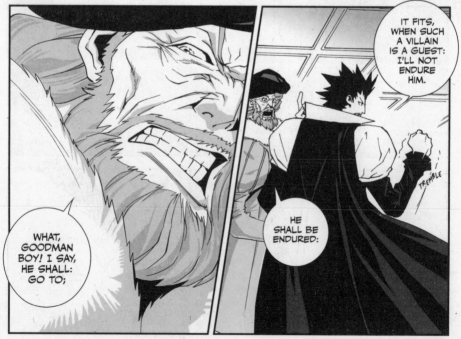

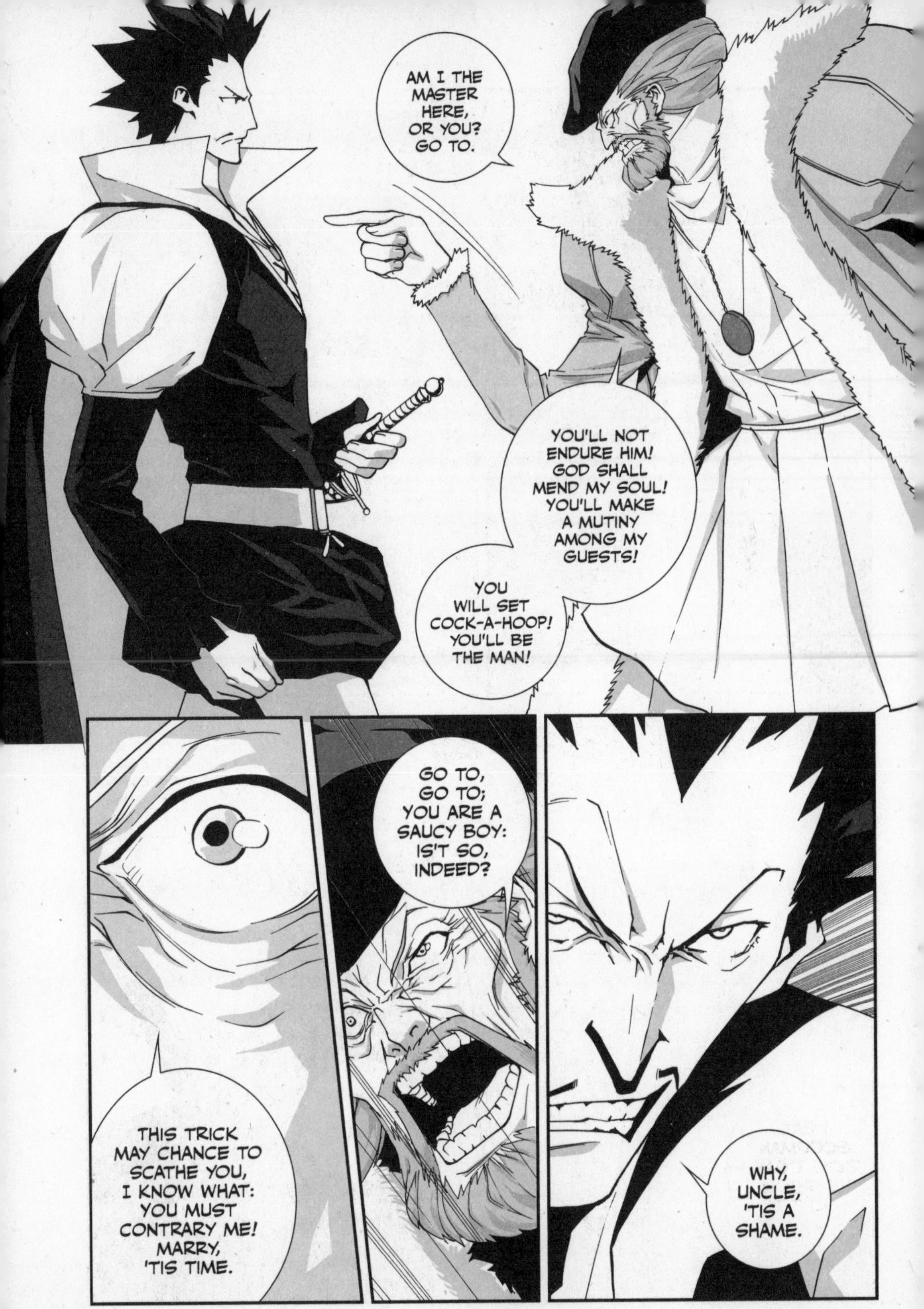
AM I THE MASTER HERE, OR YOU? GO TO.
YOU'LL NOT ENDURE HIM! GOD SHALL MEND MY SOUL! YOU'LL MAKE A MUTINY AMONG MY GUESTS!
YOU WILL SET COCK-A-HOOP! YOU'LL BE THE MAN!
WHY, UNCLE, 'TIS A SHAME.
GO TO, GO TO; YOU ARE A SAUCY BOY: IS'T SO, INDEED?
THIS TRICK MAY CHANCE TO SCATHE YOU, I KNOW WHAT: YOU MUST CONTRARY ME! MARRY, 'TIS TIME.

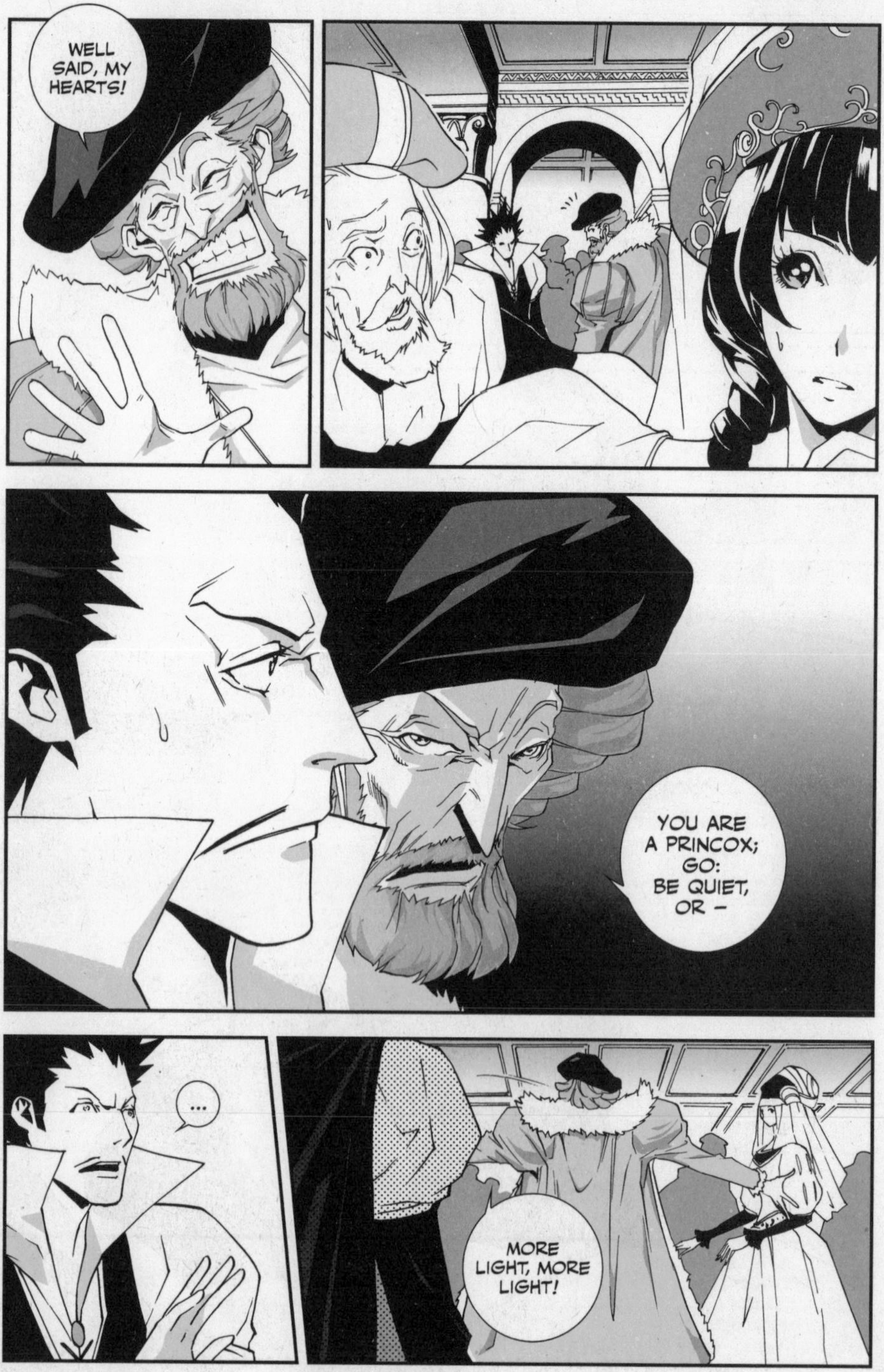
WELL SAID, MY HEARTS!
YOU ARE A PRINCOX; GO: BE QUIET, OR –
MORE LIGHT, MORE LIGHT!
...

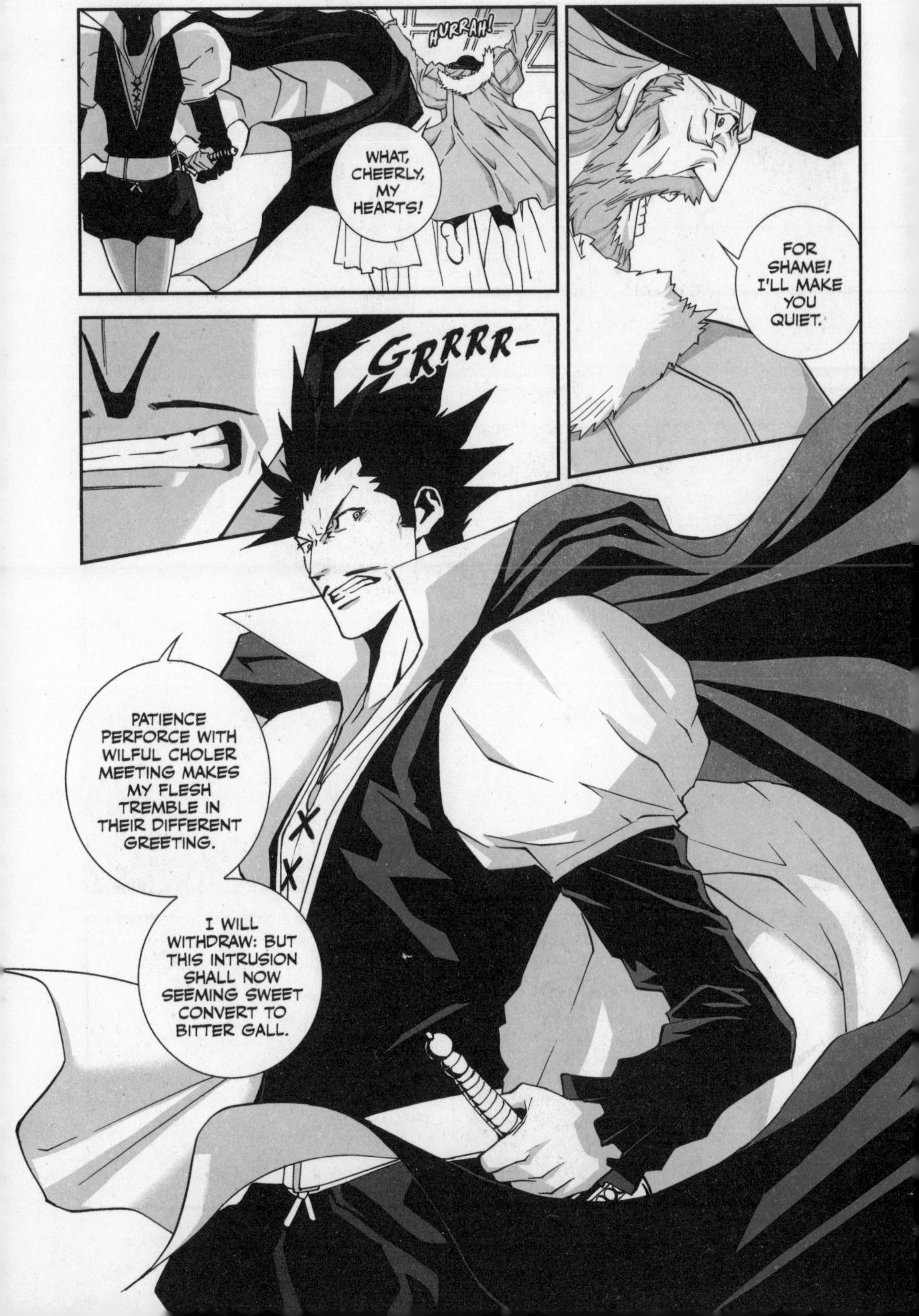
FOR SHAME! I'LL MAKE YOU QUIET.
HURRAH!
WHAT, CHEERLY, MY HEARTS!
GRRRR-
PATIENCE PERFORCE WITH WILFUL CHOLER MEETING MAKES MY FLESH TREMBLE IN THEIR DIFFERENT GREETING.
I WILL WITHDRAW: BUT THIS INTRUSION SHALL NOW SEEMING SWEET CONVERT TO BITTER GALL.

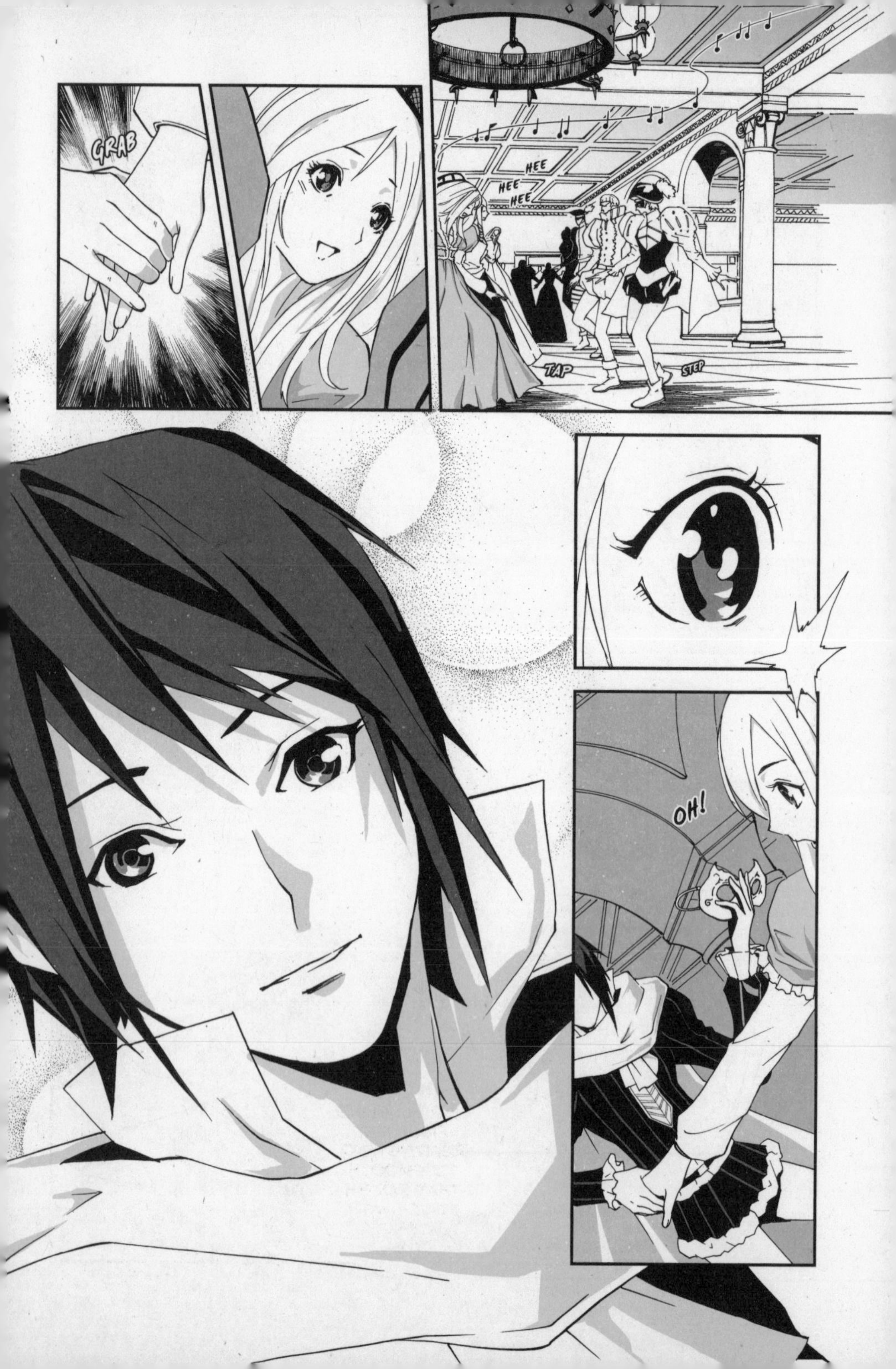
HEE
HEE
HEE
TAP
STEP
GRAB
OH!

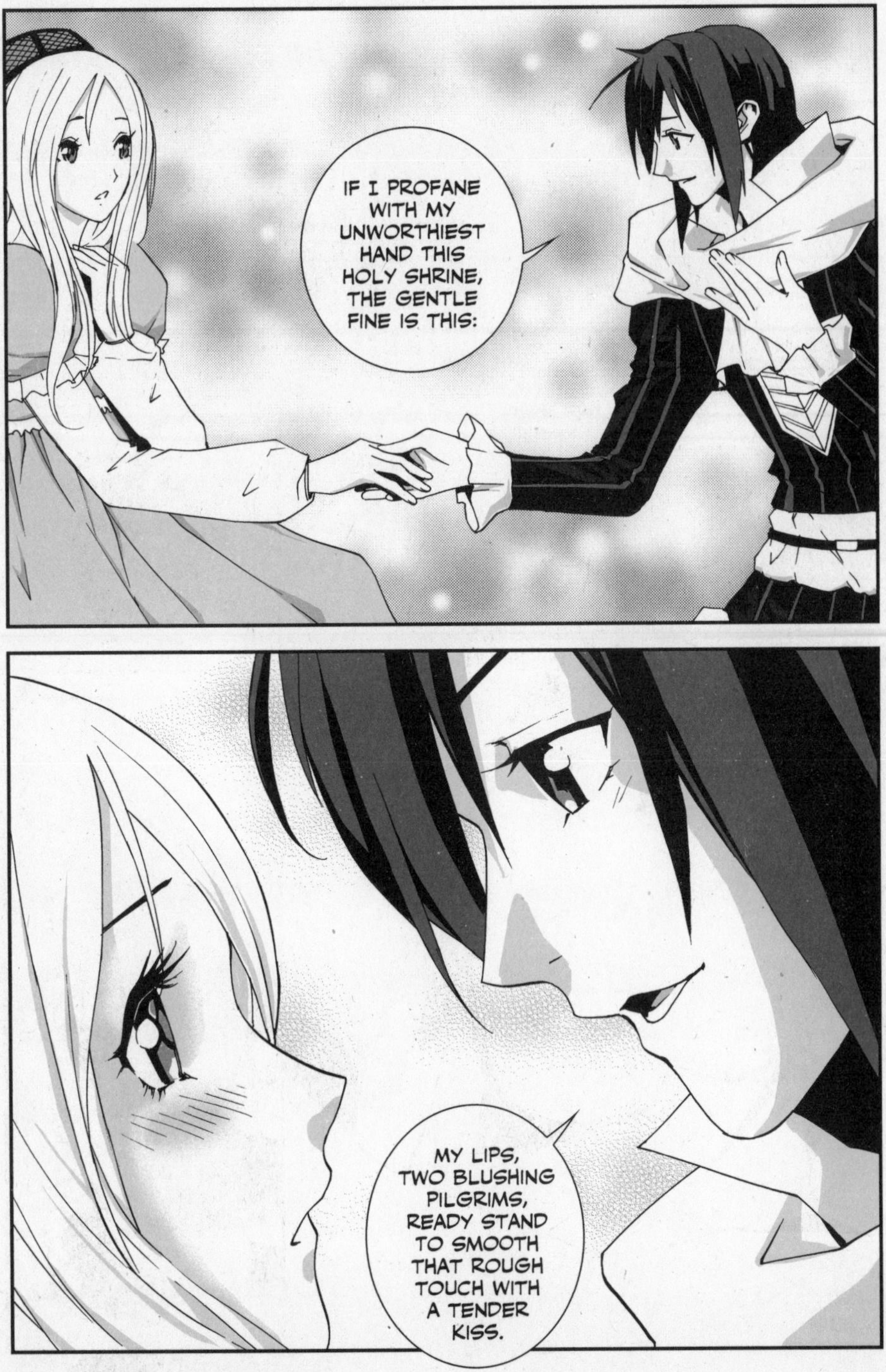
IF I PROFANE WITH MY UNWORTHIEST HAND THIS HOLY SHRINE, THE GENTLE FINE IS THIS:
MY LIPS, TWO BLUSHING PILGRIMS, READY STAND TO SMOOTH THAT ROUGH TOUCH WITH A TENDER KISS.

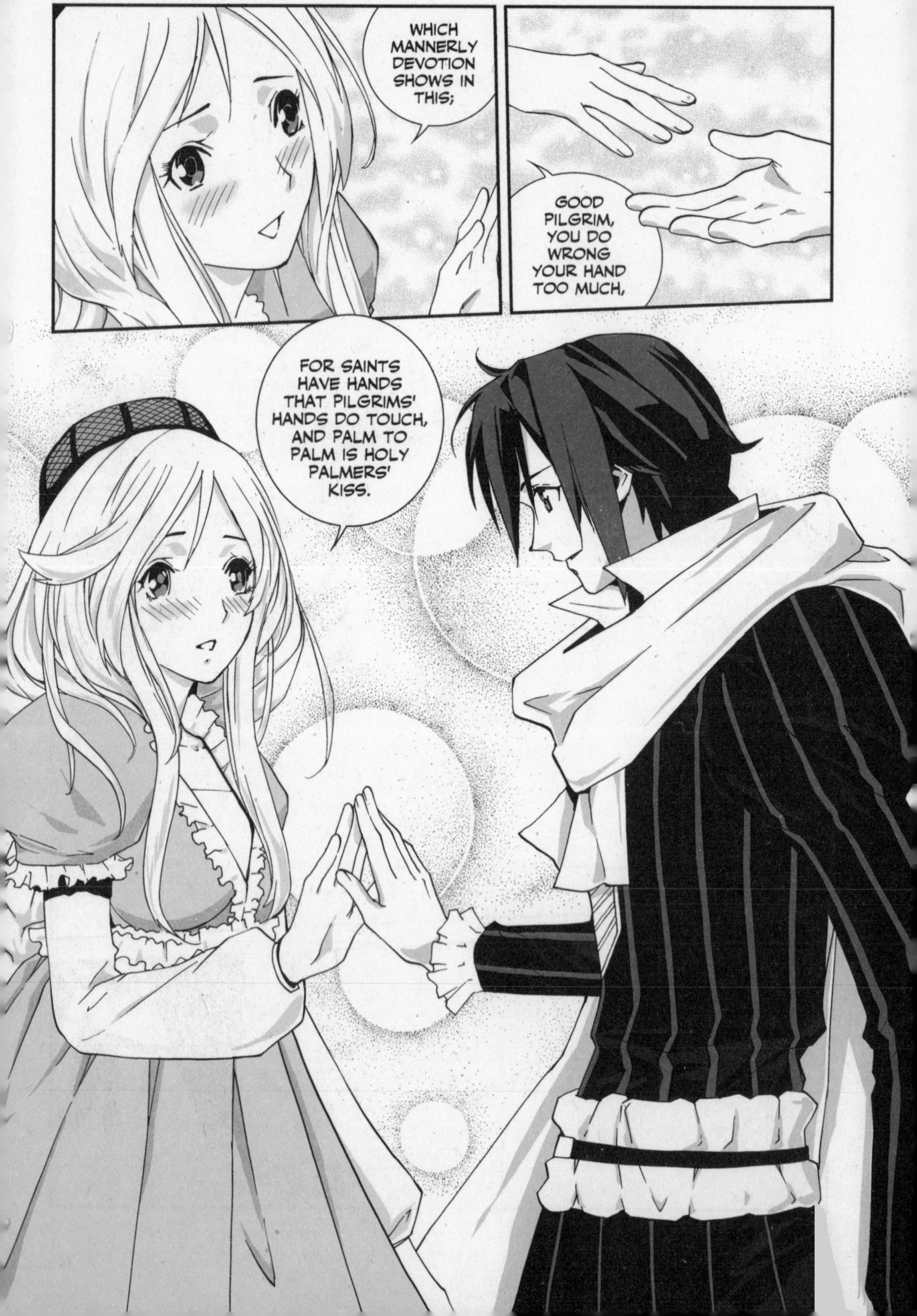
GOOD PILGRIM, YOU DO WRONG YOUR HAND TOO MUCH,
WHICH MANNERLY DEVOTION SHOWS IN THIS;
FOR SAINTS HAVE HANDS THAT PILGRIMS' HANDS DO TOUCH, AND PALM TO PALM IS HOLY PALMERS' KISS.

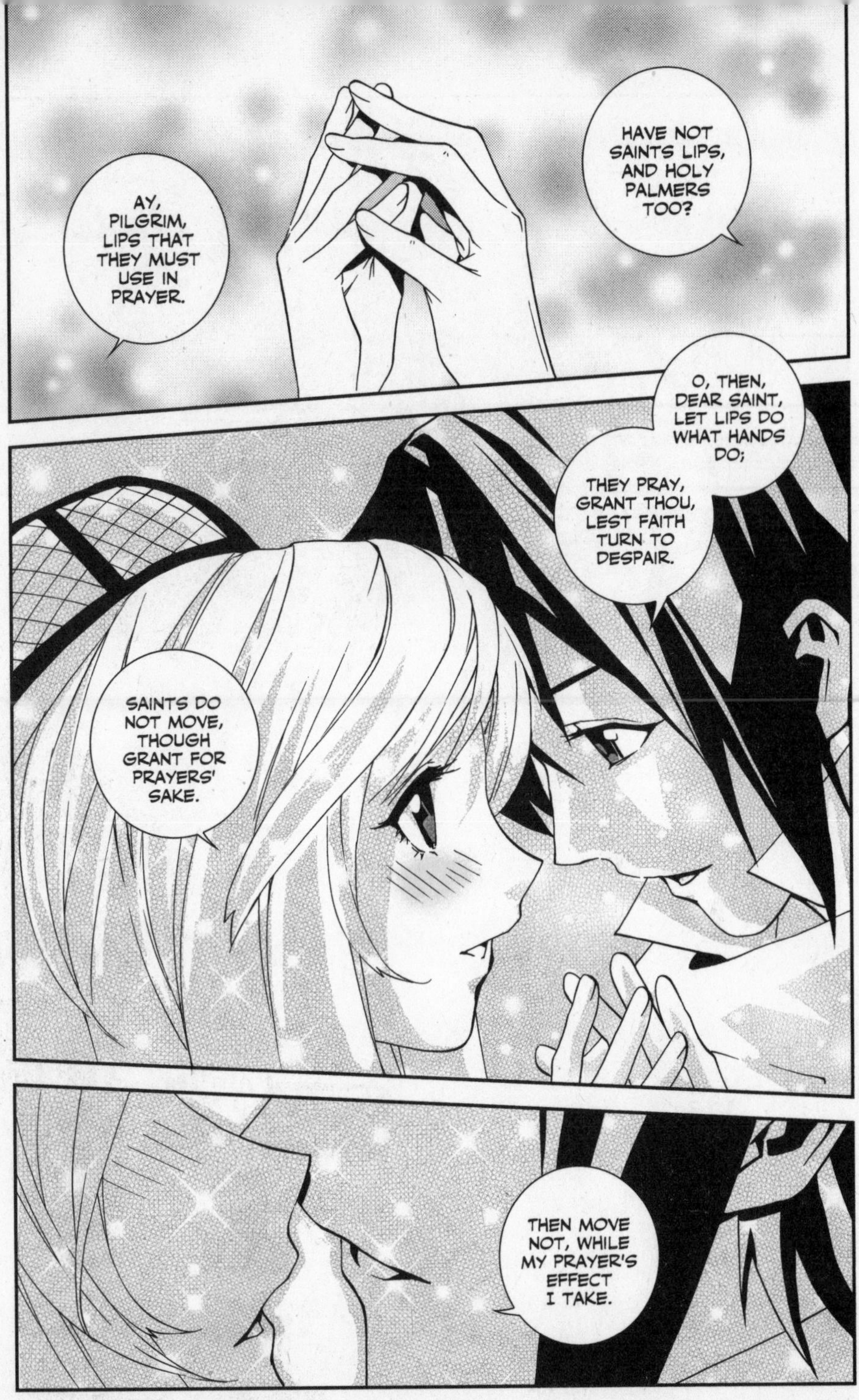
HAVE NOT SAINTS LIPS, AND HOLY PALMERS TOO?
AY, PILGRIM, LIPS THAT THEY MUST USE IN PRAYER.
O, THEN, DEAR SAINT, LET LIPS DO WHAT HANDS DO;
THEY PRAY, GRANT THOU, LEST FAITH TURN TO DESPAIR.
SAINTS DO NOT MOVE, THOUGH GRANT FOR PRAYERS' SAKE.
THEN MOVE NOT, WHILE MY PRAYER'S EFFECT I TAKE.

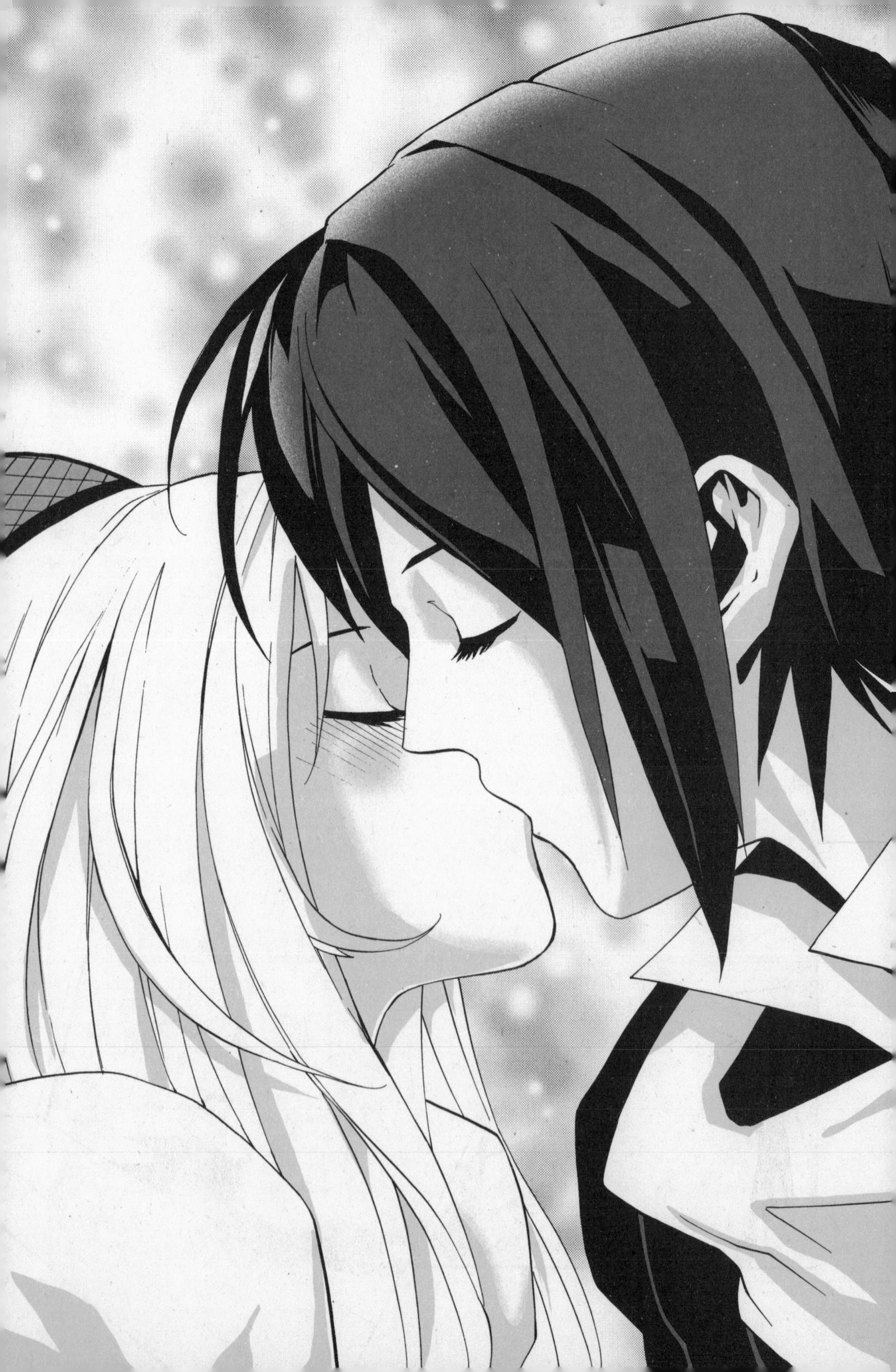

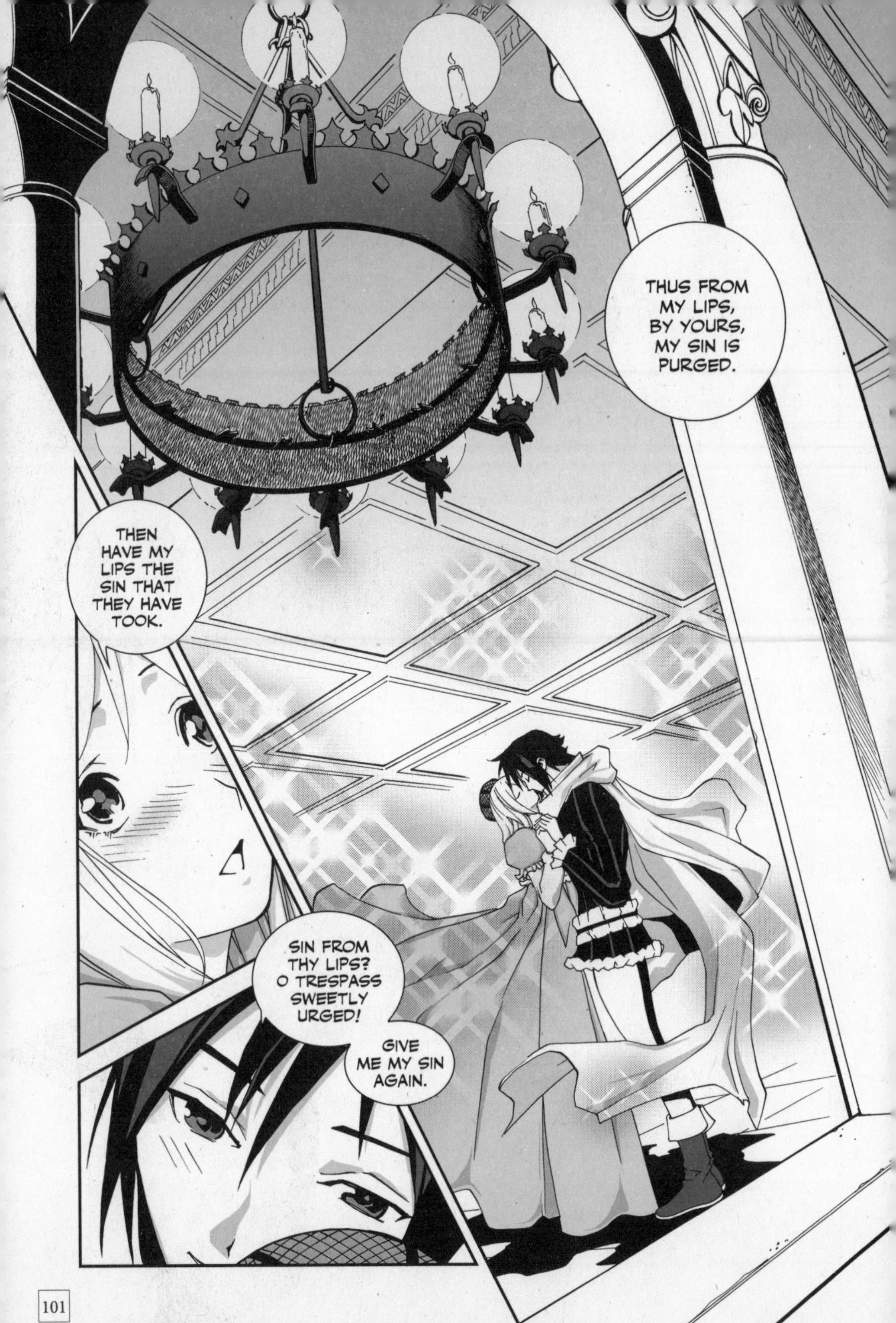
THUS FROM MY LIPS, BY YOURS, MY SIN IS PURGED.
THEN HAVE MY LIPS THE SIN THAT THEY HAVE TOOK.
SIN FROM THY LIPS? O TRESPASS SWEETLY URGED!
GIVE ME MY SIN AGAIN.

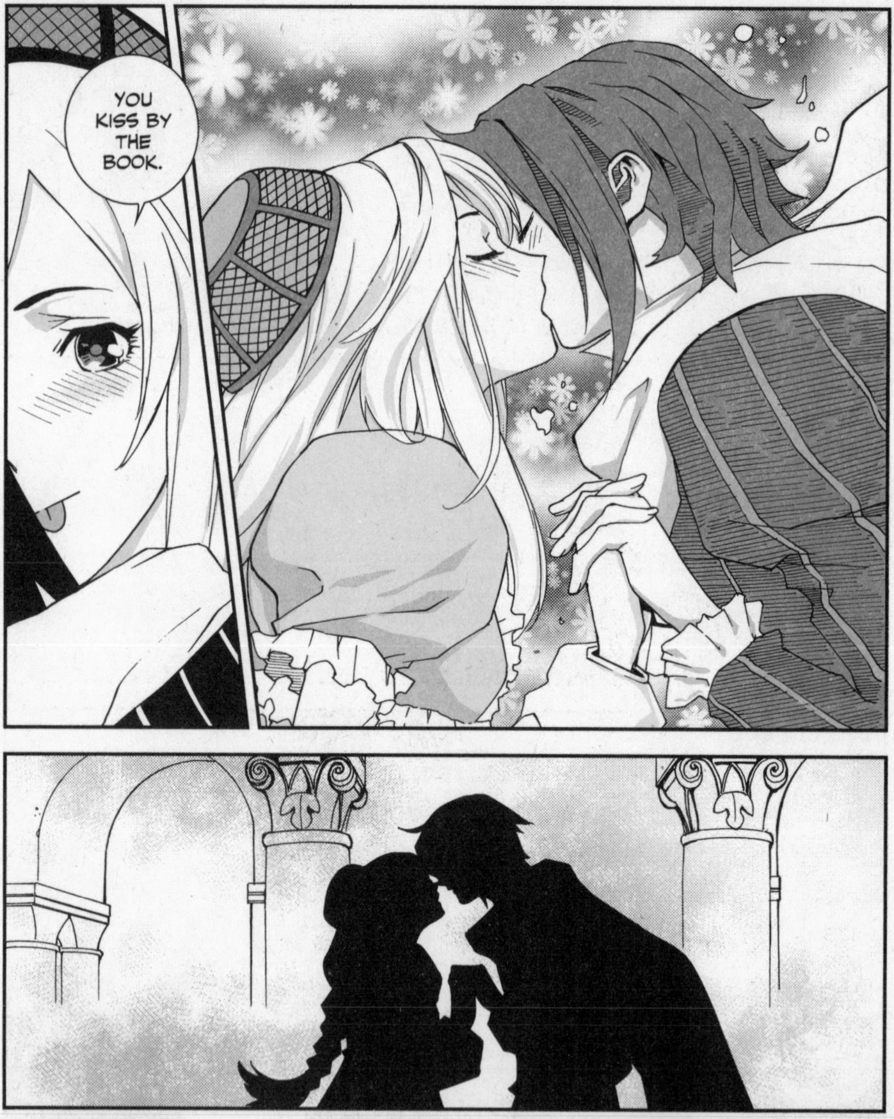
YOU KISS BY THE BOOK.
OH!
MADAM,

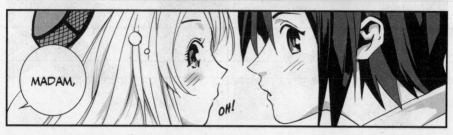

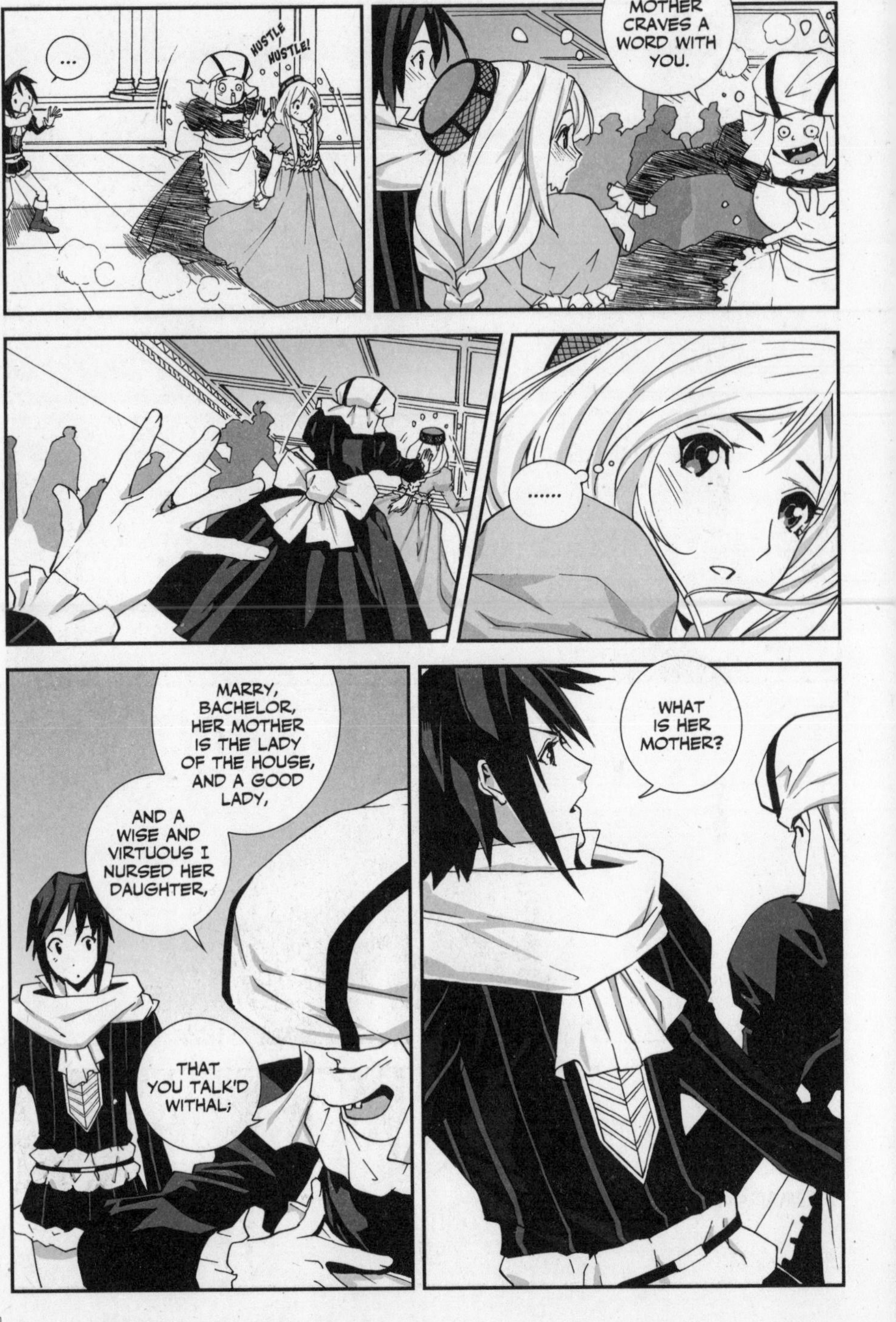
YOUR MOTHER CRAVES A WORD WITH YOU.
HUSTLE HUSTLE!
...
....
WHAT IS HER MOTHER?
MARRY, BACHELOR, HER MOTHER IS THE LADY OF THE HOUSE, AND A GOOD LADY,
AND A WISE AND VIRTUOUS I NURSED HER DAUGHTER,
THAT YOU TALK'D WITHAL;

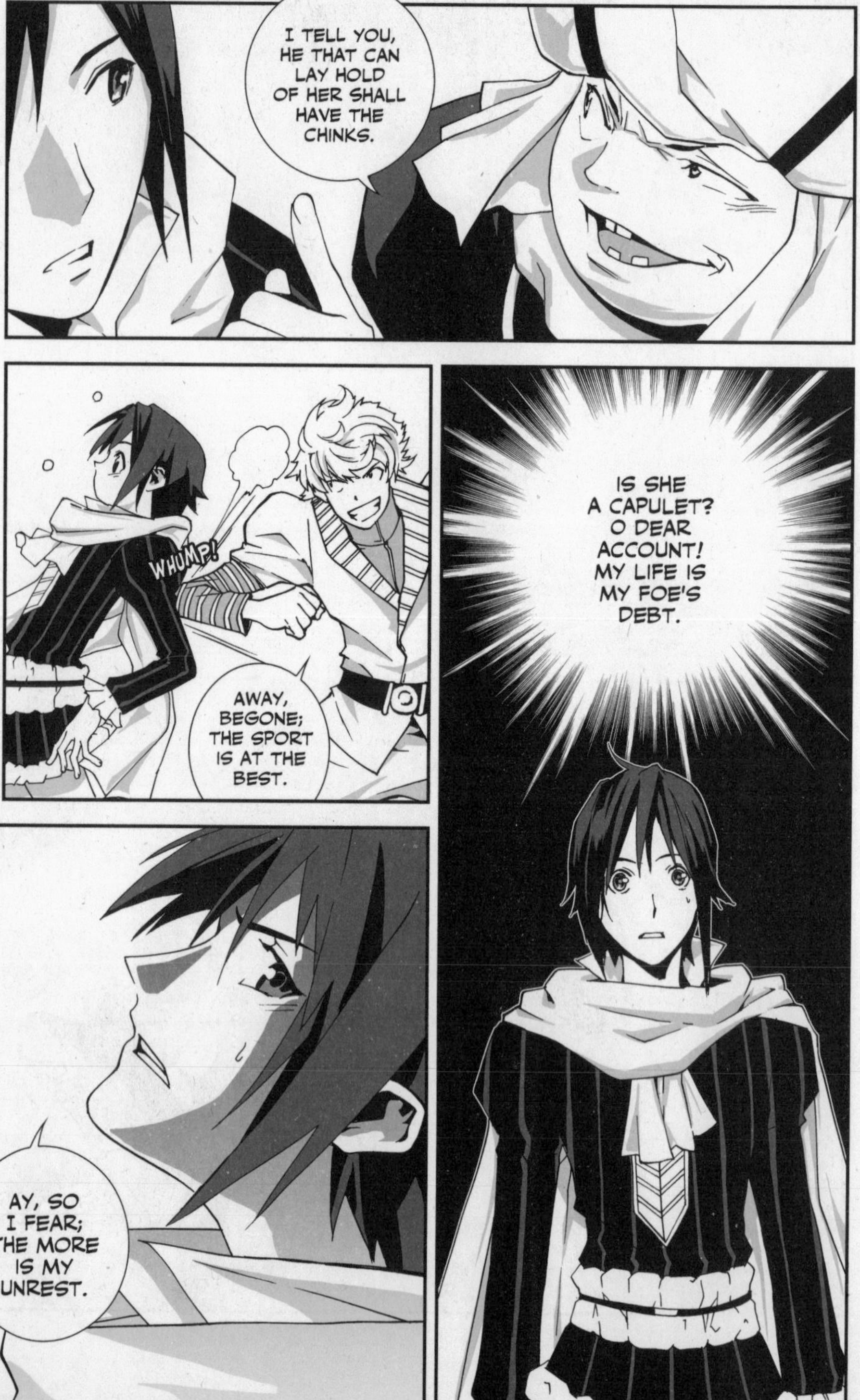
I TELL YOU, HE THAT CAN LAY HOLD OF HER SHALL HAVE THE CHINKS.
IS SHE A CAPULET? O DEAR ACCOUNT! MY LIFE IS MY FOE'S DEBT.
WHUMP!
AWAY, BEGONE; THE SPORT IS AT THE BEST.
AY, SO I FEAR; THE MORE IS MY UNREST.

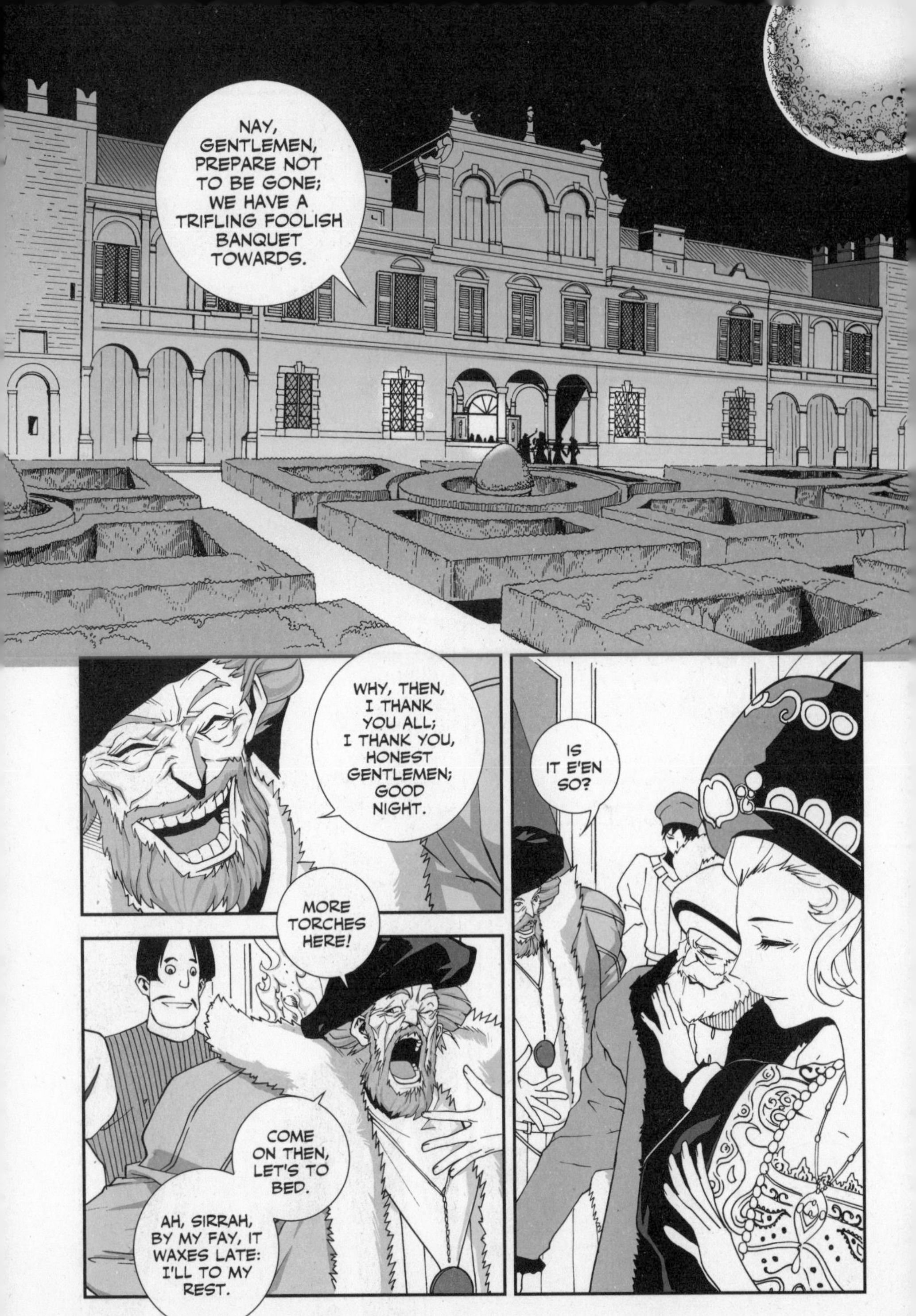
NAY, GENTLEMEN, PREPARE NOT TO BE GONE; WE HAVE A TRIFLING FOOLISH BANQUET TOWARDS.
IS IT E'EN SO?
WHY, THEN, I THANK YOU ALL; I THANK YOU, HONEST GENTLEMEN; GOOD NIGHT.
MORE TORCHES HERE!
COME ON THEN, LET'S TO BED.
AH, SIRRAH, BY MY FAY, IT WAXES LATE: I'LL TO MY REST.

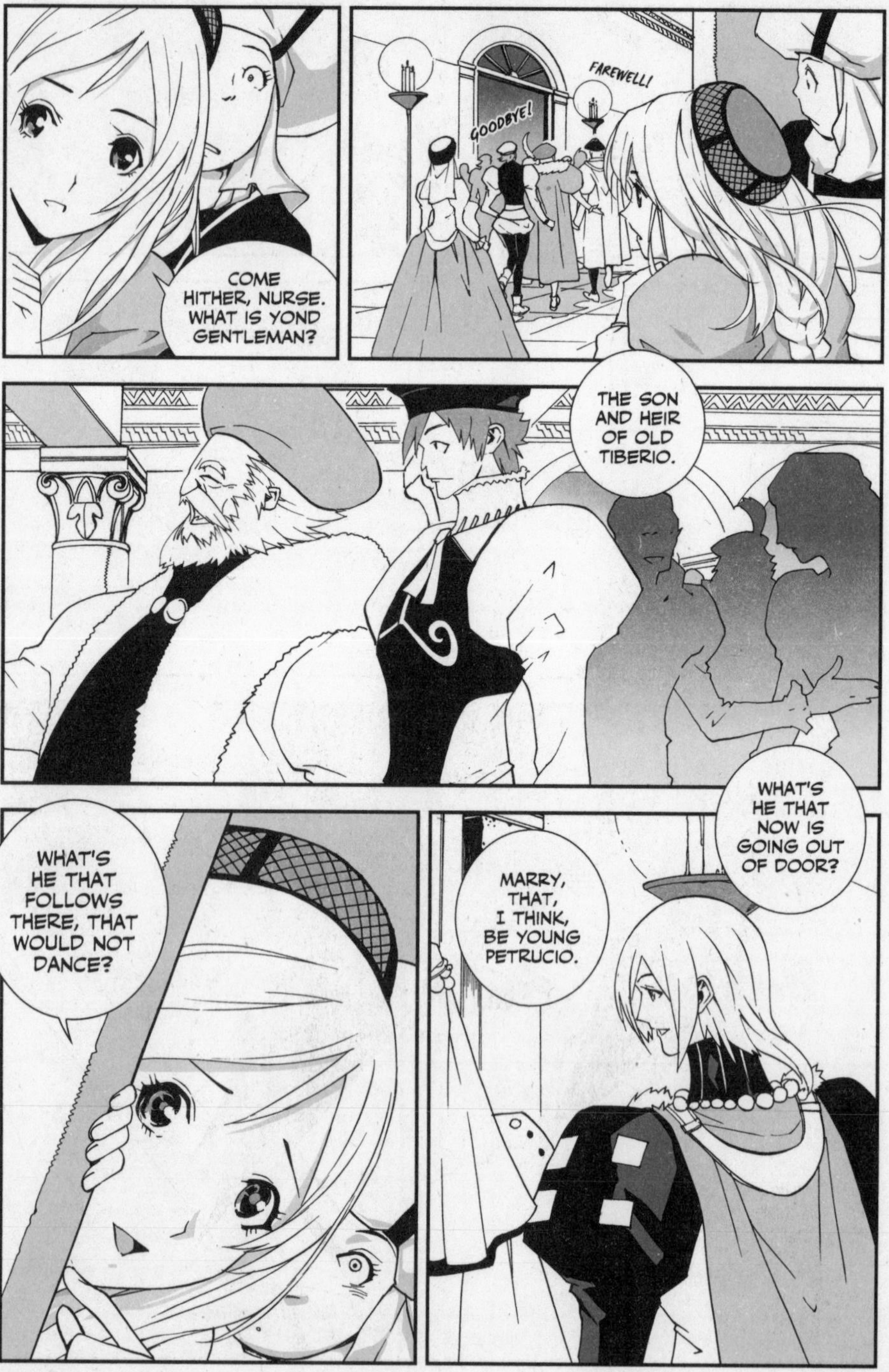
FAREWELL!
GOODBYE!
COME HITHER, NURSE. WHAT IS YOND GENTLEMAN?
THE SON AND HEIR OF OLD TIBERIO.
WHAT'S HE THAT NOW IS GOING OUT OF DOOR?
MARRY, THAT, I THINK, BE YOUNG PETRUCIO.
WHAT'S HE THAT FOLLOWS THERE, THAT WOULD NOT DANCE?

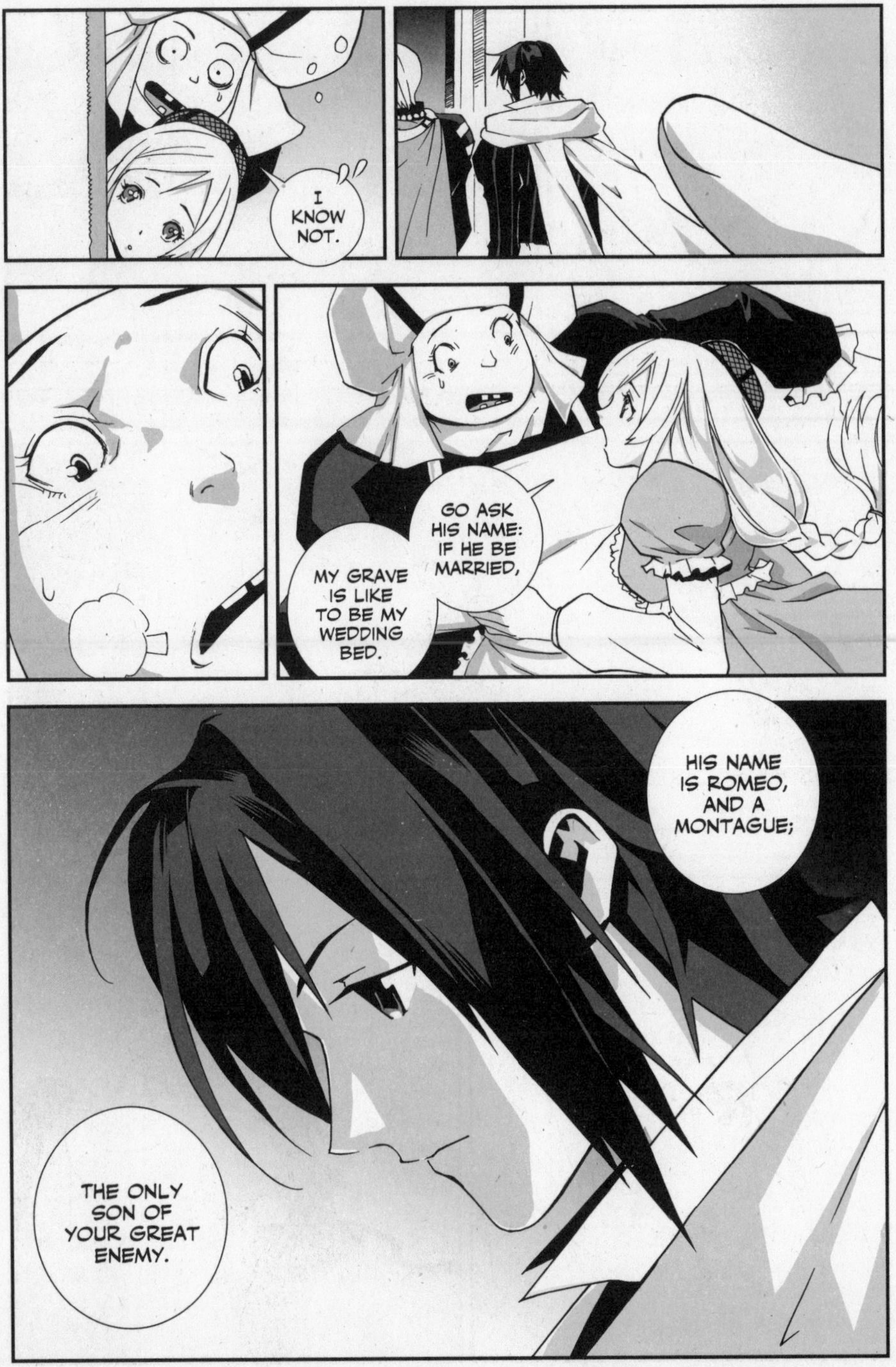
I KNOW NOT.
GO ASK HIS NAME: IF HE BE MARRIED,
MY GRAVE IS LIKE TO BE MY WEDDING BED.
HIS NAME IS ROMEO, AND A MONTAGUE;
THE ONLY SON OF YOUR GREAT ENEMY.

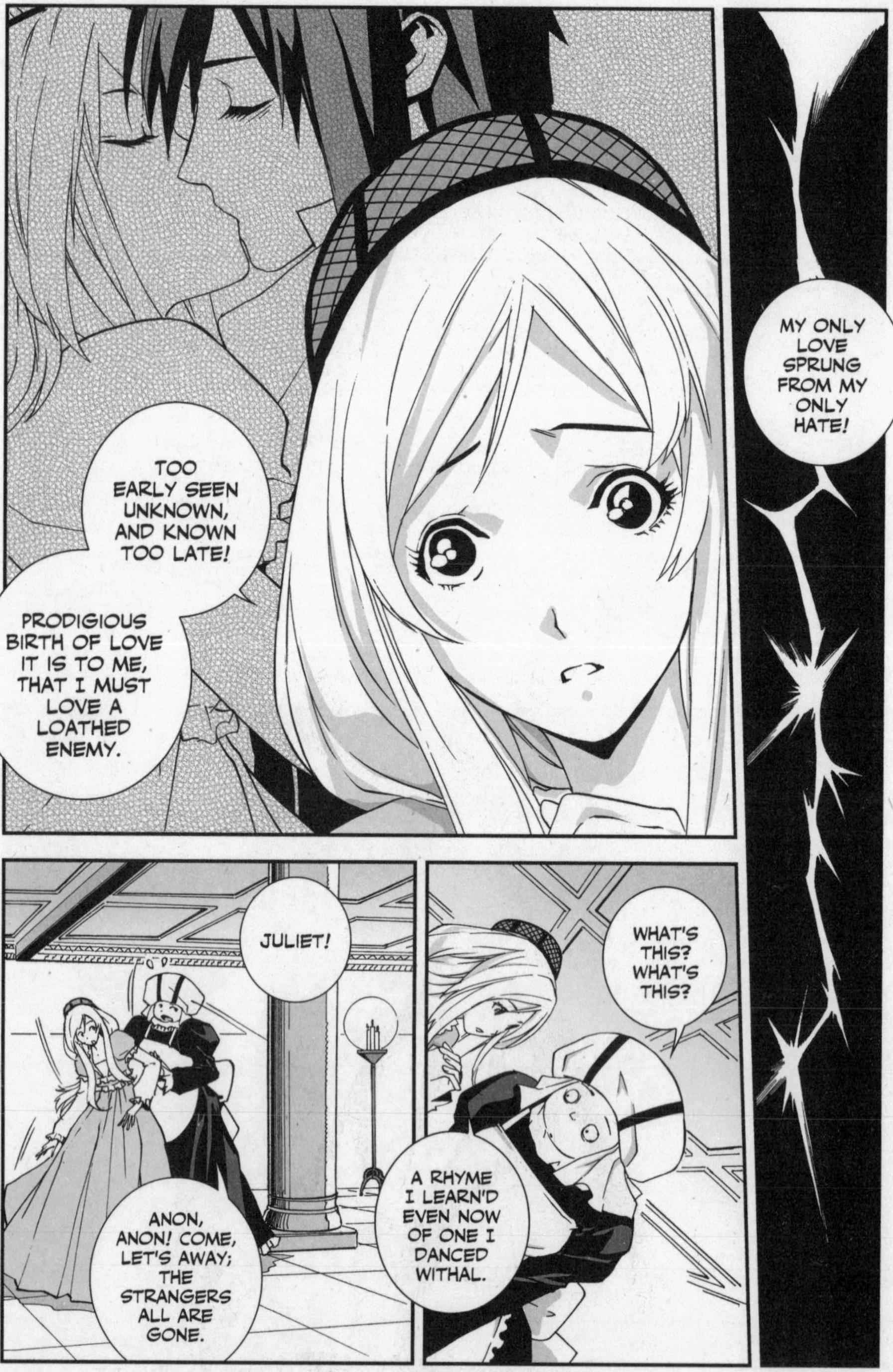
MY ONLY LOVE SPRUNG FROM MY ONLY HATE!
TOO EARLY SEEN UNKNOWN, AND KNOWN TOO LATE!
PRODIGIOUS BIRTH OF LOVE IT IS TO ME, THAT I MUST LOVE A LOATHED ENEMY.
WHAT'S THIS? WHAT'S THIS?
A RHYME I LEARN'D EVEN NOW OF ONE I DANCED WITHAL.
JULIET!
ANON, ANON! COME, LET'S AWAY; THE STRANGERS ALL ARE GONE.

ACT II

NOW OLD DESIRE DOTH IN HIS DEATH-BED LIE,
AND YOUNG AFFECTION GAPES TO BE HIS HEIR;
THAT FAIR FOR WHICH LOVE GROAN'D FOR, AND WOULD DIE,
WITH TENDER JULIET MATCH'D, IS NOW NOT FAIR.

NOW ROMEO IS BELOVED AND LOVES AGAIN,
ALIKE BEWITCHED BY THE CHARM OF LOOKS;
BUT TO HIS FOE SUPPOSED HE MUST COMPLAIN,
AND SHE STEAL LOVE'S SWEET BAIT FROM FEARFUL HOOKS:

BEING HELD A FOE, HE MAY NOT HAVE ACCESS
TO BREATHE SUCH VOWS AS LOVERS USED TO SWEAR;
AND SHE AS MUCH IN LOVE, HER MEANS MUCH LESS
TO MEET HER NEW BELOVED ANYWHERE:

BUT PASSION LENDS THEM POWER, TIME MEANS, TO MEET,
TEMPERING EXTREMITIES WITH EXTREME SWEET.

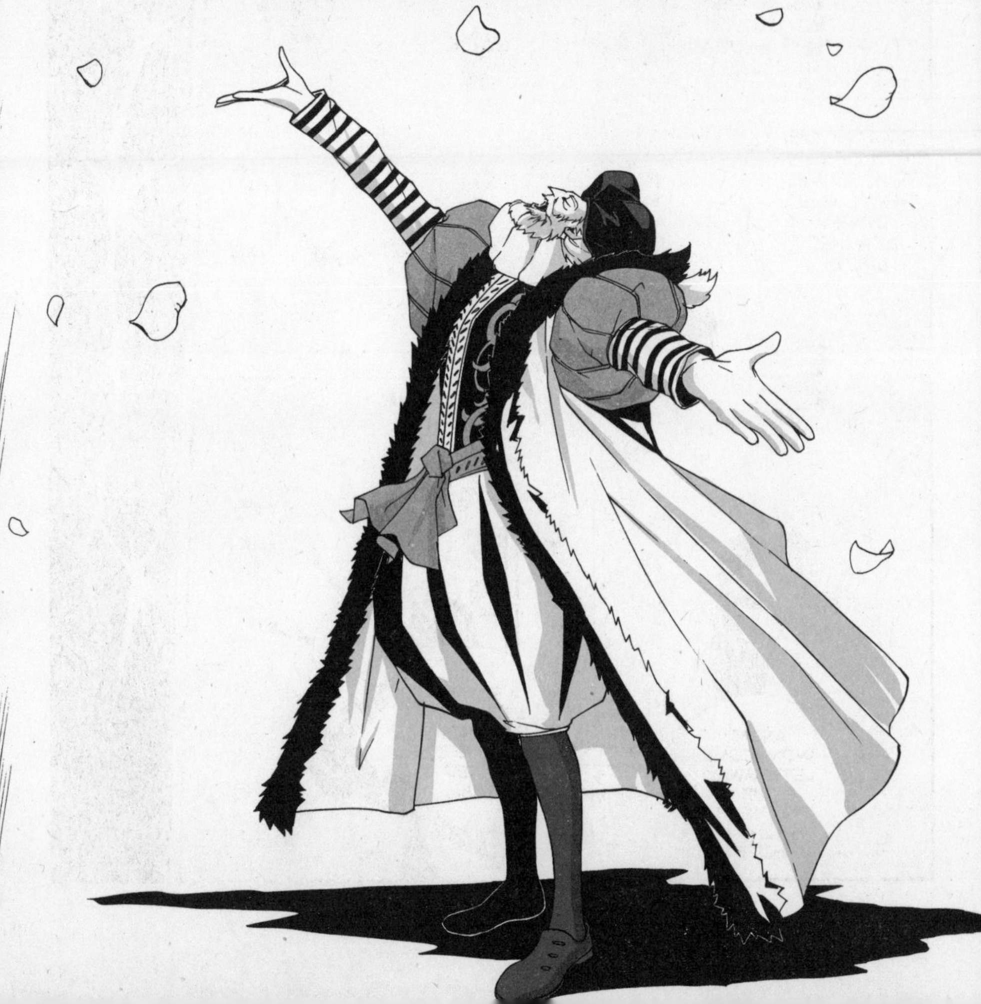

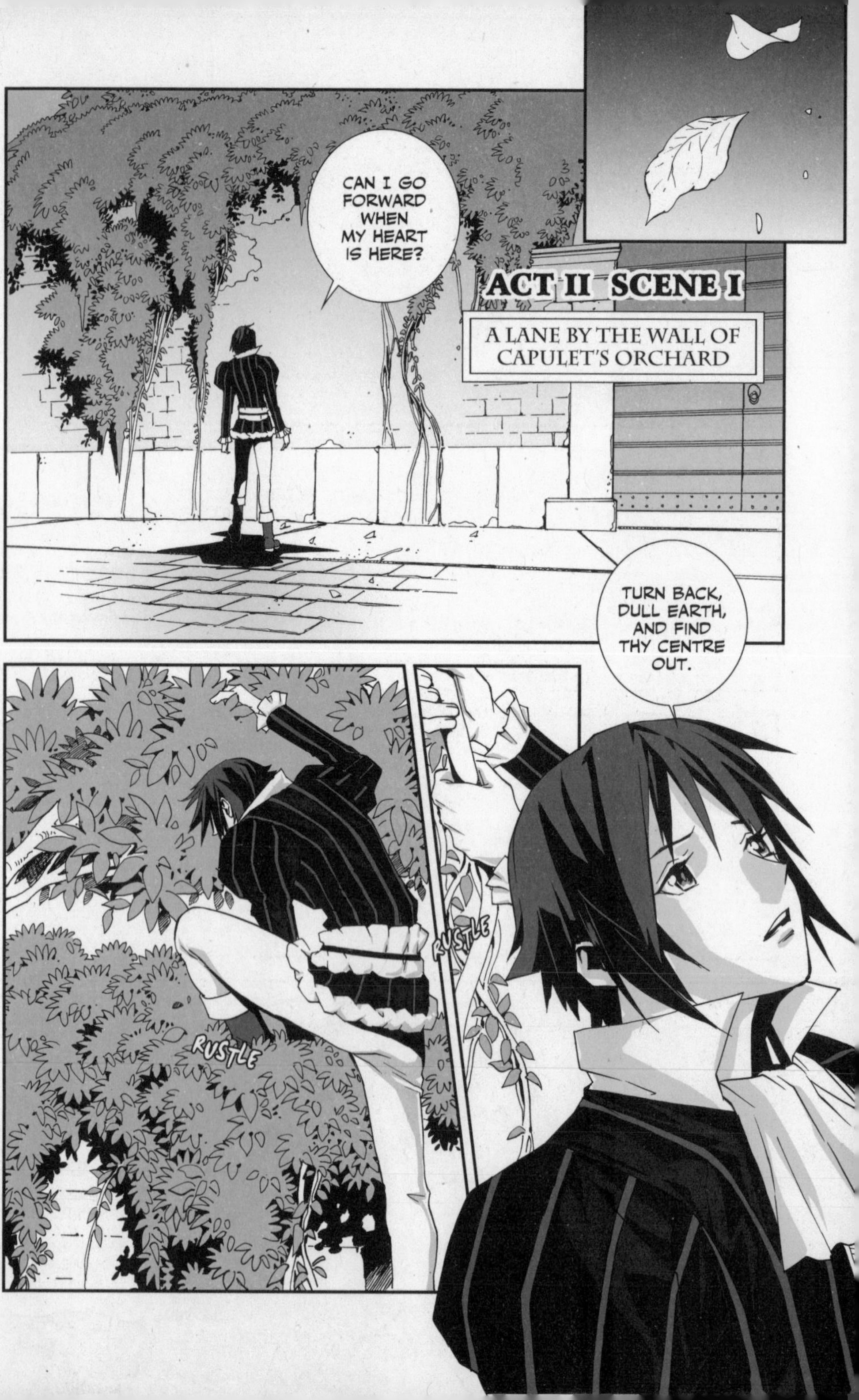
CAN I GO FORWARD WHEN MY HEART IS HERE?
ACT II SCENE I
A LANE BY THE WALL OF CAPULET'S ORCHARD
TURN BACK, DULL EARTH, AND FIND THY CENTRE OUT.
RUSTLE
RUSTLE

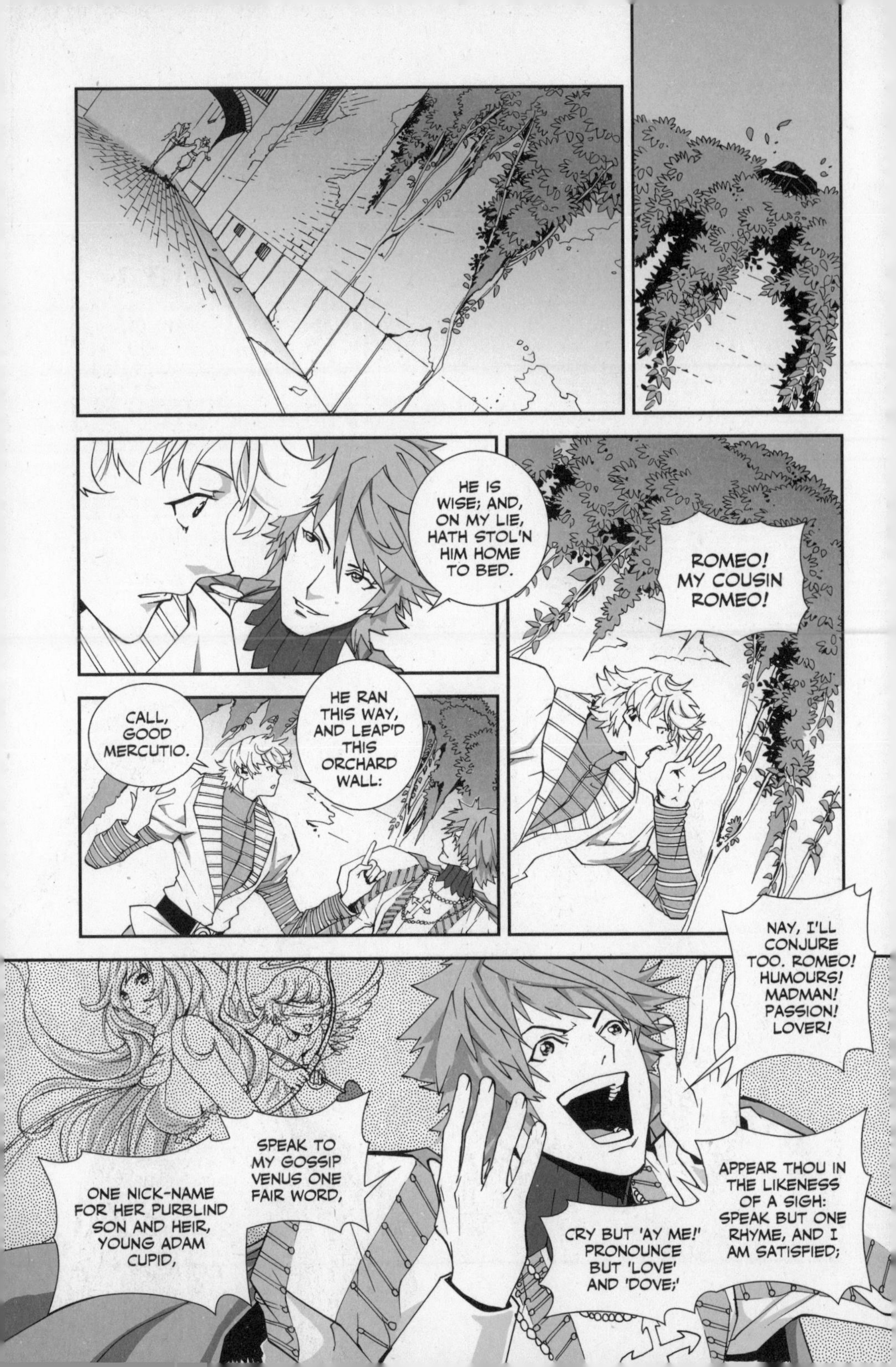
ROMEO! MY COUSIN ROMEO!
HE IS WISE; AND, ON MY LIE, HATH STOL'N HIM HOME TO BED.
HE RAN THIS WAY, AND LEAP'D THIS ORCHARD WALL:
CALL, GOOD MERCUTIO.
NAY, I'LL CONJURE TOO. ROMEO! HUMOURS! MADMAN! PASSION! LOVER!
APPEAR THOU IN THE LIKENESS OF A SIGH: SPEAK BUT ONE RHYME, AND I AM SATISFIED;
CRY BUT 'AY ME!' PRONOUNCE BUT 'LOVE' AND 'DOVE;'
SPEAK TO MY GOSSIP VENUS ONE FAIR WORD,
ONE NICK-NAME FOR HER PURBLIND SON AND HEIR, YOUNG ADAM CUPID,

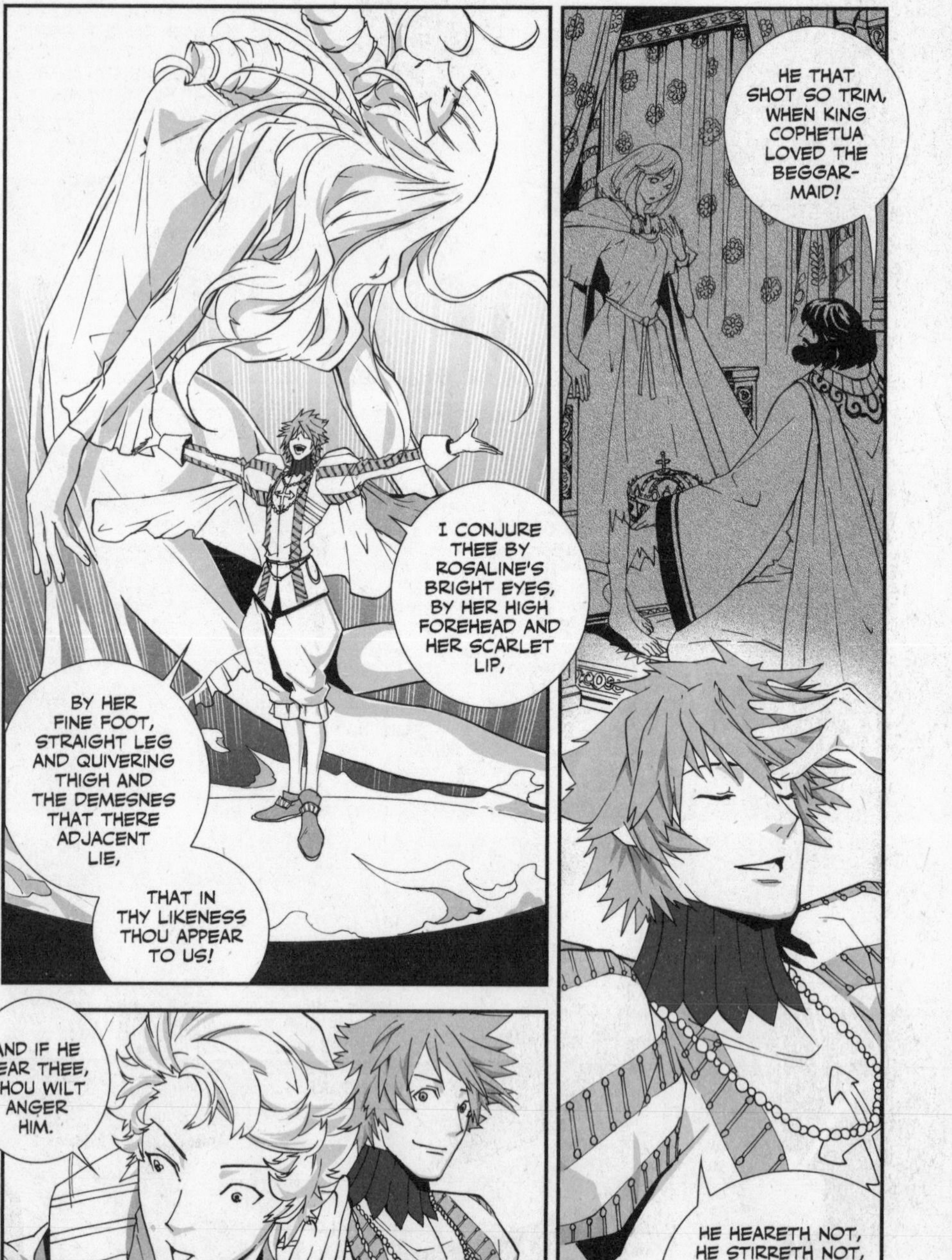
HE THAT SHOT SO TRIM, WHEN KING COPHETUA LOVED THE BEGGAR-MAID!
HE HEARETH NOT, HE STIRRETH NOT, HE MOVETH NOT; THE APE IS DEAD, AND I MUST CONJURE HIM.
I CONJURE THEE BY ROSALINE'S BRIGHT EYES, BY HER HIGH FOREHEAD AND HER SCARLET LIP,
BY HER FINE FOOT, STRAIGHT LEG AND QUIVERING THIGH AND THE DEMESNES THAT THERE ADJACENT LIE,
THAT IN THY LIKENESS THOU APPEAR TO US!
AND IF HE HEAR THEE, THOU WILT ANGER HIM.

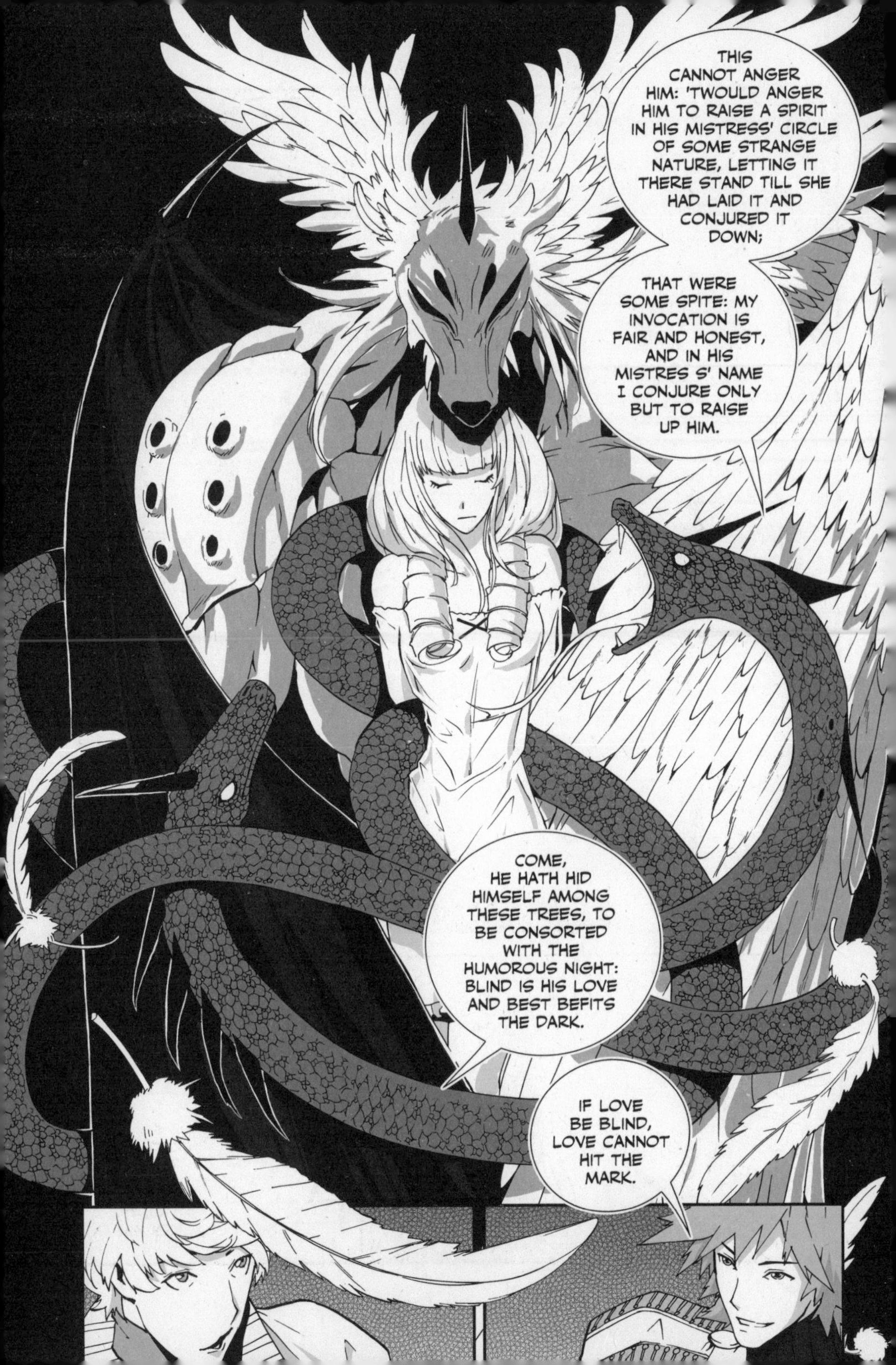
THIS CANNOT ANGER HIM: 'TWOULD ANGER HIM TO RAISE A SPIRIT IN HIS MISTRESS' CIRCLE OF SOME STRANGE NATURE, LETTING IT THERE STAND TILL SHE HAD LAID IT AND CONJURED IT DOWN;
THAT WERE SOME SPITE: MY INVOCATION IS FAIR AND HONEST, AND IN HIS MISTRES S' NAME I CONJURE ONLY BUT TO RAISE UP HIM.
COME, HE HATH HID HIMSELF AMONG THESE TREES, TO BE CONSORTED WITH THE HUMOROUS NIGHT: BLIND IS HIS LOVE AND BEST BEFITS THE DARK.
IF LOVE BE BLIND, LOVE CANNOT HIT THE MARK.

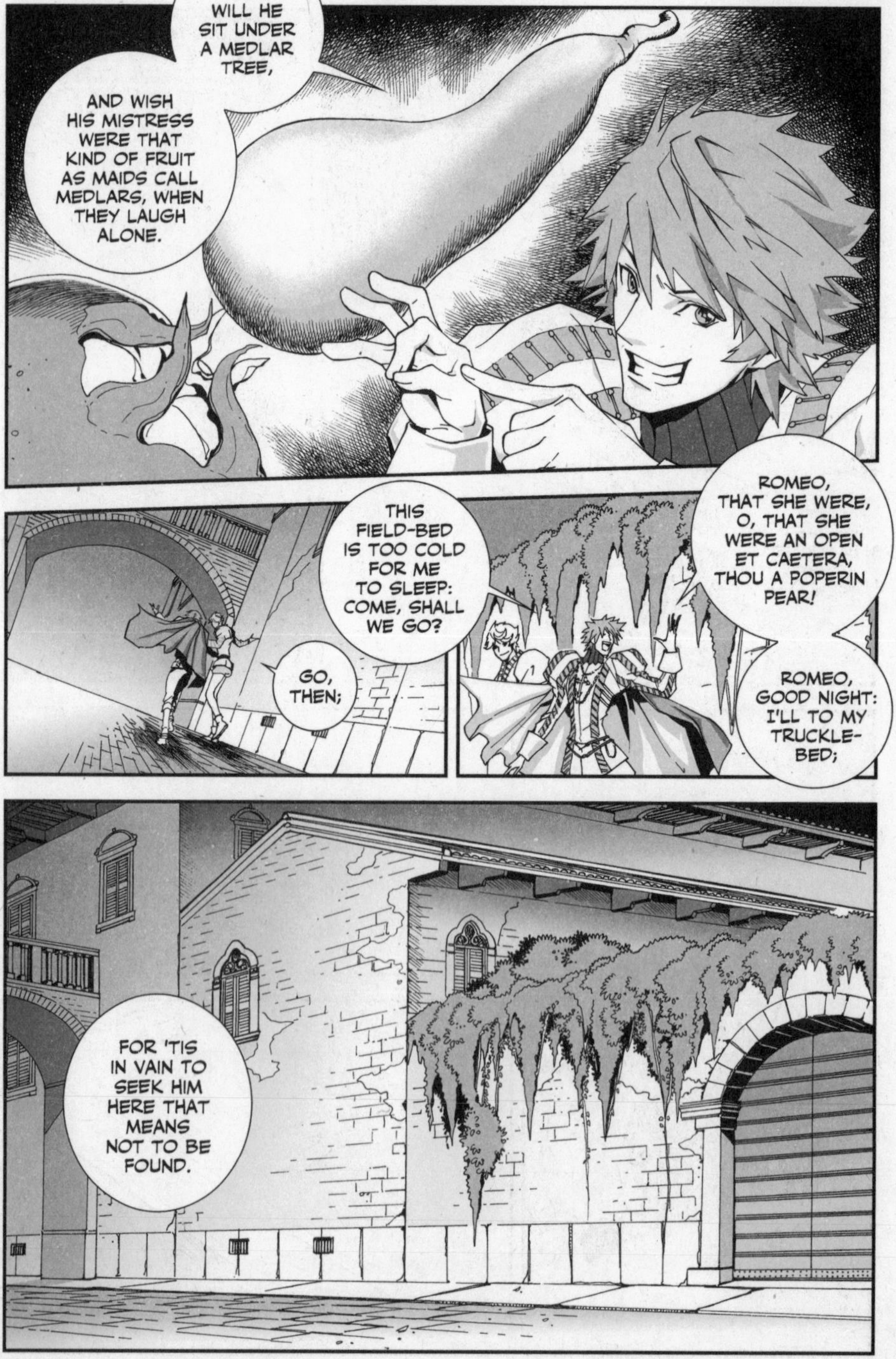
NOW WILL HE SIT UNDER A MEDLAR TREE,
AND WISH HIS MISTRESS WERE THAT KIND OF FRUIT AS MAIDS CALL MEDLARS, WHEN THEY LAUGH ALONE.
ROMEO, THAT SHE WERE, O, THAT SHE WERE AN OPEN ET CAETERA, THOU A POPERIN PEAR!
ROMEO, GOOD NIGHT: I'LL TO MY TRUCKLE-BED;
THIS FIELD-BED IS TOO COLD FOR ME TO SLEEP: COME, SHALL WE GO?
GO, THEN;
FOR 'TIS IN VAIN TO SEEK HIM HERE THAT MEANS NOT TO BE FOUND.

HE JESTS AT SCARS THAT NEVER FELT A WOUND.

ACT II
SCENE II

SIIIGH

BUT, SOFT! WHAT LIGHT THROUGH YONDER WINDOW BREAKS?

IT IS THE EAST, AND JULIET IS THE SUN.

RUSTLE...

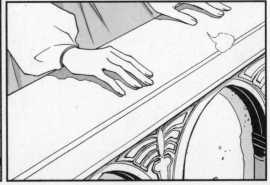

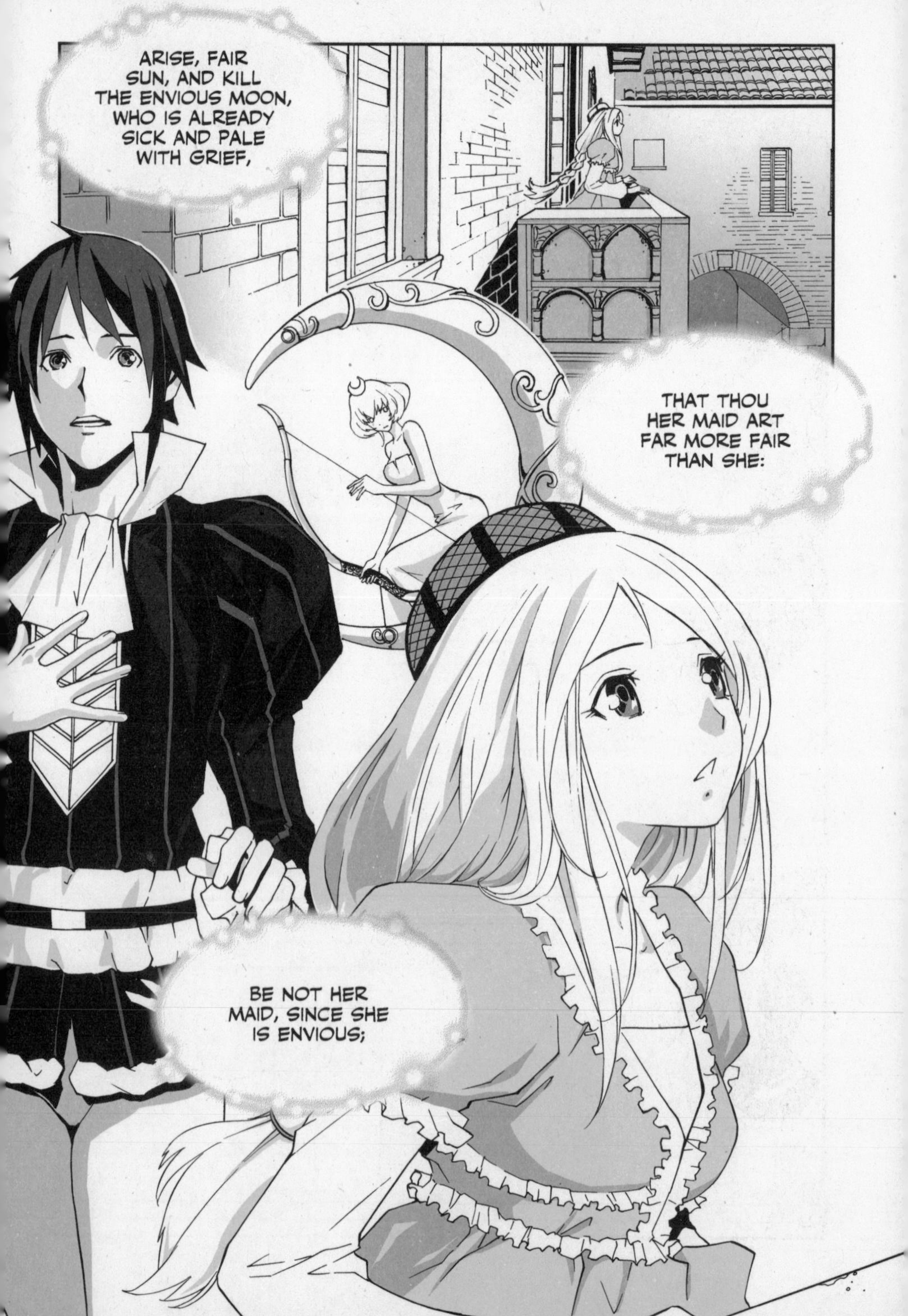
ARISE, FAIR SUN, AND KILL THE ENVIOUS MOON, WHO IS ALREADY SICK AND PALE WITH GRIEF,
THAT THOU HER MAID ART FAR MORE FAIR THAN SHE:
BE NOT HER MAID, SINCE SHE IS ENVIOUS;

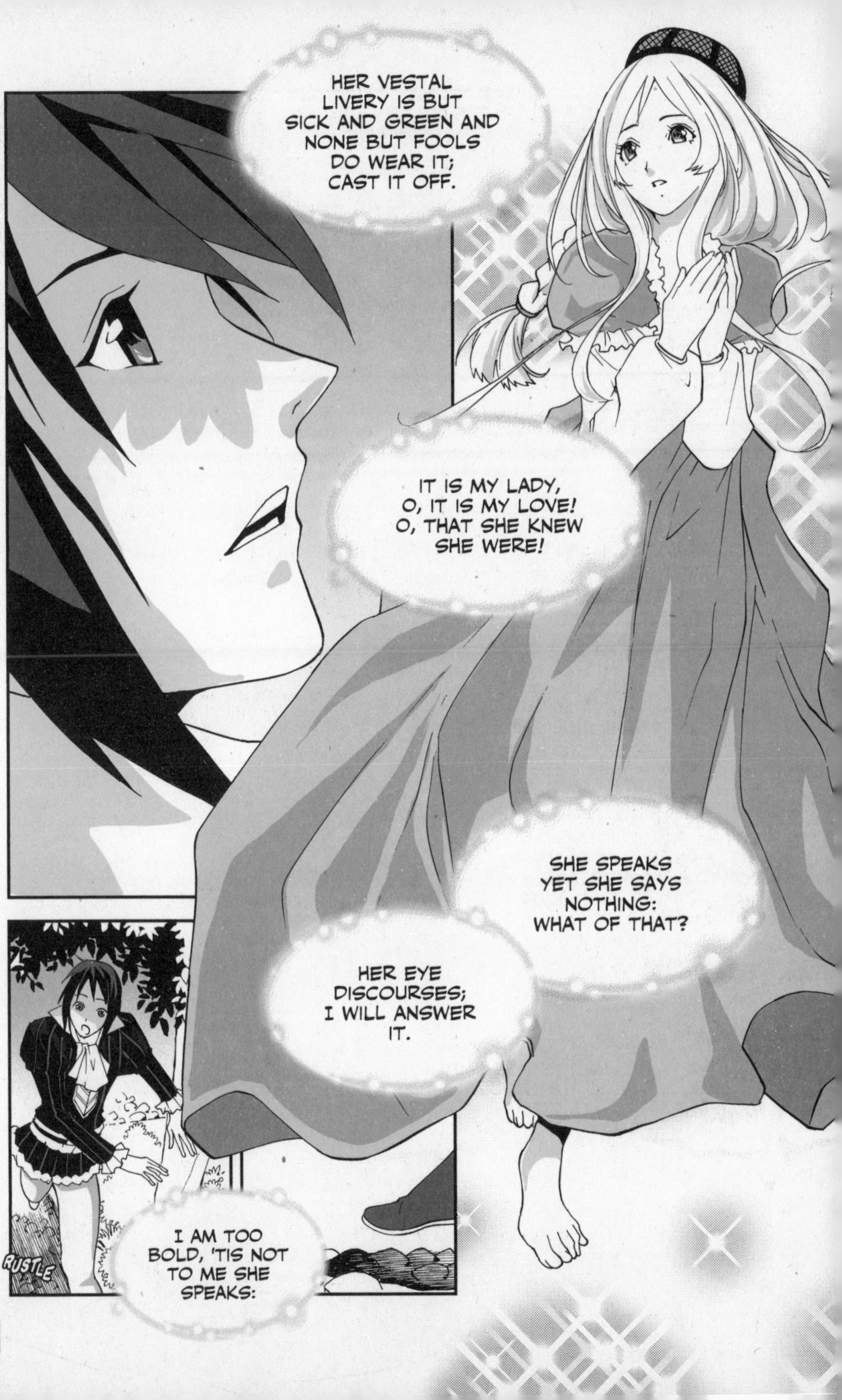
HER VESTAL LIVERY IS BUT SICK AND GREEN AND NONE BUT FOOLS DO WEAR IT; CAST IT OFF.
IT IS MY LADY, O, IT IS MY LOVE! O, THAT SHE KNEW SHE WERE!
SHE SPEAKS YET SHE SAYS NOTHING: WHAT OF THAT?
HER EYE DISCOURSES; I WILL ANSWER IT.
I AM TOO BOLD, 'TIS NOT TO ME SHE SPEAKS:
RUSTLE

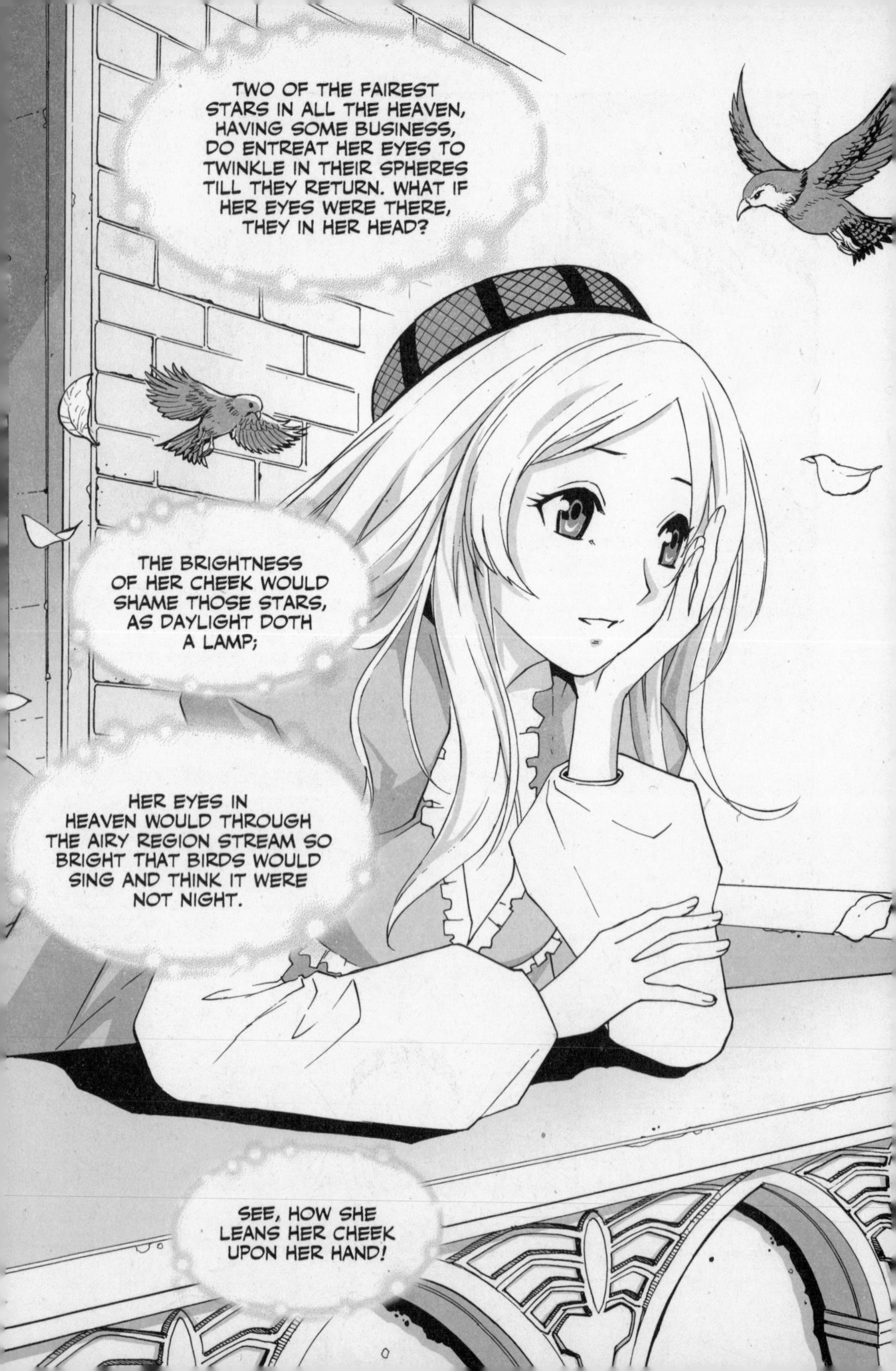
TWO OF THE FAIREST STARS IN ALL THE HEAVEN, HAVING SOME BUSINESS, DO ENTREAT HER EYES TO TWINKLE IN THEIR SPHERES TILL THEY RETURN. WHAT IF HER EYES WERE THERE, THEY IN HER HEAD?
THE BRIGHTNESS OF HER CHEEK WOULD SHAME THOSE STARS, AS DAYLIGHT DOTH A LAMP;
HER EYES IN HEAVEN WOULD THROUGH THE AIRY REGION STREAM SO BRIGHT THAT BIRDS WOULD SING AND THINK IT WERE NOT NIGHT.
SEE, HOW SHE LEANS HER CHEEK UPON HER HAND!

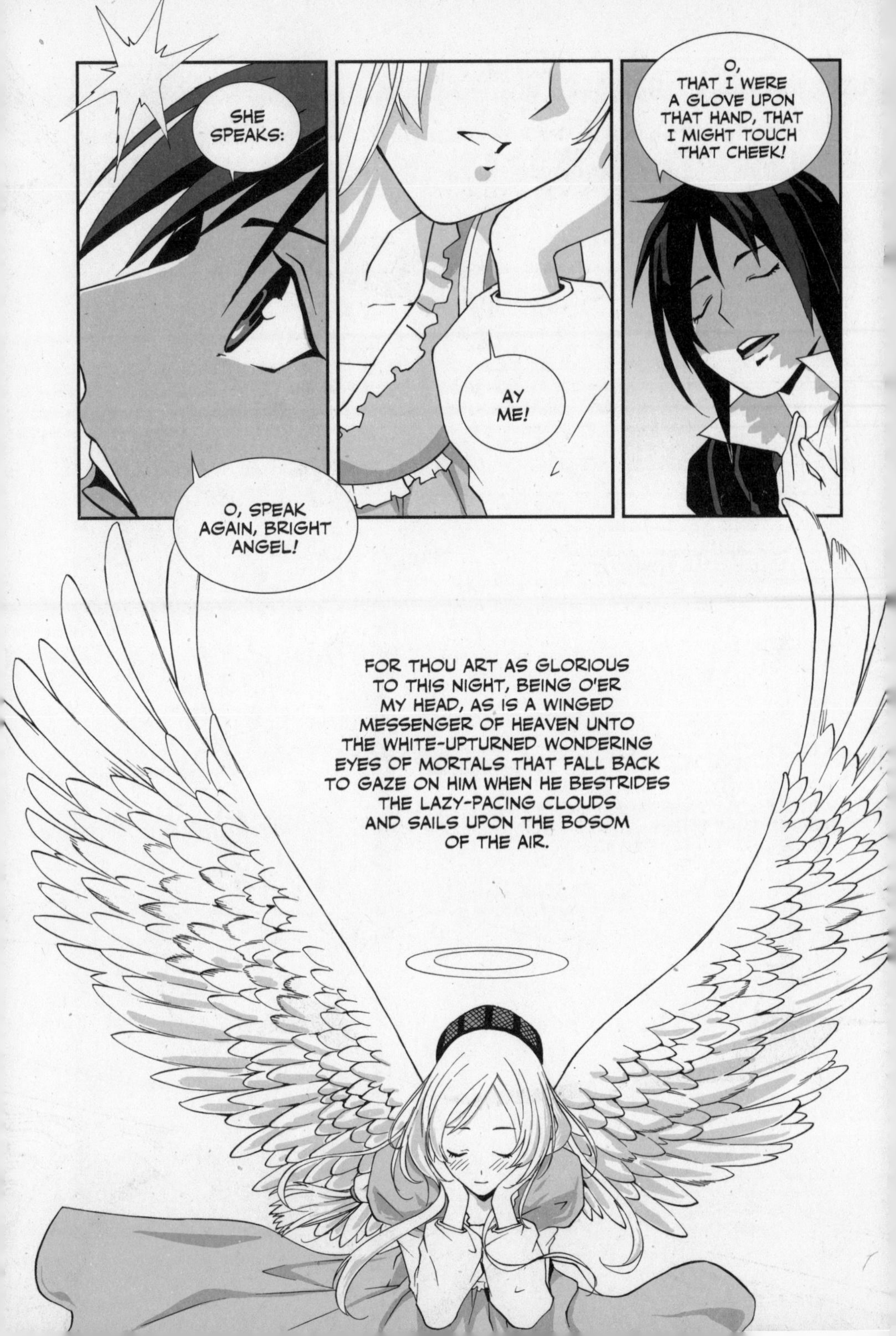
O, THAT I WERE A GLOVE UPON THAT HAND, THAT I MIGHT TOUCH THAT CHEEK!
AY ME!
SHE SPEAKS:
O, SPEAK AGAIN, BRIGHT ANGEL!
FOR THOU ART AS GLORIOUS TO THIS NIGHT, BEING O'ER MY HEAD, AS IS A WINGED MESSENGER OF HEAVEN UNTO THE WHITE-UPTURNED WONDERING EYES OF MORTALS THAT FALL BACK TO GAZE ON HIM WHEN HE BESTRIDES THE LAZY-PACING CLOUDS AND SAILS UPON THE BOSOM OF THE AIR.

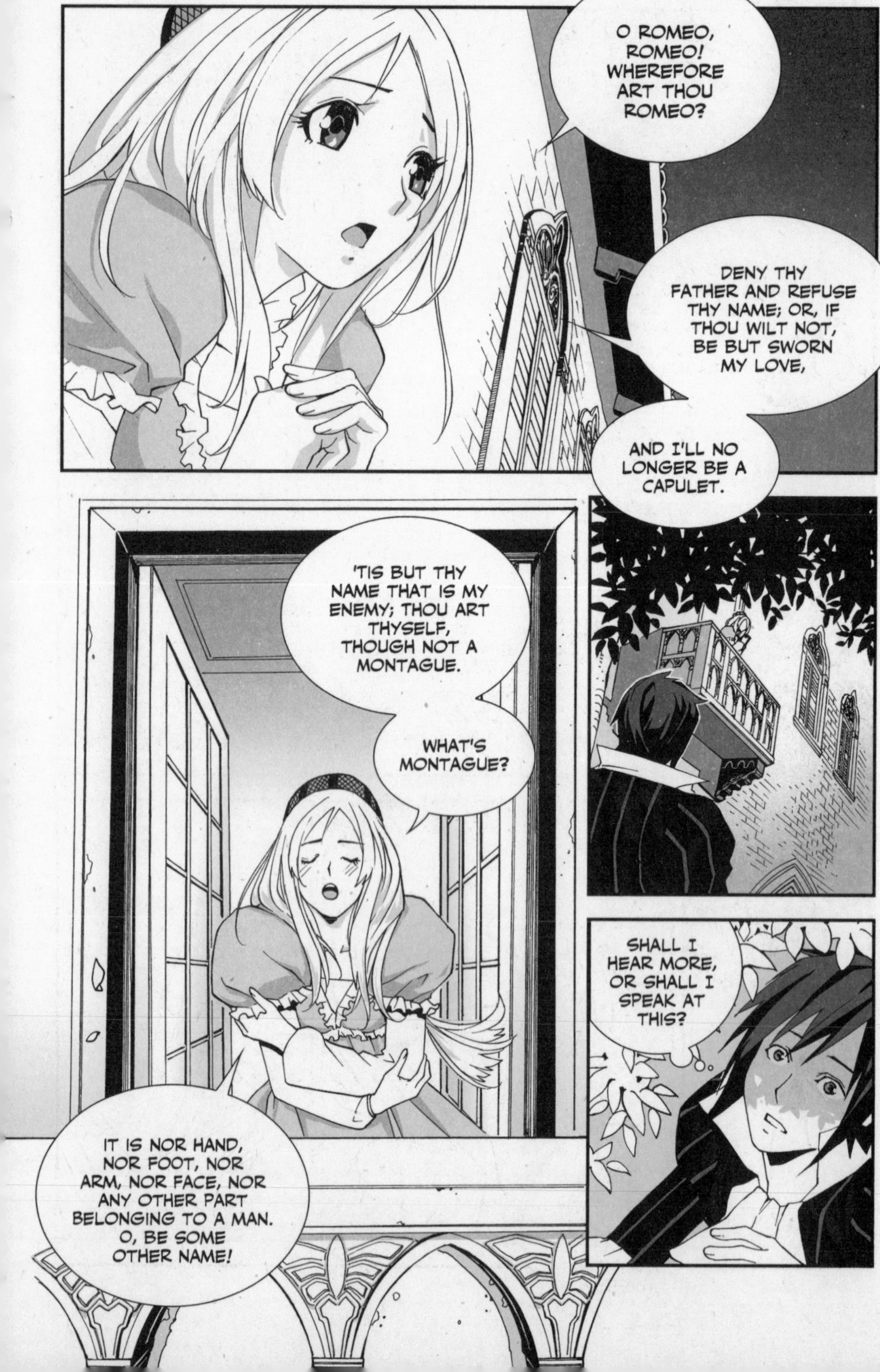
O ROMEO, ROMEO! WHEREFORE ART THOU ROMEO?
DENY THY FATHER AND REFUSE THY NAME; OR, IF THOU WILT NOT, BE BUT SWORN MY LOVE,
AND I'LL NO LONGER BE A CAPULET.
SHALL I HEAR MORE, OR SHALL I SPEAK AT THIS?
'TIS BUT THY NAME THAT IS MY ENEMY; THOU ART THYSELF, THOUGH NOT A MONTAGUE.
WHAT'S MONTAGUE?
IT IS NOR HAND, NOR FOOT, NOR ARM, NOR FACE, NOR ANY OTHER PART BELONGING TO A MAN. O, BE SOME OTHER NAME!

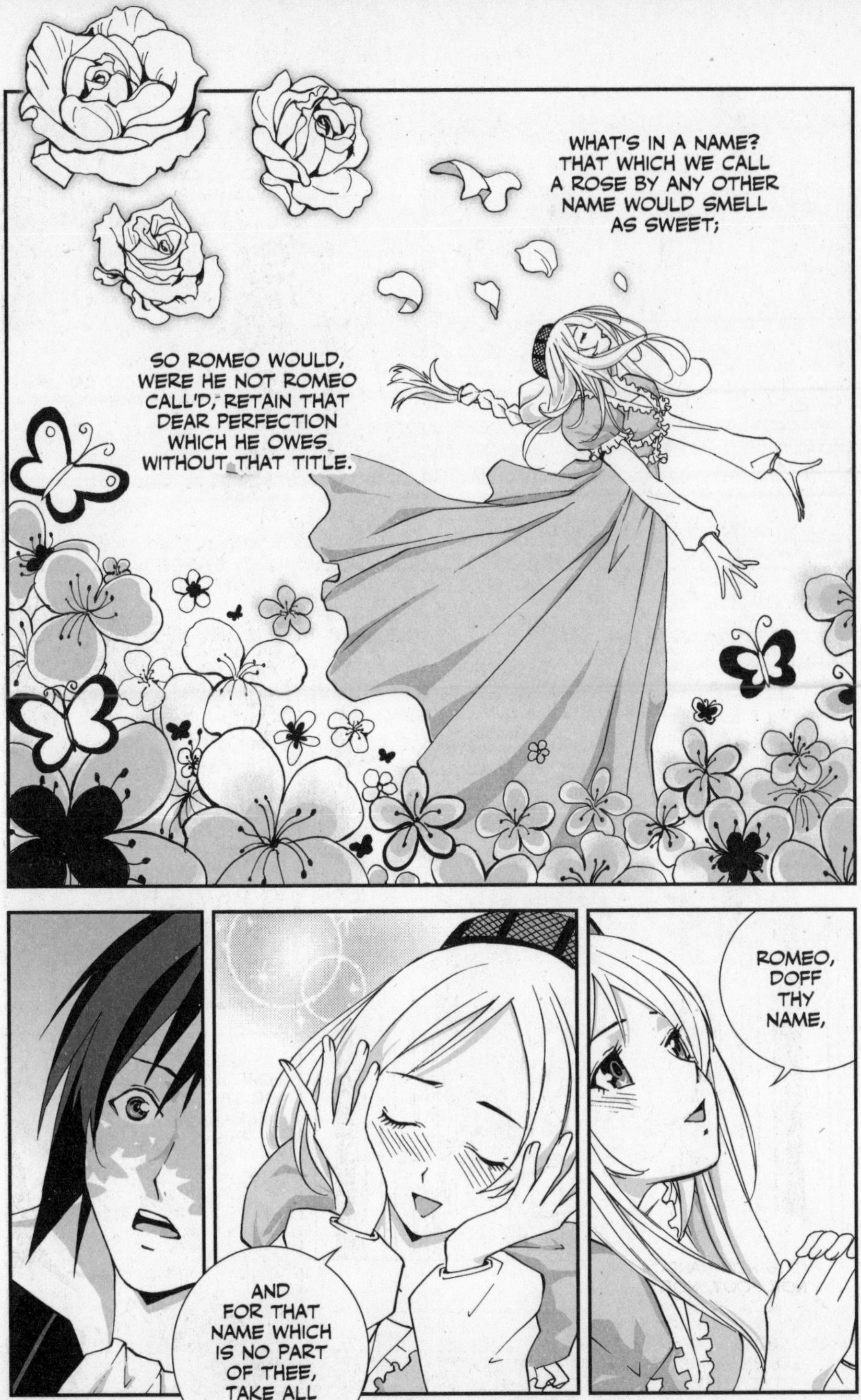
WHAT'S IN A NAME? THAT WHICH WE CALL A ROSE BY ANY OTHER NAME WOULD SMELL AS SWEET;
SO ROMEO WOULD, WERE HE NOT ROMEO CALL'D, RETAIN THAT DEAR PERFECTION WHICH HE OWES WITHOUT THAT TITLE.
ROMEO, DOFF THY NAME,
AND FOR THAT NAME WHICH IS NO PART OF THEE, TAKE ALL MYSELF.

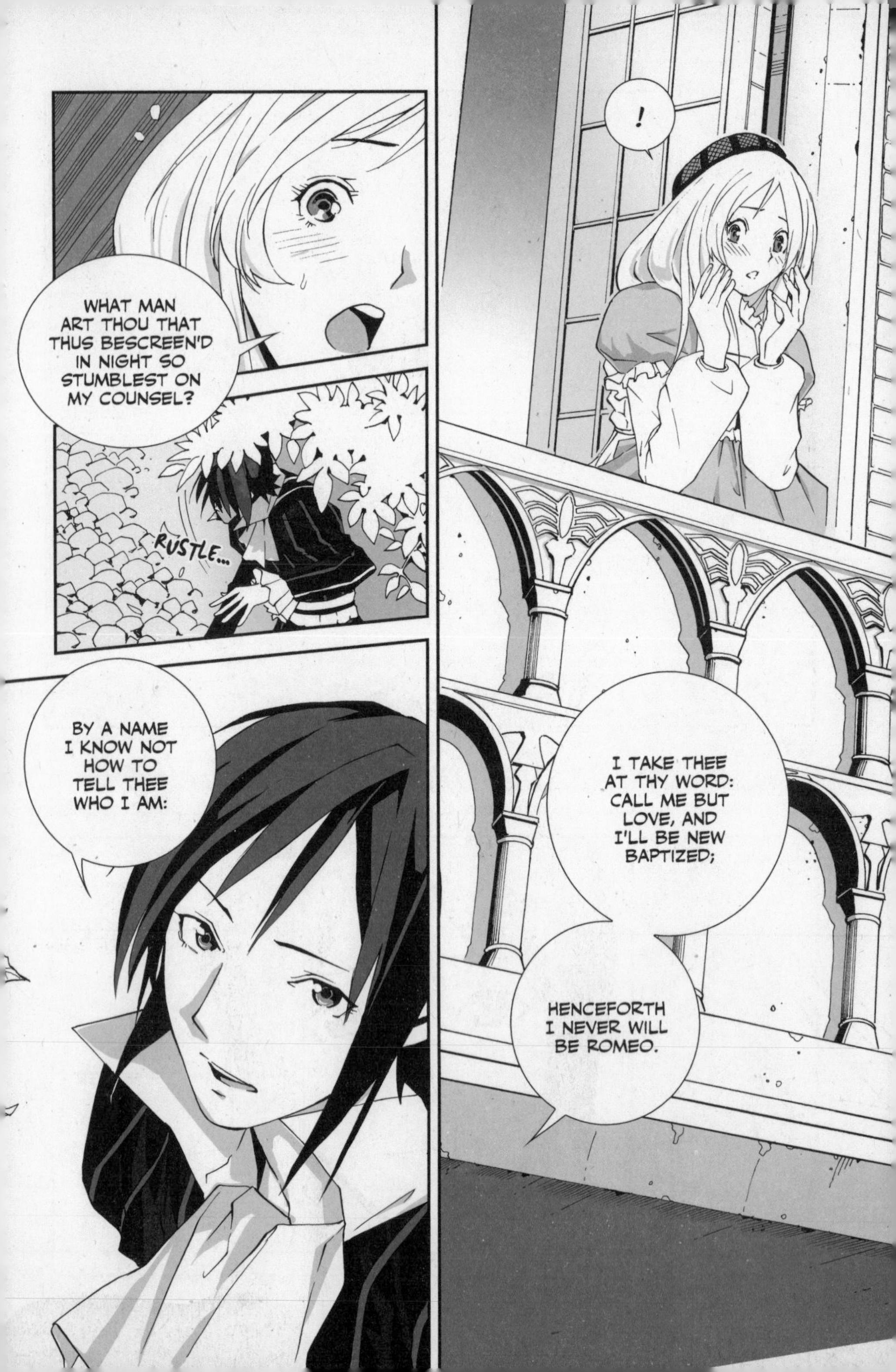
!
I TAKE THEE AT THY WORD: CALL ME BUT LOVE, AND I'LL BE NEW BAPTIZED;
HENCEFORTH I NEVER WILL BE ROMEO.
WHAT MAN ART THOU THAT THUS BESCREEN'D IN NIGHT SO STUMBLEST ON MY COUNSEL?
RUSTLE...
BY A NAME I KNOW NOT HOW TO TELL THEE WHO I AM:

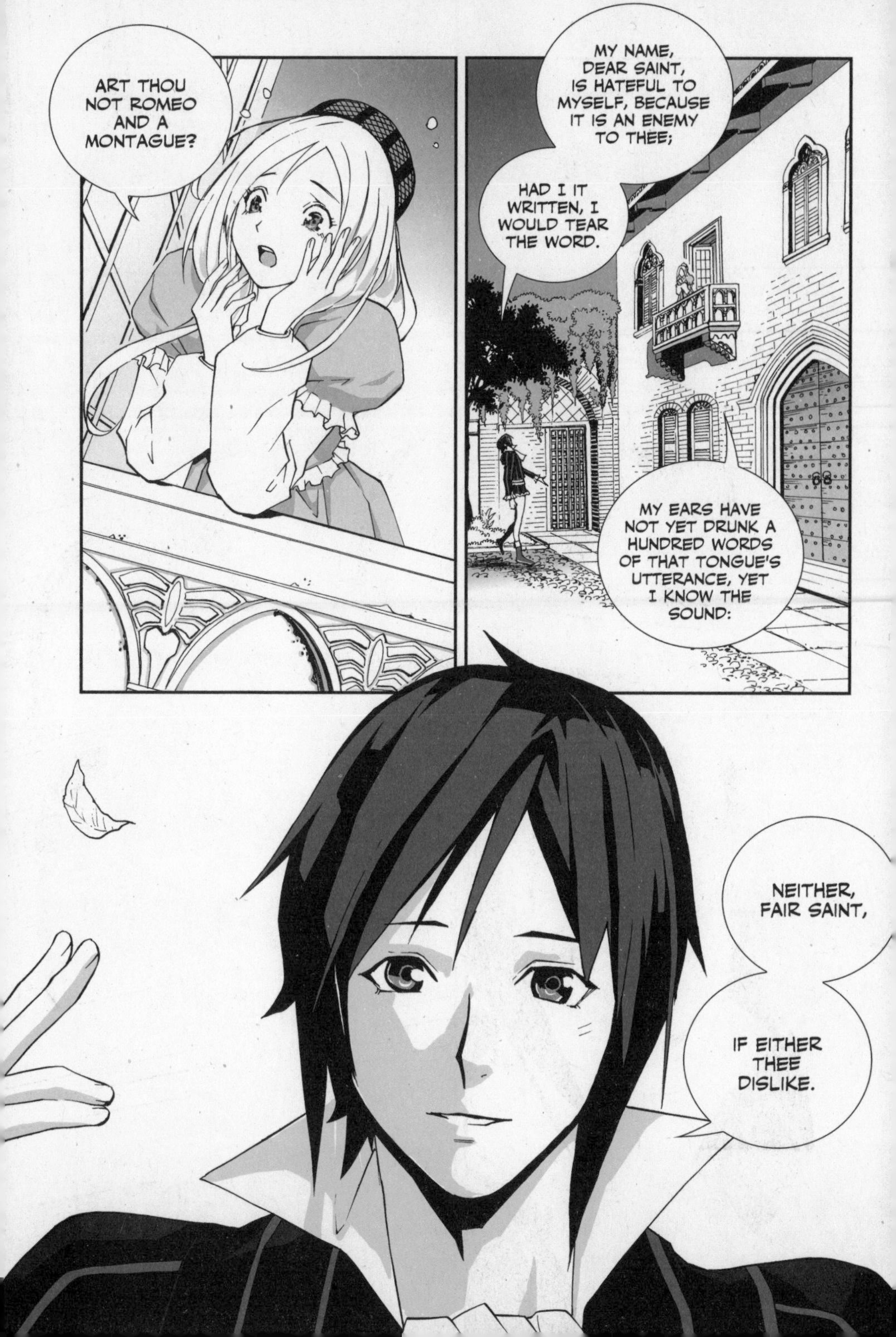
MY NAME, DEAR SAINT, IS HATEFUL TO MYSELF, BECAUSE IT IS AN ENEMY TO THEE;
HAD I IT WRITTEN, I WOULD TEAR THE WORD.
MY EARS HAVE NOT YET DRUNK A HUNDRED WORDS OF THAT TONGUE'S UTTERANCE, YET I KNOW THE SOUND:
ART THOU NOT ROMEO AND A MONTAGUE?
NEITHER, FAIR SAINT,
IF EITHER THEE DISLIKE.

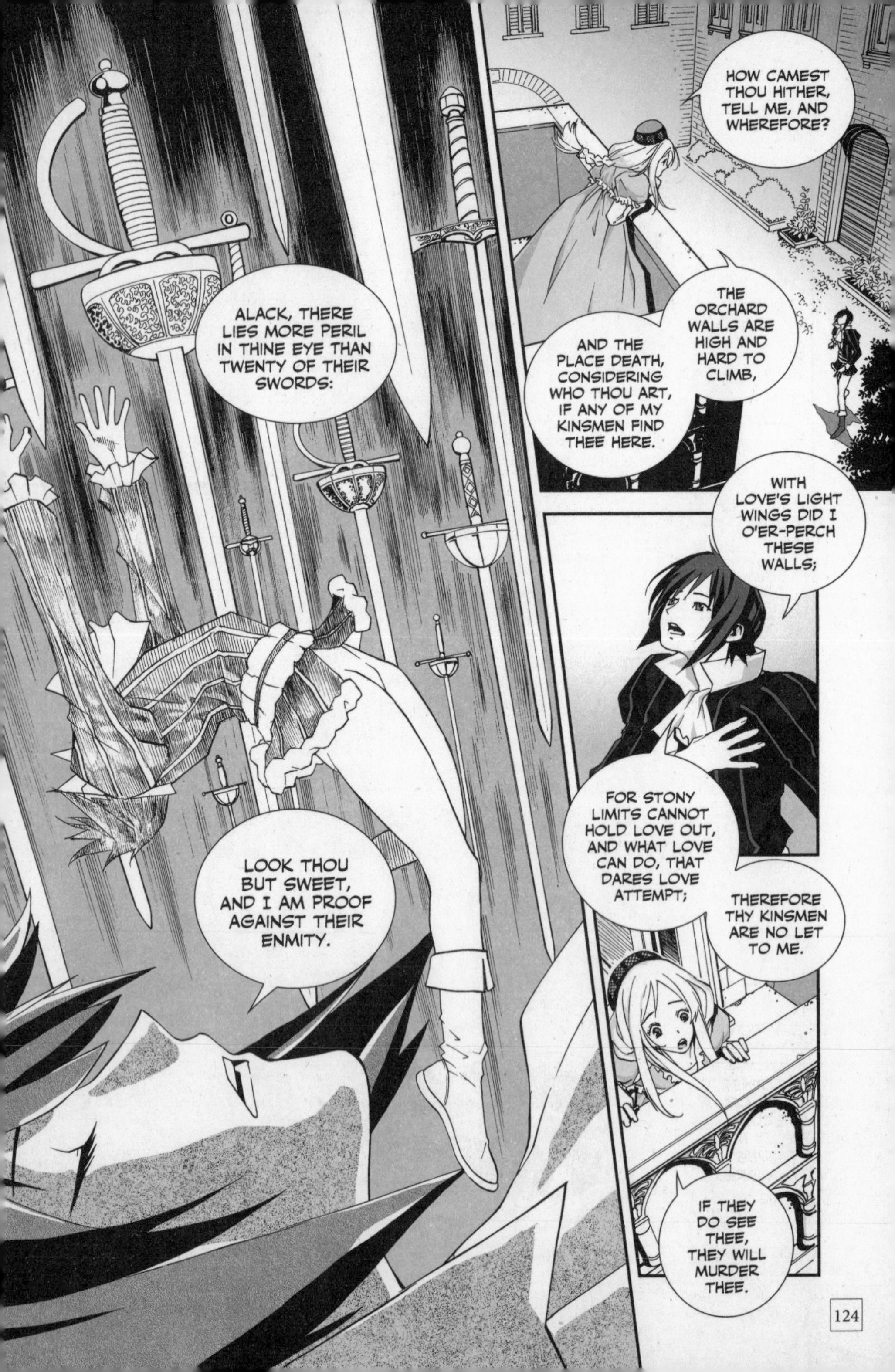
HOW CAMEST THOU HITHER, TELL ME, AND WHEREFORE?
THE ORCHARD WALLS ARE HIGH AND HARD TO CLIMB,
AND THE PLACE DEATH, CONSIDERING WHO THOU ART, IF ANY OF MY KINSMEN FIND THEE HERE.
WITH LOVE'S LIGHT WINGS DID I O'ER-PERCH THESE WALLS;
FOR STONY LIMITS CANNOT HOLD LOVE OUT, AND WHAT LOVE CAN DO, THAT DARES LOVE ATTEMPT;
THEREFORE THY KINSMEN ARE NO LET TO ME.
IF THEY DO SEE THEE, THEY WILL MURDER THEE.
ALACK, THERE LIES MORE PERIL IN THINE EYE THAN TWENTY OF THEIR SWORDS:
LOOK THOU BUT SWEET, AND I AM PROOF AGAINST THEIR ENMITY.

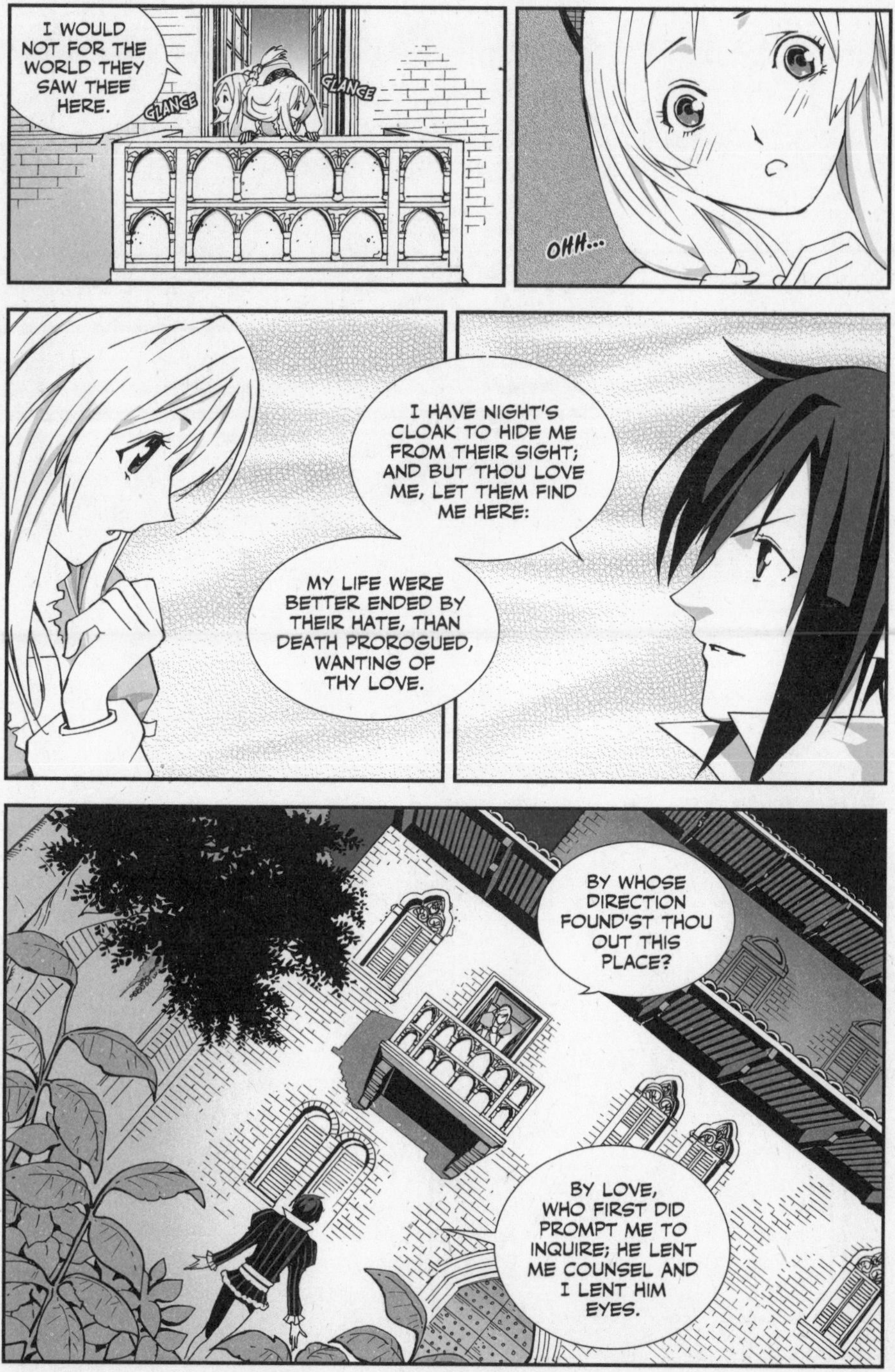
OHH...
I WOULD NOT FOR THE WORLD THEY SAW THEE HERE.
GLANCE
GLANCE
I HAVE NIGHT'S CLOAK TO HIDE ME FROM THEIR SIGHT; AND BUT THOU LOVE ME, LET THEM FIND ME HERE:
MY LIFE WERE BETTER ENDED BY THEIR HATE, THAN DEATH PROROGUED, WANTING OF THY LOVE.
BY WHOSE DIRECTION FOUND'ST THOU OUT THIS PLACE?
BY LOVE, WHO FIRST DID PROMPT ME TO INQUIRE; HE LENT ME COUNSEL AND I LENT HIM EYES.

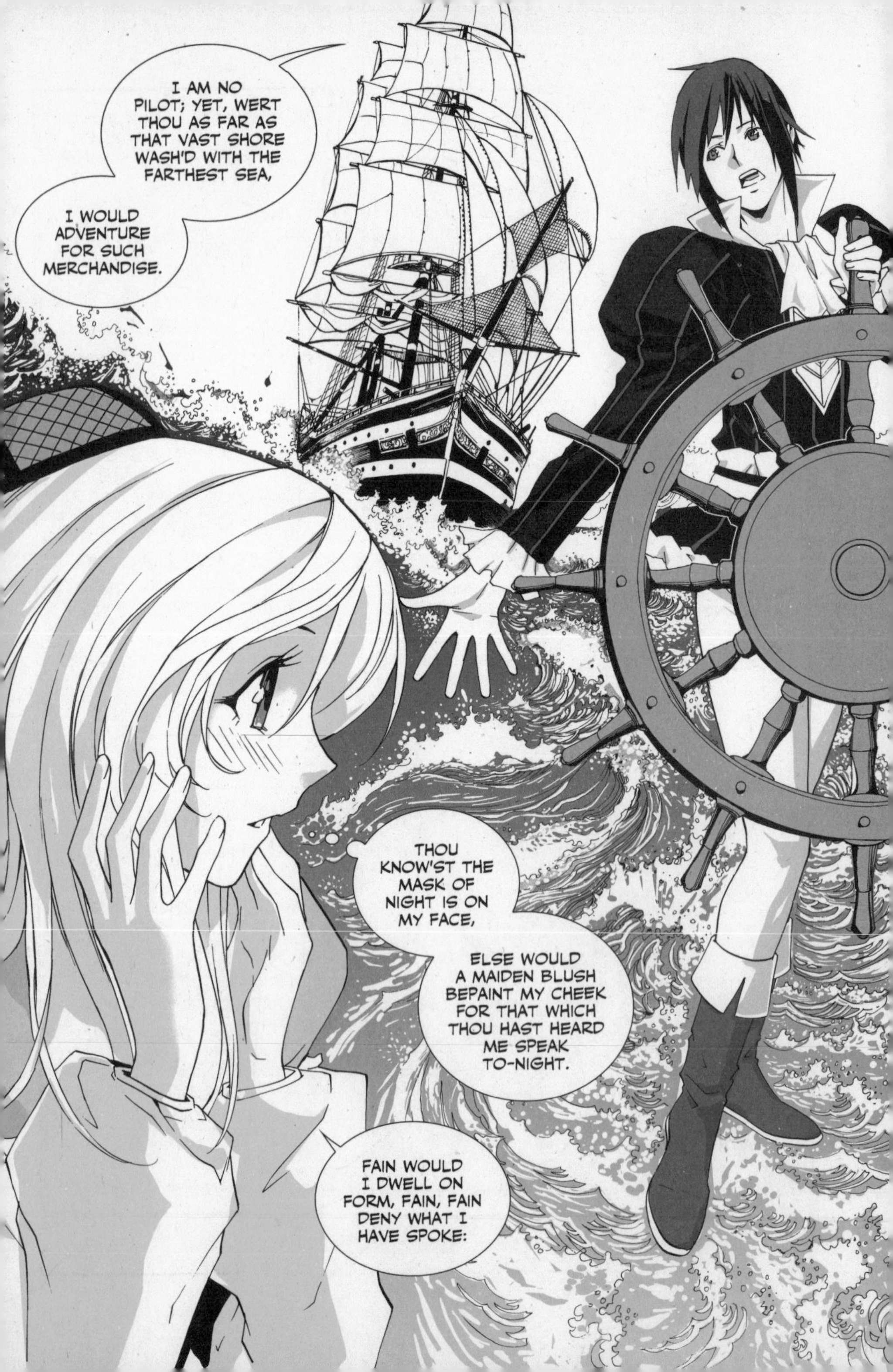
I AM NO PILOT; YET, WERT THOU AS FAR AS THAT VAST SHORE WASH'D WITH THE FARTHEST SEA,
I WOULD ADVENTURE FOR SUCH MERCHANDISE.
THOU KNOW'ST THE MASK OF NIGHT IS ON MY FACE,
ELSE WOULD A MAIDEN BLUSH BEPAINT MY CHEEK FOR THAT WHICH THOU HAST HEARD ME SPEAK TO-NIGHT.
FAIN WOULD I DWELL ON FORM, FAIN, FAIN DENY WHAT I HAVE SPOKE:

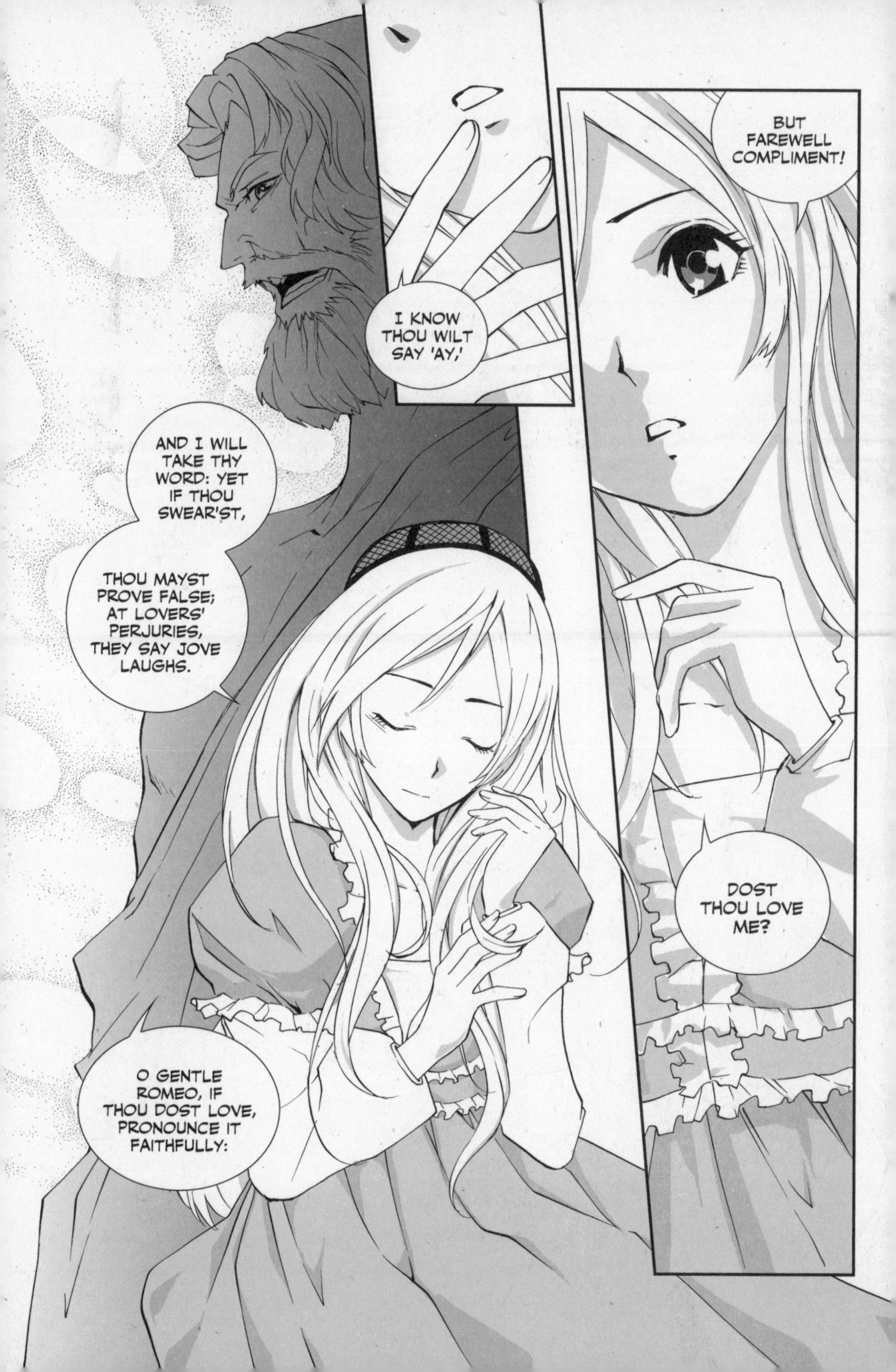
BUT FAREWELL COMPLIMENT!
DOST THOU LOVE ME?
I KNOW THOU WILT SAY 'AY,'
AND I WILL TAKE THY WORD: YET IF THOU SWEAR'ST,
THOU MAYST PROVE FALSE; AT LOVERS' PERJURIES, THEY SAY JOVE LAUGHS.
O GENTLE ROMEO, IF THOU DOST LOVE, PRONOUNCE IT FAITHFULLY:

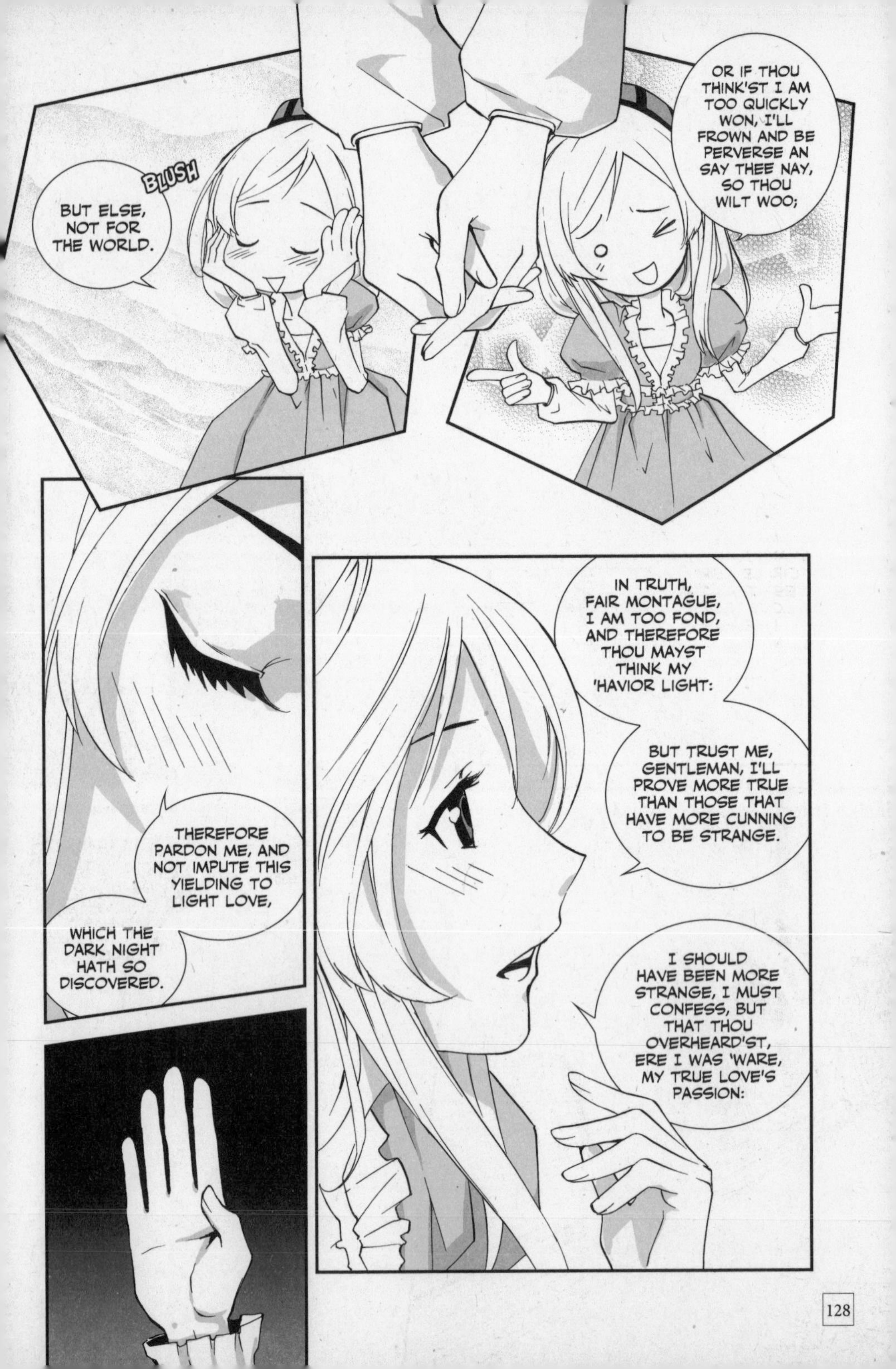
OR IF THOU THINK'ST I AM TOO QUICKLY WON, I'LL FROWN AND BE PERVERSE AN SAY THEE NAY, SO THOU WILT WOO;
BLUSH
BUT ELSE, NOT FOR THE WORLD.
IN TRUTH, FAIR MONTAGUE, I AM TOO FOND, AND THEREFORE THOU MAYST THINK MY 'HAVIOR LIGHT:
BUT TRUST ME, GENTLEMAN, I'LL PROVE MORE TRUE THAN THOSE THAT HAVE MORE CUNNING TO BE STRANGE.
I SHOULD HAVE BEEN MORE STRANGE, I MUST CONFESS, BUT THAT THOU OVERHEARD'ST, ERE I WAS 'WARE, MY TRUE LOVE'S PASSION:
THEREFORE PARDON ME, AND NOT IMPUTE THIS YIELDING TO LIGHT LOVE,
WHICH THE DARK NIGHT HATH SO DISCOVERED.

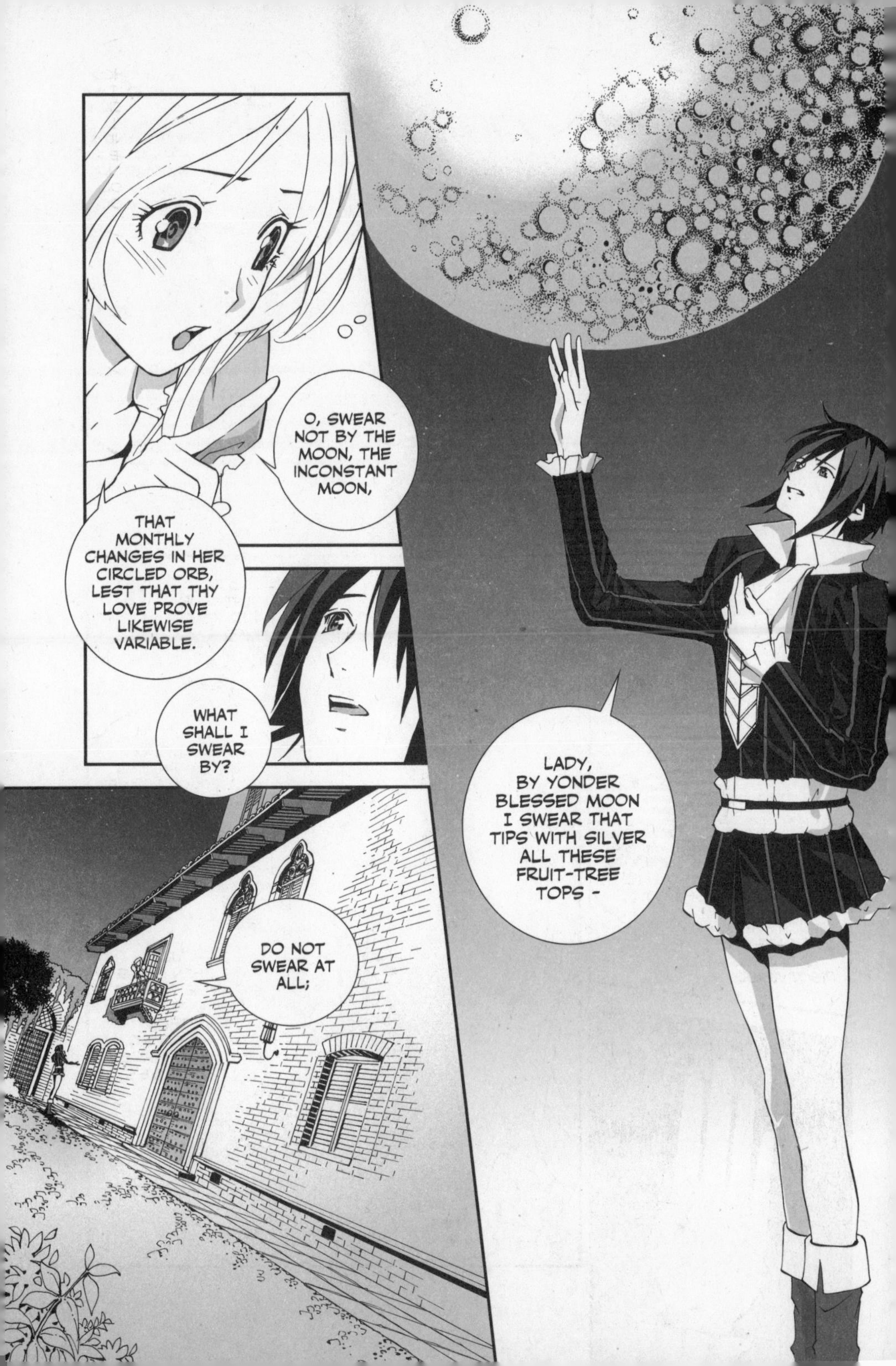
LADY, BY YONDER BLESSED MOON I SWEAR THAT TIPS WITH SILVER ALL THESE FRUIT-TREE TOPS -
O, SWEAR NOT BY THE MOON, THE INCONSTANT MOON,
THAT MONTHLY CHANGES IN HER CIRCLED ORB, LEST THAT THY LOVE PROVE LIKEWISE VARIABLE.
WHAT SHALL I SWEAR BY?
DO NOT SWEAR AT ALL;

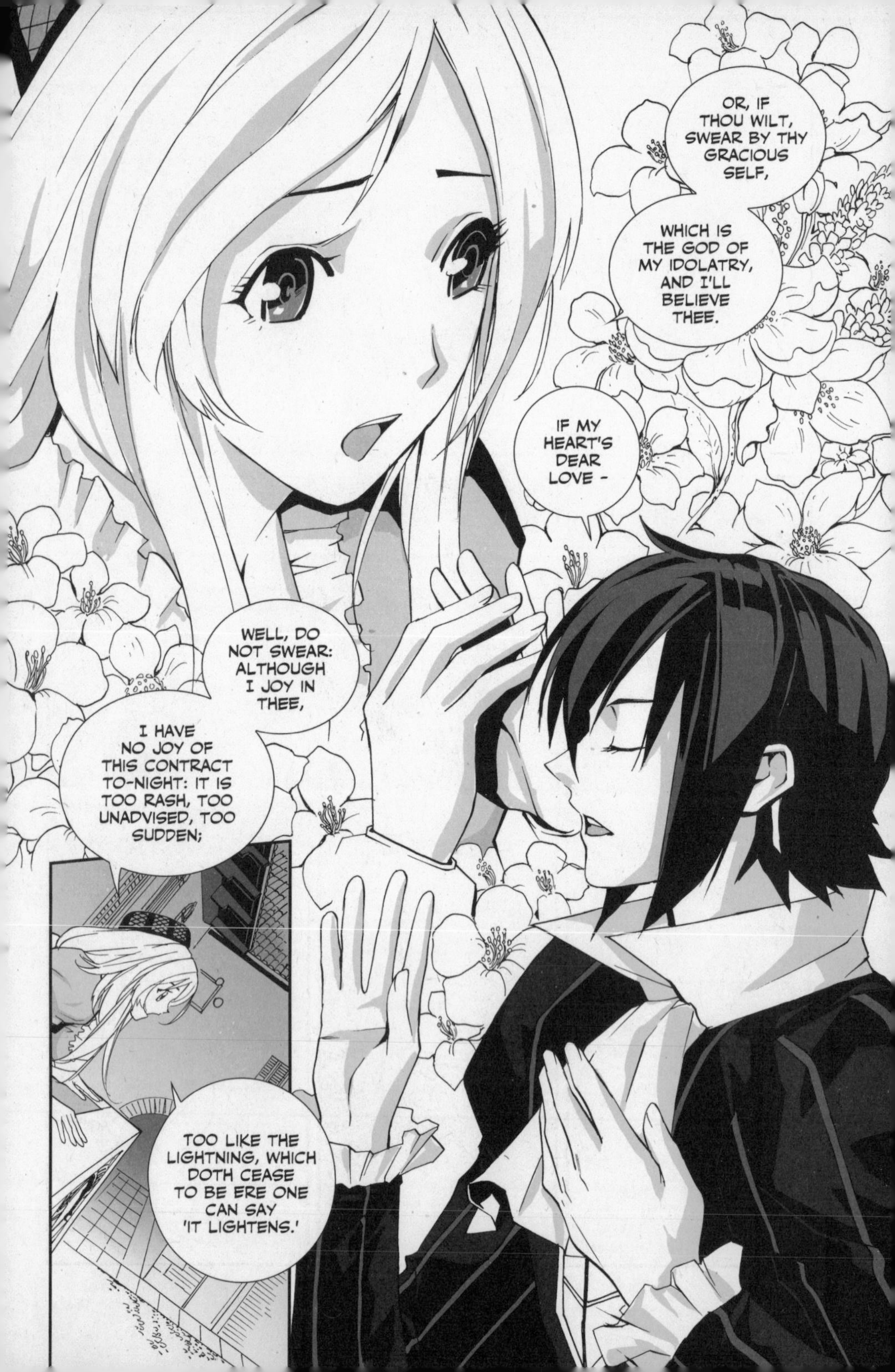
OR, IF THOU WILT, SWEAR BY THY GRACIOUS SELF,
WHICH IS THE GOD OF MY IDOLATRY, AND I'LL BELIEVE THEE.
IF MY HEART'S DEAR LOVE -
WELL, DO NOT SWEAR: ALTHOUGH I JOY IN THEE,
I HAVE NO JOY OF THIS CONTRACT TO-NIGHT: IT IS TOO RASH, TOO UNADVISED, TOO SUDDEN;
TOO LIKE THE LIGHTNING, WHICH DOTH CEASE TO BE ERE ONE CAN SAY 'IT LIGHTENS.'

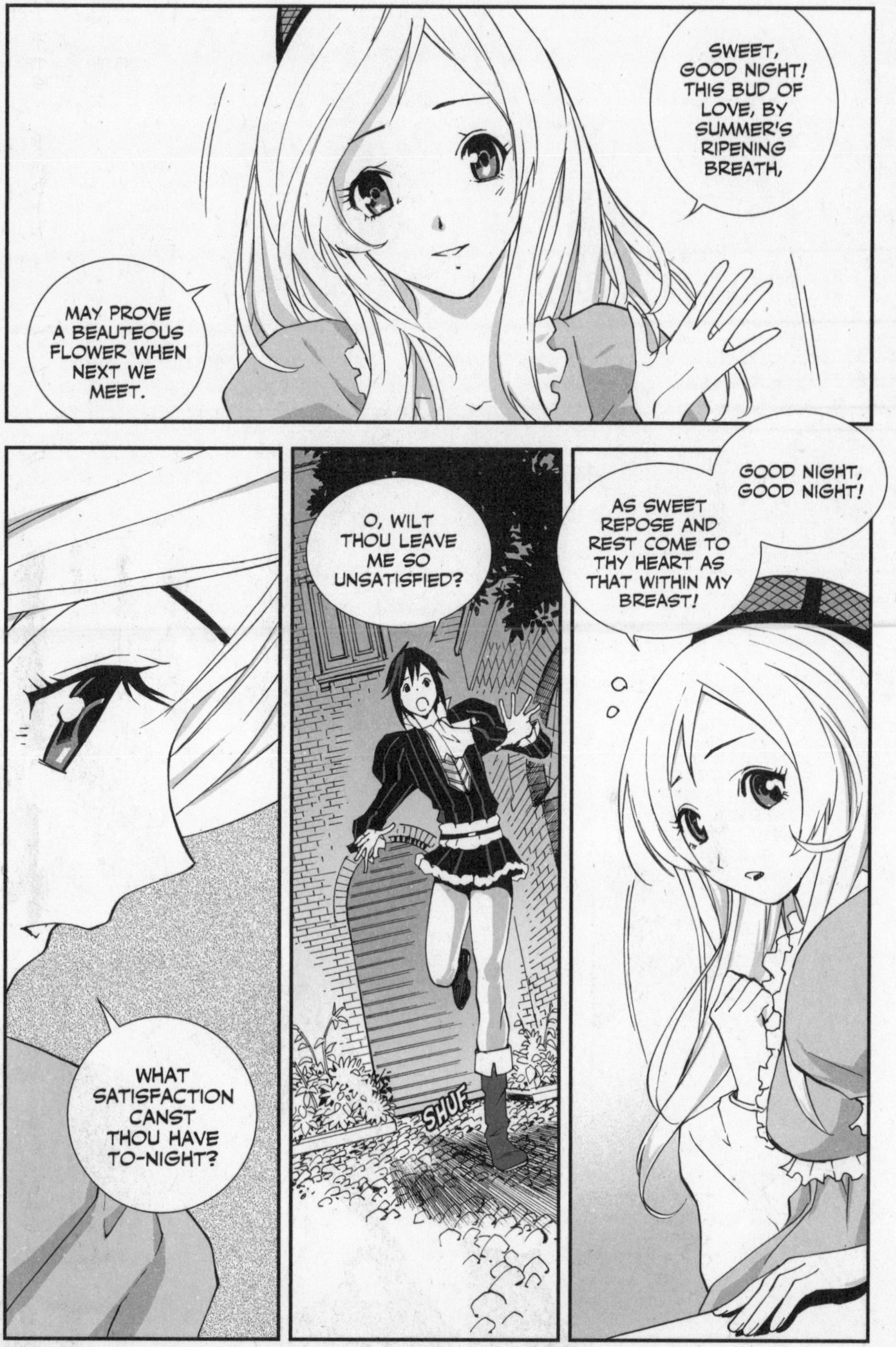
SWEET, GOOD NIGHT! THIS BUD OF LOVE, BY SUMMER'S RIPENING BREATH,
MAY PROVE A BEAUTEOUS FLOWER WHEN NEXT WE MEET.
GOOD NIGHT, GOOD NIGHT!
AS SWEET REPOSE AND REST COME TO THY HEART AS THAT WITHIN MY BREAST!
O, WILT THOU LEAVE ME SO UNSATISFIED?
SHUF
WHAT SATISFACTION CANST THOU HAVE TO-NIGHT?

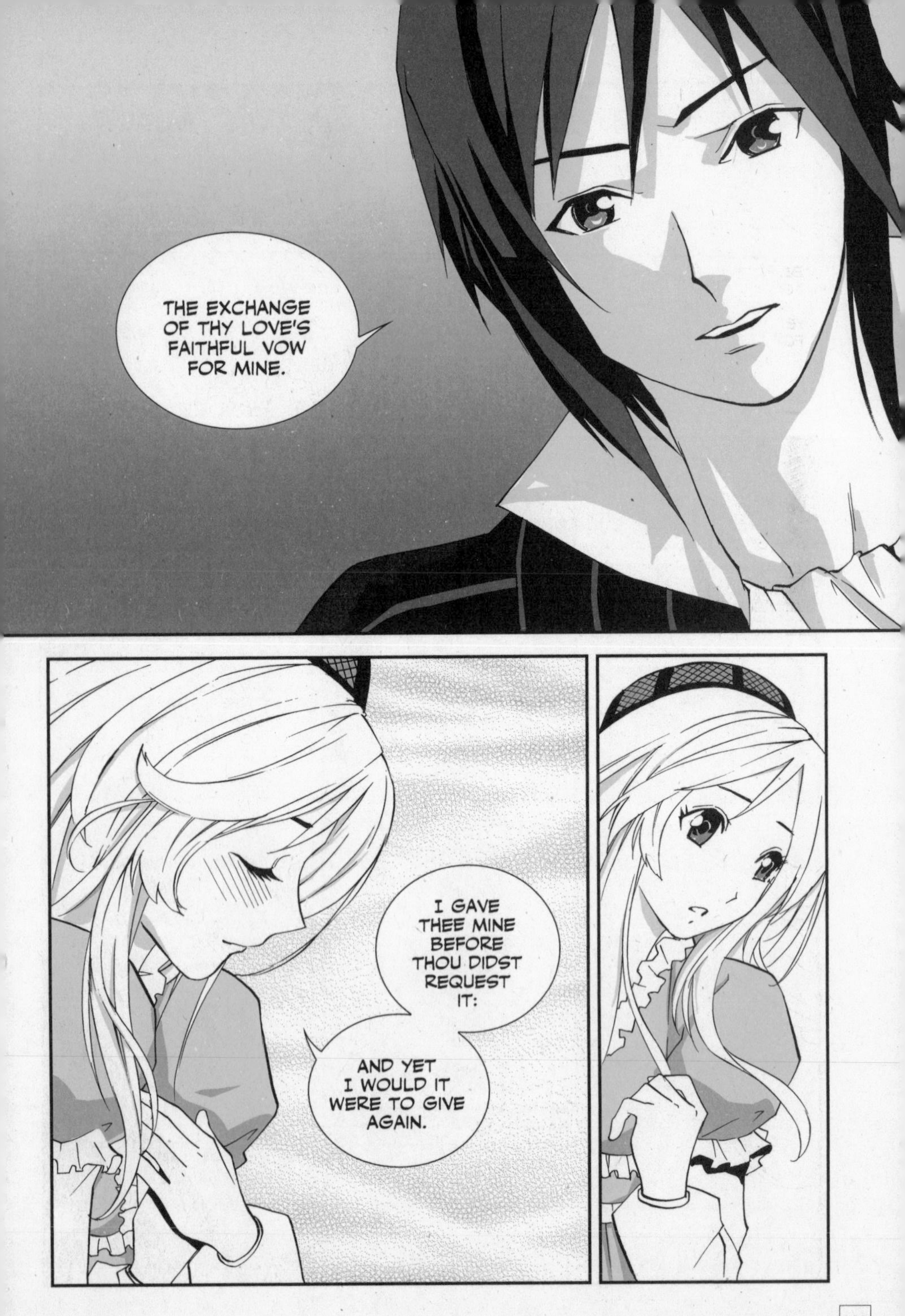
THE EXCHANGE OF THY LOVE'S FAITHFUL VOW FOR MINE.
I GAVE THEE MINE BEFORE THOU DIDST REQUEST IT:
AND YET I WOULD IT WERE TO GIVE AGAIN.

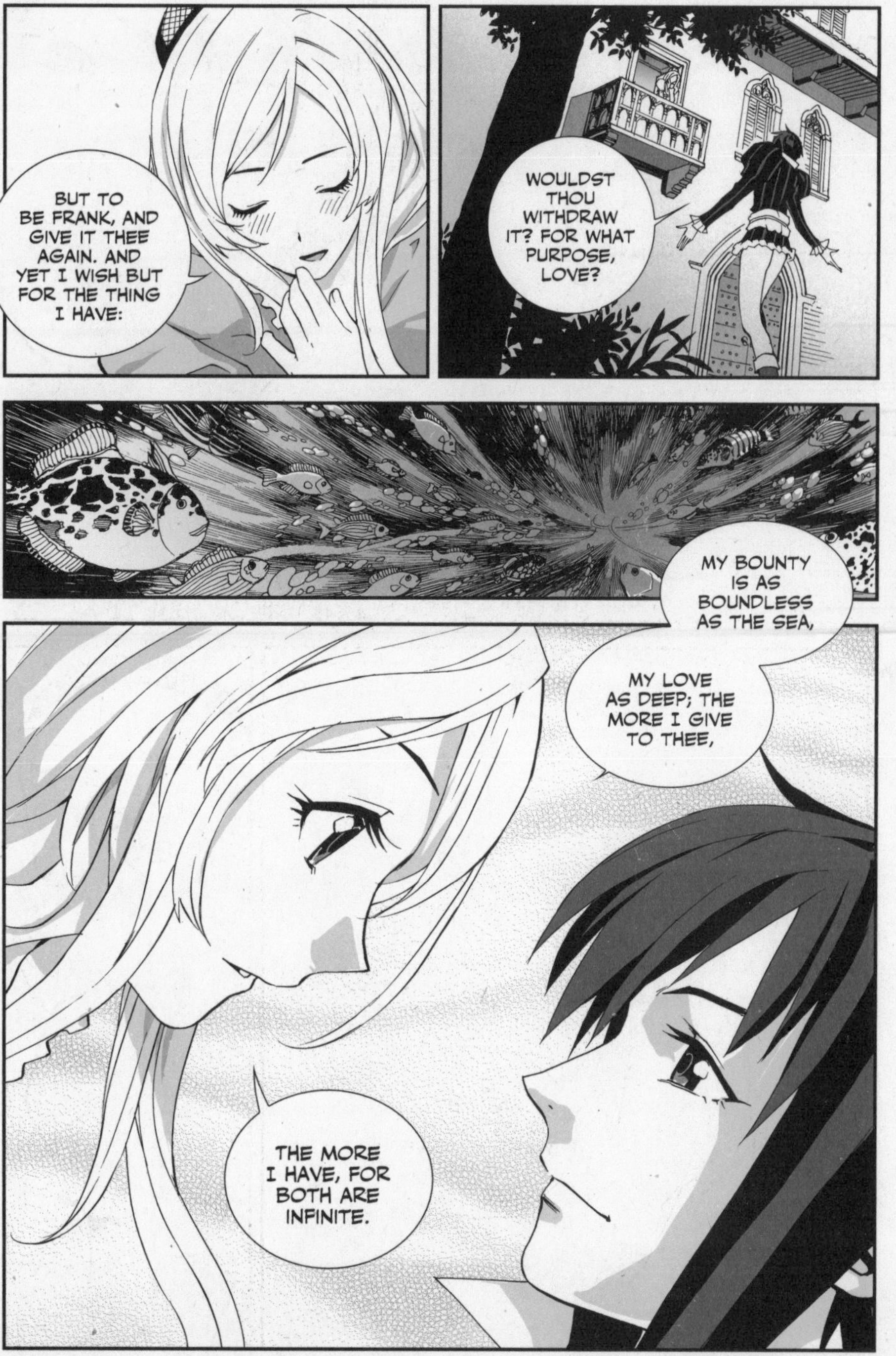
WOULDST THOU WITHDRAW IT? FOR WHAT PURPOSE, LOVE?
BUT TO BE FRANK, AND GIVE IT THEE AGAIN. AND YET I WISH BUT FOR THE THING I HAVE:
MY BOUNTY IS AS BOUNDLESS AS THE SEA,
MY LOVE AS DEEP; THE MORE I GIVE TO THEE,
THE MORE I HAVE, FOR BOTH ARE INFINITE.

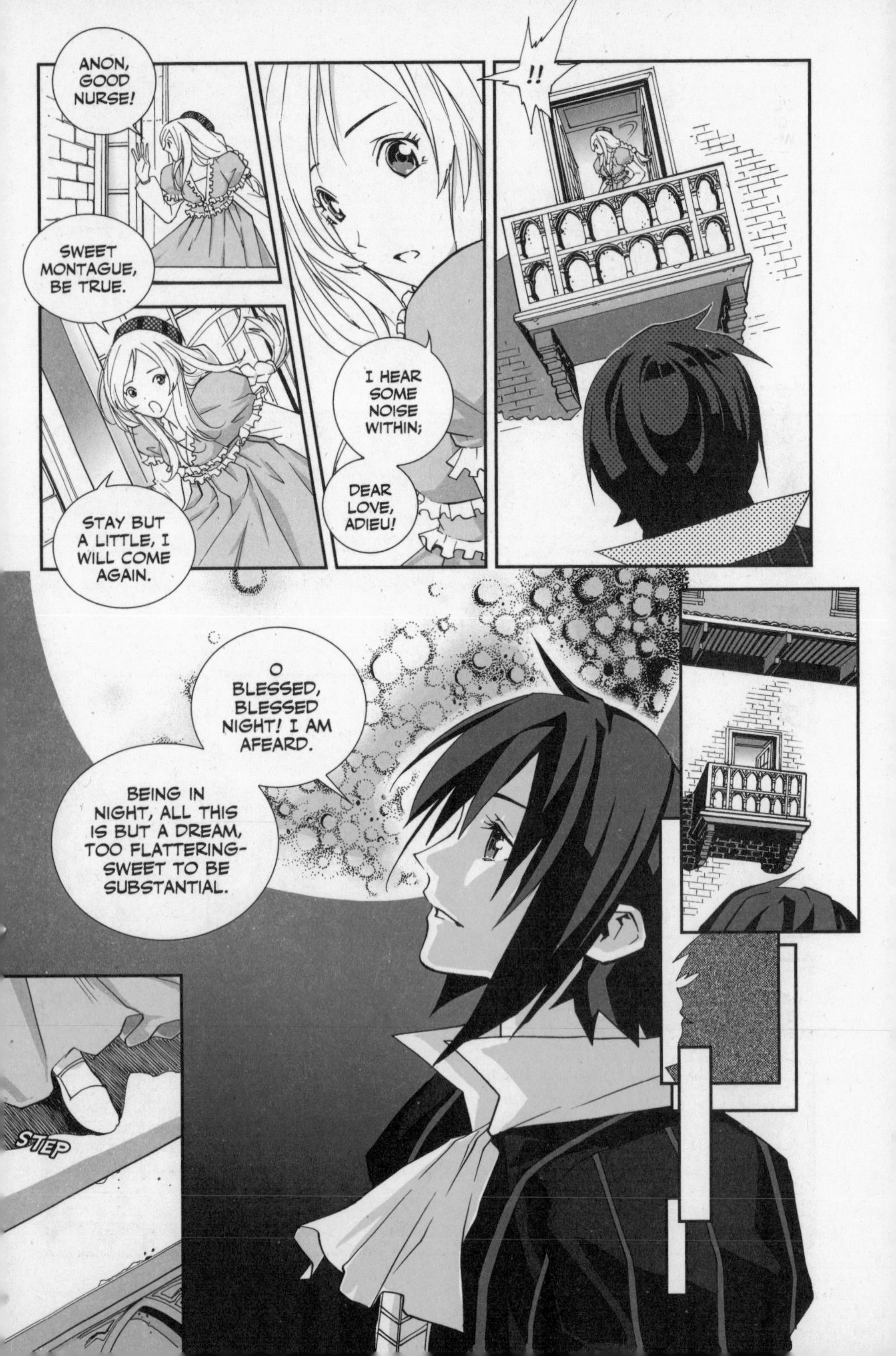
!!
I HEAR SOME NOISE WITHIN;
DEAR LOVE, ADIEU!
ANON, GOOD NURSE!
SWEET MONTAGUE, BE TRUE.
STAY BUT A LITTLE, I WILL COME AGAIN.
O BLESSED, BLESSED NIGHT! I AM AFEARD.
BEING IN NIGHT, ALL THIS IS BUT A DREAM, TOO FLATTERING-SWEET TO BE SUBSTANTIAL.
STEP

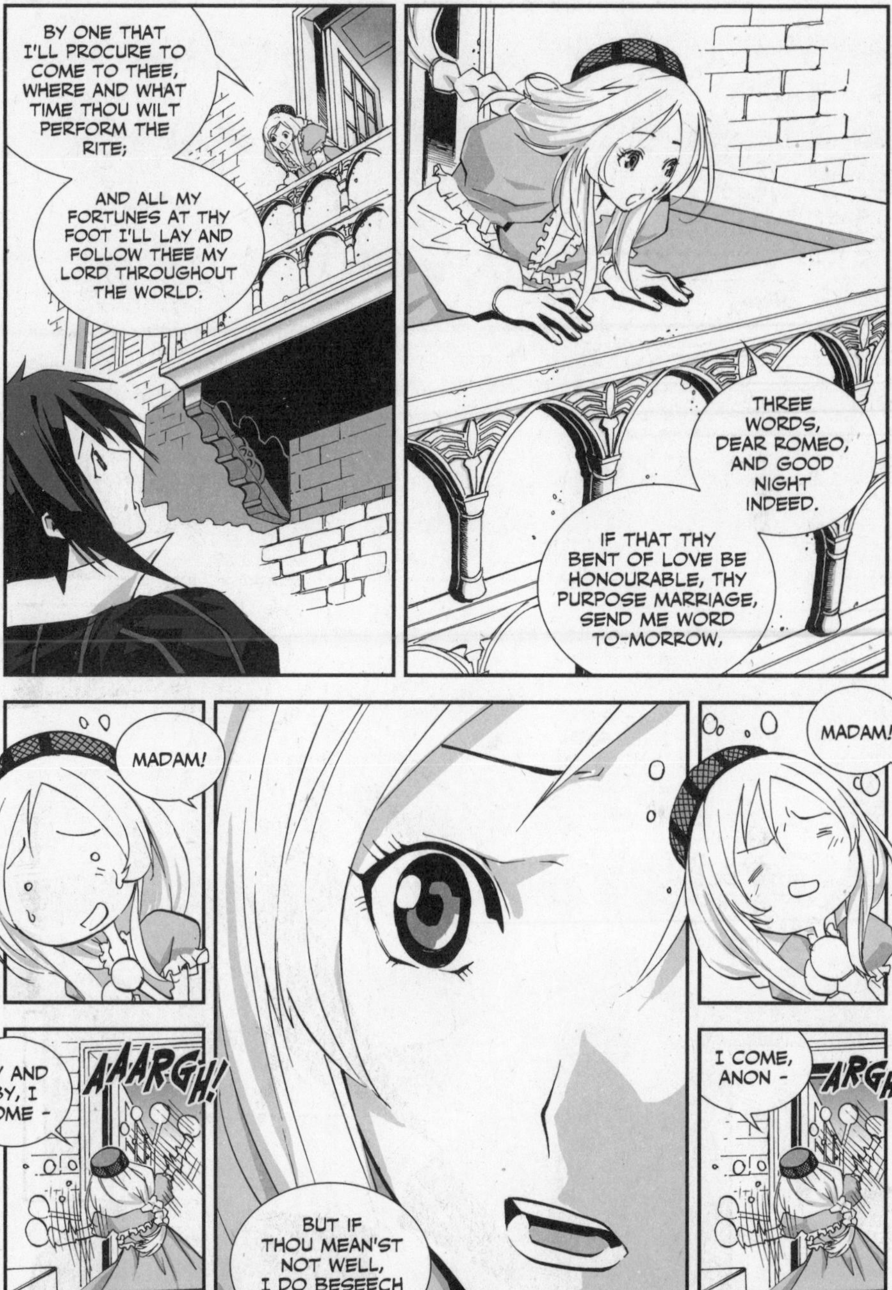
THREE WORDS, DEAR ROMEO, AND GOOD NIGHT INDEED.
IF THAT THY BENT OF LOVE BE HONOURABLE, THY PURPOSE MARRIAGE, SEND ME WORD TO-MORROW,
BY ONE THAT I'LL PROCURE TO COME TO THEE, WHERE AND WHAT TIME THOU WILT PERFORM THE RITE;
AND ALL MY FORTUNES AT THY FOOT I'LL LAY AND FOLLOW THEE MY LORD THROUGHOUT THE WORLD.
MADAM!
I COME, ANON -
ARGH!
BUT IF THOU MEAN'ST NOT WELL, I DO BESEECH THEE -
MADAM!
BY AND BY, I COME -
AAARGH!

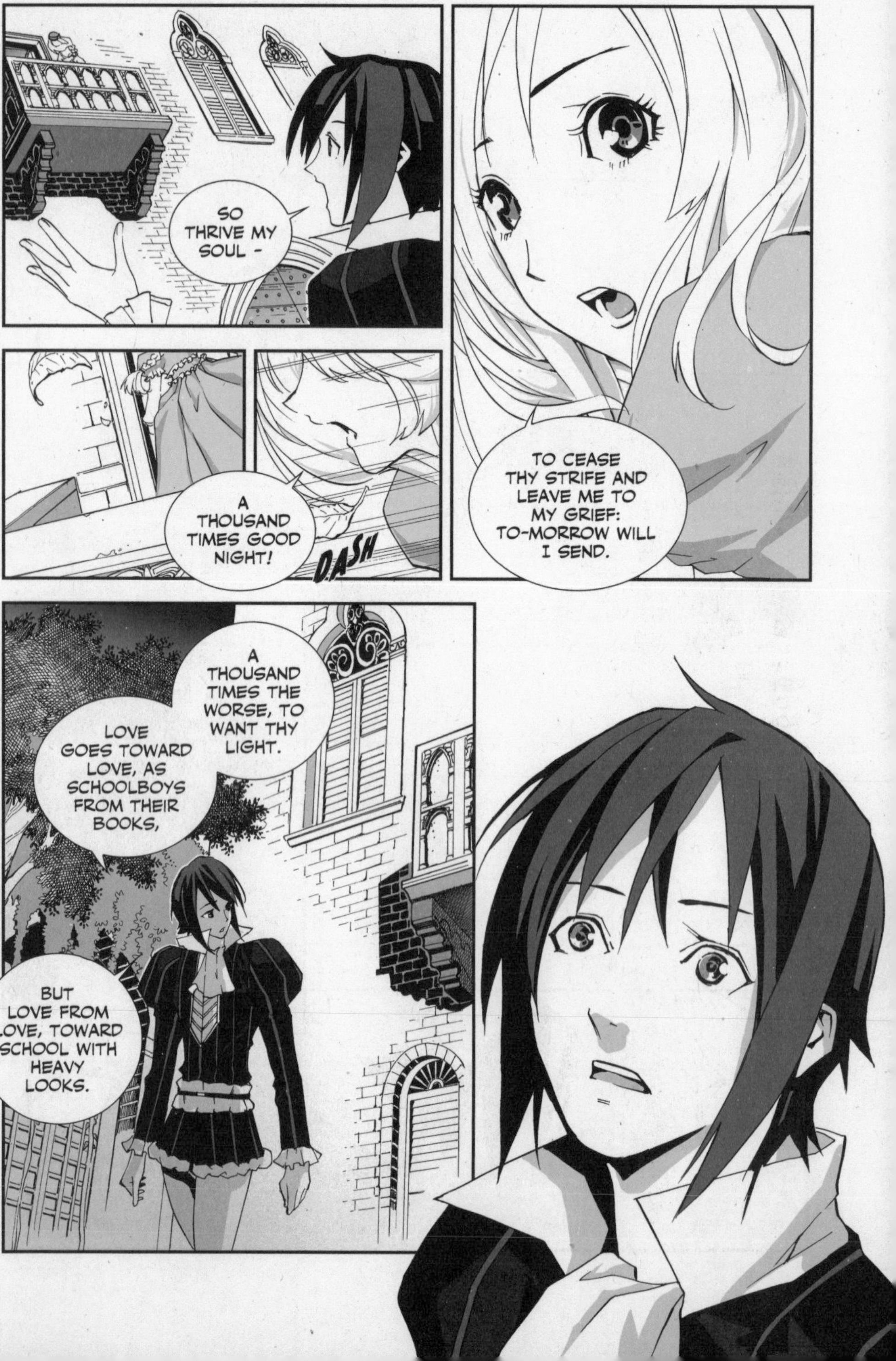
TO CEASE THY STRIFE AND LEAVE ME TO MY GRIEF: TO-MORROW WILL I SEND.
SO THRIVE MY SOUL -
A THOUSAND TIMES GOOD NIGHT!
DASH
A THOUSAND TIMES THE WORSE, TO WANT THY LIGHT.
LOVE GOES TOWARD LOVE, AS SCHOOLBOYS FROM THEIR BOOKS,
BUT LOVE FROM LOVE, TOWARD SCHOOL WITH HEAVY LOOKS.

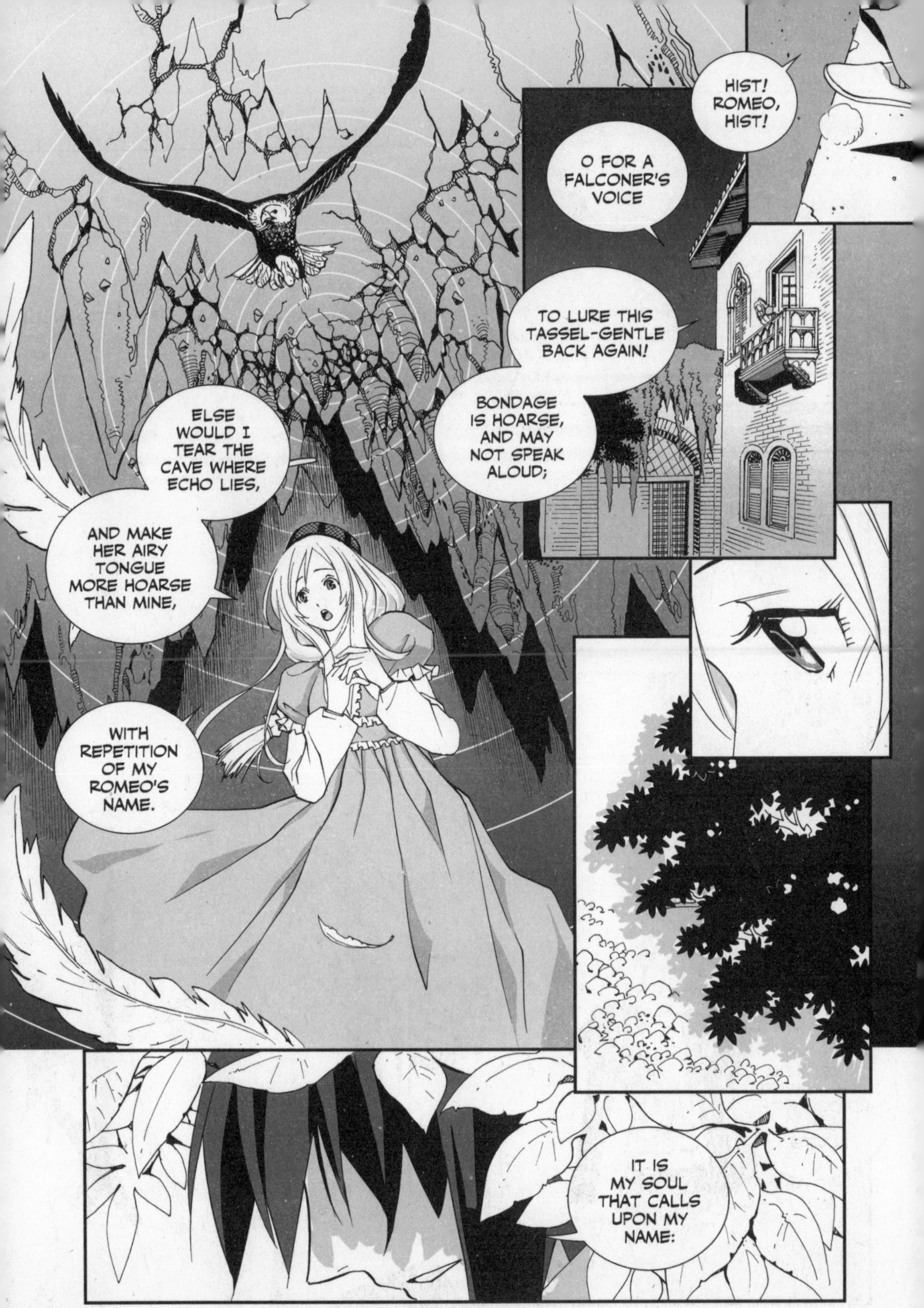
HIST! ROMEO, HIST!
O FOR A FALCONER'S VOICE
TO LURE THIS TASSEL-GENTLE BACK AGAIN!
BONDAGE IS HOARSE, AND MAY NOT SPEAK ALOUD;
ELSE WOULD I TEAR THE CAVE WHERE ECHO LIES,
AND MAKE HER AIRY TONGUE MORE HOARSE THAN MINE,
WITH REPETITION OF MY ROMEO'S NAME.
IT IS MY SOUL THAT CALLS UPON MY NAME:

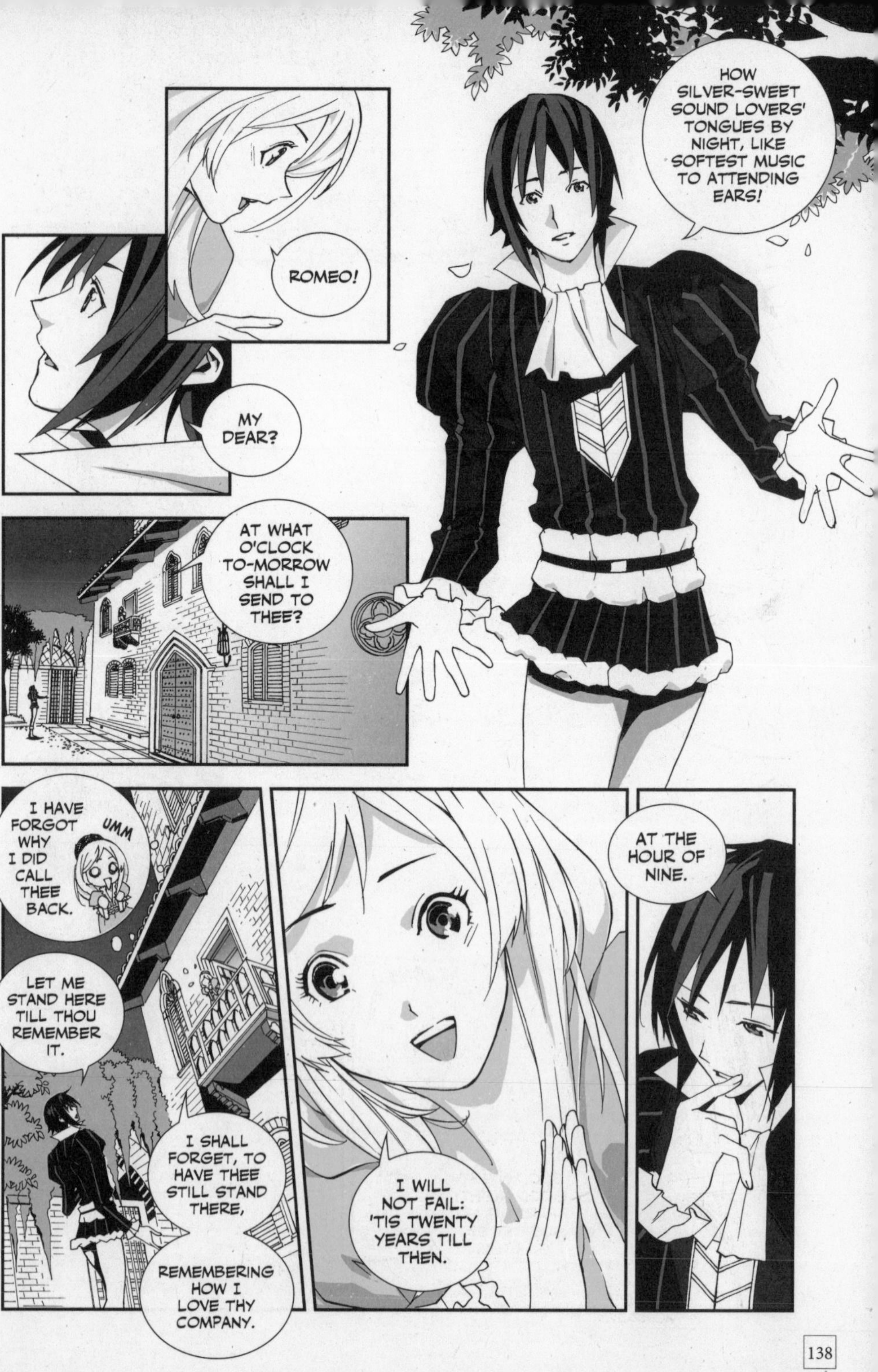
HOW SILVER-SWEET SOUND LOVERS' TONGUES BY NIGHT, LIKE SOFTEST MUSIC TO ATTENDING EARS!
ROMEO!
MY DEAR?
AT WHAT O'CLOCK TO-MORROW SHALL I SEND TO THEE?
AT THE HOUR OF NINE.
I WILL NOT FAIL: 'TIS TWENTY YEARS TILL THEN.
I HAVE FORGOT WHY I DID CALL THEE BACK.
UMM
LET ME STAND HERE TILL THOU REMEMBER IT.
I SHALL FORGET, TO HAVE THEE STILL STAND THERE,
REMEMBERING HOW I LOVE THY COMPANY.

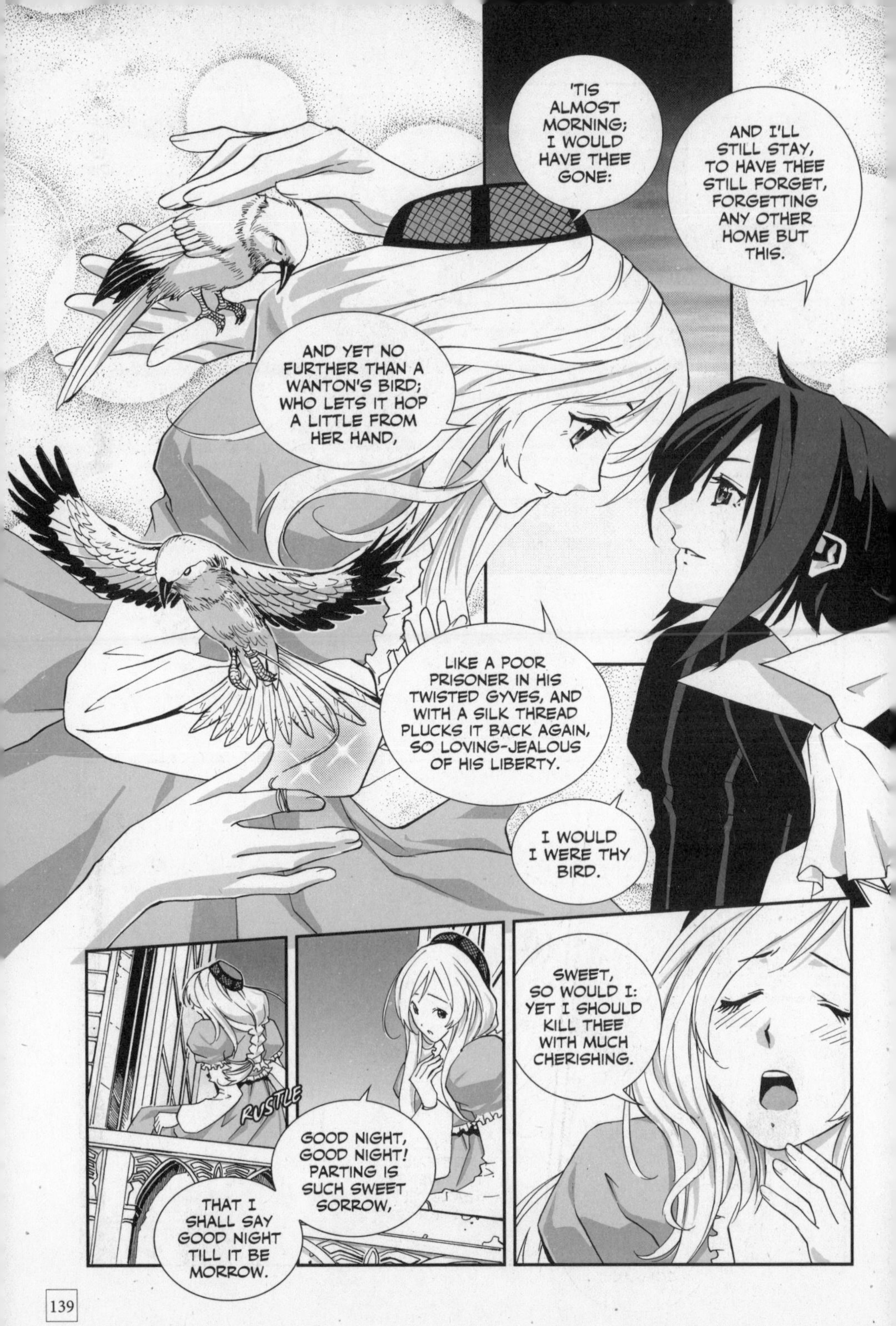
'TIS ALMOST MORNING; I WOULD HAVE THEE GONE:
AND I'LL STILL STAY, TO HAVE THEE STILL FORGET, FORGETTING ANY OTHER HOME BUT THIS.
AND YET NO FURTHER THAN A WANTON'S BIRD; WHO LETS IT HOP A LITTLE FROM HER HAND,
LIKE A POOR PRISONER IN HIS TWISTED GYVES, AND WITH A SILK THREAD PLUCKS IT BACK AGAIN, SO LOVING-JEALOUS OF HIS LIBERTY.
I WOULD I WERE THY BIRD.
SWEET, SO WOULD I: YET I SHOULD KILL THEE WITH MUCH CHERISHING.
GOOD NIGHT, GOOD NIGHT! PARTING IS SUCH SWEET SORROW,
THAT I SHALL SAY GOOD NIGHT TILL IT BE MORROW.
RUSTLE

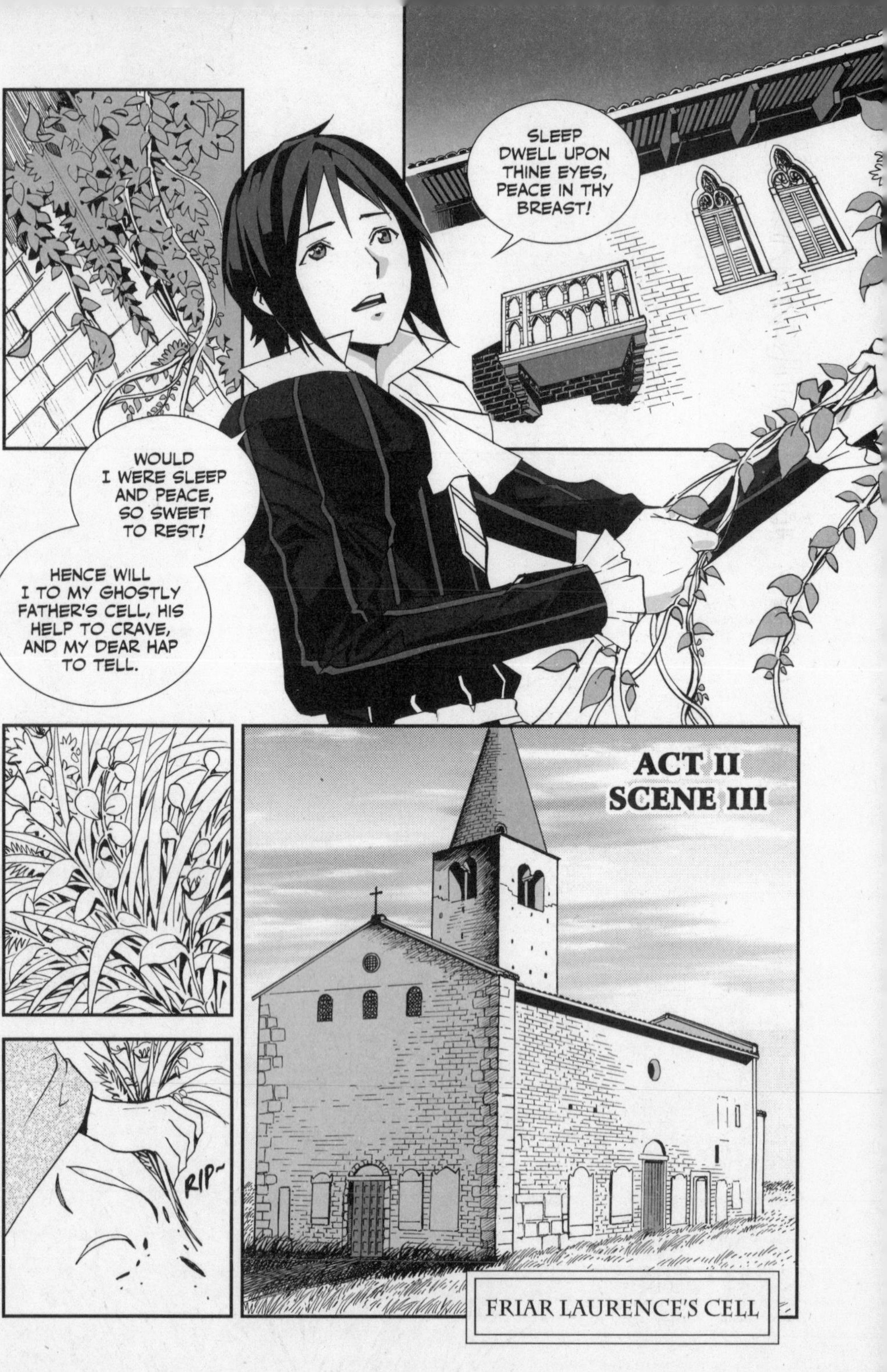
SLEEP DWELL UPON THINE EYES, PEACE IN THY BREAST!
WOULD I WERE SLEEP AND PEACE, SO SWEET TO REST!
HENCE WILL I TO MY GHOSTLY FATHER'S CELL, HIS HELP TO CRAVE, AND MY DEAR HAP TO TELL.
ACT II SCENE III
FRIAR LAURENCE'S CELL
RIP~

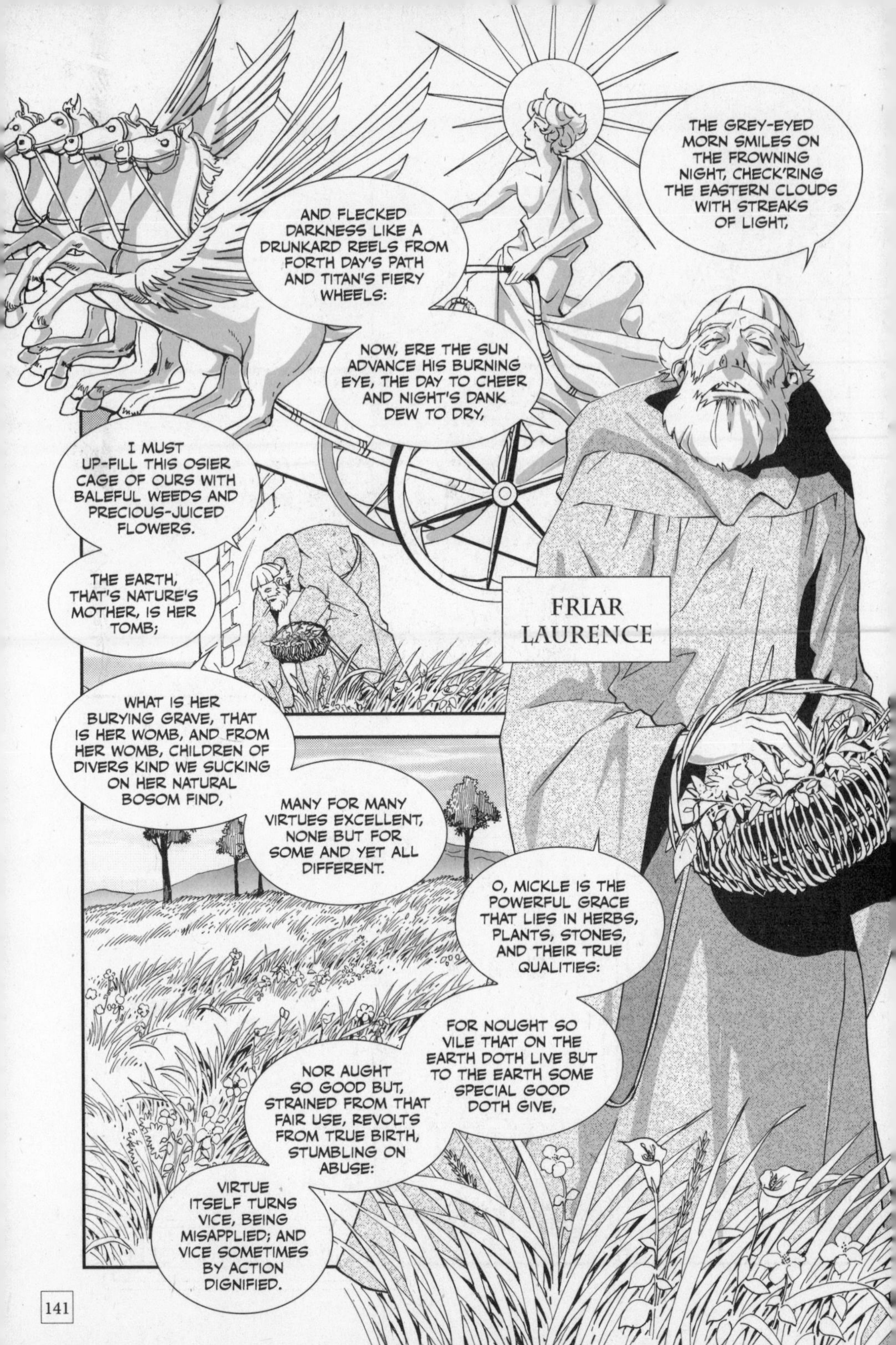
THE GREY-EYED MORN SMILES ON THE FROWNING NIGHT, CHECK'RING THE EASTERN CLOUDS WITH STREAKS OF LIGHT,
AND FLECKED DARKNESS LIKE A DRUNKARD REELS FROM FORTH DAY'S PATH AND TITAN'S FIERY WHEELS:
NOW, ERE THE SUN ADVANCE HIS BURNING EYE, THE DAY TO CHEER AND NIGHT'S DANK DEW TO DRY,
I MUST UP-FILL THIS OSIER CAGE OF OURS WITH BALEFUL WEEDS AND PRECIOUS-JUICED FLOWERS.
FRIAR LAURENCE
THE EARTH, THAT'S NATURE'S MOTHER, IS HER TOMB;
WHAT IS HER BURYING GRAVE, THAT IS HER WOMB, AND FROM HER WOMB, CHILDREN OF DIVERS KIND WE SUCKING ON HER NATURAL BOSOM FIND,
MANY FOR MANY VIRTUES EXCELLENT, NONE BUT FOR SOME AND YET ALL DIFFERENT.
O, MICKLE IS THE POWERFUL GRACE THAT LIES IN HERBS, PLANTS, STONES, AND THEIR TRUE QUALITIES:
FOR NOUGHT SO VILE THAT ON THE EARTH DOTH LIVE BUT TO THE EARTH SOME SPECIAL GOOD DOTH GIVE,
NOR AUGHT SO GOOD BUT, STRAINED FROM THAT FAIR USE, REVOLTS FROM TRUE BIRTH, STUMBLING ON ABUSE:
VIRTUE ITSELF TURNS VICE, BEING MISAPPLIED; AND VICE SOMETIMES BY ACTION DIGNIFIED.

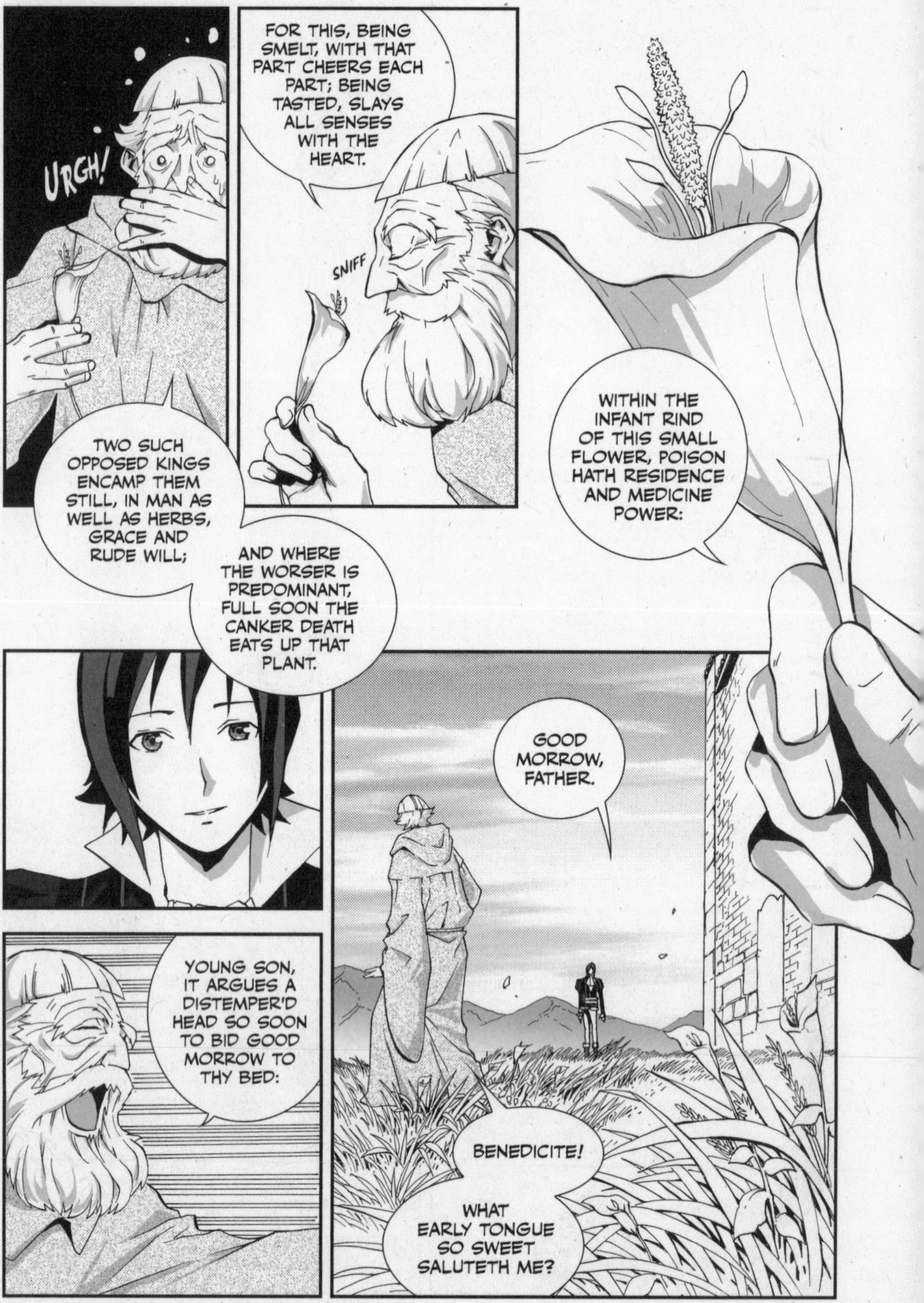
WITHIN THE INFANT RIND OF THIS SMALL FLOWER, POISON HATH RESIDENCE AND MEDICINE POWER:
FOR THIS, BEING SMELT, WITH THAT PART CHEERS EACH PART; BEING TASTED, SLAYS ALL SENSES WITH THE HEART.
SNIFF
URGH!
TWO SUCH OPPOSED KINGS ENCAMP THEM STILL, IN MAN AS WELL AS HERBS, GRACE AND RUDE WILL;
AND WHERE THE WORSER IS PREDOMINANT, FULL SOON THE CANKER DEATH EATS UP THAT PLANT.
GOOD MORROW, FATHER.
BENEDICITE!
WHAT EARLY TONGUE SO SWEET SALUTETH ME?
YOUNG SON, IT ARGUES A DISTEMPER'D HEAD SO SOON TO BID GOOD MORROW TO THY BED:

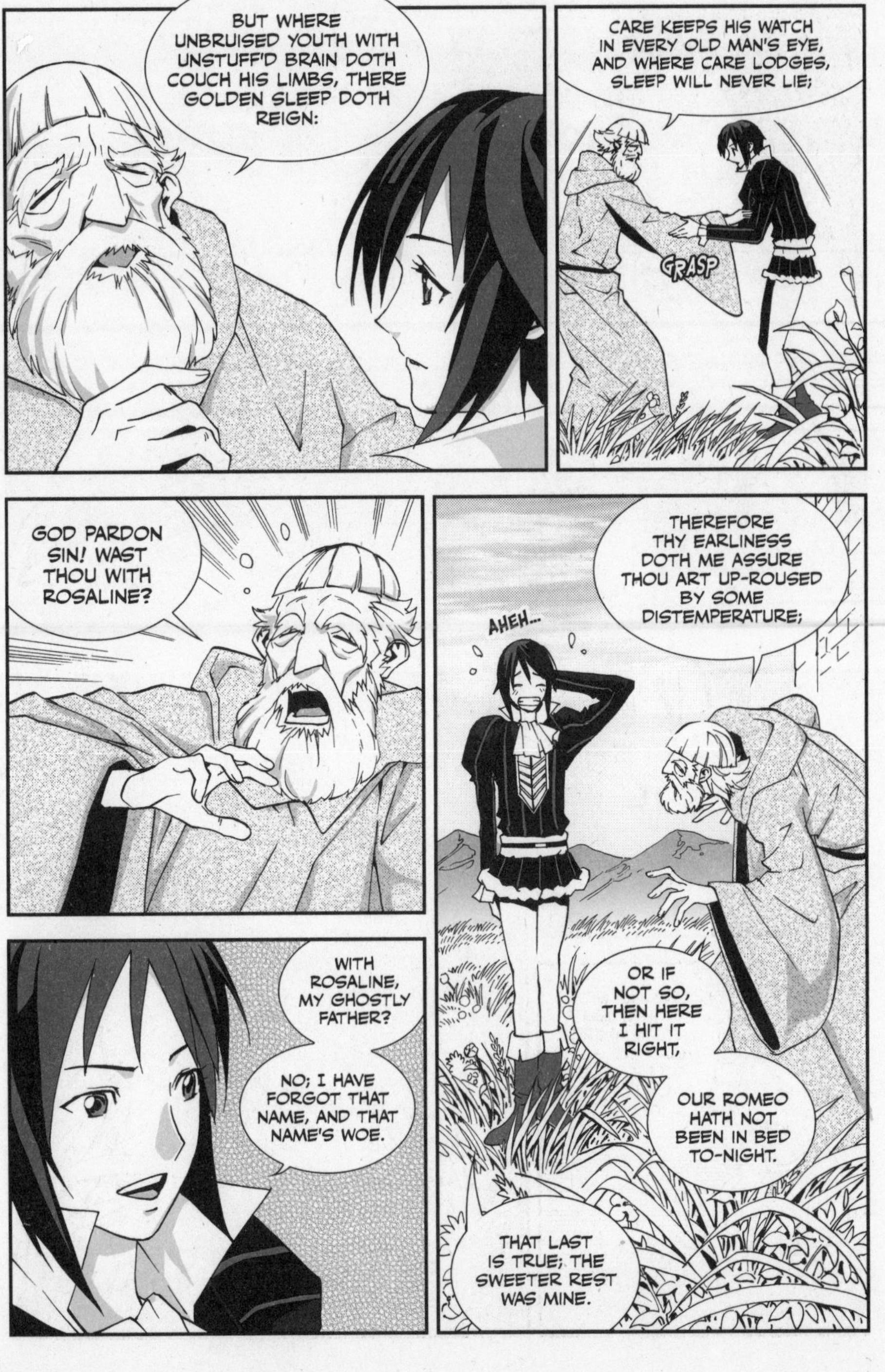
CARE KEEPS HIS WATCH IN EVERY OLD MAN'S EYE, AND WHERE CARE LODGES, SLEEP WILL NEVER LIE;
GRASP
BUT WHERE UNBRUISED YOUTH WITH UNSTUFF'D BRAIN DOTH COUCH HIS LIMBS, THERE GOLDEN SLEEP DOTH REIGN:
THEREFORE THY EARLINESS DOTH ME ASSURE THOU ART UP-ROUSED BY SOME DISTEMPERATURE;
AHEH...
OR IF NOT SO, THEN HERE I HIT IT RIGHT,
OUR ROMEO HATH NOT BEEN IN BED TO-NIGHT.
THAT LAST IS TRUE; THE SWEETER REST WAS MINE.
GOD PARDON SIN! WAST THOU WITH ROSALINE?
WITH ROSALINE, MY GHOSTLY FATHER?
NO; I HAVE FORGOT THAT NAME, AND THAT NAME'S WOE.

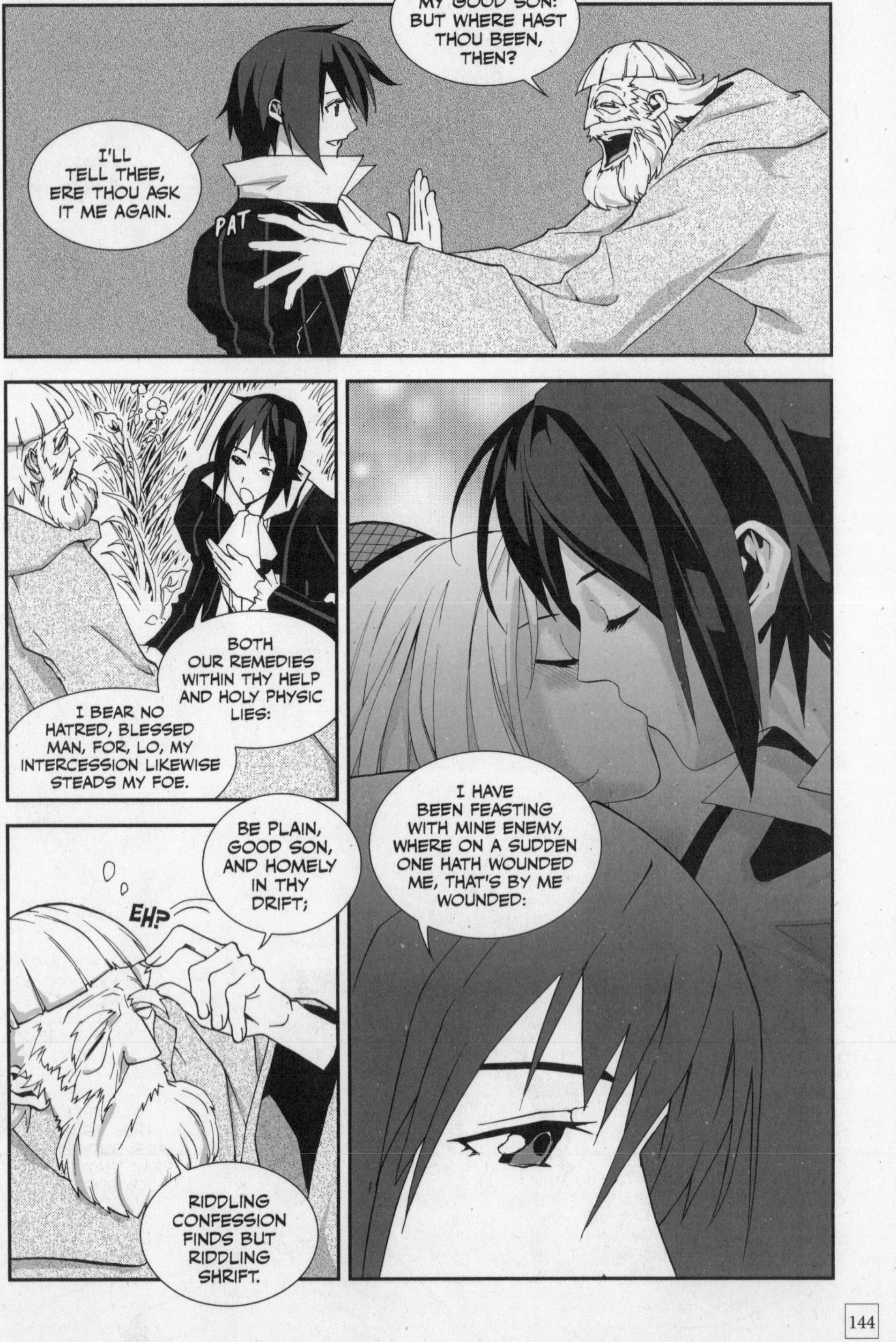
THAT'S MY GOOD SON: BUT WHERE HAST THOU BEEN, THEN?
I'LL TELL THEE, ERE THOU ASK IT ME AGAIN.
PAT
I HAVE BEEN FEASTING WITH MINE ENEMY, WHERE ON A SUDDEN ONE HATH WOUNDED ME, THAT'S BY ME WOUNDED:
BOTH OUR REMEDIES WITHIN THY HELP AND HOLY PHYSIC LIES:
I BEAR NO HATRED, BLESSED MAN, FOR, LO, MY INTERCESSION LIKEWISE STEADS MY FOE.
BE PLAIN, GOOD SON, AND HOMELY IN THY DRIFT;
EH?
RIDDLING CONFESSION FINDS BUT RIDDLING SHRIFT.

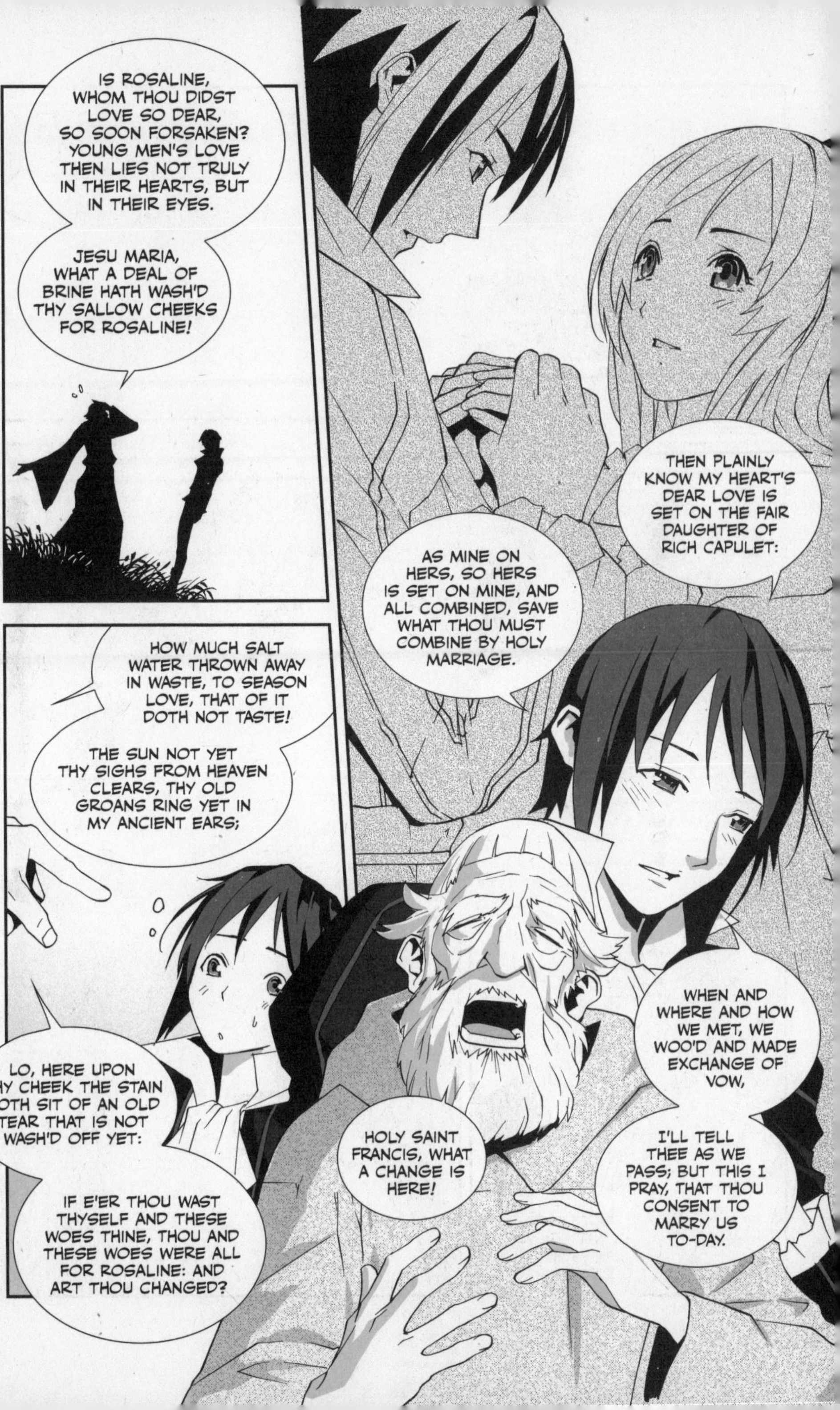
THEN PLAINLY KNOW MY HEART'S DEAR LOVE IS SET ON THE FAIR DAUGHTER OF RICH CAPULET:
AS MINE ON HERS, SO HERS IS SET ON MINE, AND ALL COMBINED, SAVE WHAT THOU MUST COMBINE BY HOLY MARRIAGE.
WHEN AND WHERE AND HOW WE MET, WE WOO'D AND MADE EXCHANGE OF VOW,
I'LL TELL THEE AS WE PASS; BUT THIS I PRAY, THAT THOU CONSENT TO MARRY US TO-DAY.
HOLY SAINT FRANCIS, WHAT A CHANGE IS HERE!
IS ROSALINE, WHOM THOU DIDST LOVE SO DEAR, SO SOON FORSAKEN? YOUNG MEN'S LOVE THEN LIES NOT TRULY IN THEIR HEARTS, BUT IN THEIR EYES.
JESU MARIA, WHAT A DEAL OF BRINE HATH WASH'D THY SALLOW CHEEKS FOR ROSALINE!
HOW MUCH SALT WATER THROWN AWAY IN WASTE, TO SEASON LOVE, THAT OF IT DOTH NOT TASTE!
THE SUN NOT YET THY SIGHS FROM HEAVEN CLEARS, THY OLD GROANS RING YET IN MY ANCIENT EARS;
LO, HERE UPON THY CHEEK THE STAIN DOTH SIT OF AN OLD TEAR THAT IS NOT WASH'D OFF YET:
IF E'ER THOU WAST THYSELF AND THESE WOES THINE, THOU AND THESE WOES WERE ALL FOR ROSALINE: AND ART THOU CHANGED?

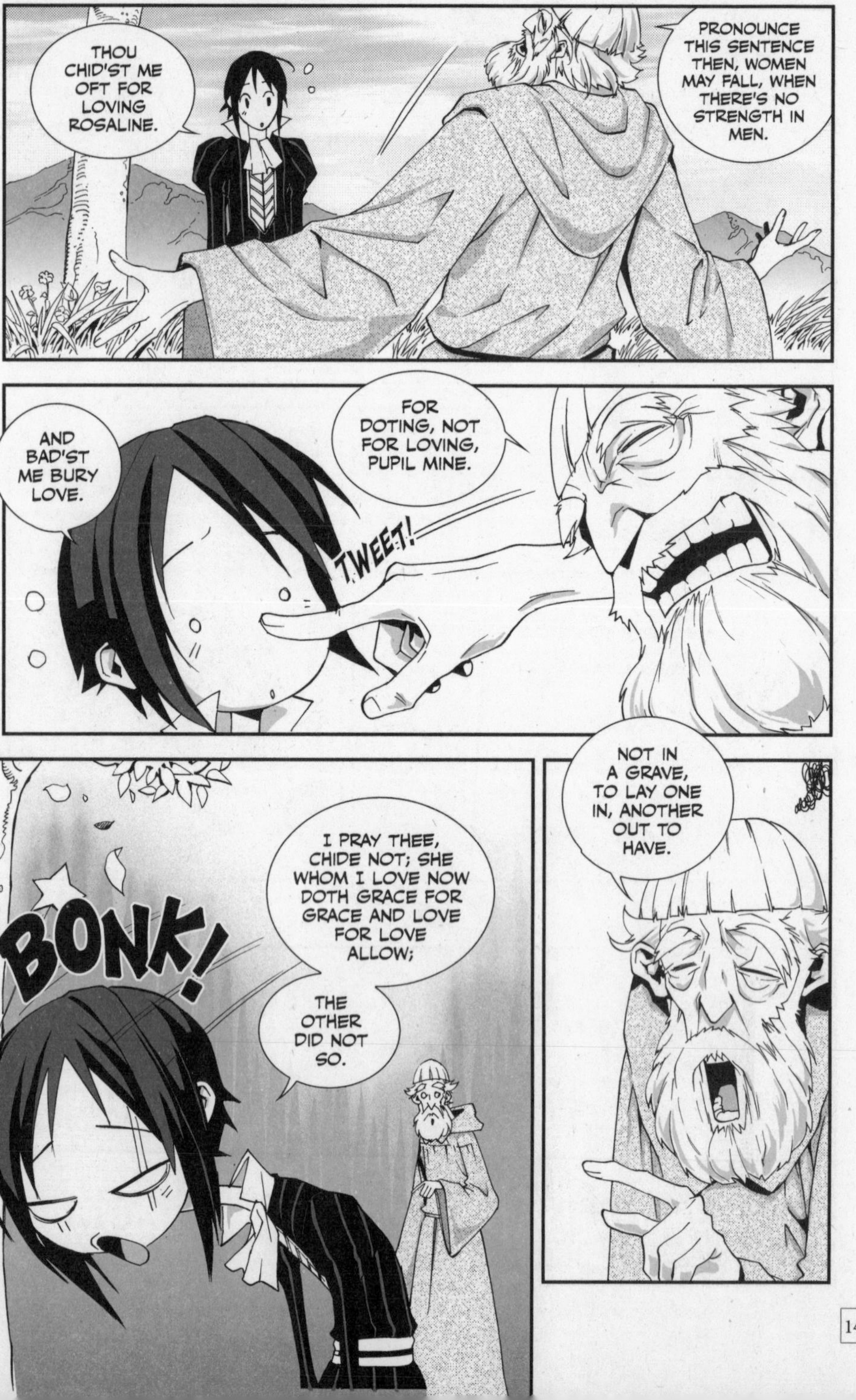
PRONOUNCE THIS SENTENCE THEN, WOMEN MAY FALL, WHEN THERE'S NO STRENGTH IN MEN.
THOU CHID'ST ME OFT FOR LOVING ROSALINE.
FOR DOTING, NOT FOR LOVING, PUPIL MINE.
TWEET!
AND BAD'ST ME BURY LOVE.
NOT IN A GRAVE, TO LAY ONE IN, ANOTHER OUT TO HAVE.
I PRAY THEE, CHIDE NOT; SHE WHOM I LOVE NOW DOTH GRACE FOR GRACE AND LOVE FOR LOVE ALLOW;
BONK!
THE OTHER DID NOT SO.

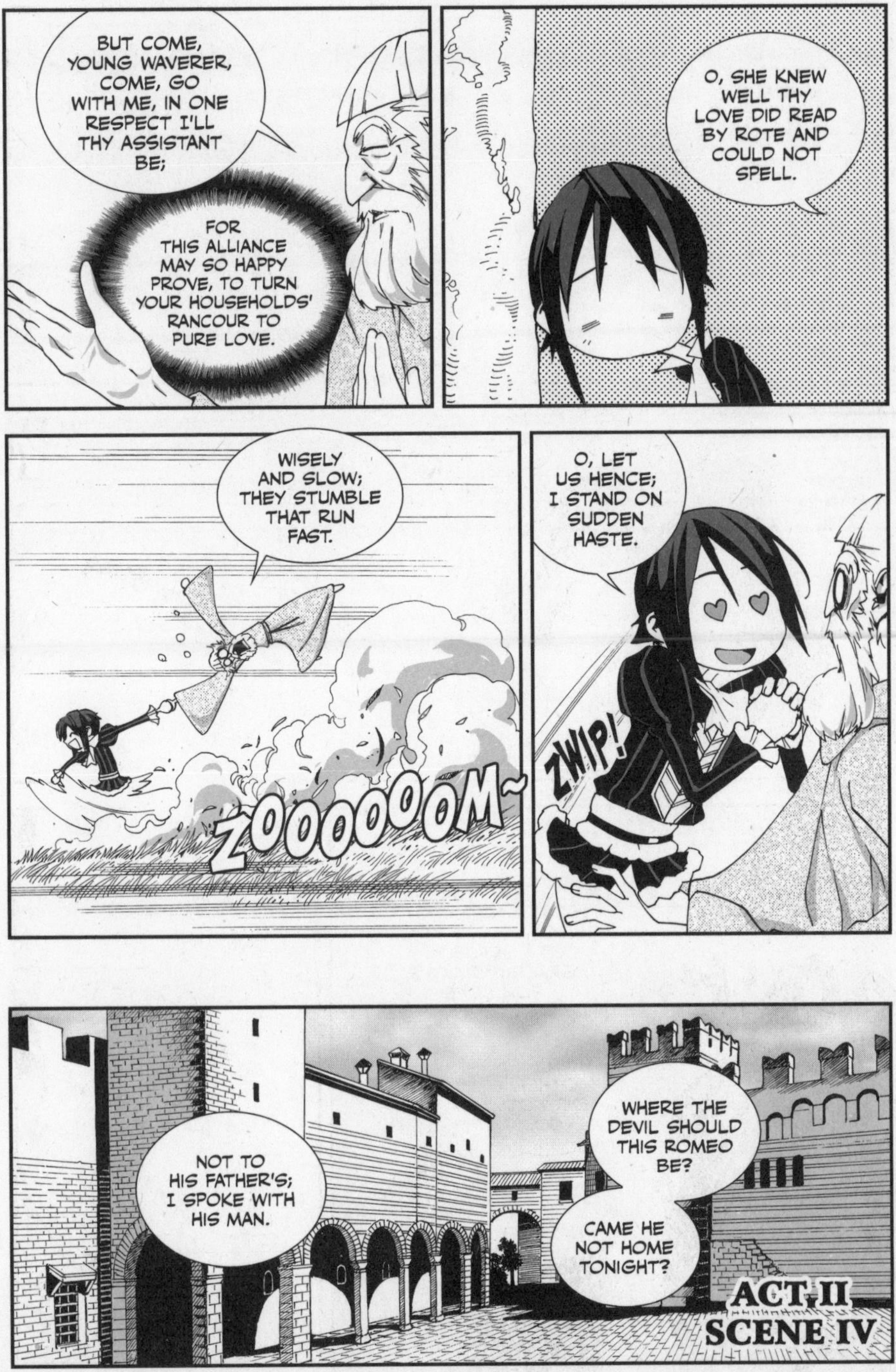
O, SHE KNEW WELL THY LOVE DID READ BY ROTE AND COULD NOT SPELL.
BUT COME, YOUNG WAVERER, COME, GO WITH ME, IN ONE RESPECT I'LL THY ASSISTANT BE;
FOR THIS ALLIANCE MAY SO HAPPY PROVE, TO TURN YOUR HOUSEHOLDS' RANCOUR TO PURE LOVE.
O, LET US HENCE; I STAND ON SUDDEN HASTE.
ZWIP!
WISELY AND SLOW; THEY STUMBLE THAT RUN FAST.
ZOOOOOOM~
WHERE THE DEVIL SHOULD THIS ROMEO BE?
CAME HE NOT HOME TONIGHT?
ACT II SCENE IV
NOT TO HIS FATHER'S; I SPOKE WITH HIS MAN.

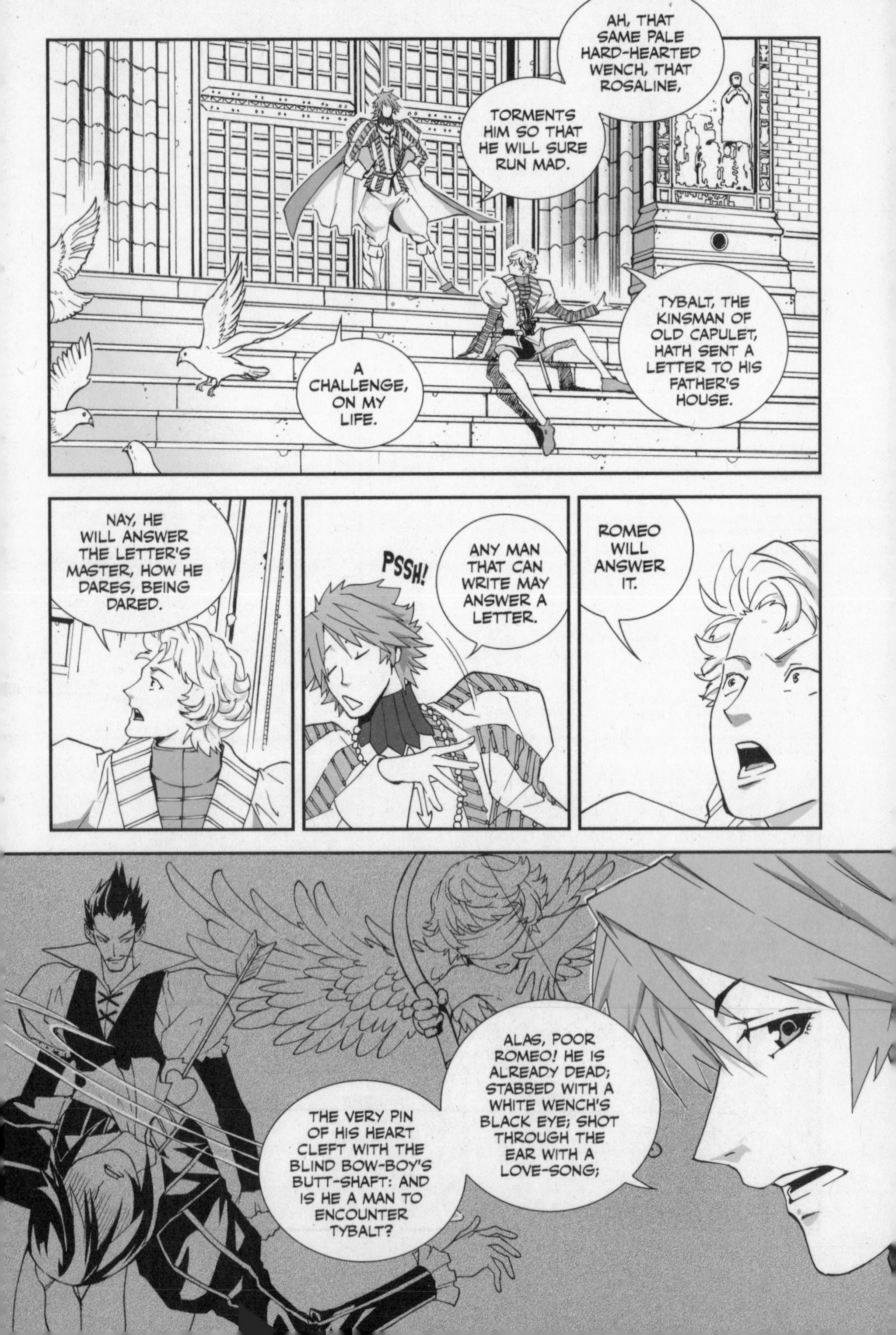
AH, THAT SAME PALE HARD-HEARTED WENCH, THAT ROSALINE,
TORMENTS HIM SO THAT HE WILL SURE RUN MAD.
TYBALT, THE KINSMAN OF OLD CAPULET, HATH SENT A LETTER TO HIS FATHER'S HOUSE.
A CHALLENGE, ON MY LIFE.
ROMEO WILL ANSWER IT.
ANY MAN THAT CAN WRITE MAY ANSWER A LETTER.
PSSH!
NAY, HE WILL ANSWER THE LETTER'S MASTER, HOW HE DARES, BEING DARED.
ALAS, POOR ROMEO! HE IS ALREADY DEAD; STABBED WITH A WHITE WENCH'S BLACK EYE; SHOT THROUGH THE EAR WITH A LOVE-SONG;
THE VERY PIN OF HIS HEART CLEFT WITH THE BLIND BOW-BOY'S BUTT-SHAFT: AND IS HE A MAN TO ENCOUNTER TYBALT?

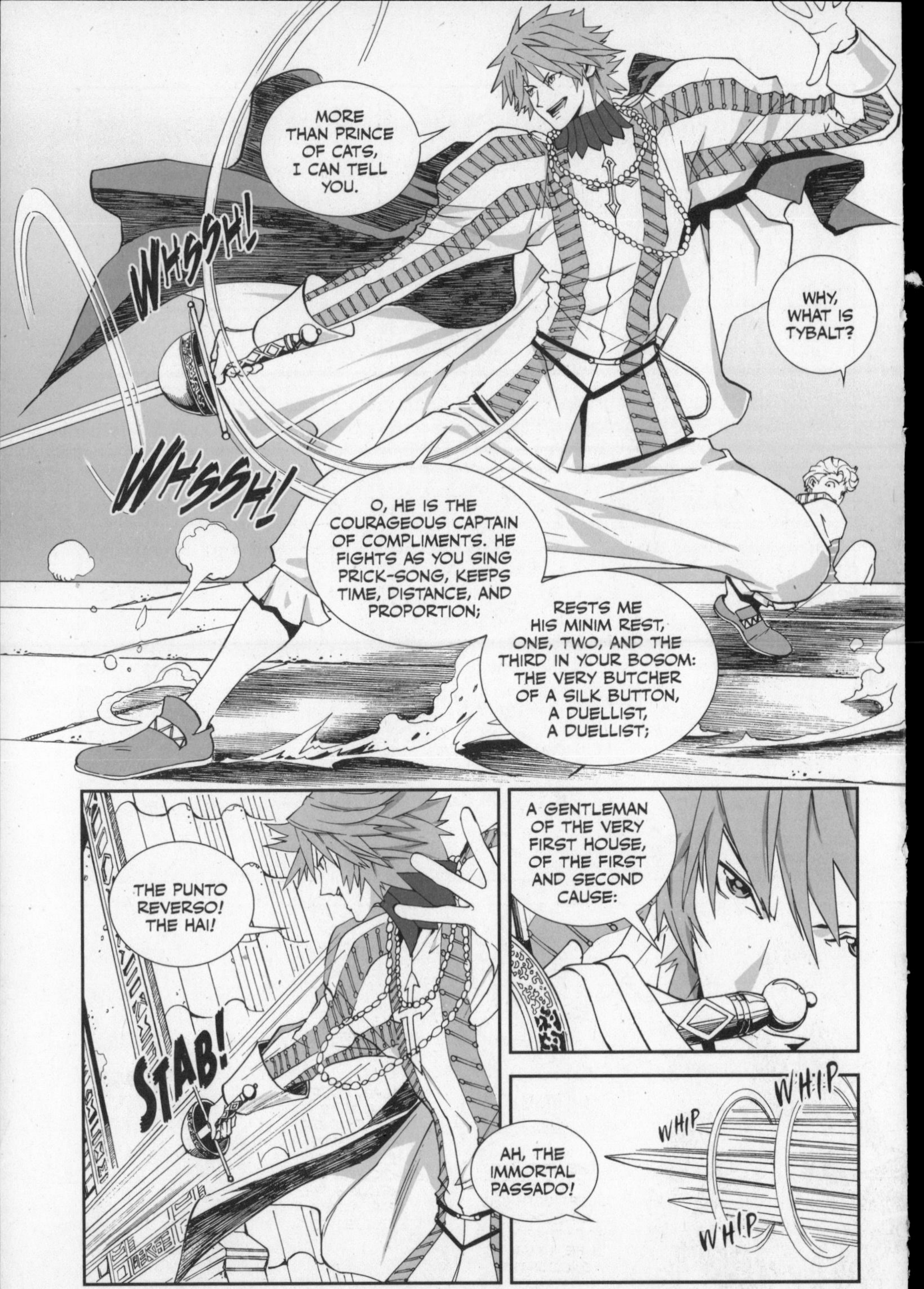
WHY, WHAT IS TYBALT?
MORE THAN PRINCE OF CATS, I CAN TELL YOU.
WHSSH!
WHSSH!
O, HE IS THE COURAGEOUS CAPTAIN OF COMPLIMENTS. HE FIGHTS AS YOU SING PRICK-SONG, KEEPS TIME, DISTANCE, AND PROPORTION;
RESTS ME HIS MINIM REST, ONE, TWO, AND THE THIRD IN YOUR BOSOM: THE VERY BUTCHER OF A SILK BUTTON, A DUELLIST, A DUELLIST;
A GENTLEMAN OF THE VERY FIRST HOUSE, OF THE FIRST AND SECOND CAUSE:
WHIP
WHIP
AH, THE IMMORTAL PASSADO!
WHIP
THE PUNTO REVERSO! THE HAI!
STAB!

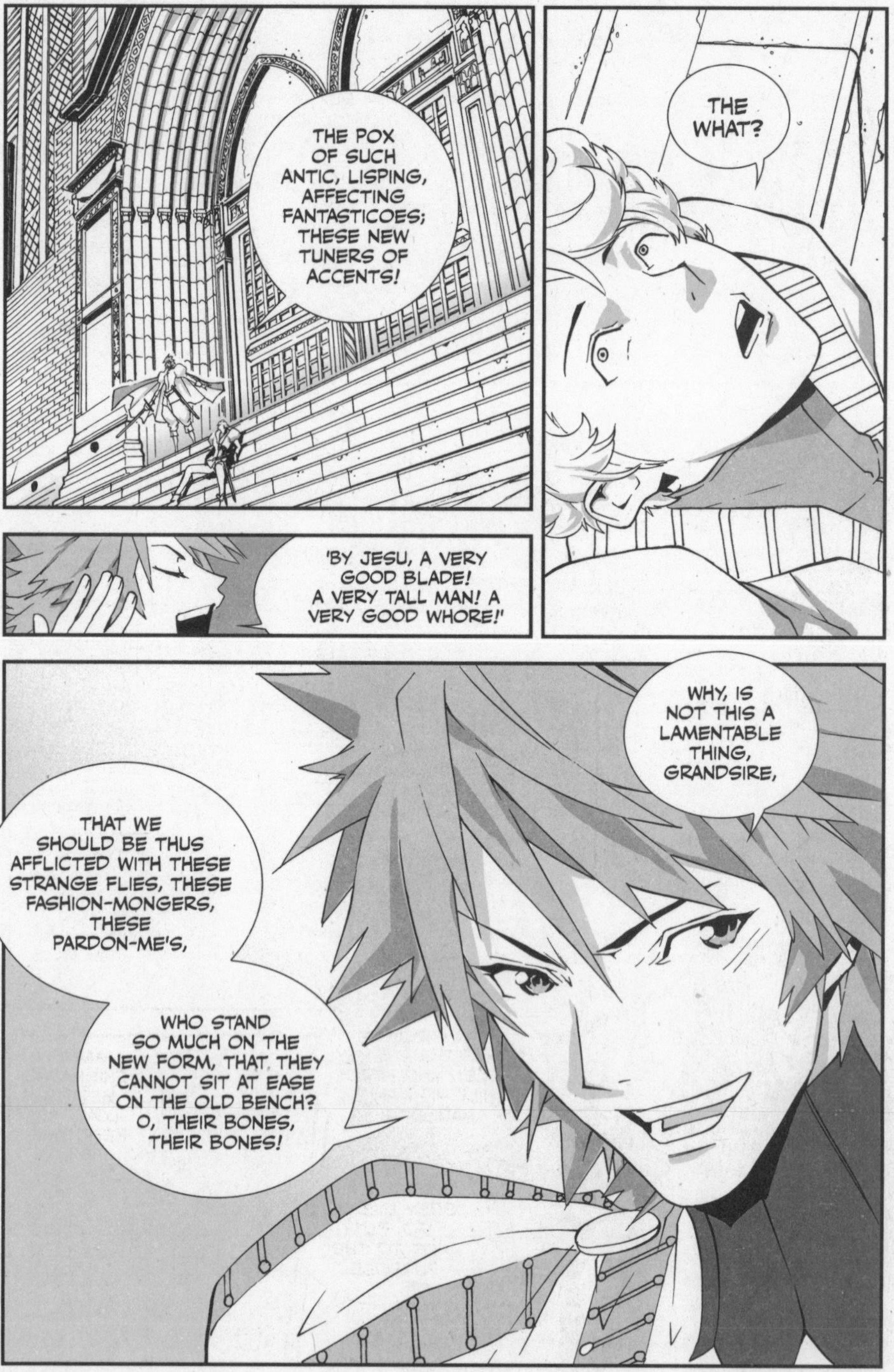
THE WHAT?
THE POX OF SUCH ANTIC, LISPING, AFFECTING FANTASTICOES; THESE NEW TUNERS OF ACCENTS!
'BY JESU, A VERY GOOD BLADE! A VERY TALL MAN! A VERY GOOD WHORE!'
WHY, IS NOT THIS A LAMENTABLE THING, GRANDSIRE,
THAT WE SHOULD BE THUS AFFLICTED WITH THESE STRANGE FLIES, THESE FASHION-MONGERS, THESE PARDON-ME'S,
WHO STAND SO MUCH ON THE NEW FORM, THAT, THEY CANNOT SIT AT EASE ON THE OLD BENCH? O, THEIR BONES, THEIR BONES!

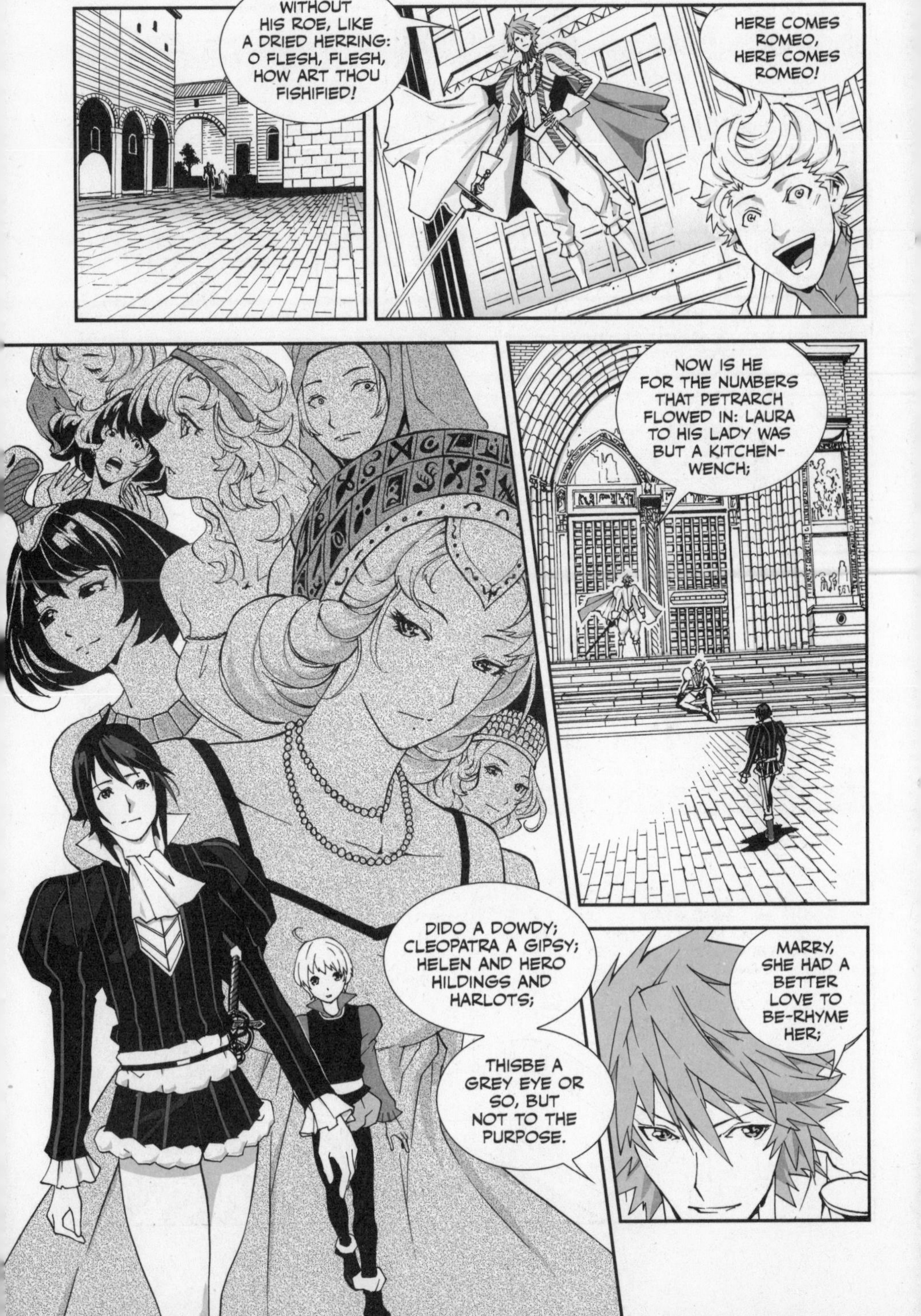
HERE COMES ROMEO, HERE COMES ROMEO!
WITHOUT HIS ROE, LIKE A DRIED HERRING: O FLESH, FLESH, HOW ART THOU FISHIFIED!
NOW IS HE FOR THE NUMBERS THAT PETRARCH FLOWED IN: LAURA TO HIS LADY WAS BUT A KITCHEN-WENCH;
MARRY, SHE HAD A BETTER LOVE TO BE-RHYME HER;
DIDO A DOWDY; CLEOPATRA A GIPSY; HELEN AND HERO HILDINGS AND HARLOTS;
THISBE A GREY EYE OR SO, BUT NOT TO THE PURPOSE.

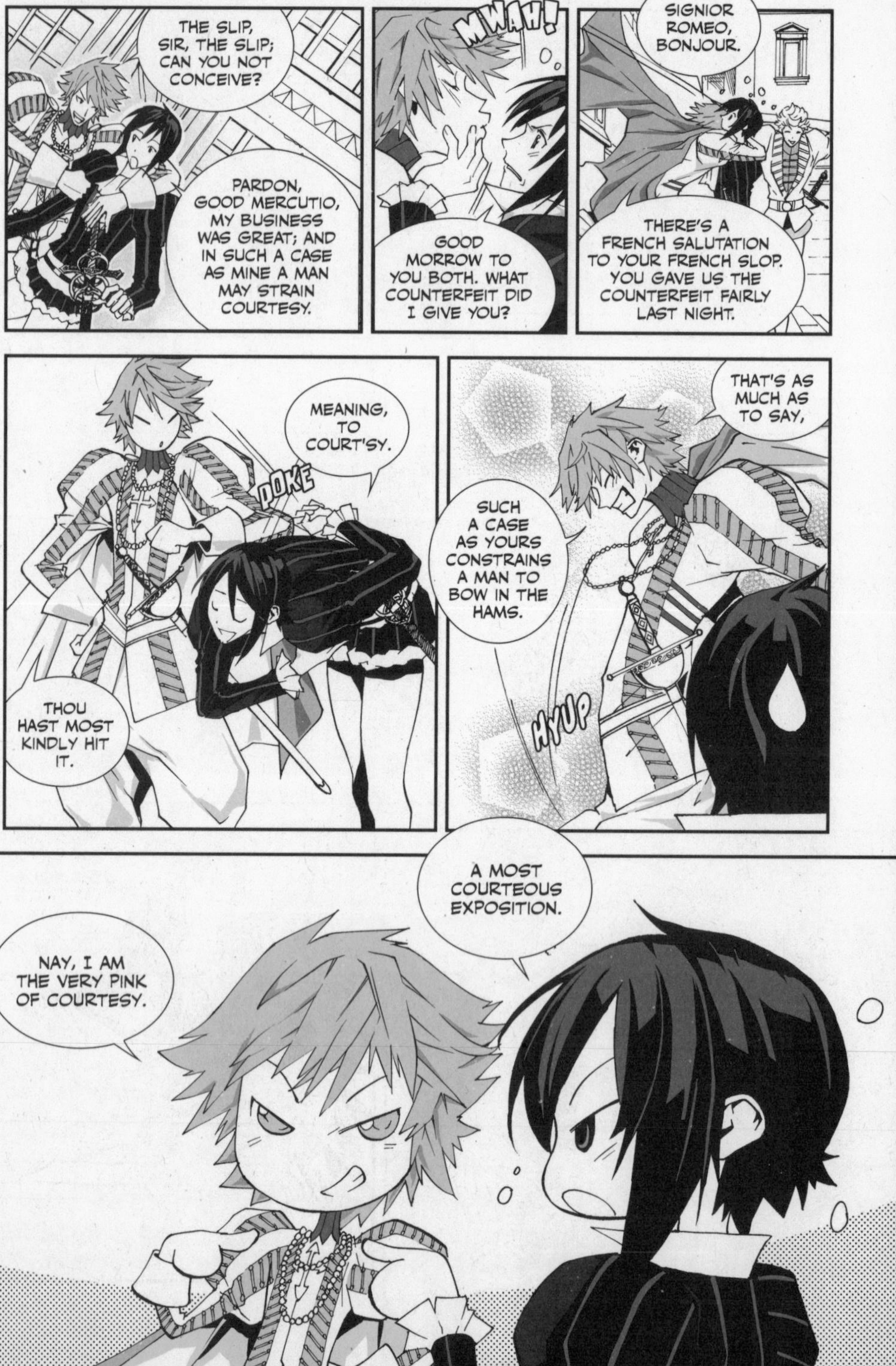
SIGNIOR ROMEO, BONJOUR.
THERE'S A FRENCH SALUTATION TO YOUR FRENCH SLOP. YOU GAVE US THE COUNTERFEIT FAIRLY LAST NIGHT.
MWAH!
GOOD MORROW TO YOU BOTH. WHAT COUNTERFEIT DID I GIVE YOU?
THE SLIP, SIR, THE SLIP; CAN YOU NOT CONCEIVE?
PARDON, GOOD MERCUTIO, MY BUSINESS WAS GREAT; AND IN SUCH A CASE AS MINE A MAN MAY STRAIN COURTESY.
THAT'S AS MUCH AS TO SAY,
SUCH A CASE AS YOURS CONSTRAINS A MAN TO BOW IN THE HAMS.
HYUP
MEANING, TO COURT'SY.
POKE
THOU HAST MOST KINDLY HIT IT.
A MOST COURTEOUS EXPOSITION.
NAY, I AM THE VERY PINK OF COURTESY.

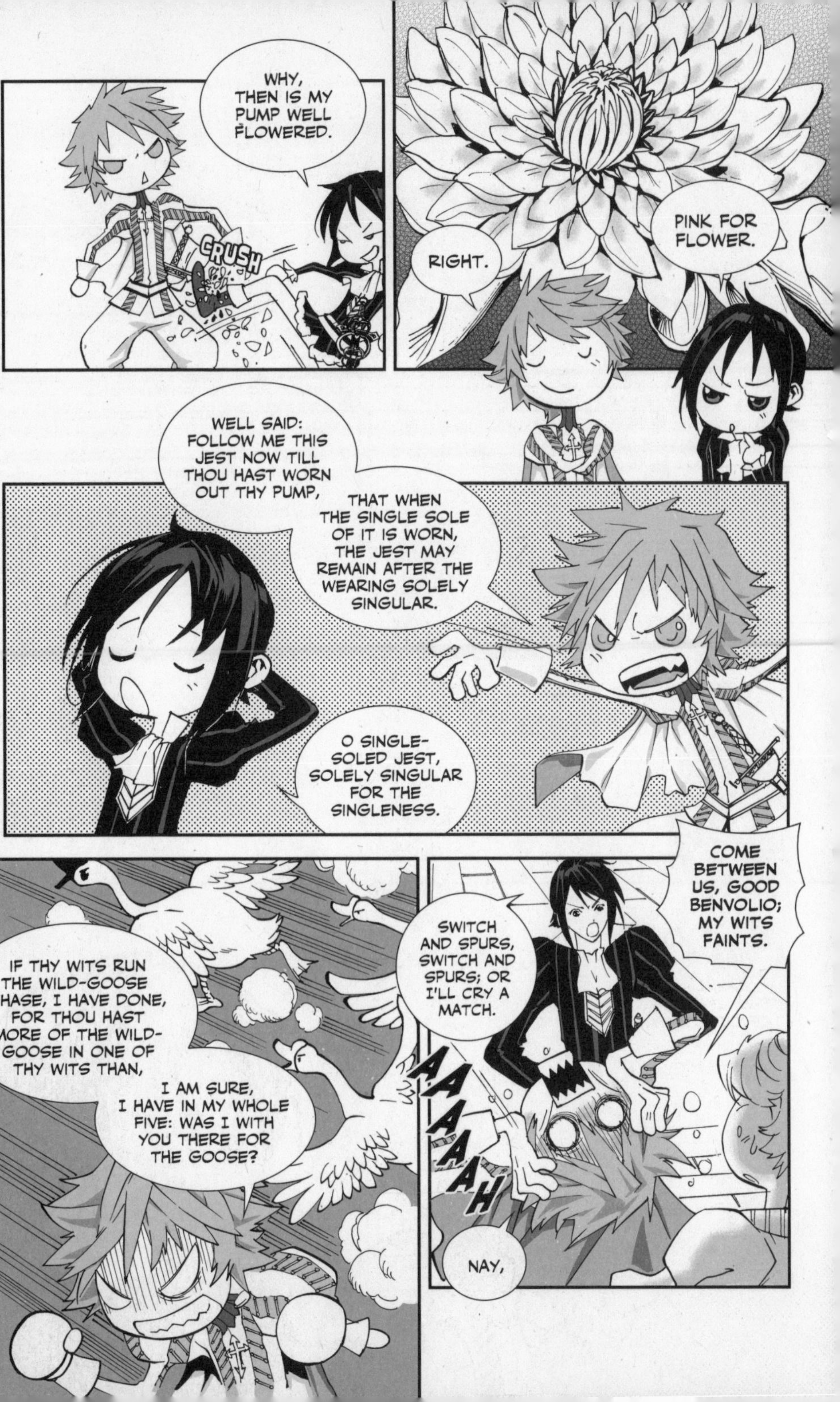
PINK FOR FLOWER.
RIGHT.
WHY, THEN IS MY PUMP WELL FLOWERED.
CRUSH
WELL SAID: FOLLOW ME THIS JEST NOW TILL THOU HAST WORN OUT THY PUMP,
THAT WHEN THE SINGLE SOLE OF IT IS WORN, THE JEST MAY REMAIN AFTER THE WEARING SOLELY SINGULAR.
O SINGLE-SOLED JEST, SOLELY SINGULAR FOR THE SINGLENESS.
COME BETWEEN US, GOOD BENVOLIO; MY WITS FAINTS.
SWITCH AND SPURS, SWITCH AND SPURS; OR I'LL CRY A MATCH.
AAAAAAH
NAY,
IF THY WITS RUN THE WILD-GOOSE CHASE, I HAVE DONE, FOR THOU HAST MORE OF THE WILD-GOOSE IN ONE OF THY WITS THAN,
I AM SURE, I HAVE IN MY WHOLE FIVE: WAS I WITH YOU THERE FOR THE GOOSE?

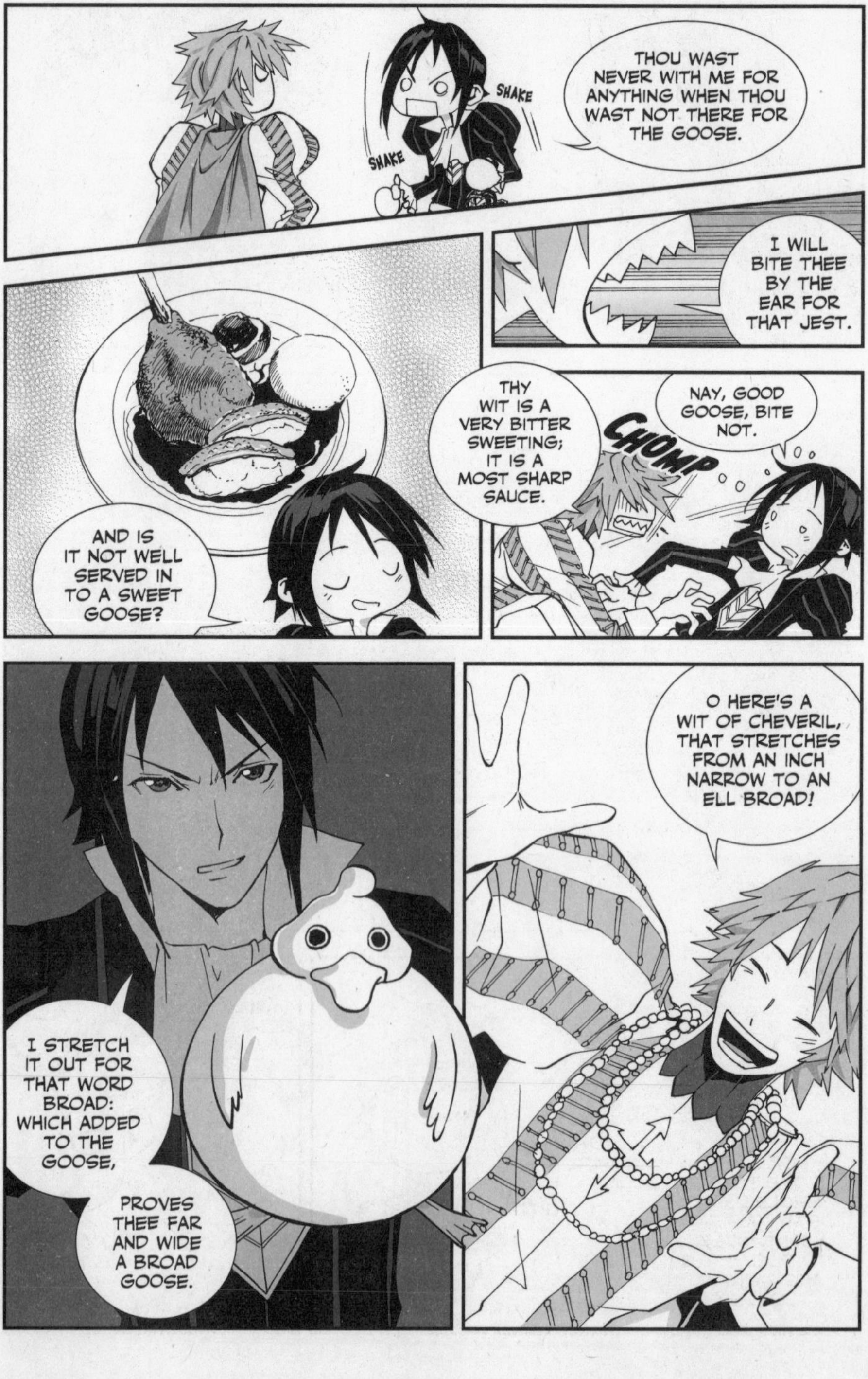
SHAKE
SHAKE
THOU WAST NEVER WITH ME FOR ANYTHING WHEN THOU WAST NOT THERE FOR THE GOOSE.
I WILL BITE THEE BY THE EAR FOR THAT JEST.
NAY, GOOD GOOSE, BITE NOT.
CHOMP
THY WIT IS A VERY BITTER SWEETING; IT IS A MOST SHARP SAUCE.
AND IS IT NOT WELL SERVED IN TO A SWEET GOOSE?
O HERE'S A WIT OF CHEVERIL, THAT STRETCHES FROM AN INCH NARROW TO AN ELL BROAD!
I STRETCH IT OUT FOR THAT WORD BROAD: WHICH ADDED TO THE GOOSE,
PROVES THEE FAR AND WIDE A BROAD GOOSE.

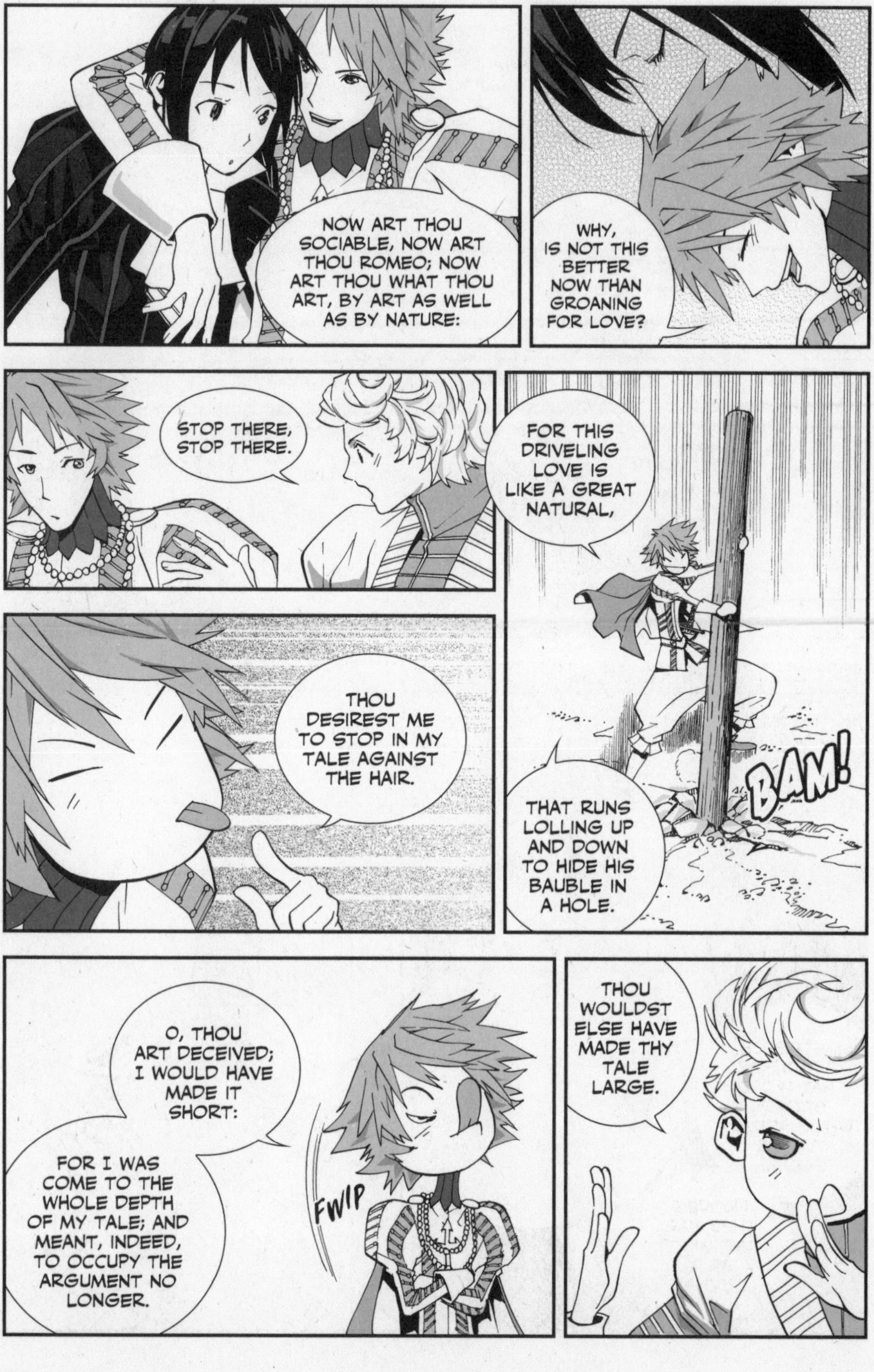
WHY, IS NOT THIS BETTER NOW THAN GROANING FOR LOVE?
NOW ART THOU SOCIABLE, NOW ART THOU ROMEO; NOW ART THOU WHAT THOU ART, BY ART AS WELL AS BY NATURE:
FOR THIS DRIVELING LOVE IS LIKE A GREAT NATURAL,
BAM!
THAT RUNS LOLLING UP AND DOWN TO HIDE HIS BAUBLE IN A HOLE.
STOP THERE, STOP THERE.
THOU DESIREST ME TO STOP IN MY TALE AGAINST THE HAIR.
THOU WOULDST ELSE HAVE MADE THY TALE LARGE.
O, THOU ART DECEIVED; I WOULD HAVE MADE IT SHORT:
FWIP
FOR I WAS COME TO THE WHOLE DEPTH OF MY TALE; AND MEANT, INDEED, TO OCCUPY THE ARGUMENT NO LONGER.

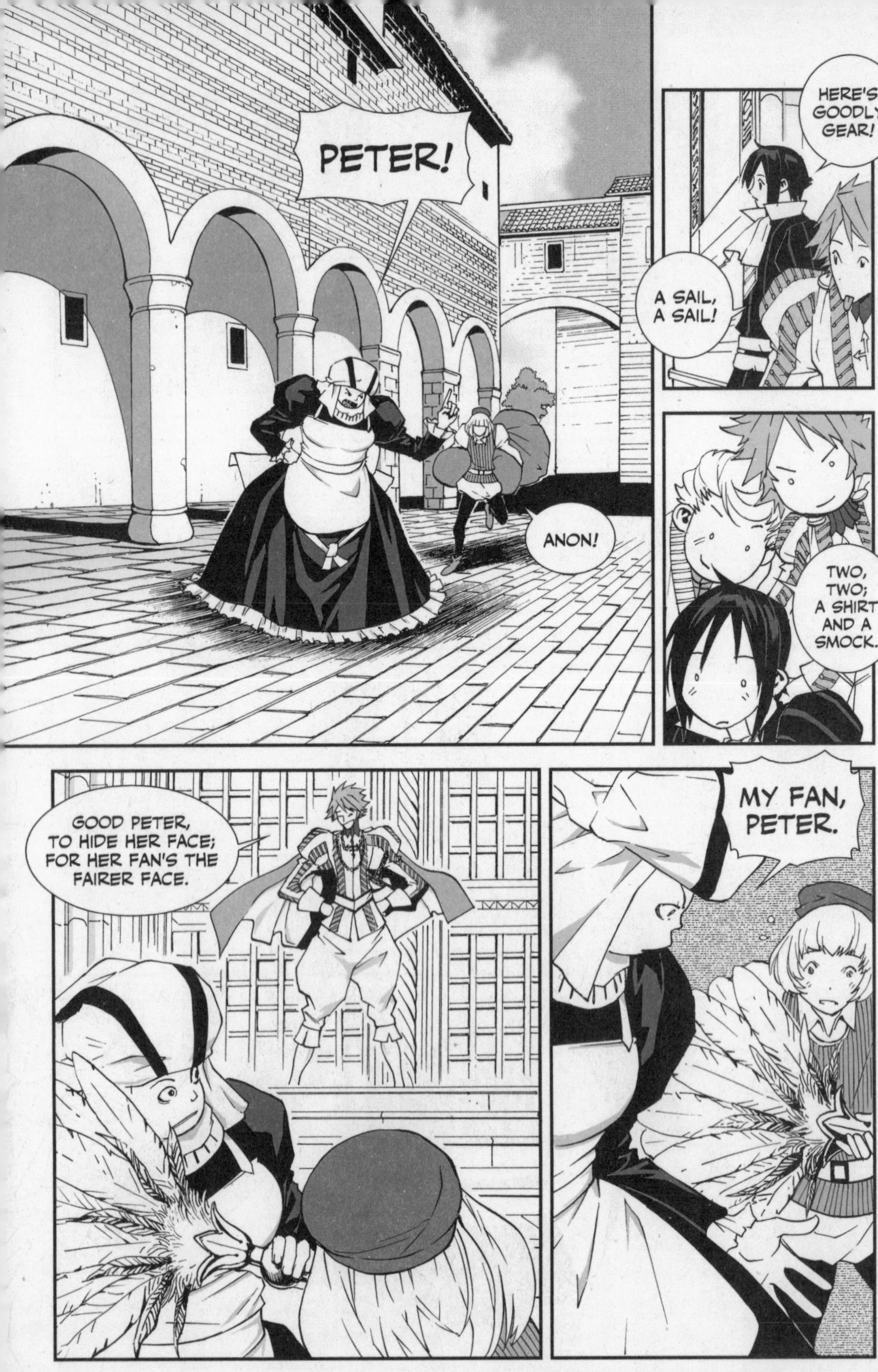
HERE'S GOODLY GEAR!
A SAIL, A SAIL!
TWO, TWO; A SHIRT AND A SMOCK.
PETER!
ANON!
MY FAN, PETER.
GOOD PETER, TO HIDE HER FACE; FOR HER FAN'S THE FAIRER FACE.

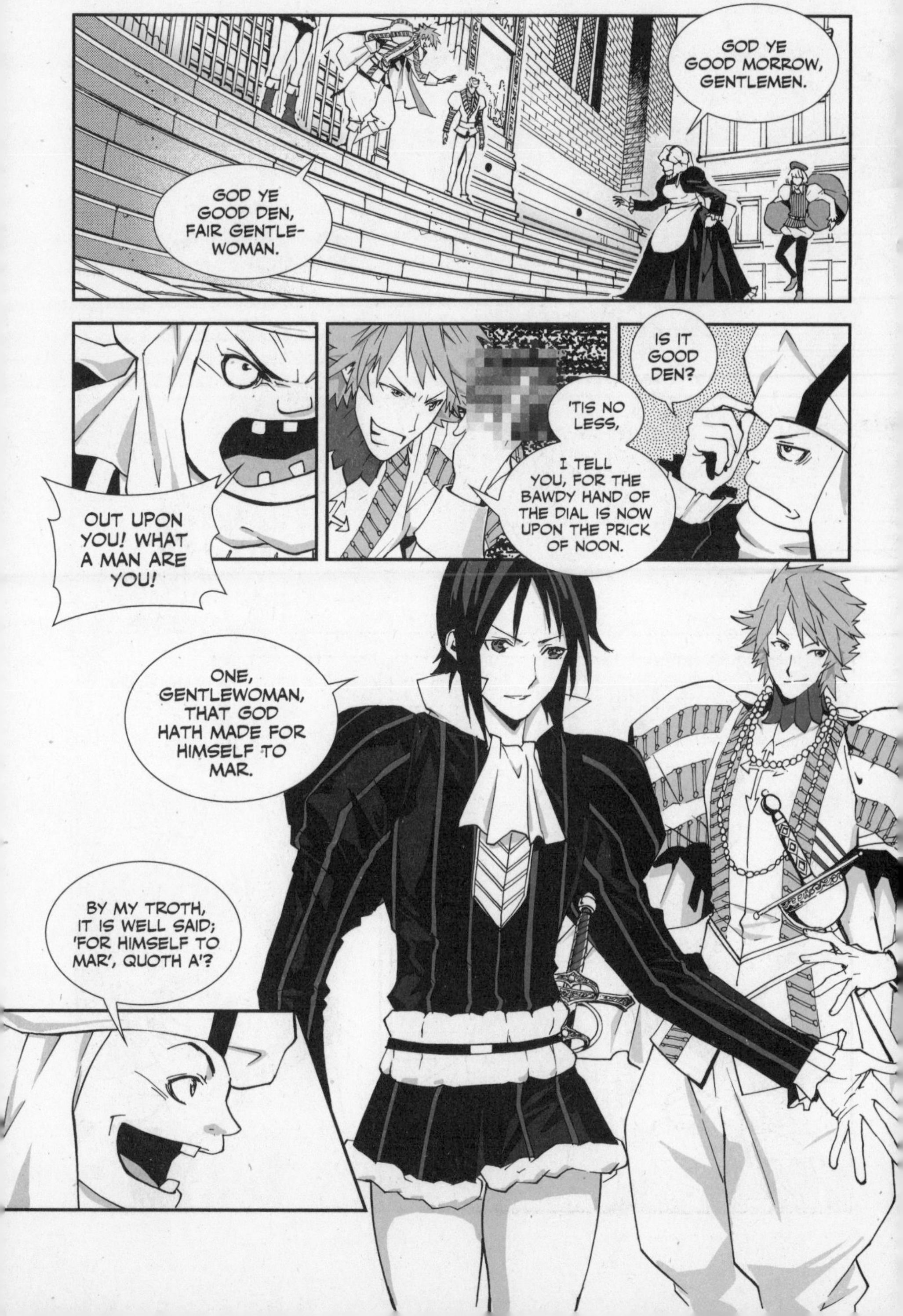
GOD YE GOOD MORROW, GENTLEMEN.
GOD YE GOOD DEN, FAIR GENTLE-WOMAN.
IS IT GOOD DEN?
'TIS NO LESS,
I TELL YOU, FOR THE BAWDY HAND OF THE DIAL IS NOW UPON THE PRICK OF NOON.
OUT UPON YOU! WHAT A MAN ARE YOU!
ONE, GENTLEWOMAN, THAT GOD HATH MADE FOR HIMSELF TO MAR.
BY MY TROTH, IT IS WELL SAID; 'FOR HIMSELF TO MAR', QUOTH A'?

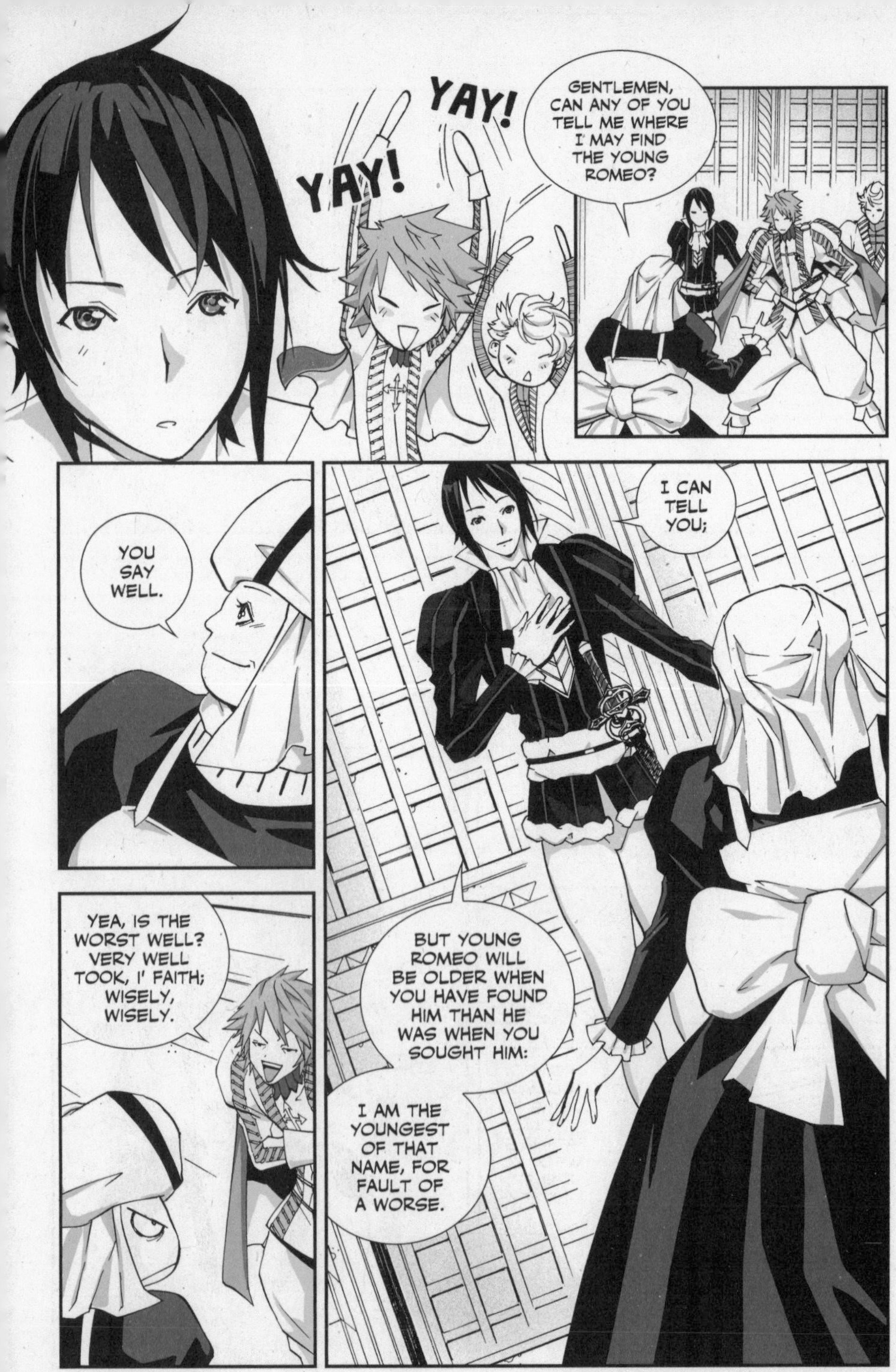
GENTLEMEN, CAN ANY OF YOU TELL ME WHERE I MAY FIND THE YOUNG ROMEO?
YAY!
YAY!
I CAN TELL YOU;
BUT YOUNG ROMEO WILL BE OLDER WHEN YOU HAVE FOUND HIM THAN HE WAS WHEN YOU SOUGHT HIM:
I AM THE YOUNGEST OF THAT NAME, FOR FAULT OF A WORSE.
YOU SAY WELL.
YEA, IS THE WORST WELL? VERY WELL TOOK, I' FAITH; WISELY, WISELY.

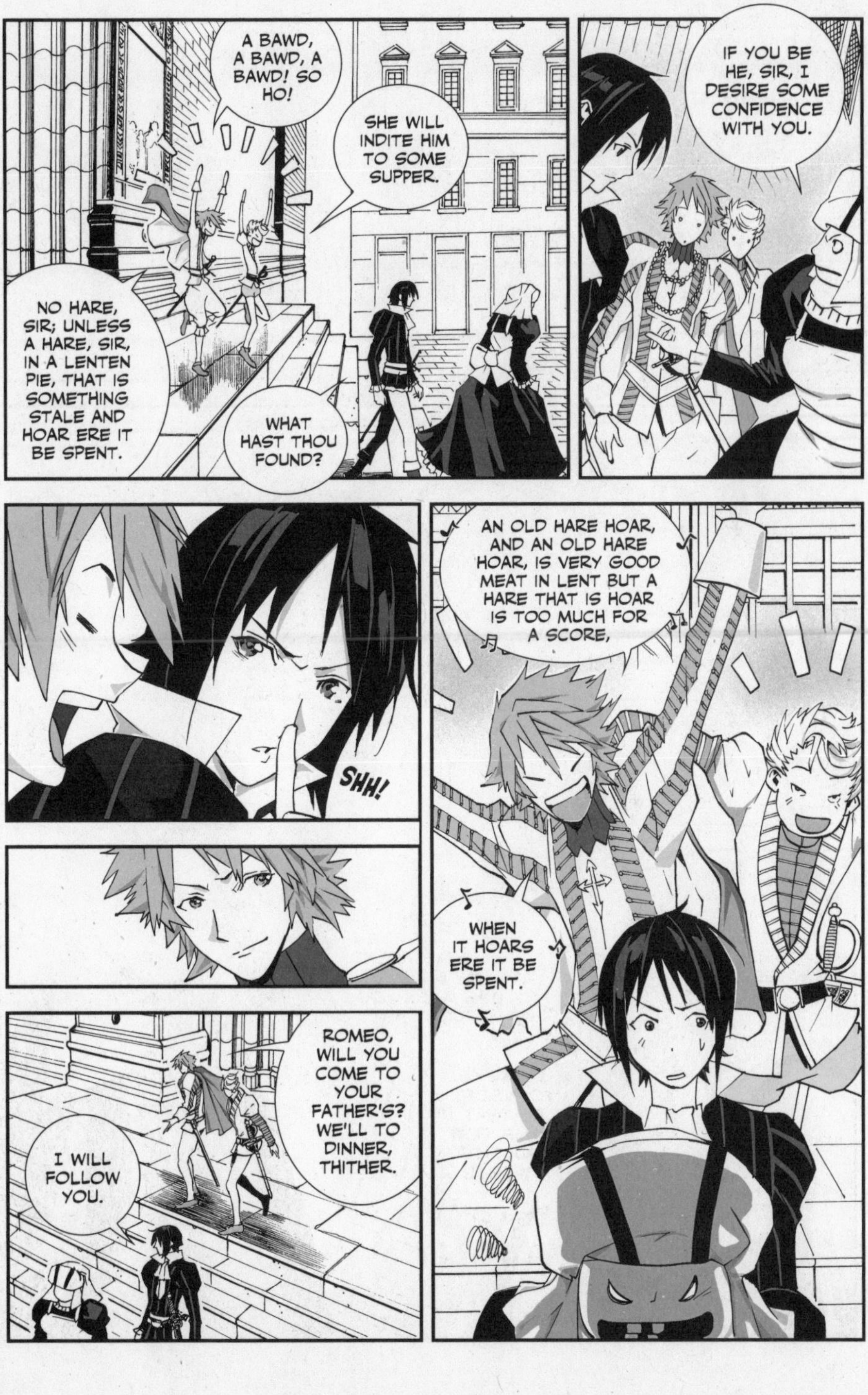
IF YOU BE HE, SIR, I DESIRE SOME CONFIDENCE WITH YOU.
SHE WILL INDITE HIM TO SOME SUPPER.
A BAWD, A BAWD, A BAWD! SO HO!
WHAT HAST THOU FOUND?
NO HARE, SIR; UNLESS A HARE, SIR, IN A LENTEN PIE, THAT IS SOMETHING STALE AND HOAR ERE IT BE SPENT.
AN OLD HARE HOAR, AND AN OLD HARE HOAR, IS VERY GOOD MEAT IN LENT BUT A HARE THAT IS HOAR IS TOO MUCH FOR A SCORE,
WHEN IT HOARS ERE IT BE SPENT.
SHH!
ROMEO, WILL YOU COME TO YOUR FATHER'S? WE'LL TO DINNER, THITHER.
I WILL FOLLOW YOU.

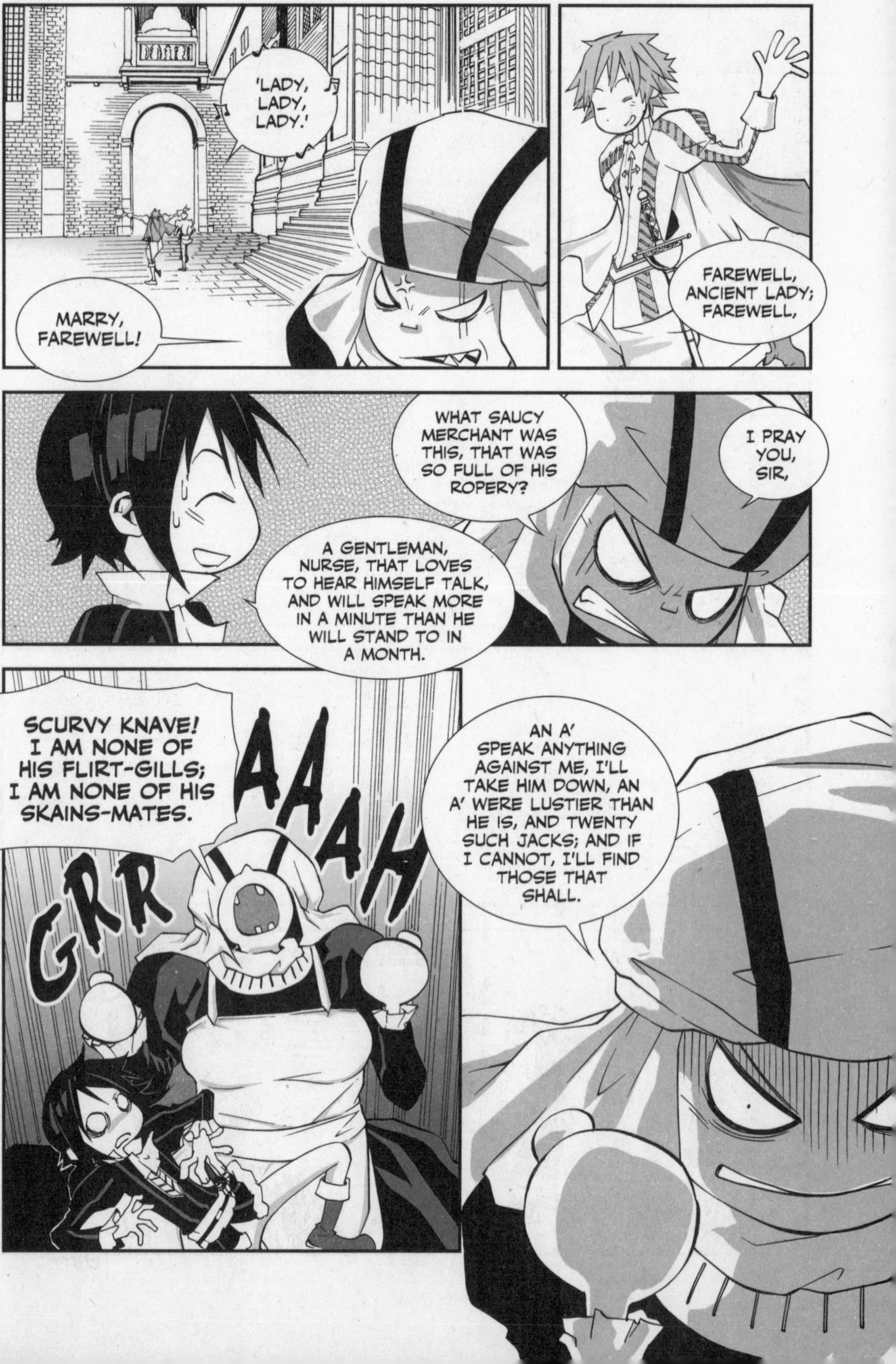
FAREWELL, ANCIENT LADY; FAREWELL,
'LADY, LADY, LADY.'
MARRY, FAREWELL!
I PRAY YOU, SIR,
WHAT SAUCY MERCHANT WAS THIS, THAT WAS SO FULL OF HIS ROPERY?
A GENTLEMAN, NURSE, THAT LOVES TO HEAR HIMSELF TALK, AND WILL SPEAK MORE IN A MINUTE THAN HE WILL STAND TO IN A MONTH.
AN A' SPEAK ANYTHING AGAINST ME, I'LL TAKE HIM DOWN, AN A' WERE LUSTIER THAN HE IS, AND TWENTY SUCH JACKS; AND IF I CANNOT, I'LL FIND THOSE THAT SHALL.
SCURVY KNAVE! I AM NONE OF HIS FLIRT-GILLS; I AM NONE OF HIS SKAINS-MATES.
GRR AAAAH

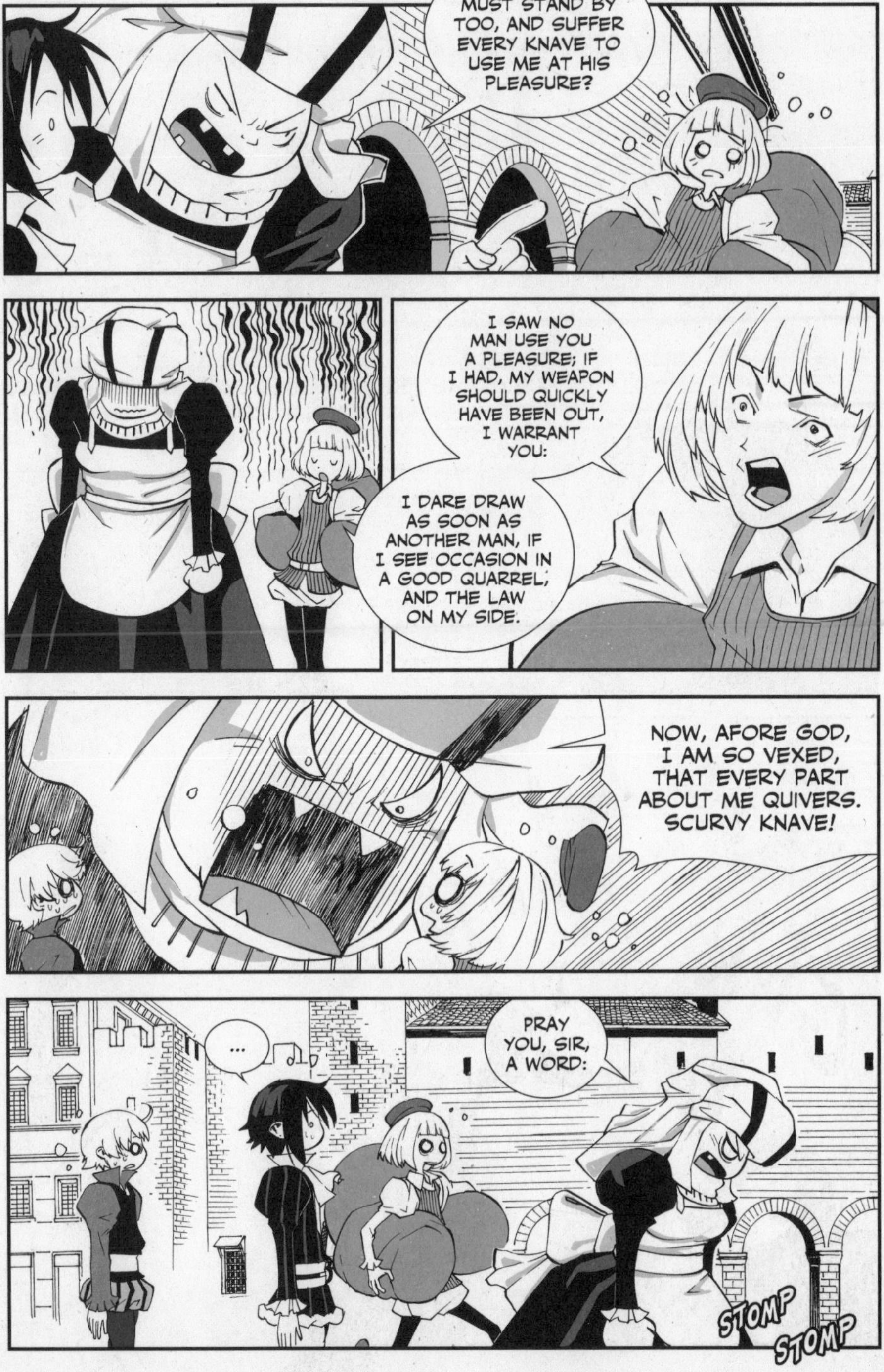
AND THOU MUST STAND BY TOO, AND SUFFER EVERY KNAVE TO USE ME AT HIS PLEASURE?
I SAW NO MAN USE YOU A PLEASURE; IF I HAD, MY WEAPON SHOULD QUICKLY HAVE BEEN OUT, I WARRANT YOU:
I DARE DRAW AS SOON AS ANOTHER MAN, IF I SEE OCCASION IN A GOOD QUARREL, AND THE LAW ON MY SIDE.
NOW, AFORE GOD, I AM SO VEXED, THAT EVERY PART ABOUT ME QUIVERS. SCURVY KNAVE!
PRAY YOU, SIR, A WORD:
...
STOMP
STOMP

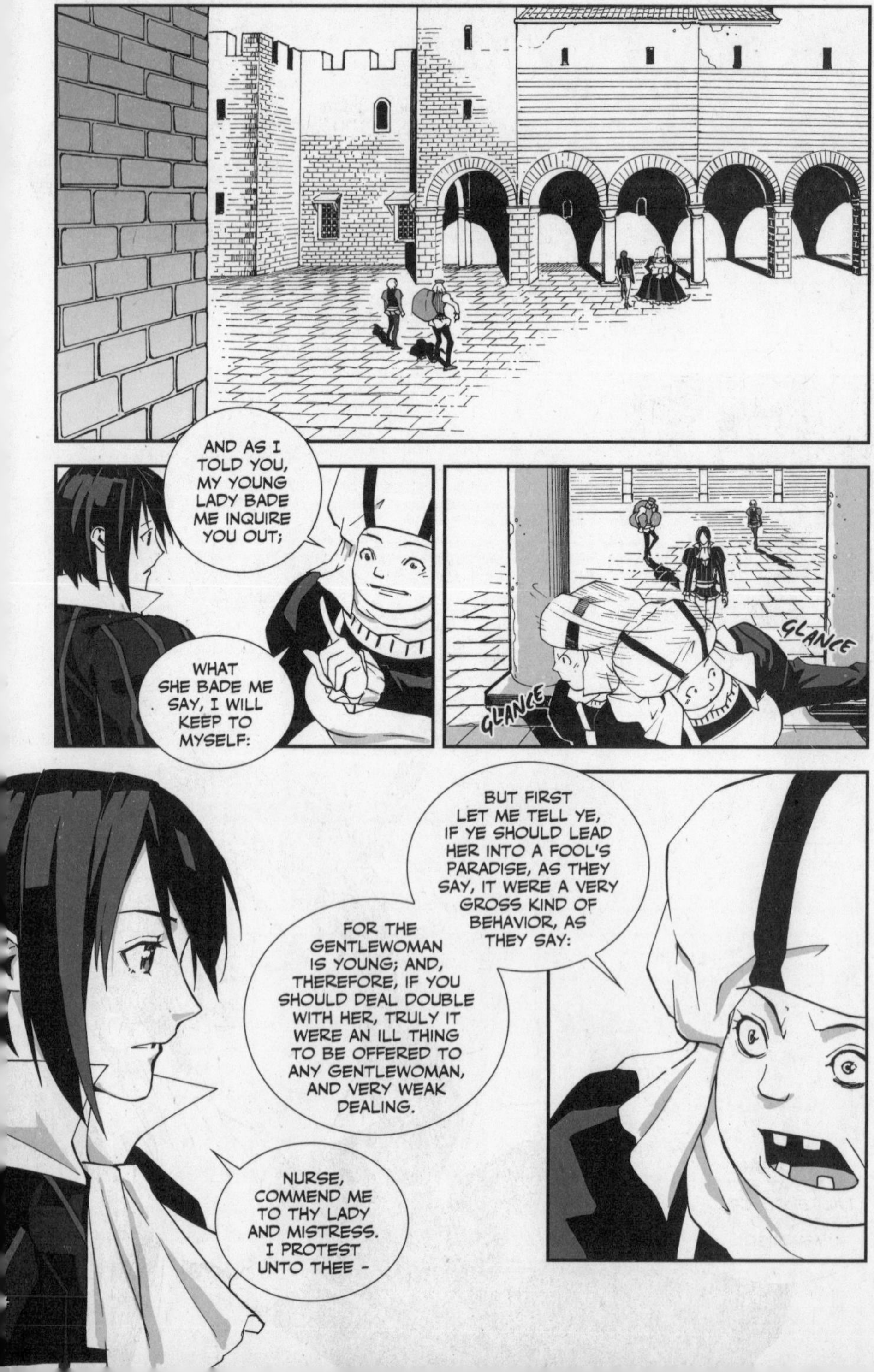
GLANCE
GLANCE
AND AS I TOLD YOU, MY YOUNG LADY BADE ME INQUIRE YOU OUT;
WHAT SHE BADE ME SAY, I WILL KEEP TO MYSELF:
BUT FIRST LET ME TELL YE, IF YE SHOULD LEAD HER INTO A FOOL'S PARADISE, AS THEY SAY, IT WERE A VERY GROSS KIND OF BEHAVIOR, AS THEY SAY:
FOR THE GENTLEWOMAN IS YOUNG; AND, THEREFORE, IF YOU SHOULD DEAL DOUBLE WITH HER, TRULY IT WERE AN ILL THING TO BE OFFERED TO ANY GENTLEWOMAN, AND VERY WEAK DEALING.
NURSE, COMMEND ME TO THY LADY AND MISTRESS. I PROTEST UNTO THEE -

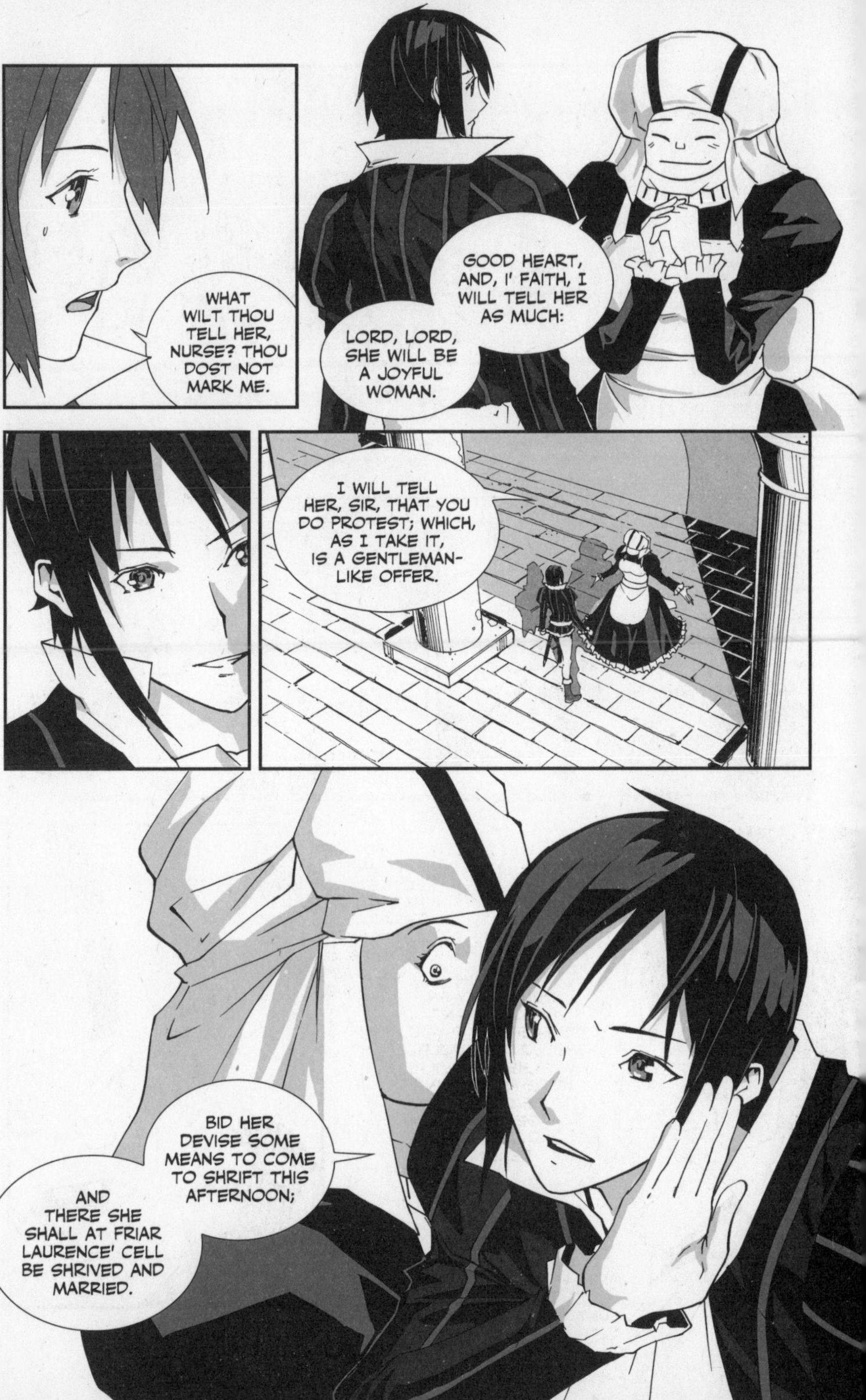
GOOD HEART, AND, I' FAITH, I WILL TELL HER AS MUCH:
LORD, LORD, SHE WILL BE A JOYFUL WOMAN.
WHAT WILT THOU TELL HER, NURSE? THOU DOST NOT MARK ME.
I WILL TELL HER, SIR, THAT YOU DO PROTEST; WHICH, AS I TAKE IT, IS A GENTLEMAN-LIKE OFFER.
BID HER DEVISE SOME MEANS TO COME TO SHRIFT THIS AFTERNOON;
AND THERE SHE SHALL AT FRIAR LAURENCE' CELL BE SHRIVED AND MARRIED.

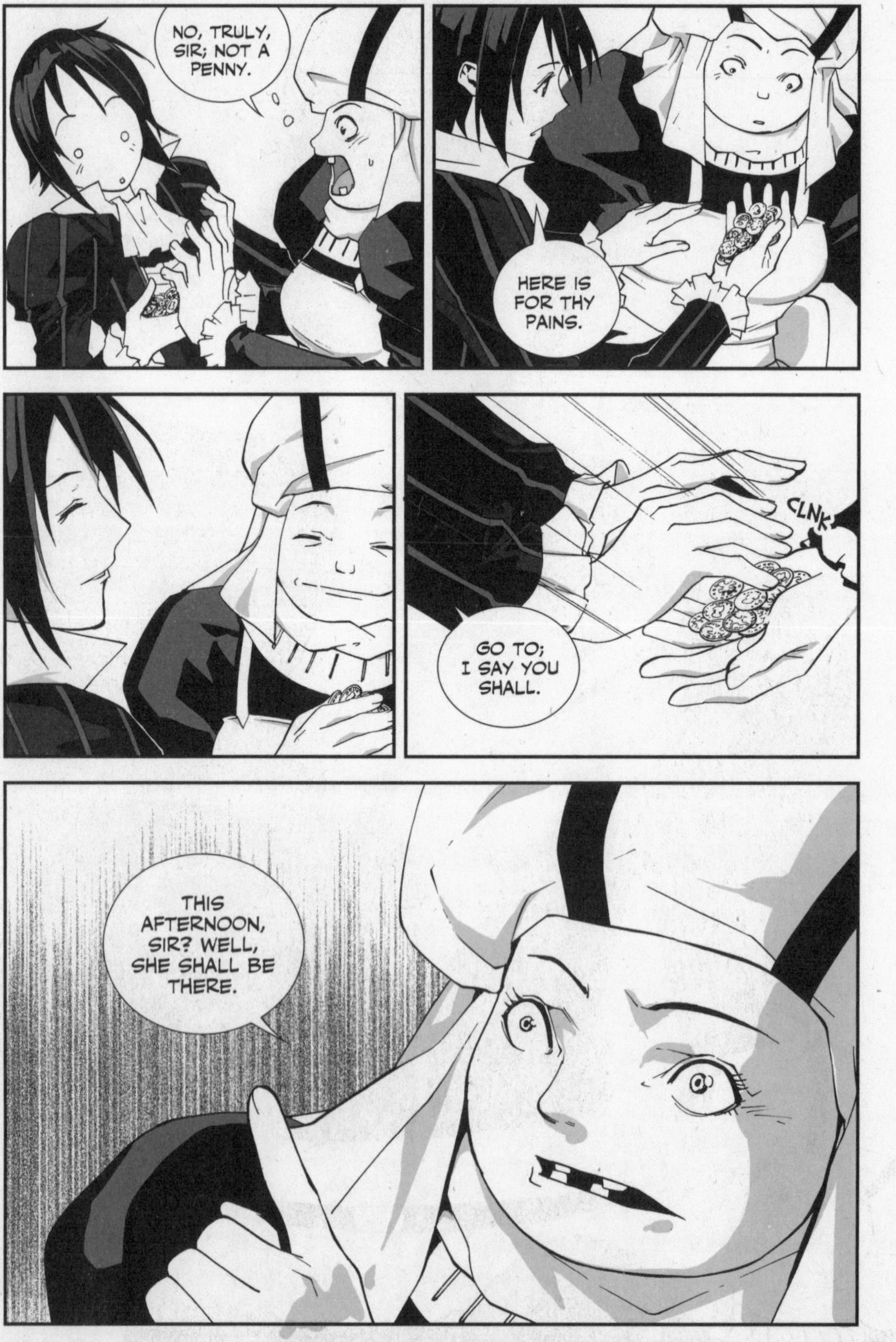
HERE IS FOR THY PAINS.
NO, TRULY, SIR; NOT A PENNY.
GO TO; I SAY YOU SHALL.
CLNK
THIS AFTERNOON, SIR? WELL, SHE SHALL BE THERE.

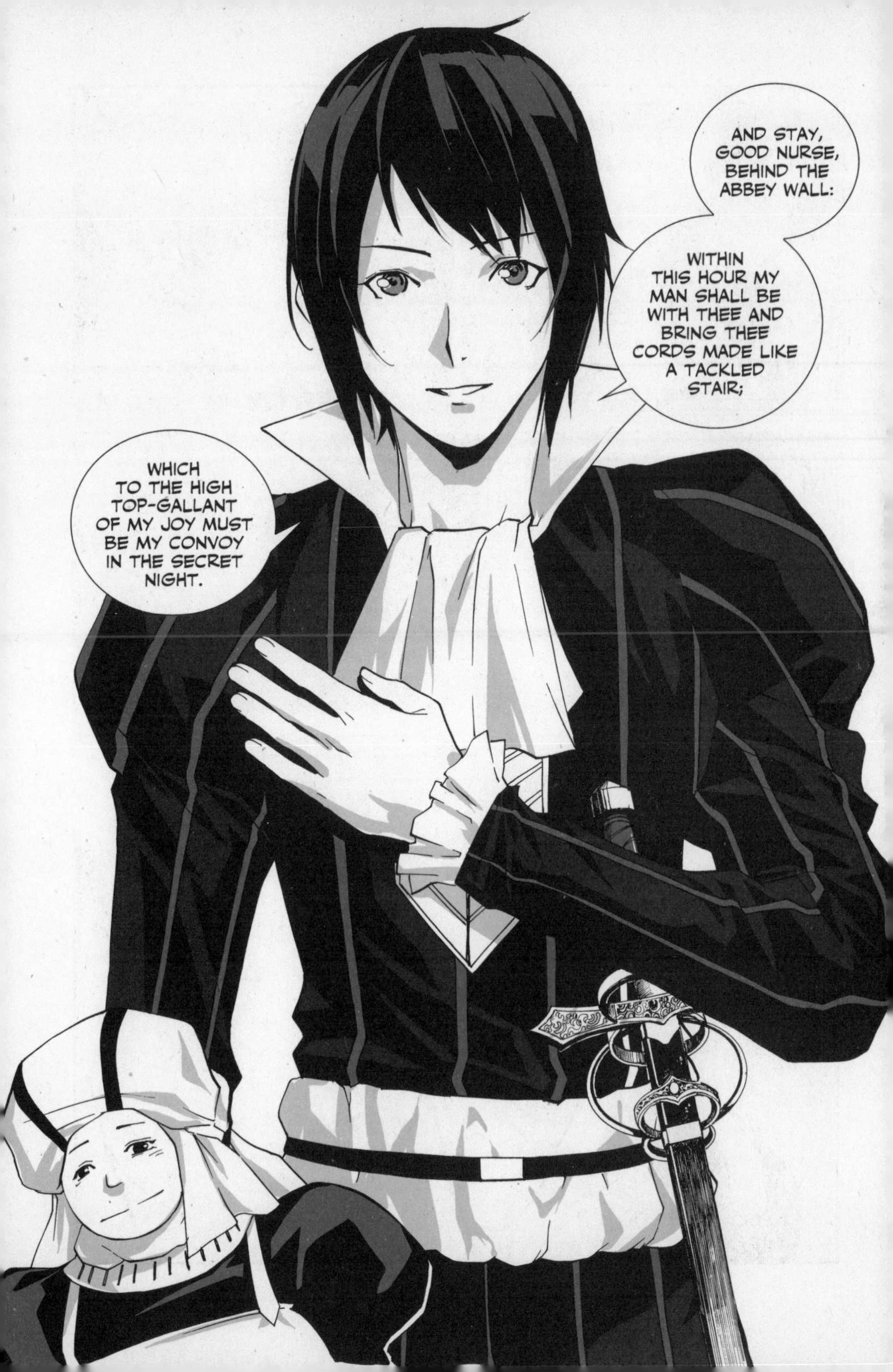
AND STAY, GOOD NURSE, BEHIND THE ABBEY WALL:
WITHIN THIS HOUR MY MAN SHALL BE WITH THEE AND BRING THEE CORDS MADE LIKE A TACKLED STAIR;
WHICH TO THE HIGH TOP-GALLANT OF MY JOY MUST BE MY CONVOY IN THE SECRET NIGHT.

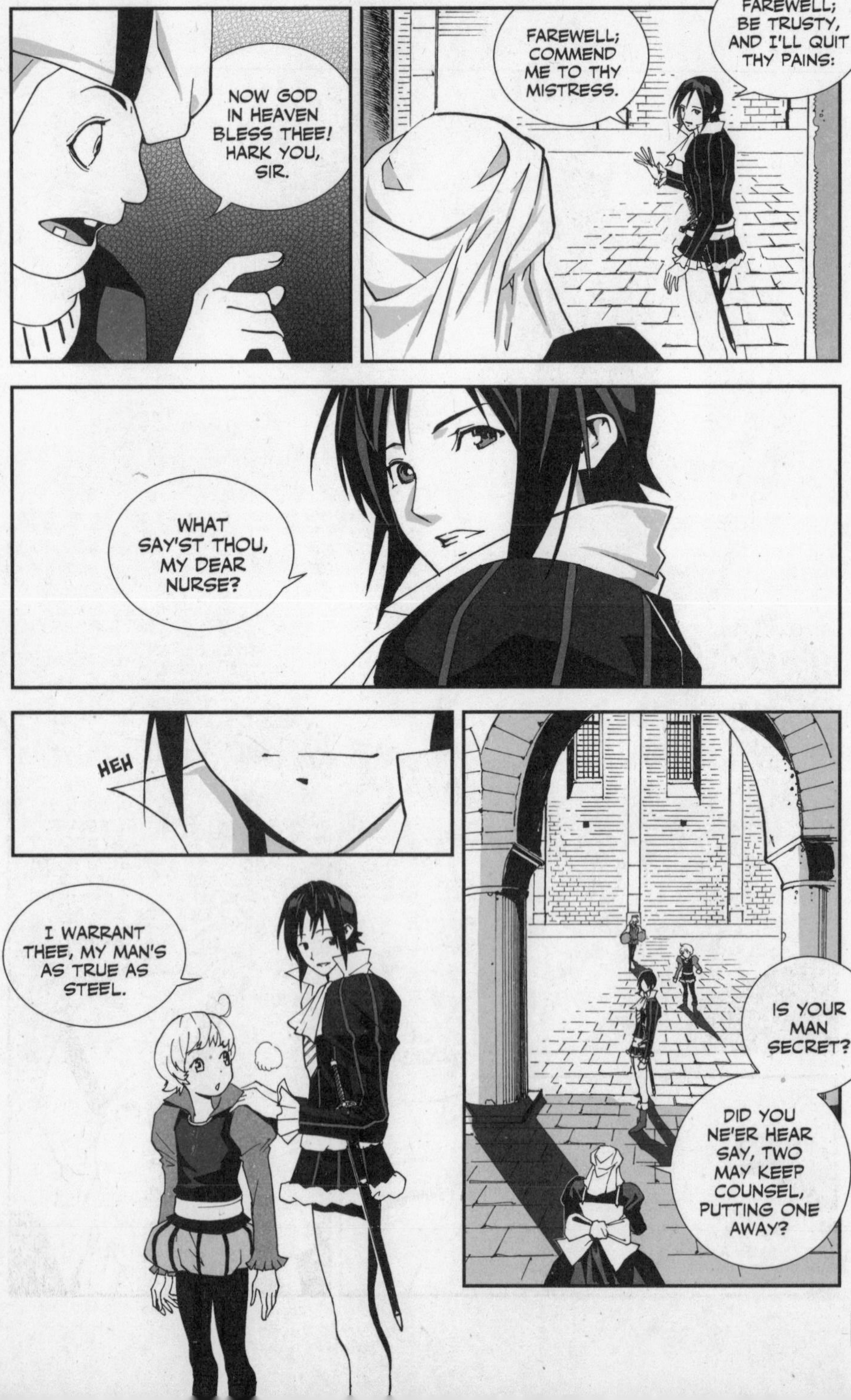
FAREWELL; BE TRUSTY, AND I'LL QUIT THY PAINS:
FAREWELL; COMMEND ME TO THY MISTRESS.
NOW GOD IN HEAVEN BLESS THEE! HARK YOU, SIR.
WHAT SAY'ST THOU, MY DEAR NURSE?
IS YOUR MAN SECRET?
DID YOU NE'ER HEAR SAY, TWO MAY KEEP COUNSEL, PUTTING ONE AWAY?
HEH
I WARRANT THEE, MY MAN'S AS TRUE AS STEEL.

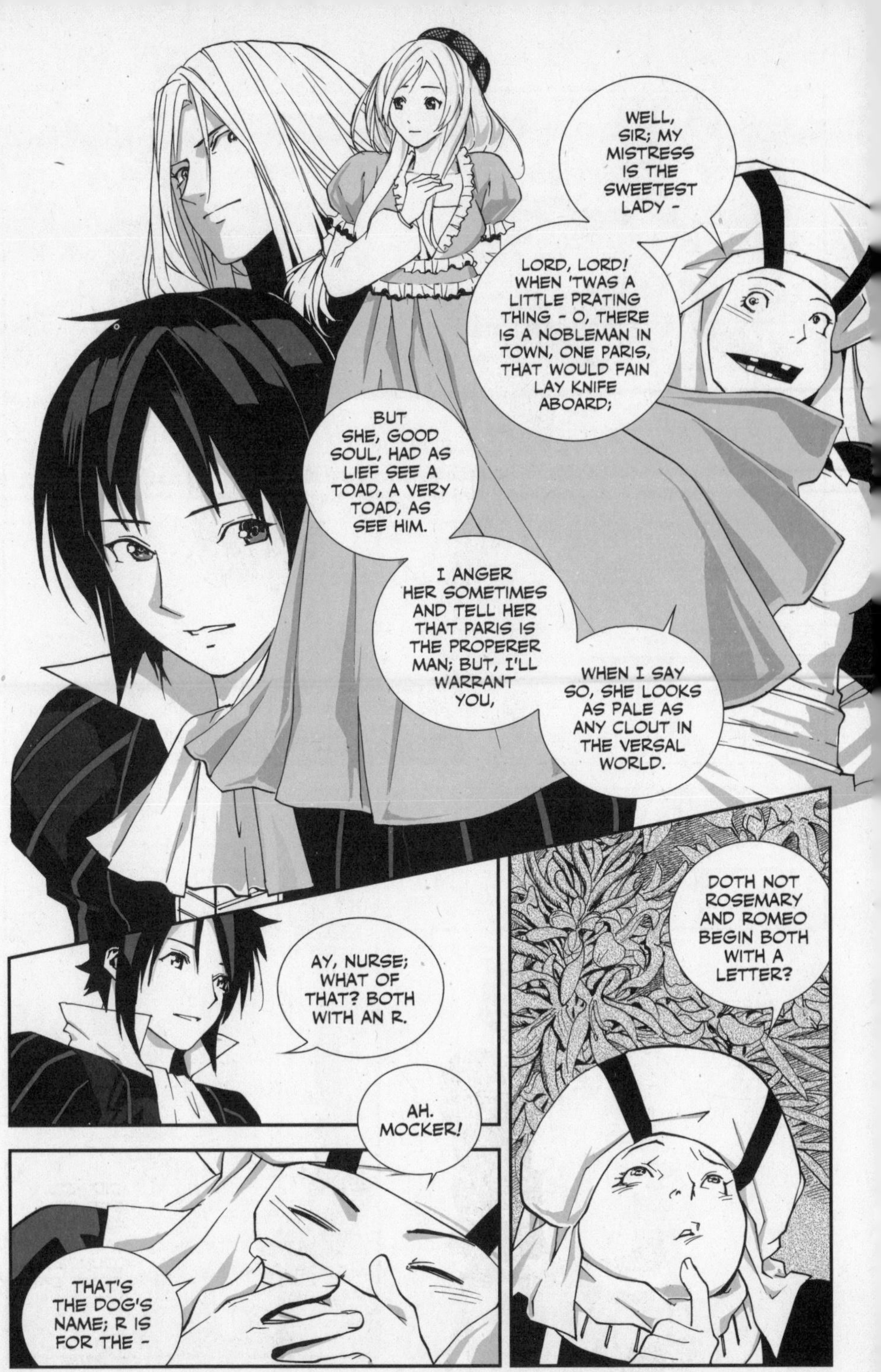
WELL, SIR; MY MISTRESS IS THE SWEETEST LADY -
LORD, LORD! WHEN 'TWAS A LITTLE PRATING THING - O, THERE IS A NOBLEMAN IN TOWN, ONE PARIS, THAT WOULD FAIN LAY KNIFE ABOARD;
BUT SHE, GOOD SOUL, HAD AS LIEF SEE A TOAD, A VERY TOAD, AS SEE HIM.
I ANGER HER SOMETIMES AND TELL HER THAT PARIS IS THE PROPERER MAN; BUT, I'LL WARRANT YOU,
WHEN I SAY SO, SHE LOOKS AS PALE AS ANY CLOUT IN THE VERSAL WORLD.
DOTH NOT ROSEMARY AND ROMEO BEGIN BOTH WITH A LETTER?
AY, NURSE; WHAT OF THAT? BOTH WITH AN R.
AH. MOCKER!
THAT'S THE DOG'S NAME; R IS FOR THE -

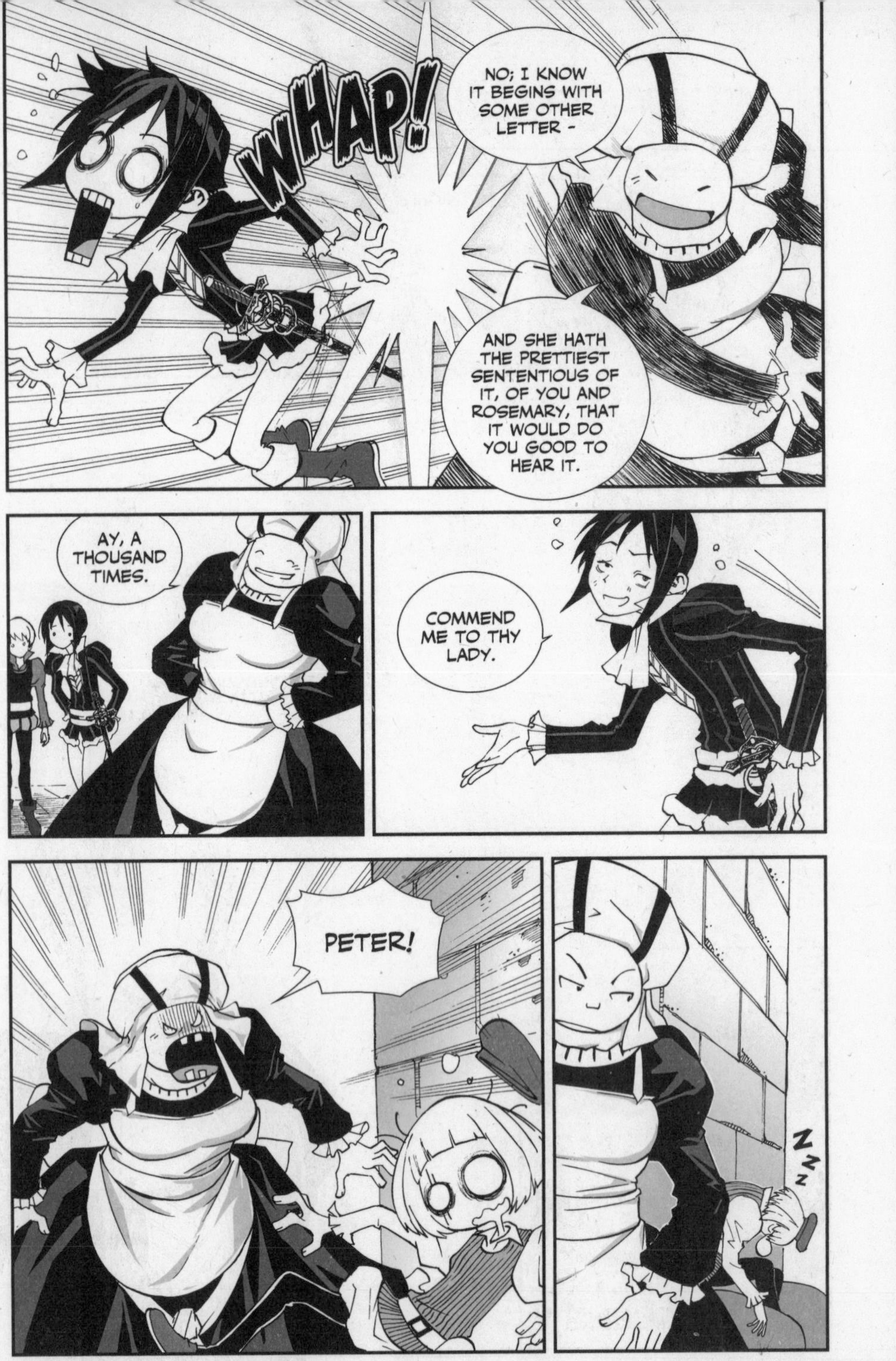
NO; I KNOW IT BEGINS WITH SOME OTHER LETTER -
WHAP!
AND SHE HATH THE PRETTIEST SENTENTIOUS OF IT, OF YOU AND ROSEMARY, THAT IT WOULD DO YOU GOOD TO HEAR IT.
COMMEND ME TO THY LADY.
AY, A THOUSAND TIMES.
ZZZ
PETER!

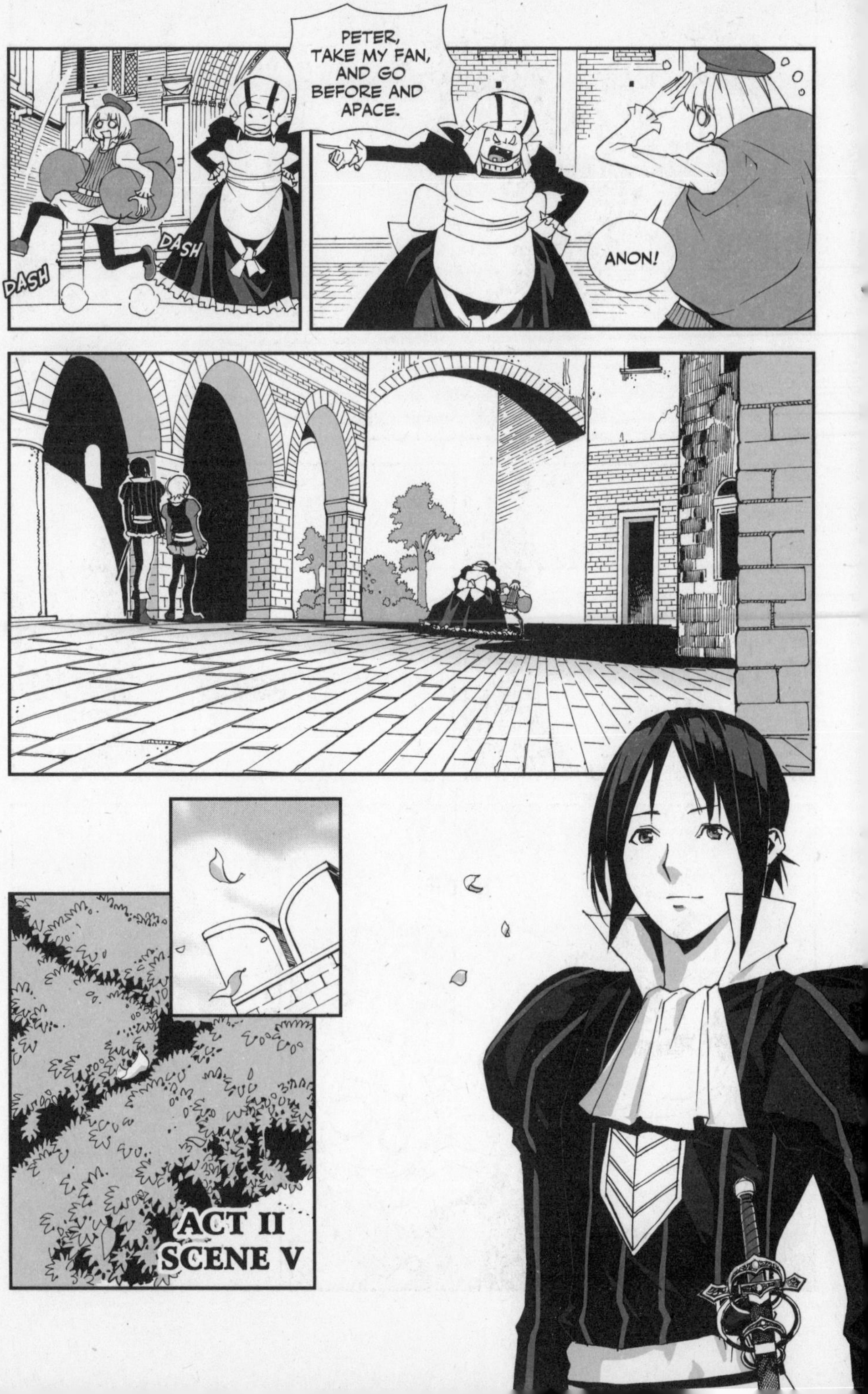
PETER, TAKE MY FAN, AND GO BEFORE AND APACE.
ANON!
DASH
DASH
ACT II
SCENE V

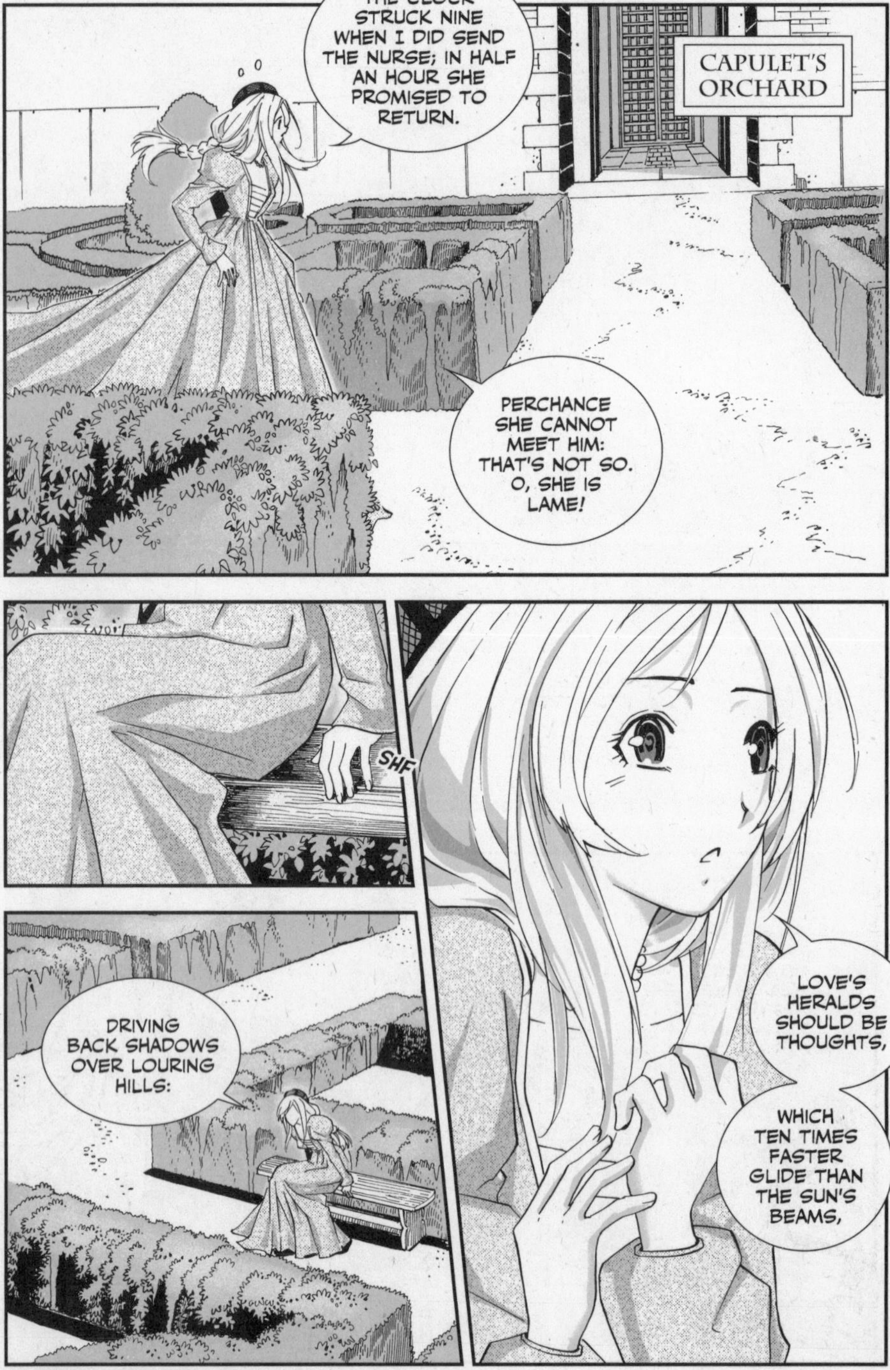
CAPULET'S ORCHARD
THE CLOCK STRUCK NINE WHEN I DID SEND THE NURSE; IN HALF AN HOUR SHE PROMISED TO RETURN.
PERCHANCE SHE CANNOT MEET HIM: THAT'S NOT SO. O, SHE IS LAME!
LOVE'S HERALDS SHOULD BE THOUGHTS,
WHICH TEN TIMES FASTER GLIDE THAN THE SUN'S BEAMS,
SHF
DRIVING BACK SHADOWS OVER LOURING HILLS:

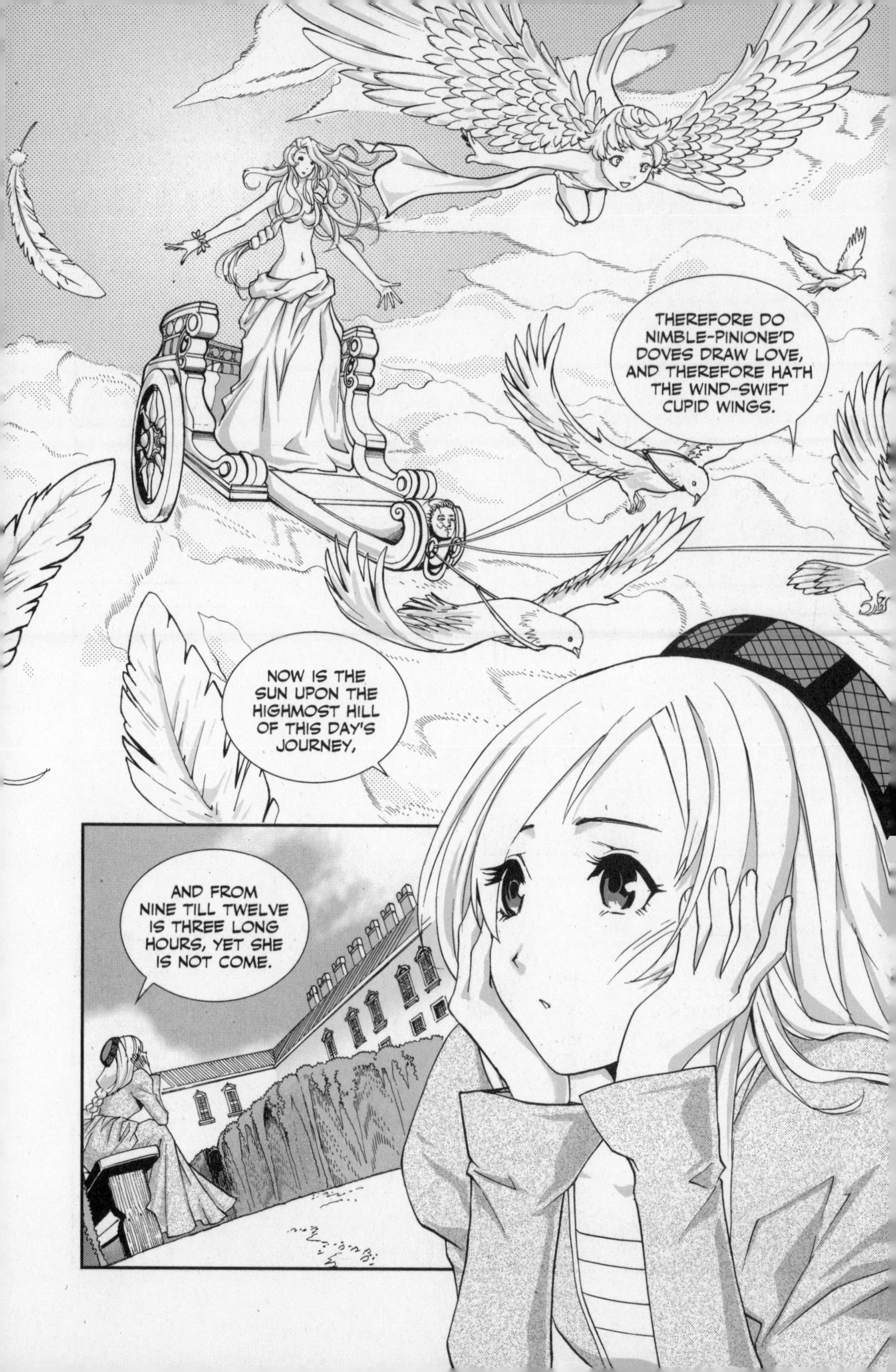
THEREFORE DO NIMBLE-PINIONE'D DOVES DRAW LOVE, AND THEREFORE HATH THE WIND-SWIFT CUPID WINGS.
NOW IS THE SUN UPON THE HIGHMOST HILL OF THIS DAY'S JOURNEY,
AND FROM NINE TILL TWELVE IS THREE LONG HOURS, YET SHE IS NOT COME.

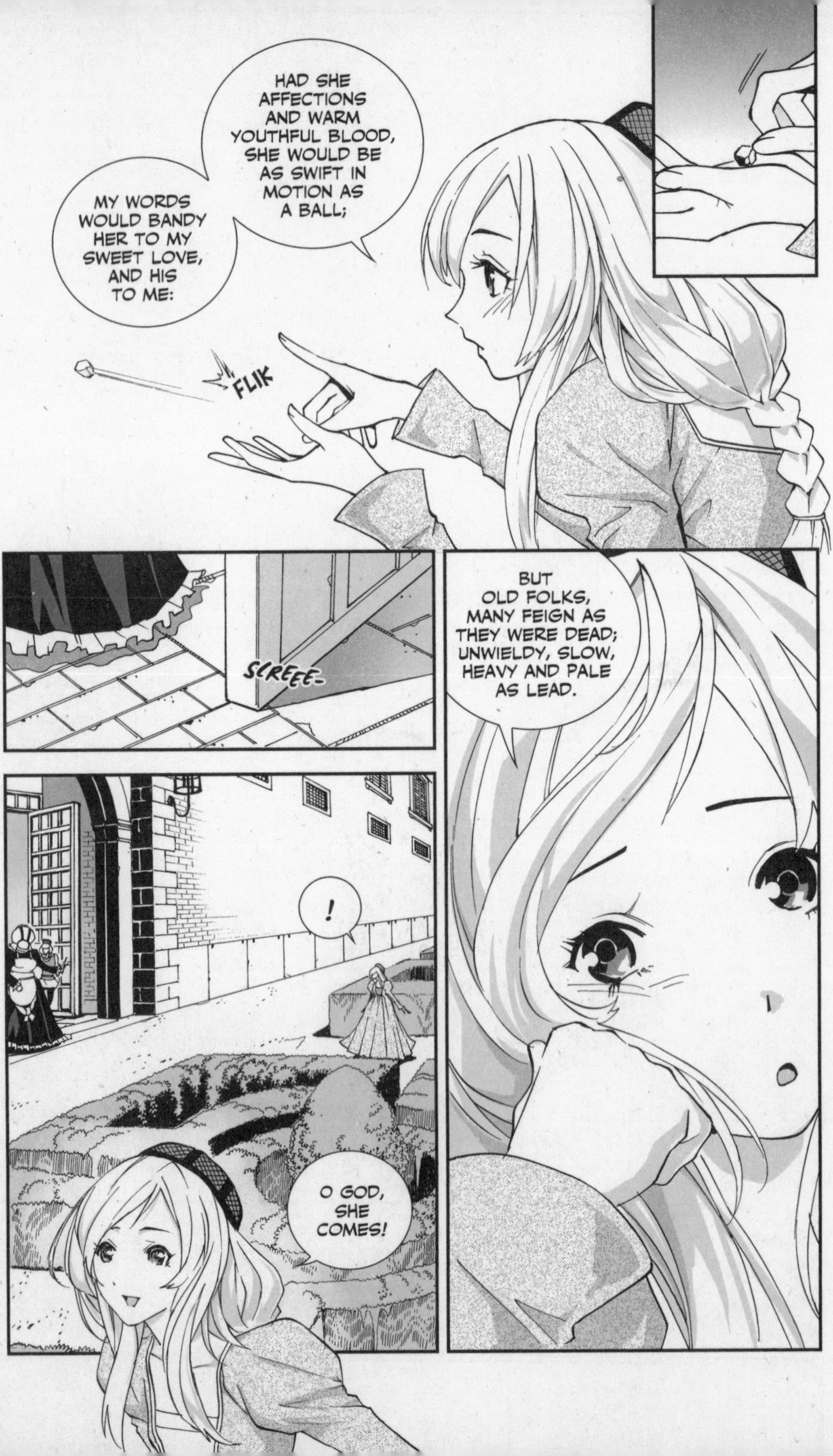
HAD SHE AFFECTIONS AND WARM YOUTHFUL BLOOD, SHE WOULD BE AS SWIFT IN MOTION AS A BALL;
MY WORDS WOULD BANDY HER TO MY SWEET LOVE, AND HIS TO ME:
FLIK
BUT OLD FOLKS, MANY FEIGN AS THEY WERE DEAD; UNWIELDY, SLOW, HEAVY AND PALE AS LEAD.
SCREEEE-
!
O GOD, SHE COMES!

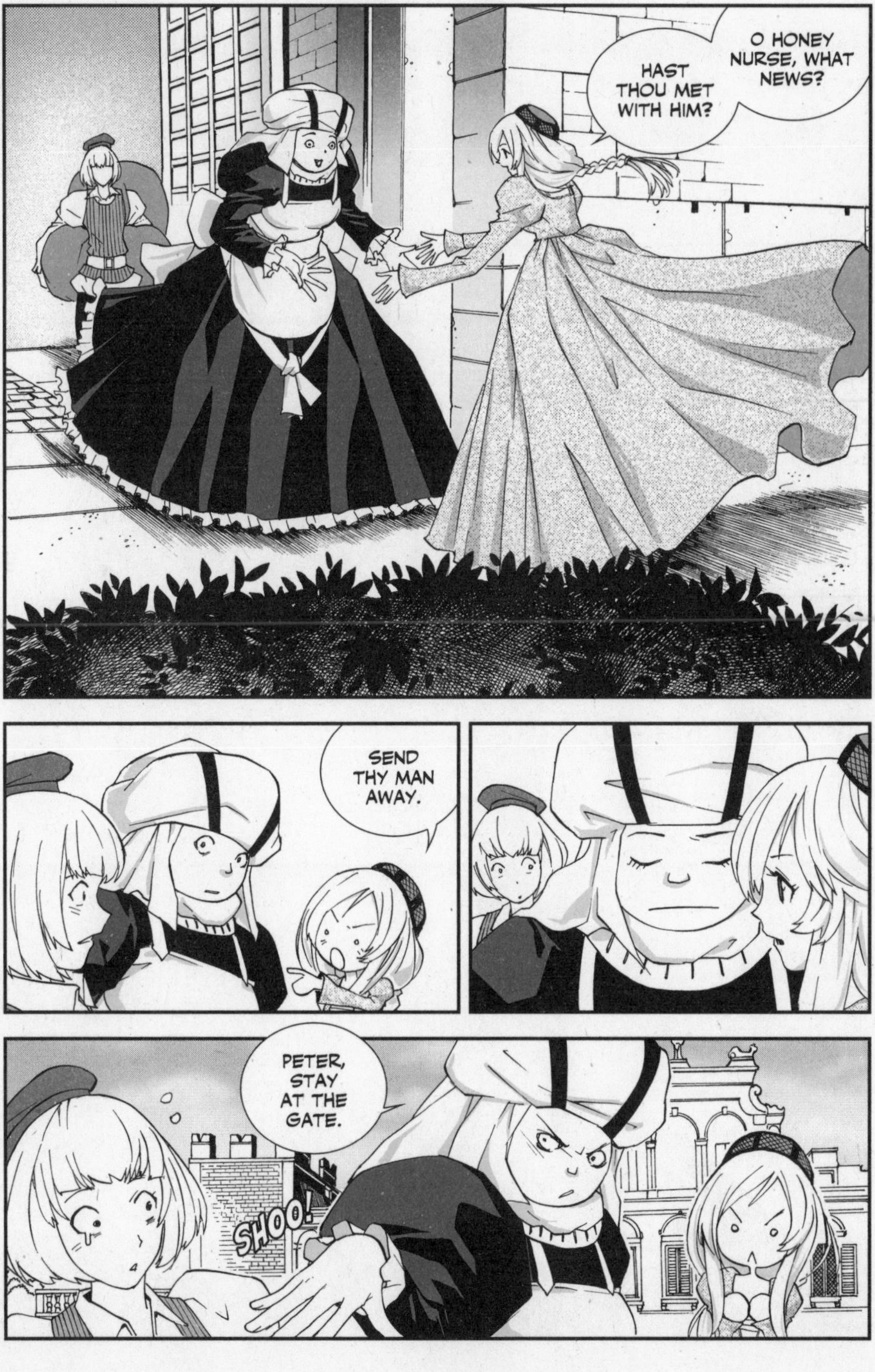
O HONEY NURSE, WHAT NEWS?
HAST THOU MET WITH HIM?
SEND THY MAN AWAY.
PETER, STAY AT THE GATE.
SHOO!

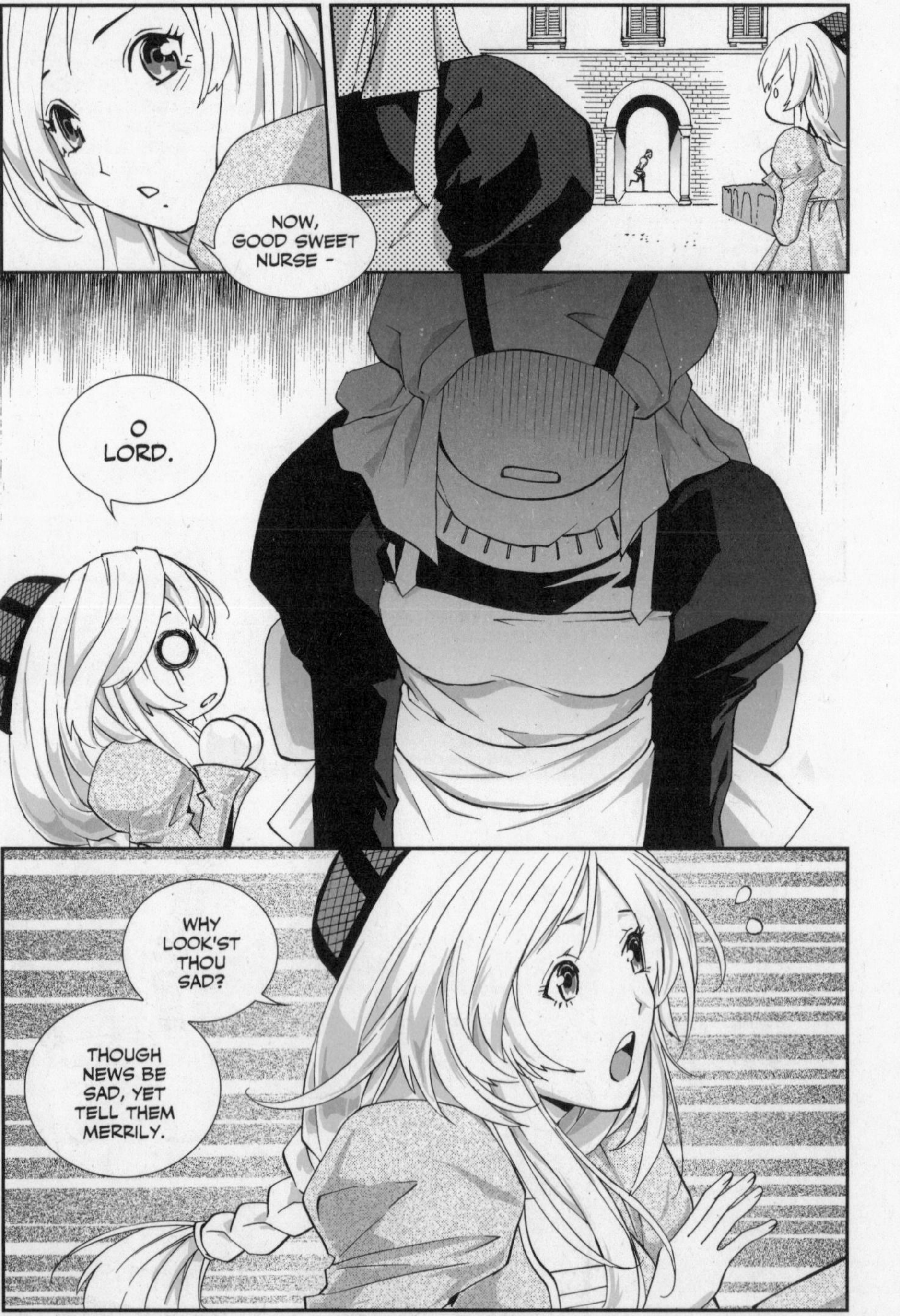
NOW, GOOD SWEET NURSE -
O LORD.
WHY LOOK'ST THOU SAD?
THOUGH NEWS BE SAD, YET TELL THEM MERRILY.

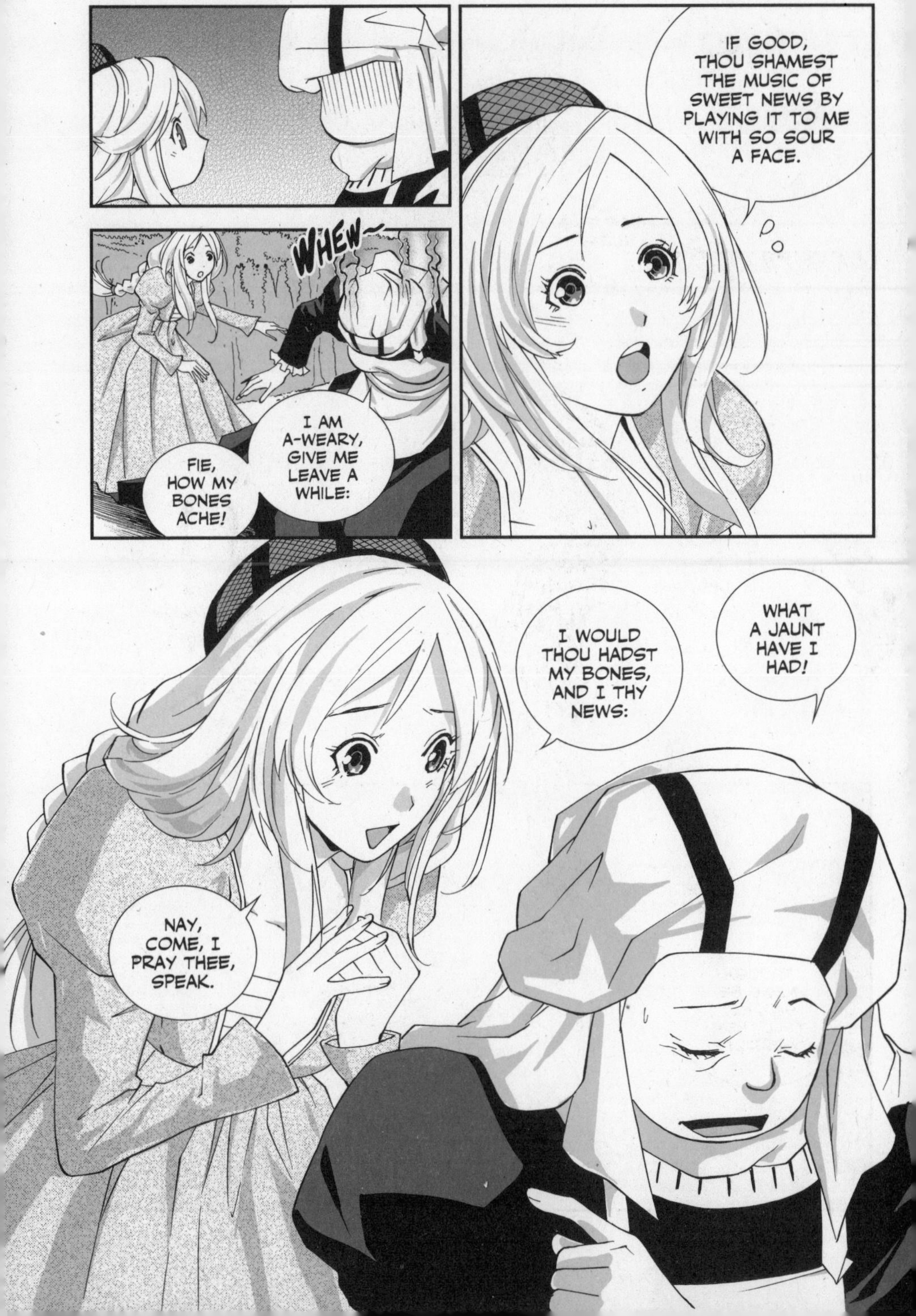
IF GOOD, THOU SHAMEST THE MUSIC OF SWEET NEWS BY PLAYING IT TO ME WITH SO SOUR A FACE.
WHEW~
I AM A-WEARY, GIVE ME LEAVE A WHILE:
FIE, HOW MY BONES ACHE!
WHAT A JAUNT HAVE I HAD!
I WOULD THOU HADST MY BONES, AND I THY NEWS:
NAY, COME, I PRAY THEE, SPEAK.

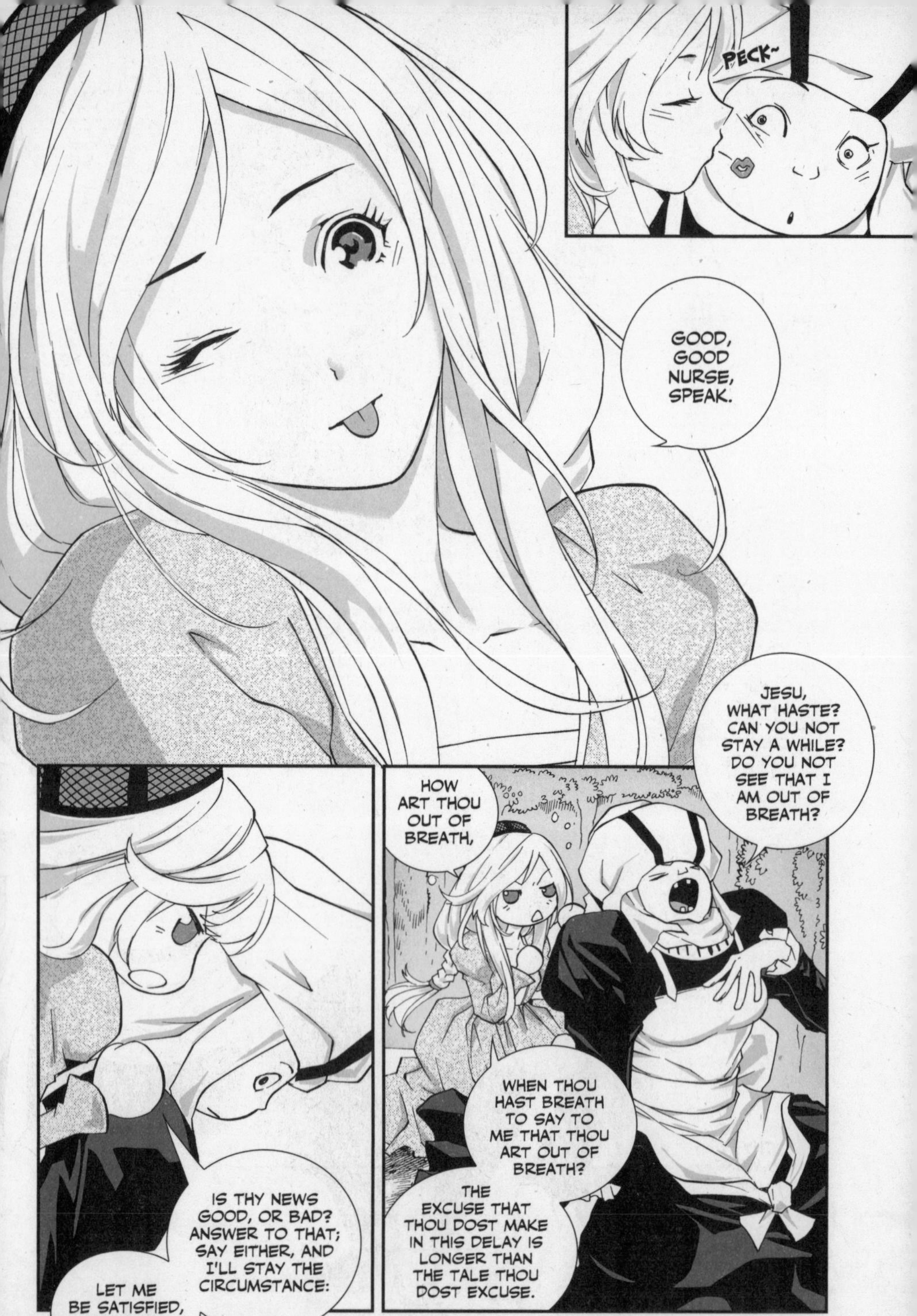
PECK~
GOOD, GOOD NURSE, SPEAK.
JESU, WHAT HASTE? CAN YOU NOT STAY A WHILE? DO YOU NOT SEE THAT I AM OUT OF BREATH?
HOW ART THOU OUT OF BREATH,
WHEN THOU HAST BREATH TO SAY TO ME THAT THOU ART OUT OF BREATH?
THE EXCUSE THAT THOU DOST MAKE IN THIS DELAY IS LONGER THAN THE TALE THOU DOST EXCUSE.
IS THY NEWS GOOD, OR BAD? ANSWER TO THAT; SAY EITHER, AND I'LL STAY THE CIRCUMSTANCE:
LET ME BE SATISFIED, IS'T GOOD OR BAD?

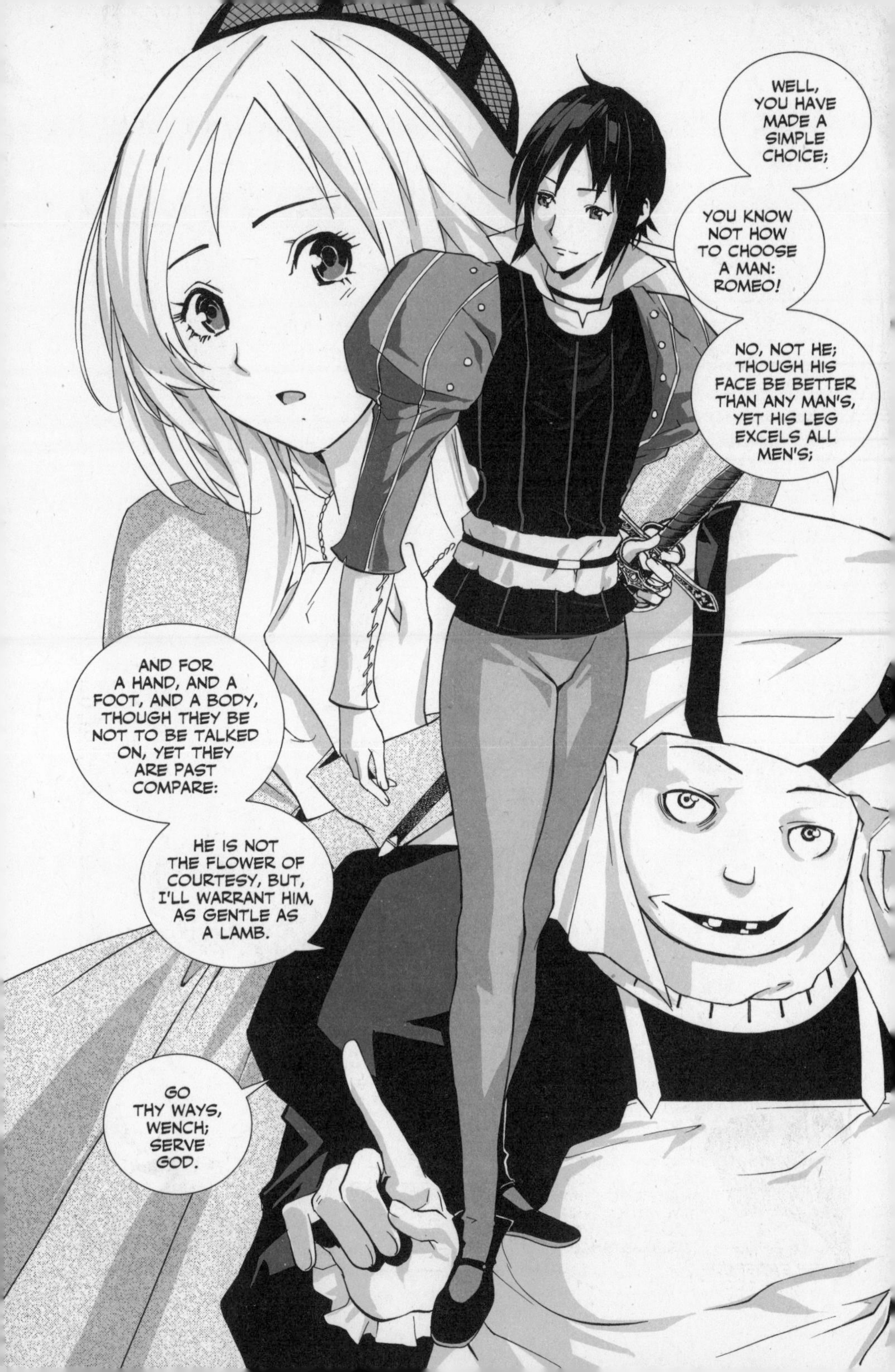
WELL, YOU HAVE MADE A SIMPLE CHOICE;
YOU KNOW NOT HOW TO CHOOSE A MAN: ROMEO!
NO, NOT HE; THOUGH HIS FACE BE BETTER THAN ANY MAN'S, YET HIS LEG EXCELS ALL MEN'S;
AND FOR A HAND, AND A FOOT, AND A BODY, THOUGH THEY BE NOT TO BE TALKED ON, YET THEY ARE PAST COMPARE:
HE IS NOT THE FLOWER OF COURTESY, BUT, I'LL WARRANT HIM, AS GENTLE AS A LAMB.
GO THY WAYS, WENCH; SERVE GOD.

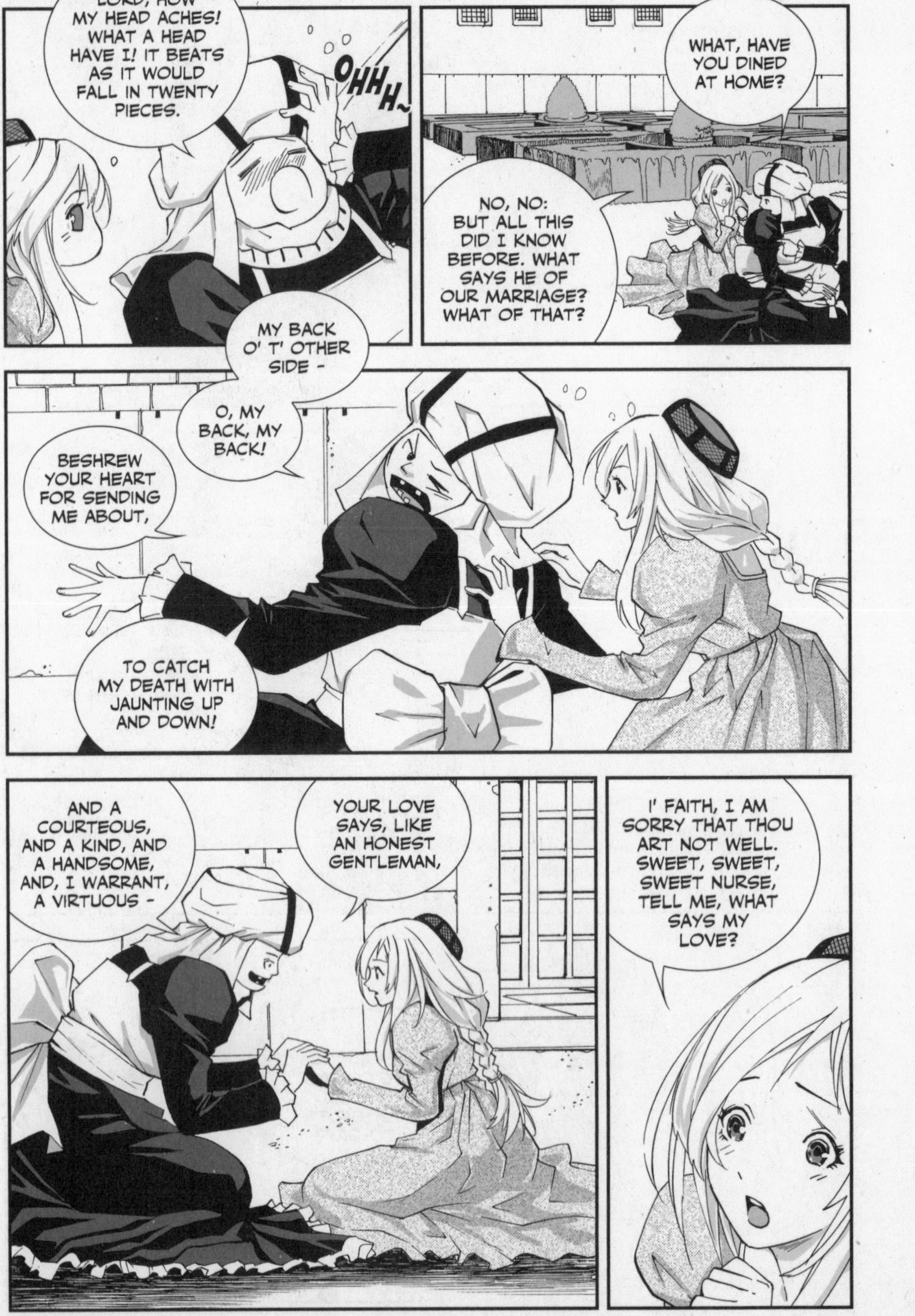
WHAT, HAVE YOU DINED AT HOME?
NO, NO: BUT ALL THIS DID I KNOW BEFORE. WHAT SAYS HE OF OUR MARRIAGE? WHAT OF THAT?
OHHH~
LORD, HOW MY HEAD ACHES! WHAT A HEAD HAVE I! IT BEATS AS IT WOULD FALL IN TWENTY PIECES.
MY BACK O' T' OTHER SIDE -
O, MY BACK, MY BACK!
BESHREW YOUR HEART FOR SENDING ME ABOUT,
TO CATCH MY DEATH WITH JAUNTING UP AND DOWN!
I' FAITH, I AM SORRY THAT THOU ART NOT WELL. SWEET, SWEET, SWEET NURSE, TELL ME, WHAT SAYS MY LOVE?
YOUR LOVE SAYS, LIKE AN HONEST GENTLEMAN,
AND A COURTEOUS, AND A KIND, AND A HANDSOME, AND, I WARRANT, A VIRTUOUS -

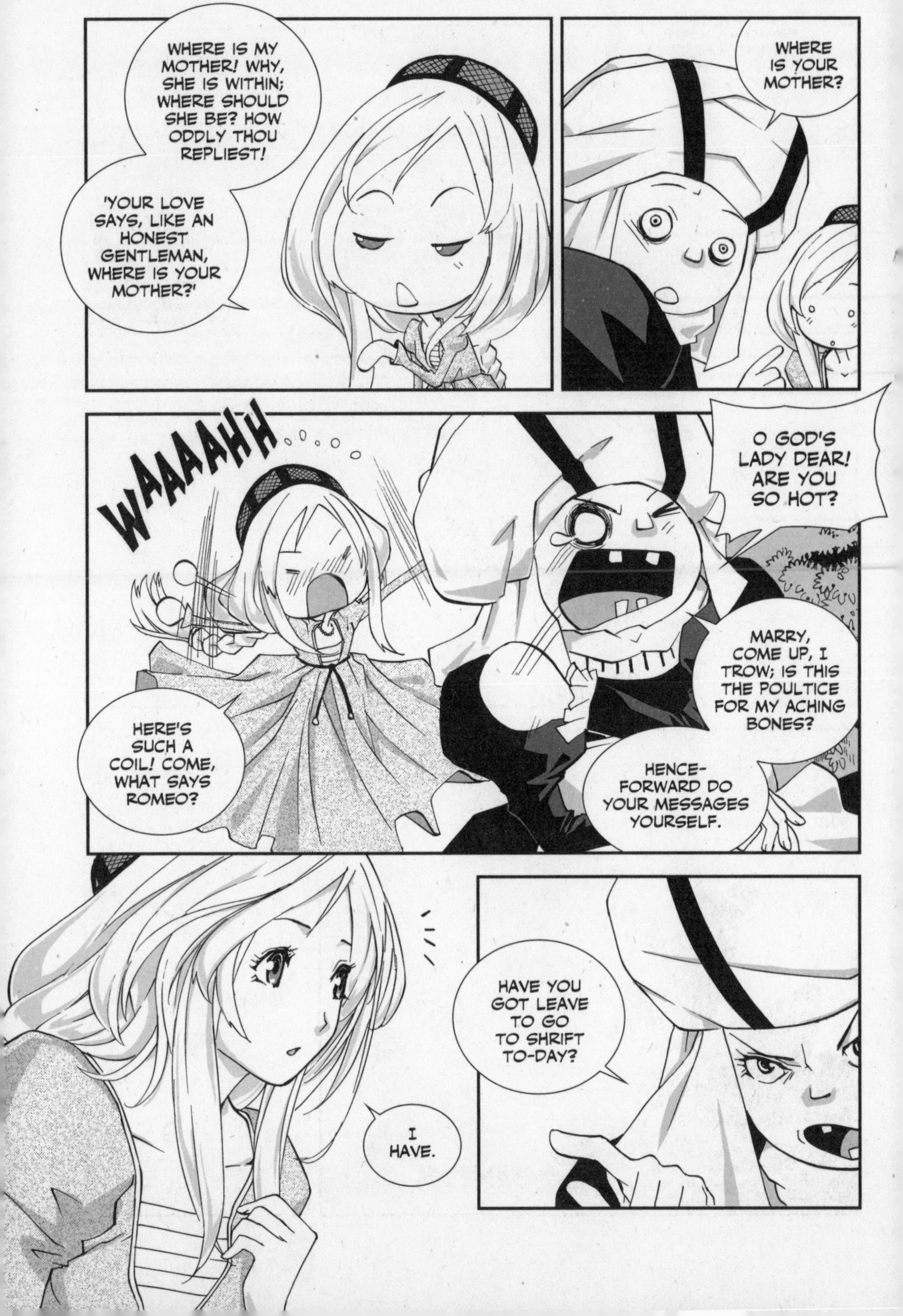
WHERE IS YOUR MOTHER?
WHERE IS MY MOTHER! WHY, SHE IS WITHIN; WHERE SHOULD SHE BE? HOW ODDLY THOU REPLIEST!
'YOUR LOVE SAYS, LIKE AN HONEST GENTLEMAN, WHERE IS YOUR MOTHER?'
O GOD'S LADY DEAR! ARE YOU SO HOT?
WAAAAHH
MARRY, COME UP, I TROW; IS THIS THE POULTICE FOR MY ACHING BONES?
HENCE-FORWARD DO YOUR MESSAGES YOURSELF.
HERE'S SUCH A COIL! COME, WHAT SAYS ROMEO?
HAVE YOU GOT LEAVE TO GO TO SHRIFT TO-DAY?
I HAVE.

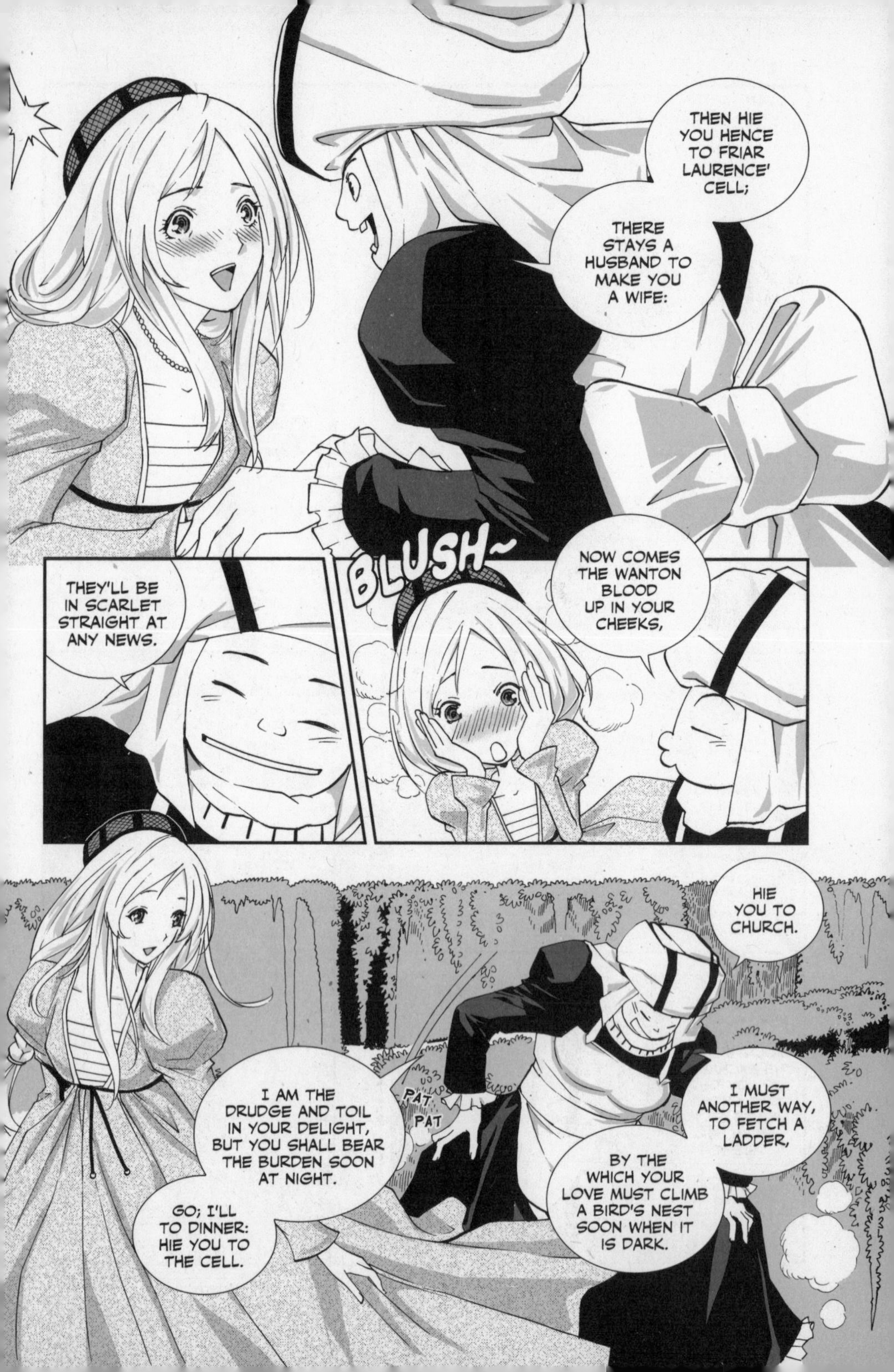
THEN HIE YOU HENCE TO FRIAR LAURENCE' CELL;
THERE STAYS A HUSBAND TO MAKE YOU A WIFE:
BLUSH~
NOW COMES THE WANTON BLOOD UP IN YOUR CHEEKS,
THEY'LL BE IN SCARLET STRAIGHT AT ANY NEWS.
HIE YOU TO CHURCH.
I MUST ANOTHER WAY, TO FETCH A LADDER,
BY THE WHICH YOUR LOVE MUST CLIMB A BIRD'S NEST SOON WHEN IT IS DARK.
PAT PAT
I AM THE DRUDGE AND TOIL IN YOUR DELIGHT, BUT YOU SHALL BEAR THE BURDEN SOON AT NIGHT.
GO; I'LL TO DINNER: HIE YOU TO THE CELL.

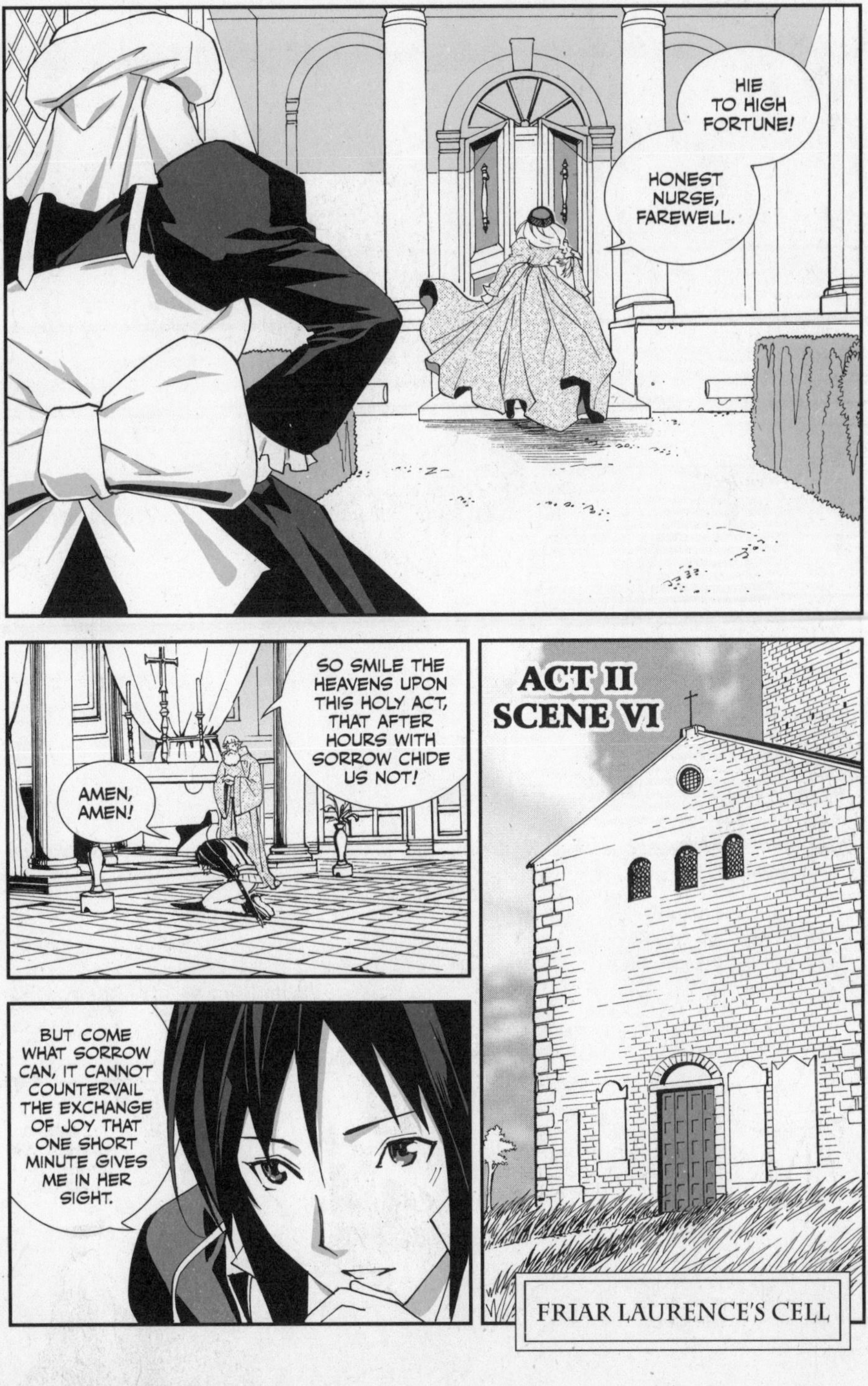
HIE TO HIGH FORTUNE!
HONEST NURSE, FAREWELL.
ACT II SCENE VI
FRIAR LAURENCE'S CELL
SO SMILE THE HEAVENS UPON THIS HOLY ACT, THAT AFTER HOURS WITH SORROW CHIDE US NOT!
AMEN, AMEN!
BUT COME WHAT SORROW CAN, IT CANNOT COUNTERVAIL THE EXCHANGE OF JOY THAT ONE SHORT MINUTE GIVES ME IN HER SIGHT.

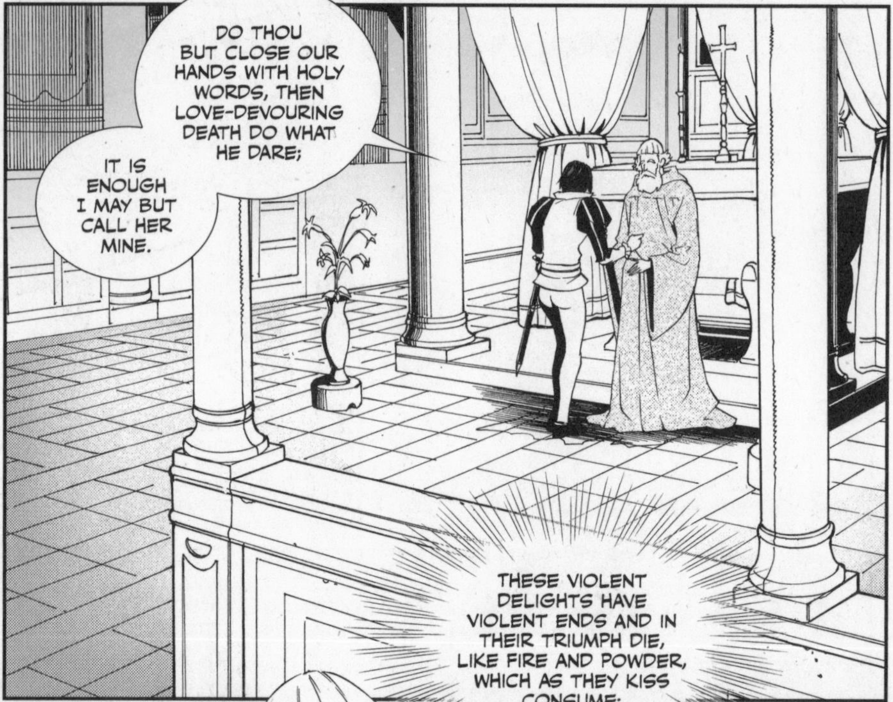
DO THOU BUT CLOSE OUR HANDS WITH HOLY WORDS, THEN LOVE-DEVOURING DEATH DO WHAT HE DARE;
IT IS ENOUGH I MAY BUT CALL HER MINE.

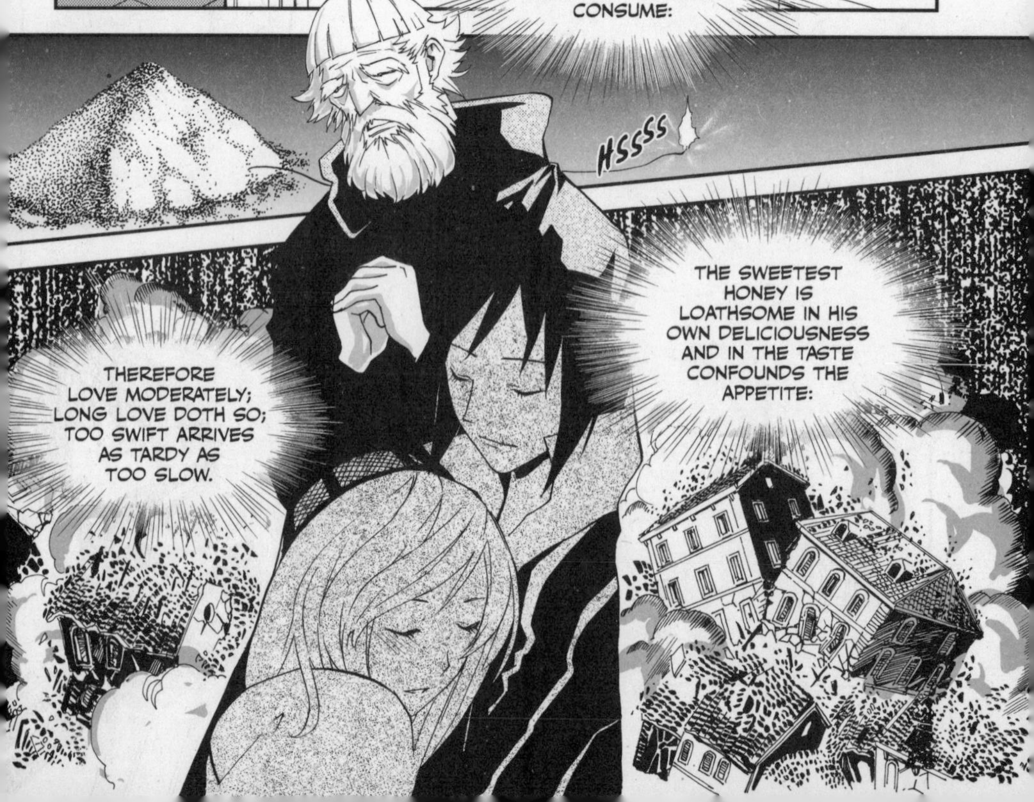
THESE VIOLENT DELIGHTS HAVE VIOLENT ENDS AND IN THEIR TRIUMPH DIE, LIKE FIRE AND POWDER, WHICH AS THEY KISS CONSUME:
HSSSS
THE SWEETEST HONEY IS LOATHSOME IN HIS OWN DELICIOUSNESS AND IN THE TASTE CONFOUNDS THE APPETITE:
THEREFORE LOVE MODERATELY; LONG LOVE DOTH SO; TOO SWIFT ARRIVES AS TARDY AS TOO SLOW.

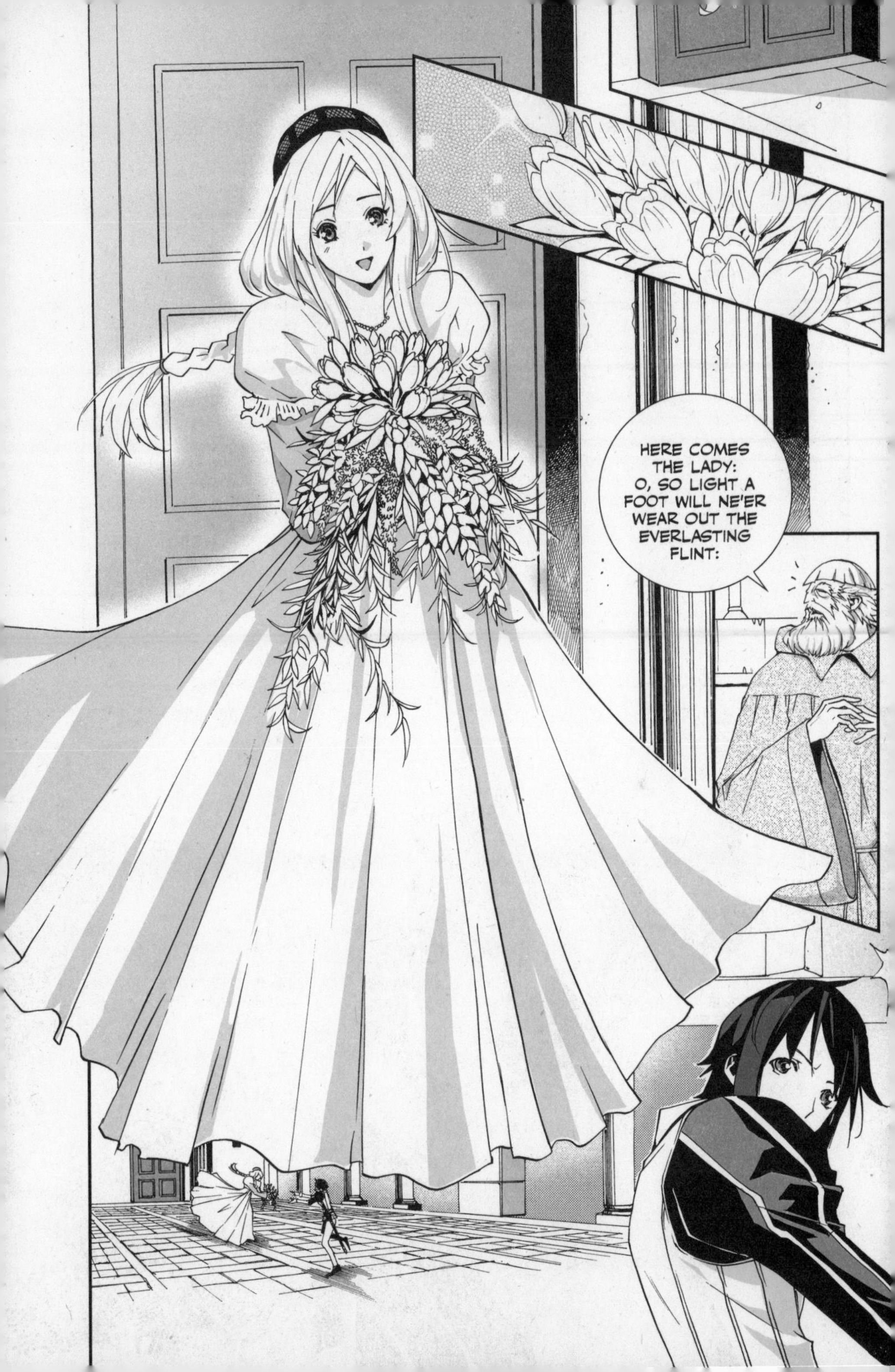
HERE COMES THE LADY: O, SO LIGHT A FOOT WILL NE'ER WEAR OUT THE EVERLASTING FLINT:

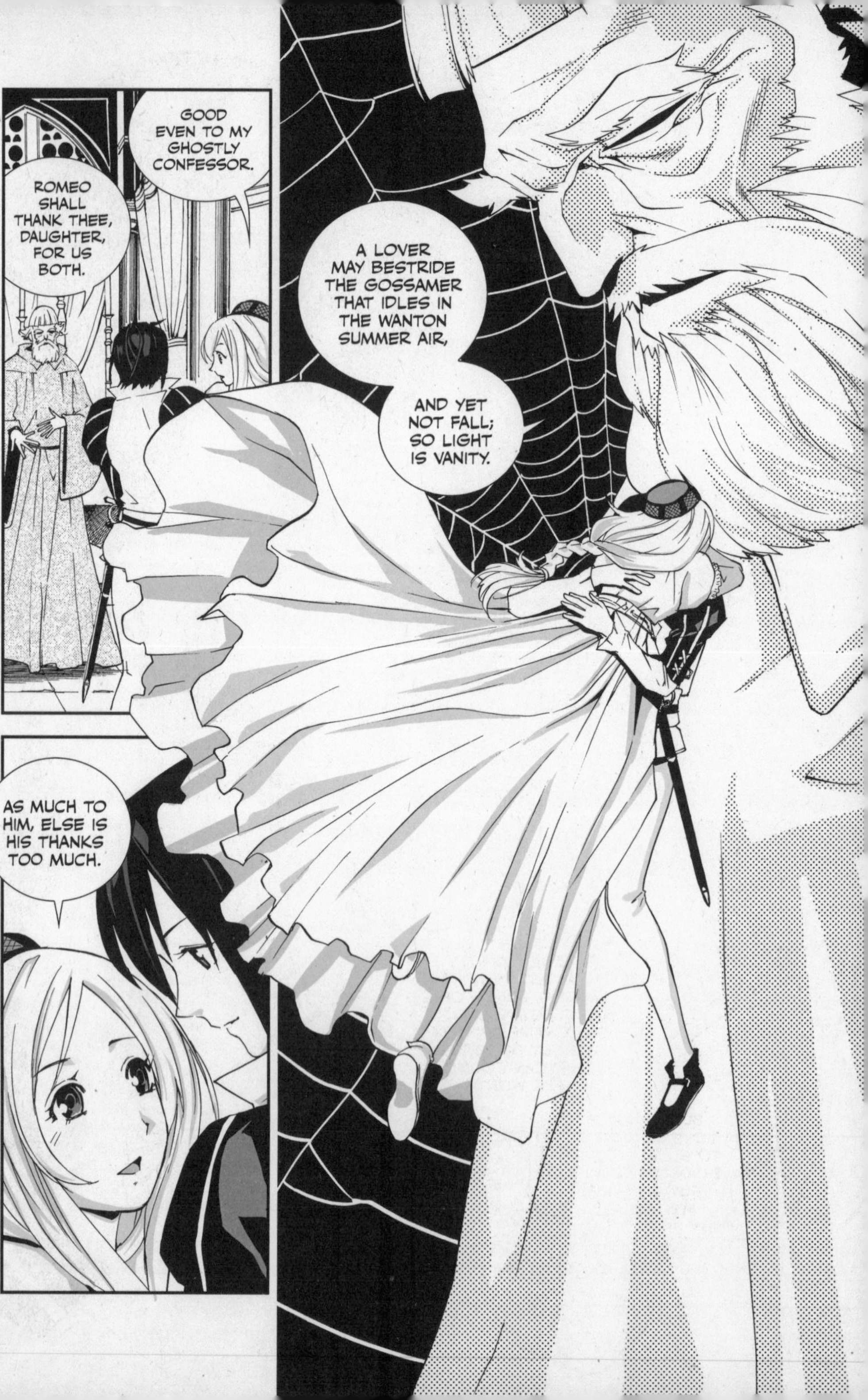
A LOVER MAY BESTRIDE THE GOSSAMER THAT IDLES IN THE WANTON SUMMER AIR,
AND YET NOT FALL; SO LIGHT IS VANITY.
GOOD EVEN TO MY GHOSTLY CONFESSOR.
ROMEO SHALL THANK THEE, DAUGHTER, FOR US BOTH.
AS MUCH TO HIM, ELSE IS HIS THANKS TOO MUCH.

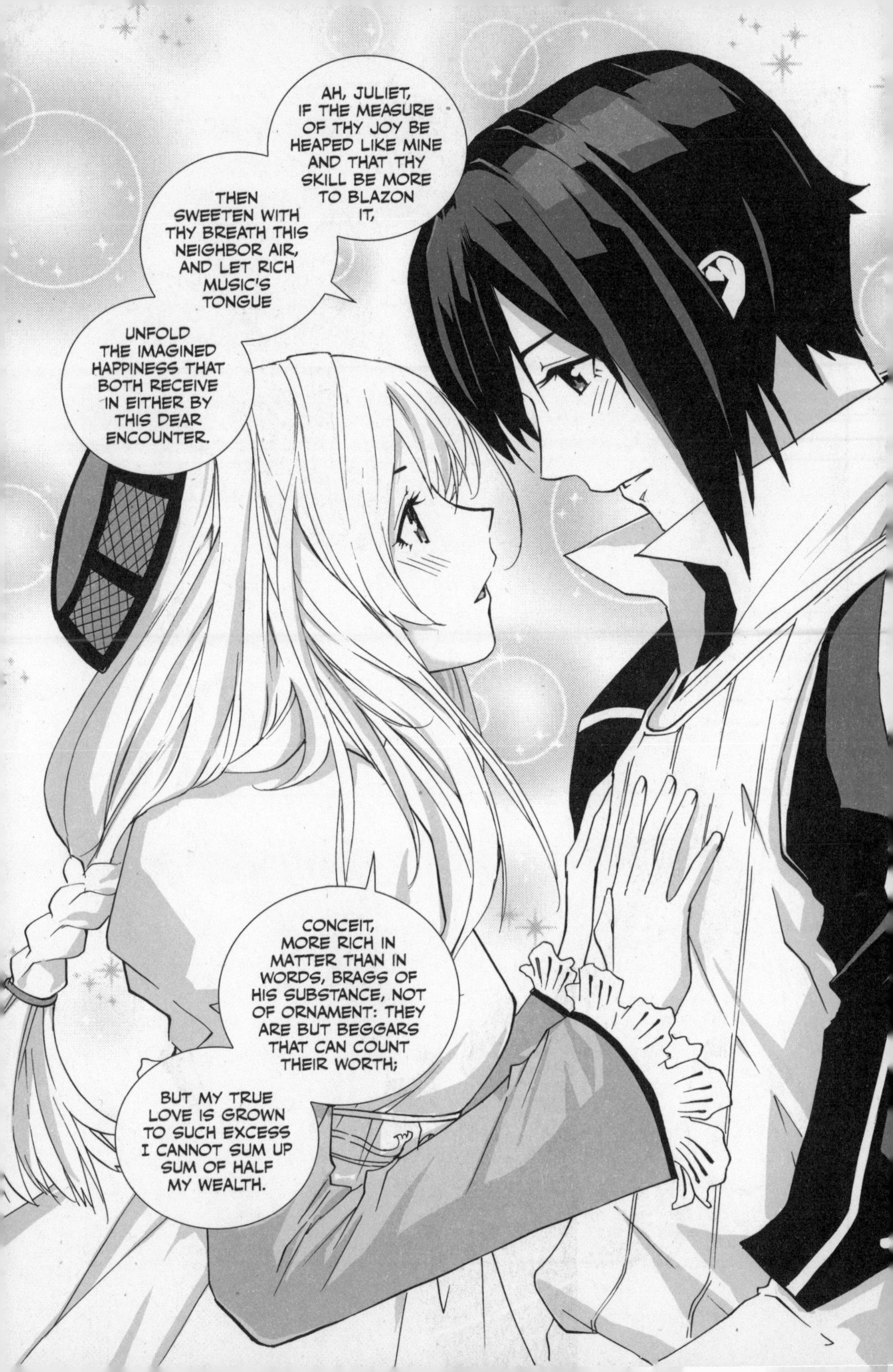
AH, JULIET, IF THE MEASURE OF THY JOY BE HEAPED LIKE MINE AND THAT THY SKILL BE MORE TO BLAZON IT,
THEN SWEETEN WITH THY BREATH THIS NEIGHBOR AIR, AND LET RICH MUSIC'S TONGUE
UNFOLD THE IMAGINED HAPPINESS THAT BOTH RECEIVE IN EITHER BY THIS DEAR ENCOUNTER.
CONCEIT, MORE RICH IN MATTER THAN IN WORDS, BRAGS OF HIS SUBSTANCE, NOT OF ORNAMENT: THEY ARE BUT BEGGARS THAT CAN COUNT THEIR WORTH;
BUT MY TRUE LOVE IS GROWN TO SUCH EXCESS I CANNOT SUM UP SUM OF HALF MY WEALTH.

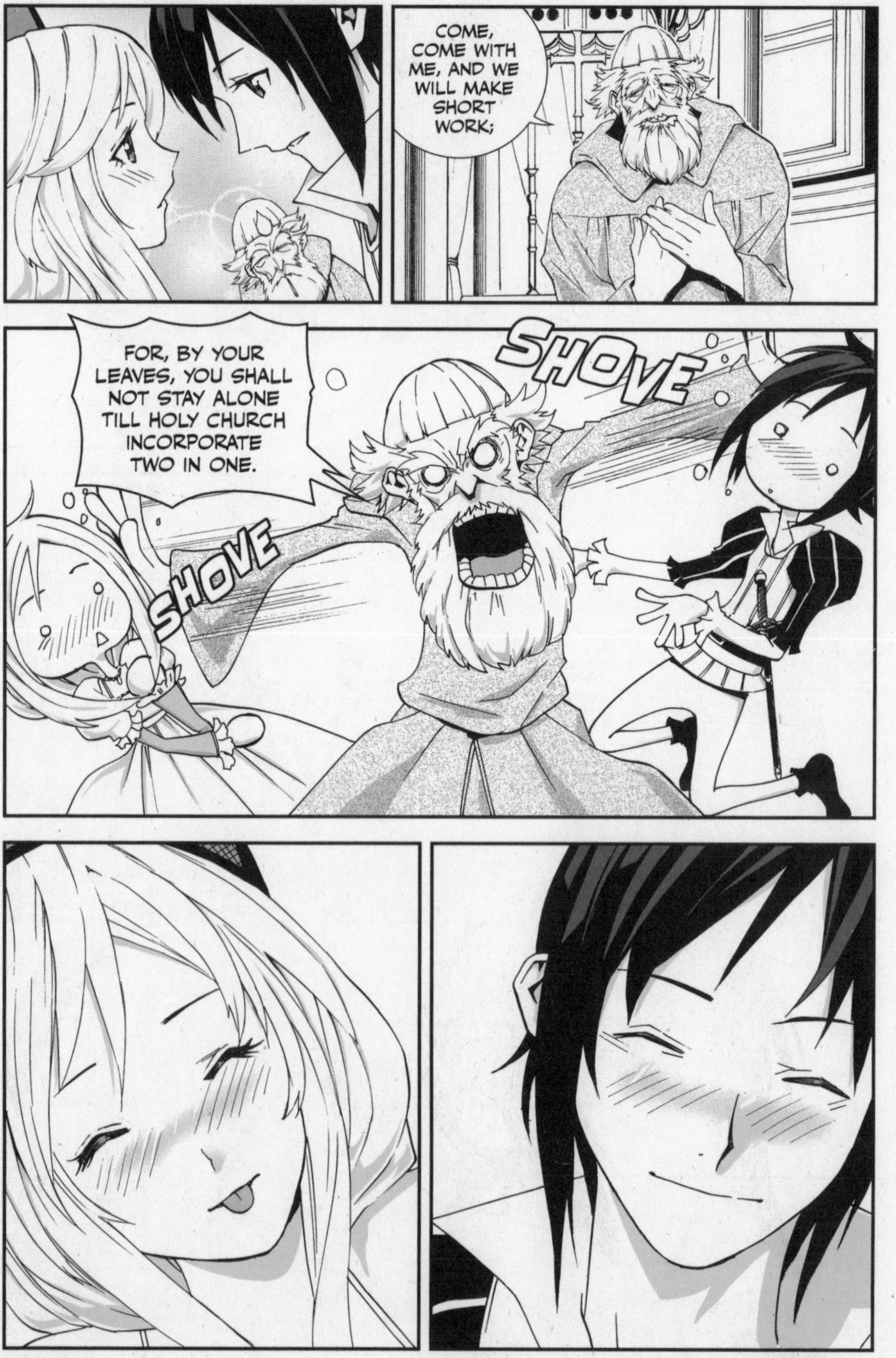
COME, COME WITH ME, AND WE WILL MAKE SHORT WORK;
SHOVE
FOR, BY YOUR LEAVES, YOU SHALL NOT STAY ALONE TILL HOLY CHURCH INCORPORATE TWO IN ONE.
SHOVE

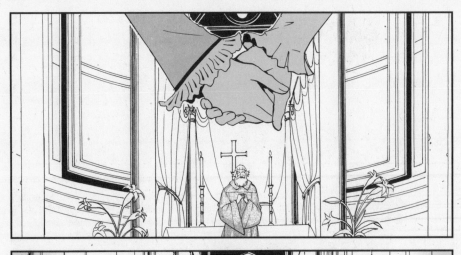

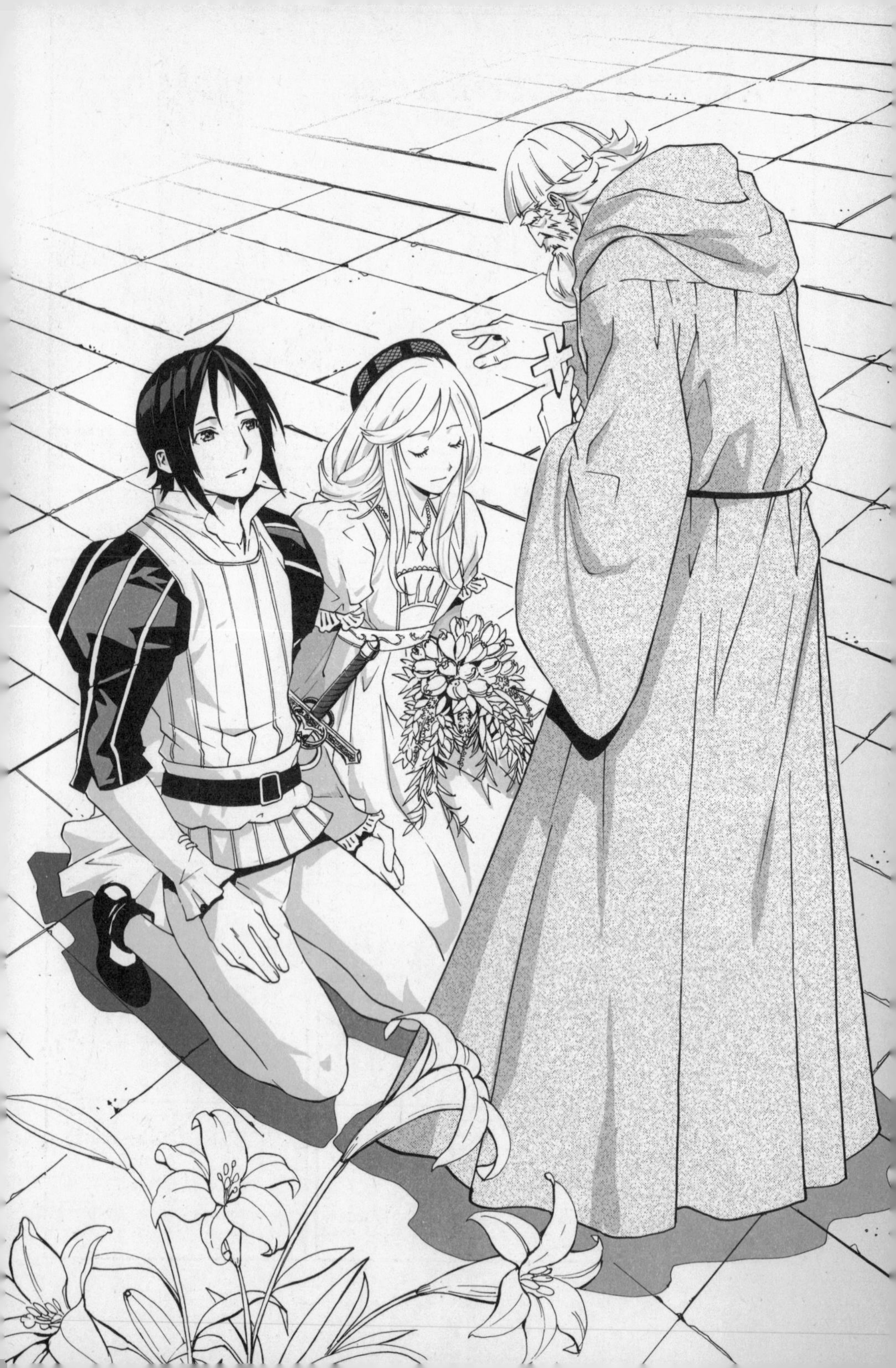

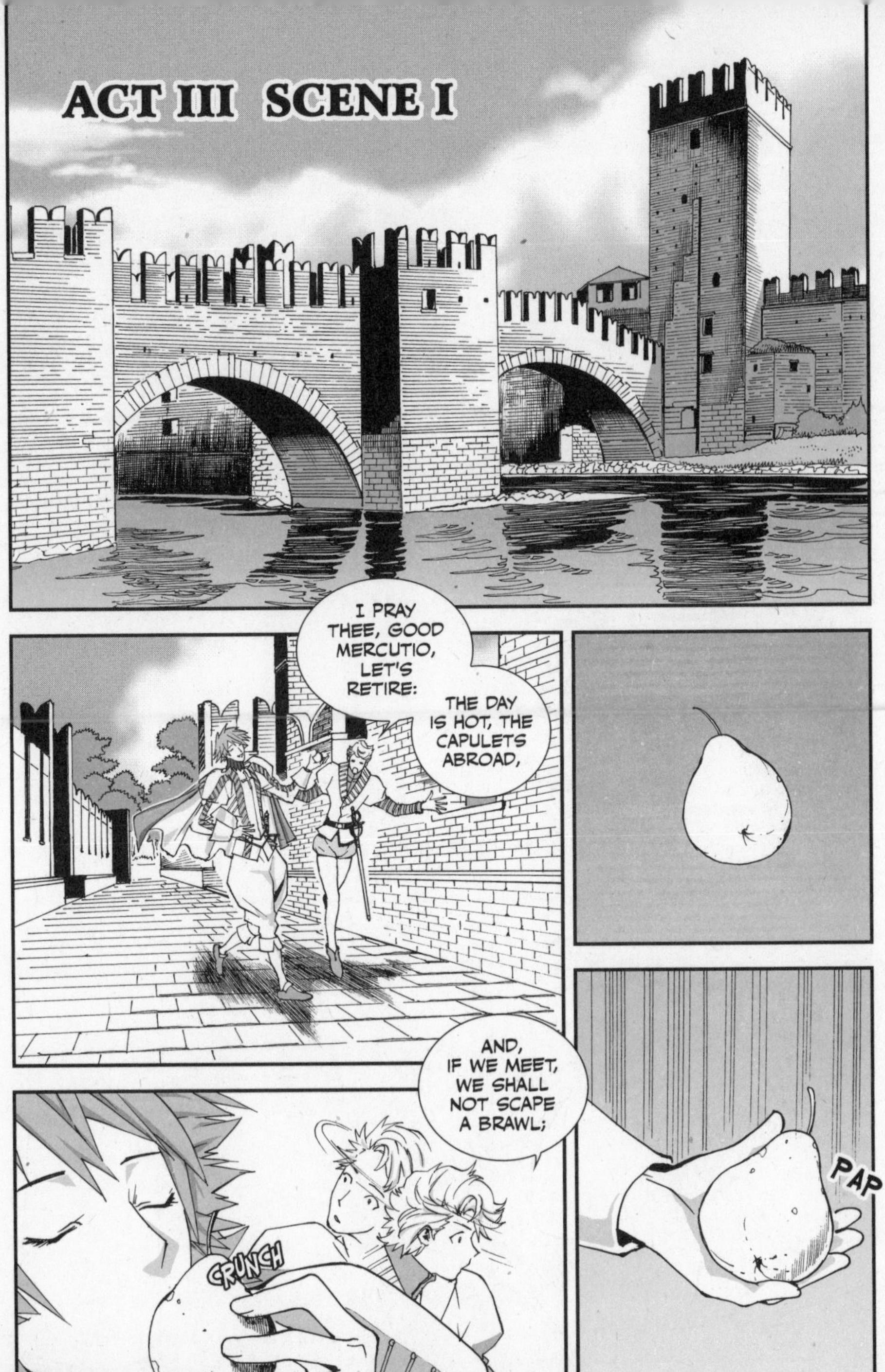
ACT III SCENE I
I PRAY THEE, GOOD MERCUTIO, LET'S RETIRE:
THE DAY IS HOT, THE CAPULETS ABROAD,
PAP
AND, IF WE MEET, WE SHALL NOT SCAPE A BRAWL;
CRUNCH

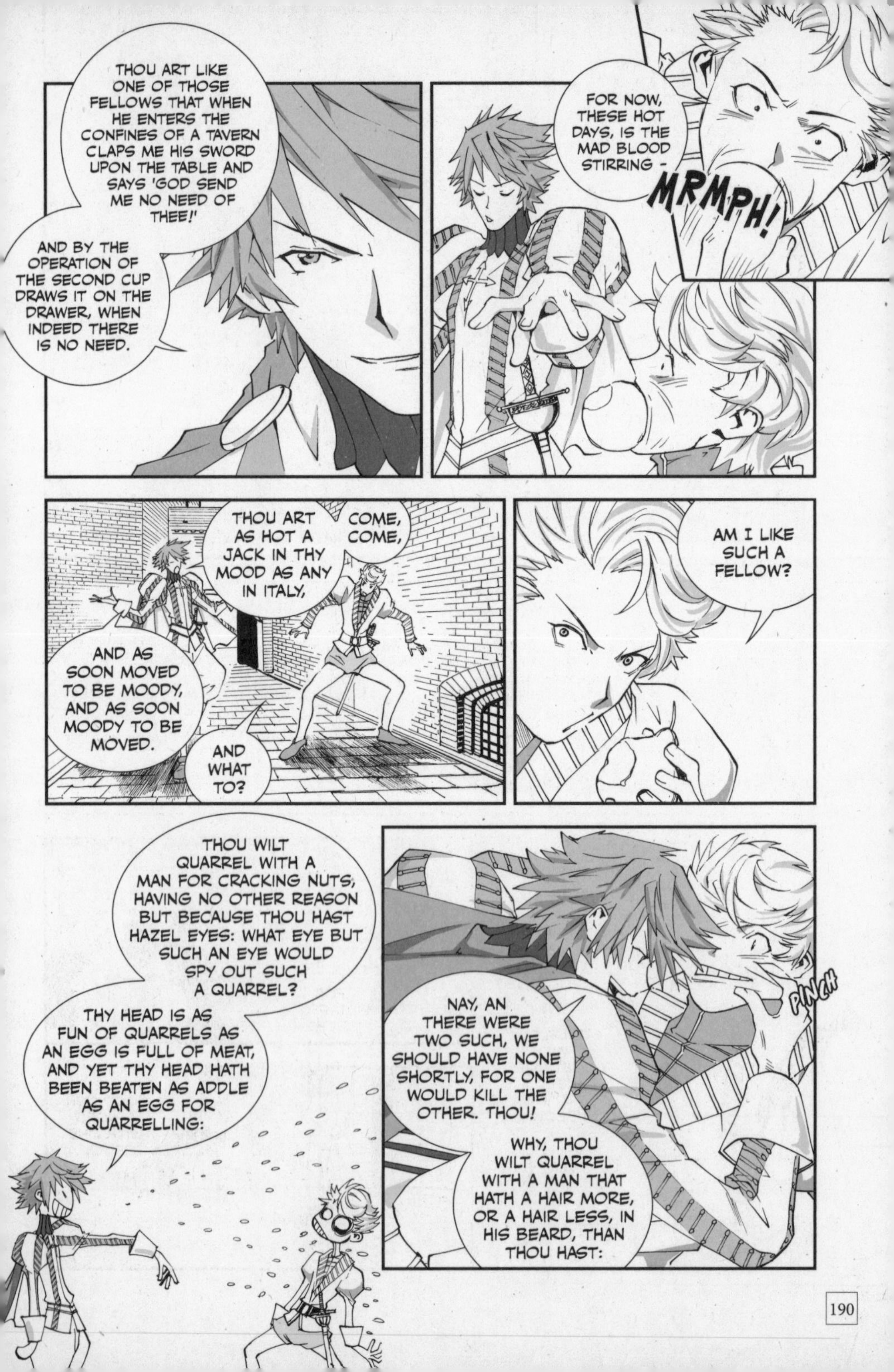

FOR NOW, THESE HOT DAYS, IS THE MAD BLOOD STIRRING -
MRMPH!
THOU ART LIKE ONE OF THOSE FELLOWS THAT WHEN HE ENTERS THE CONFINES OF A TAVERN CLAPS ME HIS SWORD UPON THE TABLE AND SAYS 'GOD SEND ME NO NEED OF THEE!'
AND BY THE OPERATION OF THE SECOND CUP DRAWS IT ON THE DRAWER, WHEN INDEED THERE IS NO NEED.
AM I LIKE SUCH A FELLOW?
COME, COME,
THOU ART AS HOT A JACK IN THY MOOD AS ANY IN ITALY,
AND AS SOON MOVED TO BE MOODY, AND AS SOON MOODY TO BE MOVED.
AND WHAT TO?
NAY, AN THERE WERE TWO SUCH, WE SHOULD HAVE NONE SHORTLY, FOR ONE WOULD KILL THE OTHER. THOU!
PINCH
WHY, THOU WILT QUARREL WITH A MAN THAT HATH A HAIR MORE, OR A HAIR LESS, IN HIS BEARD, THAN THOU HAST:
THOU WILT QUARREL WITH A MAN FOR CRACKING NUTS, HAVING NO OTHER REASON BUT BECAUSE THOU HAST HAZEL EYES: WHAT EYE BUT SUCH AN EYE WOULD SPY OUT SUCH A QUARREL?
THY HEAD IS AS FUN OF QUARRELS AS AN EGG IS FULL OF MEAT, AND YET THY HEAD HATH BEEN BEATEN AS ADDLE AS AN EGG FOR QUARRELLING:

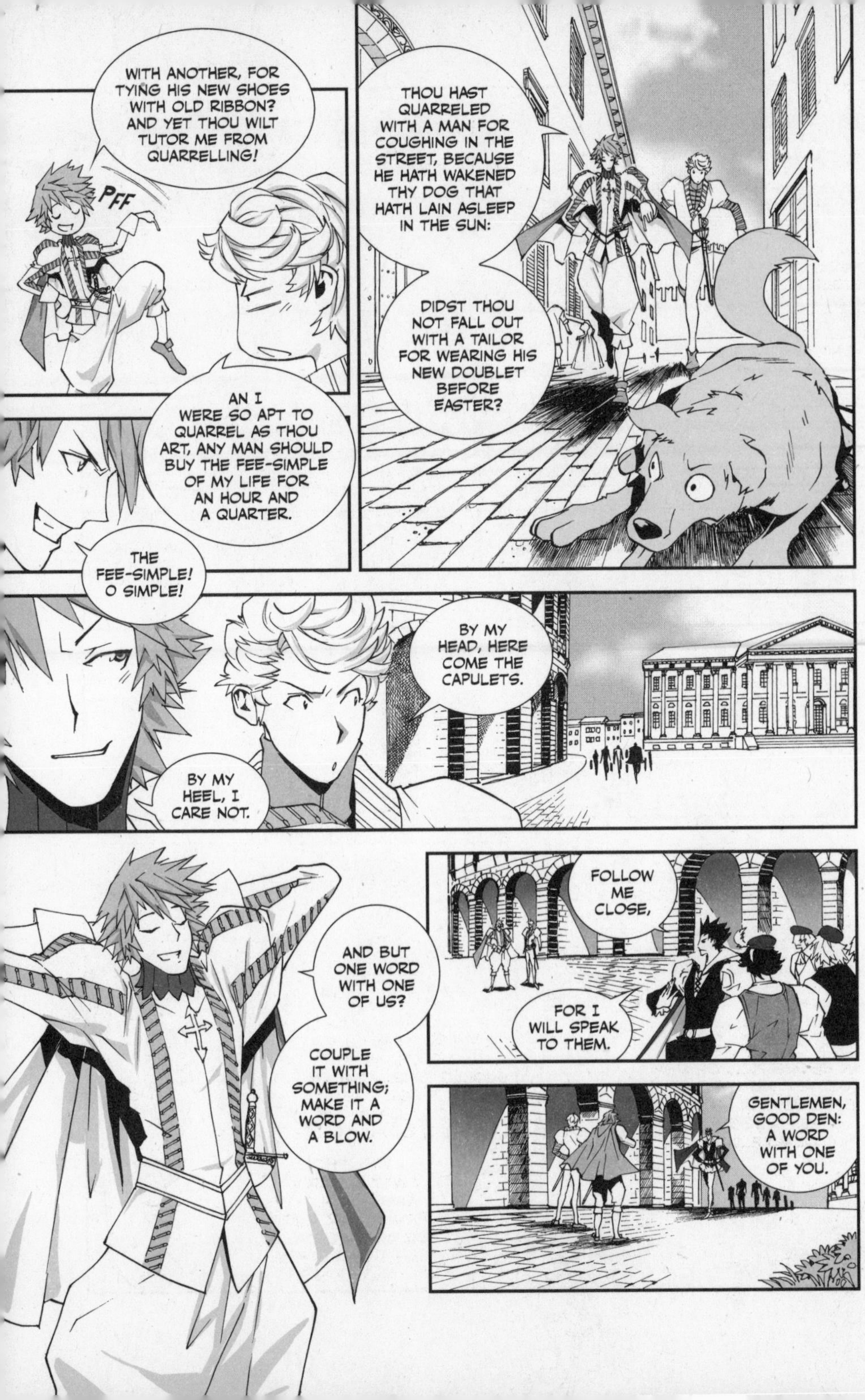
THOU HAST QUARRELED WITH A MAN FOR COUGHING IN THE STREET, BECAUSE HE HATH WAKENED THY DOG THAT HATH LAIN ASLEEP IN THE SUN:
DIDST THOU NOT FALL OUT WITH A TAILOR FOR WEARING HIS NEW DOUBLET BEFORE EASTER?
WITH ANOTHER, FOR TYING HIS NEW SHOES WITH OLD RIBBON? AND YET THOU WILT TUTOR ME FROM QUARRELLING!
PFF
AN I WERE SO APT TO QUARREL AS THOU ART, ANY MAN SHOULD BUY THE FEE-SIMPLE OF MY LIFE FOR AN HOUR AND A QUARTER.
THE FEE-SIMPLE! O SIMPLE!
BY MY HEAD, HERE COME THE CAPULETS.
BY MY HEEL, I CARE NOT.
FOLLOW ME CLOSE,
FOR I WILL SPEAK TO THEM.
GENTLEMEN, GOOD DEN: A WORD WITH ONE OF YOU.
AND BUT ONE WORD WITH ONE OF US?
COUPLE IT WITH SOMETHING; MAKE IT A WORD AND A BLOW.

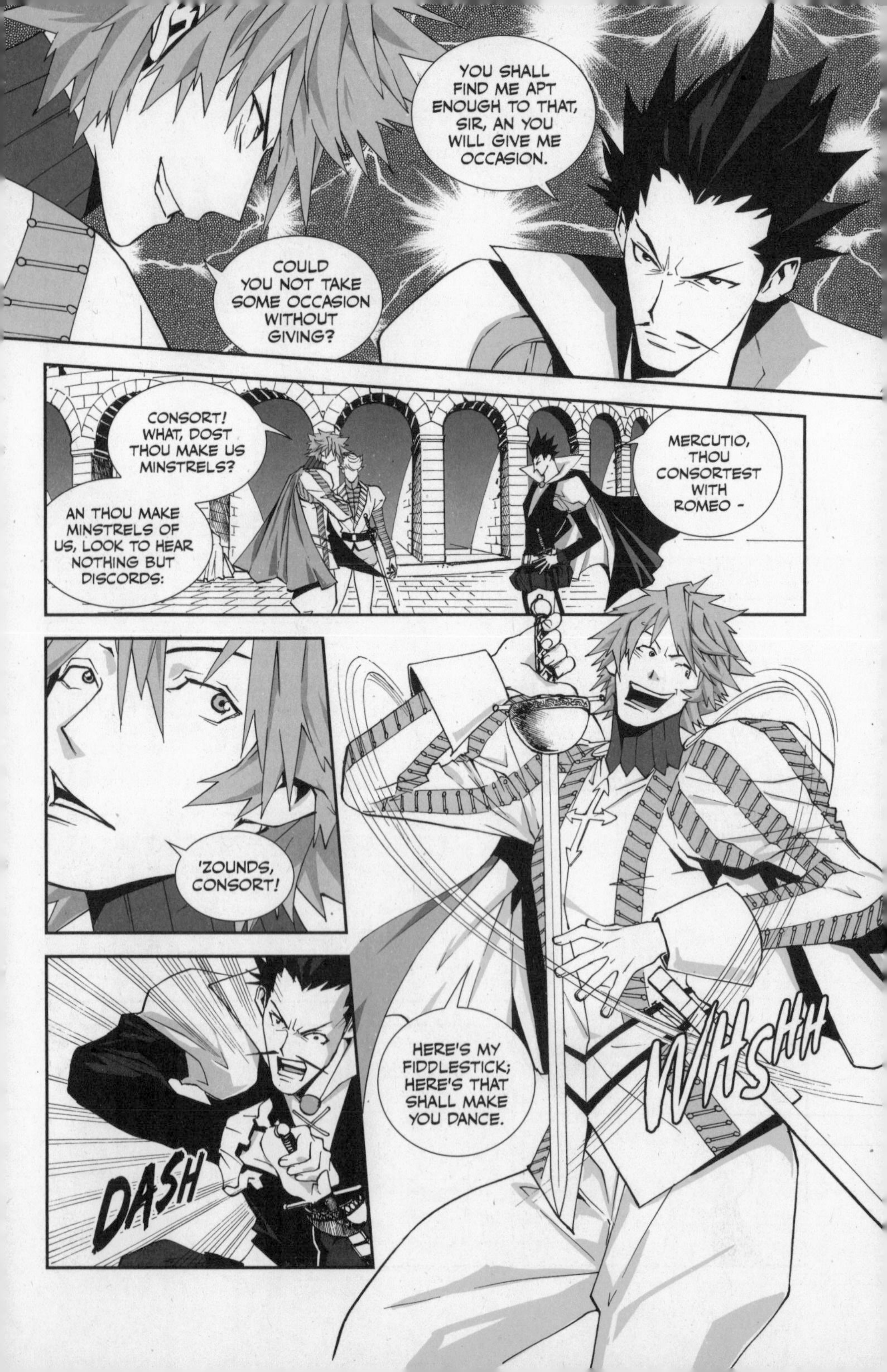
YOU SHALL FIND ME APT ENOUGH TO THAT, SIR, AN YOU WILL GIVE ME OCCASION.
COULD YOU NOT TAKE SOME OCCASION WITHOUT GIVING?
MERCUTIO, THOU CONSORTEST WITH ROMEO -
CONSORT! WHAT, DOST THOU MAKE US MINSTRELS?
AN THOU MAKE MINSTRELS OF US, LOOK TO HEAR NOTHING BUT DISCORDS:
HERE'S MY FIDDLESTICK; HERE'S THAT SHALL MAKE YOU DANCE.
WHSHH
'ZOUNDS, CONSORT!
DASH

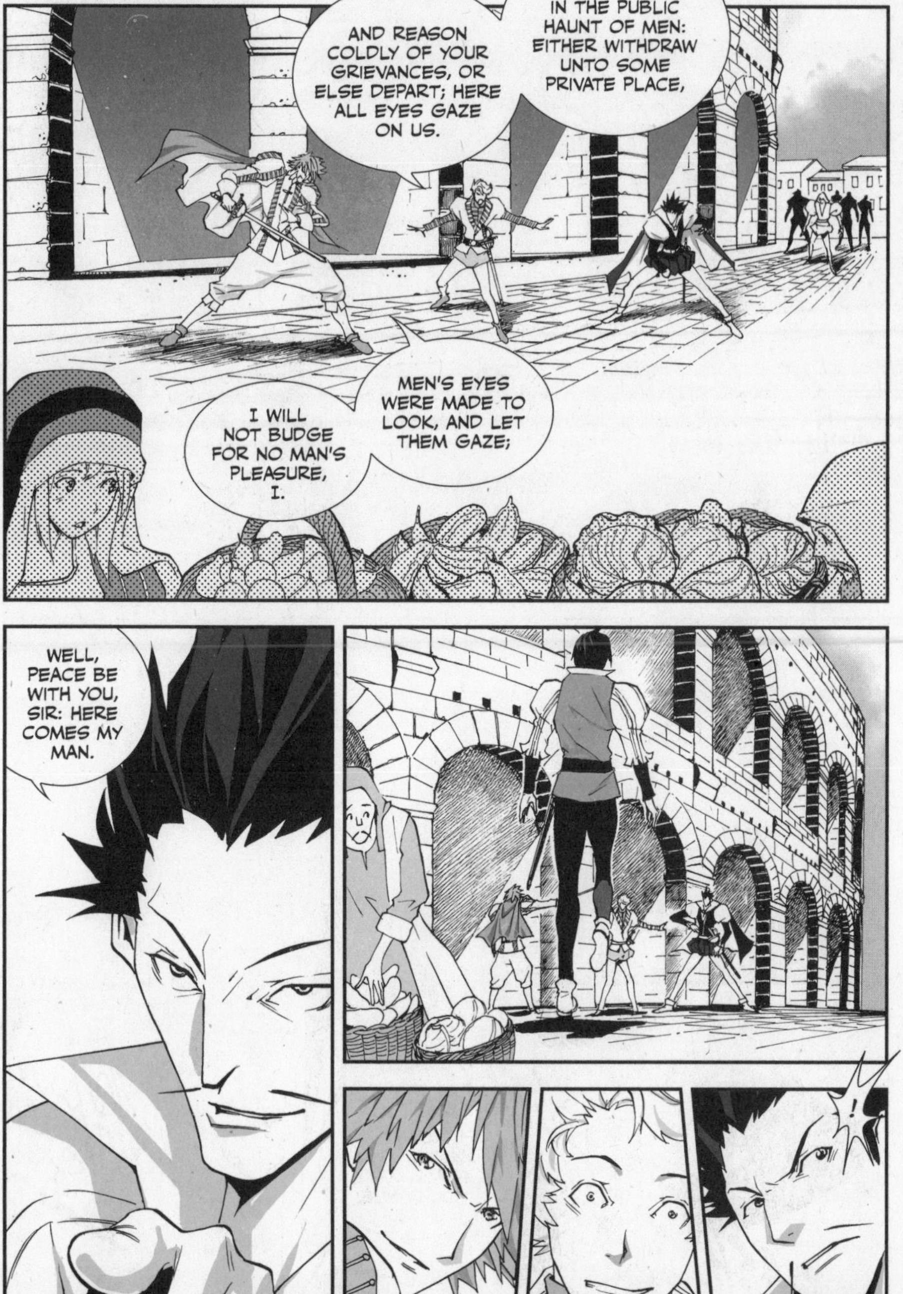
WE TALK HERE IN THE PUBLIC HAUNT OF MEN: EITHER WITHDRAW UNTO SOME PRIVATE PLACE,
AND REASON COLDLY OF YOUR GRIEVANCES, OR ELSE DEPART; HERE ALL EYES GAZE ON US.
MEN'S EYES WERE MADE TO LOOK, AND LET THEM GAZE;
I WILL NOT BUDGE FOR NO MAN'S PLEASURE, I.
!
WELL, PEACE BE WITH YOU, SIR: HERE COMES MY MAN.

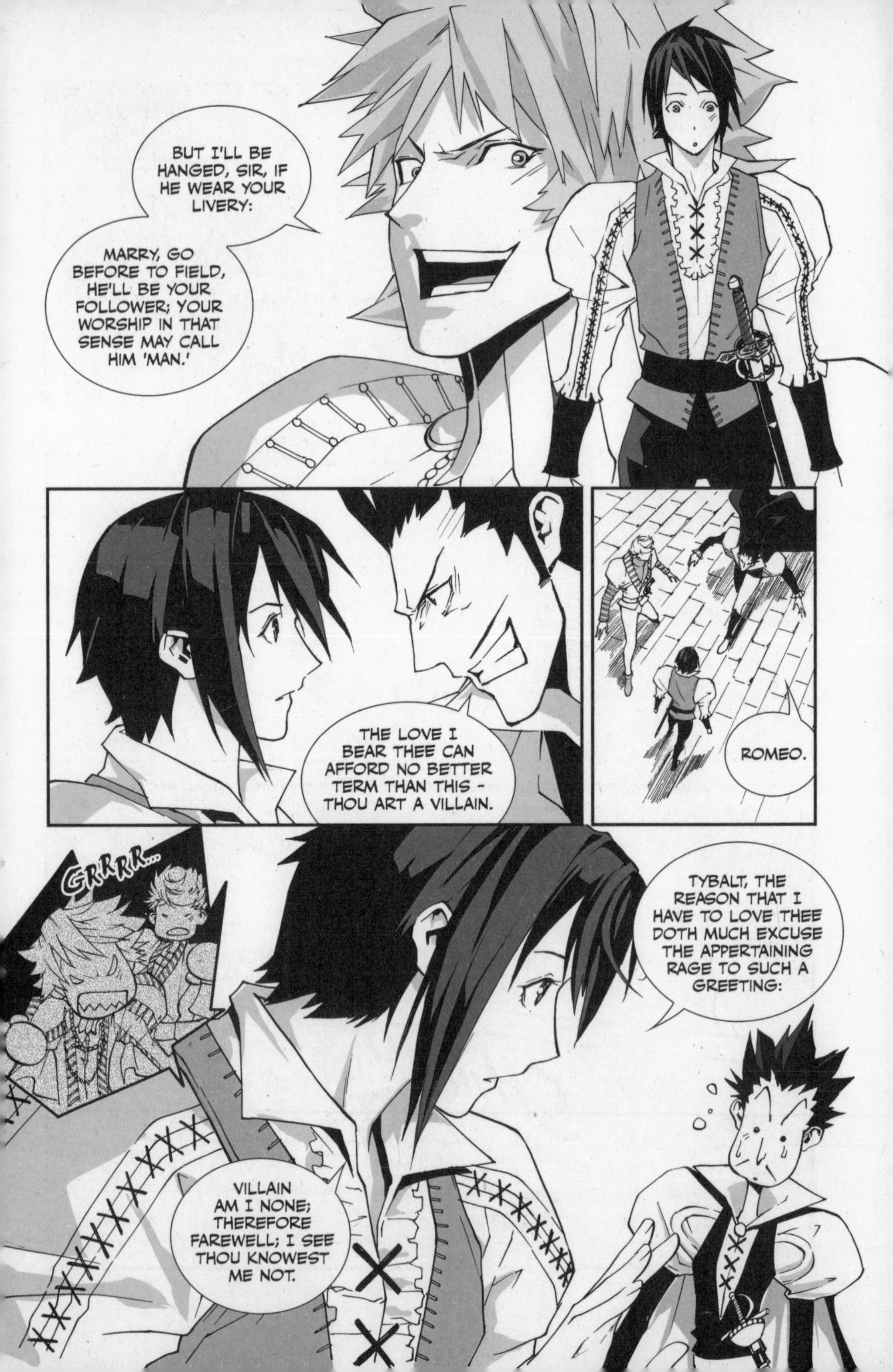
BUT I'LL BE HANGED, SIR, IF HE WEAR YOUR LIVERY:
MARRY, GO BEFORE TO FIELD, HE'LL BE YOUR FOLLOWER; YOUR WORSHIP IN THAT SENSE MAY CALL HIM 'MAN.'
ROMEO.
THE LOVE I BEAR THEE CAN AFFORD NO BETTER TERM THAN THIS - THOU ART A VILLAIN.
TYBALT, THE REASON THAT I HAVE TO LOVE THEE DOTH MUCH EXCUSE THE APPERTAINING RAGE TO SUCH A GREETING:
GRRRR...
VILLAIN AM I NONE; THEREFORE FAREWELL; I SEE THOU KNOWEST ME NOT.

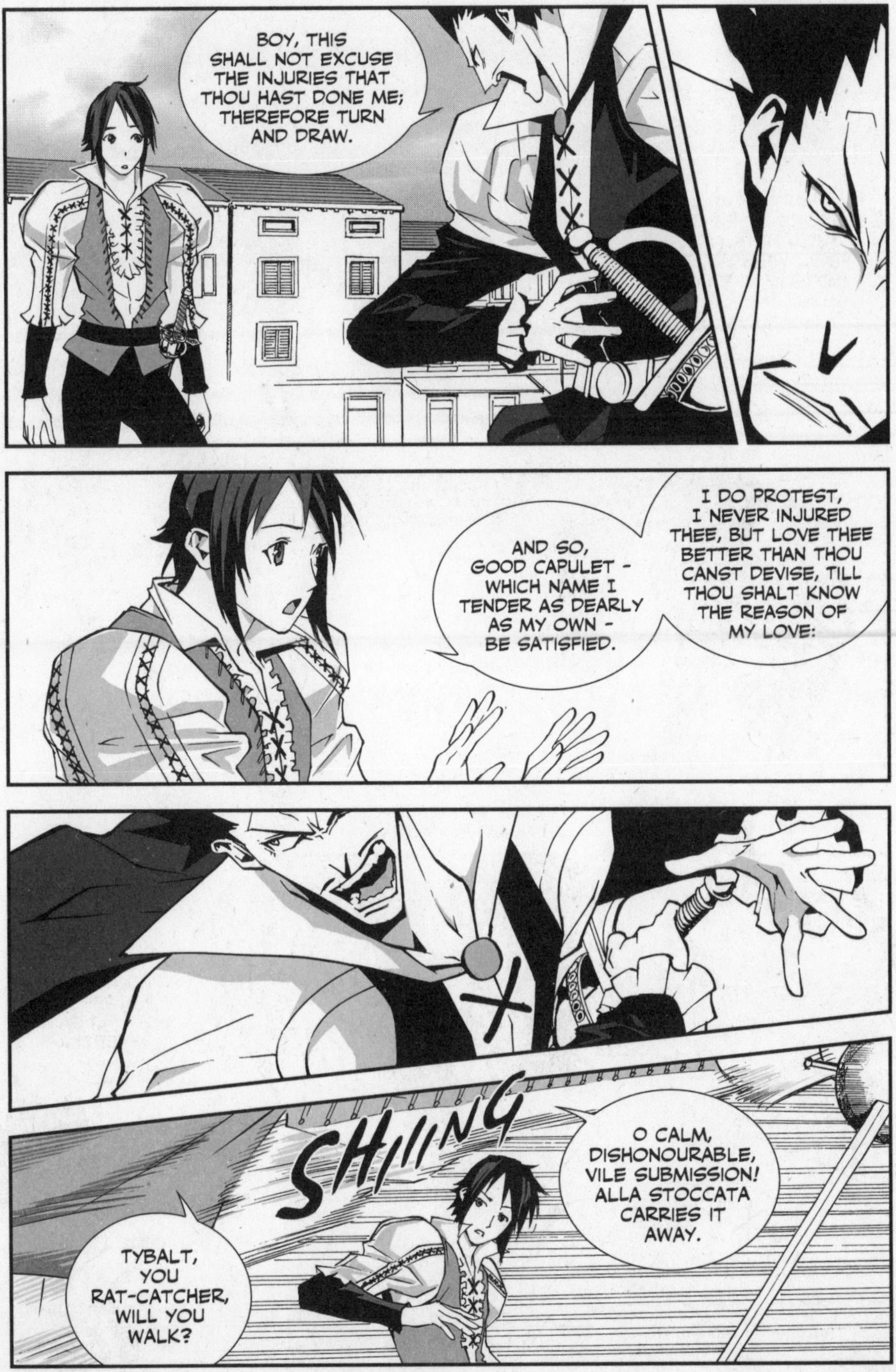
BOY, THIS SHALL NOT EXCUSE THE INJURIES THAT THOU HAST DONE ME; THEREFORE TURN AND DRAW.
I DO PROTEST, I NEVER INJURED THEE, BUT LOVE THEE BETTER THAN THOU CANST DEVISE, TILL THOU SHALT KNOW THE REASON OF MY LOVE:
AND SO, GOOD CAPULET - WHICH NAME I TENDER AS DEARLY AS MY OWN - BE SATISFIED.
SHIIING
O CALM, DISHONOURABLE, VILE SUBMISSION! ALLA STOCCATA CARRIES IT AWAY.
TYBALT, YOU RAT-CATCHER, WILL YOU WALK?

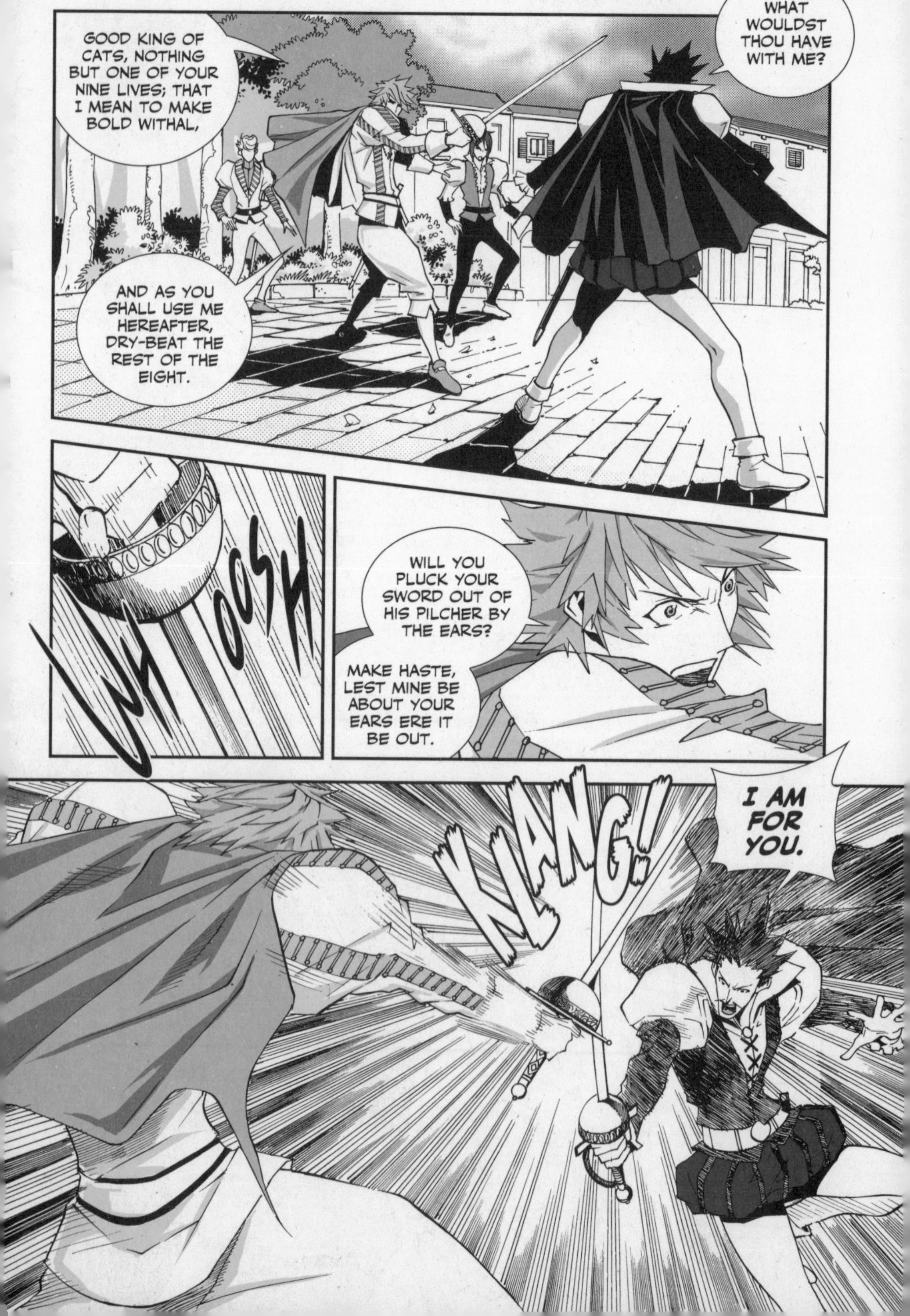
WHAT WOULDST THOU HAVE WITH ME?
GOOD KING OF CATS, NOTHING BUT ONE OF YOUR NINE LIVES; THAT I MEAN TO MAKE BOLD WITHAL,
AND AS YOU SHALL USE ME HEREAFTER, DRY-BEAT THE REST OF THE EIGHT.
WILL YOU PLUCK YOUR SWORD OUT OF HIS PILCHER BY THE EARS?
MAKE HASTE, LEST MINE BE ABOUT YOUR EARS ERE IT BE OUT.
WHOOSH
I AM FOR YOU.
KLANG!!

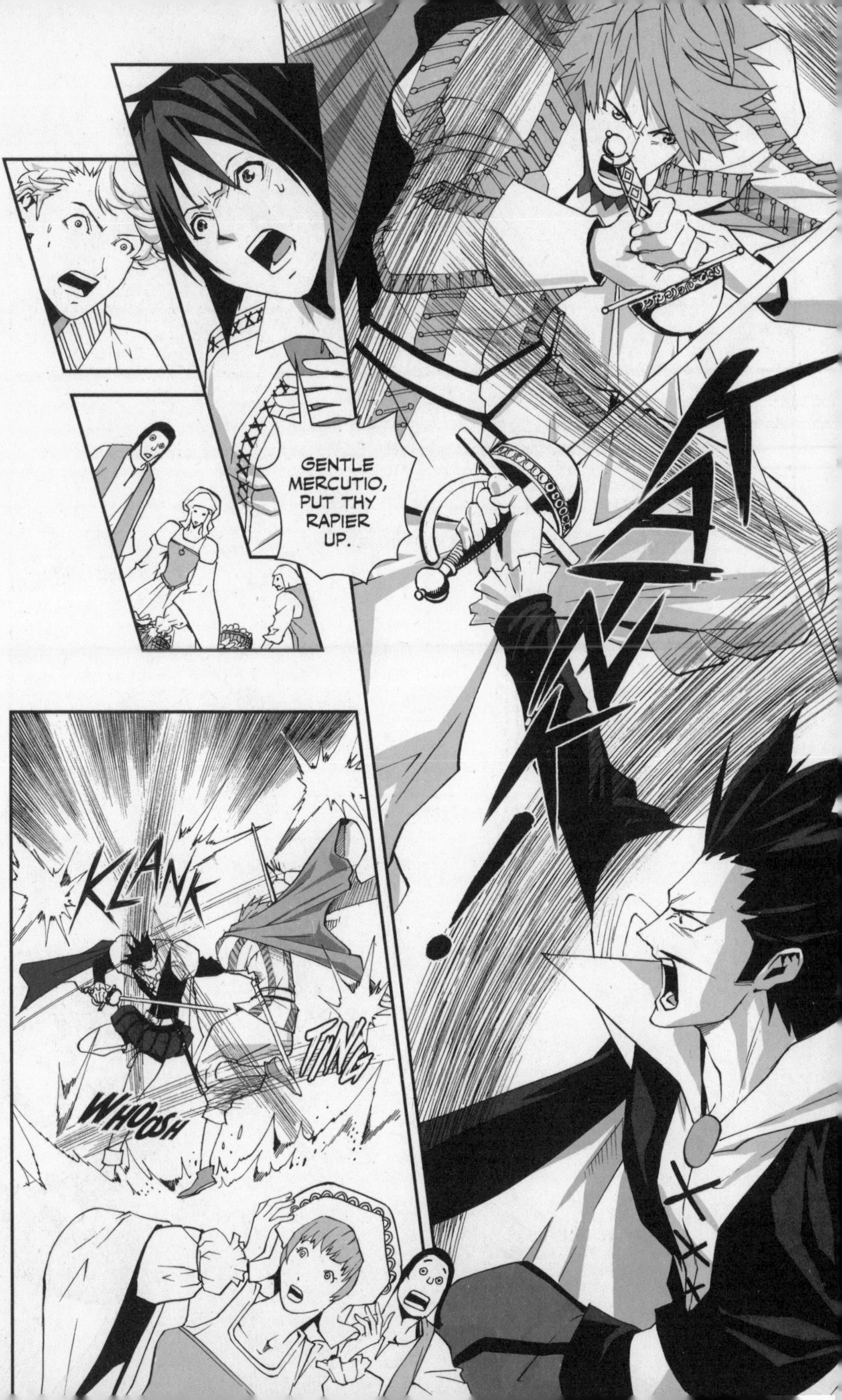
GENTLE MERCUTIO, PUT THY RAPIER UP.
KLANK
TING
WHOOSH

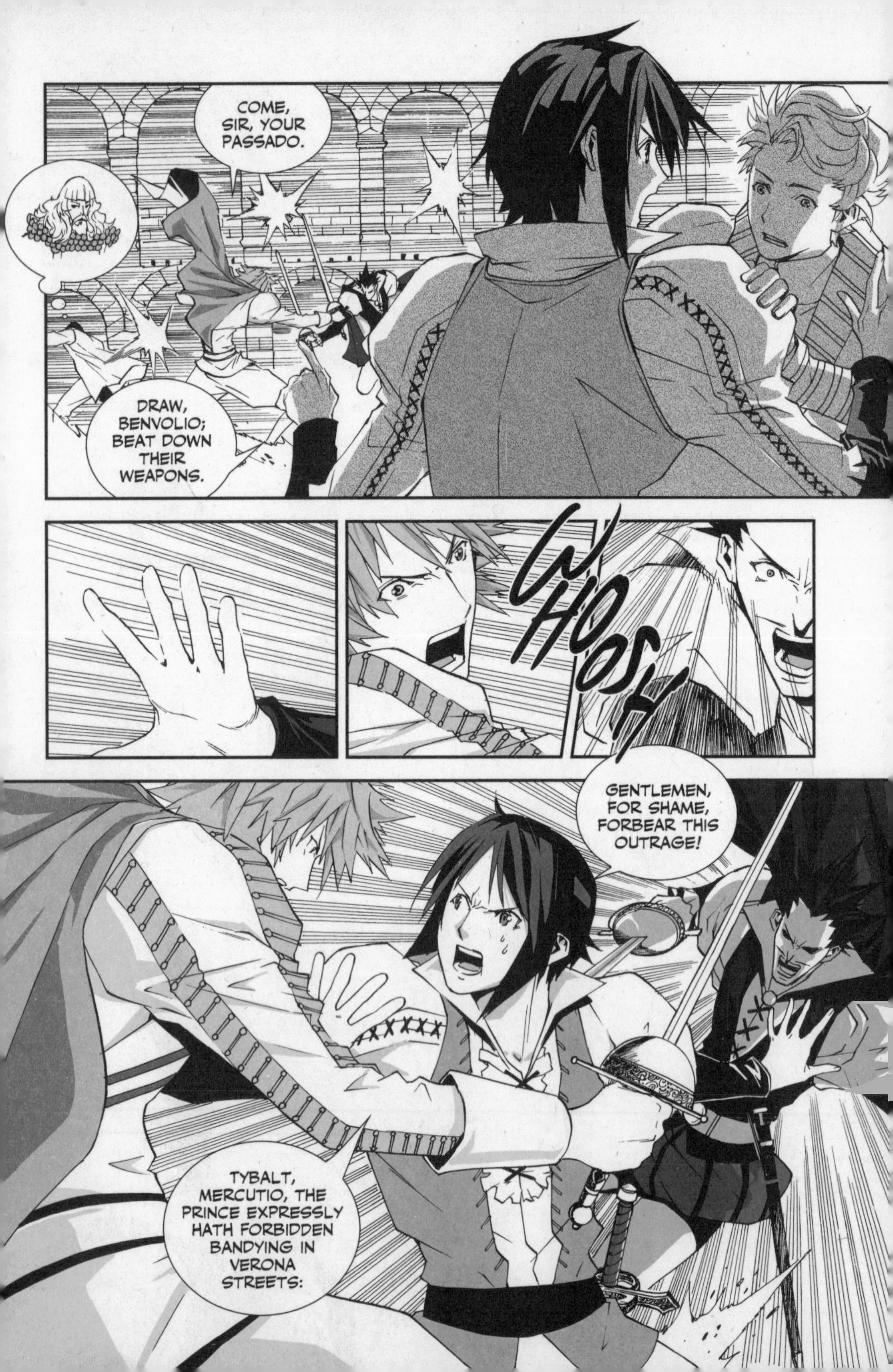
COME, SIR, YOUR PASSADO.
DRAW, BENVOLIO; BEAT DOWN THEIR WEAPONS.
WHOOSH
GENTLEMEN, FOR SHAME, FORBEAR THIS OUTRAGE!
TYBALT, MERCUTIO, THE PRINCE EXPRESSLY HATH FORBIDDEN BANDYING IN VERONA STREETS:

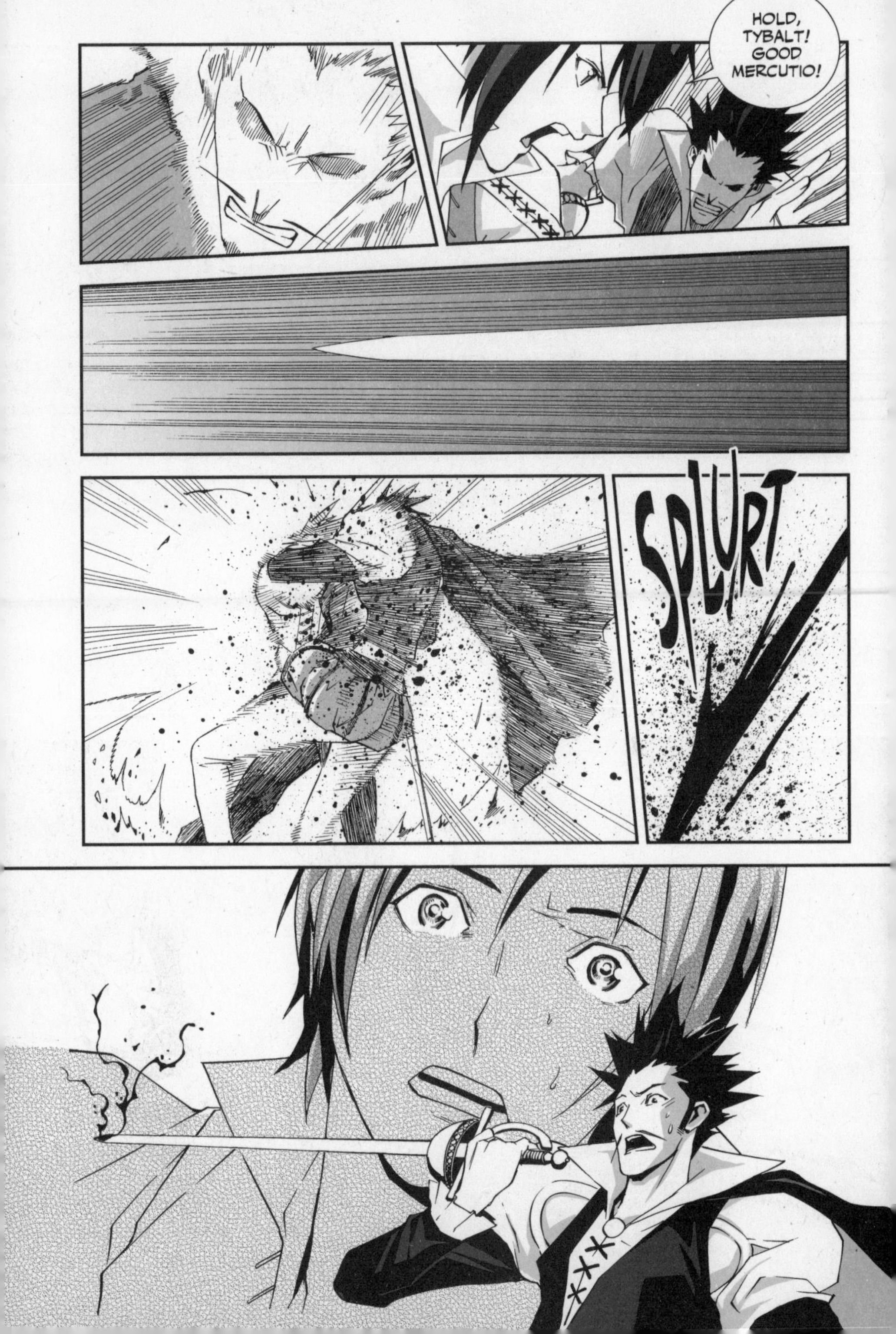
HOLD, TYBALT! GOOD MERCUTIO!
SPLURT

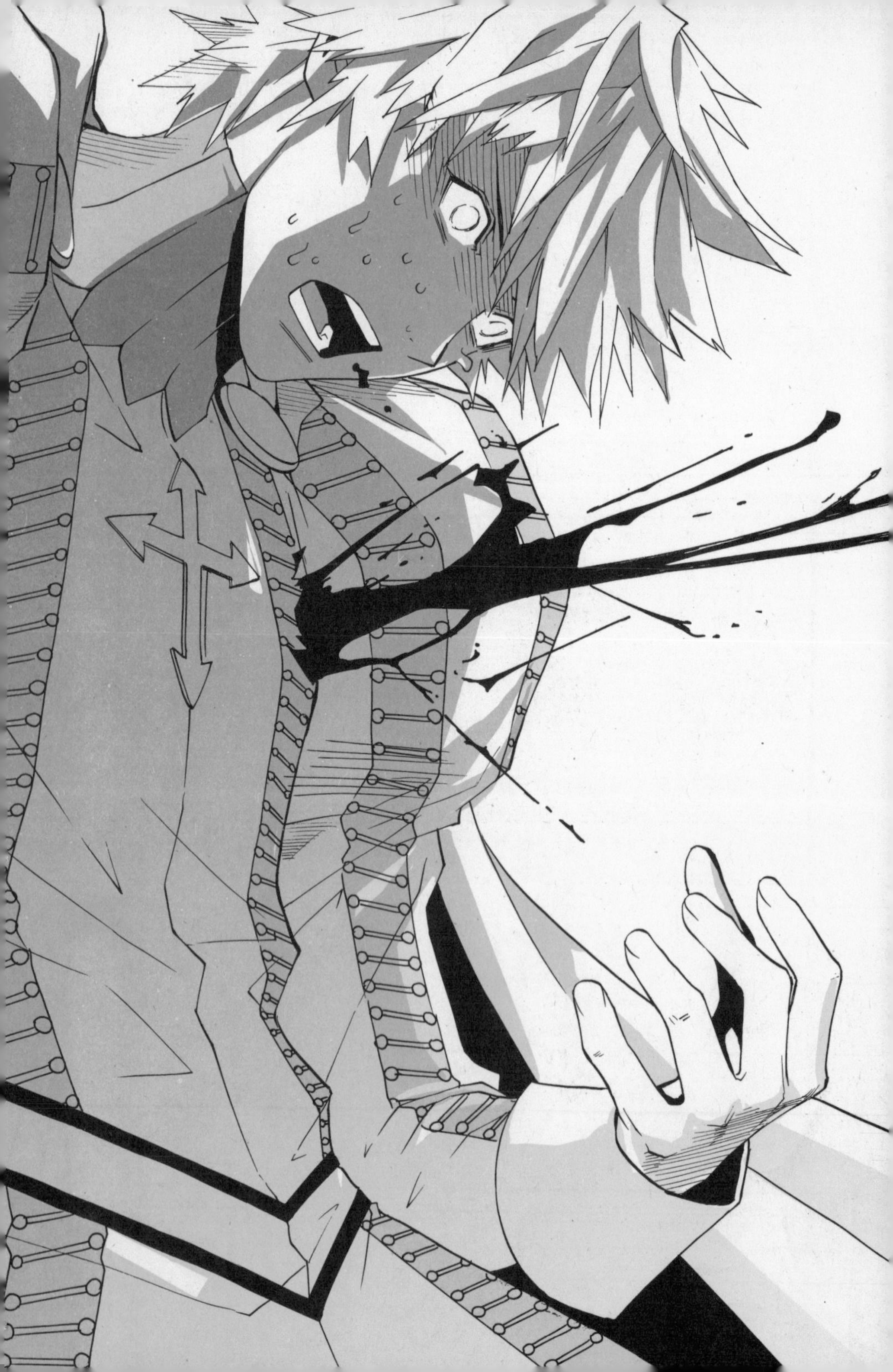

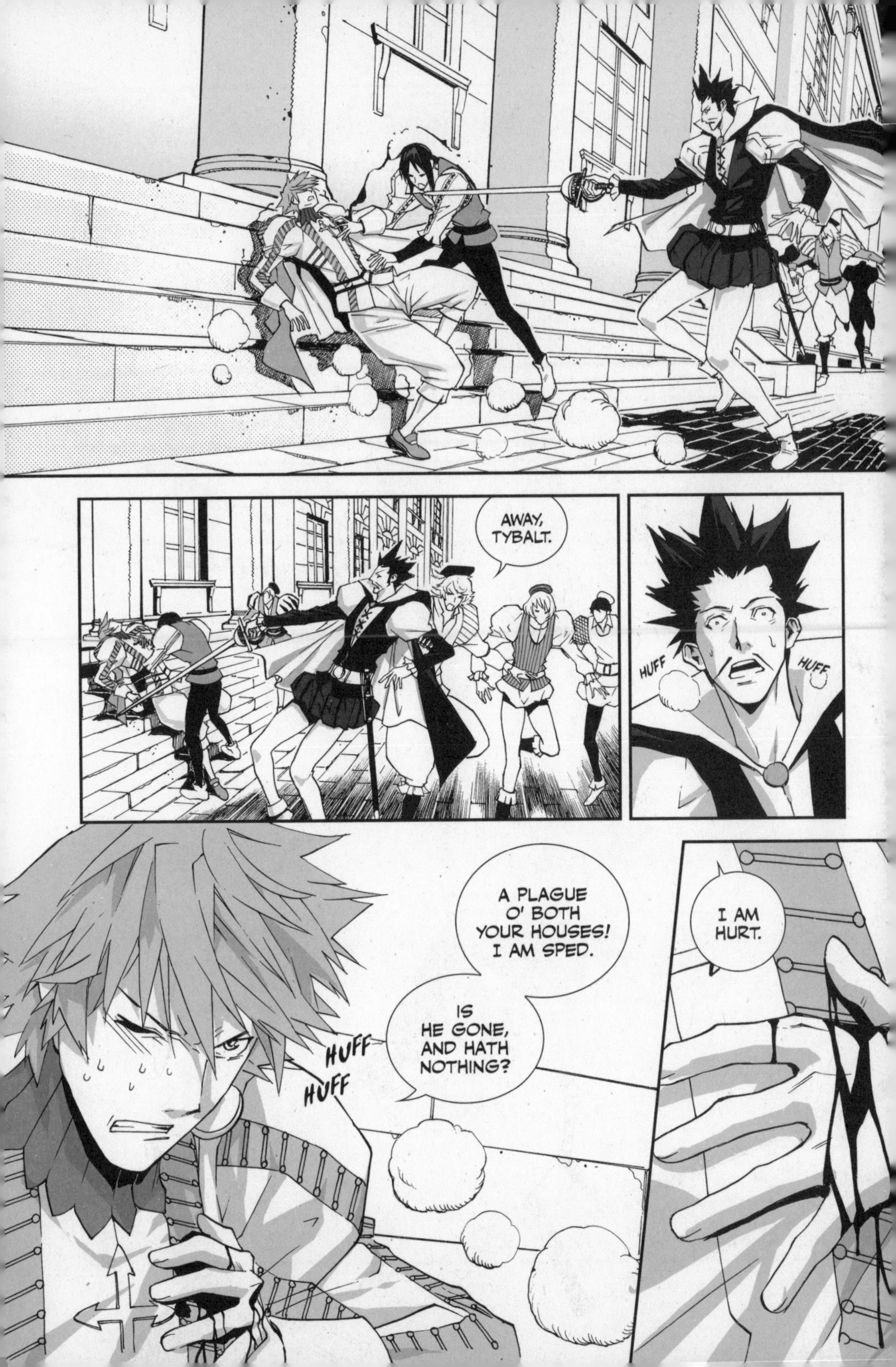
HUFF
HUFF
AWAY, TYBALT.
I AM HURT.
A PLAGUE O' BOTH YOUR HOUSES! I AM SPED.
IS HE GONE, AND HATH NOTHING?
HUFF
HUFF

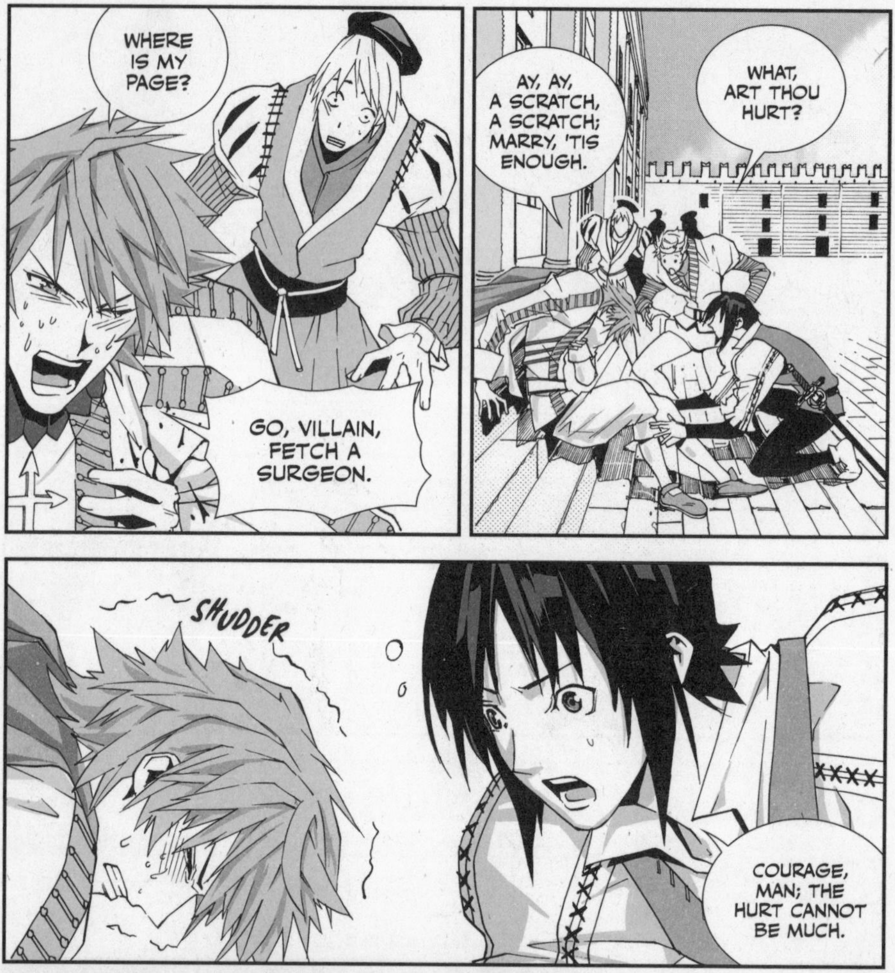
WHAT, ART THOU HURT?
AY, AY, A SCRATCH, A SCRATCH; MARRY, 'TIS ENOUGH.
WHERE IS MY PAGE?
GO, VILLAIN, FETCH A SURGEON.
SHUDDER
COURAGE, MAN; THE HURT CANNOT BE MUCH.
KOFF
THUD

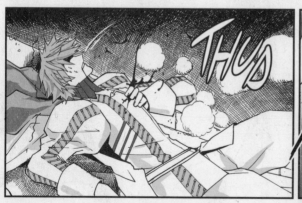

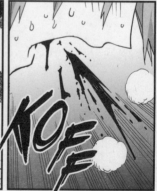

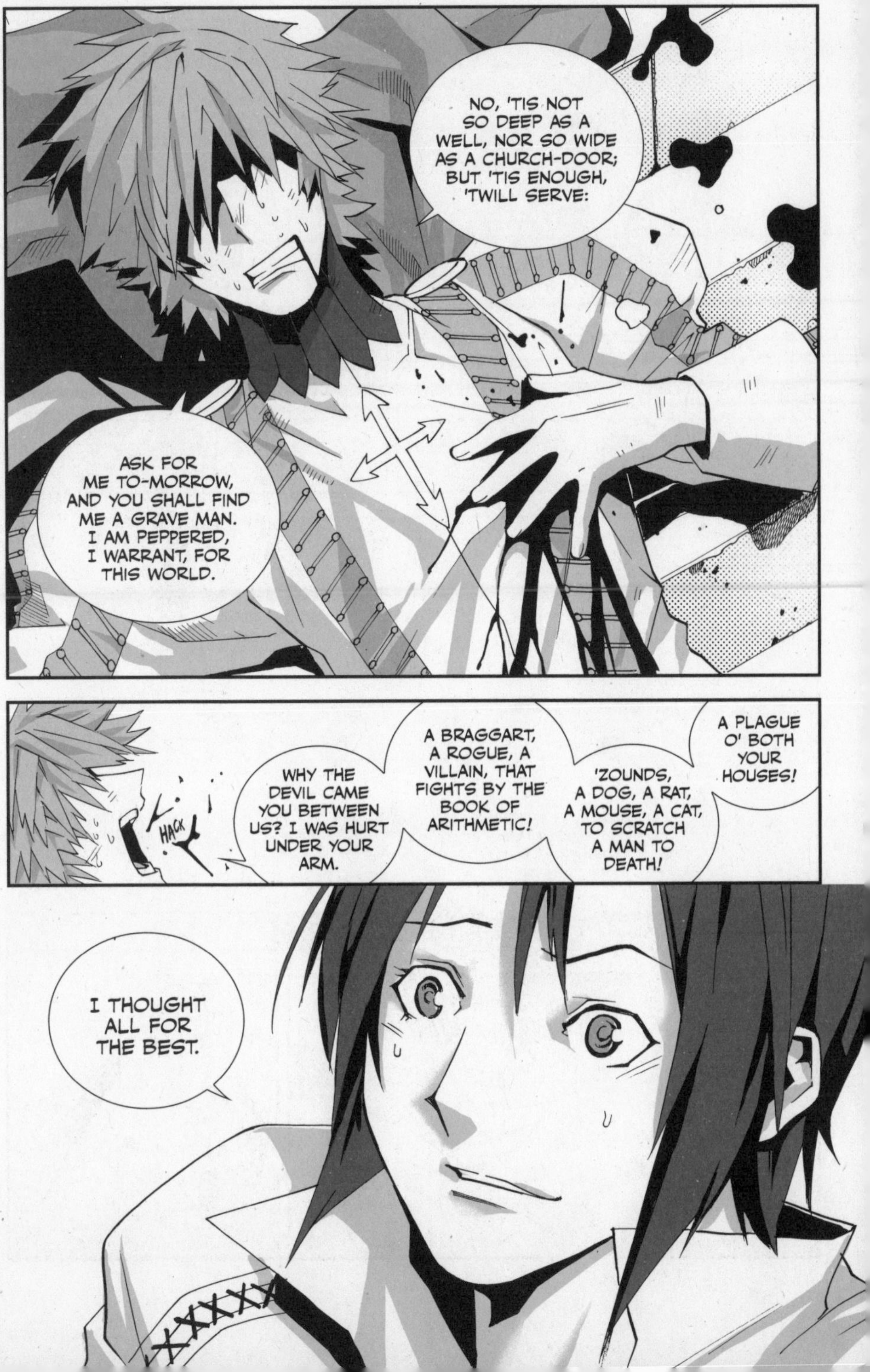
NO, 'TIS NOT SO DEEP AS A WELL, NOR SO WIDE AS A CHURCH-DOOR; BUT 'TIS ENOUGH, 'TWILL SERVE:
ASK FOR ME TO-MORROW, AND YOU SHALL FIND ME A GRAVE MAN. I AM PEPPERED, I WARRANT, FOR THIS WORLD.
A PLAGUE O' BOTH YOUR HOUSES!
'ZOUNDS, A DOG, A RAT, A MOUSE, A CAT, TO SCRATCH A MAN TO DEATH!
A BRAGGART, A ROGUE, A VILLAIN, THAT FIGHTS BY THE BOOK OF ARITHMETIC!
WHY THE DEVIL CAME YOU BETWEEN US? I WAS HURT UNDER YOUR ARM.
HACK
I THOUGHT ALL FOR THE BEST.

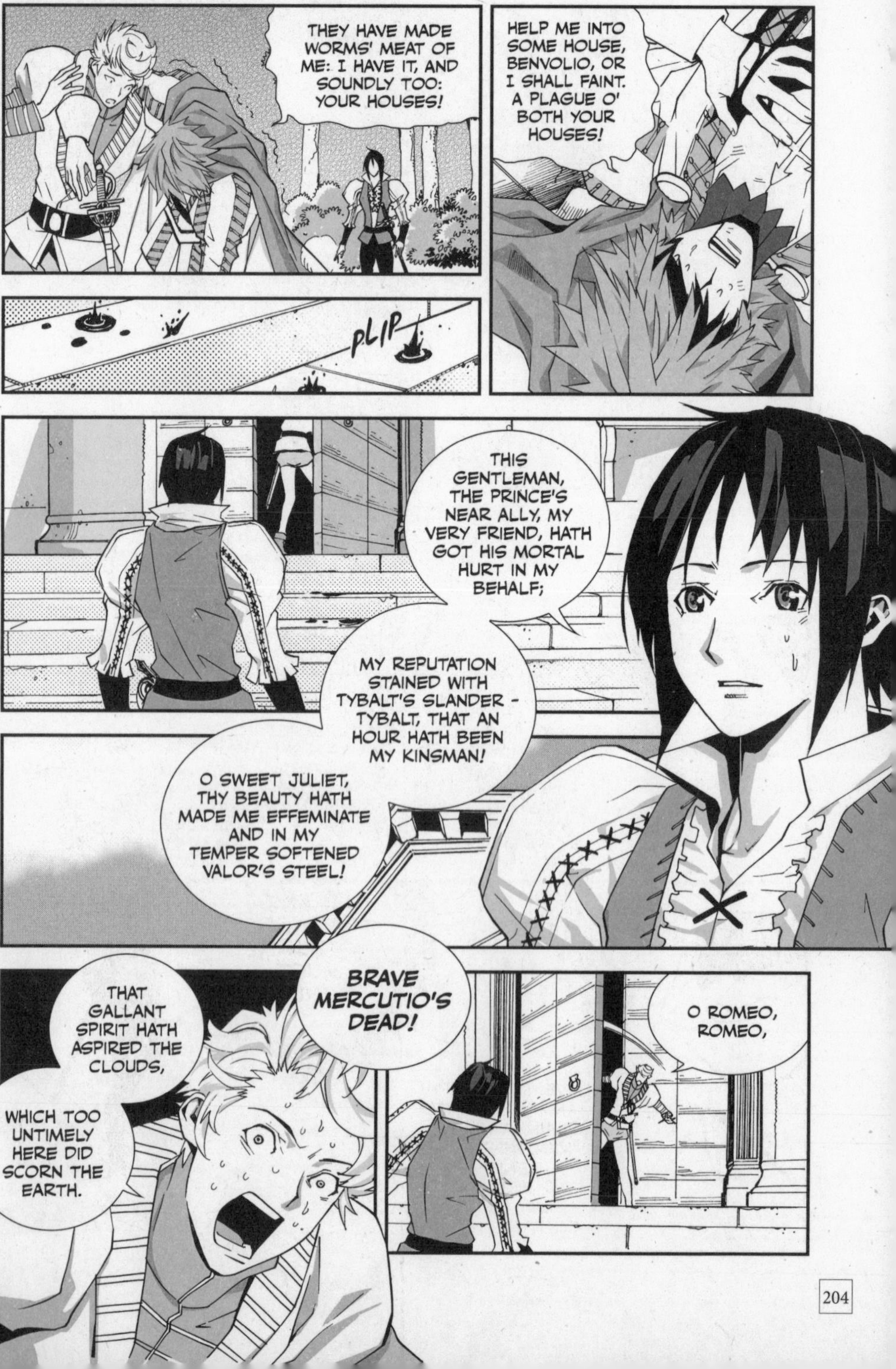
HELP ME INTO SOME HOUSE, BENVOLIO, OR I SHALL FAINT. A PLAGUE O' BOTH YOUR HOUSES!
THEY HAVE MADE WORMS' MEAT OF ME: I HAVE IT, AND SOUNDLY TOO: YOUR HOUSES!
PLIP
THIS GENTLEMAN, THE PRINCE'S NEAR ALLY, MY VERY FRIEND, HATH GOT HIS MORTAL HURT IN MY BEHALF;
MY REPUTATION STAINED WITH TYBALT'S SLANDER - TYBALT, THAT AN HOUR HATH BEEN MY KINSMAN!
O SWEET JULIET, THY BEAUTY HATH MADE ME EFFEMINATE AND IN MY TEMPER SOFTENED VALOR'S STEEL!
O ROMEO, ROMEO,
BRAVE MERCUTIO'S DEAD!
THAT GALLANT SPIRIT HATH ASPIRED THE CLOUDS,
WHICH TOO UNTIMELY HERE DID SCORN THE EARTH.

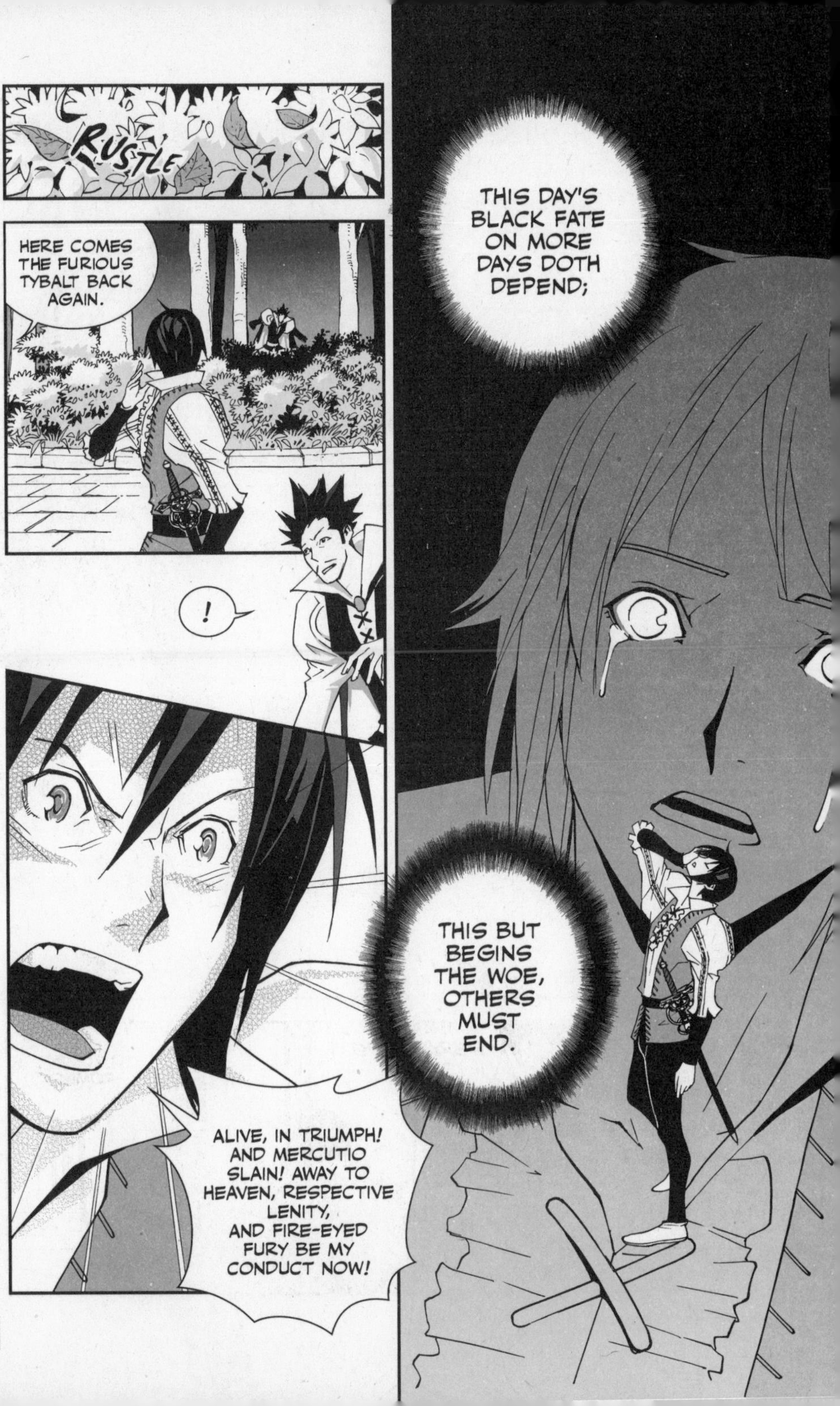
THIS DAY'S BLACK FATE ON MORE DAYS DOTH DEPEND;
THIS BUT BEGINS THE WOE, OTHERS MUST END.
RUSTLE
HERE COMES THE FURIOUS TYBALT BACK AGAIN.
!
ALIVE, IN TRIUMPH! AND MERCUTIO SLAIN! AWAY TO HEAVEN, RESPECTIVE LENITY, AND FIRE-EYED FURY BE MY CONDUCT NOW!

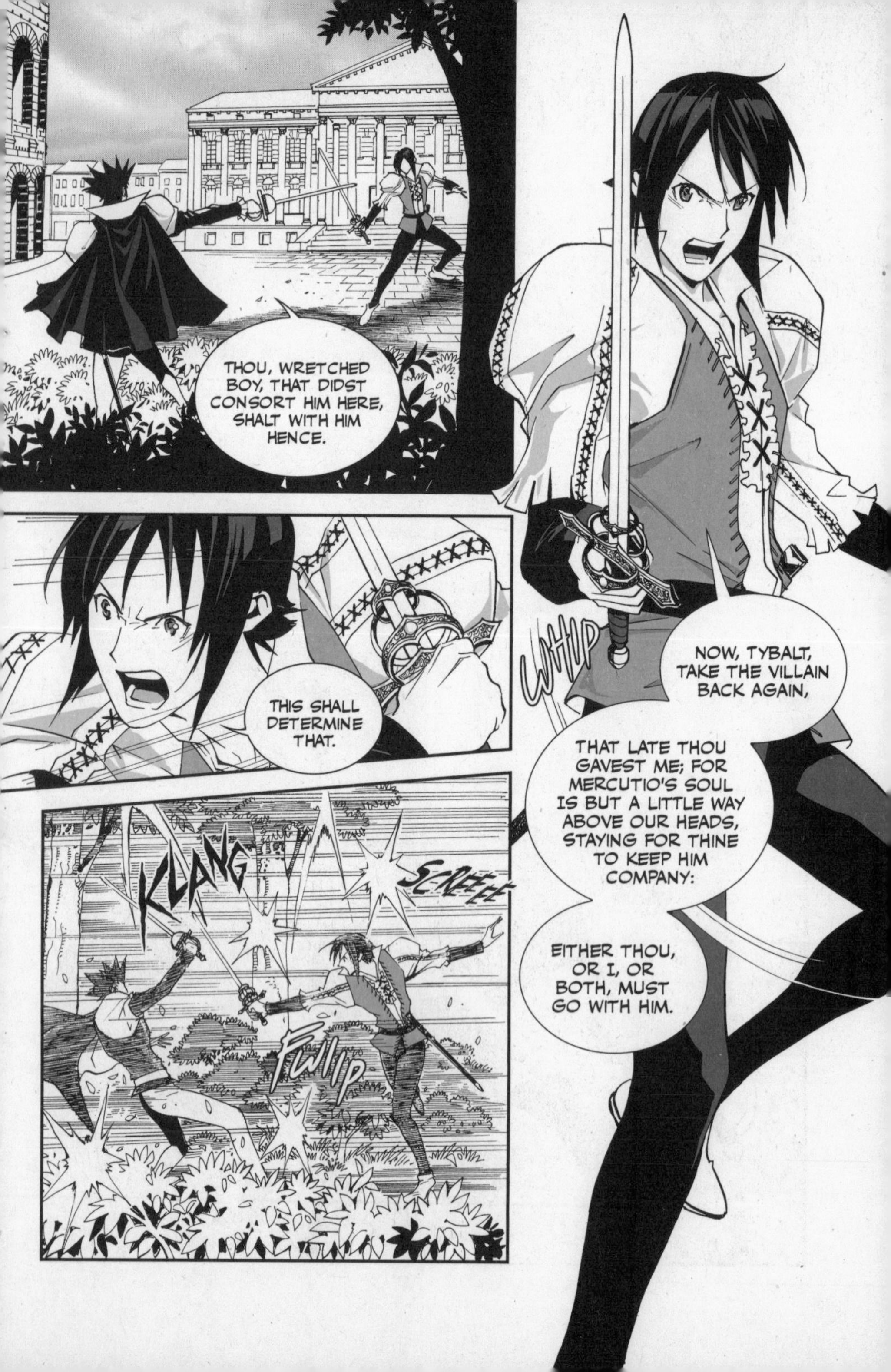
WHIP
NOW, TYBALT, TAKE THE VILLAIN BACK AGAIN,
THAT LATE THOU GAVEST ME; FOR MERCUTIO'S SOUL IS BUT A LITTLE WAY ABOVE OUR HEADS, STAYING FOR THINE TO KEEP HIM COMPANY:
EITHER THOU, OR I, OR BOTH, MUST GO WITH HIM.
THOU, WRETCHED BOY, THAT DIDST CONSORT HIM HERE, SHALT WITH HIM HENCE.
THIS SHALL DETERMINE THAT.
SCREEEE
KLANG
FWLIP

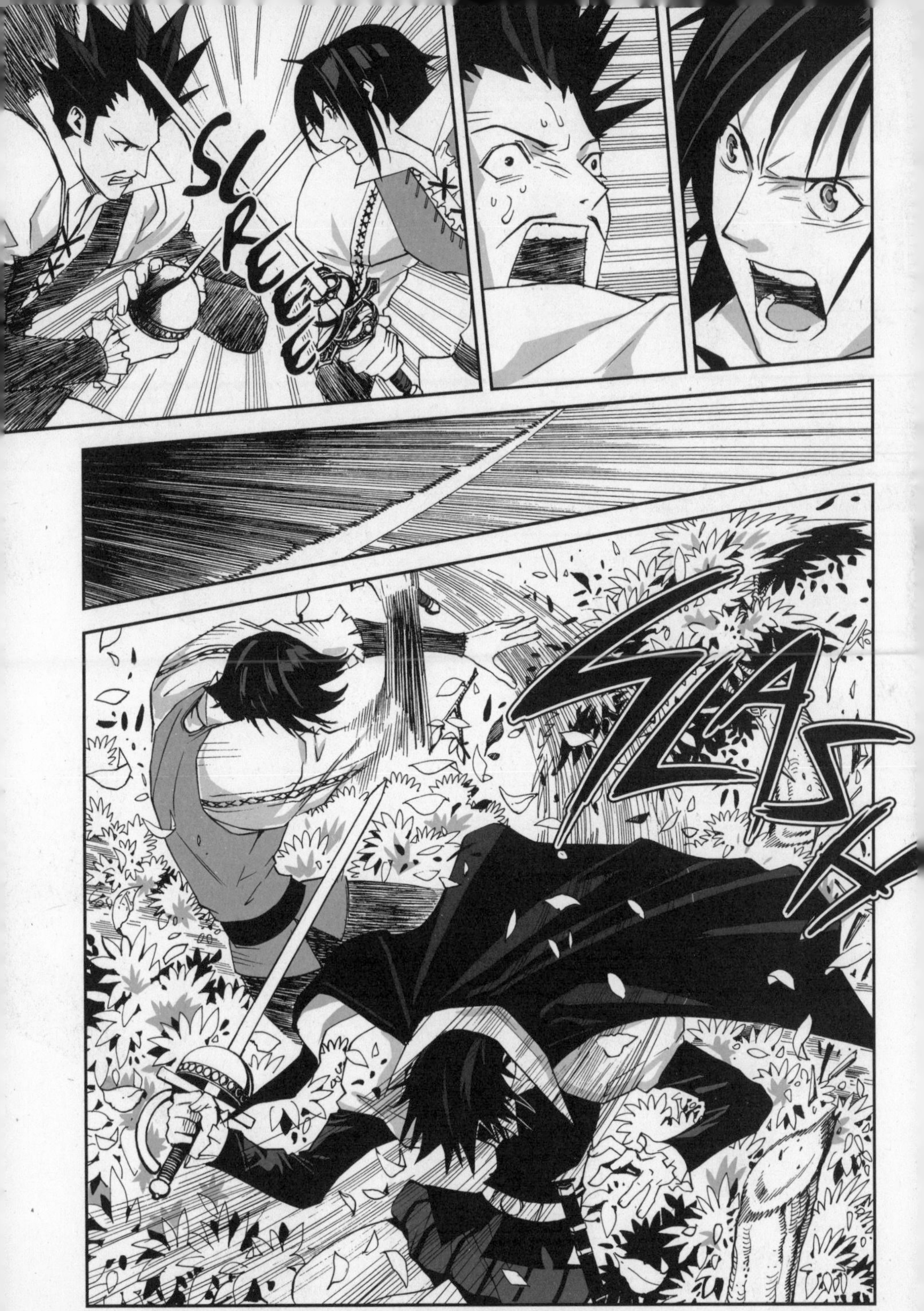
SLREEEE
ZLASH

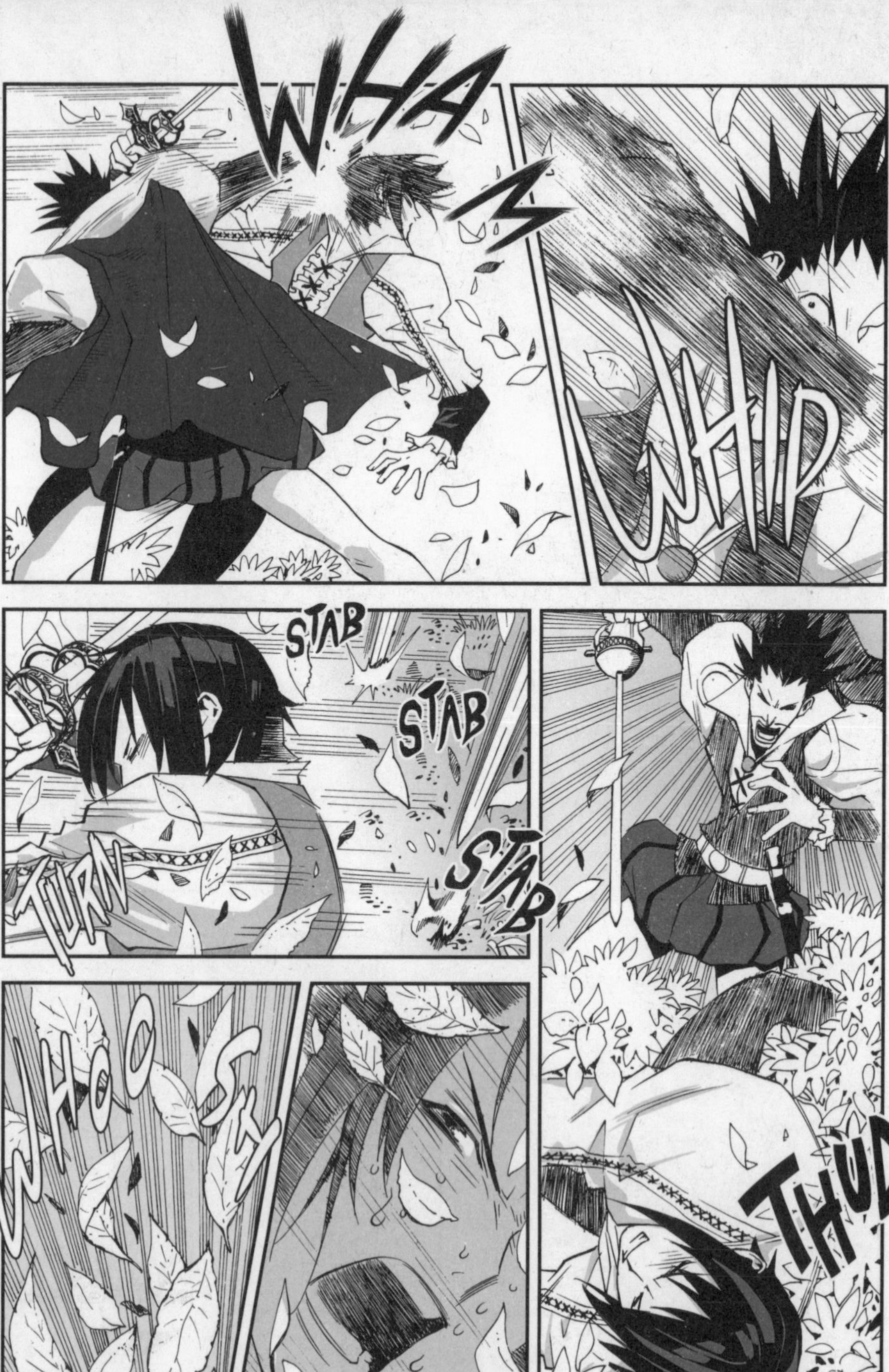
WHIP
WHAM
THUD
STAB
STAB
STAB
TURN
WHOOSH

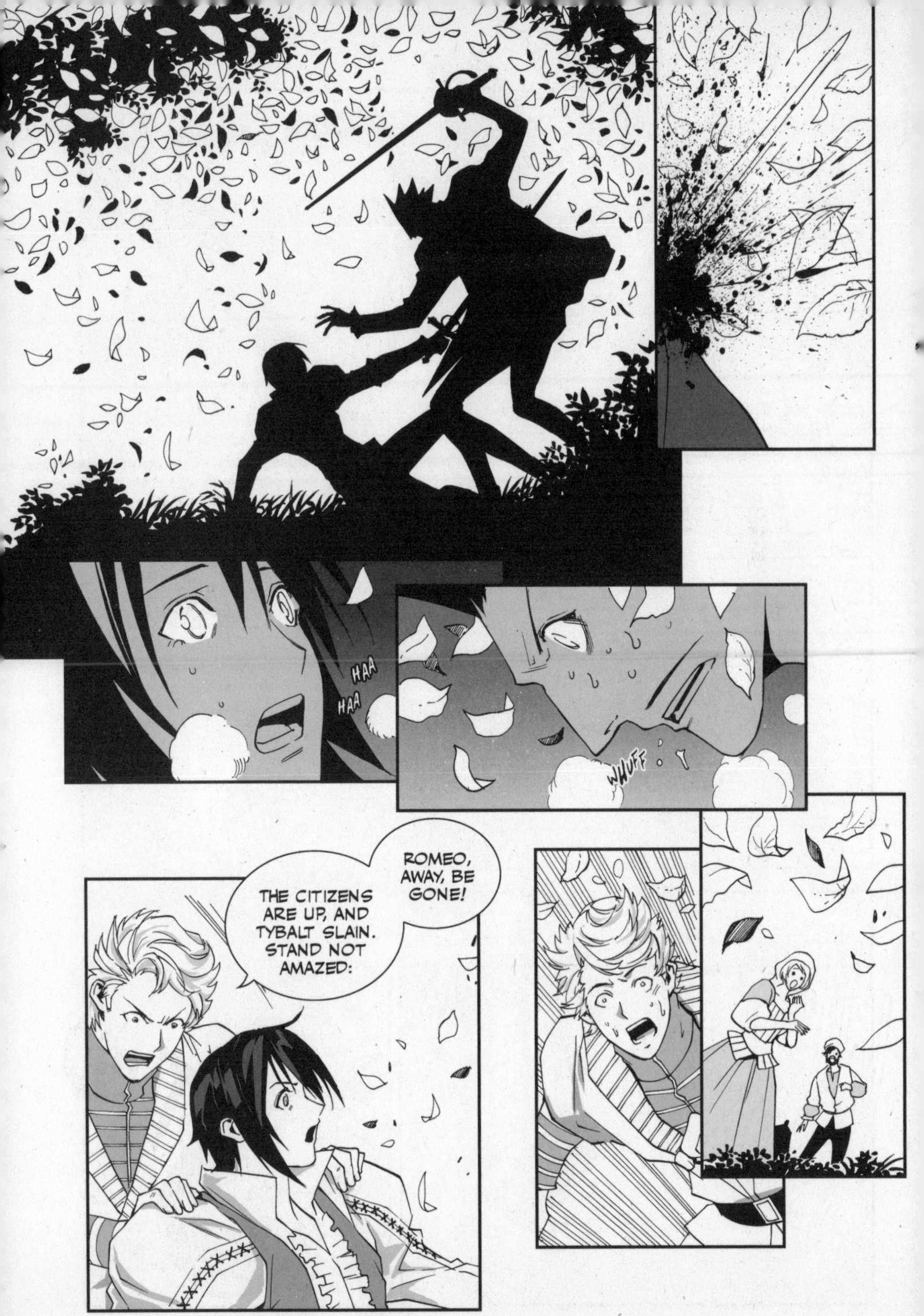
WHUFF
HAA
HAA
ROMEO, AWAY, BE GONE!
THE CITIZENS ARE UP, AND TYBALT SLAIN. STAND NOT AMAZED:

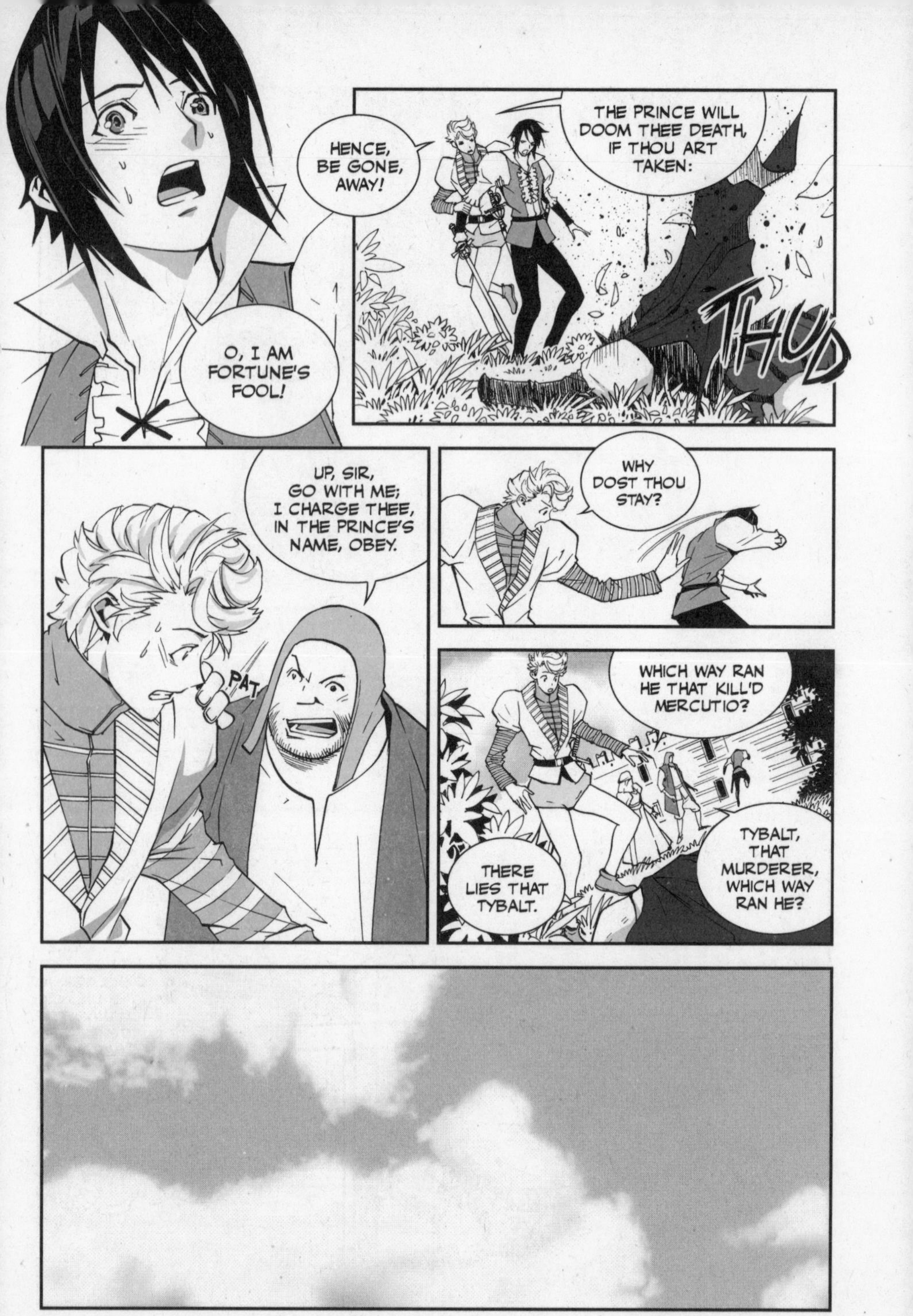
THE PRINCE WILL DOOM THEE DEATH, IF THOU ART TAKEN:
HENCE, BE GONE, AWAY!
THUD
O, I AM FORTUNE'S FOOL!
WHY DOST THOU STAY?
WHICH WAY RAN HE THAT KILL'D MERCUTIO?
TYBALT, THAT MURDERER, WHICH WAY RAN HE?
THERE LIES THAT TYBALT.
UP, SIR, GO WITH ME; I CHARGE THEE, IN THE PRINCE'S NAME, OBEY.
PAT

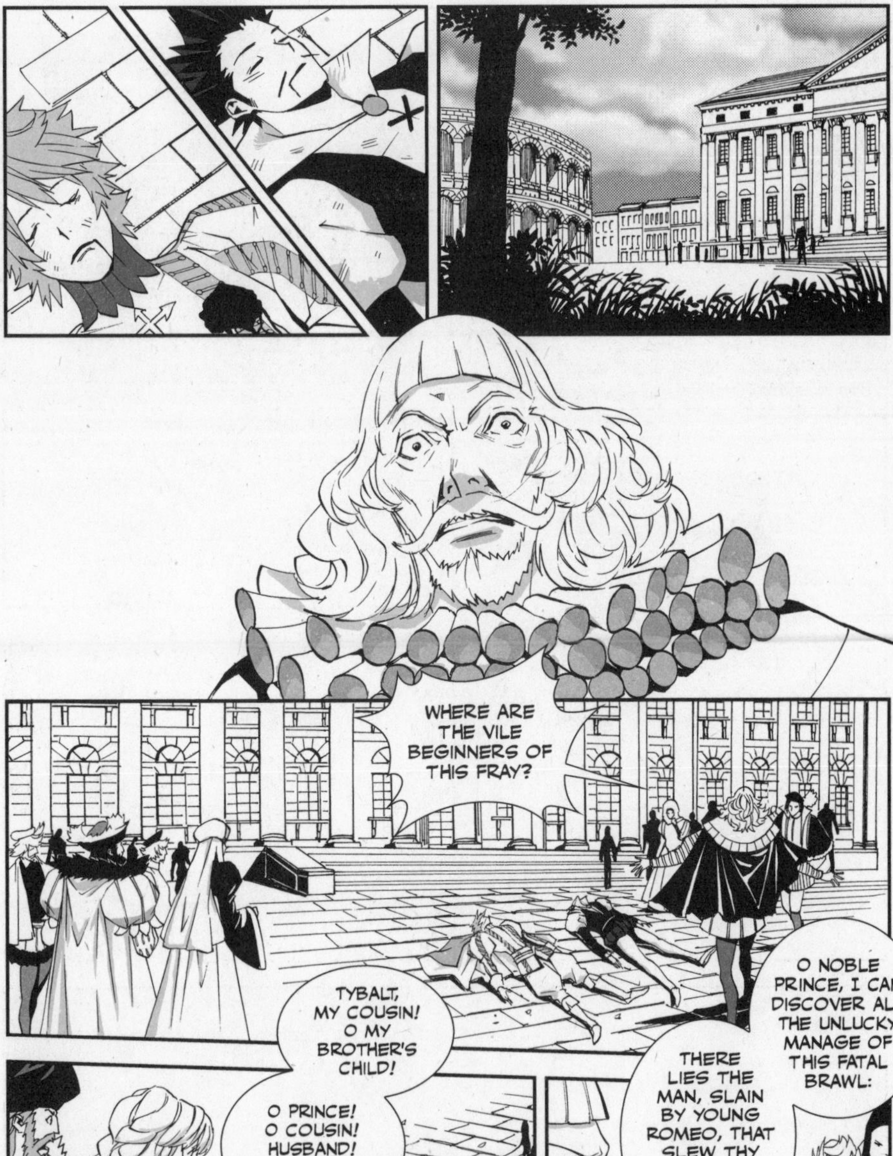
WHERE ARE THE VILE BEGINNERS OF THIS FRAY?
O NOBLE PRINCE, I CAN DISCOVER ALL THE UNLUCKY MANAGE OF THIS FATAL BRAWL:
THERE LIES THE MAN, SLAIN BY YOUNG ROMEO, THAT SLEW THY KINSMAN, BRAVE MERCUTIO.
TYBALT, MY COUSIN! O MY BROTHER'S CHILD!
O PRINCE! O COUSIN! HUSBAND! O, THE BLOOD IS SPILT
O MY DEAR KINSMAN!

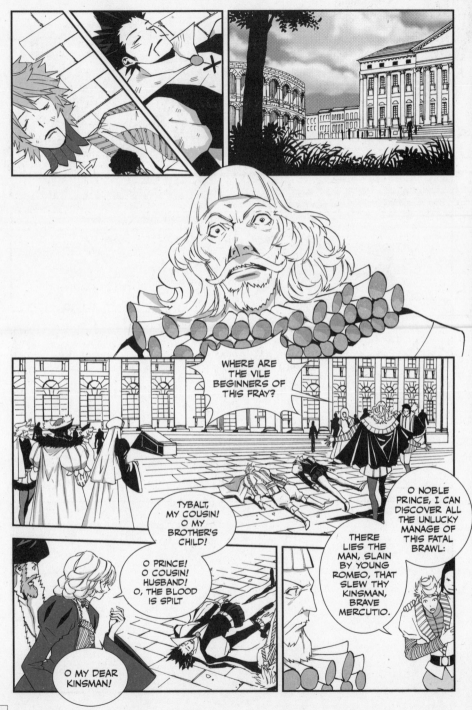

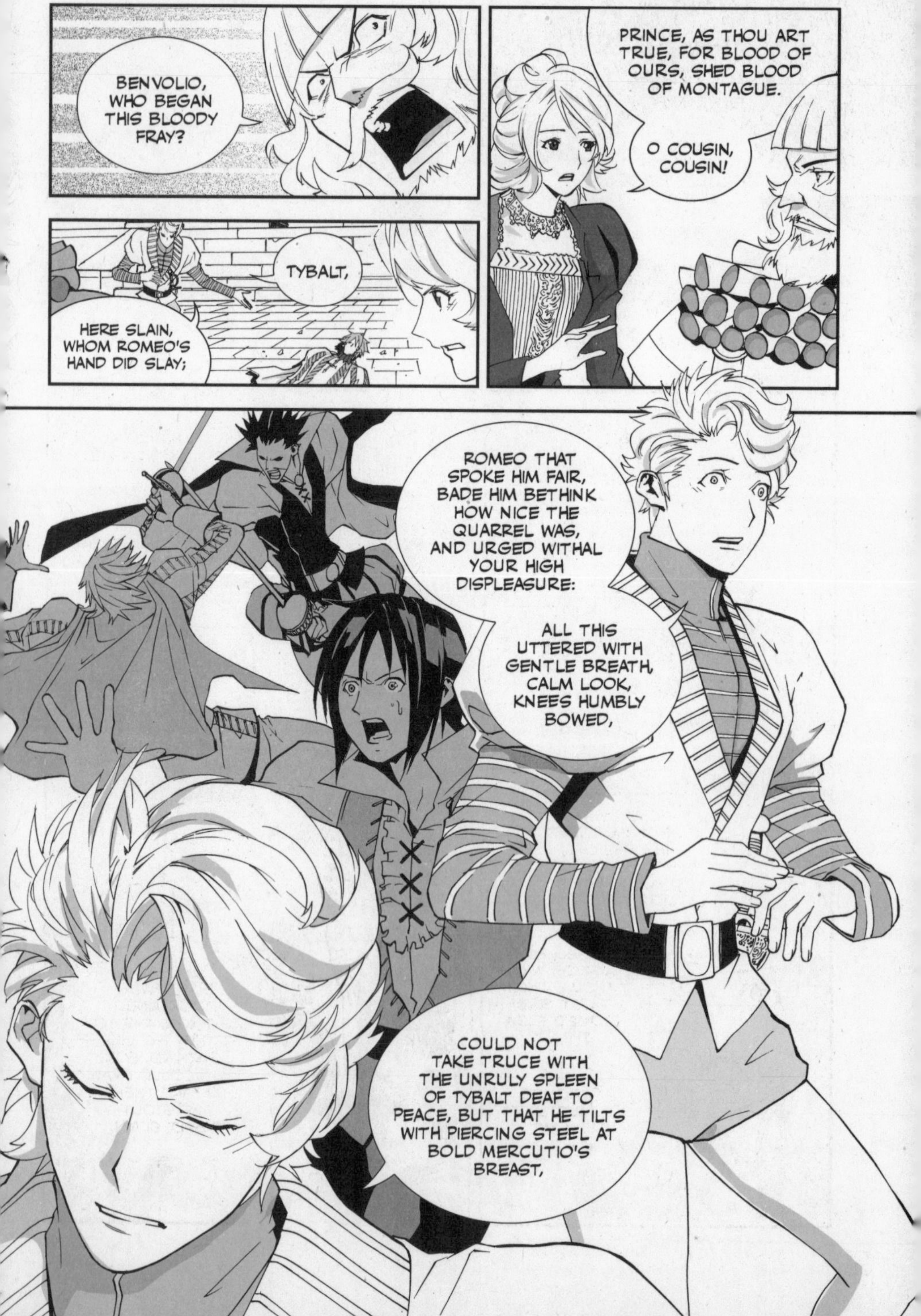
PRINCE, AS THOU ART TRUE, FOR BLOOD OF OURS, SHED BLOOD OF MONTAGUE.
O COUSIN, COUSIN!
BENVOLIO, WHO BEGAN THIS BLOODY FRAY?
TYBALT,
HERE SLAIN, WHOM ROMEO'S HAND DID SLAY;
ROMEO THAT SPOKE HIM FAIR, BADE HIM BETHINK HOW NICE THE QUARREL WAS, AND URGED WITHAL YOUR HIGH DISPLEASURE:
ALL THIS UTTERED WITH GENTLE BREATH, CALM LOOK, KNEES HUMBLY BOWED,
COULD NOT TAKE TRUCE WITH THE UNRULY SPLEEN OF TYBALT DEAF TO PEACE, BUT THAT HE TILTS WITH PIERCING STEEL AT BOLD MERCUTIO'S BREAST,

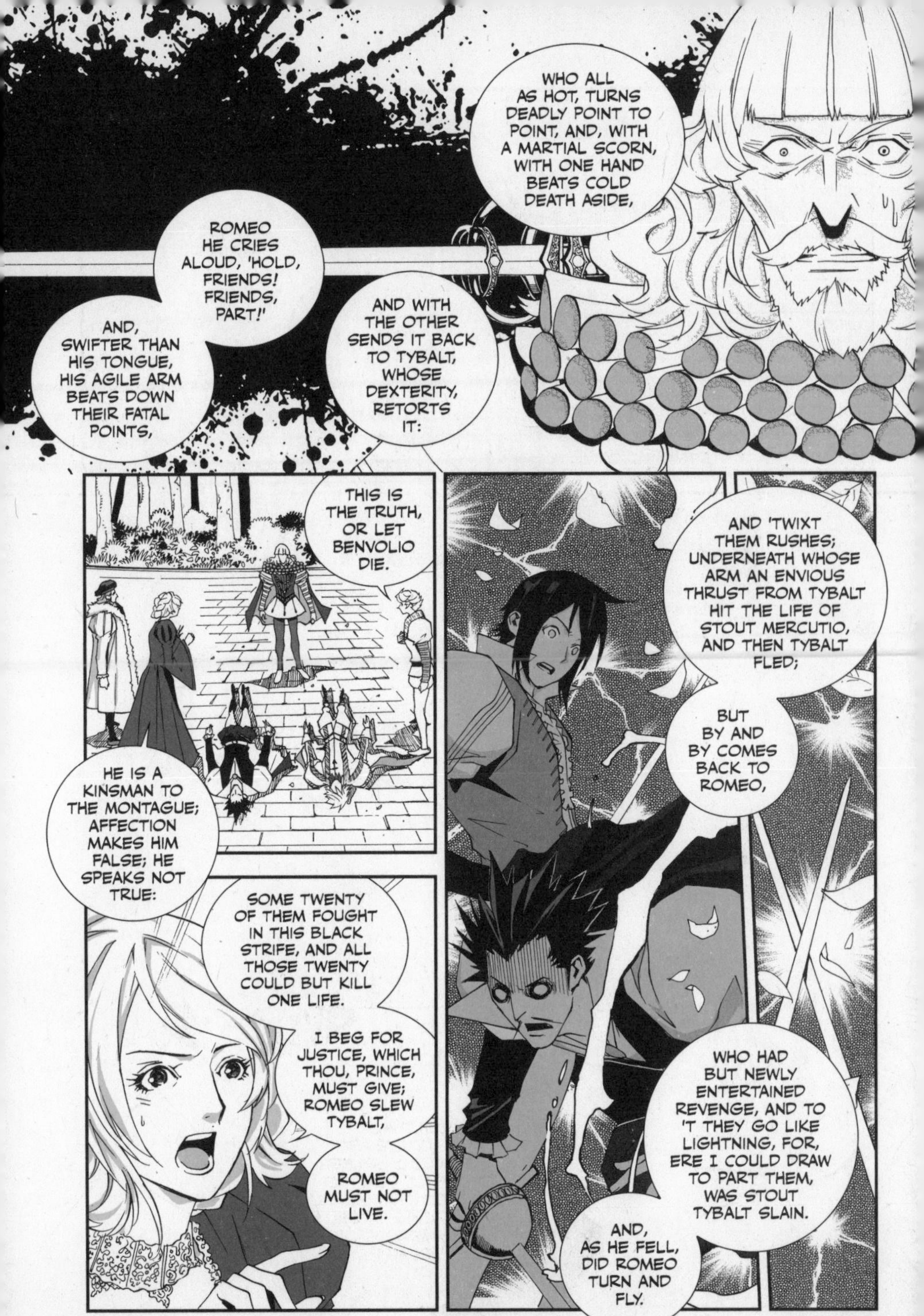
WHO ALL AS HOT, TURNS DEADLY POINT TO POINT, AND, WITH A MARTIAL SCORN, WITH ONE HAND BEATS COLD DEATH ASIDE,
AND WITH THE OTHER SENDS IT BACK TO TYBALT, WHOSE DEXTERITY, RETORTS IT:
ROMEO HE CRIES ALOUD, 'HOLD, FRIENDS! FRIENDS, PART!'
AND, SWIFTER THAN HIS TONGUE, HIS AGILE ARM BEATS DOWN THEIR FATAL POINTS,
AND 'TWIXT THEM RUSHES; UNDERNEATH WHOSE ARM AN ENVIOUS THRUST FROM TYBALT HIT THE LIFE OF STOUT MERCUTIO, AND THEN TYBALT FLED;
BUT BY AND BY COMES BACK TO ROMEO,
WHO HAD BUT NEWLY ENTERTAINED REVENGE, AND TO 'T THEY GO LIKE LIGHTNING, FOR, ERE I COULD DRAW TO PART THEM, WAS STOUT TYBALT SLAIN.
AND, AS HE FELL, DID ROMEO TURN AND FLY.
THIS IS THE TRUTH, OR LET BENVOLIO DIE.
HE IS A KINSMAN TO THE MONTAGUE; AFFECTION MAKES HIM FALSE; HE SPEAKS NOT TRUE:
SOME TWENTY OF THEM FOUGHT IN THIS BLACK STRIFE, AND ALL THOSE TWENTY COULD BUT KILL ONE LIFE.
I BEG FOR JUSTICE, WHICH THOU, PRINCE, MUST GIVE; ROMEO SLEW TYBALT,
ROMEO MUST NOT LIVE.

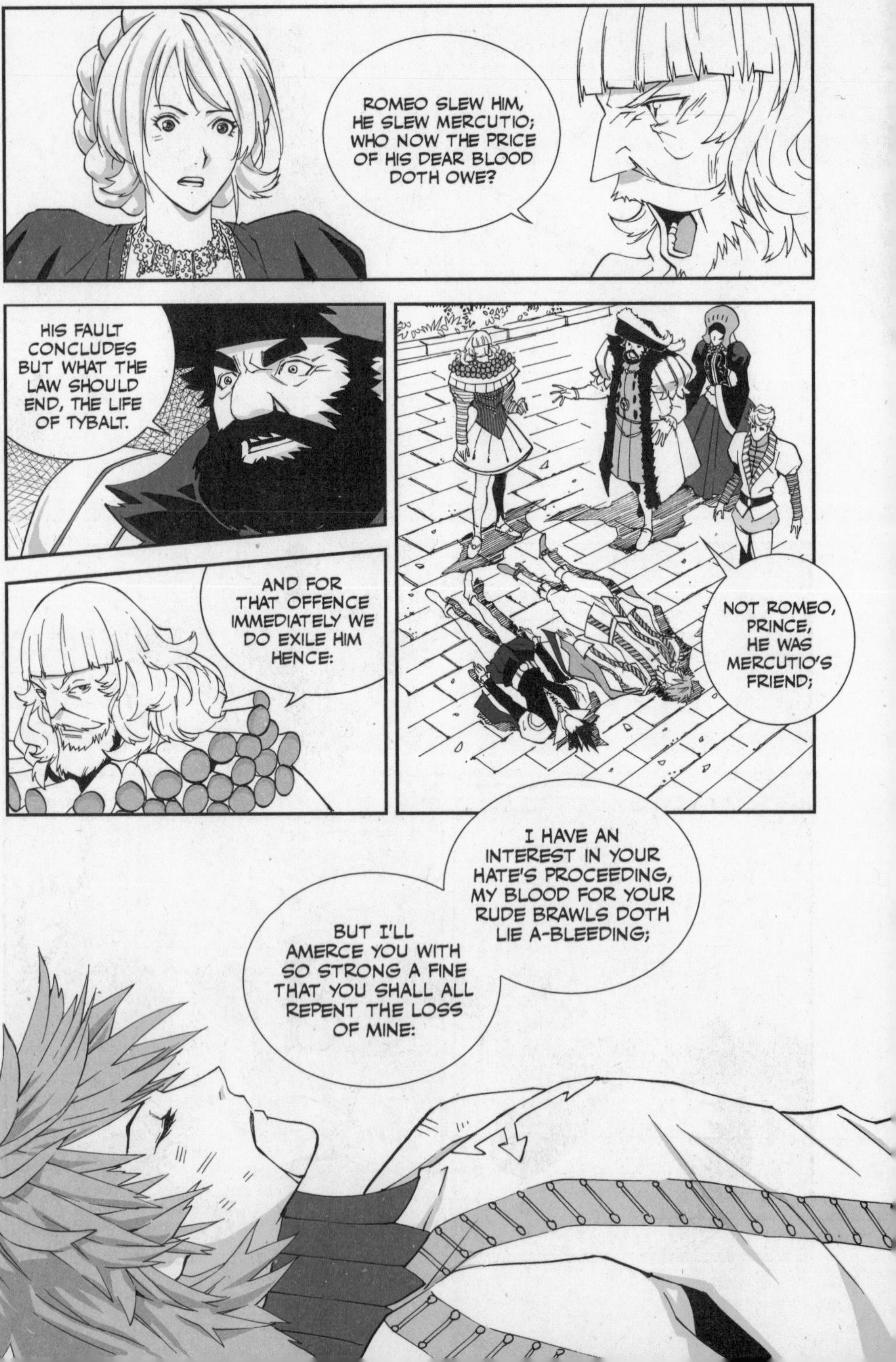
ROMEO SLEW HIM, HE SLEW MERCUTIO; WHO NOW THE PRICE OF HIS DEAR BLOOD DOTH OWE?
NOT ROMEO, PRINCE, HE WAS MERCUTIO'S FRIEND;
HIS FAULT CONCLUDES BUT WHAT THE LAW SHOULD END, THE LIFE OF TYBALT.
AND FOR THAT OFFENCE IMMEDIATELY WE DO EXILE HIM HENCE:
I HAVE AN INTEREST IN YOUR HATE'S PROCEEDING, MY BLOOD FOR YOUR RUDE BRAWLS DOTH LIE A-BLEEDING;
BUT I'LL AMERCE YOU WITH SO STRONG A FINE THAT YOU SHALL ALL REPENT THE LOSS OF MINE:

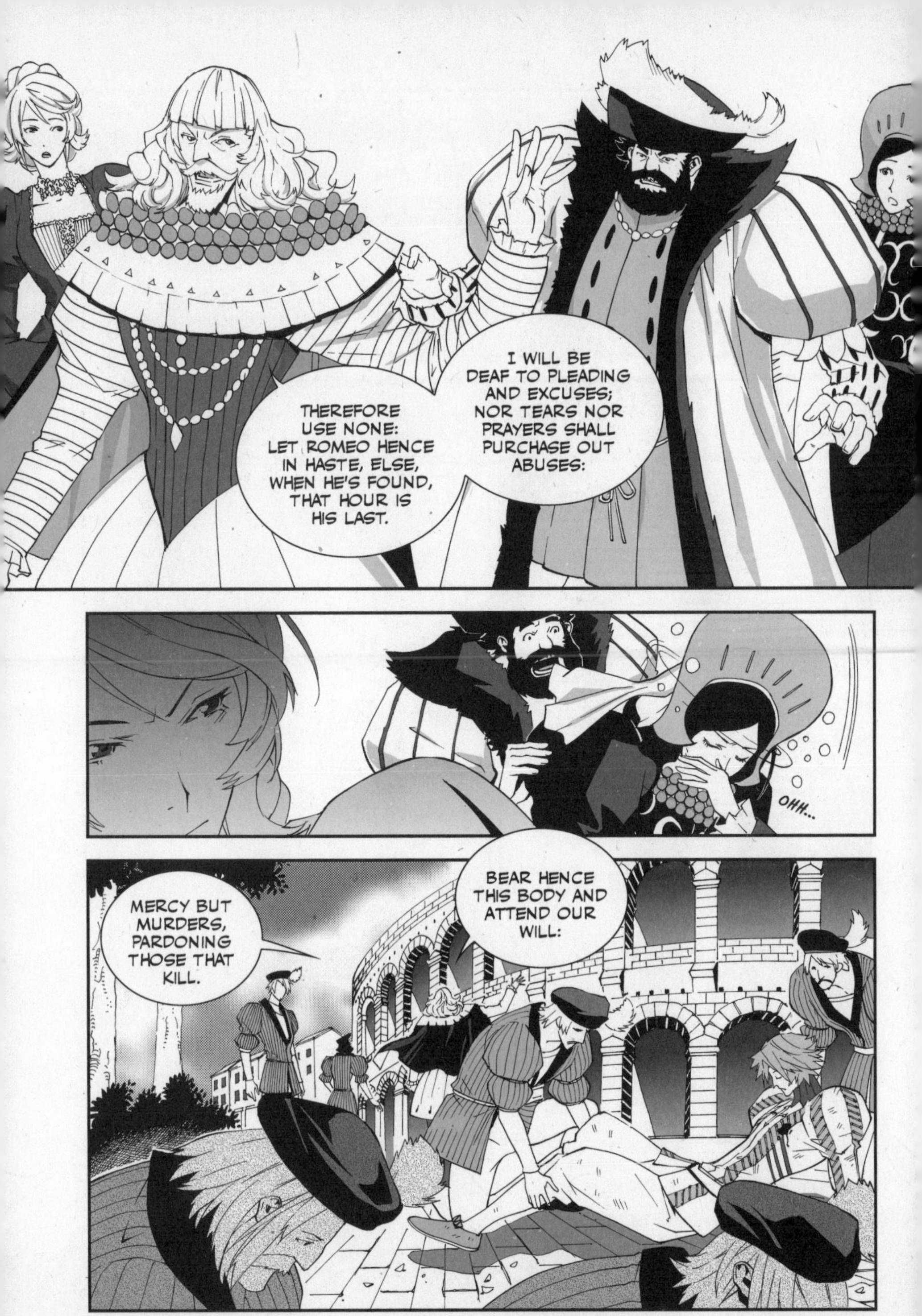
I WILL BE DEAF TO PLEADING AND EXCUSES; NOR TEARS NOR PRAYERS SHALL PURCHASE OUT ABUSES:
THEREFORE USE NONE: LET ROMEO HENCE IN HASTE, ELSE, WHEN HE'S FOUND, THAT HOUR IS HIS LAST.
OHH...
BEAR HENCE THIS BODY AND ATTEND OUR WILL:
MERCY BUT MURDERS, PARDONING THOSE THAT KILL.

ACT III SCENE II

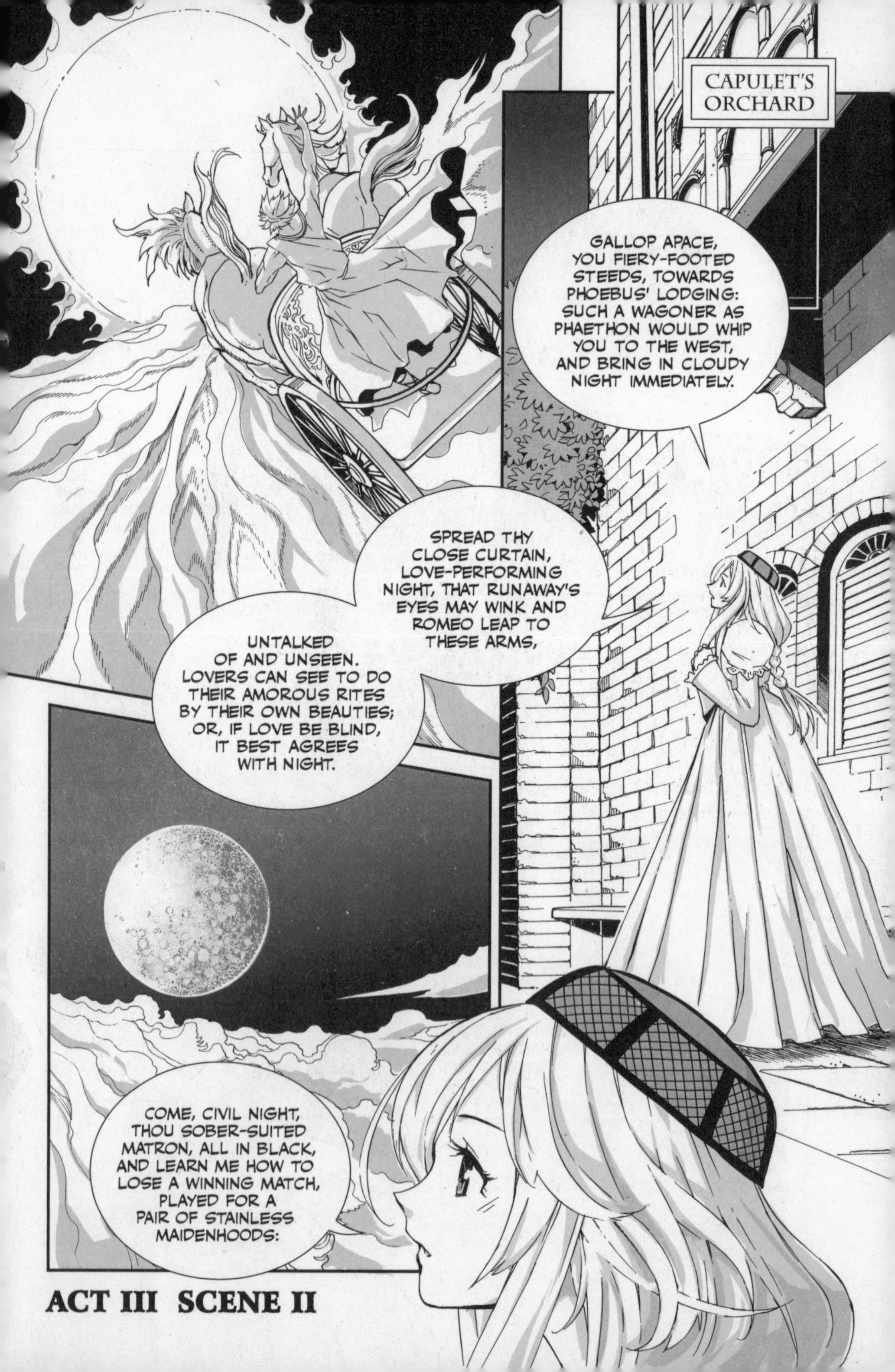
CAPULET'S ORCHARD
GALLOP APACE, YOU FIERY-FOOTED STEEDS, TOWARDS PHOEBUS' LODGING: SUCH A WAGONER AS PHAETHON WOULD WHIP YOU TO THE WEST, AND BRING IN CLOUDY NIGHT IMMEDIATELY.
SPREAD THY CLOSE CURTAIN, LOVE-PERFORMING NIGHT, THAT RUNAWAY'S EYES MAY WINK AND ROMEO LEAP TO THESE ARMS,
UNTALKED OF AND UNSEEN. LOVERS CAN SEE TO DO THEIR AMOROUS RITES BY THEIR OWN BEAUTIES; OR, IF LOVE BE BLIND, IT BEST AGREES WITH NIGHT.
COME, CIVIL NIGHT, THOU SOBER-SUITED MATRON, ALL IN BLACK, AND LEARN ME HOW TO LOSE A WINNING MATCH, PLAYED FOR A PAIR OF STAINLESS MAIDENHOODS:

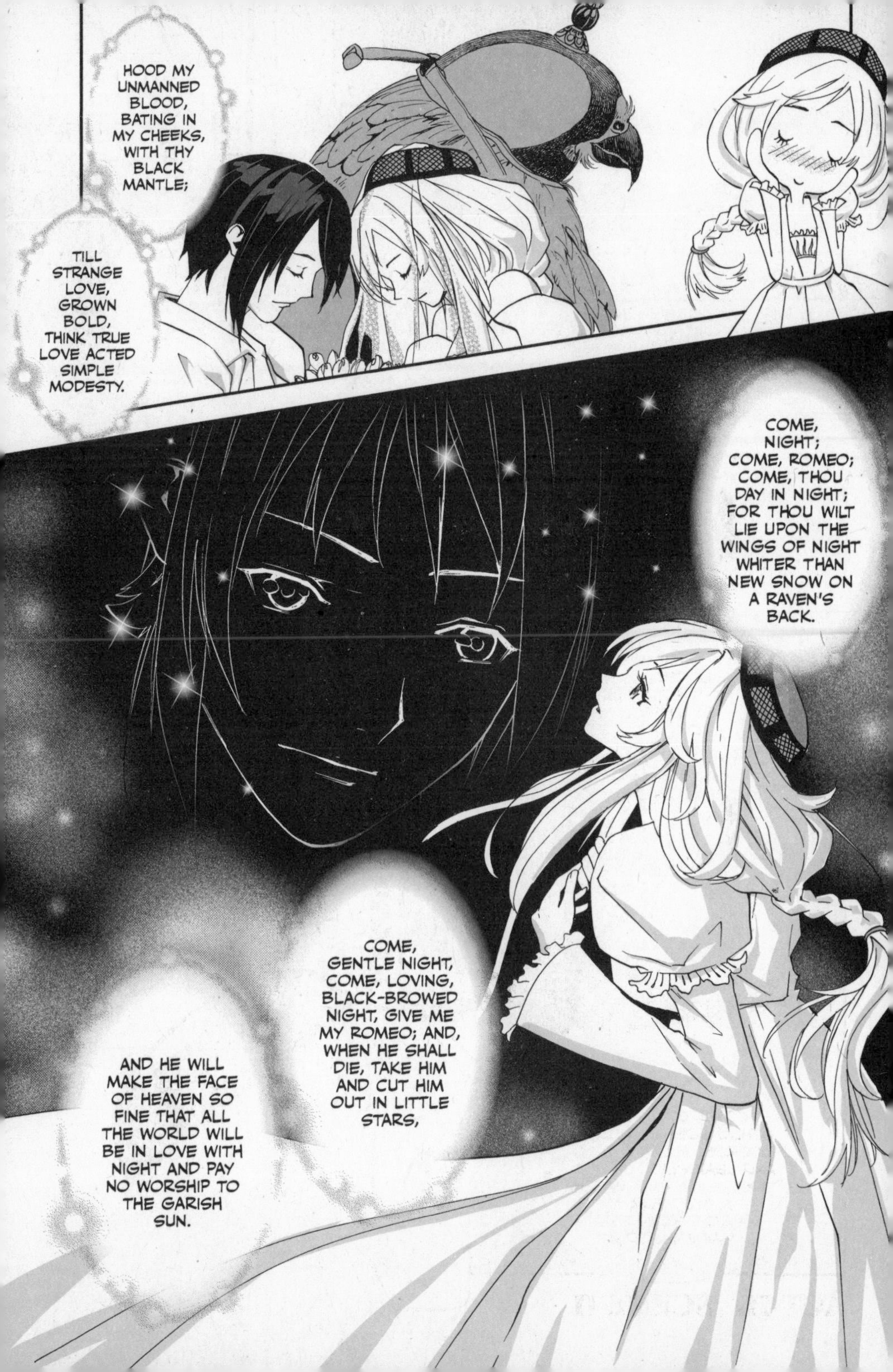
HOOD MY UNMANNED BLOOD, BATING IN MY CHEEKS, WITH THY BLACK MANTLE;
TILL STRANGE LOVE, GROWN BOLD, THINK TRUE LOVE ACTED SIMPLE MODESTY.
COME, NIGHT; COME, ROMEO; COME, THOU DAY IN NIGHT; FOR THOU WILT LIE UPON THE WINGS OF NIGHT WHITER THAN NEW SNOW ON A RAVEN'S BACK.
COME, GENTLE NIGHT, COME, LOVING, BLACK-BROWED NIGHT, GIVE ME MY ROMEO; AND, WHEN HE SHALL DIE, TAKE HIM AND CUT HIM OUT IN LITTLE STARS,
AND HE WILL MAKE THE FACE OF HEAVEN SO FINE THAT ALL THE WORLD WILL BE IN LOVE WITH NIGHT AND PAY NO WORSHIP TO THE GARISH SUN.

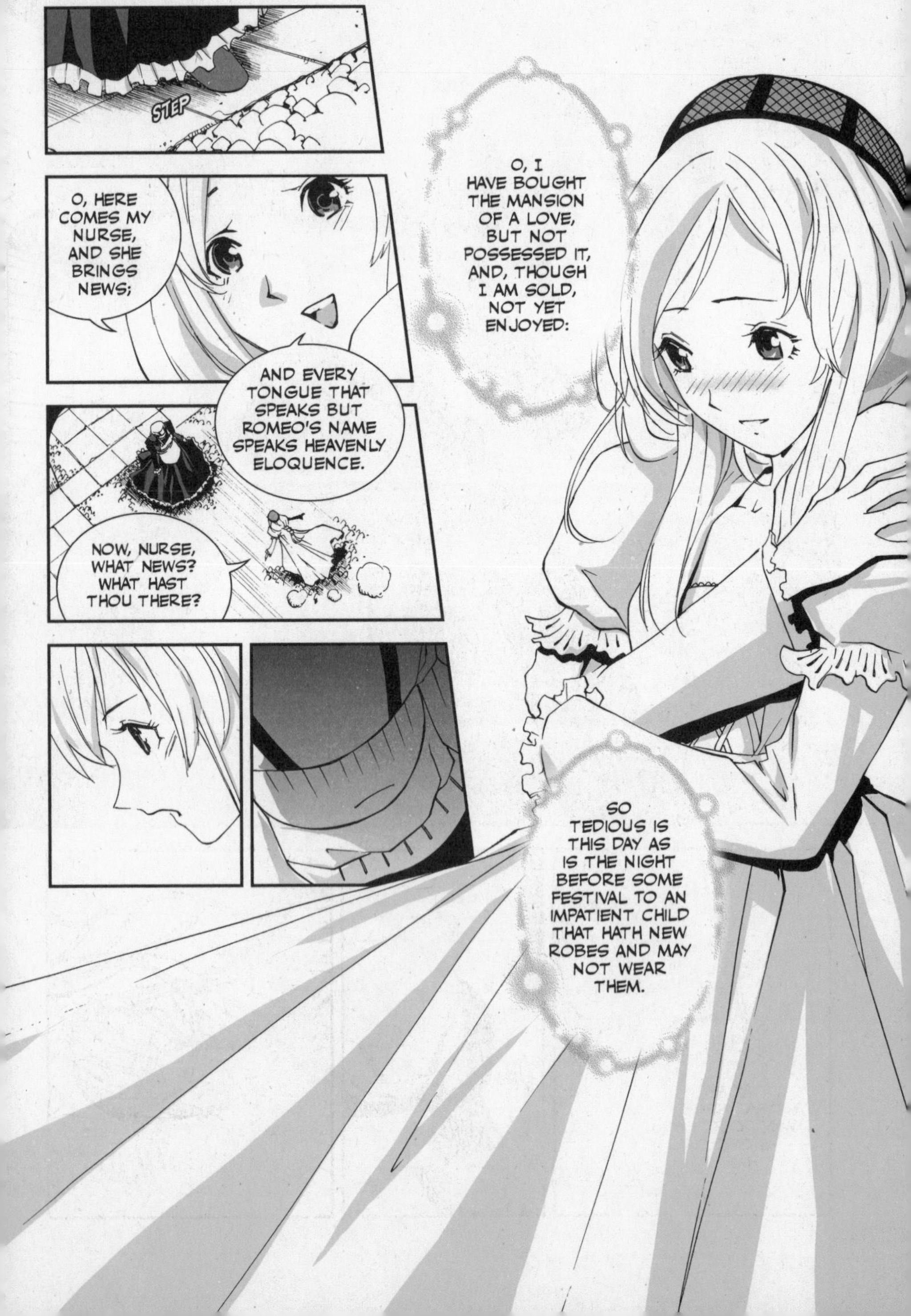
O, I HAVE BOUGHT THE MANSION OF A LOVE, BUT NOT POSSESSED IT, AND, THOUGH I AM SOLD, NOT YET ENJOYED:
SO TEDIOUS IS THIS DAY AS IS THE NIGHT BEFORE SOME FESTIVAL TO AN IMPATIENT CHILD THAT HATH NEW ROBES AND MAY NOT WEAR THEM.
STEP
O, HERE COMES MY NURSE, AND SHE BRINGS NEWS;
AND EVERY TONGUE THAT SPEAKS BUT ROMEO'S NAME SPEAKS HEAVENLY ELOQUENCE.
NOW, NURSE, WHAT NEWS? WHAT HAST THOU THERE?

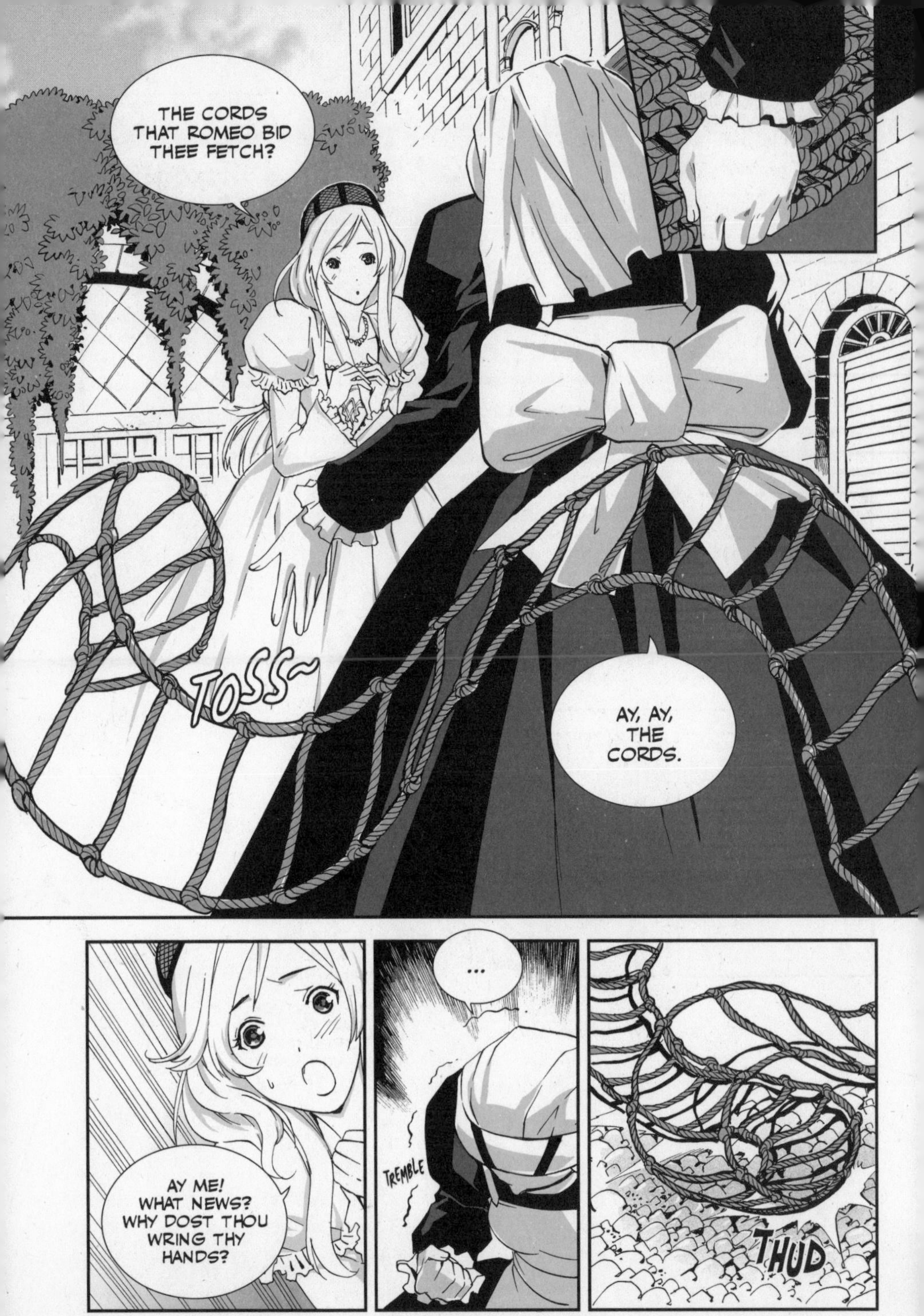
THE CORDS THAT ROMEO BID THEE FETCH?
AY, AY, THE CORDS.
TOSS~
THUD
...
TREMBLE
AY ME! WHAT NEWS? WHY DOST THOU WRING THY HANDS?

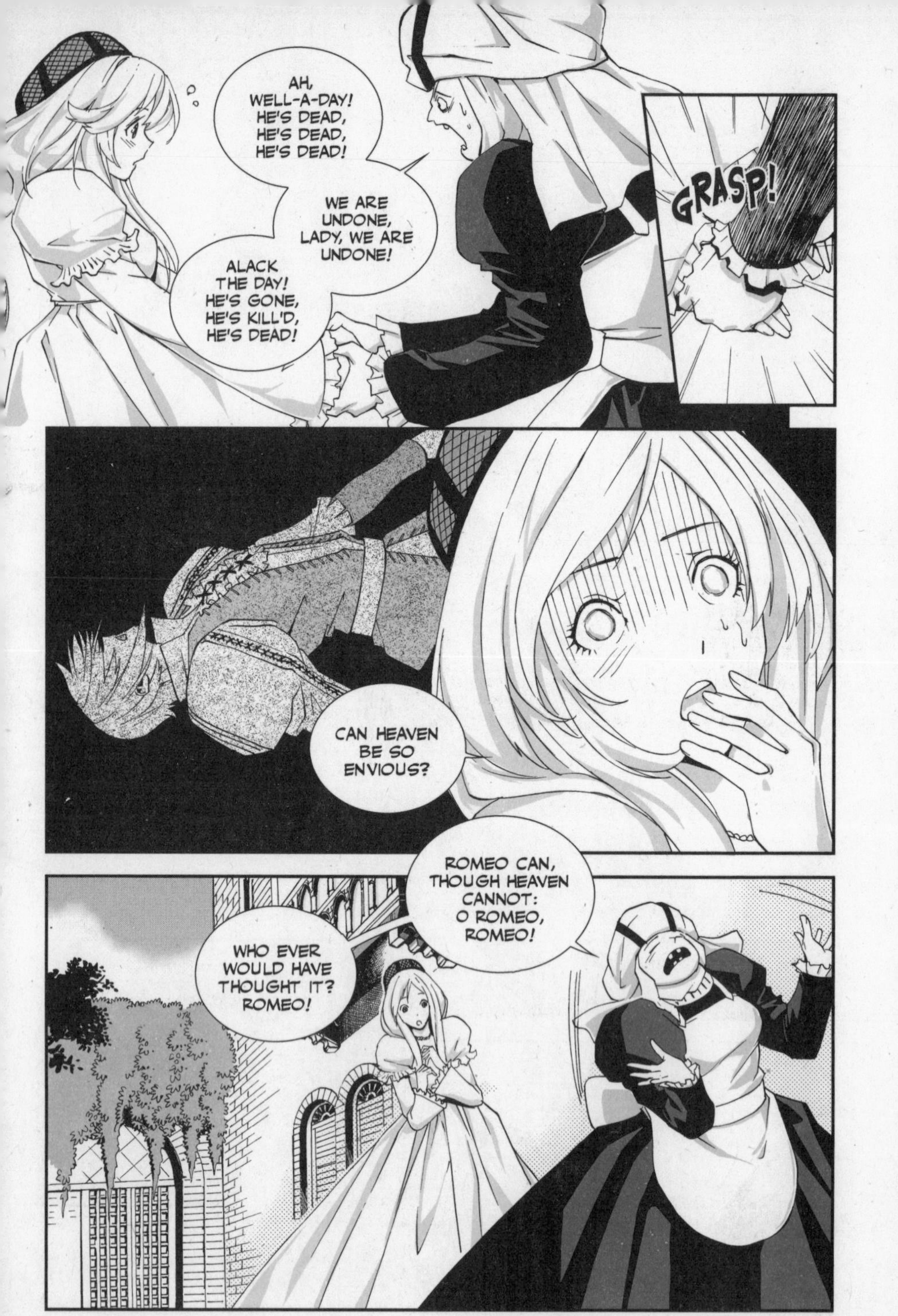
GRASP!
AH, WELL-A-DAY! HE'S DEAD, HE'S DEAD, HE'S DEAD!
WE ARE UNDONE, LADY, WE ARE UNDONE!
ALACK THE DAY! HE'S GONE, HE'S KILL'D, HE'S DEAD!
CAN HEAVEN BE SO ENVIOUS?
ROMEO CAN, THOUGH HEAVEN CANNOT: O ROMEO, ROMEO!
WHO EVER WOULD HAVE THOUGHT IT? ROMEO!

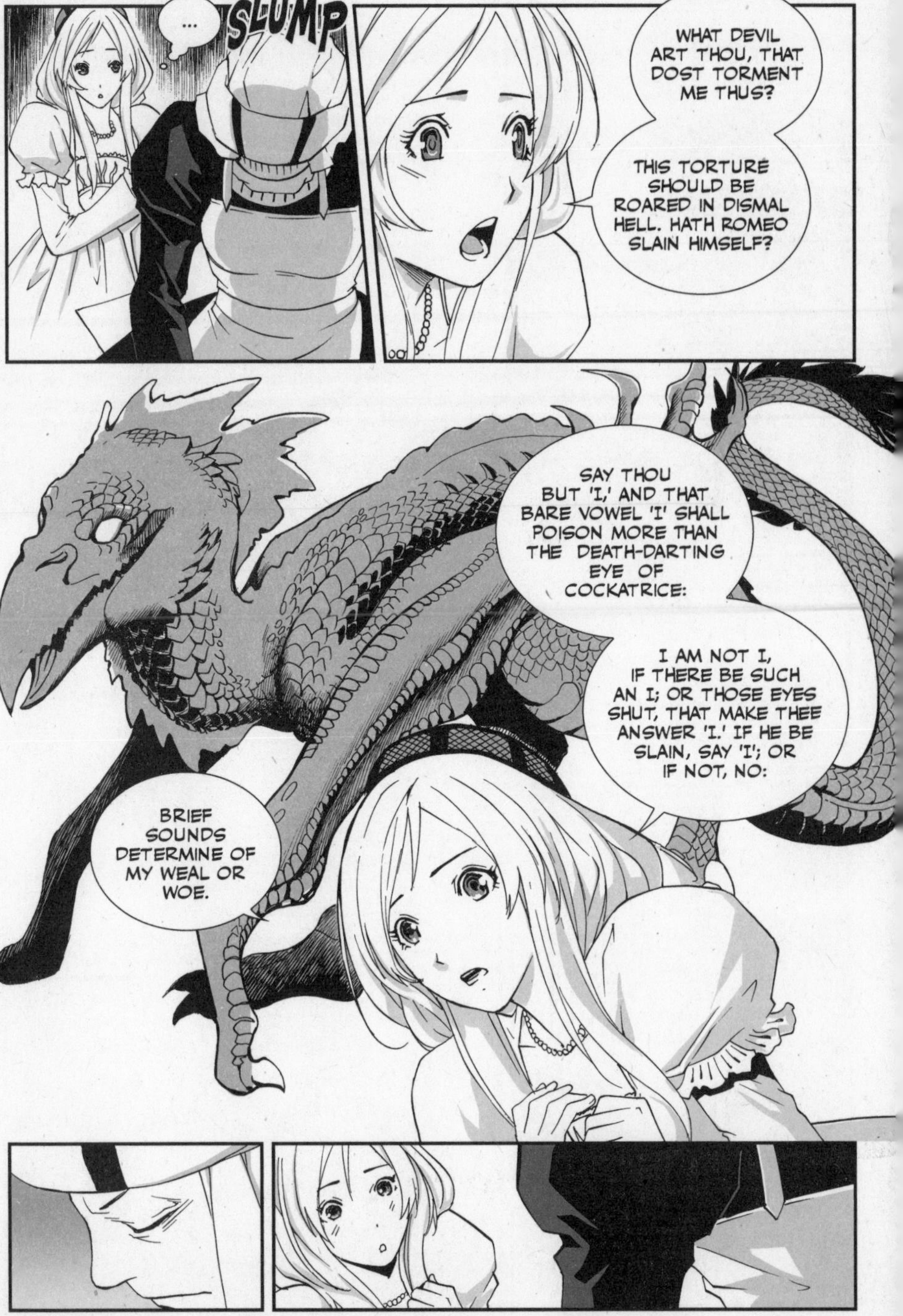
WHAT DEVIL ART THOU, THAT DOST TORMENT ME THUS?
THIS TORTURE SHOULD BE ROARED IN DISMAL HELL. HATH ROMEO SLAIN HIMSELF?
...
SLUMP
SAY THOU BUT 'I,' AND THAT BARE VOWEL 'I' SHALL POISON MORE THAN THE DEATH-DARTING EYE OF COCKATRICE:
I AM NOT I, IF THERE BE SUCH AN I; OR THOSE EYES SHUT, THAT MAKE THEE ANSWER 'I.' IF HE BE SLAIN, SAY 'I'; OR IF NOT, NO:
BRIEF SOUNDS DETERMINE OF MY WEAL OR WOE.

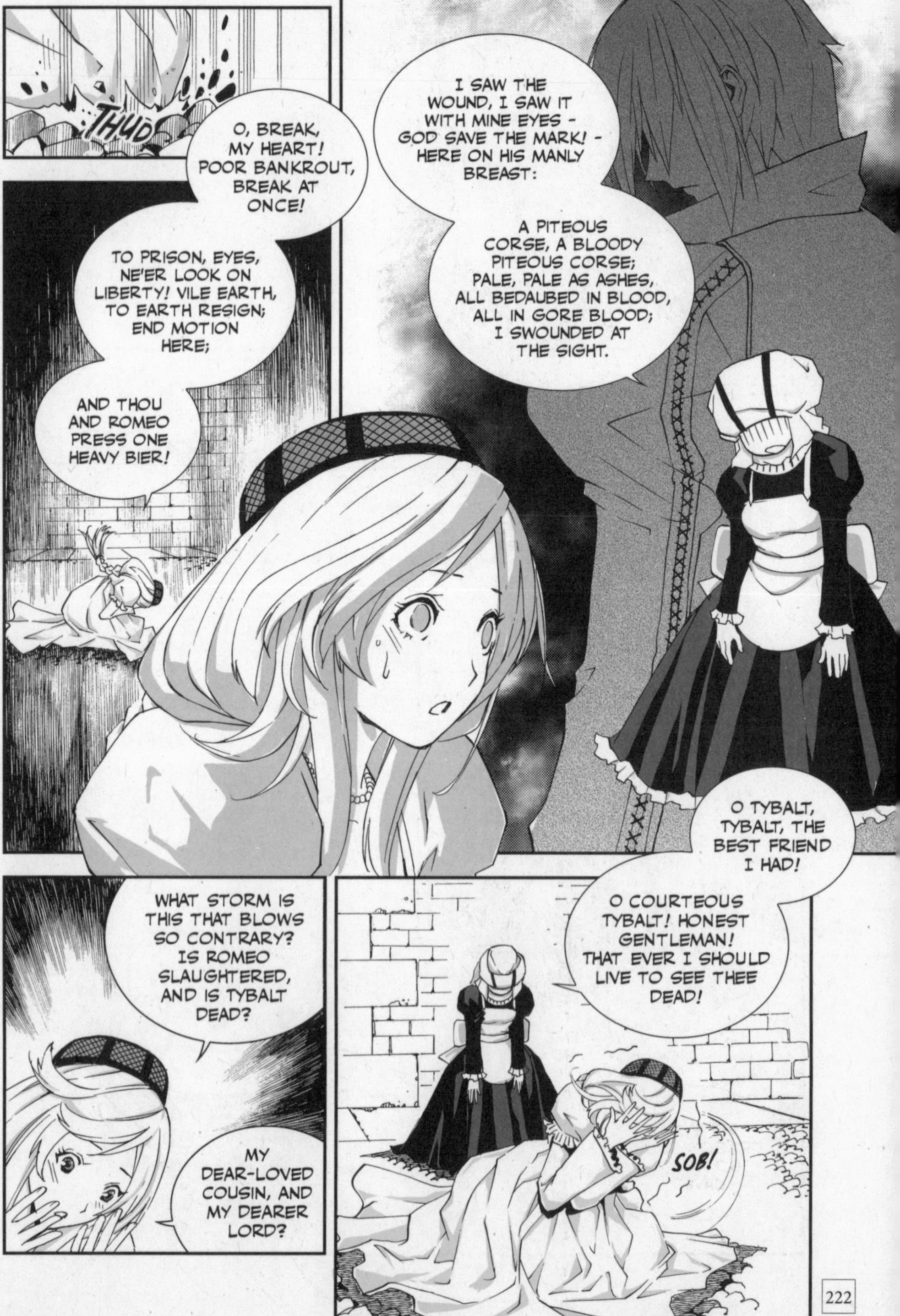
I SAW THE WOUND, I SAW IT WITH MINE EYES - GOD SAVE THE MARK! - HERE ON HIS MANLY BREAST:
A PITEOUS CORSE, A BLOODY PITEOUS CORSE; PALE, PALE AS ASHES, ALL BEDAUBED IN BLOOD, ALL IN GORE BLOOD; I SWOUNDED AT THE SIGHT.
THUD
O, BREAK, MY HEART! POOR BANKROUT, BREAK AT ONCE!
TO PRISON, EYES, NE'ER LOOK ON LIBERTY! VILE EARTH, TO EARTH RESIGN; END MOTION HERE;
AND THOU AND ROMEO PRESS ONE HEAVY BIER!
O TYBALT, TYBALT, THE BEST FRIEND I HAD!
O COURTEOUS TYBALT! HONEST GENTLEMAN! THAT EVER I SHOULD LIVE TO SEE THEE DEAD!
SOB!
WHAT STORM IS THIS THAT BLOWS SO CONTRARY? IS ROMEO SLAUGHTERED, AND IS TYBALT DEAD?
MY DEAR-LOVED COUSIN, AND MY DEARER LORD?

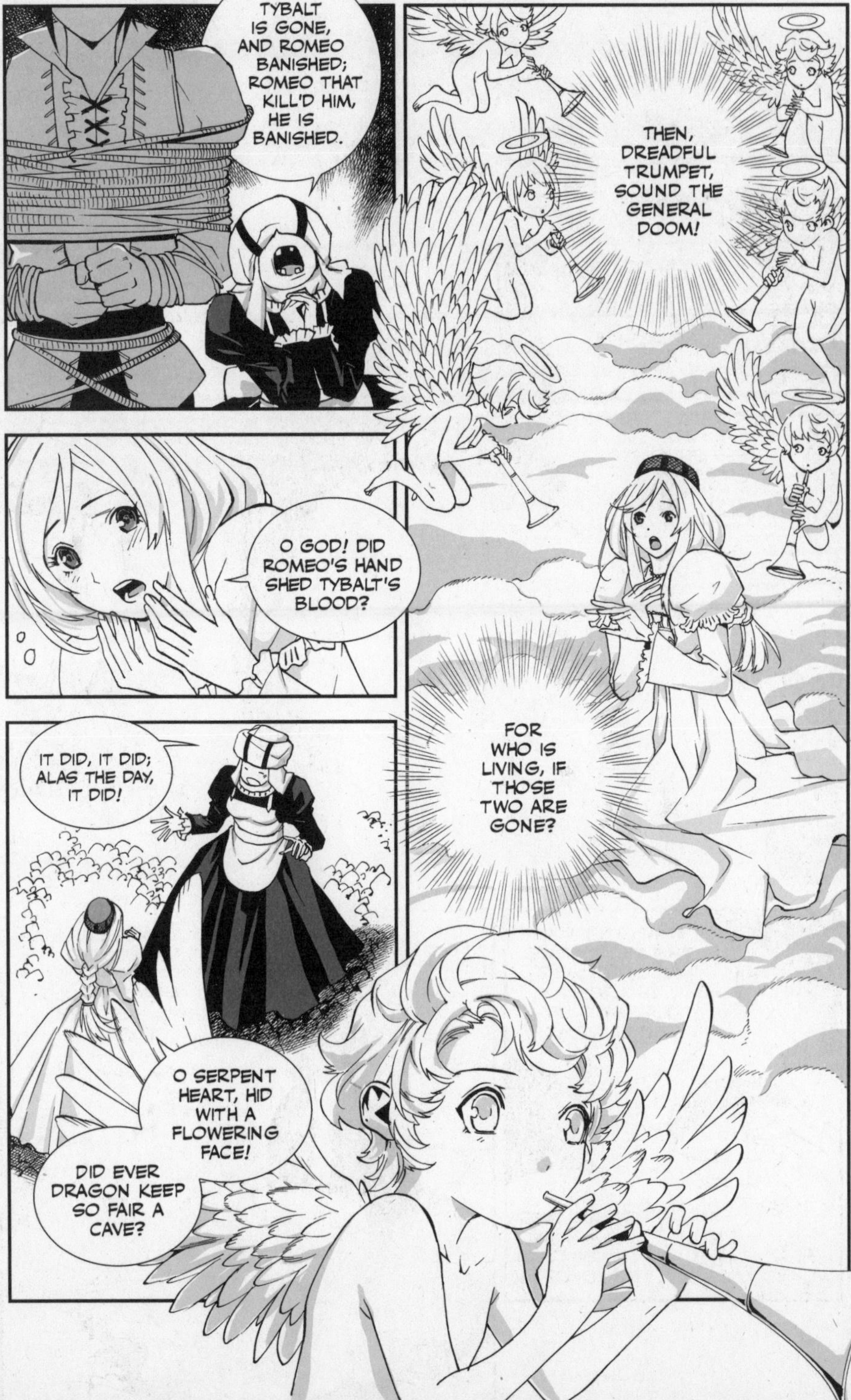
THEN, DREADFUL TRUMPET, SOUND THE GENERAL DOOM!
FOR WHO IS LIVING, IF THOSE TWO ARE GONE?
TYBALT IS GONE, AND ROMEO BANISHED; ROMEO THAT KILL'D HIM, HE IS BANISHED.
O GOD! DID ROMEO'S HAND SHED TYBALT'S BLOOD?
IT DID, IT DID; ALAS THE DAY, IT DID!
O SERPENT HEART, HID WITH A FLOWERING FACE!
DID EVER DRAGON KEEP SO FAIR A CAVE?

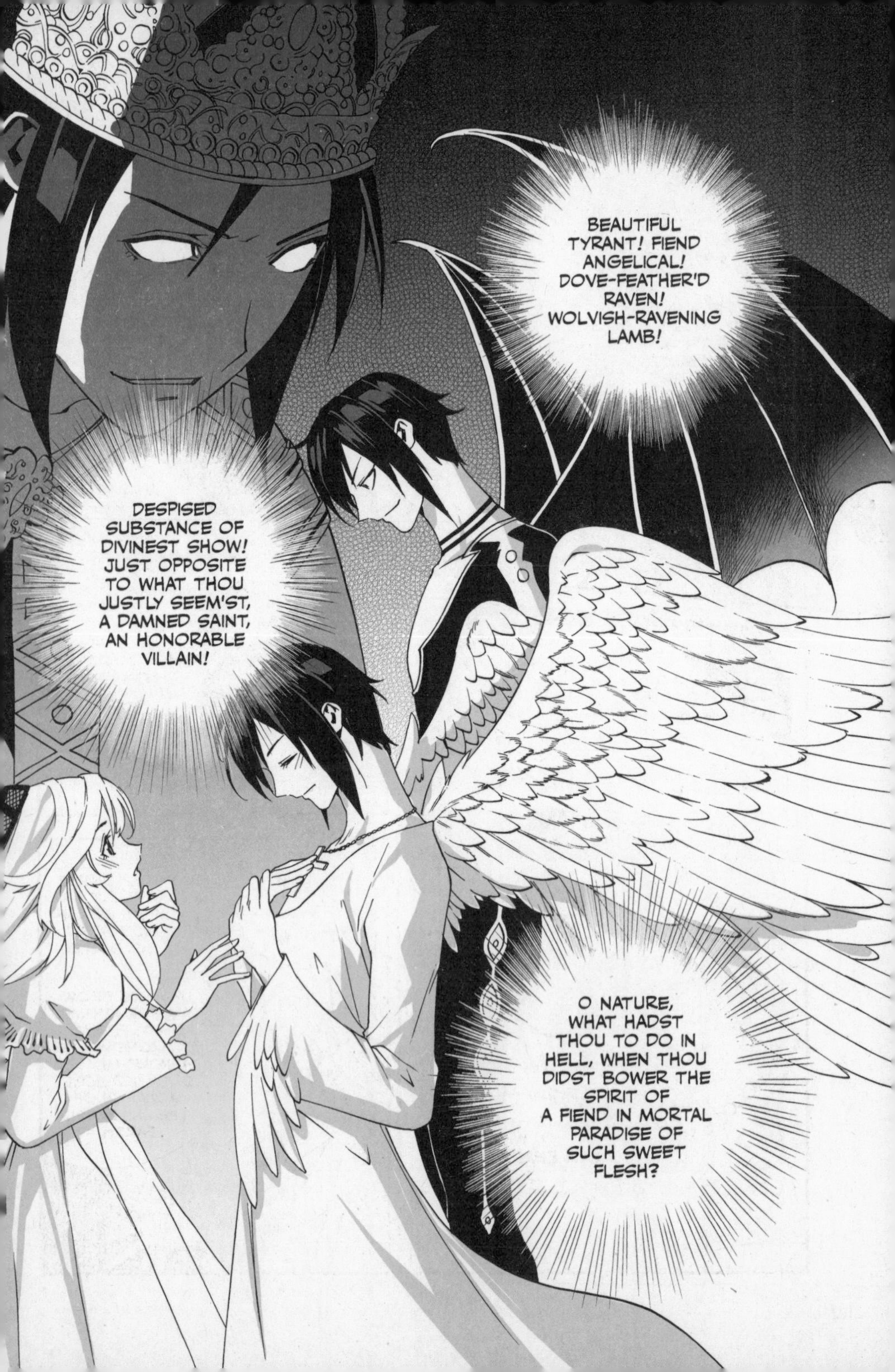
BEAUTIFUL TYRANT! FIEND ANGELICAL! DOVE-FEATHER'D RAVEN! WOLVISH-RAVENING LAMB!
DESPISED SUBSTANCE OF DIVINEST SHOW! JUST OPPOSITE TO WHAT THOU JUSTLY SEEM'ST, A DAMNED SAINT, AN HONORABLE VILLAIN!
O NATURE, WHAT HADST THOU TO DO IN HELL, WHEN THOU DIDST BOWER THE SPIRIT OF A FIEND IN MORTAL PARADISE OF SUCH SWEET FLESH?

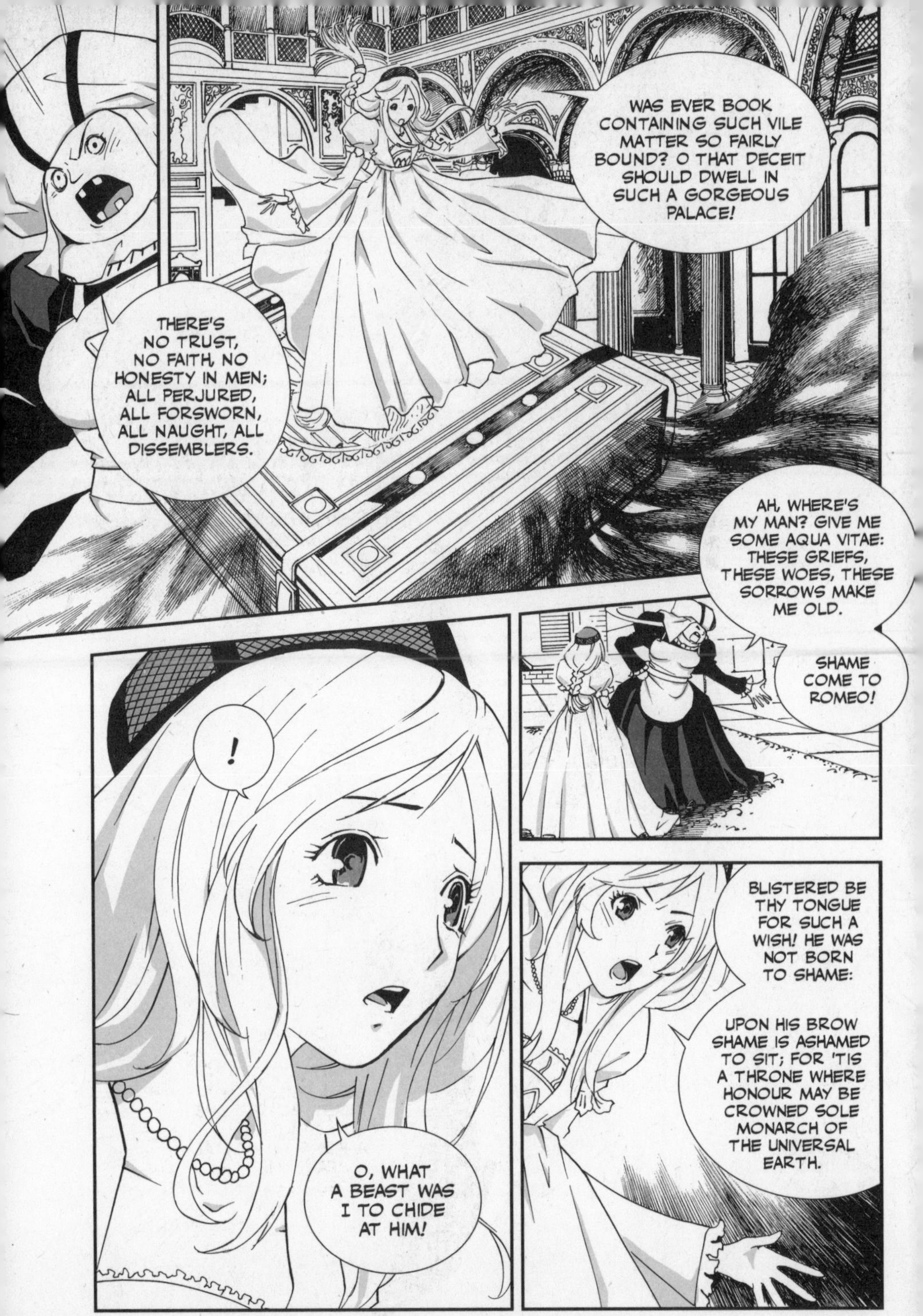
WAS EVER BOOK CONTAINING SUCH VILE MATTER SO FAIRLY BOUND? O THAT DECEIT SHOULD DWELL IN SUCH A GORGEOUS PALACE!
THERE'S NO TRUST, NO FAITH, NO HONESTY IN MEN; ALL PERJURED, ALL FORSWORN, ALL NAUGHT, ALL DISSEMBLERS.
AH, WHERE'S MY MAN? GIVE ME SOME AQUA VITAE: THESE GRIEFS, THESE WOES, THESE SORROWS MAKE ME OLD.
SHAME COME TO ROMEO!
BLISTERED BE THY TONGUE FOR SUCH A WISH! HE WAS NOT BORN TO SHAME:
UPON HIS BROW SHAME IS ASHAMED TO SIT; FOR 'TIS A THRONE WHERE HONOUR MAY BE CROWNED SOLE MONARCH OF THE UNIVERSAL EARTH.
!
O, WHAT A BEAST WAS I TO CHIDE AT HIM!

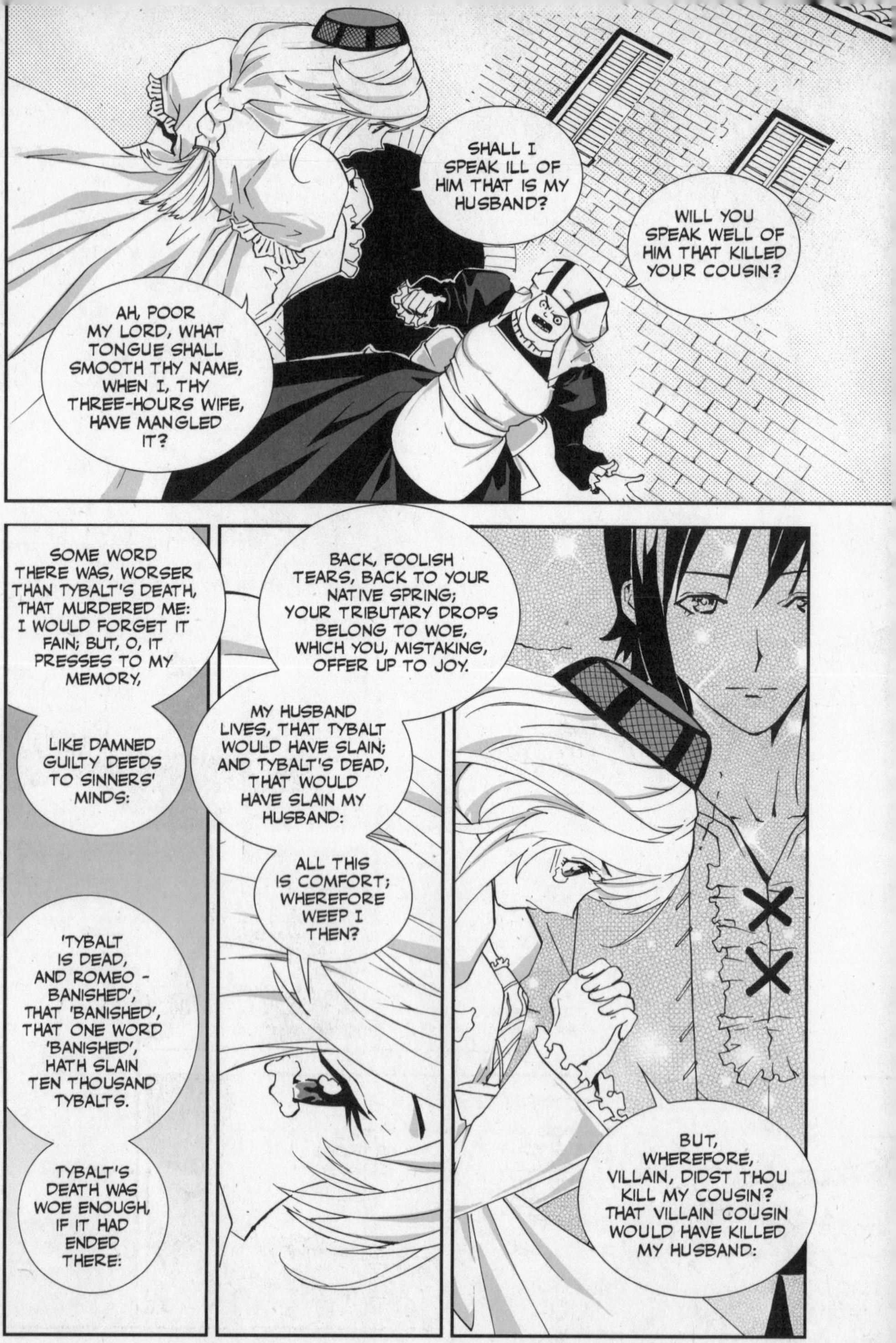
WILL YOU SPEAK WELL OF HIM THAT KILLED YOUR COUSIN?
SHALL I SPEAK ILL OF HIM THAT IS MY HUSBAND?
AH, POOR MY LORD, WHAT TONGUE SHALL SMOOTH THY NAME, WHEN I, THY THREE-HOURS WIFE, HAVE MANGLED IT?
BUT, WHEREFORE, VILLAIN, DIDST THOU KILL MY COUSIN? THAT VILLAIN COUSIN WOULD HAVE KILLED MY HUSBAND:
BACK, FOOLISH TEARS, BACK TO YOUR NATIVE SPRING; YOUR TRIBUTARY DROPS BELONG TO WOE, WHICH YOU, MISTAKING, OFFER UP TO JOY.
MY HUSBAND LIVES, THAT TYBALT WOULD HAVE SLAIN; AND TYBALT'S DEAD, THAT WOULD HAVE SLAIN MY HUSBAND:
ALL THIS IS COMFORT; WHEREFORE WEEP I THEN?
SOME WORD THERE WAS, WORSER THAN TYBALT'S DEATH, THAT MURDERED ME: I WOULD FORGET IT FAIN; BUT, O, IT PRESSES TO MY MEMORY,
LIKE DAMNED GUILTY DEEDS TO SINNERS' MINDS:
'TYBALT IS DEAD, AND ROMEO - BANISHED', THAT 'BANISHED', THAT ONE WORD 'BANISHED', HATH SLAIN TEN THOUSAND TYBALTS.
TYBALT'S DEATH WAS WOE ENOUGH, IF IT HAD ENDED THERE:

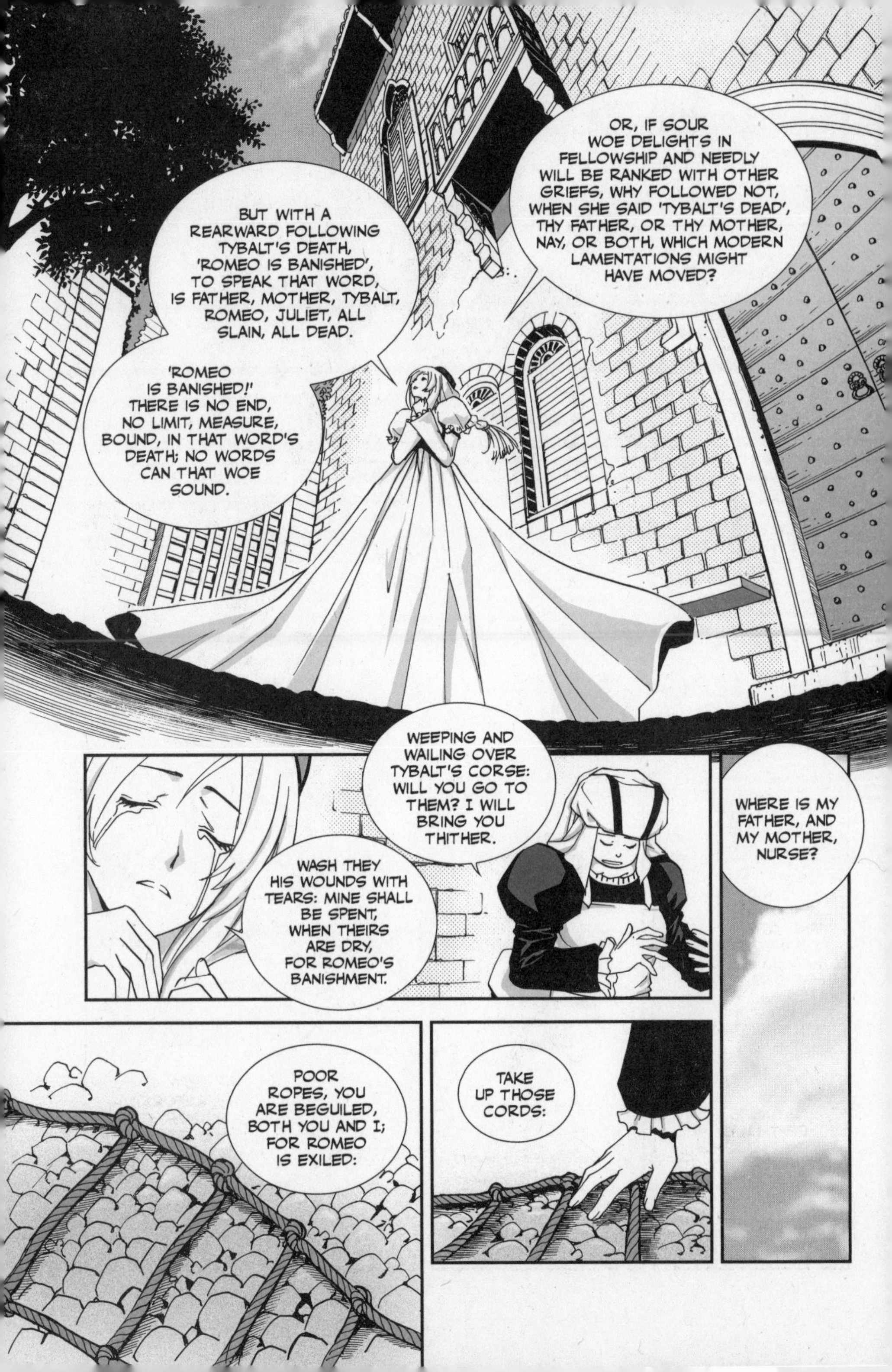
OR, IF SOUR WOE DELIGHTS IN FELLOWSHIP AND NEEDLY WILL BE RANKED WITH OTHER GRIEFS, WHY FOLLOWED NOT, WHEN SHE SAID 'TYBALT'S DEAD', THY FATHER, OR THY MOTHER, NAY, OR BOTH, WHICH MODERN LAMENTATIONS MIGHT HAVE MOVED?
BUT WITH A REARWARD FOLLOWING TYBALT'S DEATH, 'ROMEO IS BANISHED', TO SPEAK THAT WORD, IS FATHER, MOTHER, TYBALT, ROMEO, JULIET, ALL SLAIN, ALL DEAD.
'ROMEO IS BANISHED!' THERE IS NO END, NO LIMIT, MEASURE, BOUND, IN THAT WORD'S DEATH; NO WORDS CAN THAT WOE SOUND.
WHERE IS MY FATHER, AND MY MOTHER, NURSE?
WEEPING AND WAILING OVER TYBALT'S CORSE: WILL YOU GO TO THEM? I WILL BRING YOU THITHER.
WASH THEY HIS WOUNDS WITH TEARS: MINE SHALL BE SPENT, WHEN THEIRS ARE DRY, FOR ROMEO'S BANISHMENT.
TAKE UP THOSE CORDS:
POOR ROPES, YOU ARE BEGUILED, BOTH YOU AND I; FOR ROMEO IS EXILED:

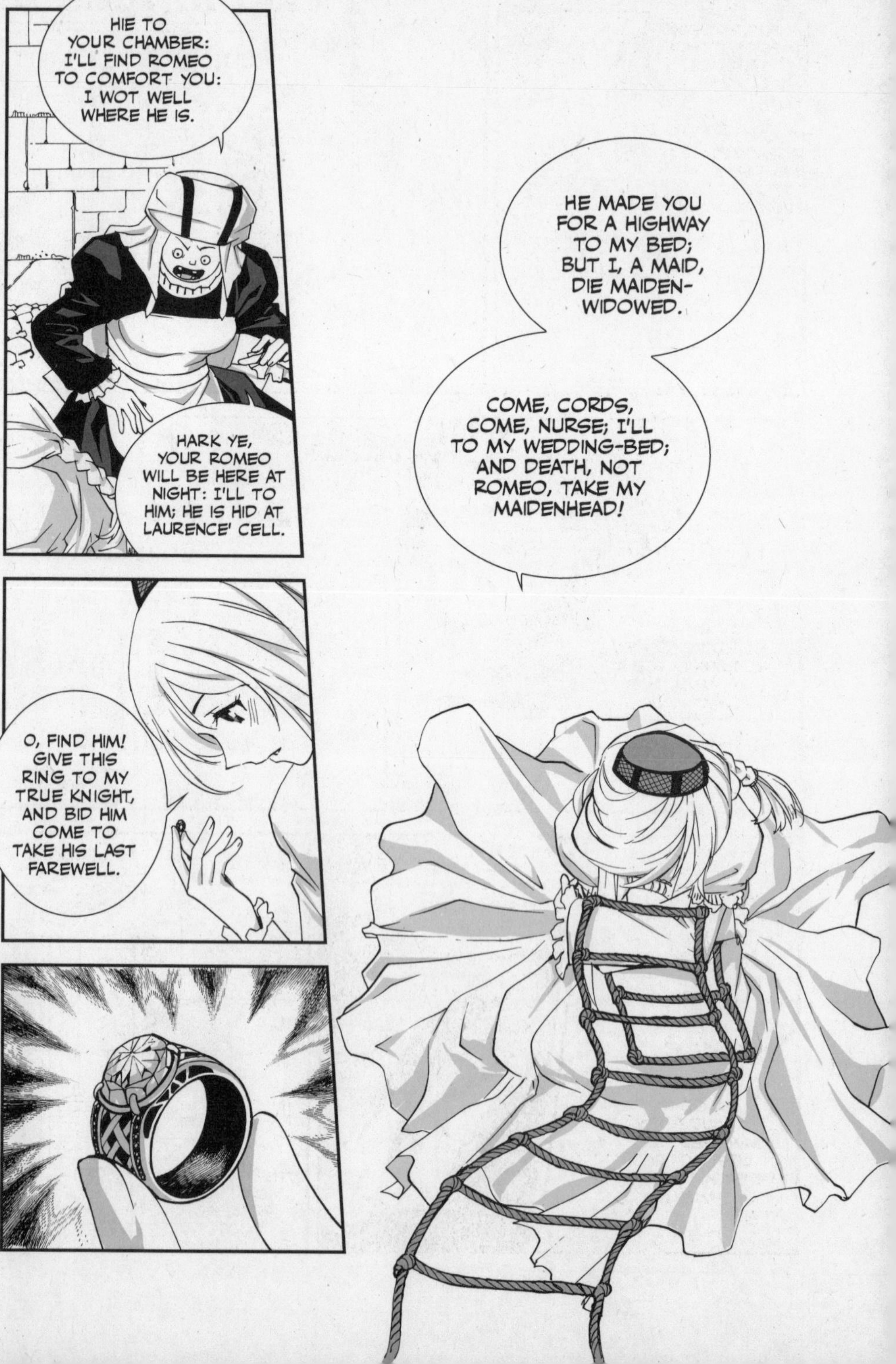

HE MADE YOU FOR A HIGHWAY TO MY BED; BUT I, A MAID, DIE MAIDEN-WIDOWED.
COME, CORDS, COME, NURSE; I'LL TO MY WEDDING-BED; AND DEATH, NOT ROMEO, TAKE MY MAIDENHEAD!
HIE TO YOUR CHAMBER: I'LL FIND ROMEO TO COMFORT YOU: I WOT WELL WHERE HE IS.
HARK YE, YOUR ROMEO WILL BE HERE AT NIGHT: I'LL TO HIM; HE IS HID AT LAURENCE' CELL.
O, FIND HIM! GIVE THIS RING TO MY TRUE KNIGHT, AND BID HIM COME TO TAKE HIS LAST FAREWELL.

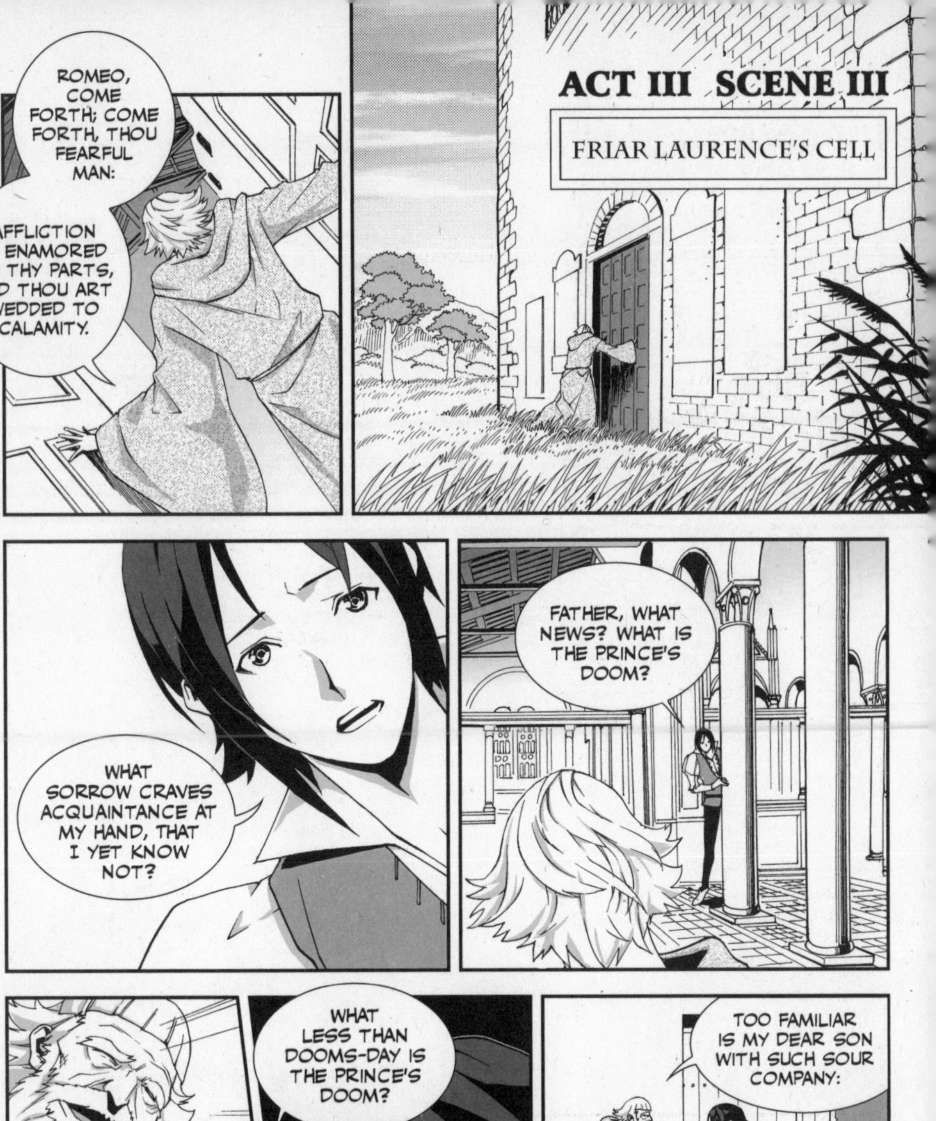
ACT III SCENE III
FRIAR LAURENCE'S CELL
ROMEO, COME FORTH; COME FORTH, THOU FEARFUL MAN:
AFFLICTION IS ENAMORED OF THY PARTS, AND THOU ART WEDDED TO CALAMITY.
FATHER, WHAT NEWS? WHAT IS THE PRINCE'S DOOM?
WHAT SORROW CRAVES ACQUAINTANCE AT MY HAND, THAT I YET KNOW NOT?
TOO FAMILIAR IS MY DEAR SON WITH SUCH SOUR COMPANY:
I BRING THEE TIDINGS OF THE PRINCE'S DOOM.
WHAT LESS THAN DOOMS-DAY IS THE PRINCE'S DOOM?
A GENTLER JUDGMENT VANISHED FROM HIS LIPS, NOT BODY'S DEATH, BUT BODY'S BANISHMENT.

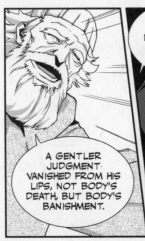

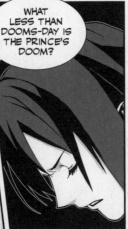

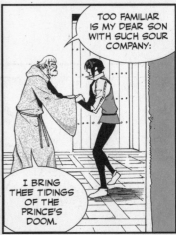

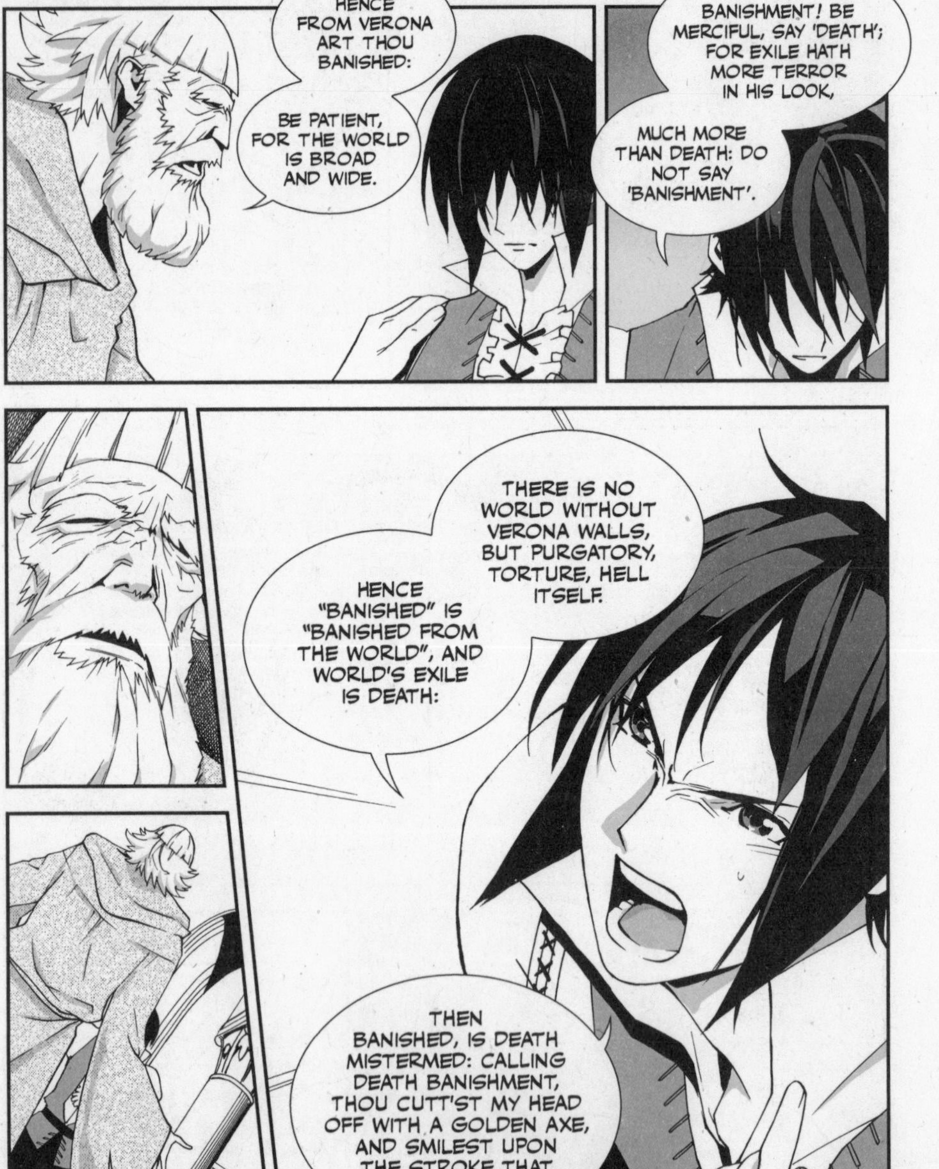
HA, BANISHMENT! BE MERCIFUL, SAY 'DEATH'; FOR EXILE HATH MORE TERROR IN HIS LOOK,
MUCH MORE THAN DEATH: DO NOT SAY 'BANISHMENT'.
HENCE FROM VERONA ART THOU BANISHED:
BE PATIENT, FOR THE WORLD IS BROAD AND WIDE.
THERE IS NO WORLD WITHOUT VERONA WALLS, BUT PURGATORY, TORTURE, HELL ITSELF.
HENCE "BANISHED" IS "BANISHED FROM THE WORLD", AND WORLD'S EXILE IS DEATH:
THEN BANISHED, IS DEATH MISTERMED: CALLING DEATH BANISHMENT, THOU CUTT'ST MY HEAD OFF WITH A GOLDEN AXE, AND SMILEST UPON THE STROKE THAT MURDERS ME.
O DEADLY SIN! O RUDE UNTHANKFULNESS! THY FAULT OUR LAW CALLS DEATH;

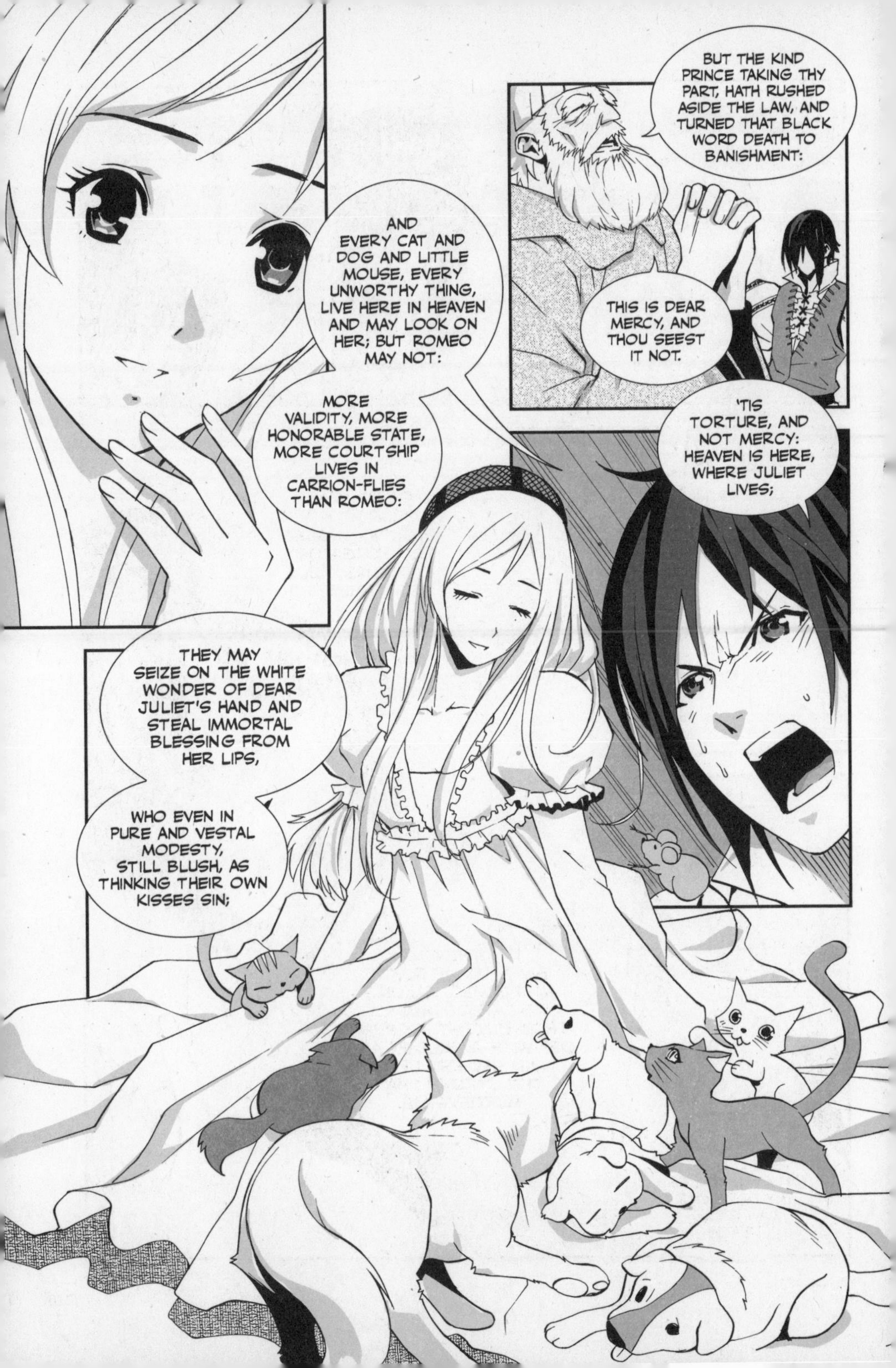
BUT THE KIND PRINCE TAKING THY PART, HATH RUSHED ASIDE THE LAW, AND TURNED THAT BLACK WORD DEATH TO BANISHMENT:
THIS IS DEAR MERCY, AND THOU SEEST IT NOT.
'TIS TORTURE, AND NOT MERCY: HEAVEN IS HERE, WHERE JULIET LIVES;
AND EVERY CAT AND DOG AND LITTLE MOUSE, EVERY UNWORTHY THING, LIVE HERE IN HEAVEN AND MAY LOOK ON HER; BUT ROMEO MAY NOT:
MORE VALIDITY, MORE HONORABLE STATE, MORE COURTSHIP LIVES IN CARRION-FLIES THAN ROMEO:
THEY MAY SEIZE ON THE WHITE WONDER OF DEAR JULIET'S HAND AND STEAL IMMORTAL BLESSING FROM HER LIPS,
WHO EVEN IN PURE AND VESTAL MODESTY, STILL BLUSH, AS THINKING THEIR OWN KISSES SIN;

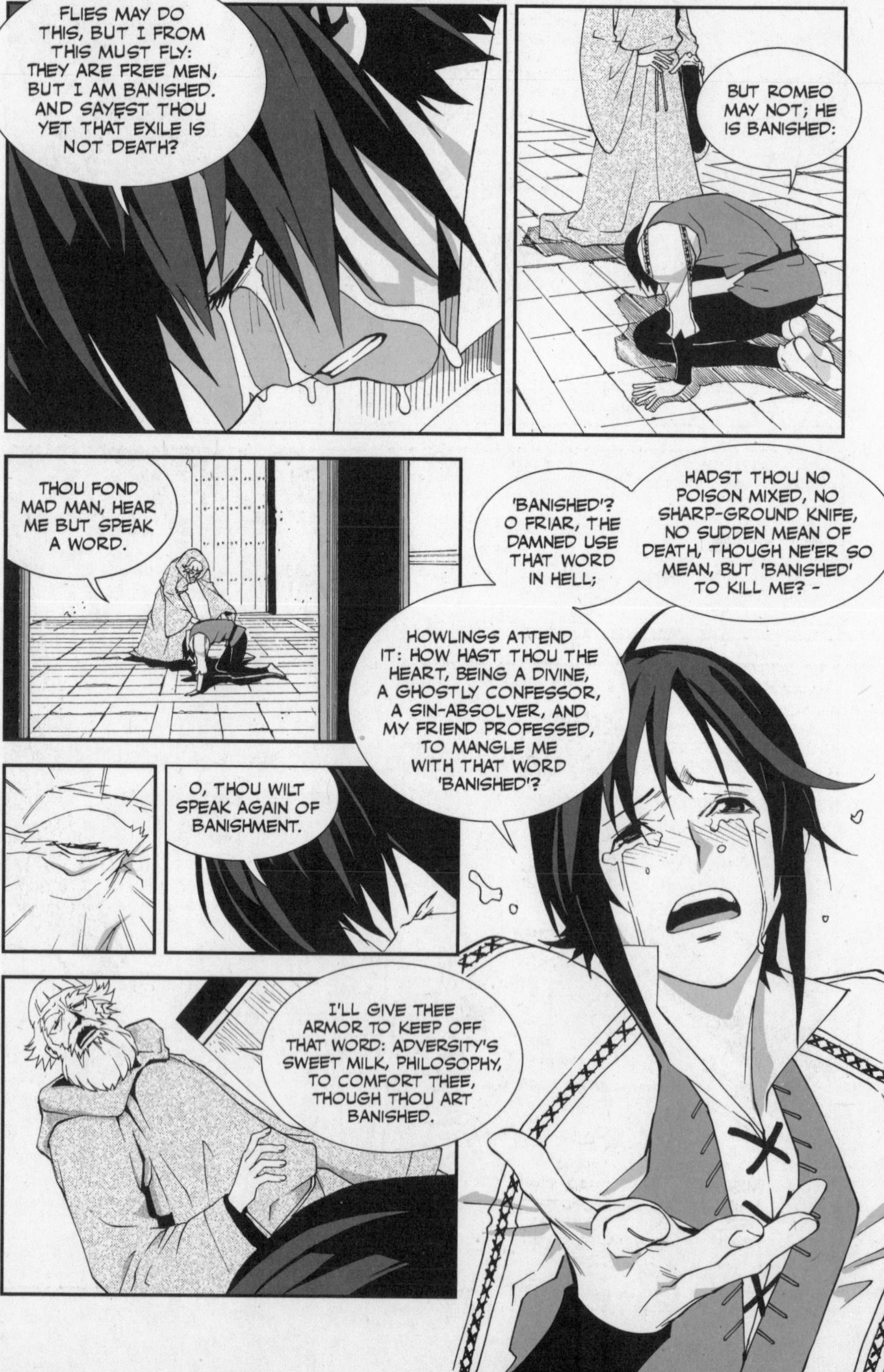
BUT ROMEO MAY NOT; HE IS BANISHED:
FLIES MAY DO THIS, BUT I FROM THIS MUST FLY: THEY ARE FREE MEN, BUT I AM BANISHED. AND SAYEST THOU YET THAT EXILE IS NOT DEATH?
HADST THOU NO POISON MIXED, NO SHARP-GROUND KNIFE, NO SUDDEN MEAN OF DEATH, THOUGH NE'ER SO MEAN, BUT 'BANISHED' TO KILL ME? -
'BANISHED'? O FRIAR, THE DAMNED USE THAT WORD IN HELL;
HOWLINGS ATTEND IT: HOW HAST THOU THE HEART, BEING A DIVINE, A GHOSTLY CONFESSOR, A SIN-ABSOLVER, AND MY FRIEND PROFESSED, TO MANGLE ME WITH THAT WORD 'BANISHED'?
THOU FOND MAD MAN, HEAR ME BUT SPEAK A WORD.
O, THOU WILT SPEAK AGAIN OF BANISHMENT.
I'LL GIVE THEE ARMOR TO KEEP OFF THAT WORD: ADVERSITY'S SWEET MILK, PHILOSOPHY, TO COMFORT THEE, THOUGH THOU ART BANISHED.

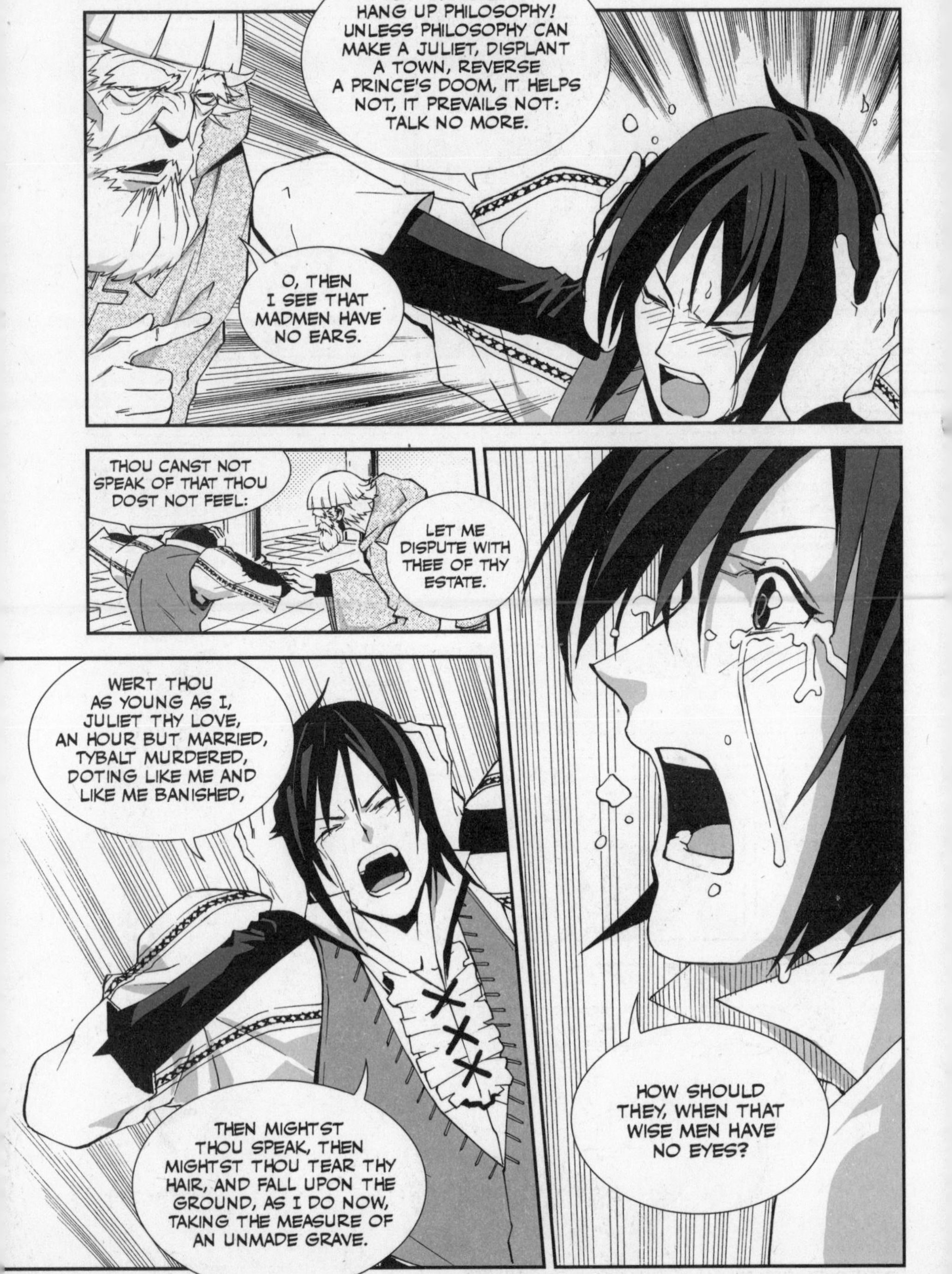
YET 'BANISHED'? HANG UP PHILOSOPHY! UNLESS PHILOSOPHY CAN MAKE A JULIET, DISPLANT A TOWN, REVERSE A PRINCE'S DOOM, IT HELPS NOT, IT PREVAILS NOT: TALK NO MORE.
O, THEN I SEE THAT MADMEN HAVE NO EARS.
HOW SHOULD THEY, WHEN THAT WISE MEN HAVE NO EYES?
LET ME DISPUTE WITH THEE OF THY ESTATE.
THOU CANST NOT SPEAK OF THAT THOU DOST NOT FEEL:
WERT THOU AS YOUNG AS I, JULIET THY LOVE, AN HOUR BUT MARRIED, TYBALT MURDERED, DOTING LIKE ME AND LIKE ME BANISHED,
THEN MIGHTST THOU SPEAK, THEN MIGHTST THOU TEAR THY HAIR, AND FALL UPON THE GROUND, AS I DO NOW, TAKING THE MEASURE OF AN UNMADE GRAVE.

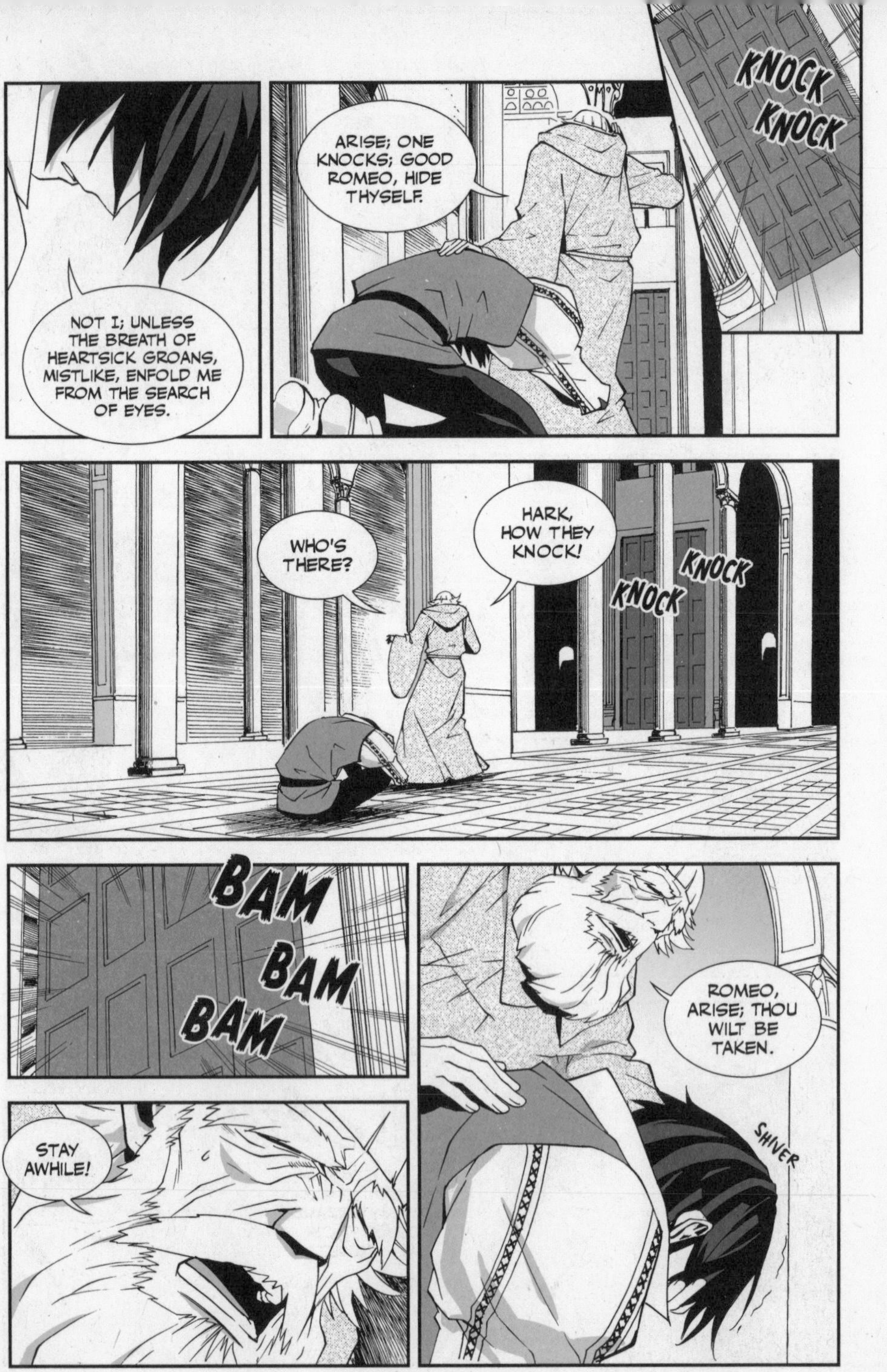
KNOCK
KNOCK
ARISE; ONE KNOCKS; GOOD ROMEO, HIDE THYSELF.
NOT I; UNLESS THE BREATH OF HEARTSICK GROANS, MISTLIKE, ENFOLD ME FROM THE SEARCH OF EYES.
HARK, HOW THEY KNOCK!
KNOCK
KNOCK
WHO'S THERE?
ROMEO, ARISE; THOU WILT BE TAKEN.
SHIVER
BAM
BAM
BAM
STAY AWHILE!

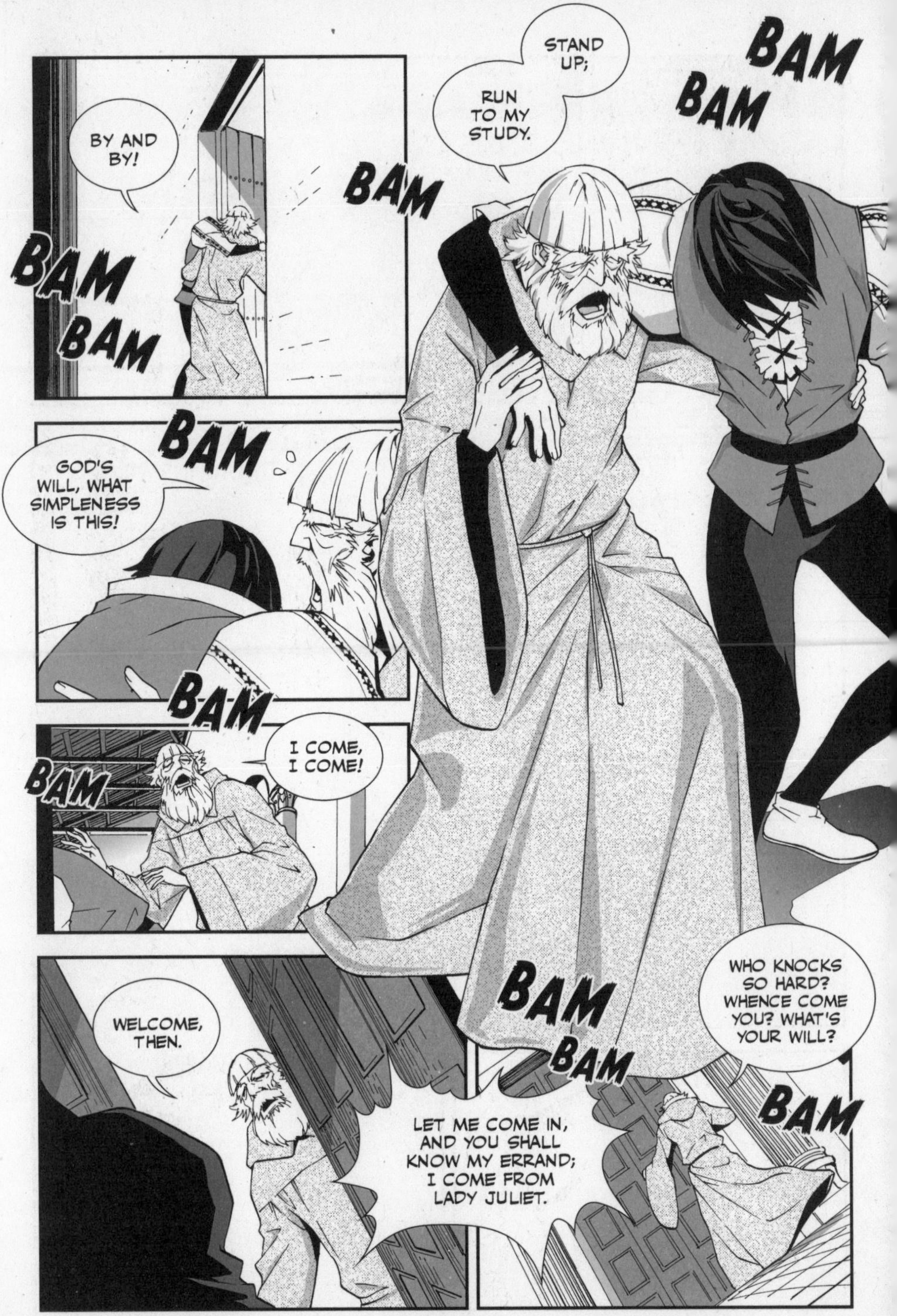
BAM
BAM
STAND UP;
RUN TO MY STUDY.
BAM
BAM
BAM
BY AND BY!
BAM
GOD'S WILL, WHAT SIMPLENESS IS THIS!
BAM
BAM
I COME, I COME!
WHO KNOCKS SO HARD? WHENCE COME YOU? WHAT'S YOUR WILL?
BAM
BAM
BAM
LET ME COME IN, AND YOU SHALL KNOW MY ERRAND; I COME FROM LADY JULIET.
WELCOME, THEN.

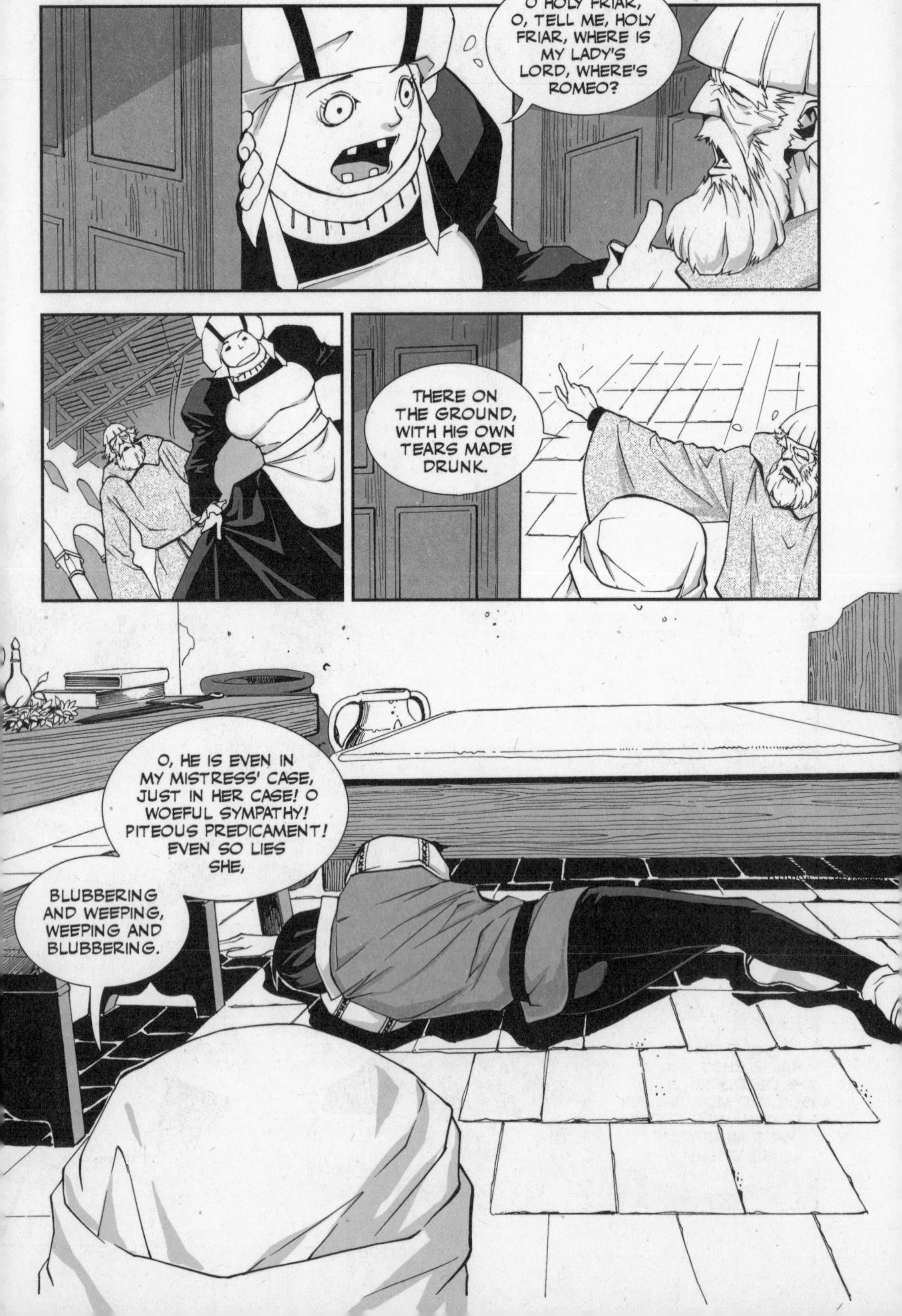
O HOLY FRIAR, O, TELL ME, HOLY FRIAR, WHERE IS MY LADY'S LORD, WHERE'S ROMEO?
THERE ON THE GROUND, WITH HIS OWN TEARS MADE DRUNK.
O, HE IS EVEN IN MY MISTRESS' CASE, JUST IN HER CASE! O WOEFUL SYMPATHY! PITEOUS PREDICAMENT! EVEN SO LIES SHE,
BLUBBERING AND WEEPING, WEEPING AND BLUBBERING.

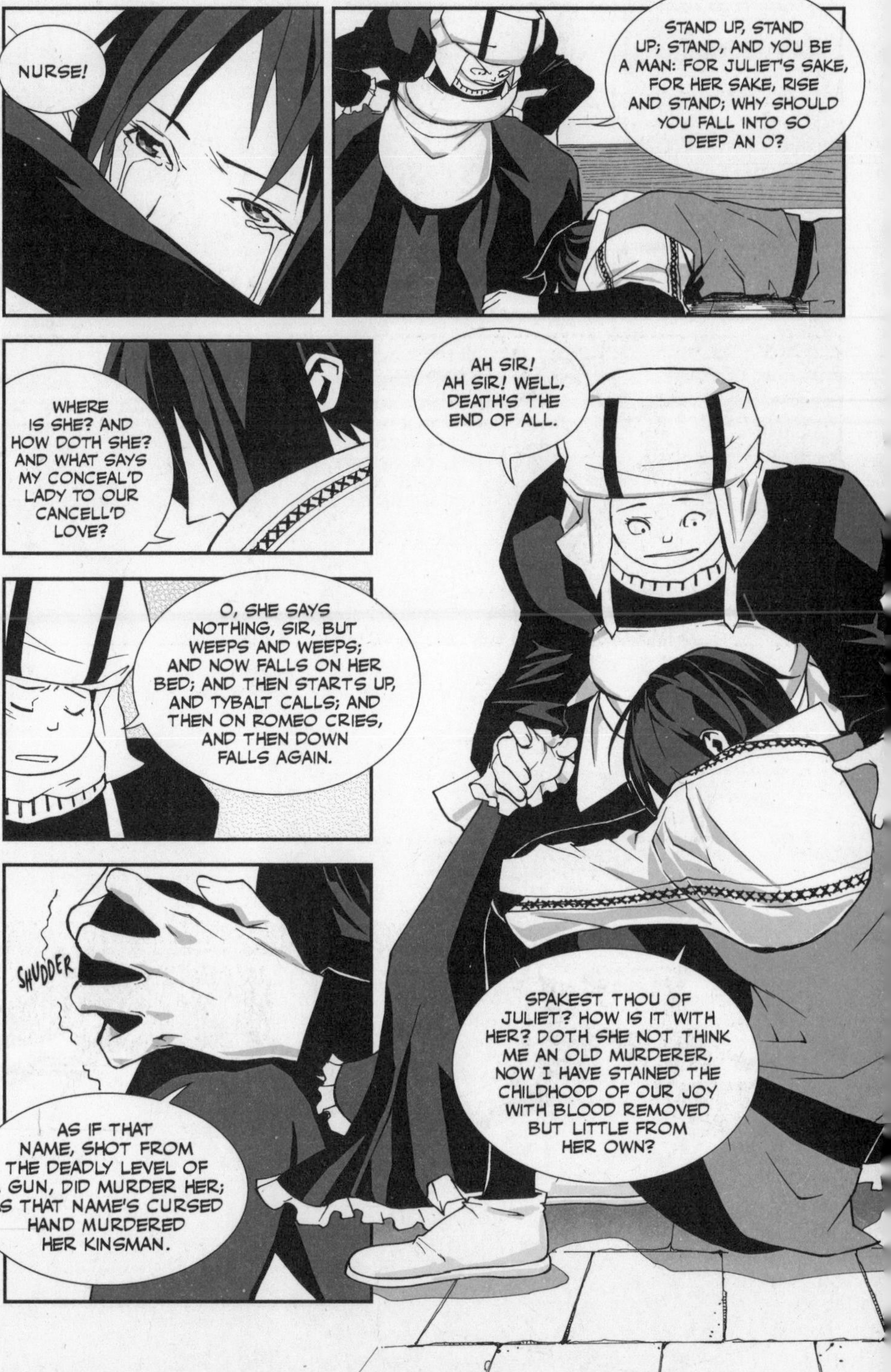
STAND UP, STAND UP; STAND, AND YOU BE A MAN: FOR JULIET'S SAKE, FOR HER SAKE, RISE AND STAND; WHY SHOULD YOU FALL INTO SO DEEP AN O?
NURSE!
AH SIR! AH SIR! WELL, DEATH'S THE END OF ALL.
SPAKEST THOU OF JULIET? HOW IS IT WITH HER? DOTH SHE NOT THINK ME AN OLD MURDERER, NOW I HAVE STAINED THE CHILDHOOD OF OUR JOY WITH BLOOD REMOVED BUT LITTLE FROM HER OWN?
WHERE IS SHE? AND HOW DOTH SHE? AND WHAT SAYS MY CONCEAL'D LADY TO OUR CANCELL'D LOVE?
O, SHE SAYS NOTHING, SIR, BUT WEEPS AND WEEPS; AND NOW FALLS ON HER BED; AND THEN STARTS UP, AND TYBALT CALLS; AND THEN ON ROMEO CRIES, AND THEN DOWN FALLS AGAIN.
SHUDDER
AS IF THAT NAME, SHOT FROM THE DEADLY LEVEL OF A GUN, DID MURDER HER; AS THAT NAME'S CURSED HAND MURDERED HER KINSMAN.

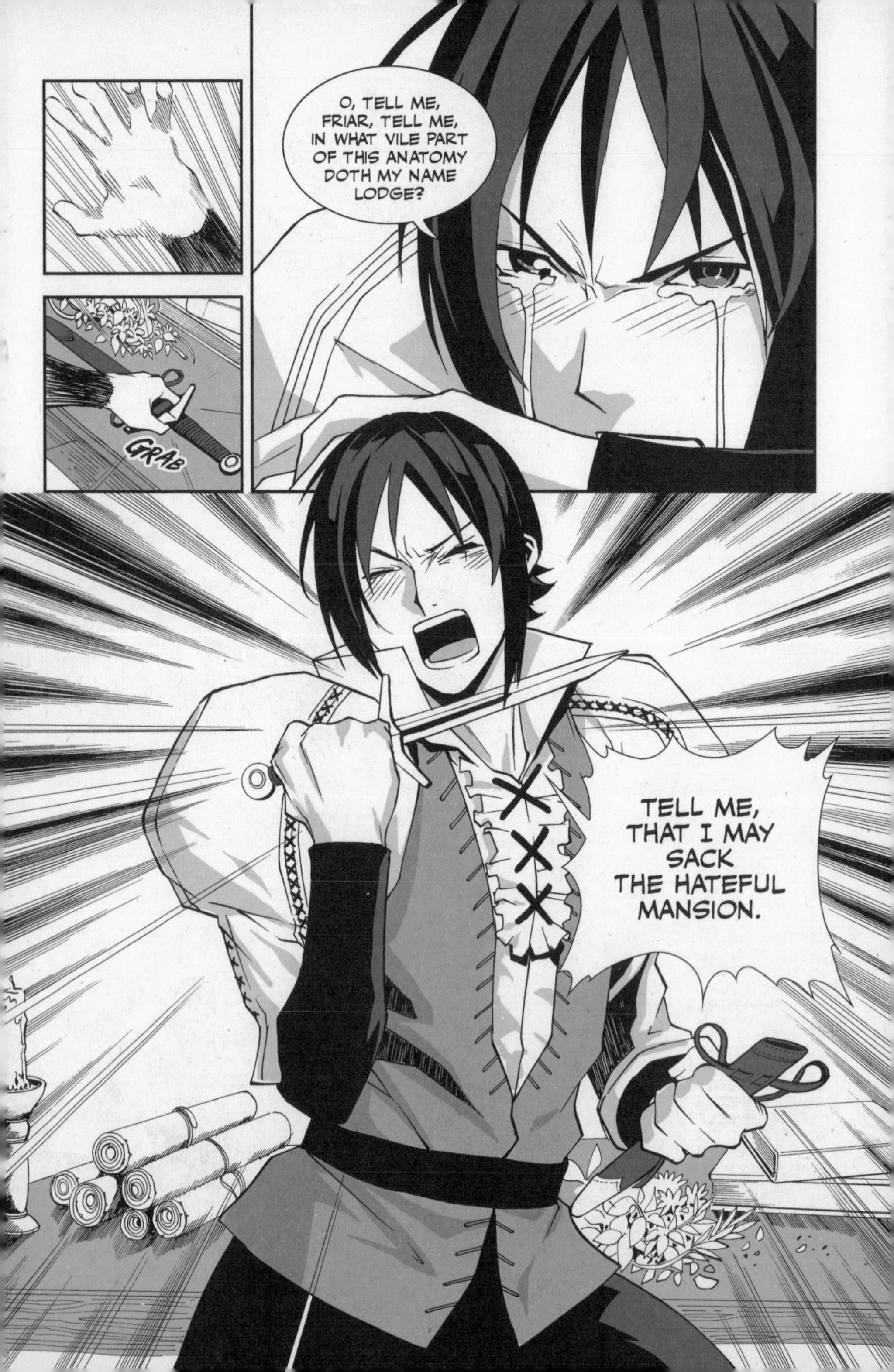
O, TELL ME, FRIAR, TELL ME, IN WHAT VILE PART OF THIS ANATOMY DOTH MY NAME LODGE?
GRAB
TELL ME, THAT I MAY SACK THE HATEFUL MANSION.

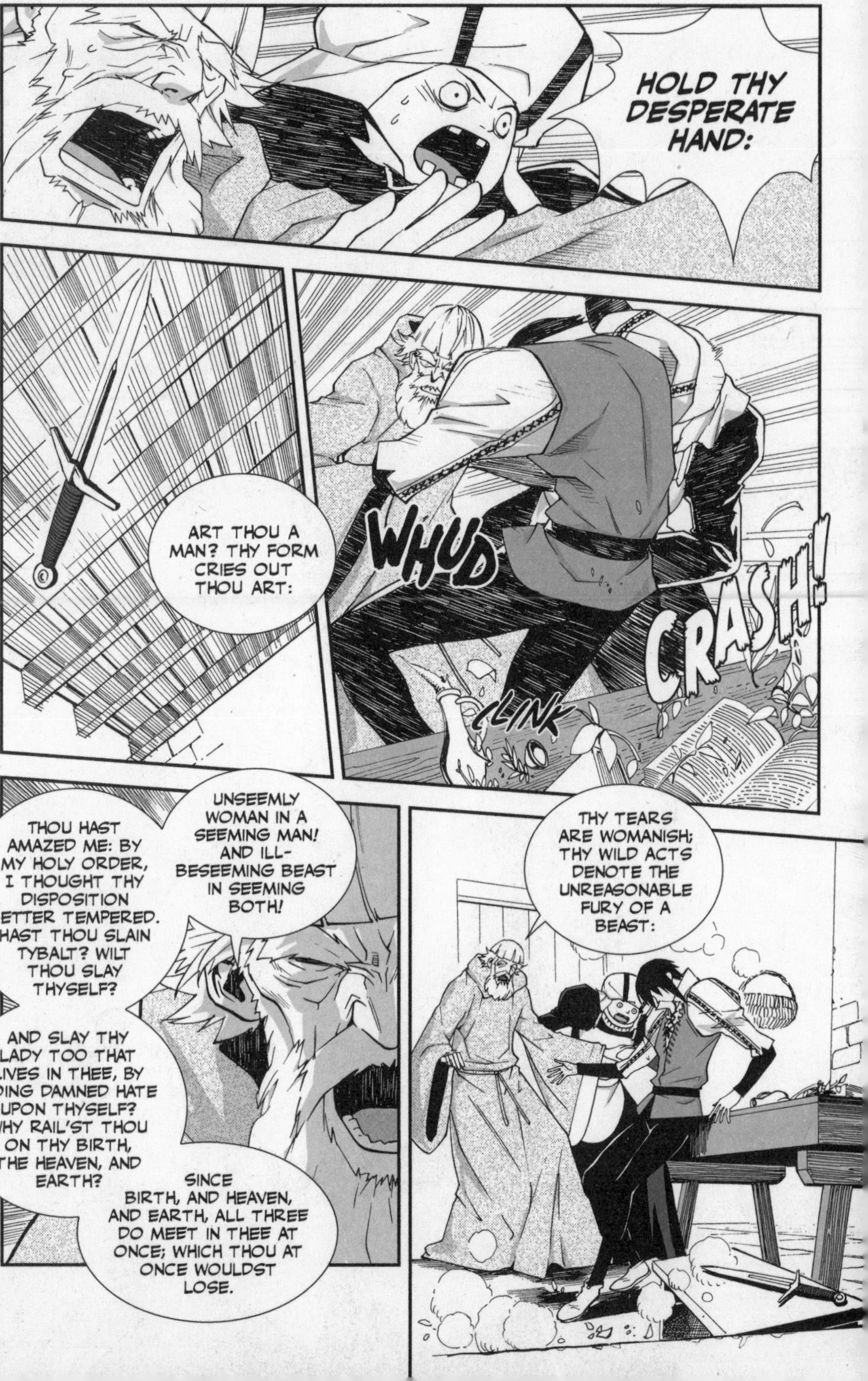

HOLD THY DESPERATE HAND:
WHUD
CRASH!
CLINK
ART THOU A MAN? THY FORM CRIES OUT THOU ART:
THY TEARS ARE WOMANISH; THY WILD ACTS DENOTE THE UNREASONABLE FURY OF A BEAST:
UNSEEMLY WOMAN IN A SEEMING MAN! AND ILL-BESEEMING BEAST IN SEEMING BOTH!
THOU HAST AMAZED ME: BY MY HOLY ORDER, I THOUGHT THY DISPOSITION BETTER TEMPERED. HAST THOU SLAIN TYBALT? WILT THOU SLAY THYSELF?
AND SLAY THY LADY TOO THAT LIVES IN THEE, BY DOING DAMNED HATE UPON THYSELF? WHY RAIL'ST THOU ON THY BIRTH, THE HEAVEN, AND EARTH?
SINCE BIRTH, AND HEAVEN, AND EARTH, ALL THREE DO MEET IN THEE AT ONCE; WHICH THOU AT ONCE WOULDST LOSE.

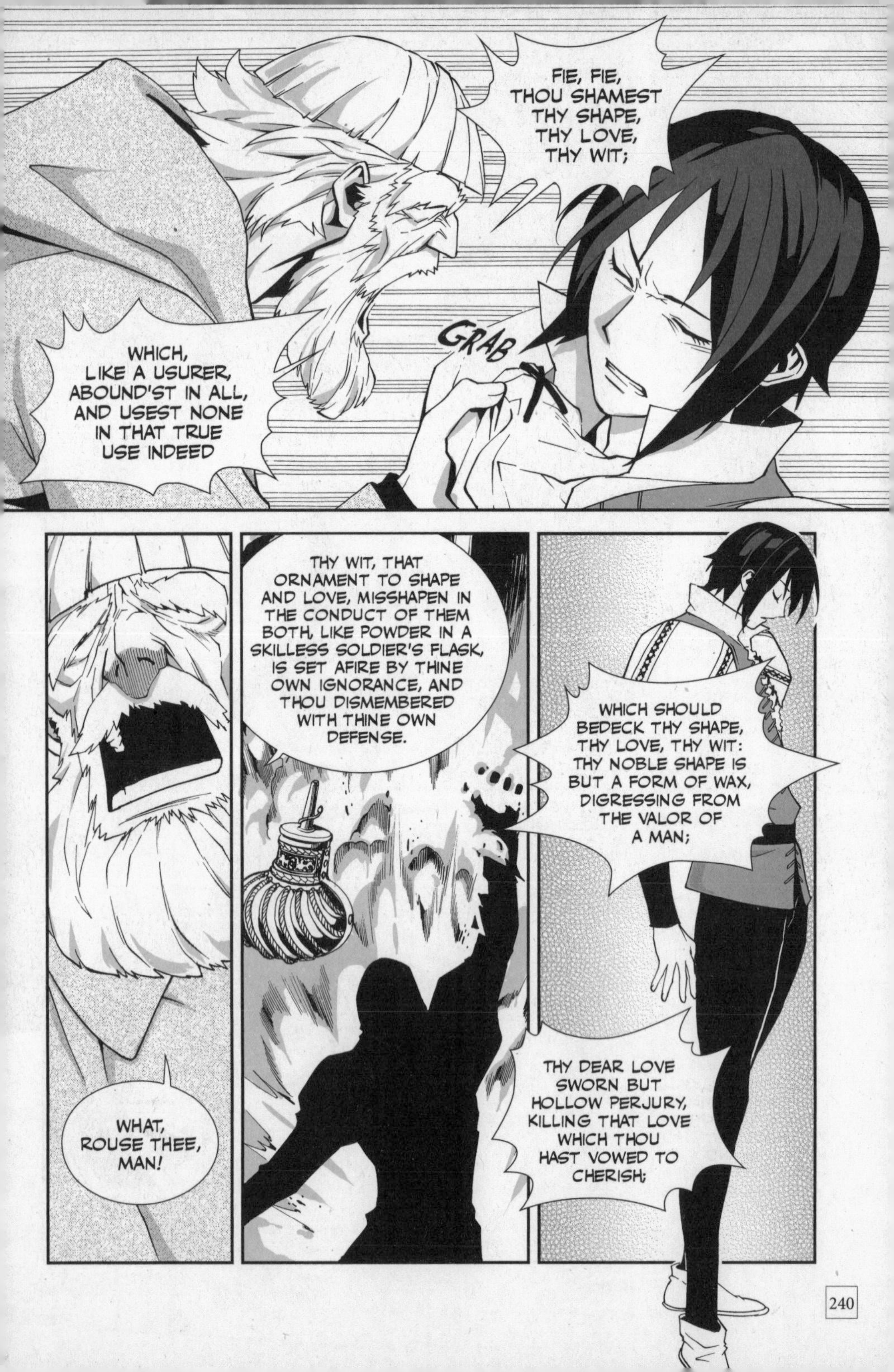
FIE, FIE, THOU SHAMEST THY SHAPE, THY LOVE, THY WIT;
GRAB
WHICH, LIKE A USURER, ABOUND'ST IN ALL, AND USEST NONE IN THAT TRUE USE INDEED
WHICH SHOULD BEDECK THY SHAPE, THY LOVE, THY WIT: THY NOBLE SHAPE IS BUT A FORM OF WAX, DIGRESSING FROM THE VALOR OF A MAN;
THY DEAR LOVE SWORN BUT HOLLOW PERJURY, KILLING THAT LOVE WHICH THOU HAST VOWED TO CHERISH;
THY WIT, THAT ORNAMENT TO SHAPE AND LOVE, MISSHAPEN IN THE CONDUCT OF THEM BOTH, LIKE POWDER IN A SKILLESS SOLDIER'S FLASK, IS SET AFIRE BY THINE OWN IGNORANCE, AND THOU DISMEMBERED WITH THINE OWN DEFENSE.
...
WHAT, ROUSE THEE, MAN!

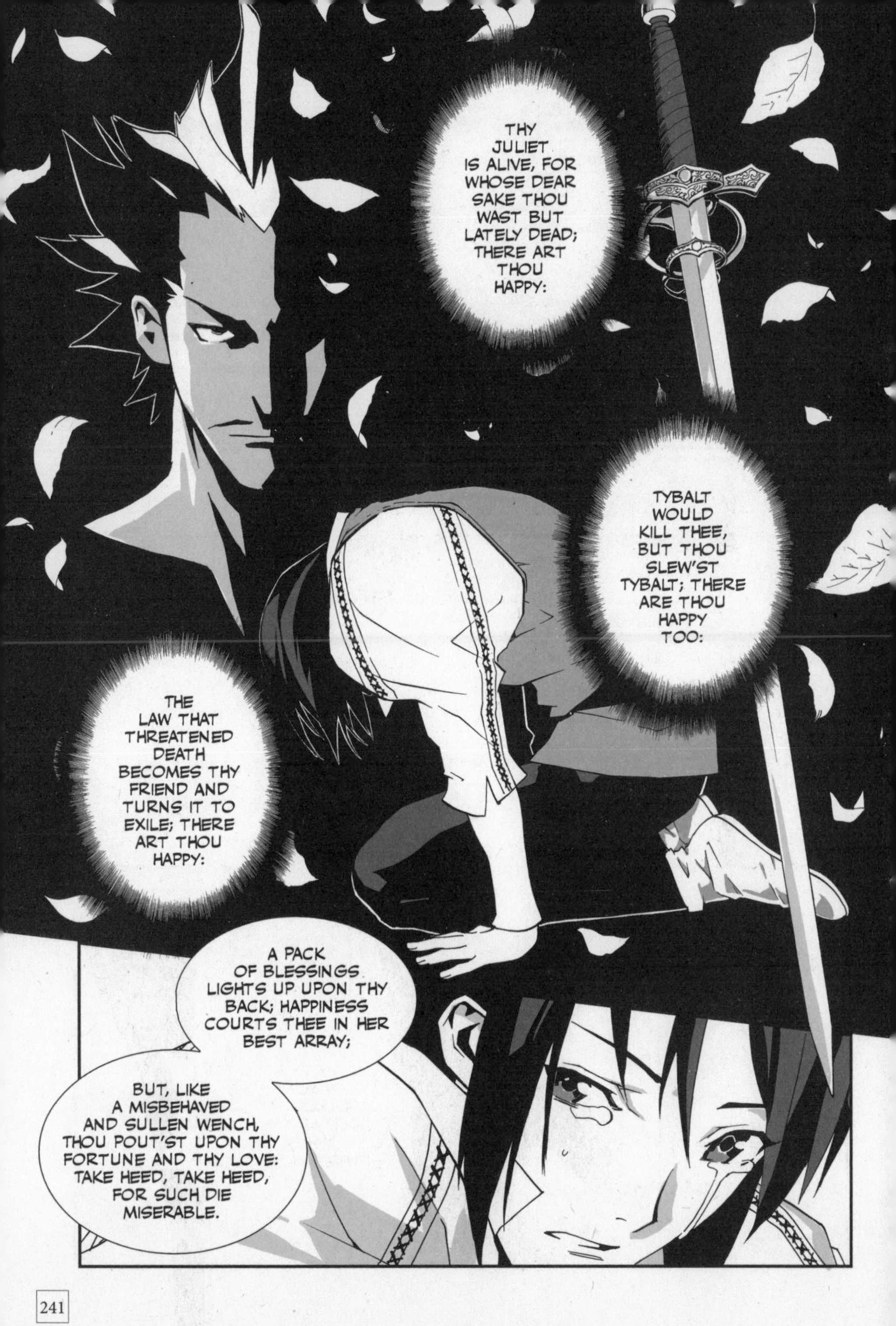
THY JULIET IS ALIVE, FOR WHOSE DEAR SAKE THOU WAST BUT LATELY DEAD; THERE ART THOU HAPPY:
TYBALT WOULD KILL THEE, BUT THOU SLEW'ST TYBALT; THERE ARE THOU HAPPY TOO:
THE LAW THAT THREATENED DEATH BECOMES THY FRIEND AND TURNS IT TO EXILE; THERE ART THOU HAPPY:
A PACK OF BLESSINGS LIGHTS UP UPON THY BACK; HAPPINESS COURTS THEE IN HER BEST ARRAY;
BUT, LIKE A MISBEHAVED AND SULLEN WENCH, THOU POUT'ST UPON THY FORTUNE AND THY LOVE: TAKE HEED, TAKE HEED, FOR SUCH DIE MISERABLE.

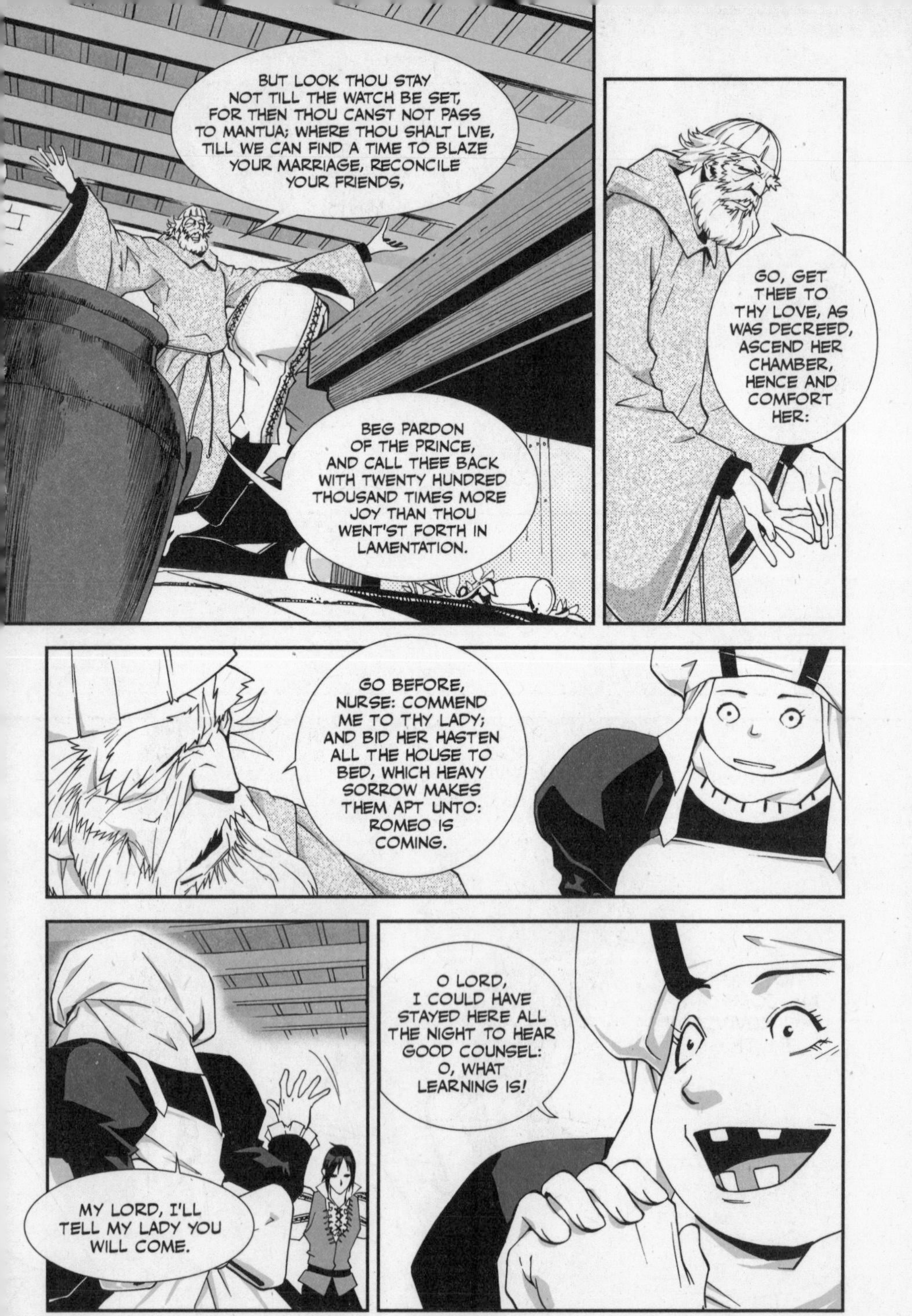
GO, GET THEE TO THY LOVE, AS WAS DECREED, ASCEND HER CHAMBER, HENCE AND COMFORT HER:
BUT LOOK THOU STAY NOT TILL THE WATCH BE SET, FOR THEN THOU CANST NOT PASS TO MANTUA; WHERE THOU SHALT LIVE, TILL WE CAN FIND A TIME TO BLAZE YOUR MARRIAGE, RECONCILE YOUR FRIENDS,
BEG PARDON OF THE PRINCE, AND CALL THEE BACK WITH TWENTY HUNDRED THOUSAND TIMES MORE JOY THAN THOU WENT'ST FORTH IN LAMENTATION.
GO BEFORE, NURSE: COMMEND ME TO THY LADY; AND BID HER HASTEN ALL THE HOUSE TO BED, WHICH HEAVY SORROW MAKES THEM APT UNTO: ROMEO IS COMING.
O LORD, I COULD HAVE STAYED HERE ALL THE NIGHT TO HEAR GOOD COUNSEL: O, WHAT LEARNING IS!
MY LORD, I'LL TELL MY LADY YOU WILL COME.

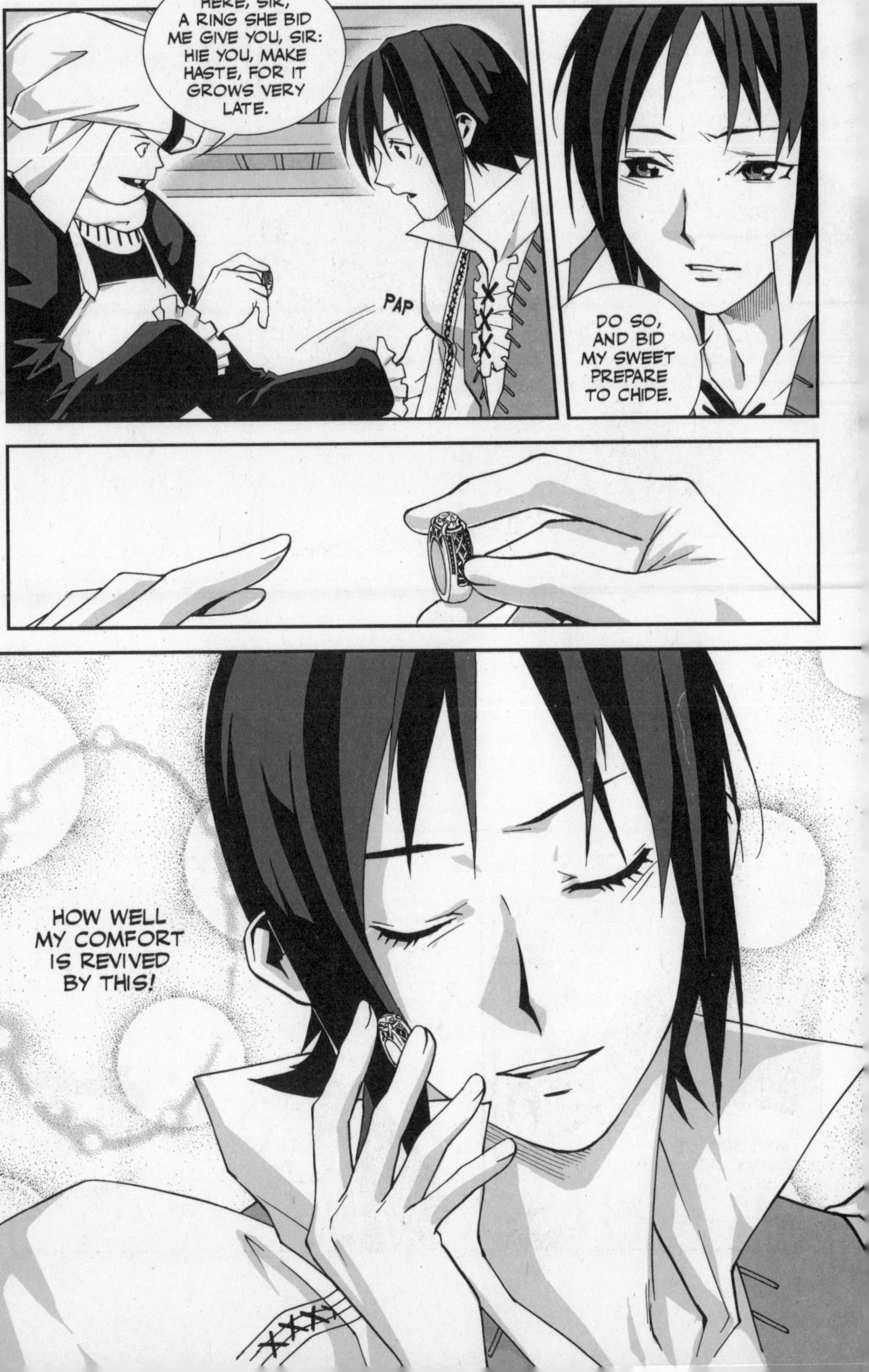
DO SO, AND BID MY SWEET PREPARE TO CHIDE.
HERE, SIR, A RING SHE BID ME GIVE YOU, SIR: HIE YOU, MAKE HASTE, FOR IT GROWS VERY LATE.
PAP
HOW WELL MY COMFORT IS REVIVED BY THIS!

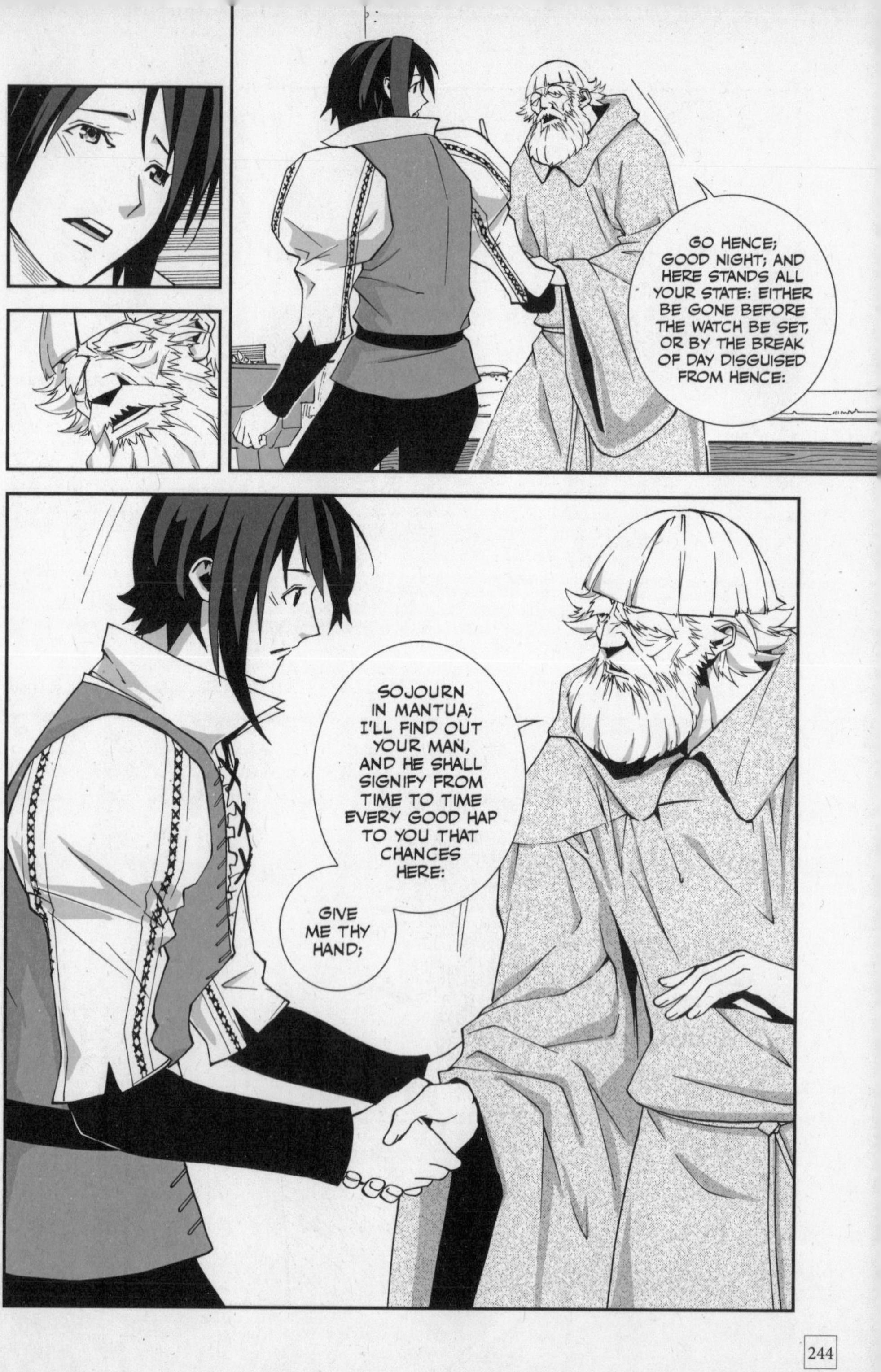
GO HENCE; GOOD NIGHT; AND HERE STANDS ALL YOUR STATE: EITHER BE GONE BEFORE THE WATCH BE SET, OR BY THE BREAK OF DAY DISGUISED FROM HENCE:
SOJOURN IN MANTUA; I'LL FIND OUT YOUR MAN, AND HE SHALL SIGNIFY FROM TIME TO TIME EVERY GOOD HAP TO YOU THAT CHANCES HERE:
GIVE ME THY HAND;

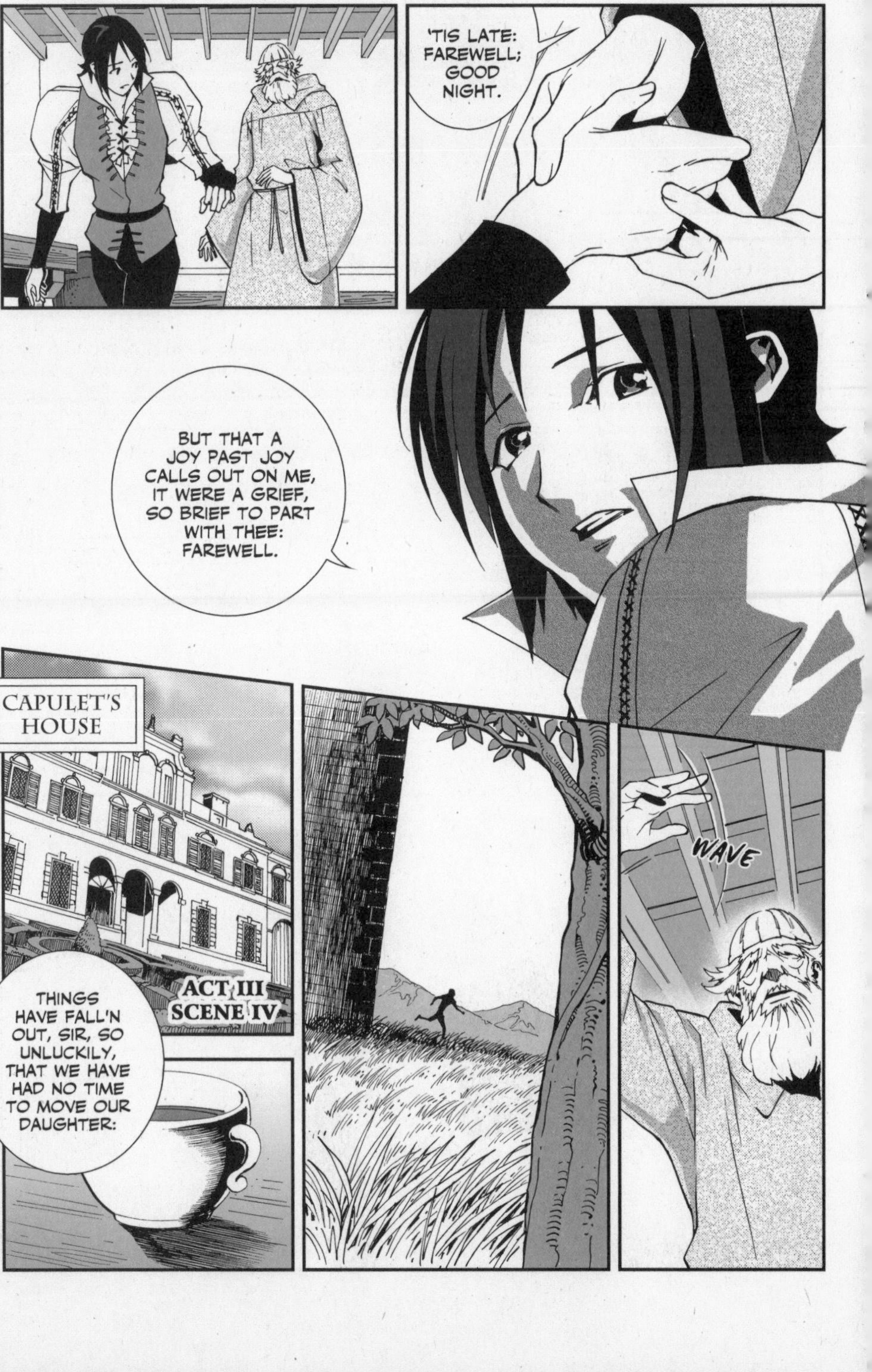
'TIS LATE: FAREWELL; GOOD NIGHT.
BUT THAT A JOY PAST JOY CALLS OUT ON ME, IT WERE A GRIEF, SO BRIEF TO PART WITH THEE: FAREWELL.
WAVE
CAPULET'S HOUSE
ACT III SCENE IV
THINGS HAVE FALL'N OUT, SIR, SO UNLUCKILY, THAT WE HAVE HAD NO TIME TO MOVE OUR DAUGHTER:

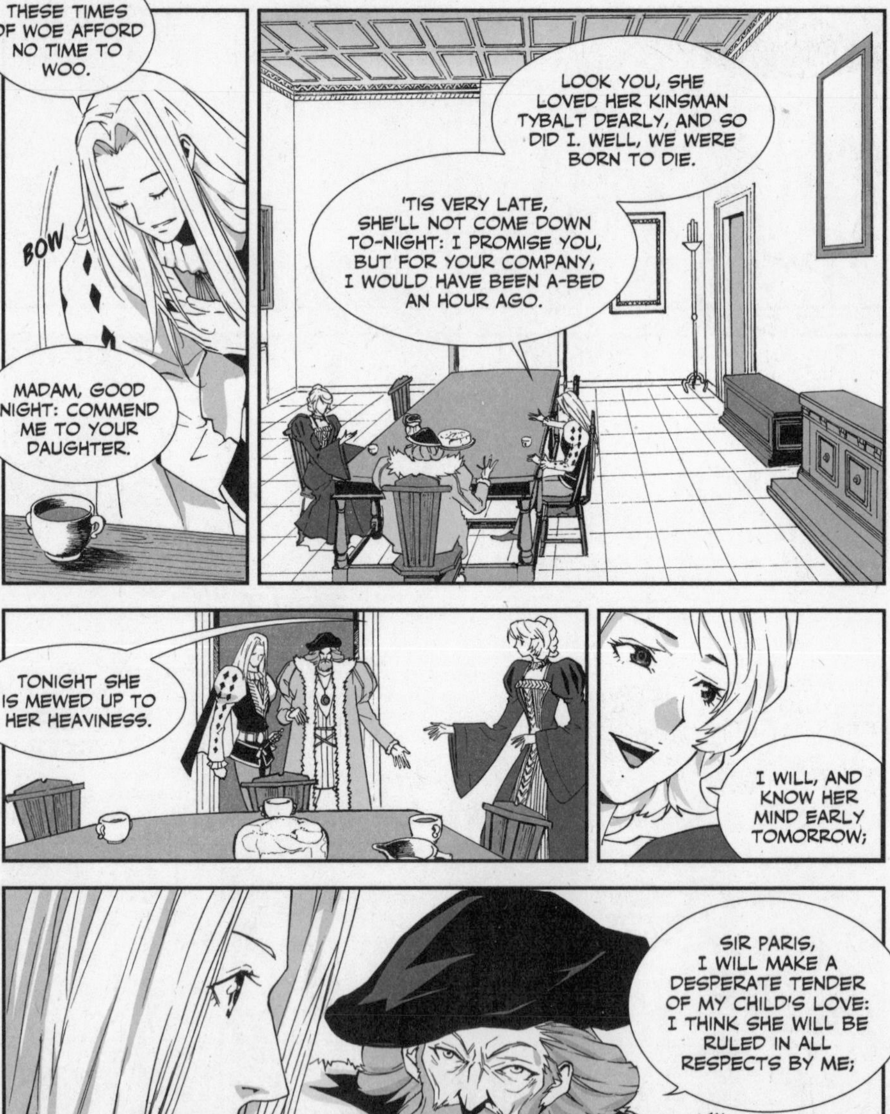
LOOK YOU, SHE LOVED HER KINSMAN TYBALT DEARLY, AND SO DID I. WELL, WE WERE BORN TO DIE.
'TIS VERY LATE, SHE'LL NOT COME DOWN TO-NIGHT: I PROMISE YOU, BUT FOR YOUR COMPANY, I WOULD HAVE BEEN A-BED AN HOUR AGO.
THESE TIMES OF WOE AFFORD NO TIME TO WOO.
BOW
MADAM, GOOD NIGHT: COMMEND ME TO YOUR DAUGHTER.
I WILL, AND KNOW HER MIND EARLY TOMORROW;
TONIGHT SHE IS MEWED UP TO HER HEAVINESS.
SIR PARIS, I WILL MAKE A DESPERATE TENDER OF MY CHILD'S LOVE: I THINK SHE WILL BE RULED IN ALL RESPECTS BY ME;

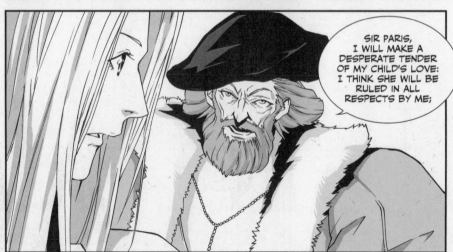

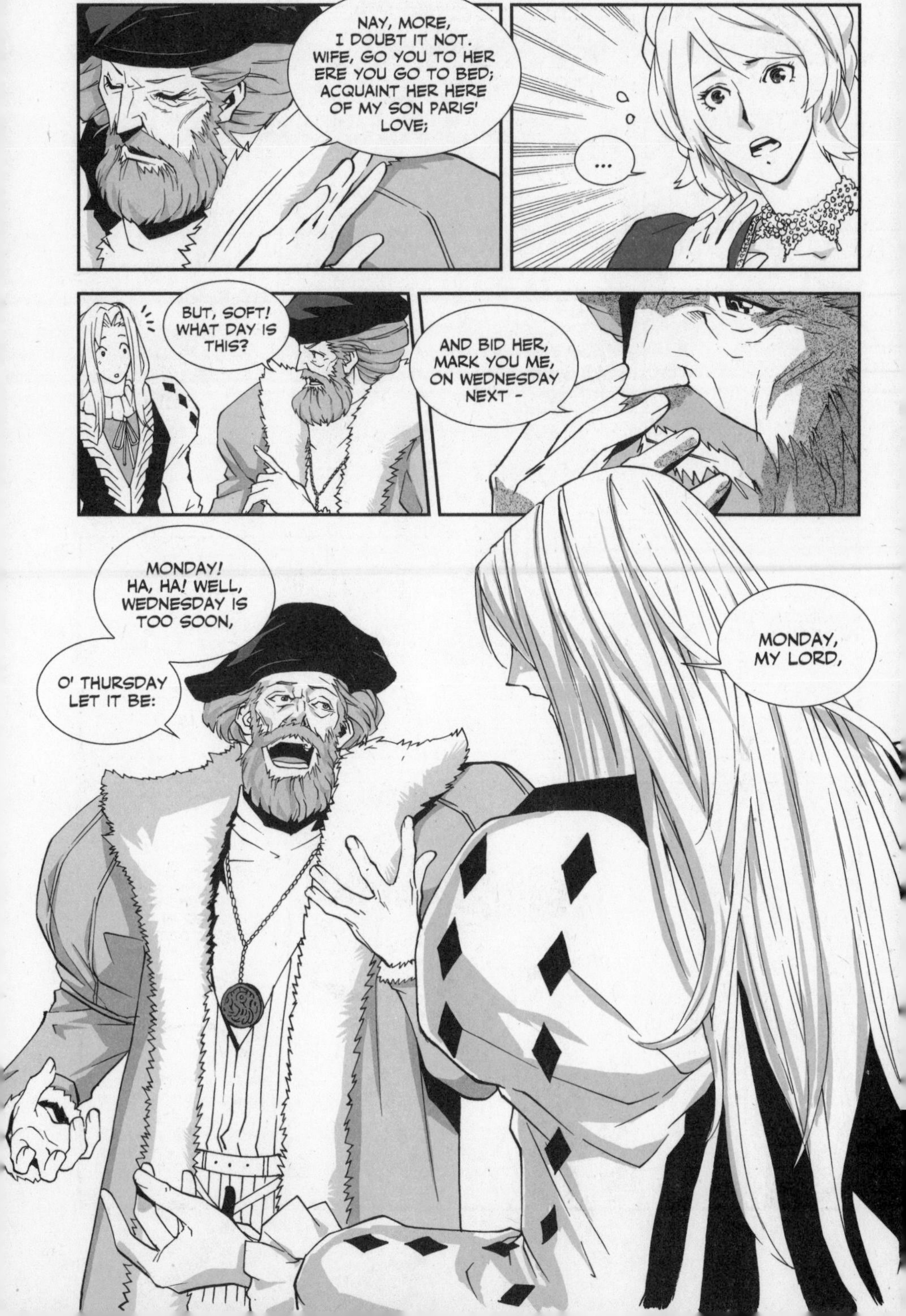
...
NAY, MORE, I DOUBT IT NOT. WIFE, GO YOU TO HER ERE YOU GO TO BED; ACQUAINT HER HERE OF MY SON PARIS' LOVE;
AND BID HER, MARK YOU ME, ON WEDNESDAY NEXT -
BUT, SOFT! WHAT DAY IS THIS?
MONDAY, MY LORD,
MONDAY! HA, HA! WELL, WEDNESDAY IS TOO SOON,
O' THURSDAY LET IT BE:

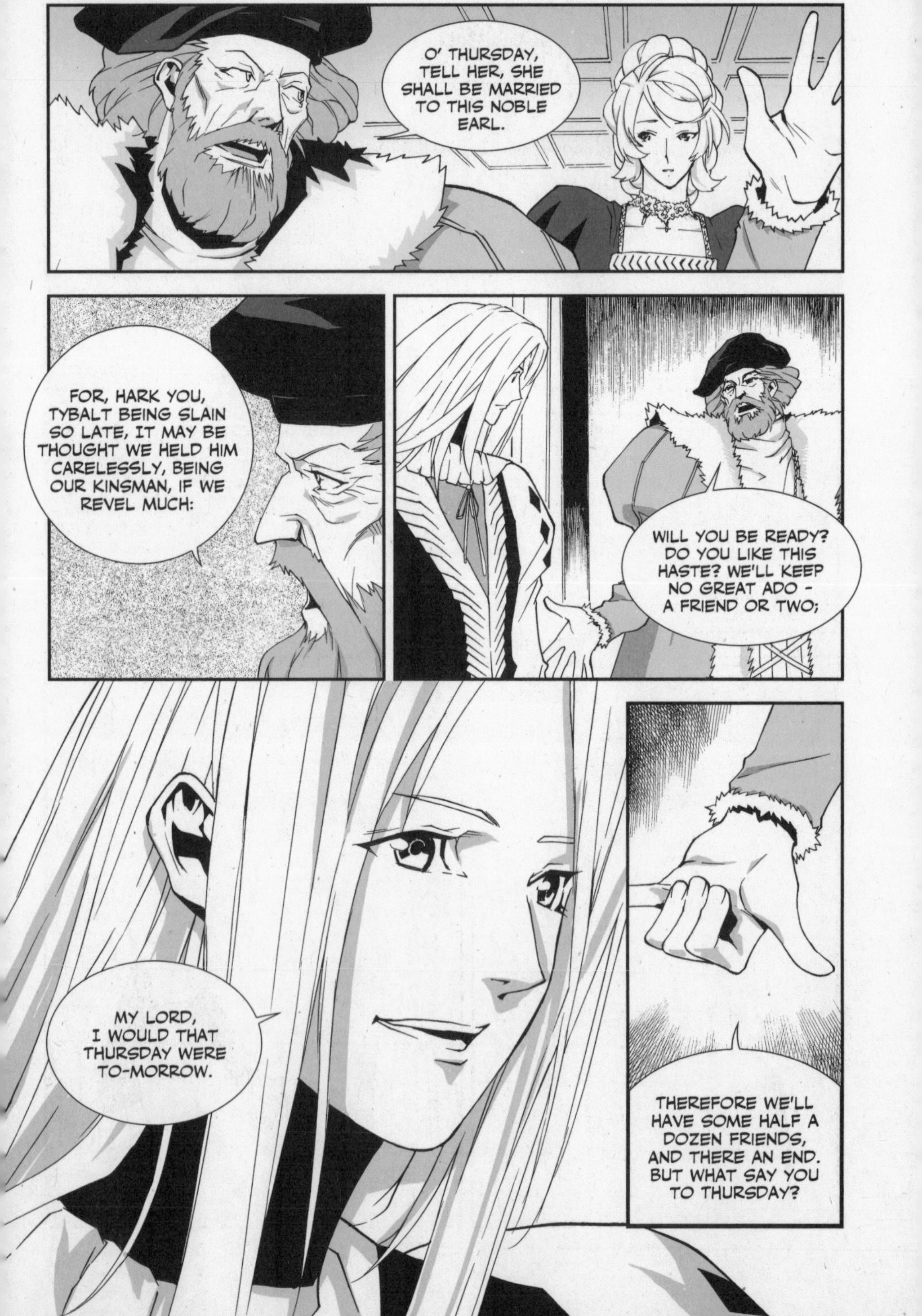
O' THURSDAY, TELL HER, SHE SHALL BE MARRIED TO THIS NOBLE EARL.
WILL YOU BE READY? DO YOU LIKE THIS HASTE? WE'LL KEEP NO GREAT ADO - A FRIEND OR TWO;
FOR, HARK YOU, TYBALT BEING SLAIN SO LATE, IT MAY BE THOUGHT WE HELD HIM CARELESSLY, BEING OUR KINSMAN, IF WE REVEL MUCH:
THEREFORE WE'LL HAVE SOME HALF A DOZEN FRIENDS, AND THERE AN END. BUT WHAT SAY YOU TO THURSDAY?
MY LORD, I WOULD THAT THURSDAY WERE TO-MORROW.

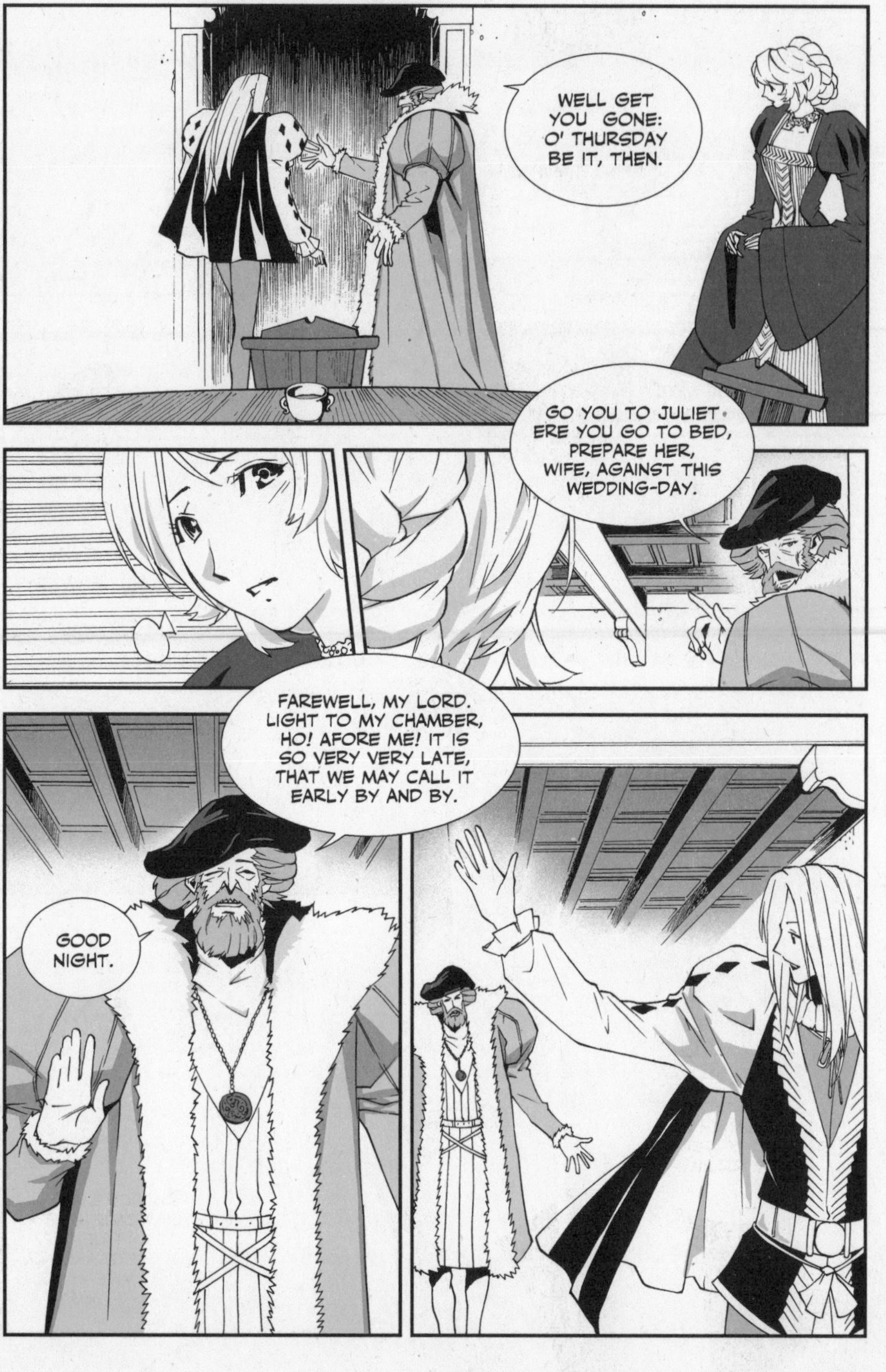
WELL GET YOU GONE: O' THURSDAY BE IT, THEN.
GO YOU TO JULIET ERE YOU GO TO BED, PREPARE HER, WIFE, AGAINST THIS WEDDING-DAY.
FAREWELL, MY LORD. LIGHT TO MY CHAMBER, HO! AFORE ME! IT IS SO VERY VERY LATE, THAT WE MAY CALL IT EARLY BY AND BY.
GOOD NIGHT.

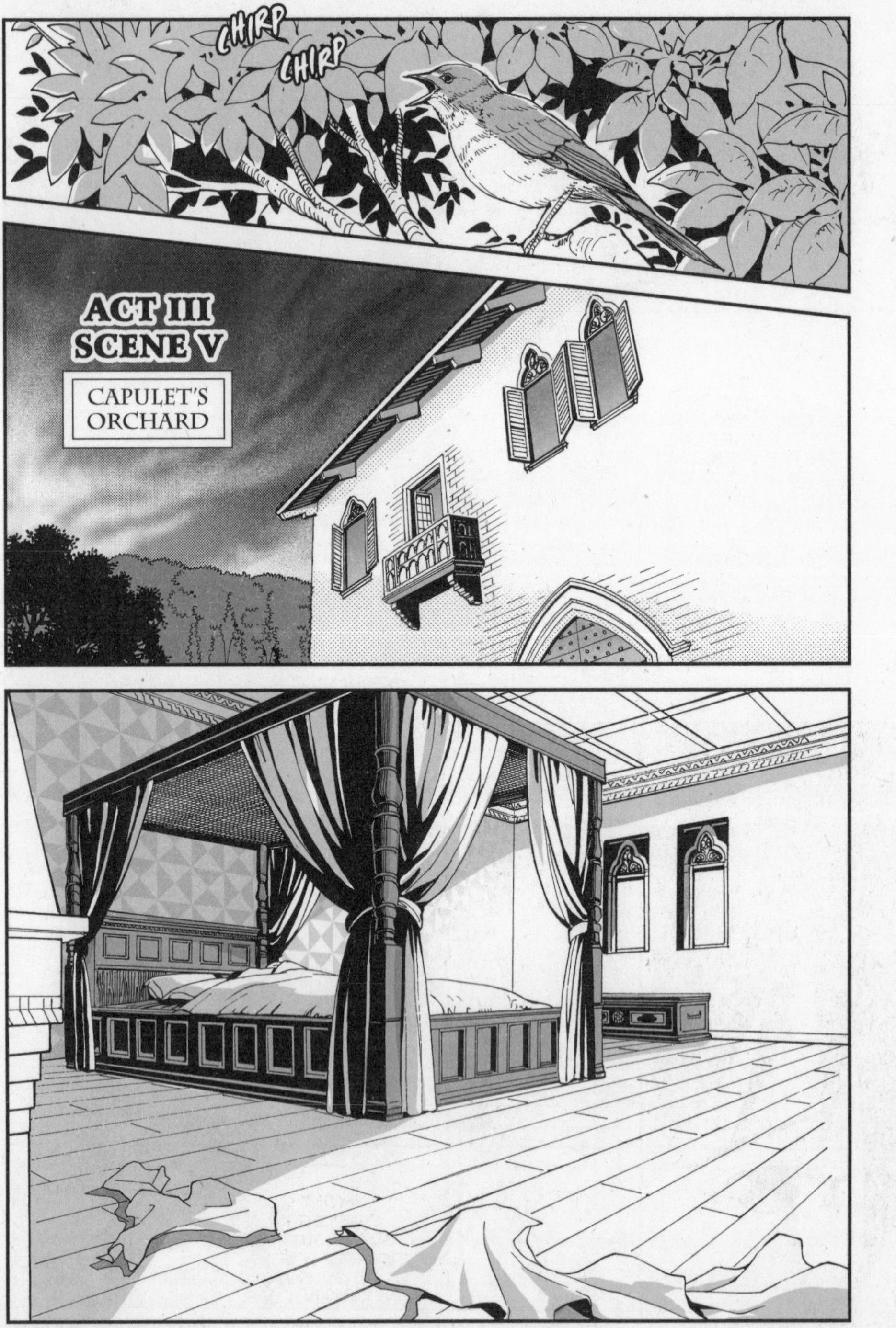
CHIRP
CHIRP
ACT III
SCENE V
CAPULET'S
ORCHARD

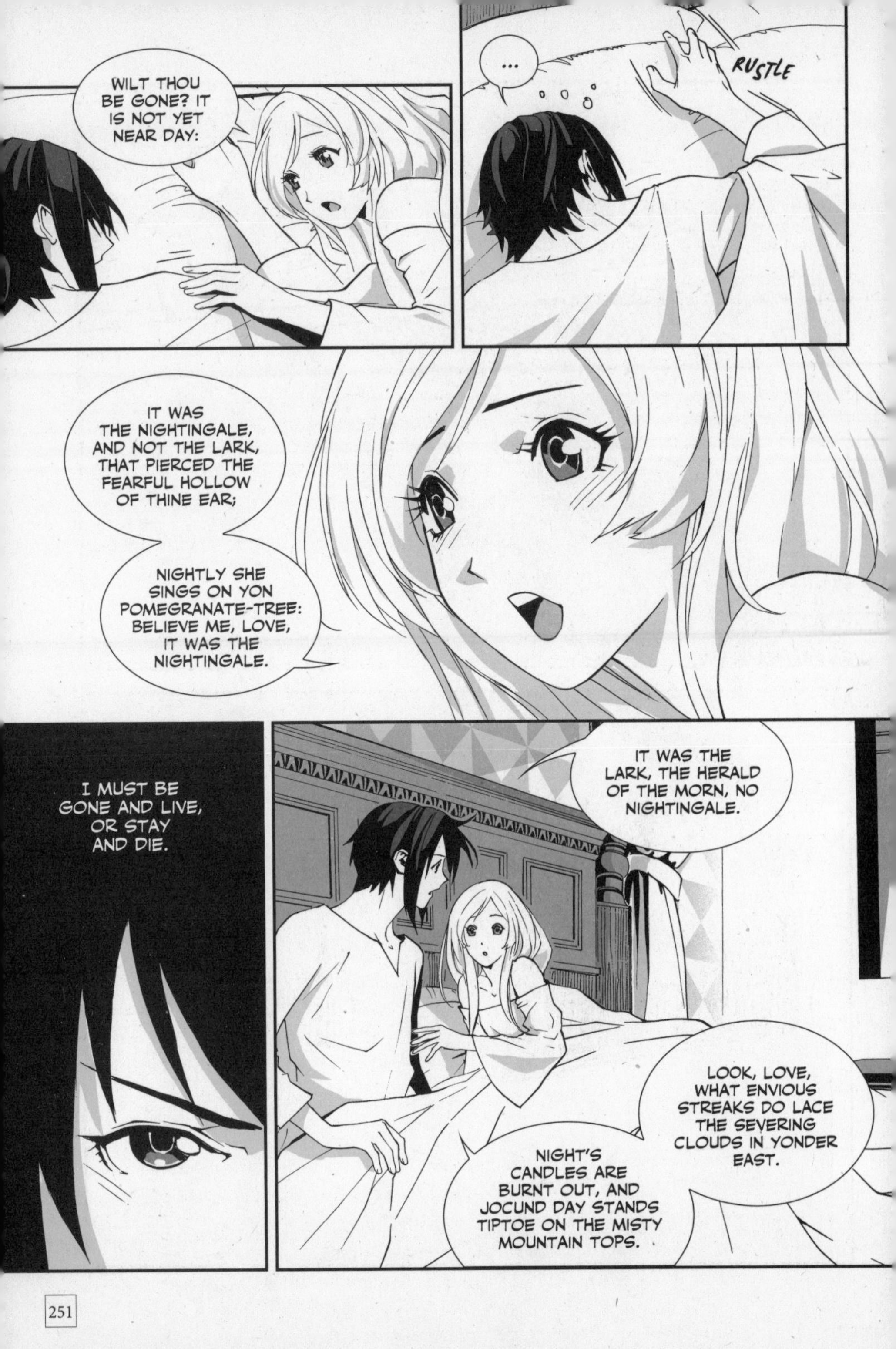
...
RUSTLE
WILT THOU BE GONE? IT IS NOT YET NEAR DAY:
IT WAS THE NIGHTINGALE, AND NOT THE LARK, THAT PIERCED THE FEARFUL HOLLOW OF THINE EAR;
NIGHTLY SHE SINGS ON YON POMEGRANATE-TREE: BELIEVE ME, LOVE, IT WAS THE NIGHTINGALE.
IT WAS THE LARK, THE HERALD OF THE MORN, NO NIGHTINGALE.
LOOK, LOVE, WHAT ENVIOUS STREAKS DO LACE THE SEVERING CLOUDS IN YONDER EAST.
NIGHT'S CANDLES ARE BURNT OUT, AND JOCUND DAY STANDS TIPTOE ON THE MISTY MOUNTAIN TOPS.
I MUST BE GONE AND LIVE, OR STAY AND DIE.

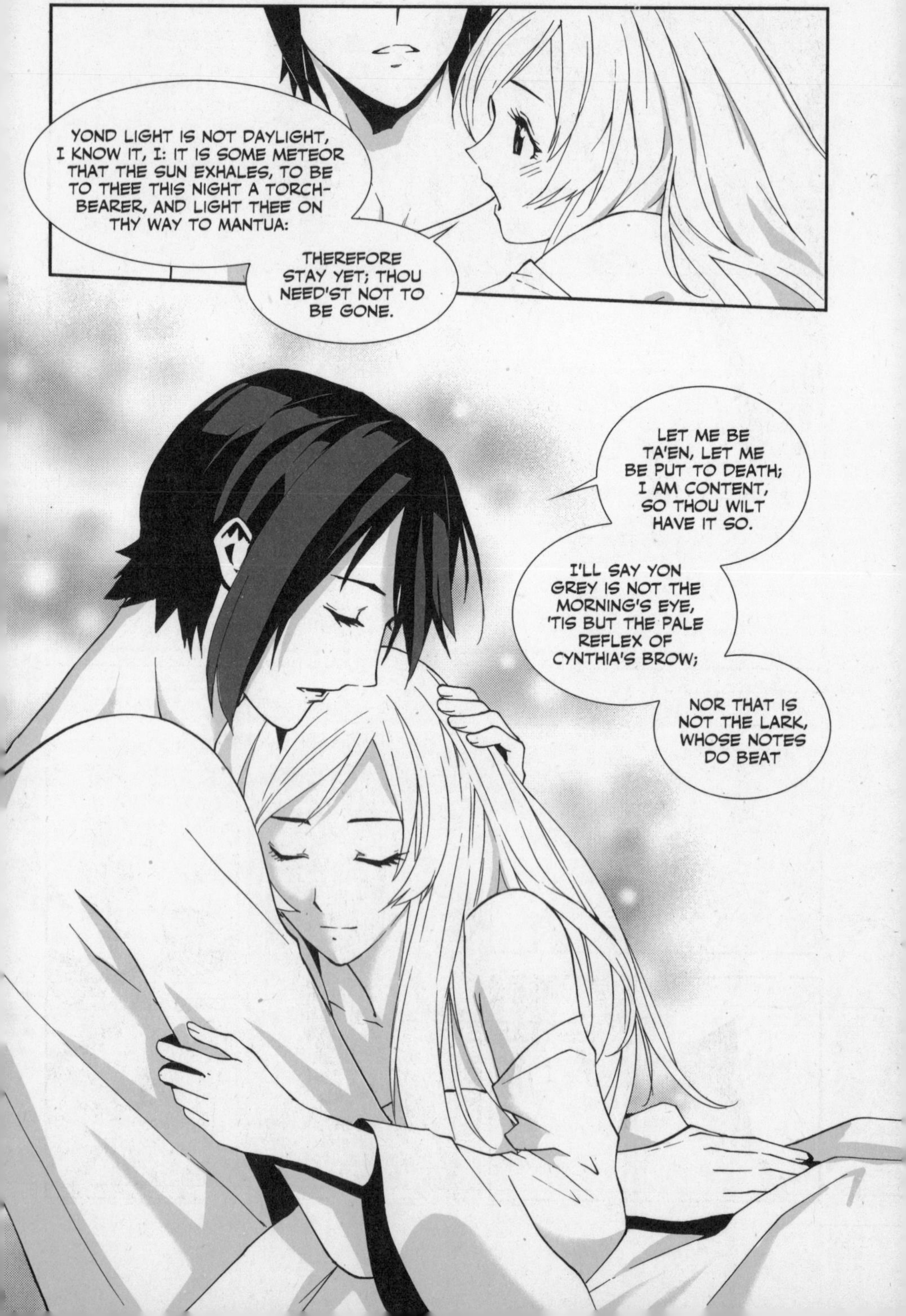
YOND LIGHT IS NOT DAYLIGHT, I KNOW IT, I: IT IS SOME METEOR THAT THE SUN EXHALES, TO BE TO THEE THIS NIGHT A TORCH-BEARER, AND LIGHT THEE ON THY WAY TO MANTUA:
THEREFORE STAY YET; THOU NEED'ST NOT TO BE GONE.
LET ME BE TA'EN, LET ME BE PUT TO DEATH; I AM CONTENT, SO THOU WILT HAVE IT SO.
I'LL SAY YON GREY IS NOT THE MORNING'S EYE, 'TIS BUT THE PALE REFLEX OF CYNTHIA'S BROW;
NOR THAT IS NOT THE LARK, WHOSE NOTES DO BEAT

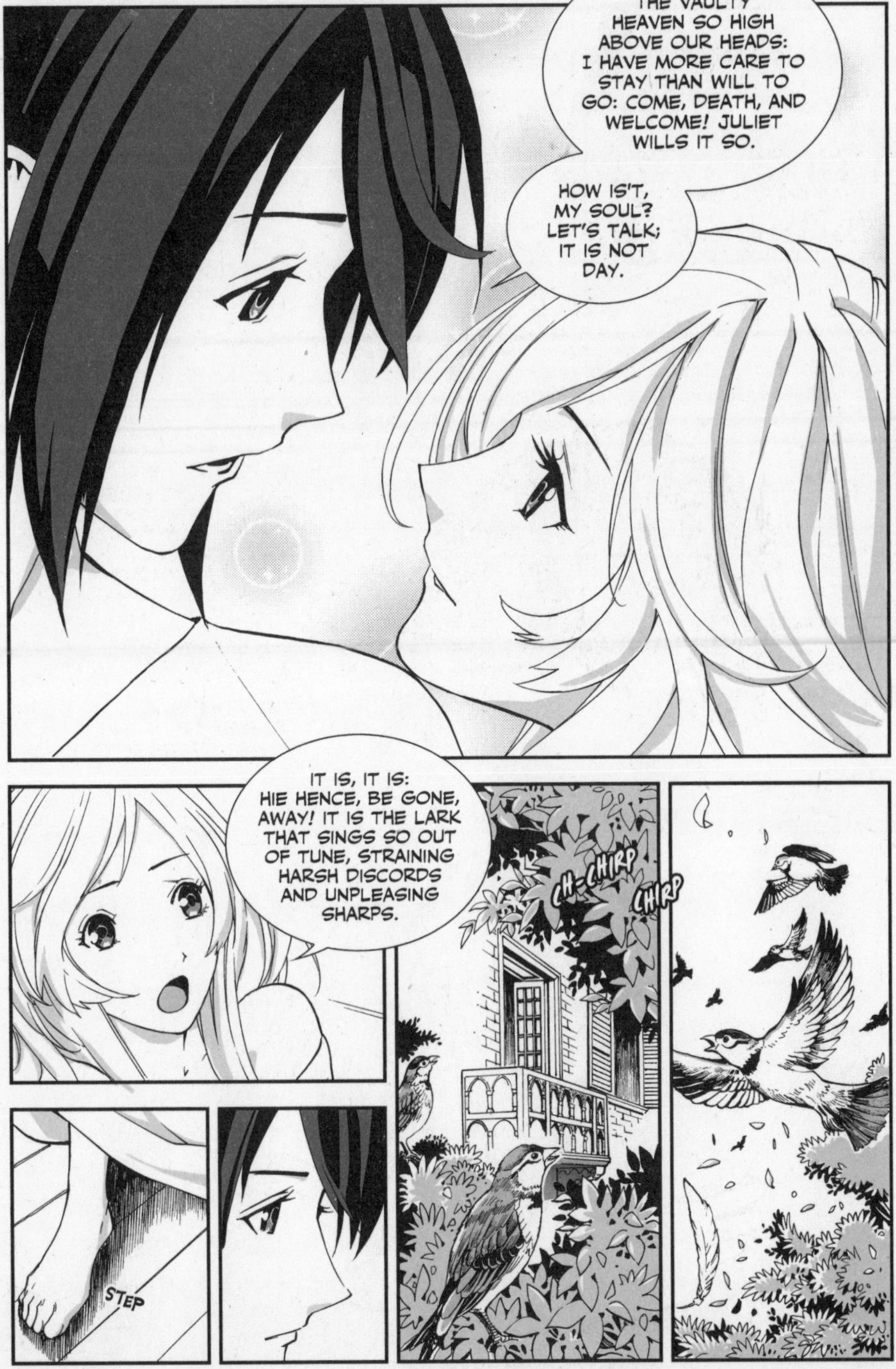
THE VAULTY HEAVEN SO HIGH ABOVE OUR HEADS: I HAVE MORE CARE TO STAY THAN WILL TO GO: COME, DEATH, AND WELCOME! JULIET WILLS IT SO.
HOW IS'T, MY SOUL? LET'S TALK; IT IS NOT DAY.
CHIRP
CH-CHIRP
IT IS, IT IS: HIE HENCE, BE GONE, AWAY! IT IS THE LARK THAT SINGS SO OUT OF TUNE, STRAINING HARSH DISCORDS AND UNPLEASING SHARPS.
STEP

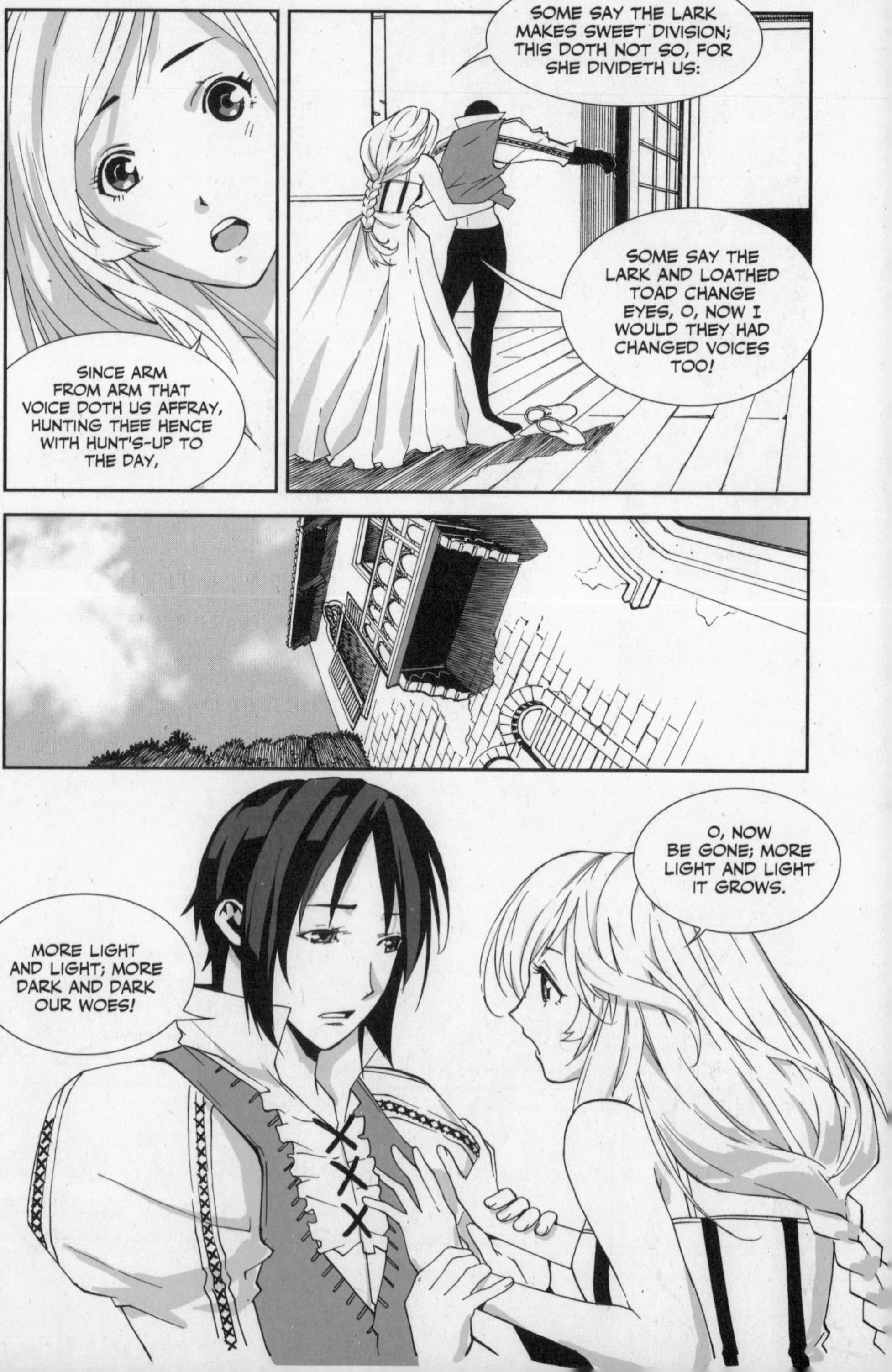
SOME SAY THE LARK MAKES SWEET DIVISION; THIS DOTH NOT SO, FOR SHE DIVIDETH US:
SOME SAY THE LARK AND LOATHED TOAD CHANGE EYES, O, NOW I WOULD THEY HAD CHANGED VOICES TOO!
SINCE ARM FROM ARM THAT VOICE DOTH US AFFRAY, HUNTING THEE HENCE WITH HUNT'S-UP TO THE DAY,
O, NOW BE GONE; MORE LIGHT AND LIGHT IT GROWS.
MORE LIGHT AND LIGHT; MORE DARK AND DARK OUR WOES!

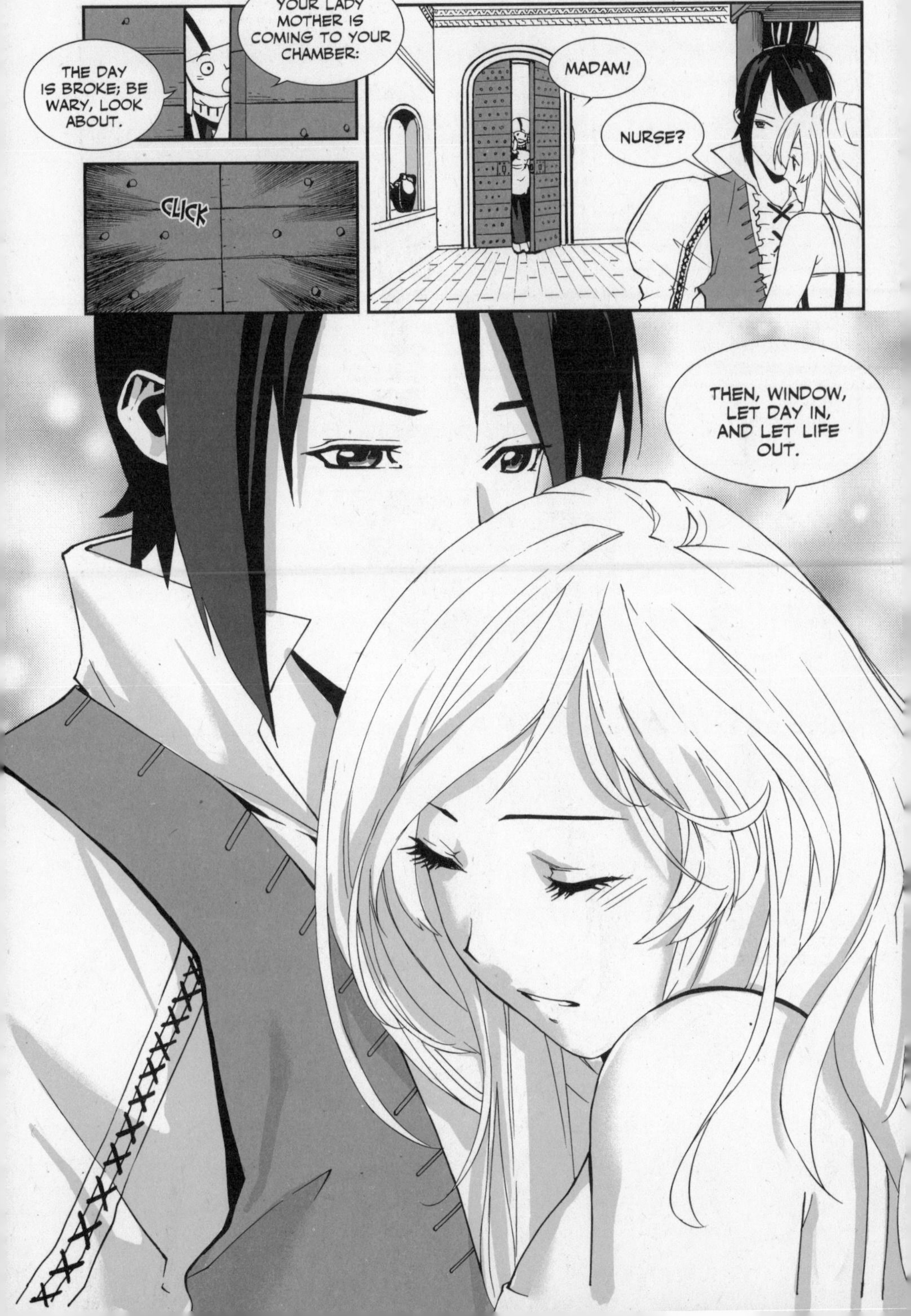
MADAM!
NURSE?
YOUR LADY MOTHER IS COMING TO YOUR CHAMBER:
THE DAY IS BROKE; BE WARY, LOOK ABOUT.
CLICK
THEN, WINDOW, LET DAY IN, AND LET LIFE OUT.

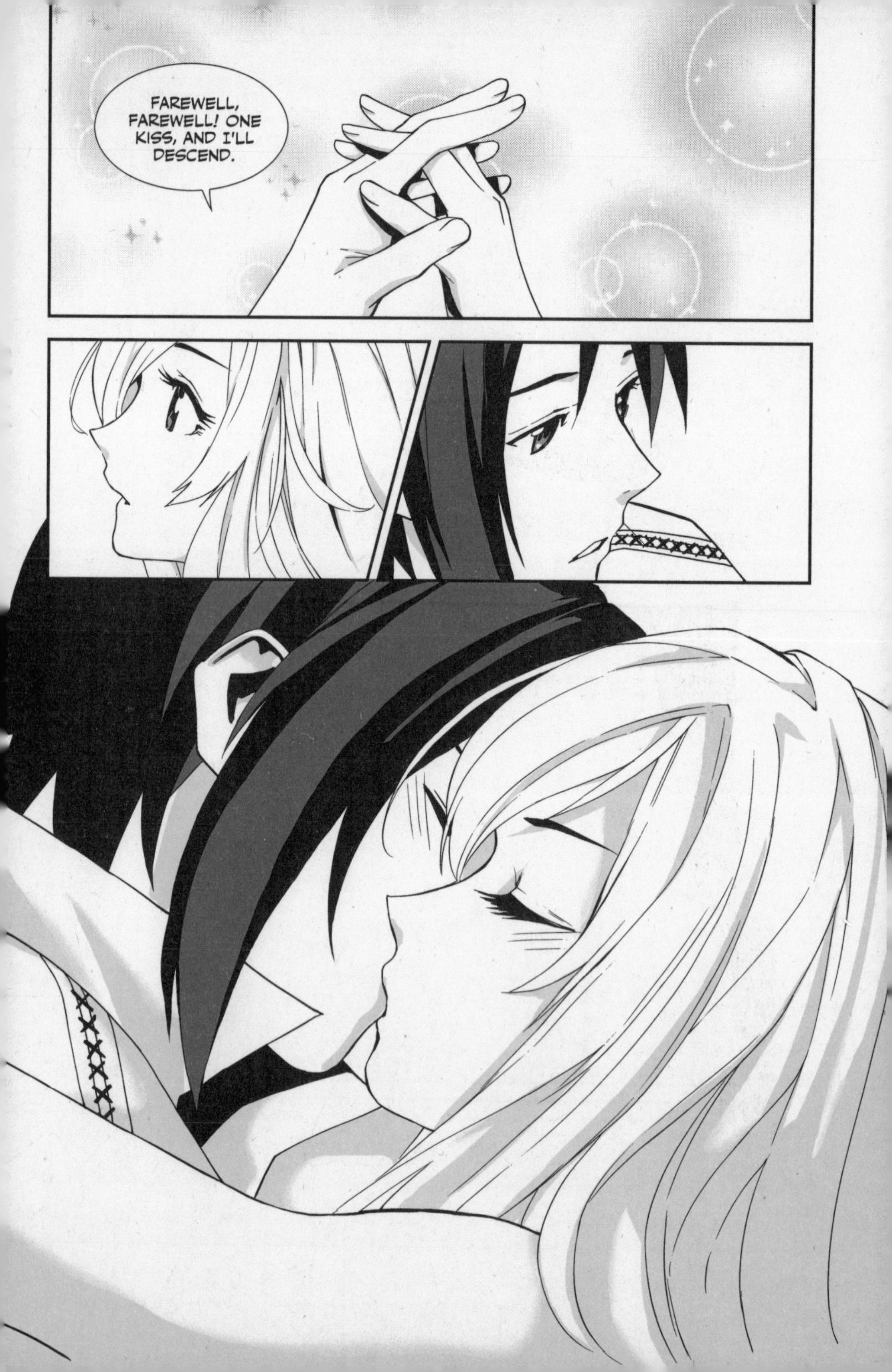
FAREWELL, FAREWELL! ONE KISS, AND I'LL DESCEND.

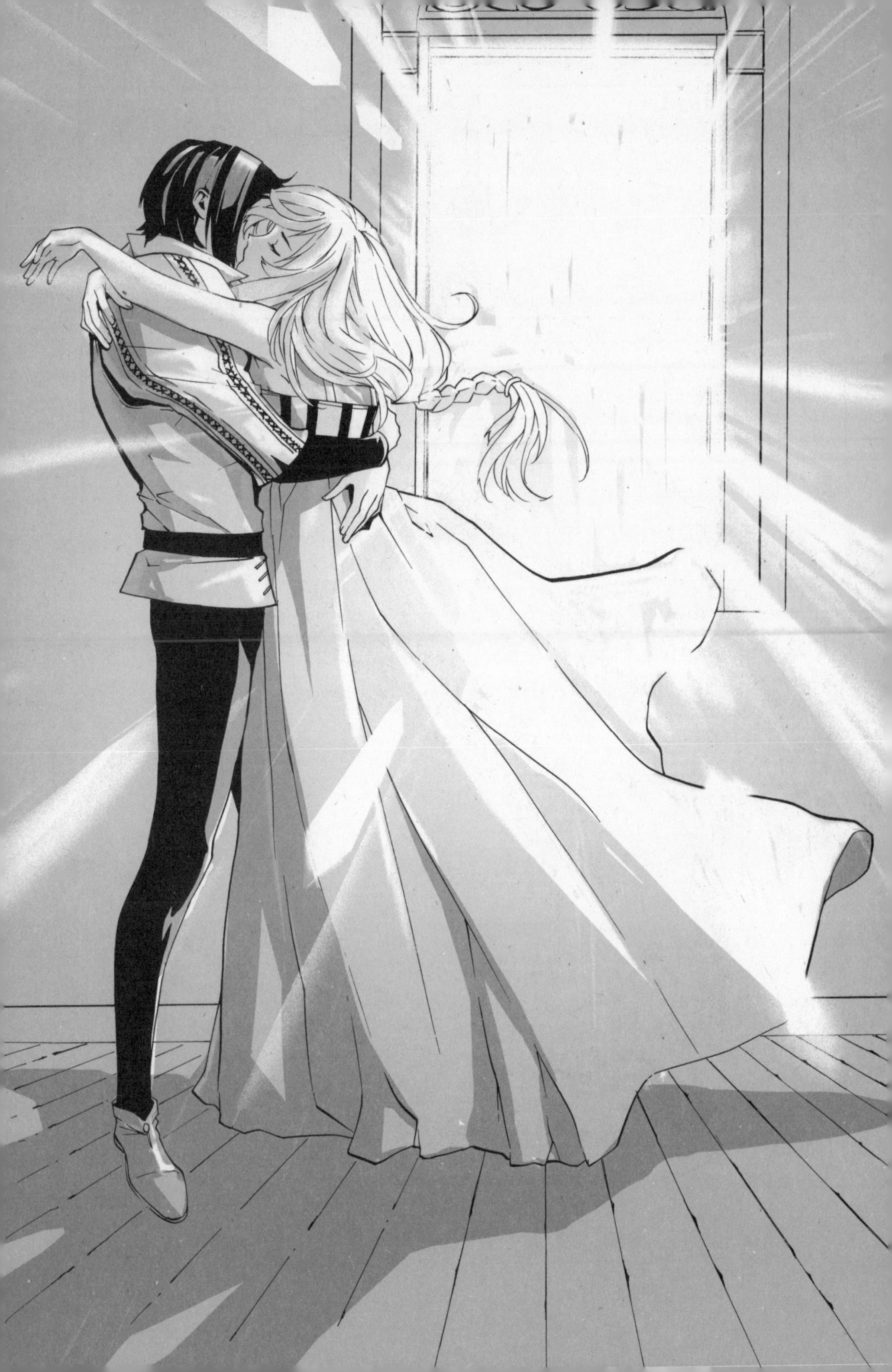

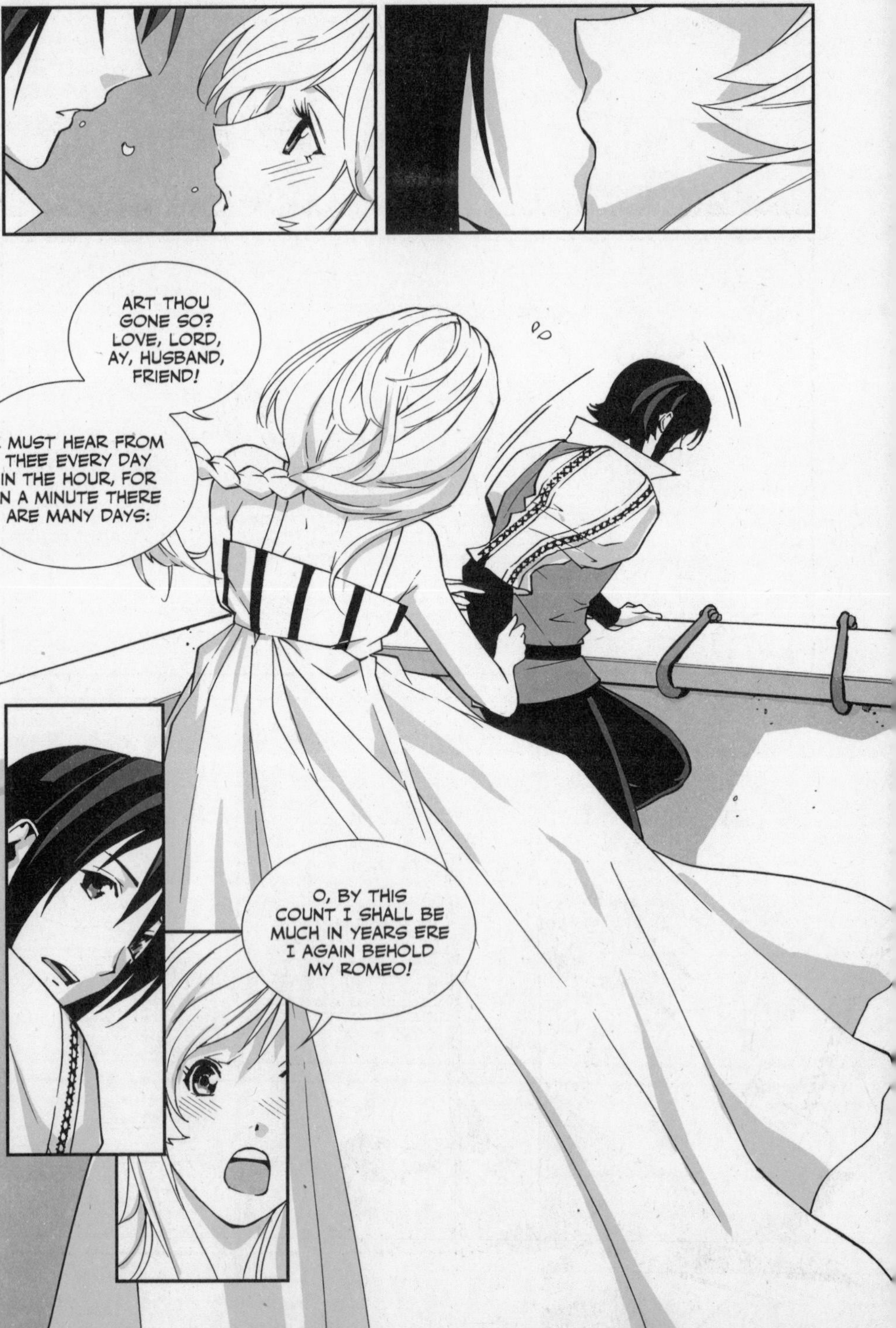
ART THOU GONE SO? LOVE, LORD, AY, HUSBAND, FRIEND!
I MUST HEAR FROM THEE EVERY DAY IN THE HOUR, FOR IN A MINUTE THERE ARE MANY DAYS:
O, BY THIS COUNT I SHALL BE MUCH IN YEARS ERE I AGAIN BEHOLD MY ROMEO!

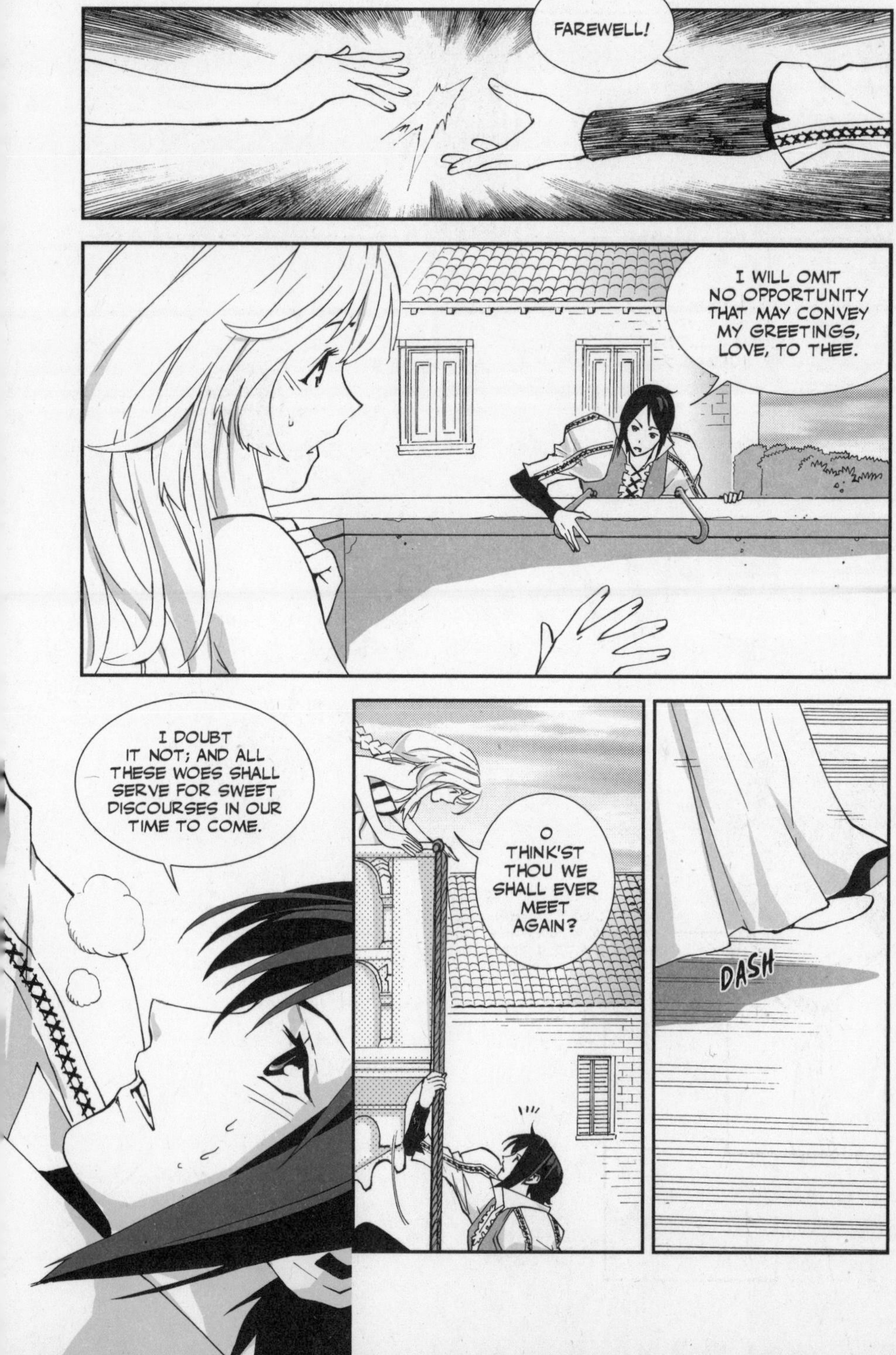
FAREWELL!
I WILL OMIT NO OPPORTUNITY THAT MAY CONVEY MY GREETINGS, LOVE, TO THEE.
DASH
O THINK'ST THOU WE SHALL EVER MEET AGAIN?
I DOUBT IT NOT; AND ALL THESE WOES SHALL SERVE FOR SWEET DISCOURSES IN OUR TIME TO COME.

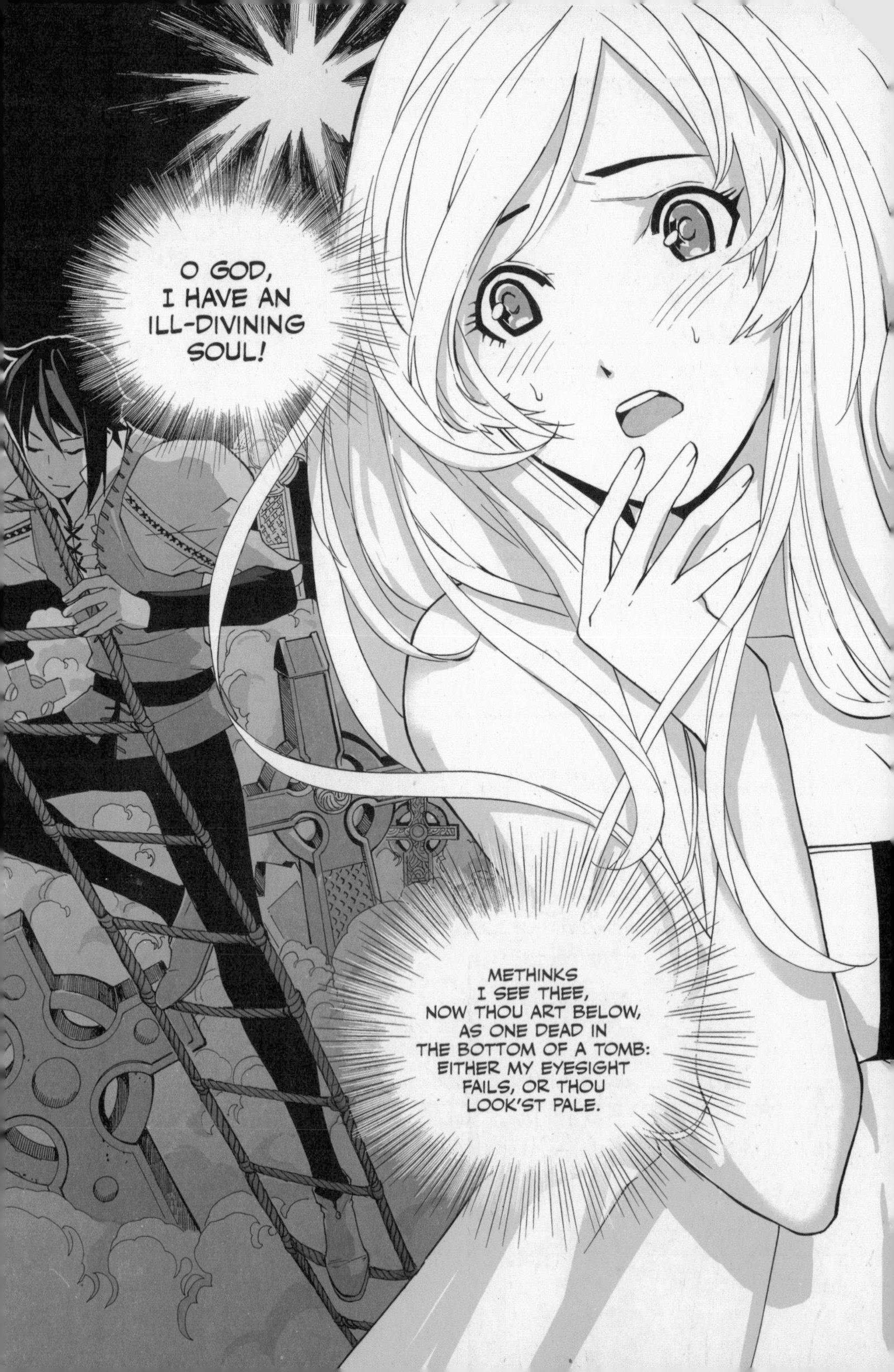
O GOD, I HAVE AN ILL-DIVINING SOUL!
METHINKS I SEE THEE, NOW THOU ART BELOW, AS ONE DEAD IN THE BOTTOM OF A TOMB: EITHER MY EYESIGHT FAILS, OR THOU LOOK'ST PALE.

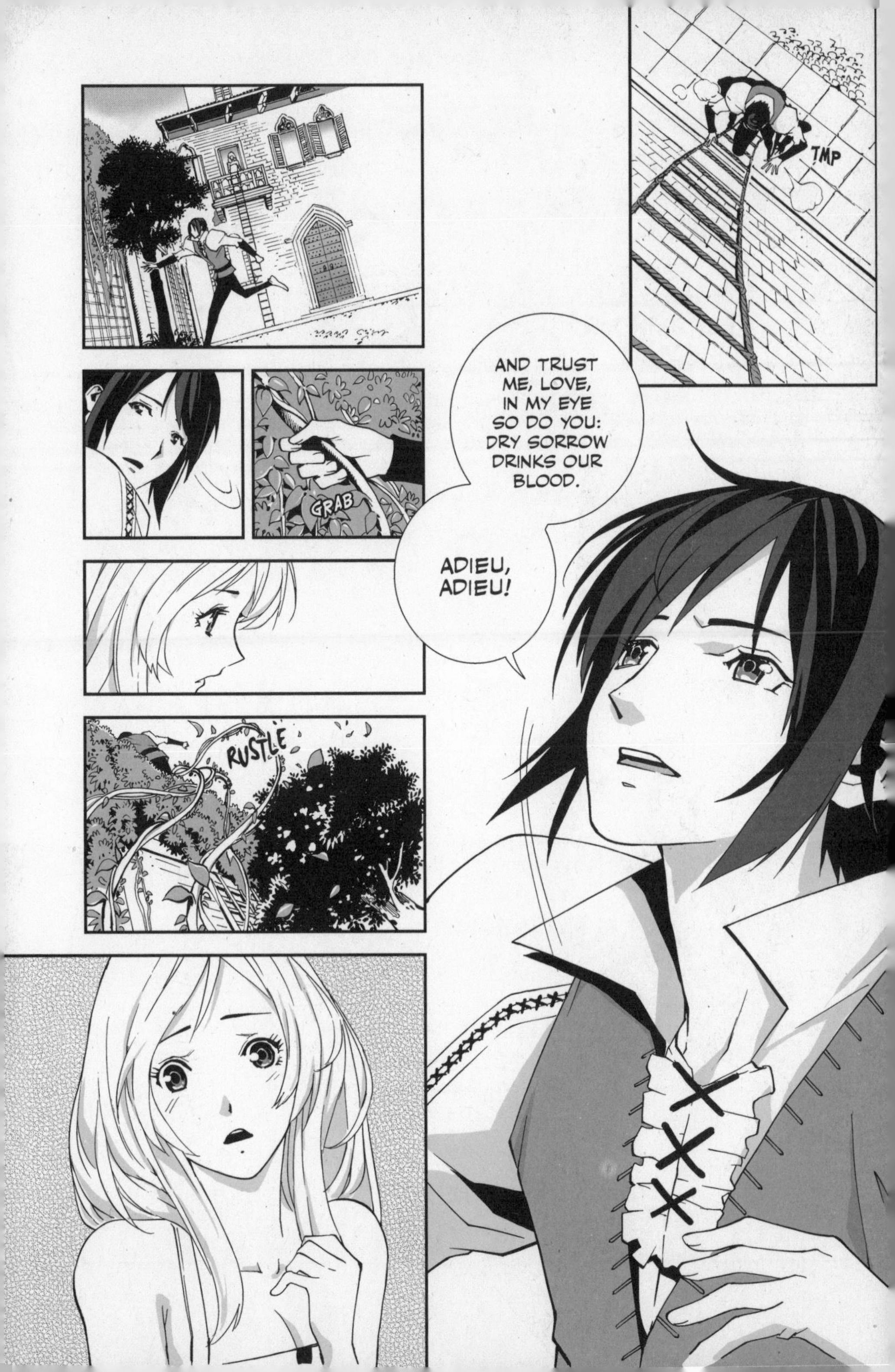
TMP
AND TRUST ME, LOVE, IN MY EYE SO DO YOU: DRY SORROW DRINKS OUR BLOOD.
ADIEU, ADIEU!
GRAB
RUSTLE

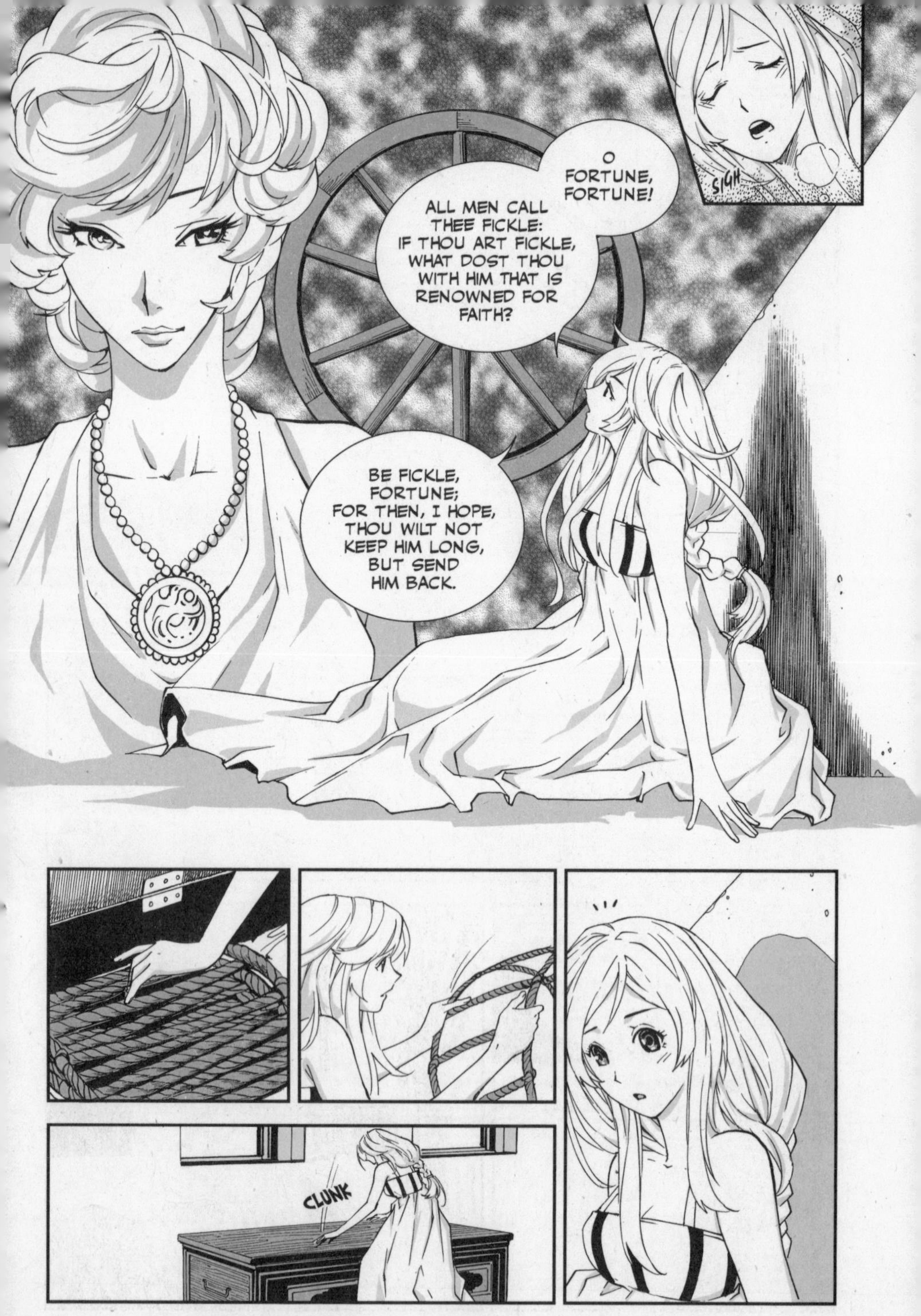
SIGH
O FORTUNE, FORTUNE!
ALL MEN CALL THEE FICKLE: IF THOU ART FICKLE, WHAT DOST THOU WITH HIM THAT IS RENOWNED FOR FAITH?
BE FICKLE, FORTUNE; FOR THEN, I HOPE, THOU WILT NOT KEEP HIM LONG, BUT SEND HIM BACK.
CLUNK

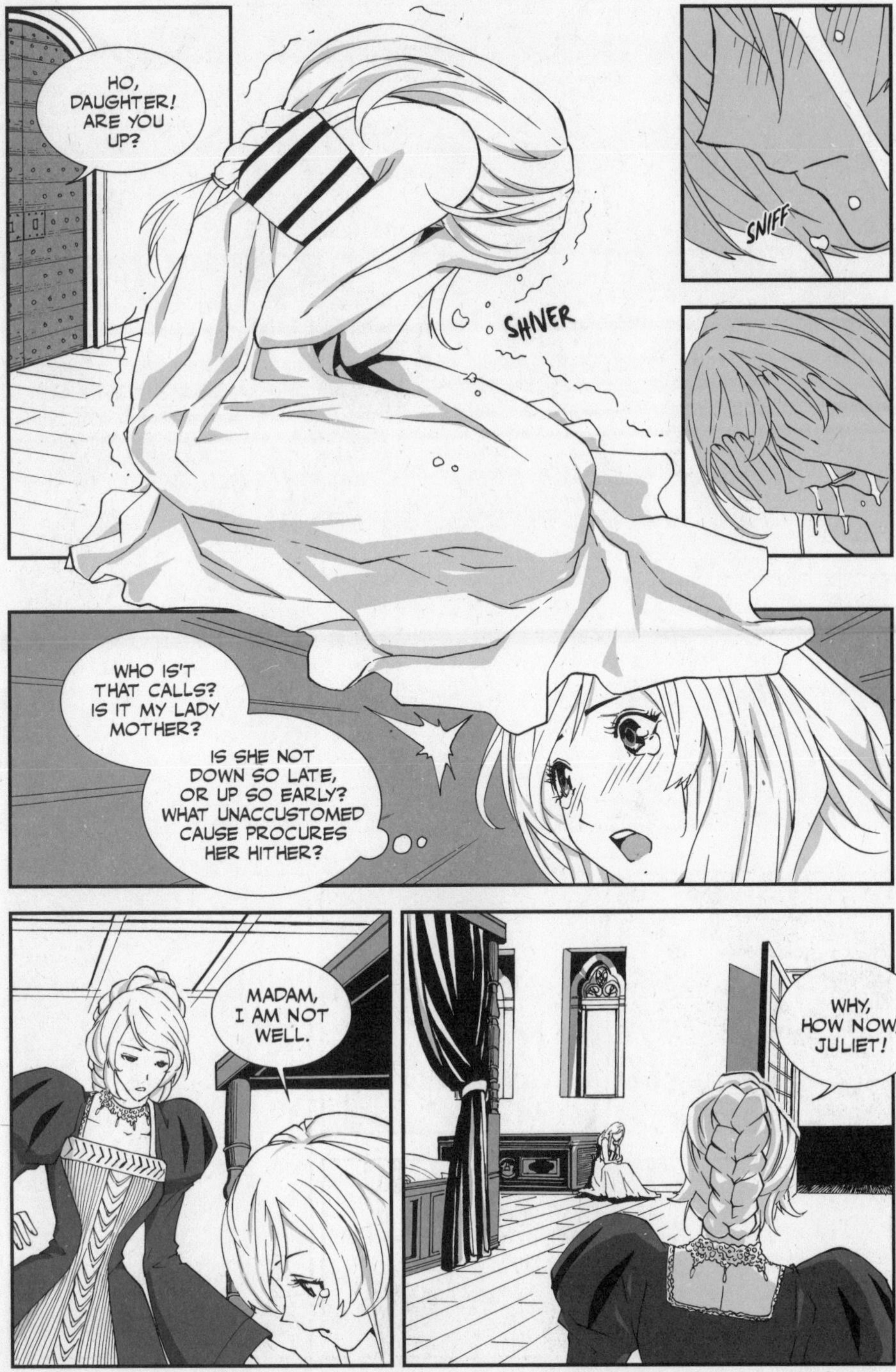
SNIFF
HO, DAUGHTER! ARE YOU UP?
SHIVER
WHO IS'T THAT CALLS? IS IT MY LADY MOTHER?
IS SHE NOT DOWN SO LATE, OR UP SO EARLY? WHAT UNACCUSTOMED CAUSE PROCURES HER HITHER?
WHY, HOW NOW, JULIET!
MADAM, I AM NOT WELL.

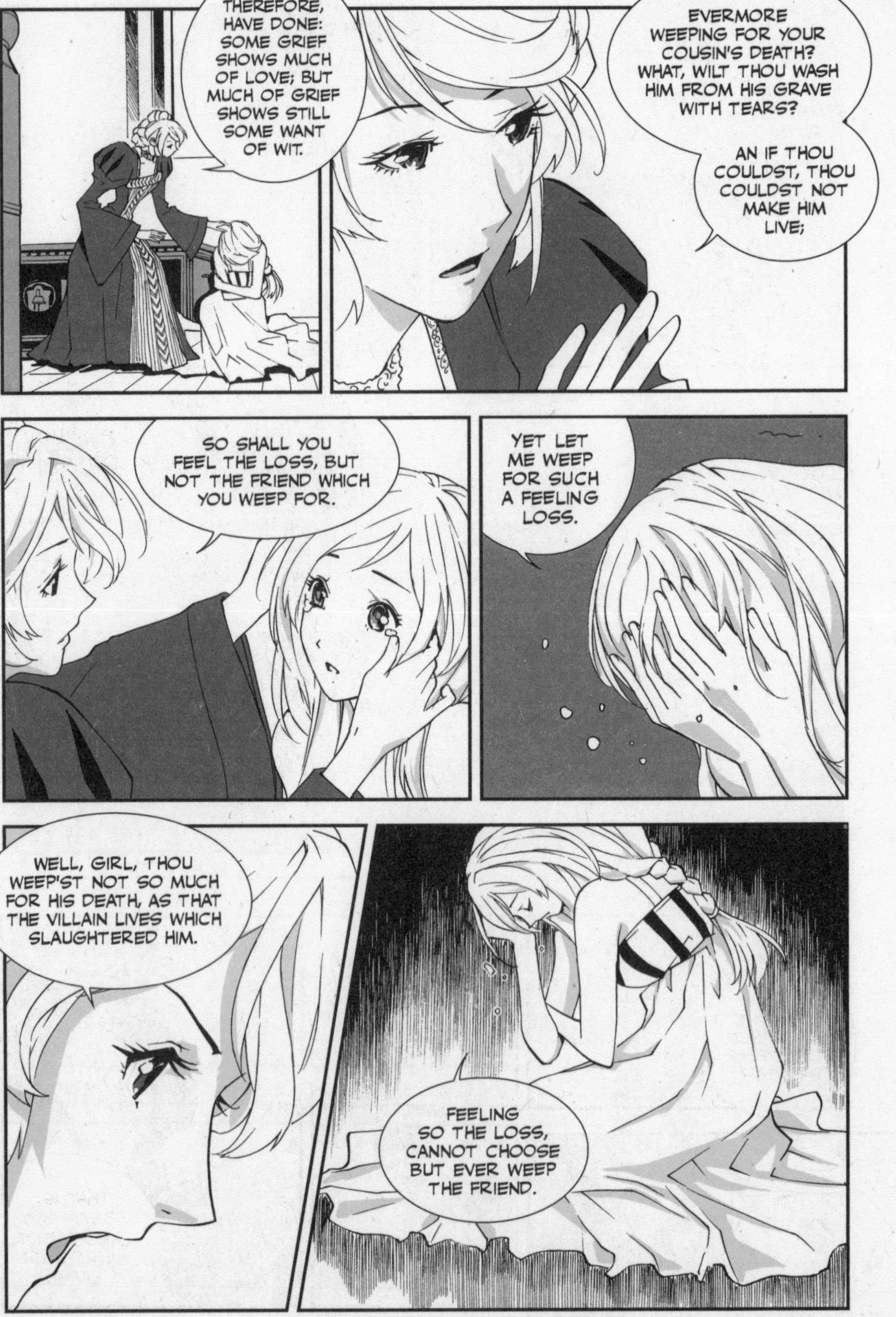
EVERMORE WEEPING FOR YOUR COUSIN'S DEATH? WHAT, WILT THOU WASH HIM FROM HIS GRAVE WITH TEARS?
AN IF THOU COULDST, THOU COULDST NOT MAKE HIM LIVE;
THEREFORE, HAVE DONE: SOME GRIEF SHOWS MUCH OF LOVE; BUT MUCH OF GRIEF SHOWS STILL SOME WANT OF WIT.
YET LET ME WEEP FOR SUCH A FEELING LOSS.
SO SHALL YOU FEEL THE LOSS, BUT NOT THE FRIEND WHICH YOU WEEP FOR.
FEELING SO THE LOSS, CANNOT CHOOSE BUT EVER WEEP THE FRIEND.
WELL, GIRL, THOU WEEP'ST NOT SO MUCH FOR HIS DEATH, AS THAT THE VILLAIN LIVES WHICH SLAUGHTERED HIM.

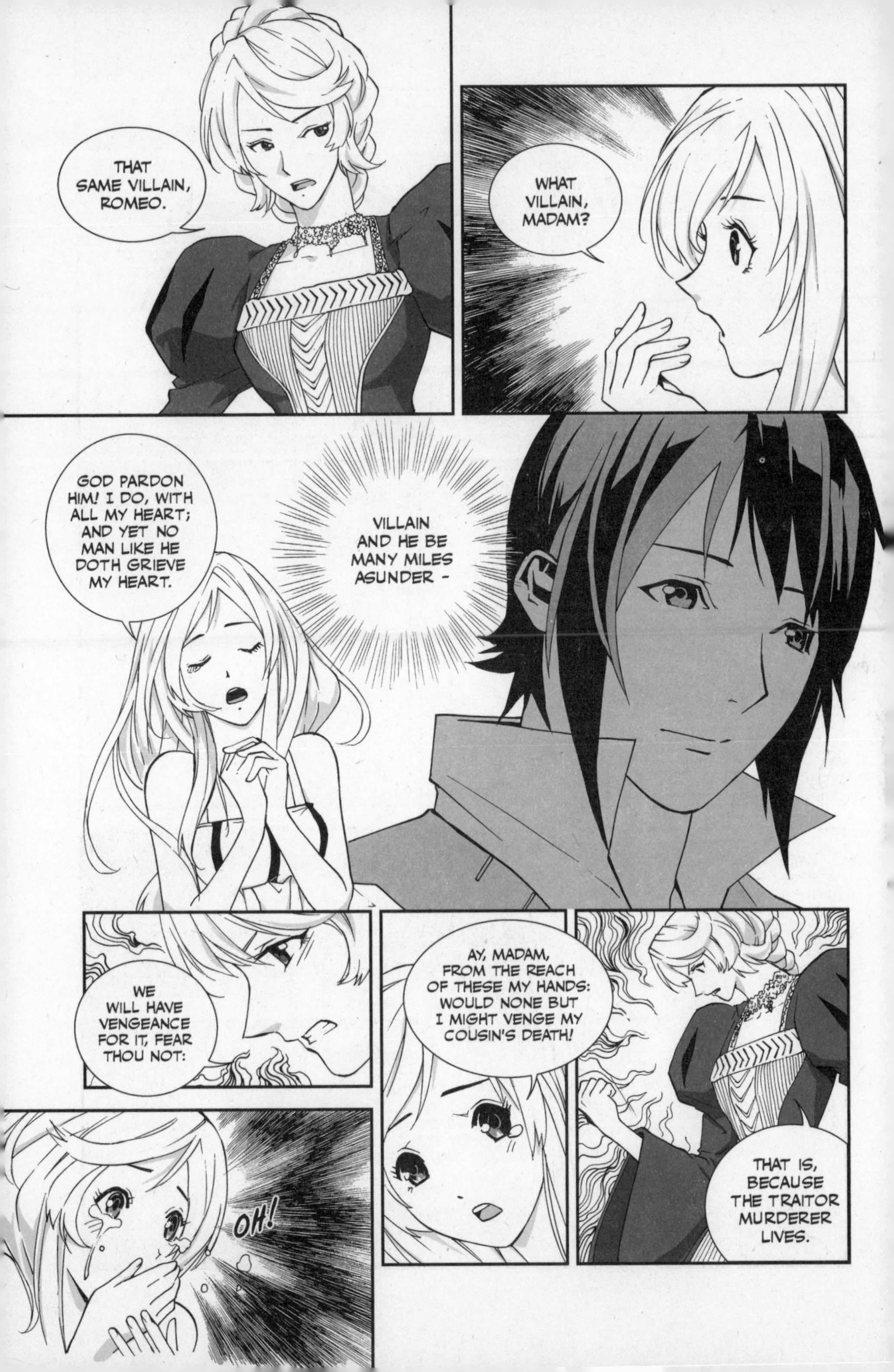
WHAT VILLAIN, MADAM?
THAT SAME VILLAIN, ROMEO.
VILLAIN AND HE BE MANY MILES ASUNDER -
GOD PARDON HIM! I DO, WITH ALL MY HEART; AND YET NO MAN LIKE HE DOTH GRIEVE MY HEART.
THAT IS, BECAUSE THE TRAITOR MURDERER LIVES.
AY, MADAM, FROM THE REACH OF THESE MY HANDS: WOULD NONE BUT I MIGHT VENGE MY COUSIN'S DEATH!
WE WILL HAVE VENGEANCE FOR IT, FEAR THOU NOT:
OH!

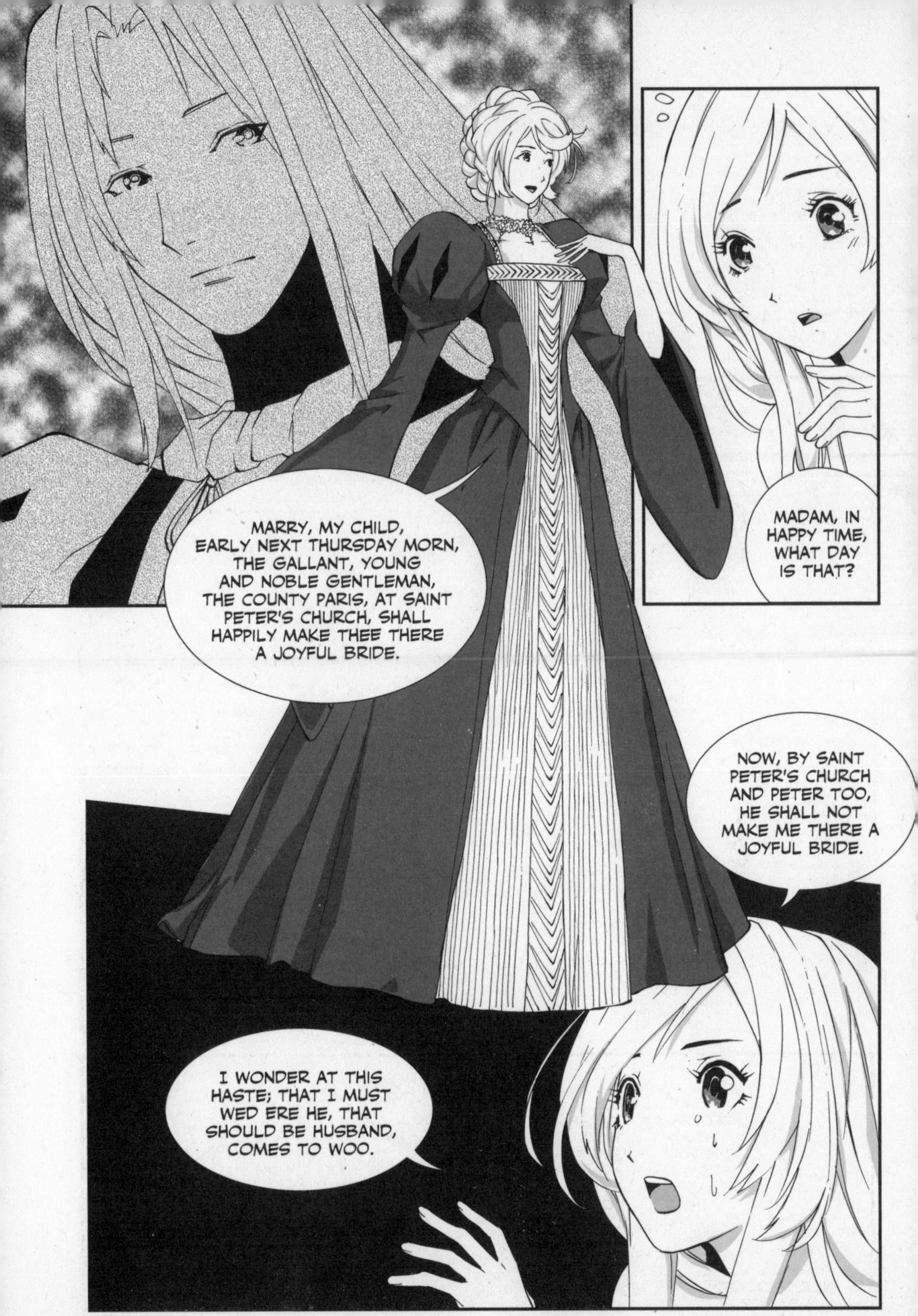
MADAM, IN HAPPY TIME, WHAT DAY IS THAT?
MARRY, MY CHILD, EARLY NEXT THURSDAY MORN, THE GALLANT, YOUNG AND NOBLE GENTLEMAN, THE COUNTY PARIS, AT SAINT PETER'S CHURCH, SHALL HAPPILY MAKE THEE THERE A JOYFUL BRIDE.
NOW, BY SAINT PETER'S CHURCH AND PETER TOO, HE SHALL NOT MAKE ME THERE A JOYFUL BRIDE.
I WONDER AT THIS HASTE; THAT I MUST WED ERE HE, THAT SHOULD BE HUSBAND, COMES TO WOO.

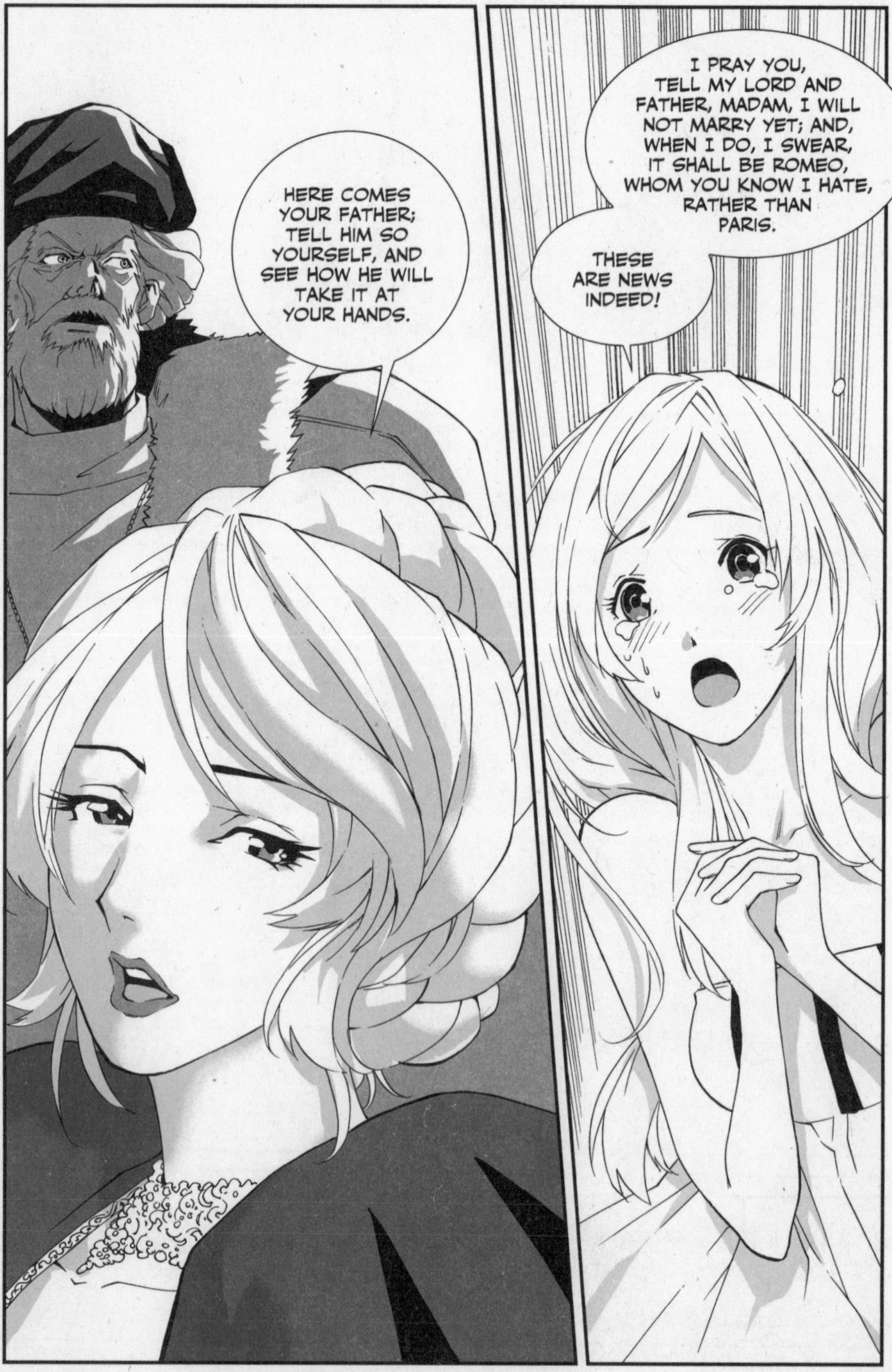
I PRAY YOU, TELL MY LORD AND FATHER, MADAM, I WILL NOT MARRY YET; AND, WHEN I DO, I SWEAR, IT SHALL BE ROMEO, WHOM YOU KNOW I HATE, RATHER THAN PARIS.
THESE ARE NEWS INDEED!
HERE COMES YOUR FATHER; TELL HIM SO YOURSELF, AND SEE HOW HE WILL TAKE IT AT YOUR HANDS.

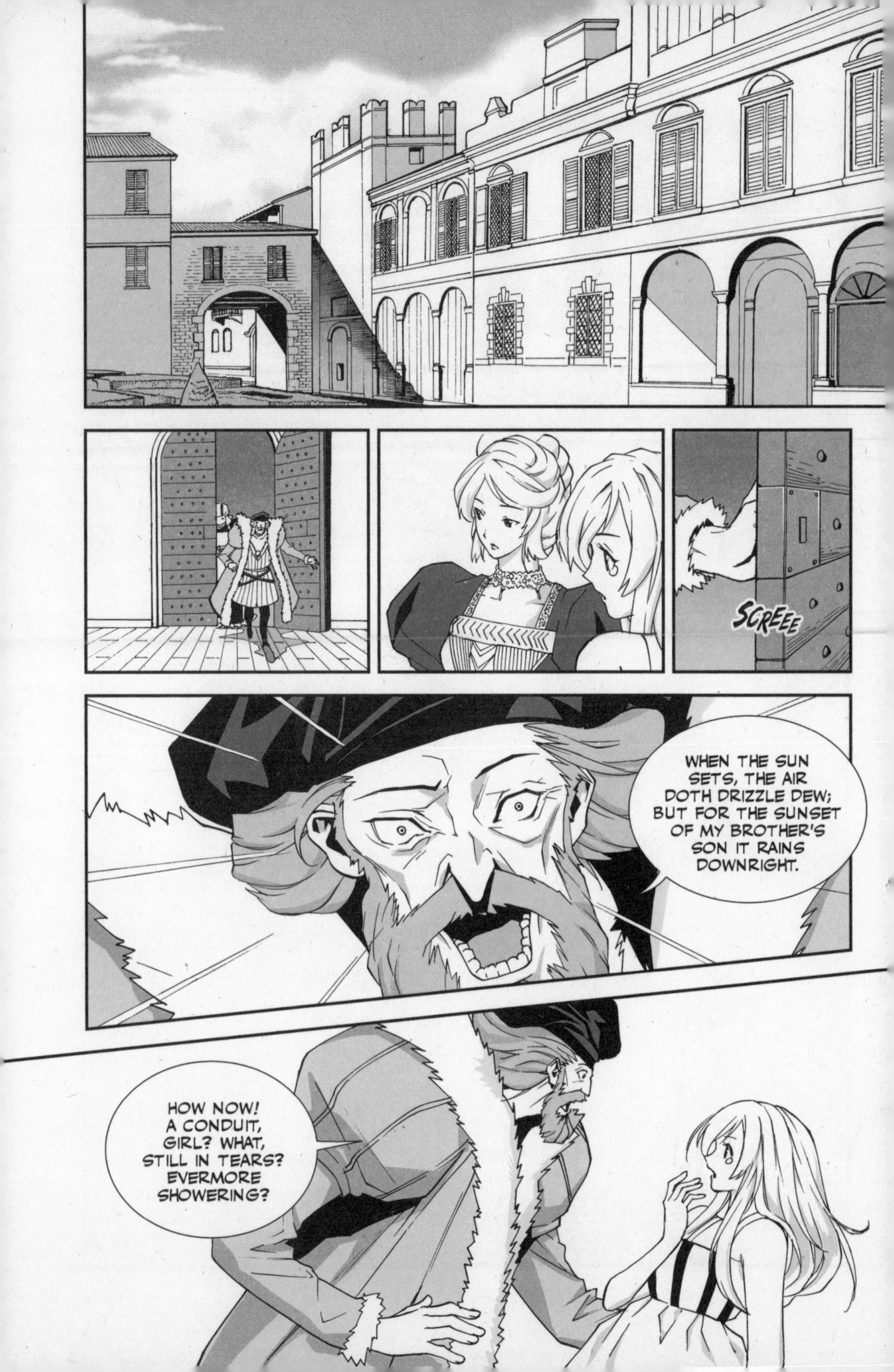
SCREEE
WHEN THE SUN SETS, THE AIR DOTH DRIZZLE DEW; BUT FOR THE SUNSET OF MY BROTHER'S SON IT RAINS DOWNRIGHT.
HOW NOW! A CONDUIT, GIRL? WHAT, STILL IN TEARS? EVERMORE SHOWERING?

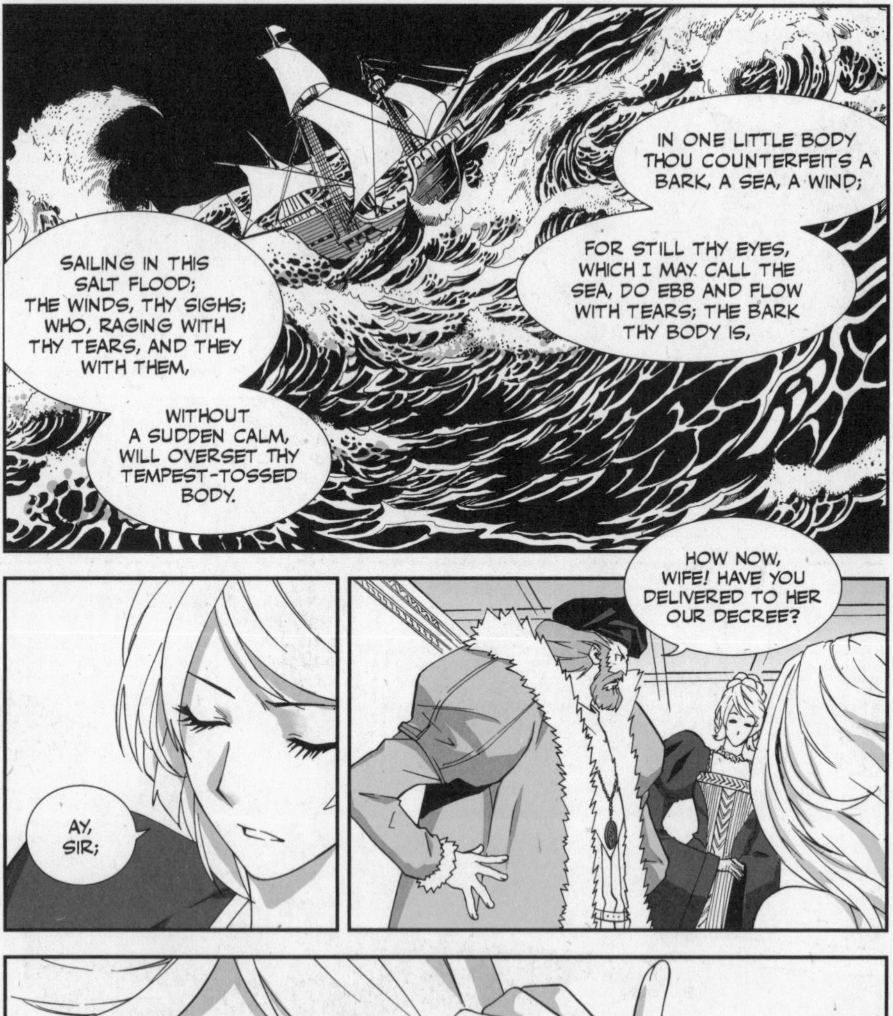
IN ONE LITTLE BODY THOU COUNTERFEITS A BARK, A SEA, A WIND;
FOR STILL THY EYES, WHICH I MAY CALL THE SEA, DO EBB AND FLOW WITH TEARS; THE BARK THY BODY IS,
SAILING IN THIS SALT FLOOD; THE WINDS, THY SIGHS; WHO, RAGING WITH THY TEARS, AND THEY WITH THEM,
WITHOUT A SUDDEN CALM, WILL OVERSET THY TEMPEST-TOSSED BODY.
HOW NOW, WIFE! HAVE YOU DELIVERED TO HER OUR DECREE?
AY, SIR;
BUT SHE WILL NONE, SHE GIVES YOU THANKS.
I WOULD THE FOOL WERE MARRIED TO HER GRAVE!

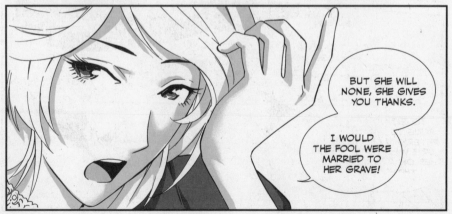

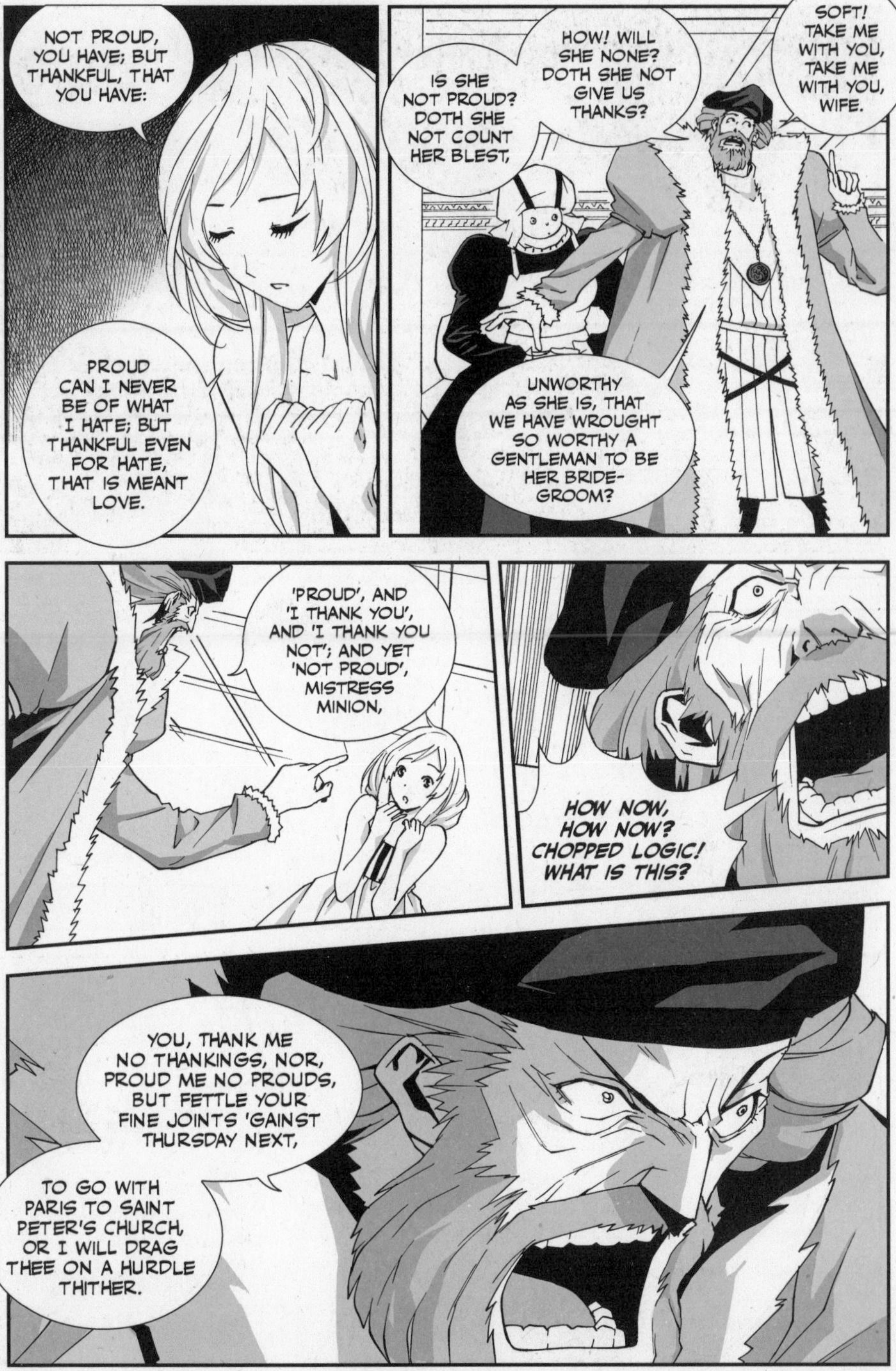
SOFT! TAKE ME WITH YOU, TAKE ME WITH YOU, WIFE.
HOW! WILL SHE NONE? DOTH SHE NOT GIVE US THANKS?
IS SHE NOT PROUD? DOTH SHE NOT COUNT HER BLEST,
UNWORTHY AS SHE IS, THAT WE HAVE WROUGHT SO WORTHY A GENTLEMAN TO BE HER BRIDE-GROOM?
NOT PROUD, YOU HAVE; BUT THANKFUL, THAT YOU HAVE:
PROUD CAN I NEVER BE OF WHAT I HATE; BUT THANKFUL EVEN FOR HATE, THAT IS MEANT LOVE.
HOW NOW, HOW NOW? CHOPPED LOGIC! WHAT IS THIS?
'PROUD', AND 'I THANK YOU', AND 'I THANK YOU NOT'; AND YET 'NOT PROUD', MISTRESS MINION,
YOU, THANK ME NO THANKINGS, NOR, PROUD ME NO PROUDS, BUT FETTLE YOUR FINE JOINTS 'GAINST THURSDAY NEXT,
TO GO WITH PARIS TO SAINT PETER'S CHURCH, OR I WILL DRAG THEE ON A HURDLE THITHER.

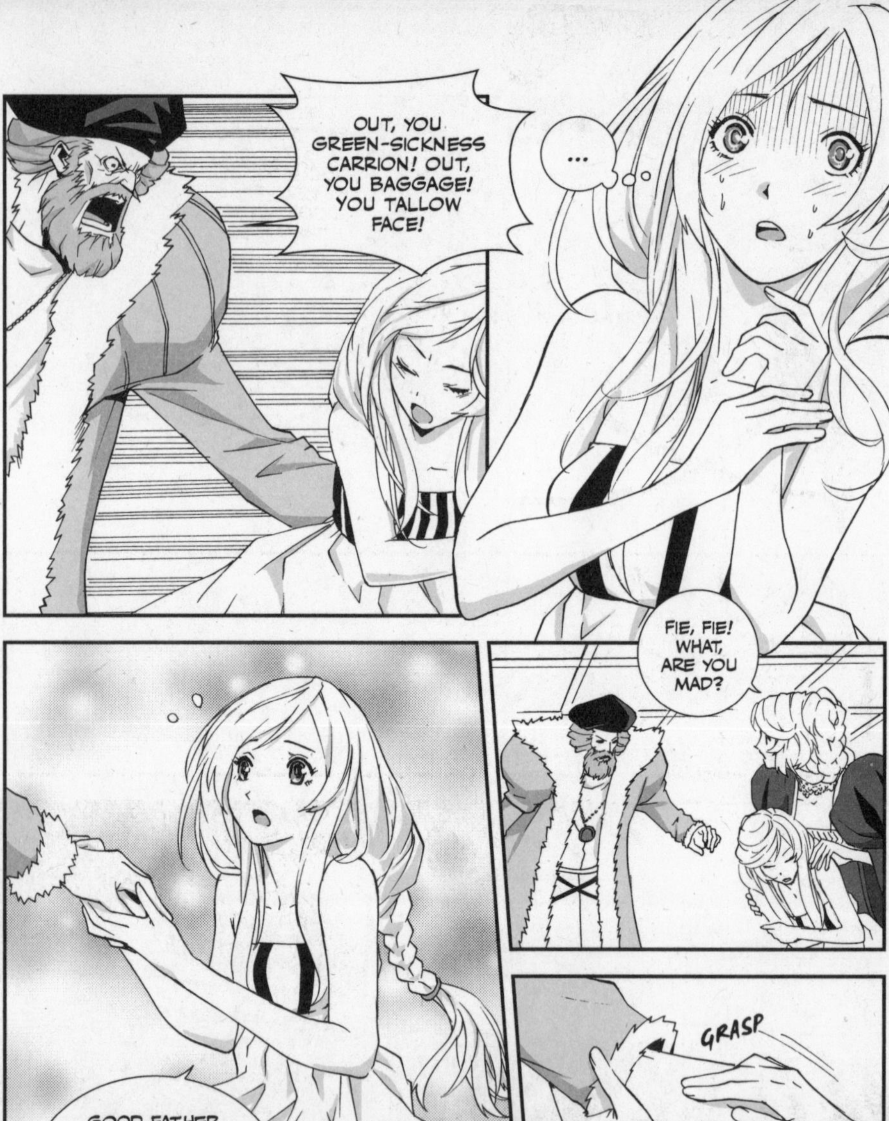
...
OUT, YOU GREEN-SICKNESS CARRION! OUT, YOU BAGGAGE! YOU TALLOW FACE!
FIE, FIE! WHAT, ARE YOU MAD?
GRASP
GOOD FATHER, I BESEECH YOU ON MY KNEES, HEAR ME WITH PATIENCE BUT TO SPEAK A WORD.

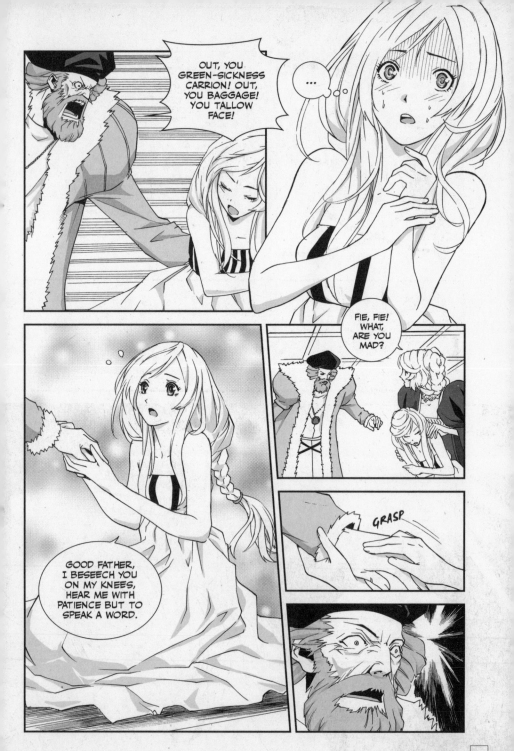

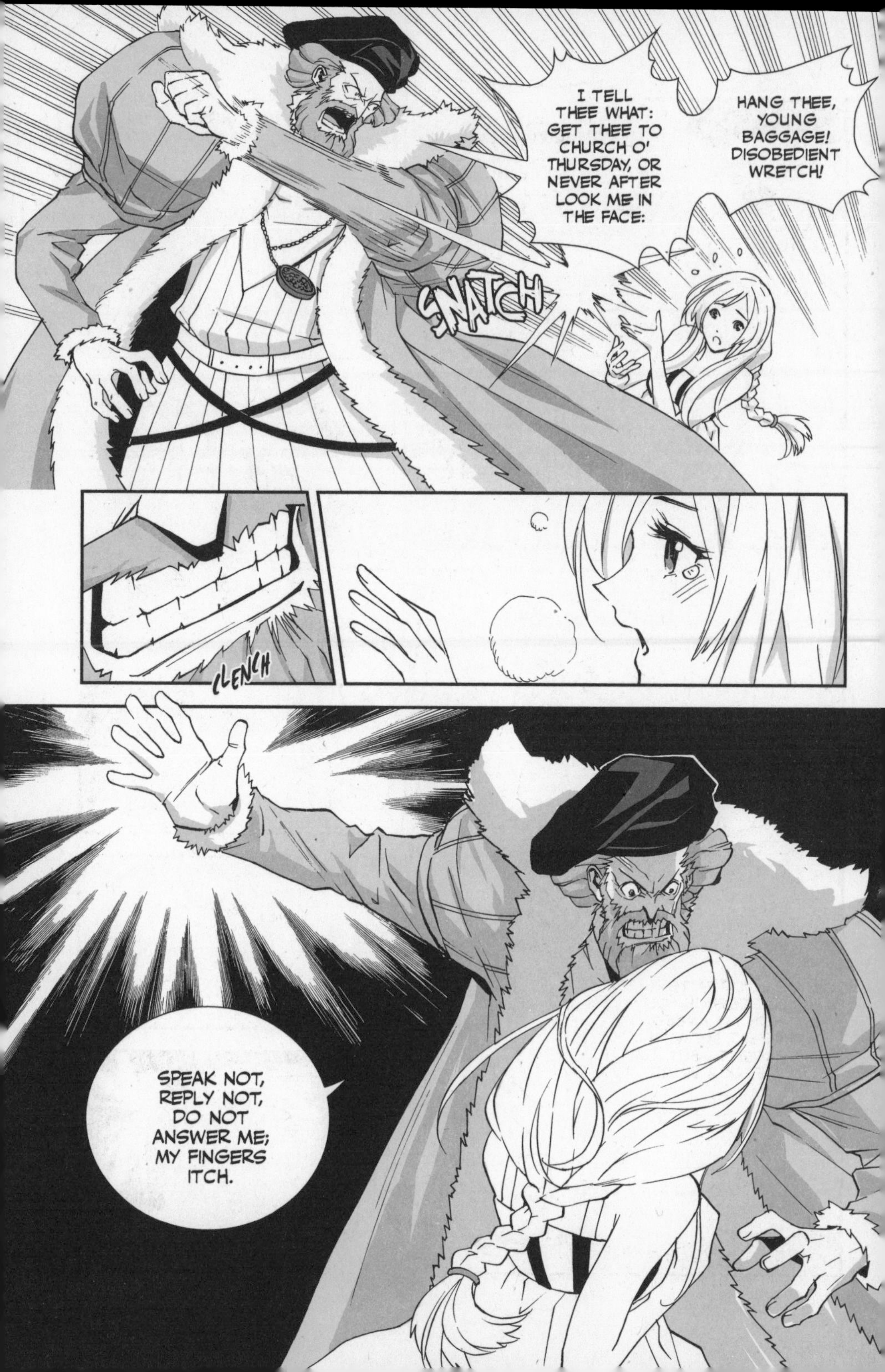
HANG THEE, YOUNG BAGGAGE! DISOBEDIENT WRETCH!
I TELL THEE WHAT: GET THEE TO CHURCH O' THURSDAY, OR NEVER AFTER LOOK ME IN THE FACE:
SNATCH
CLENCH
SPEAK NOT, REPLY NOT, DO NOT ANSWER ME; MY FINGERS ITCH.

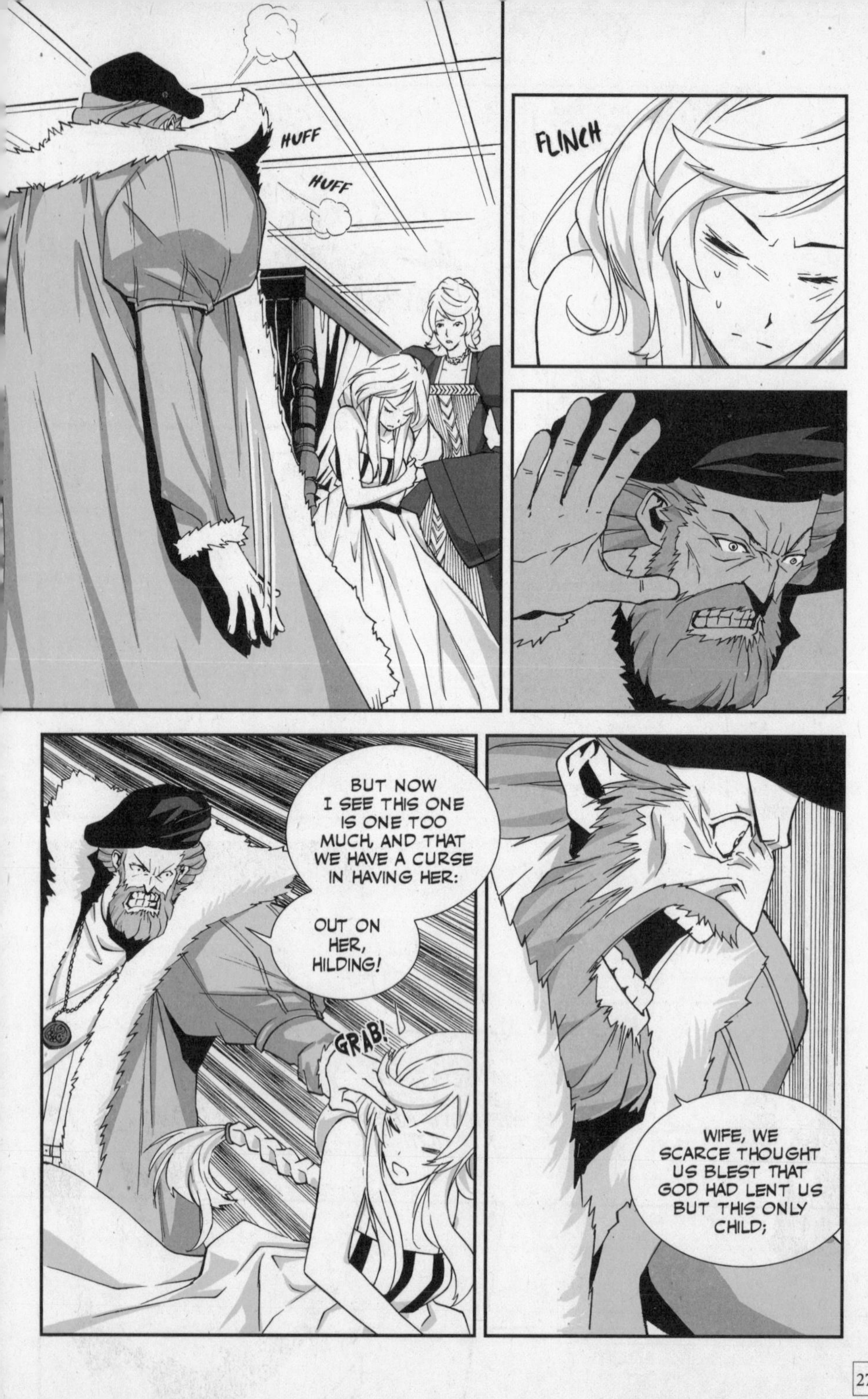
FLINCH
HUFF
HUFF
WIFE, WE SCARCE THOUGHT US BLEST THAT GOD HAD LENT US BUT THIS ONLY CHILD;
BUT NOW I SEE THIS ONE IS ONE TOO MUCH, AND THAT WE HAVE A CURSE IN HAVING HER:
OUT ON HER, HILDING!
GRAB!

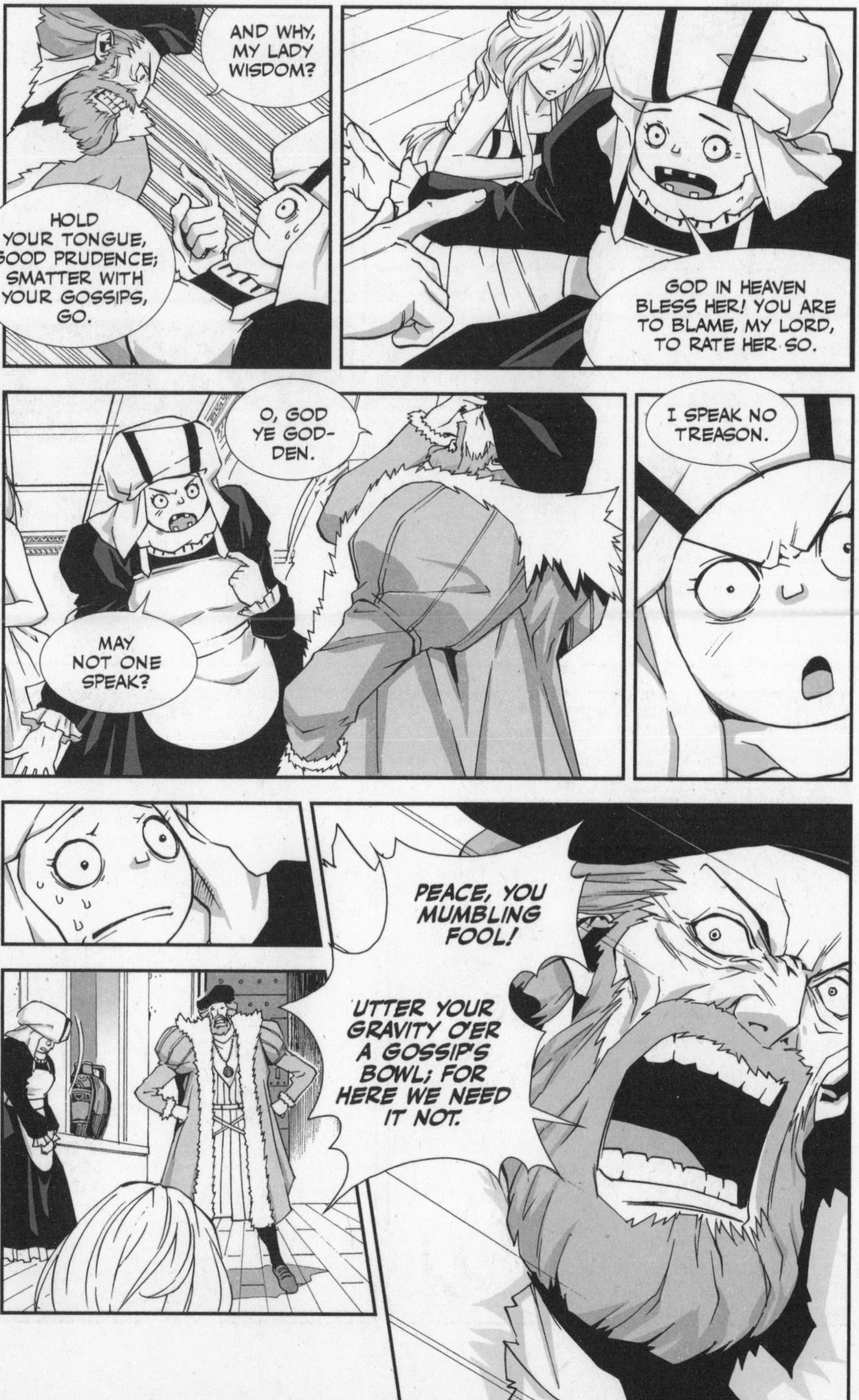
GOD IN HEAVEN BLESS HER! YOU ARE TO BLAME, MY LORD, TO RATE HER SO.
AND WHY, MY LADY WISDOM?
HOLD YOUR TONGUE, GOOD PRUDENCE; SMATTER WITH YOUR GOSSIPS, GO.
I SPEAK NO TREASON.
O, GOD YE GOD-DEN.
MAY NOT ONE SPEAK?
PEACE, YOU MUMBLING FOOL!
UTTER YOUR GRAVITY O'ER A GOSSIP'S BOWL; FOR HERE WE NEED IT NOT.

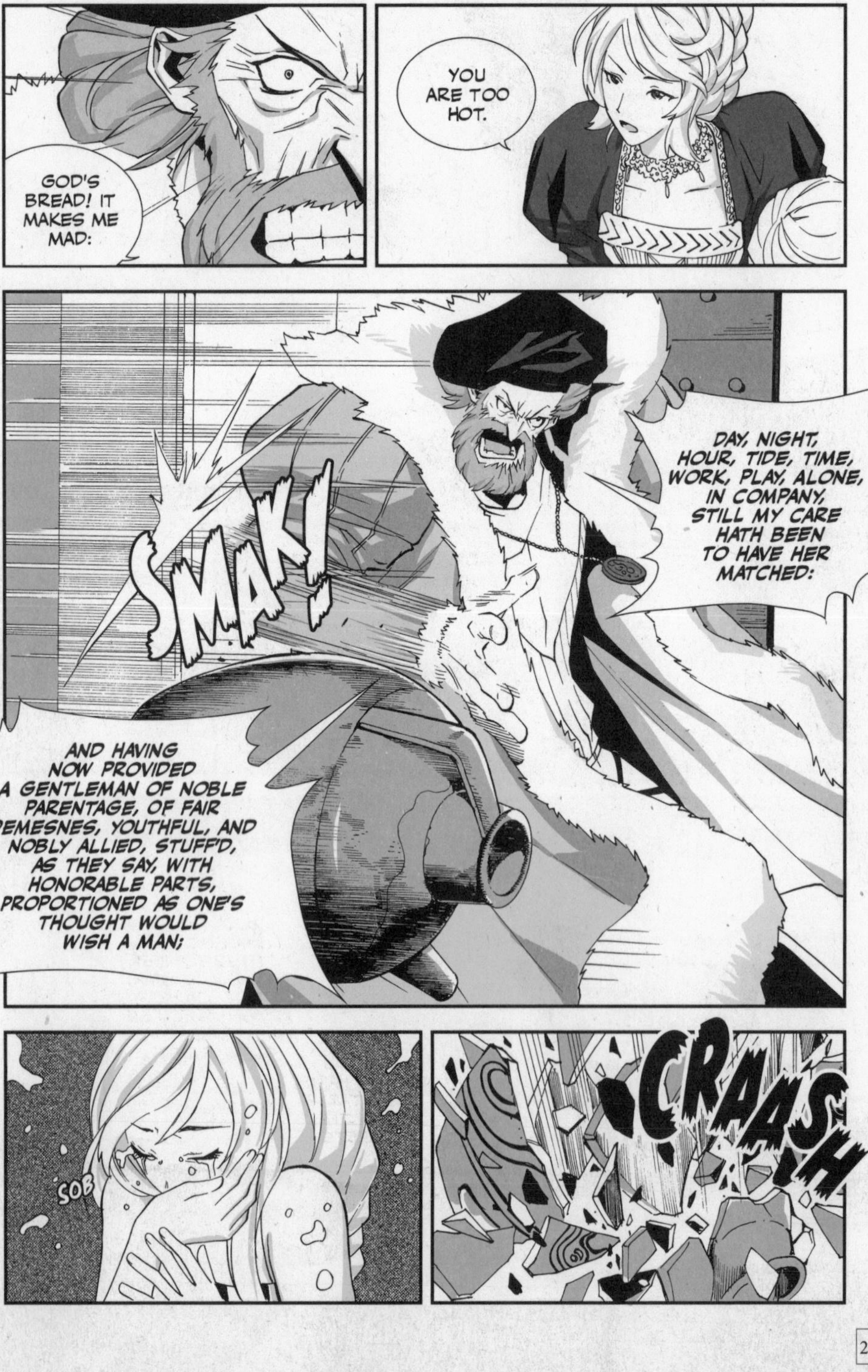
YOU ARE TOO HOT.
GOD'S BREAD! IT MAKES ME MAD:
DAY, NIGHT, HOUR, TIDE, TIME, WORK, PLAY, ALONE, IN COMPANY, STILL MY CARE HATH BEEN TO HAVE HER MATCHED:
SMAK!
AND HAVING NOW PROVIDED A GENTLEMAN OF NOBLE PARENTAGE, OF FAIR DEMESNES, YOUTHFUL, AND NOBLY ALLIED, STUFF'D, AS THEY SAY, WITH HONORABLE PARTS, PROPORTIONED AS ONE'S THOUGHT WOULD WISH A MAN;
CRASH
SOB

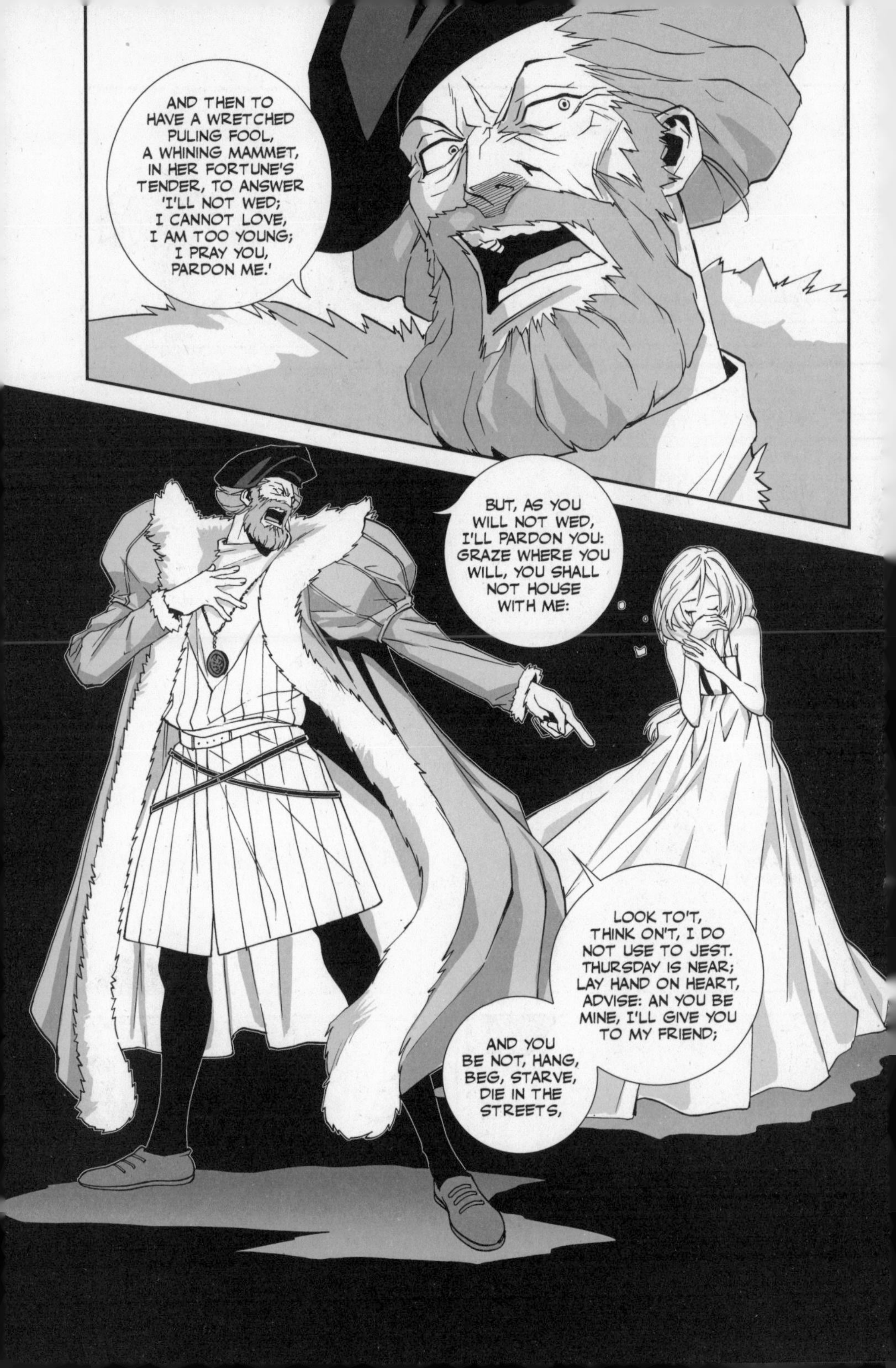

AND THEN TO HAVE A WRETCHED PULING FOOL, A WHINING MAMMET, IN HER FORTUNE'S TENDER, TO ANSWER 'I'LL NOT WED; I CANNOT LOVE, I AM TOO YOUNG; I PRAY YOU, PARDON ME.'
BUT, AS YOU WILL NOT WED, I'LL PARDON YOU: GRAZE WHERE YOU WILL, YOU SHALL NOT HOUSE WITH ME:
LOOK TO'T, THINK ON'T, I DO NOT USE TO JEST. THURSDAY IS NEAR; LAY HAND ON HEART, ADVISE: AN YOU BE MINE, I'LL GIVE YOU TO MY FRIEND;
AND YOU BE NOT, HANG, BEG, STARVE, DIE IN THE STREETS,

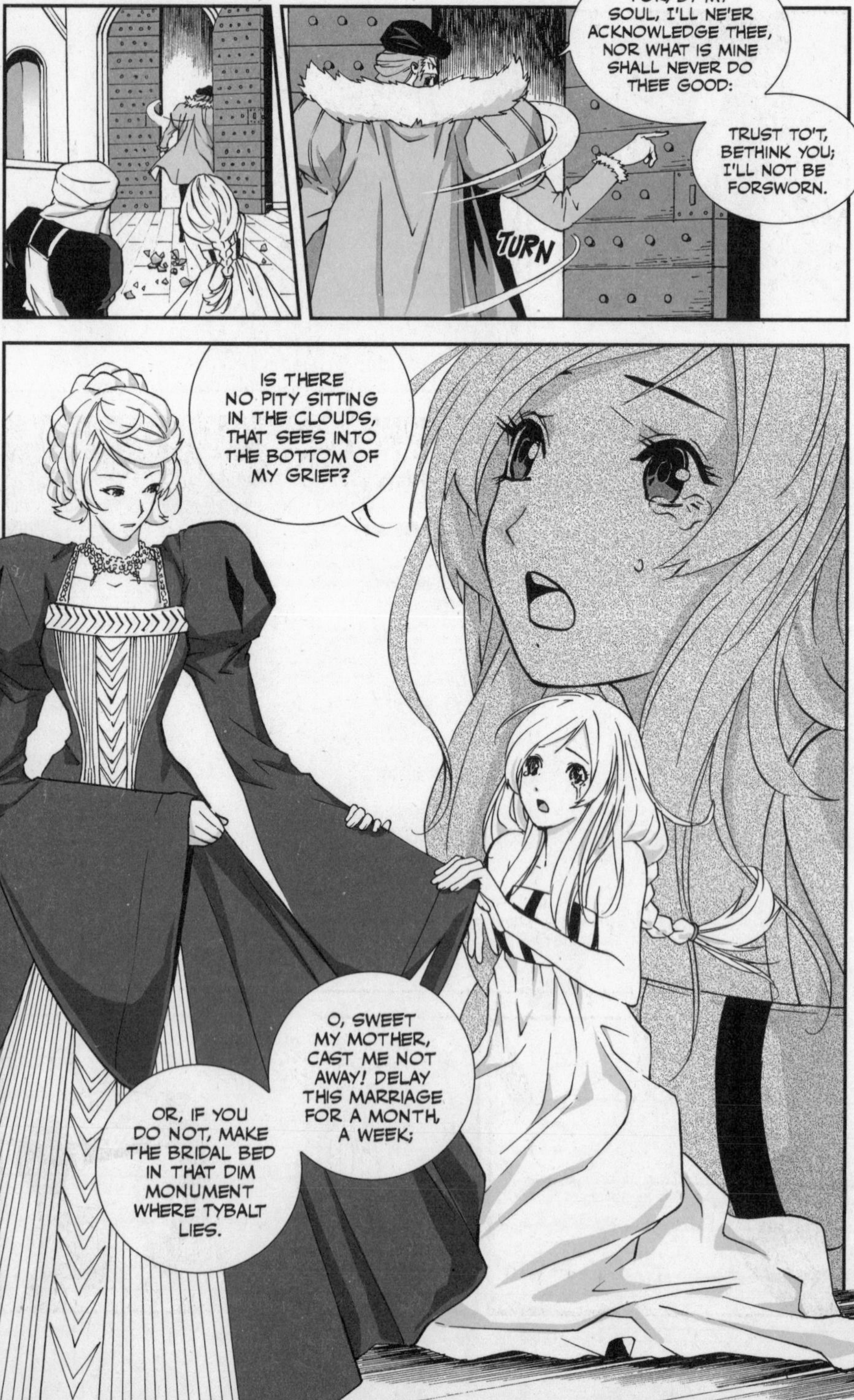
FOR, BY MY SOUL, I'LL NE'ER ACKNOWLEDGE THEE, NOR WHAT IS MINE SHALL NEVER DO THEE GOOD:
TRUST TO'T, BETHINK YOU; I'LL NOT BE FORSWORN.
TURN
IS THERE NO PITY SITTING IN THE CLOUDS, THAT SEES INTO THE BOTTOM OF MY GRIEF?
O, SWEET MY MOTHER, CAST ME NOT AWAY! DELAY THIS MARRIAGE FOR A MONTH, A WEEK;
OR, IF YOU DO NOT, MAKE THE BRIDAL BED IN THAT DIM MONUMENT WHERE TYBALT LIES.

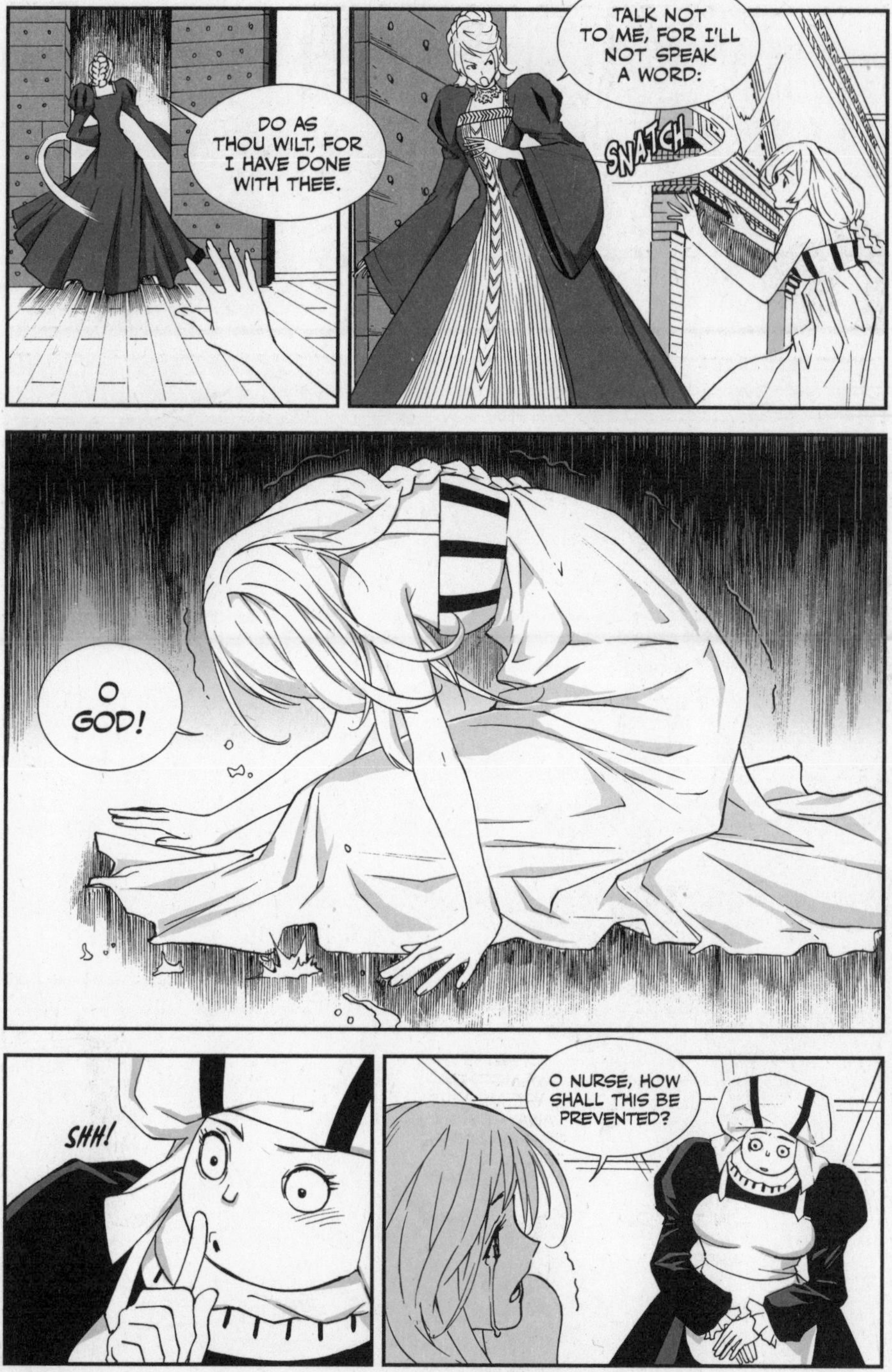
TALK NOT TO ME, FOR I'LL NOT SPEAK A WORD:
SNATCH
DO AS THOU WILT, FOR I HAVE DONE WITH THEE.
O GOD!
O NURSE, HOW SHALL THIS BE PREVENTED?
SHH!

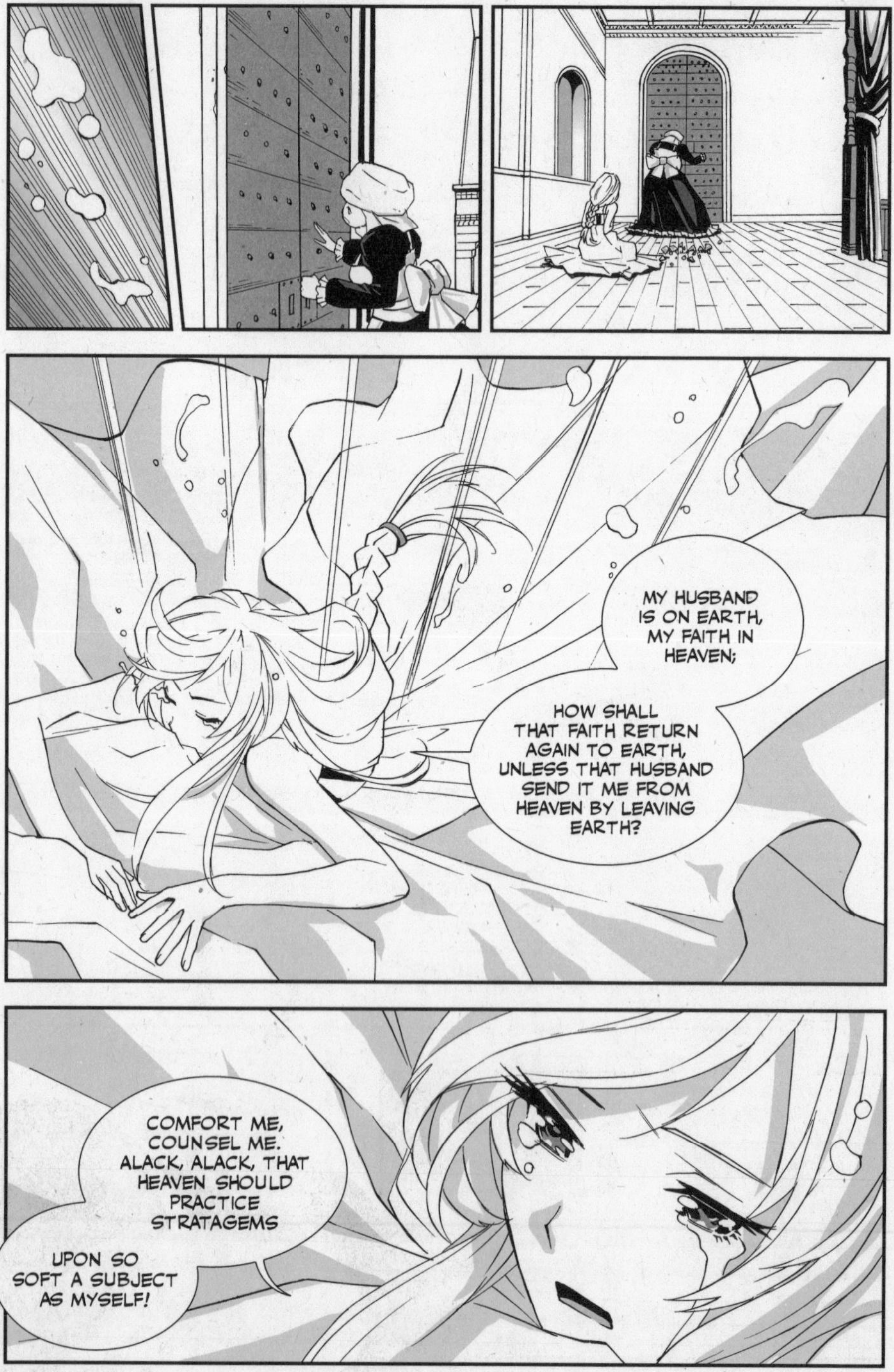
MY HUSBAND IS ON EARTH, MY FAITH IN HEAVEN;
HOW SHALL THAT FAITH RETURN AGAIN TO EARTH, UNLESS THAT HUSBAND SEND IT ME FROM HEAVEN BY LEAVING EARTH?
COMFORT ME, COUNSEL ME. ALACK, ALACK, THAT HEAVEN SHOULD PRACTICE STRATAGEMS
UPON SO SOFT A SUBJECT AS MYSELF!

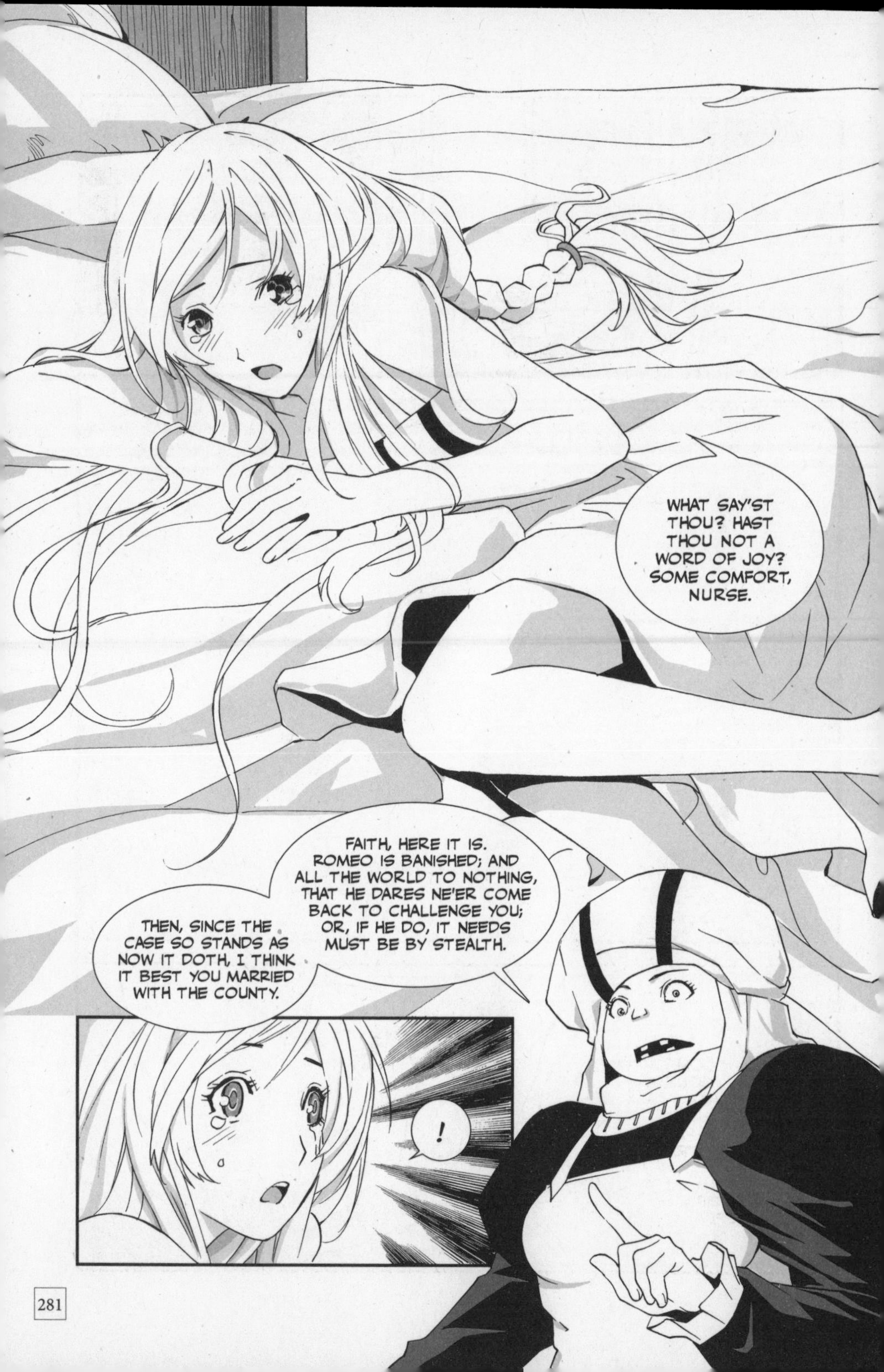
WHAT SAY'ST THOU? HAST THOU NOT A WORD OF JOY? SOME COMFORT, NURSE.
FAITH, HERE IT IS. ROMEO IS BANISHED; AND ALL THE WORLD TO NOTHING, THAT HE DARES NE'ER COME BACK TO CHALLENGE YOU; OR, IF HE DO, IT NEEDS MUST BE BY STEALTH.
THEN, SINCE THE CASE SO STANDS AS NOW IT DOTH, I THINK IT BEST YOU MARRIED WITH THE COUNTY.
!

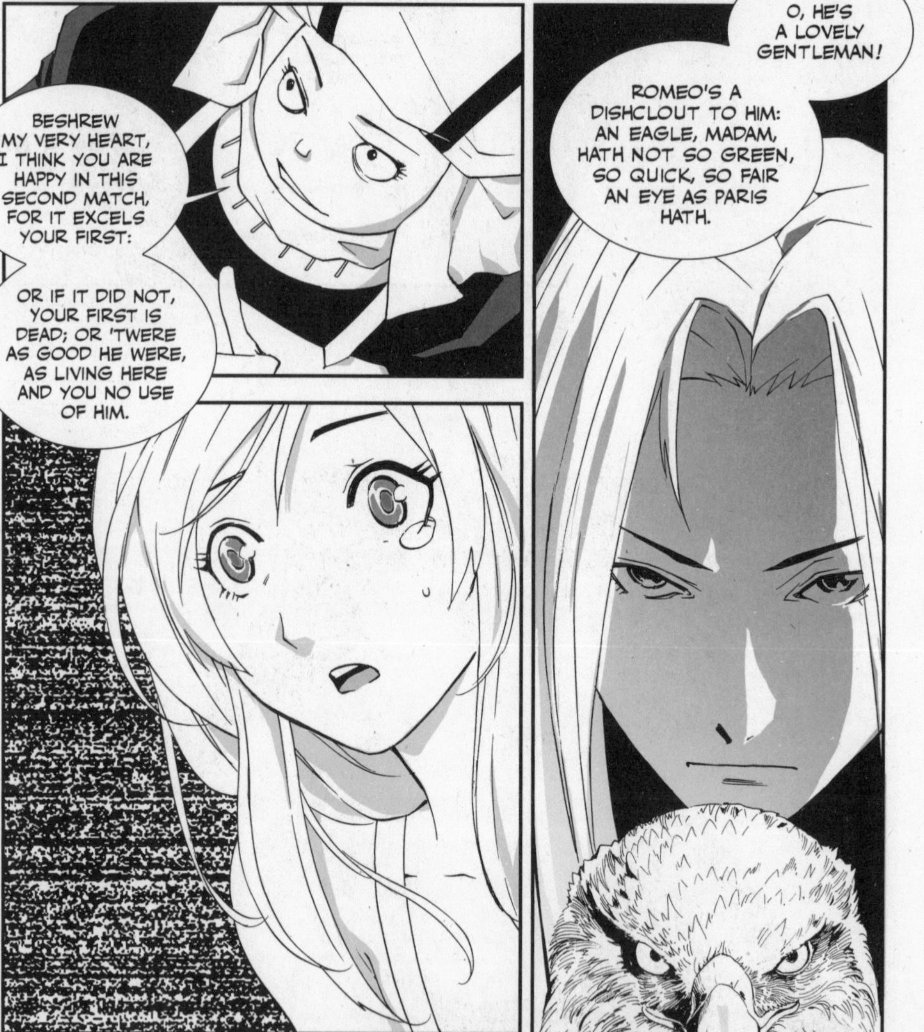
O, HE'S A LOVELY GENTLEMAN!
ROMEO'S A DISHCLOUT TO HIM: AN EAGLE, MADAM, HATH NOT SO GREEN, SO QUICK, SO FAIR AN EYE AS PARIS HATH.
BESHREW MY VERY HEART, I THINK YOU ARE HAPPY IN THIS SECOND MATCH, FOR IT EXCELS YOUR FIRST:
OR IF IT DID NOT, YOUR FIRST IS DEAD; OR 'TWERE AS GOOD HE WERE, AS LIVING HERE AND YOU NO USE OF HIM.
HE HE

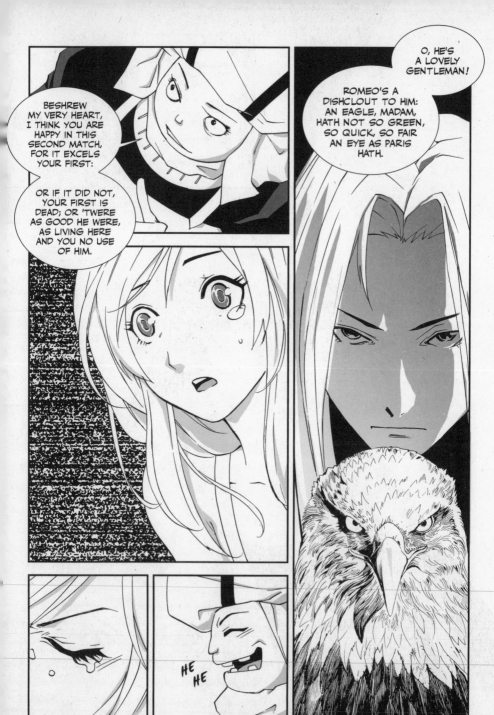

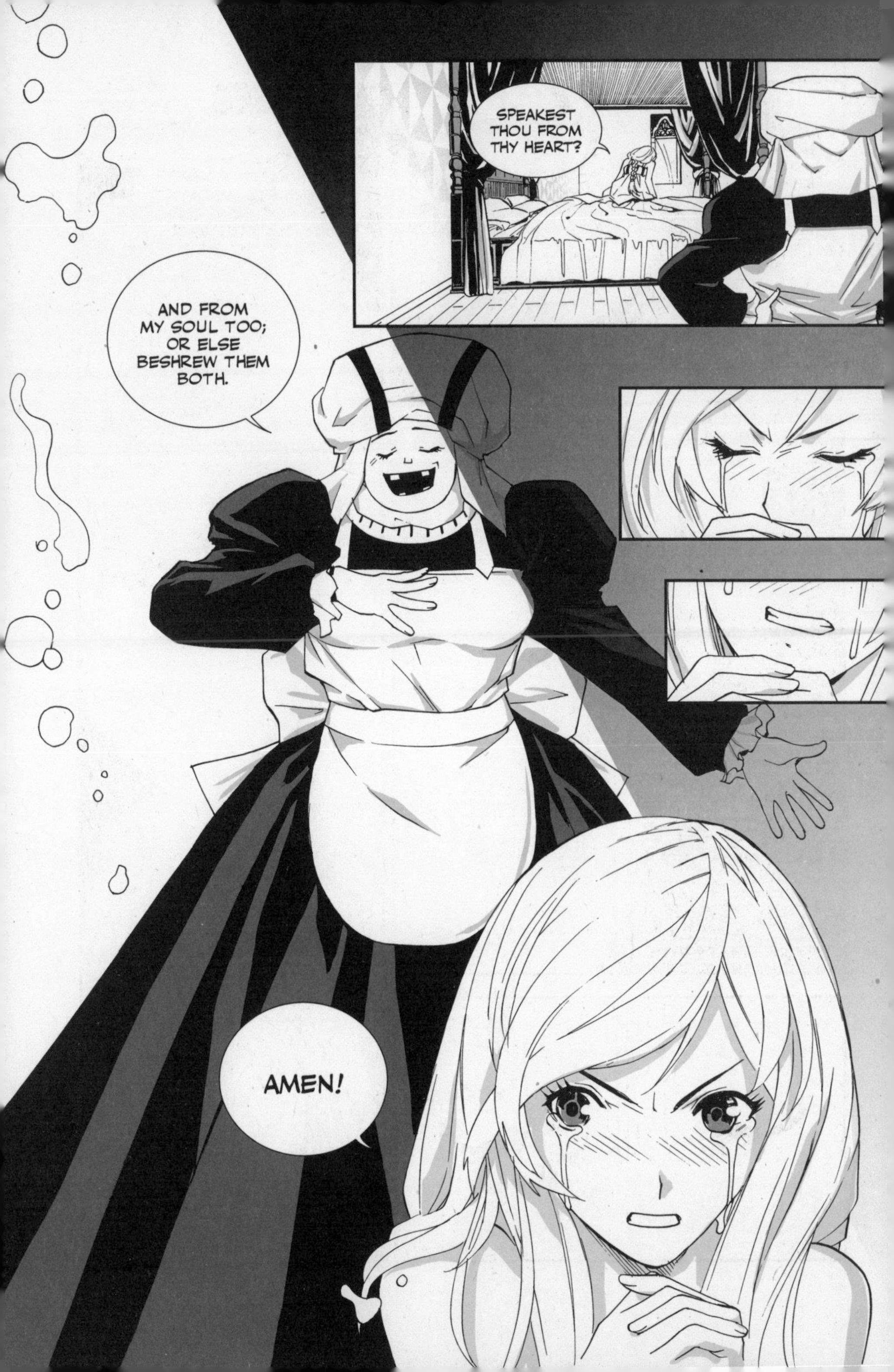
SPEAKEST THOU FROM THY HEART?
AND FROM MY SOUL TOO; OR ELSE BESHREW THEM BOTH.
AMEN!

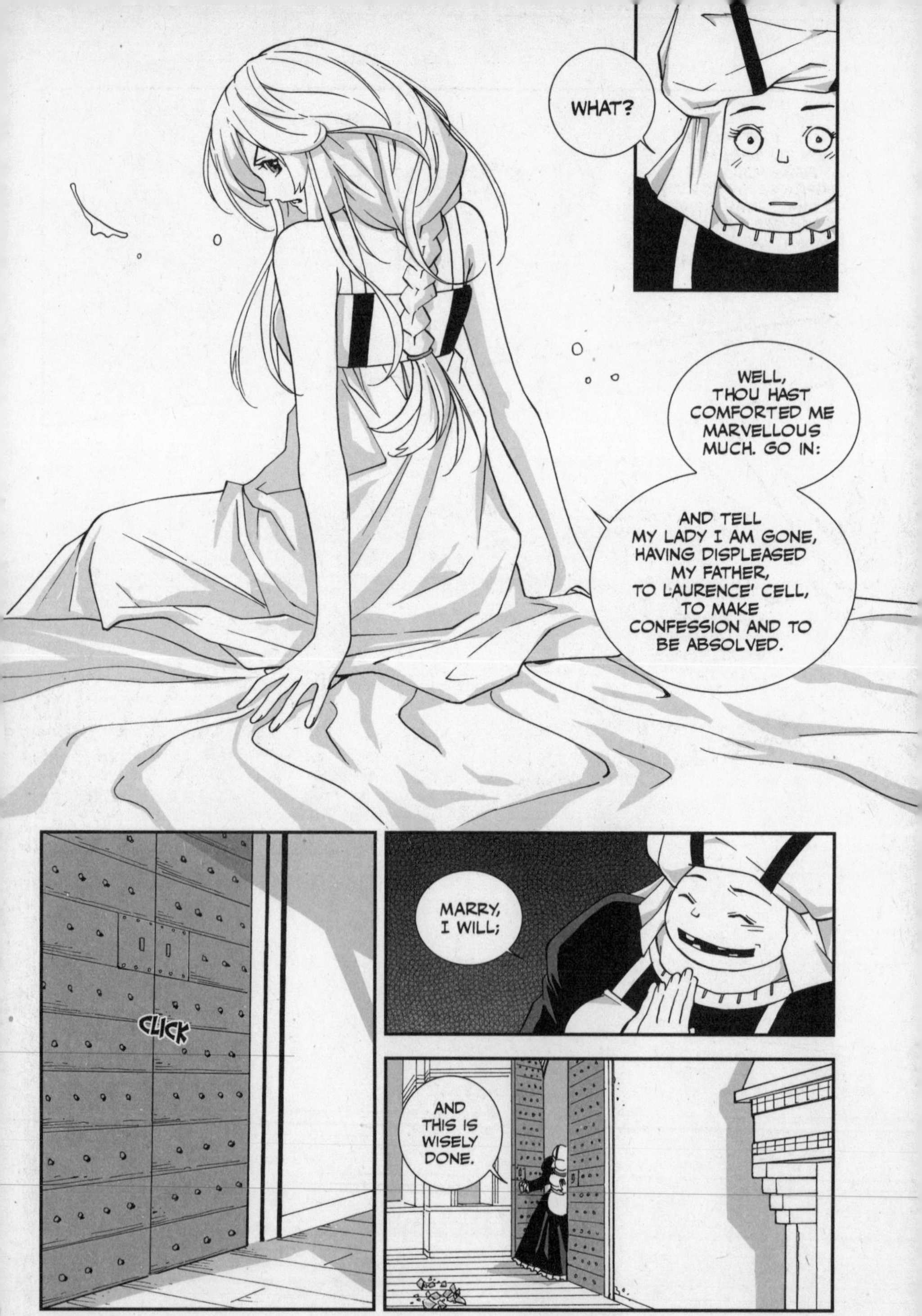
WHAT?
WELL, THOU HAST COMFORTED ME MARVELLOUS MUCH. GO IN:
AND TELL MY LADY I AM GONE, HAVING DISPLEASED MY FATHER, TO LAURENCE' CELL, TO MAKE CONFESSION AND TO BE ABSOLVED.
MARRY, I WILL;
AND THIS IS WISELY DONE.
CLICK

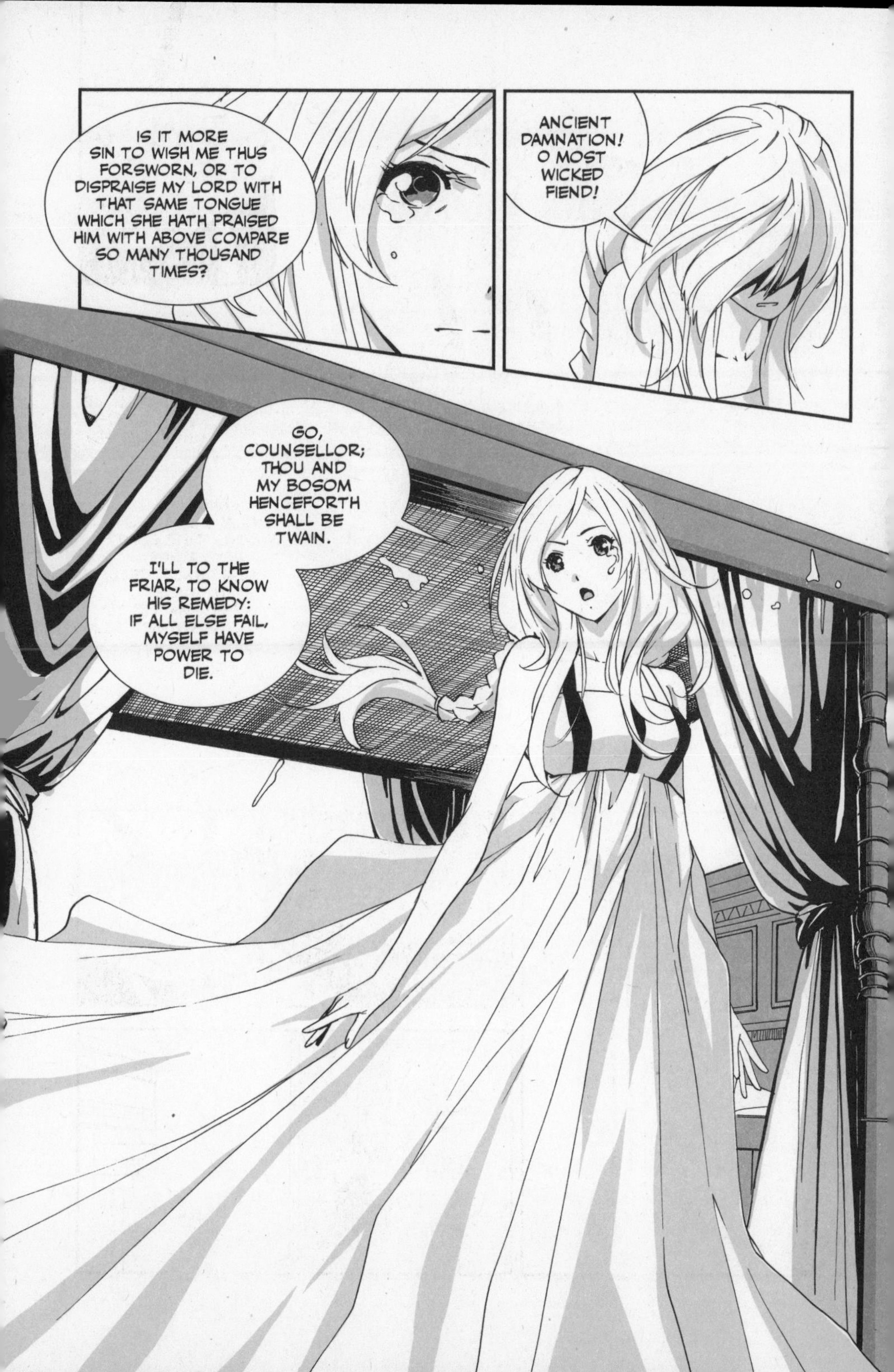
ANCIENT DAMNATION! O MOST WICKED FIEND!
IS IT MORE SIN TO WISH ME THUS FORSWORN, OR TO DISPRAISE MY LORD WITH THAT SAME TONGUE WHICH SHE HATH PRAISED HIM WITH ABOVE COMPARE SO MANY THOUSAND TIMES?
GO, COUNSELLOR; THOU AND MY BOSOM HENCEFORTH SHALL BE TWAIN.
I'LL TO THE FRIAR, TO KNOW HIS REMEDY: IF ALL ELSE FAIL, MYSELF HAVE POWER TO DIE.

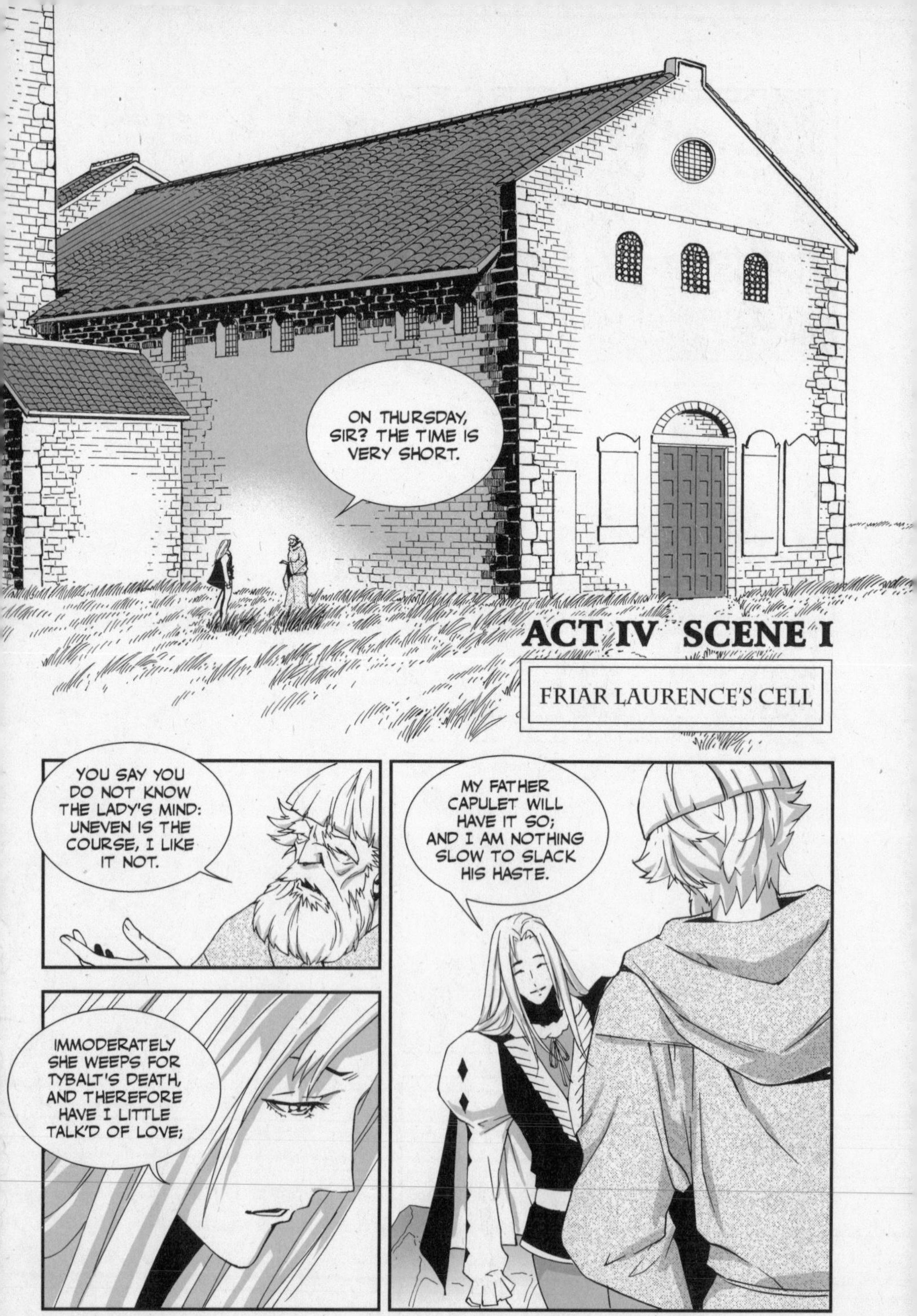
ON THURSDAY, SIR? THE TIME IS VERY SHORT.
ACT IV SCENE I
FRIAR LAURENCE'S CELL
MY FATHER CAPULET WILL HAVE IT SO; AND I AM NOTHING SLOW TO SLACK HIS HASTE.
YOU SAY YOU DO NOT KNOW THE LADY'S MIND: UNEVEN IS THE COURSE, I LIKE IT NOT.
IMMODERATELY SHE WEEPS FOR TYBALT'S DEATH, AND THEREFORE HAVE I LITTLE TALK'D OF LOVE;

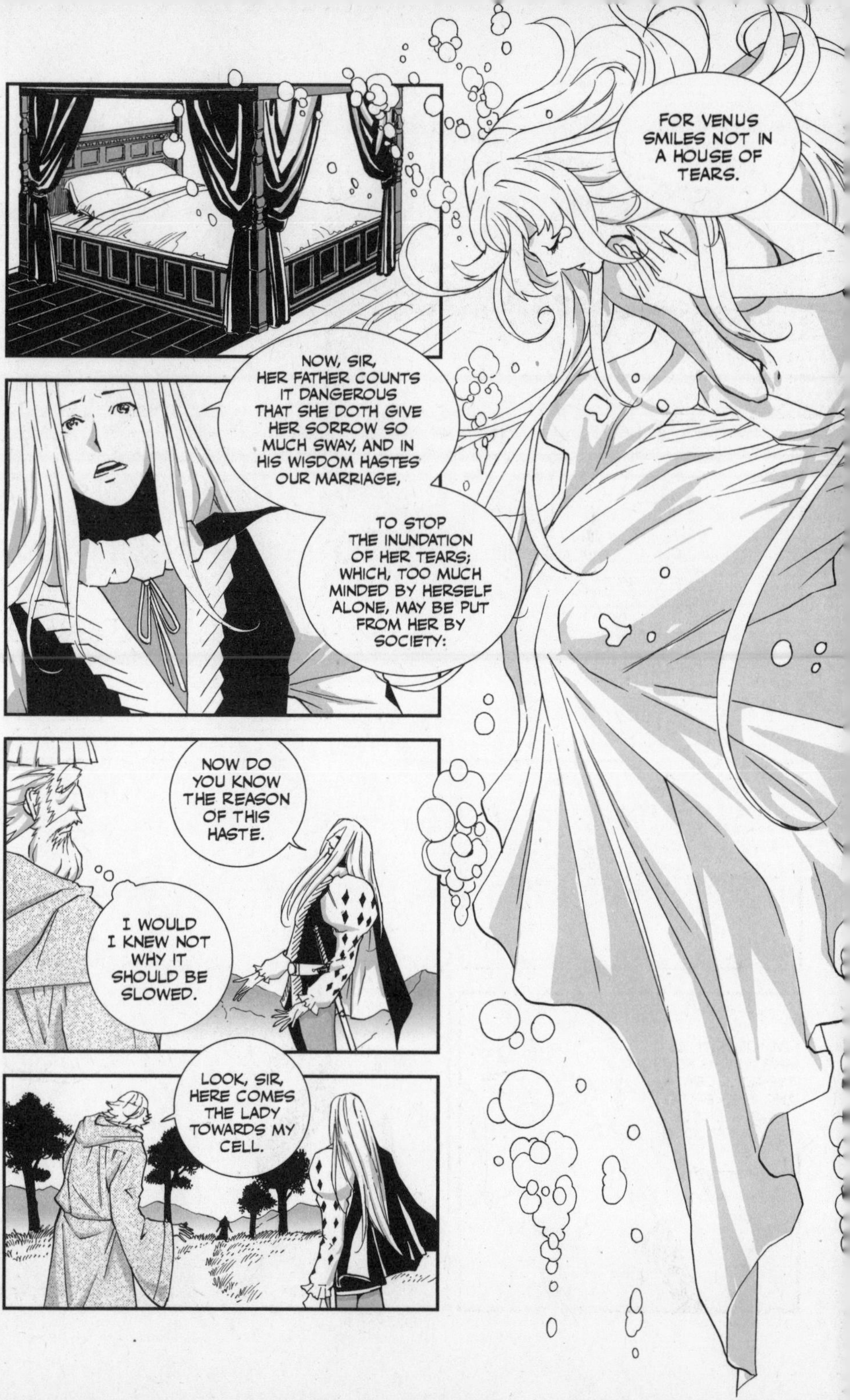
FOR VENUS SMILES NOT IN A HOUSE OF TEARS.
NOW, SIR, HER FATHER COUNTS IT DANGEROUS THAT SHE DOTH GIVE HER SORROW SO MUCH SWAY, AND IN HIS WISDOM HASTES OUR MARRIAGE,
TO STOP THE INUNDATION OF HER TEARS; WHICH, TOO MUCH MINDED BY HERSELF ALONE, MAY BE PUT FROM HER BY SOCIETY:
NOW DO YOU KNOW THE REASON OF THIS HASTE.
I WOULD I KNEW NOT WHY IT SHOULD BE SLOWED.
LOOK, SIR, HERE COMES THE LADY TOWARDS MY CELL.

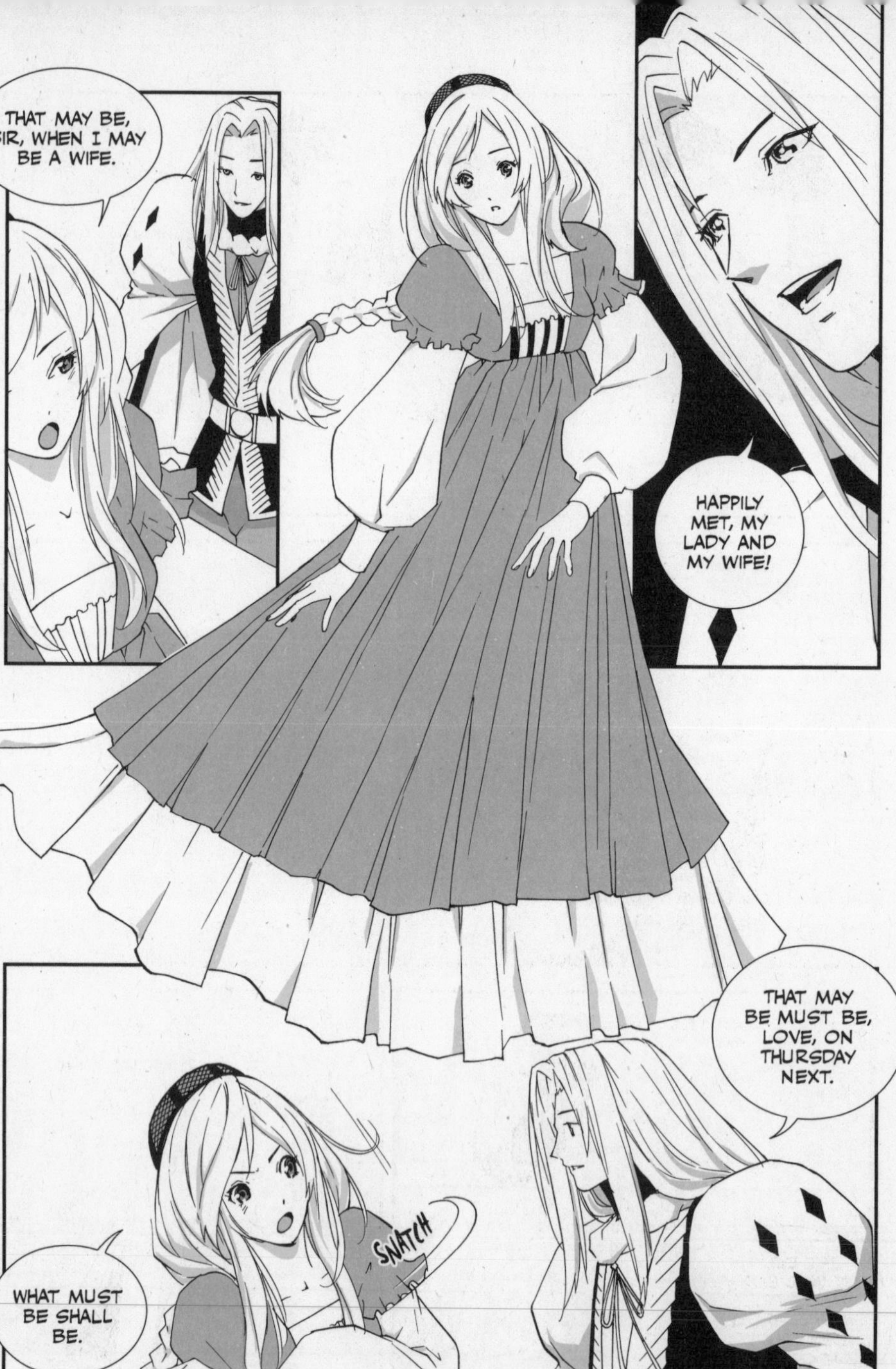
HAPPILY MET, MY LADY AND MY WIFE!
THAT MAY BE, SIR, WHEN I MAY BE A WIFE.
THAT MAY BE MUST BE, LOVE, ON THURSDAY NEXT.
SNATCH
WHAT MUST BE SHALL BE.

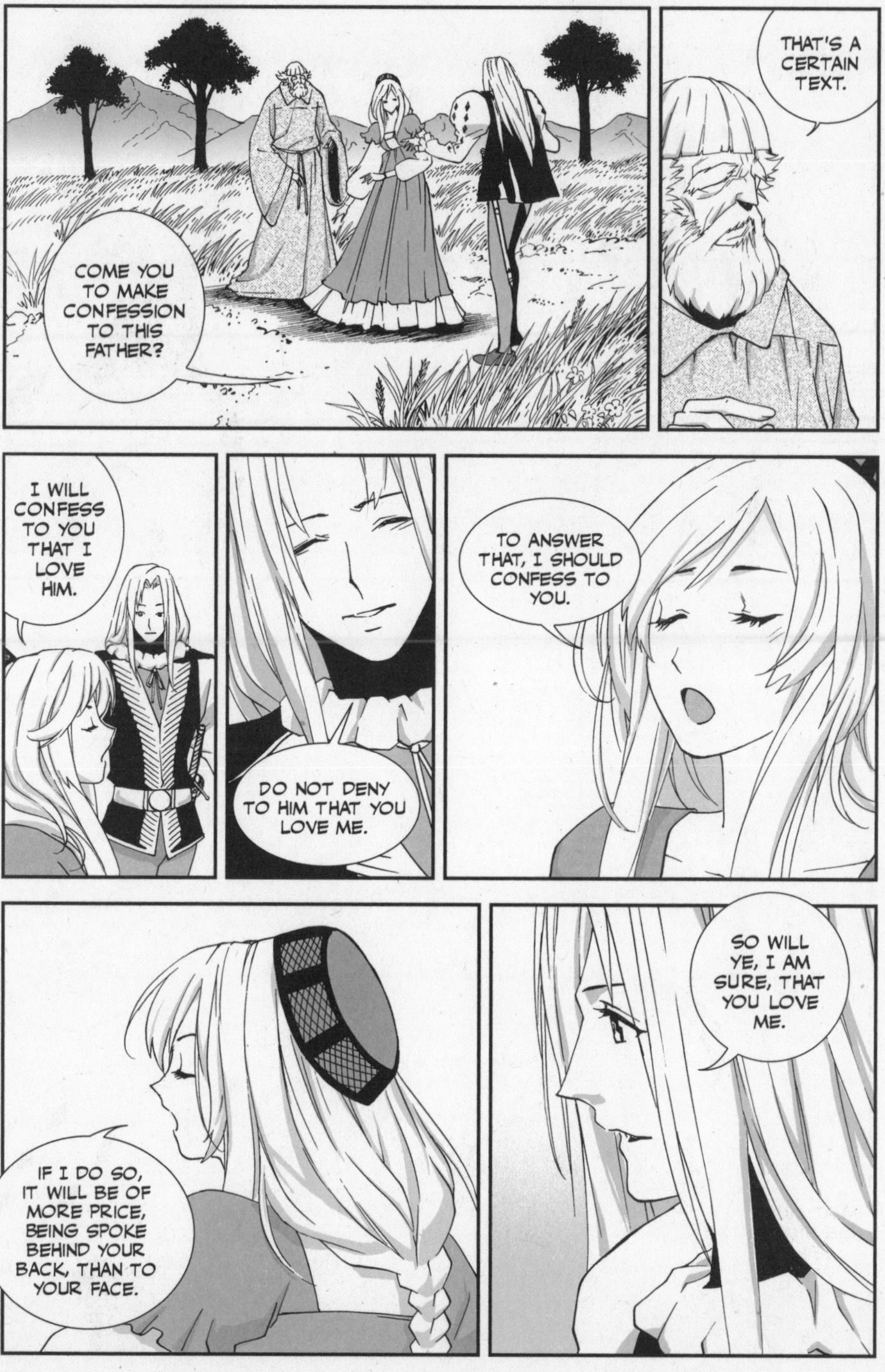
THAT'S A CERTAIN TEXT.
COME YOU TO MAKE CONFESSION TO THIS FATHER?
TO ANSWER THAT, I SHOULD CONFESS TO YOU.
DO NOT DENY TO HIM THAT YOU LOVE ME.
I WILL CONFESS TO YOU THAT I LOVE HIM.
SO WILL YE, I AM SURE, THAT YOU LOVE ME.
IF I DO SO, IT WILL BE OF MORE PRICE, BEING SPOKE BEHIND YOUR BACK, THAN TO YOUR FACE.

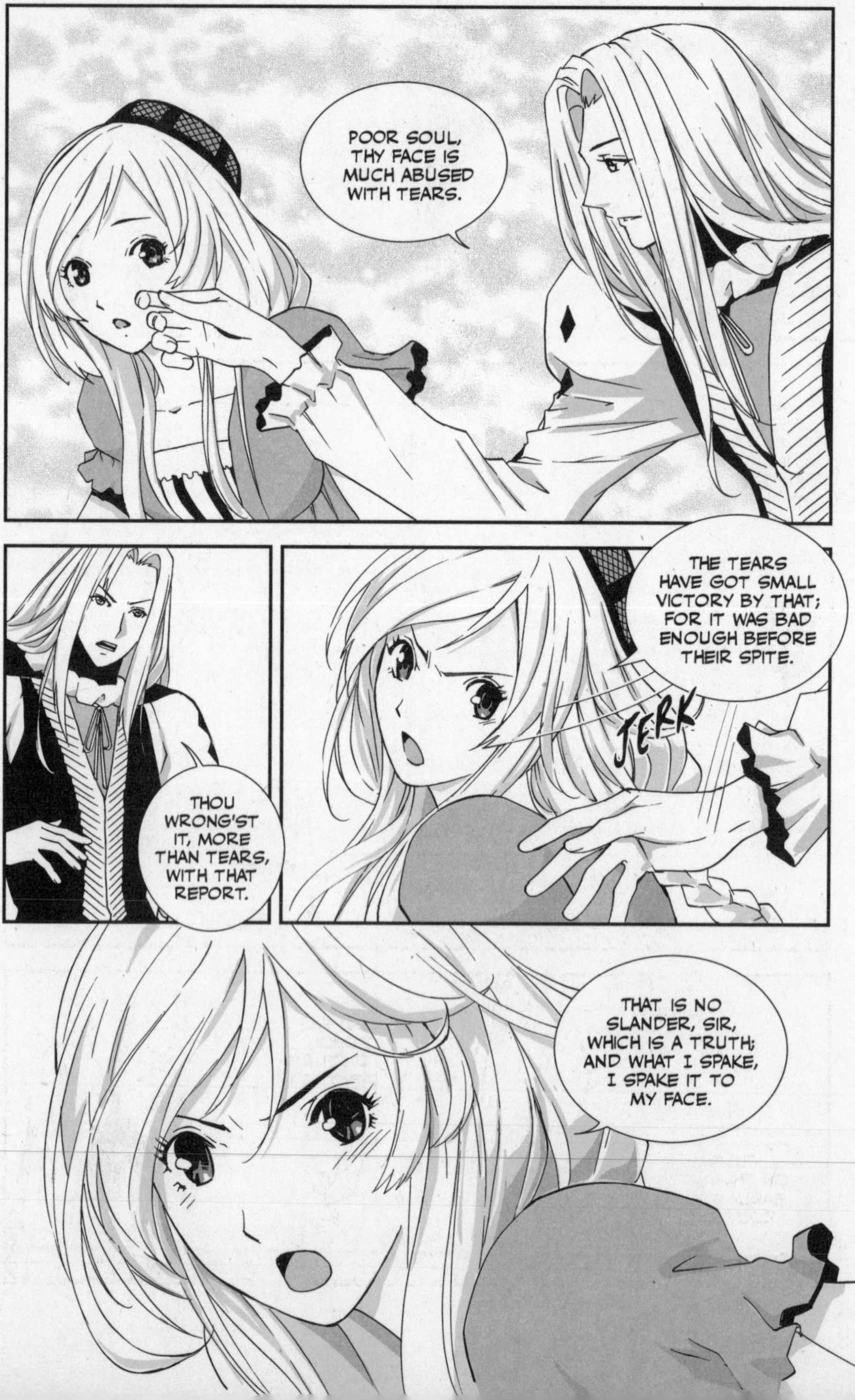
POOR SOUL, THY FACE IS MUCH ABUSED WITH TEARS.
THE TEARS HAVE GOT SMALL VICTORY BY THAT; FOR IT WAS BAD ENOUGH BEFORE THEIR SPITE.
JERK
THOU WRONG'ST IT, MORE THAN TEARS, WITH THAT REPORT.
THAT IS NO SLANDER, SIR, WHICH IS A TRUTH; AND WHAT I SPAKE, I SPAKE IT TO MY FACE.

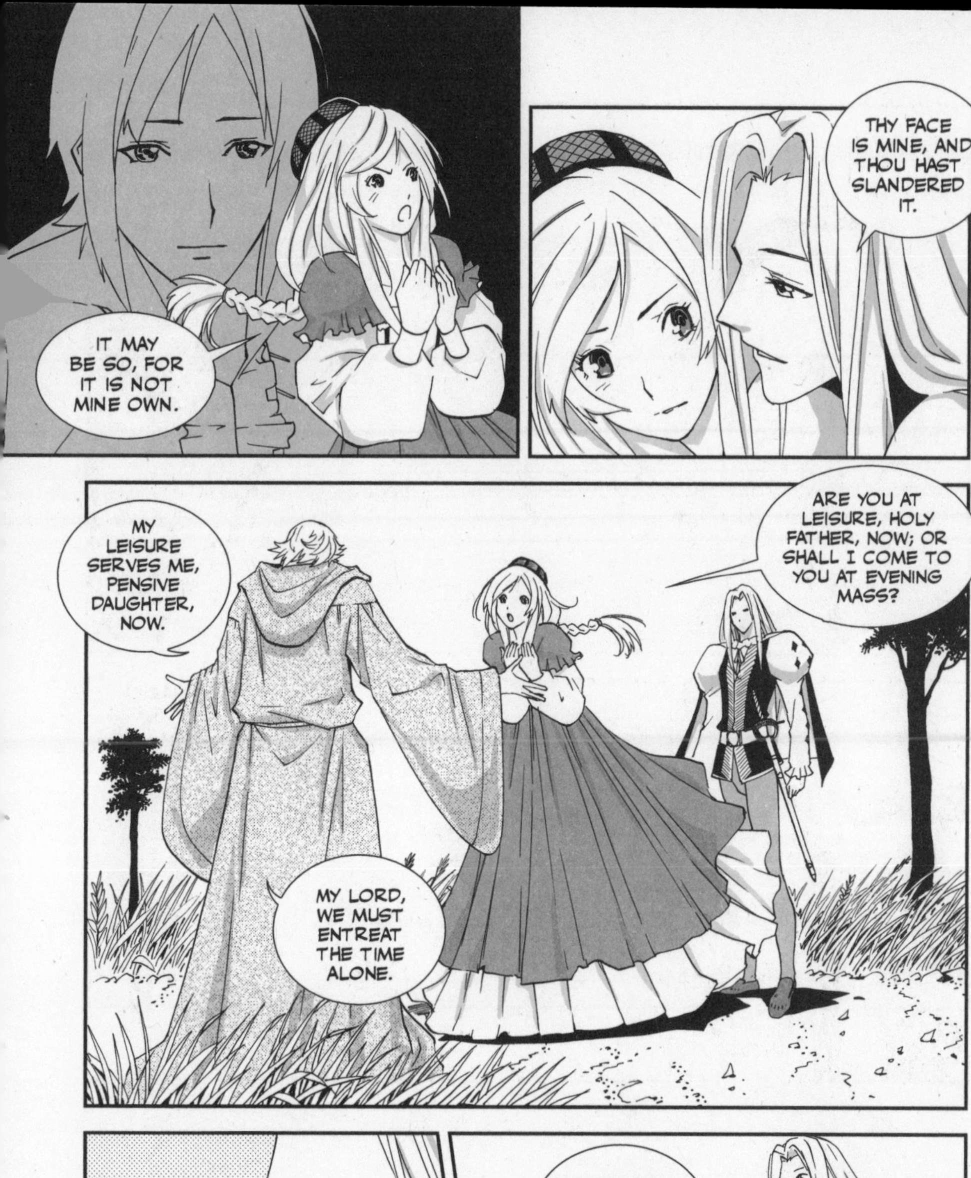
THY FACE IS MINE, AND THOU HAST SLANDERED IT.
IT MAY BE SO, FOR IT IS NOT MINE OWN.
ARE YOU AT LEISURE, HOLY FATHER, NOW; OR SHALL I COME TO YOU AT EVENING MASS?
MY LEISURE SERVES ME, PENSIVE DAUGHTER, NOW.
MY LORD, WE MUST ENTREAT THE TIME ALONE.
GOD SHIELD I SHOULD DISTURB DEVOTION!
JULIET, ON THURSDAY EARLY WILL I ROUSE YE:

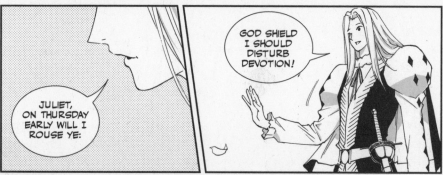

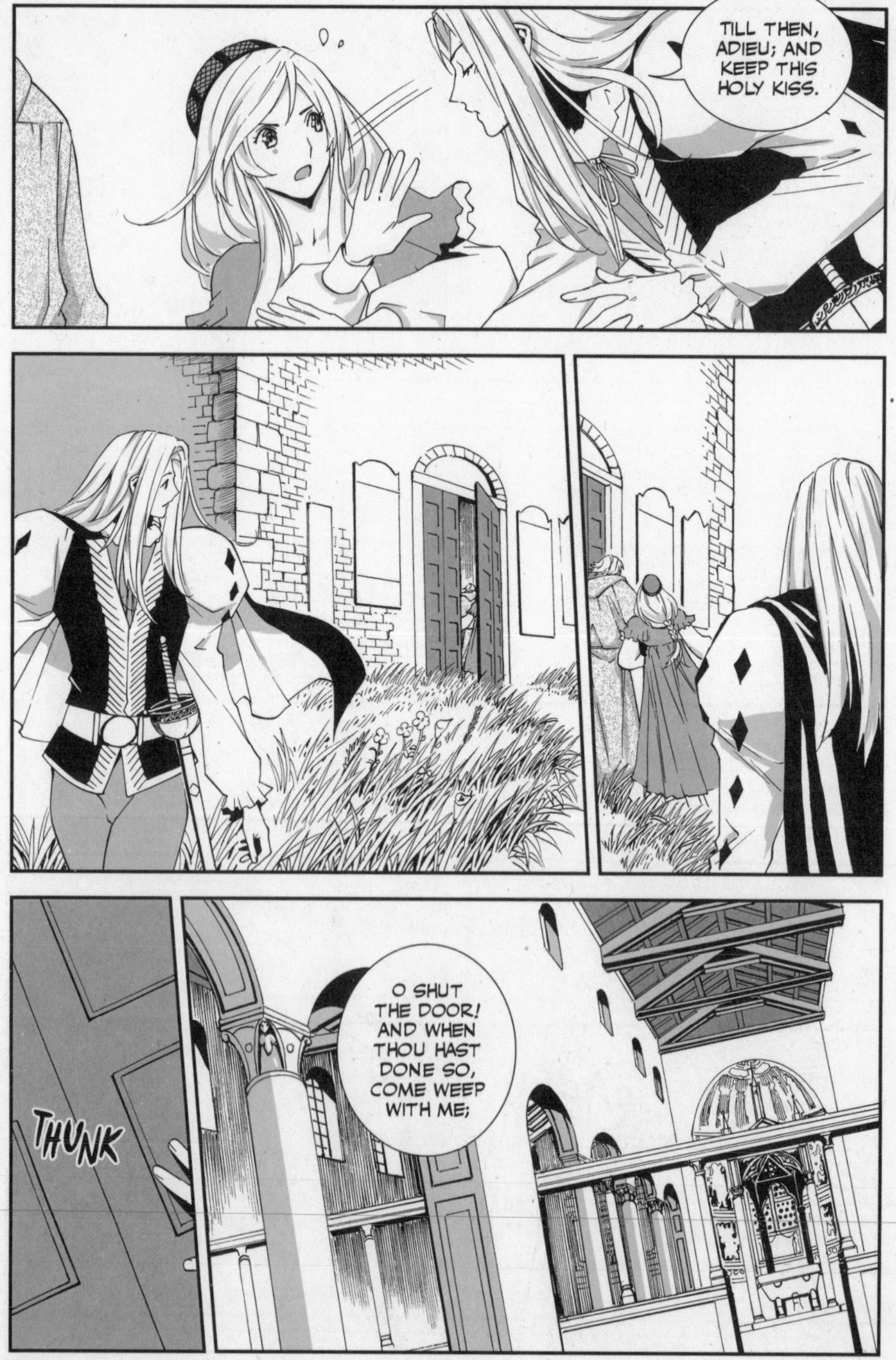
TILL THEN, ADIEU; AND KEEP THIS HOLY KISS.
O SHUT THE DOOR! AND WHEN THOU HAST DONE SO, COME WEEP WITH ME;
THUNK

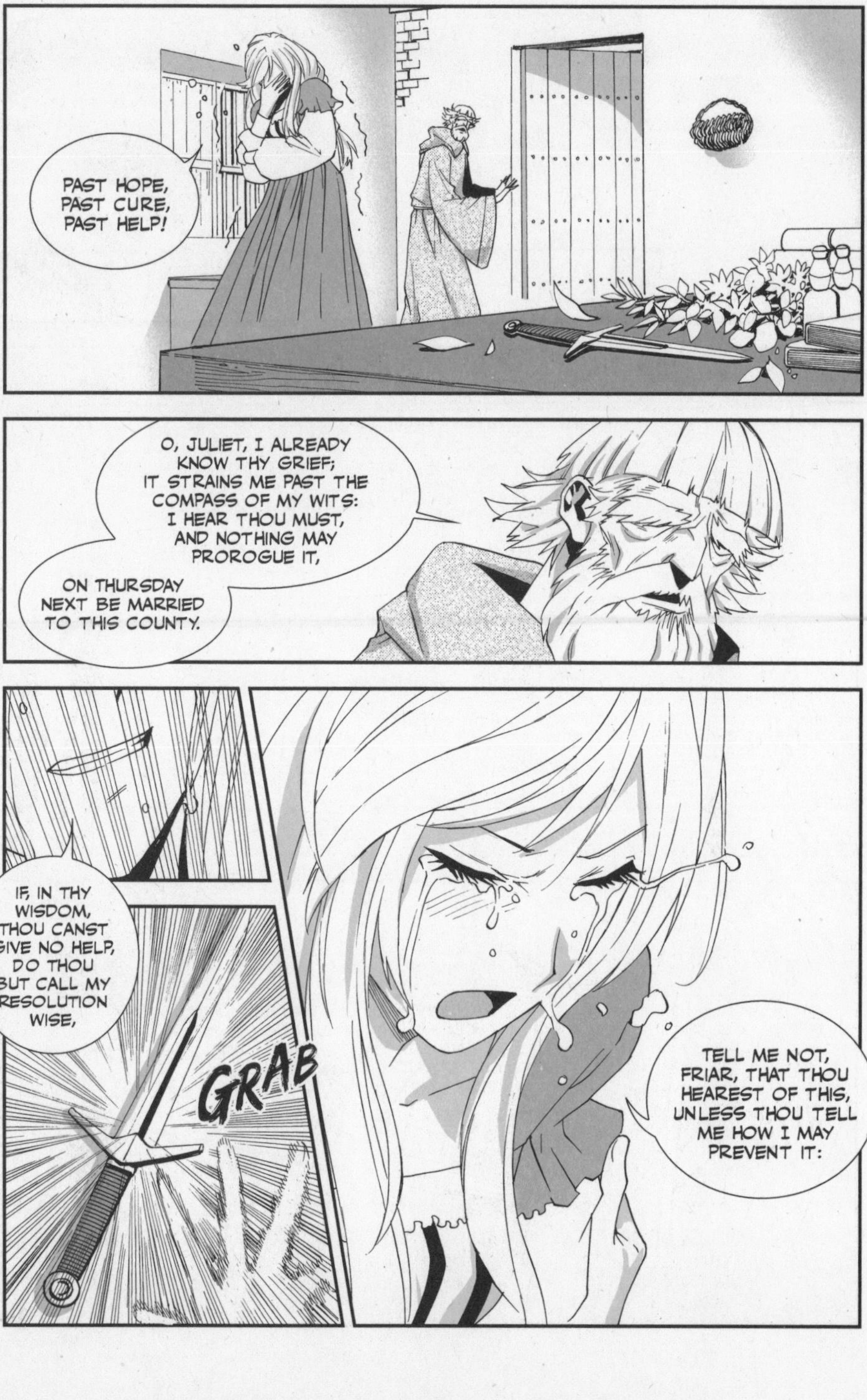
PAST HOPE, PAST CURE, PAST HELP!
O, JULIET, I ALREADY KNOW THY GRIEF; IT STRAINS ME PAST THE COMPASS OF MY WITS: I HEAR THOU MUST, AND NOTHING MAY PROROGUE IT,
ON THURSDAY NEXT BE MARRIED TO THIS COUNTY.
TELL ME NOT, FRIAR, THAT THOU HEAREST OF THIS, UNLESS THOU TELL ME HOW I MAY PREVENT IT:
IF, IN THY WISDOM, THOU CANST GIVE NO HELP, DO THOU BUT CALL MY RESOLUTION WISE,
GRAB

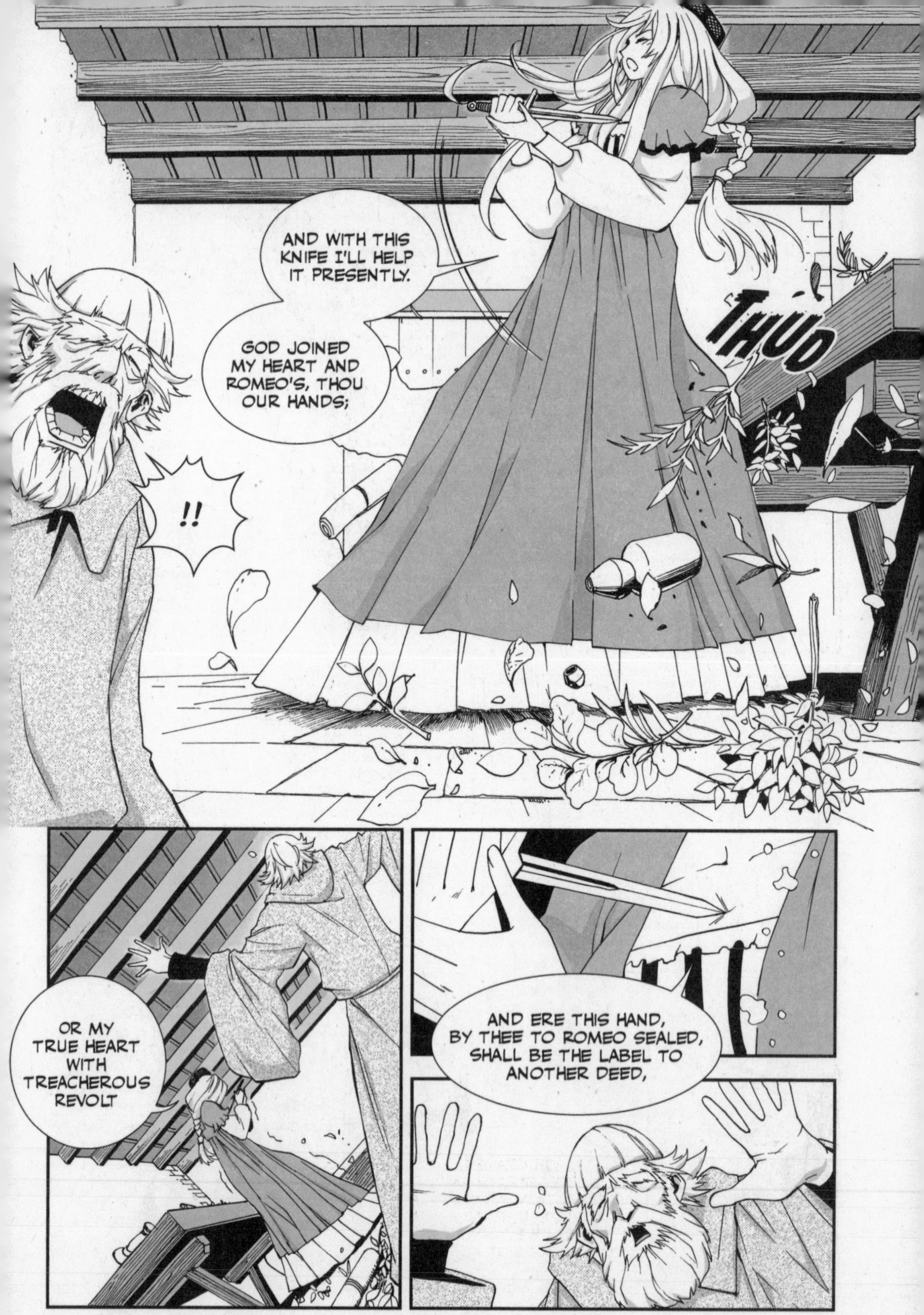
AND WITH THIS KNIFE I'LL HELP IT PRESENTLY.
THUD
GOD JOINED MY HEART AND ROMEO'S, THOU OUR HANDS;
!!
AND ERE THIS HAND, BY THEE TO ROMEO SEALED, SHALL BE THE LABEL TO ANOTHER DEED,
OR MY TRUE HEART WITH TREACHEROUS REVOLT

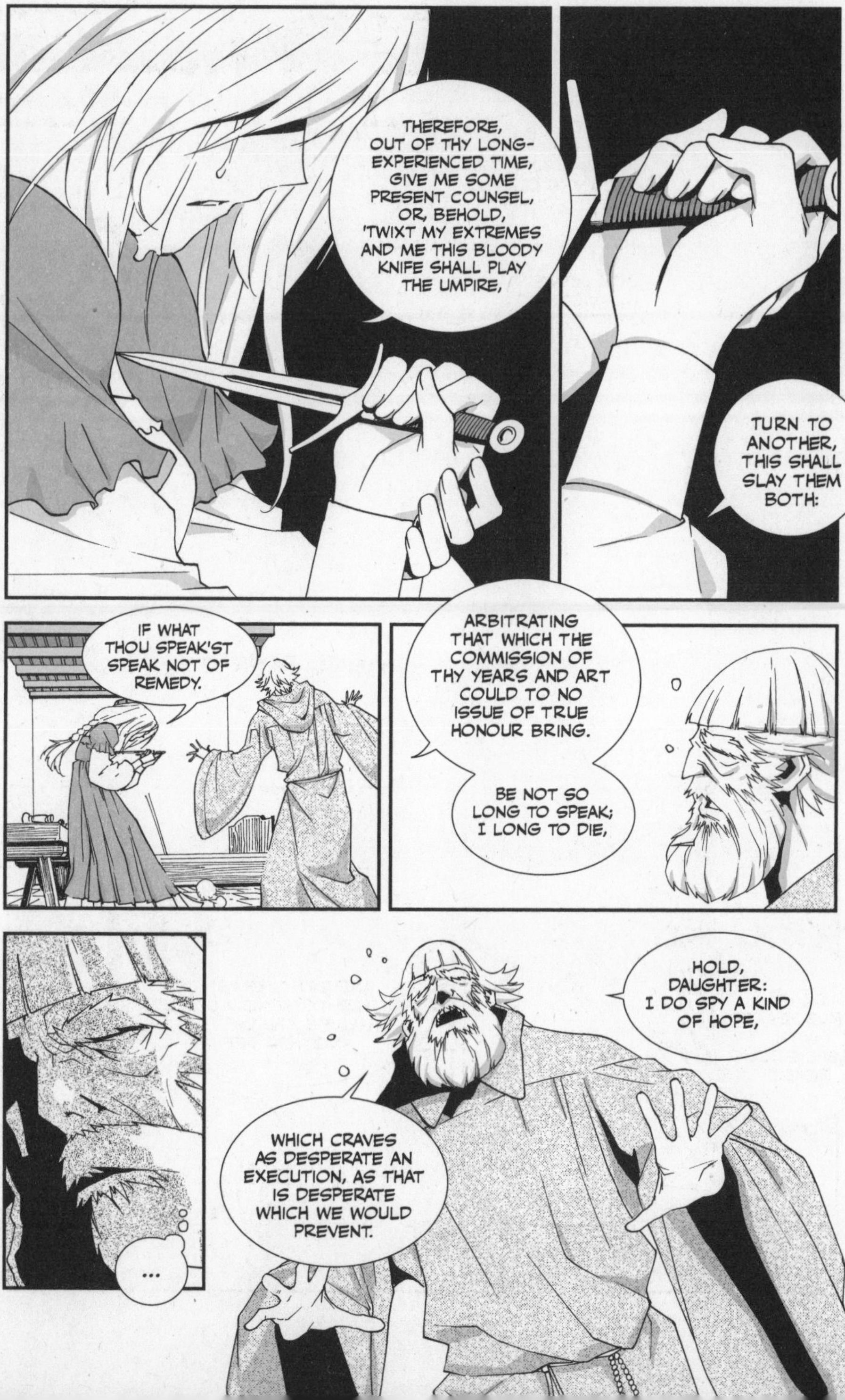
TURN TO ANOTHER, THIS SHALL SLAY THEM BOTH:
THEREFORE, OUT OF THY LONG-EXPERIENCED TIME, GIVE ME SOME PRESENT COUNSEL, OR, BEHOLD, 'TWIXT MY EXTREMES AND ME THIS BLOODY KNIFE SHALL PLAY THE UMPIRE,
ARBITRATING THAT WHICH THE COMMISSION OF THY YEARS AND ART COULD TO NO ISSUE OF TRUE HONOUR BRING.
BE NOT SO LONG TO SPEAK; I LONG TO DIE,
IF WHAT THOU SPEAK'ST SPEAK NOT OF REMEDY.
HOLD, DAUGHTER: I DO SPY A KIND OF HOPE,
WHICH CRAVES AS DESPERATE AN EXECUTION, AS THAT IS DESPERATE WHICH WE WOULD PREVENT.
...

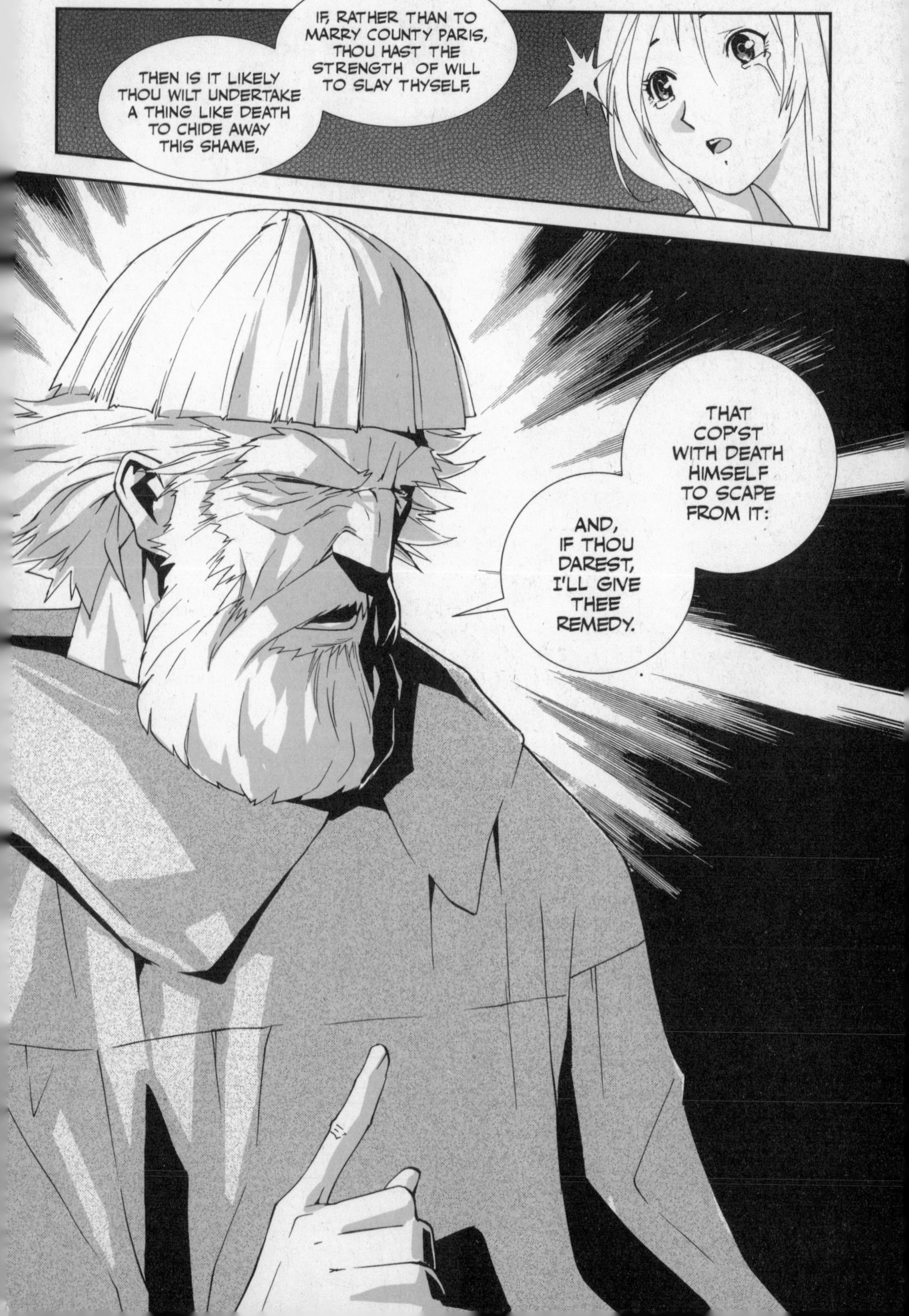
IF, RATHER THAN TO MARRY COUNTY PARIS, THOU HAST THE STRENGTH OF WILL TO SLAY THYSELF,
THEN IS IT LIKELY THOU WILT UNDERTAKE A THING LIKE DEATH TO CHIDE AWAY THIS SHAME,
THAT COP'ST WITH DEATH HIMSELF TO SCAPE FROM IT:
AND, IF THOU DAREST, I'LL GIVE THEE REMEDY.

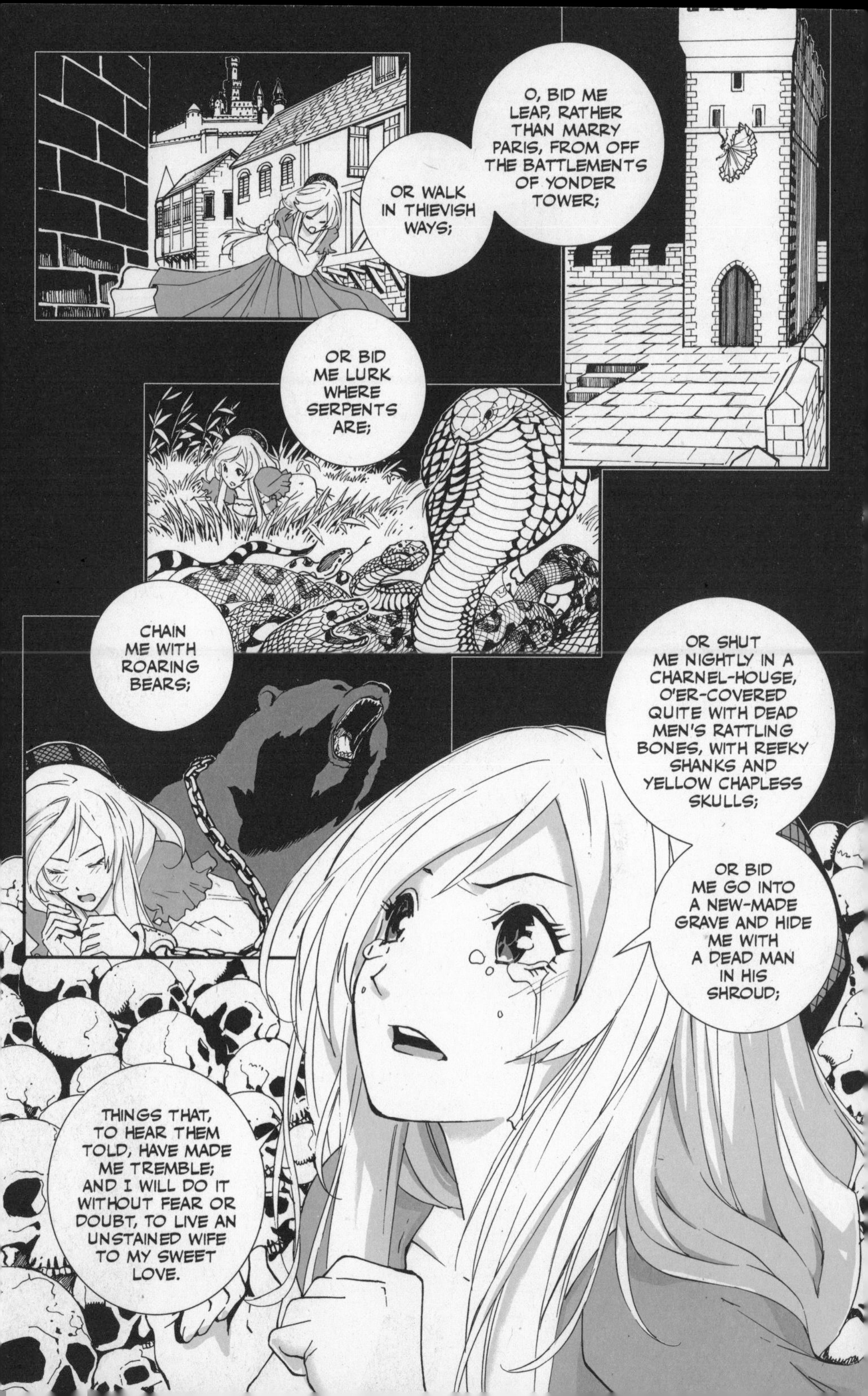
O, BID ME LEAP, RATHER THAN MARRY PARIS, FROM OFF THE BATTLEMENTS OF YONDER TOWER;
OR WALK IN THIEVISH WAYS;
OR BID ME LURK WHERE SERPENTS ARE;
CHAIN ME WITH ROARING BEARS;
OR SHUT ME NIGHTLY IN A CHARNEL-HOUSE, O'ER-COVERED QUITE WITH DEAD MEN'S RATTLING BONES, WITH REEKY SHANKS AND YELLOW CHAPLESS SKULLS;
OR BID ME GO INTO A NEW-MADE GRAVE AND HIDE ME WITH A DEAD MAN IN HIS SHROUD;
THINGS THAT, TO HEAR THEM TOLD, HAVE MADE ME TREMBLE; AND I WILL DO IT WITHOUT FEAR OR DOUBT, TO LIVE AN UNSTAINED WIFE TO MY SWEET LOVE.

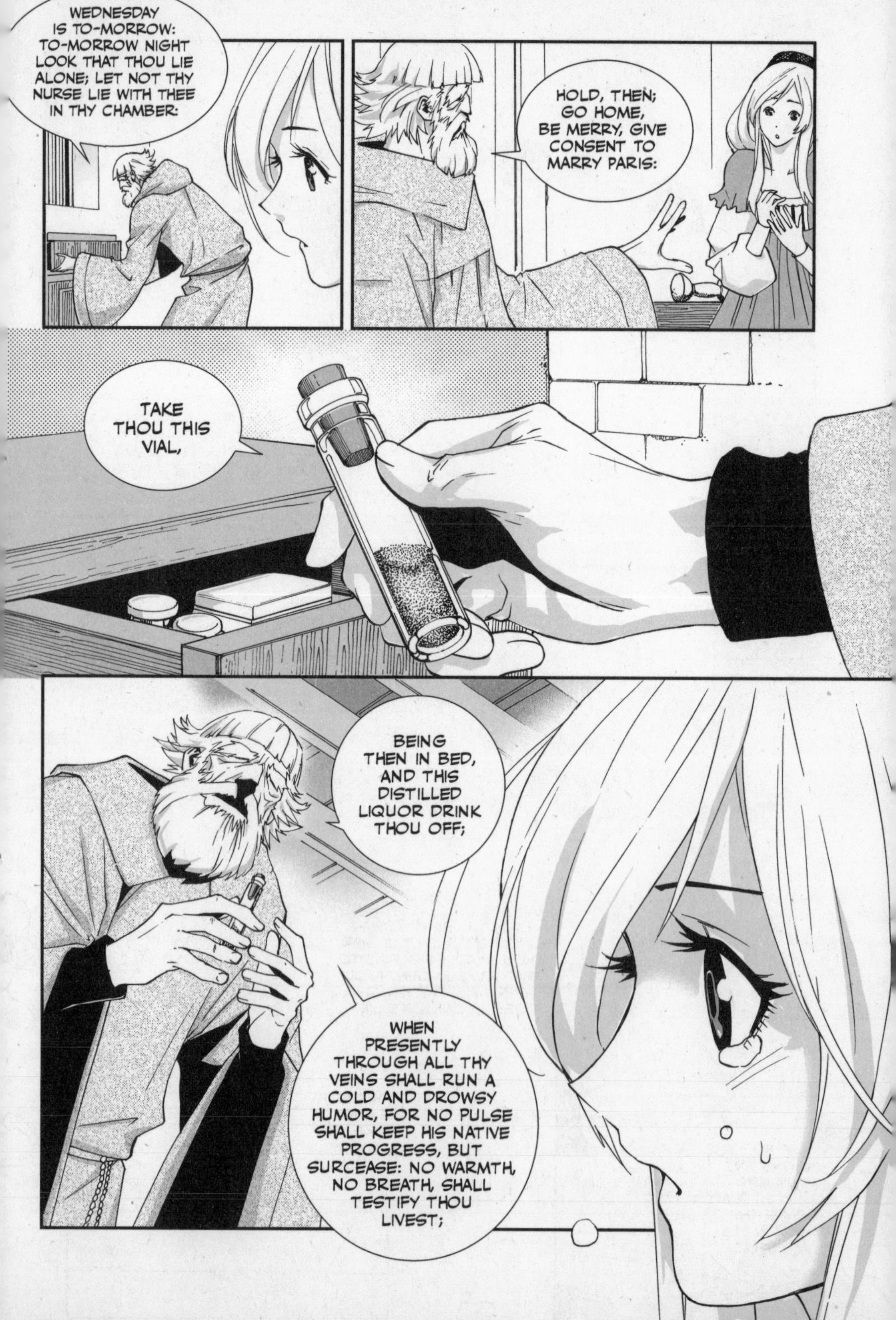
HOLD, THEN; GO HOME, BE MERRY, GIVE CONSENT TO MARRY PARIS:
WEDNESDAY IS TO-MORROW: TO-MORROW NIGHT LOOK THAT THOU LIE ALONE; LET NOT THY NURSE LIE WITH THEE IN THY CHAMBER:
TAKE THOU THIS VIAL,
BEING THEN IN BED, AND THIS DISTILLED LIQUOR DRINK THOU OFF;
WHEN PRESENTLY THROUGH ALL THY VEINS SHALL RUN A COLD AND DROWSY HUMOR, FOR NO PULSE SHALL KEEP HIS NATIVE PROGRESS, BUT SURCEASE: NO WARMTH, NO BREATH, SHALL TESTIFY THOU LIVEST;

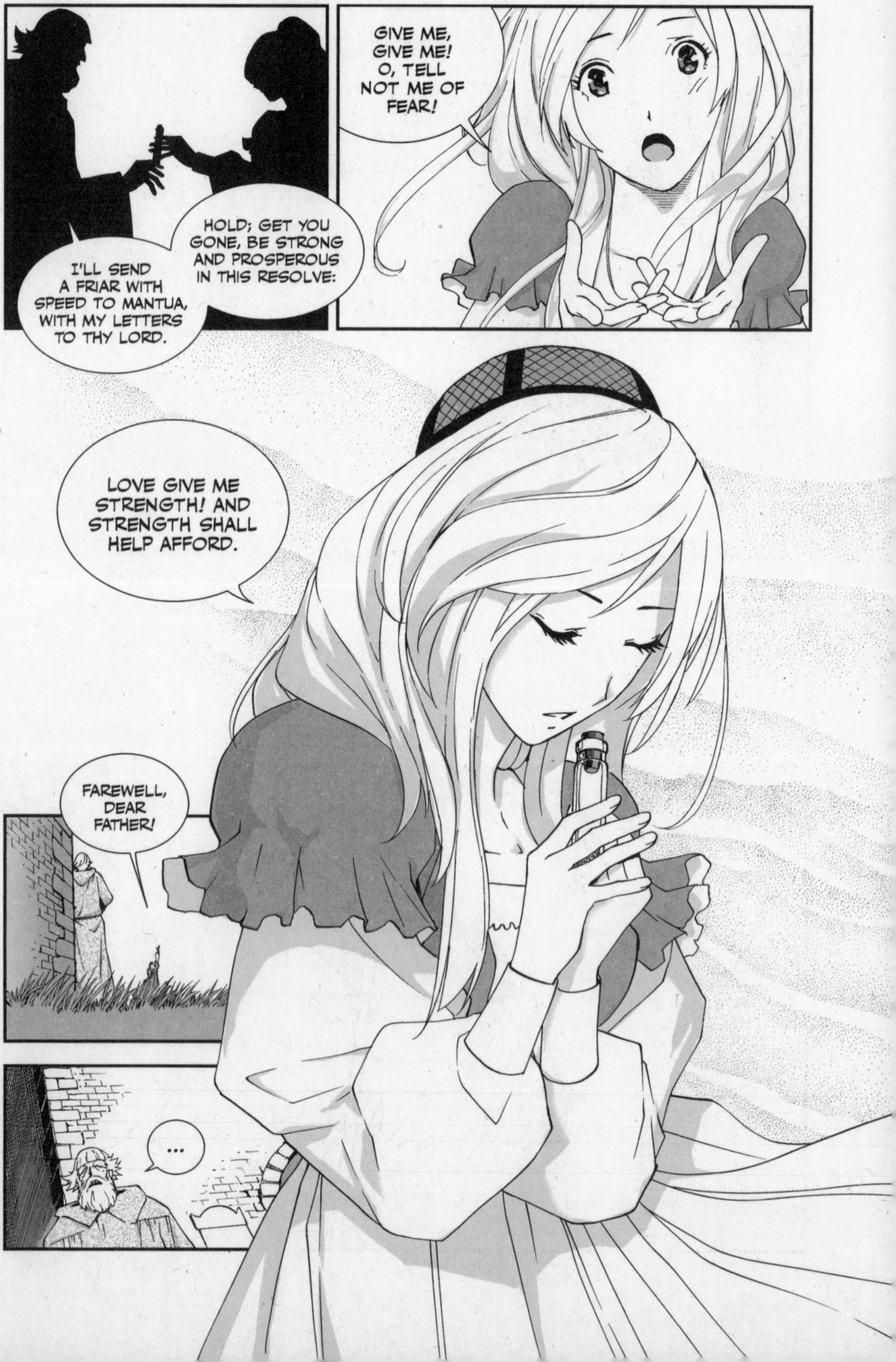
GIVE ME, GIVE ME! O, TELL NOT ME OF FEAR!
HOLD; GET YOU GONE, BE STRONG AND PROSPEROUS IN THIS RESOLVE:
I'LL SEND A FRIAR WITH SPEED TO MANTUA, WITH MY LETTERS TO THY LORD.
LOVE GIVE ME STRENGTH! AND STRENGTH SHALL HELP AFFORD.
FAREWELL, DEAR FATHER!
...

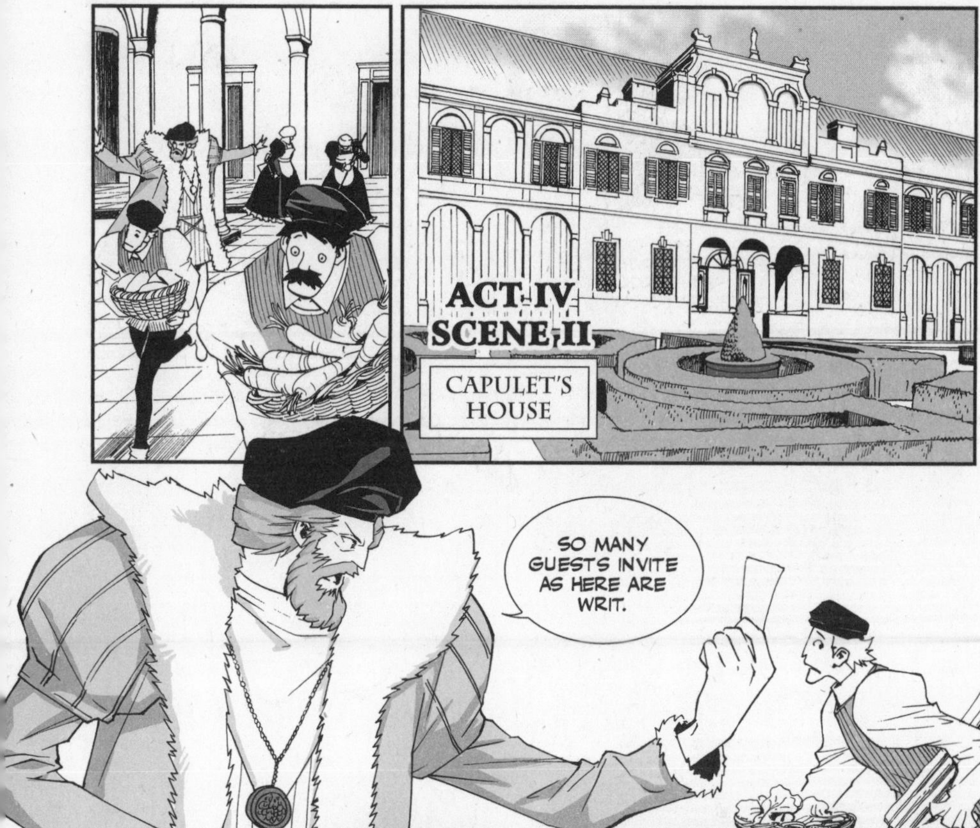
ACT IV SCENE II
CAPULET'S HOUSE
SO MANY GUESTS INVITE AS HERE ARE WRIT.
SIRRAH, GO HIRE ME TWENTY CUNNING COOKS.
YOU SHALL HAVE NONE ILL, SIR; FOR I'LL TRY IF THEY CAN LICK THEIR FINGERS.

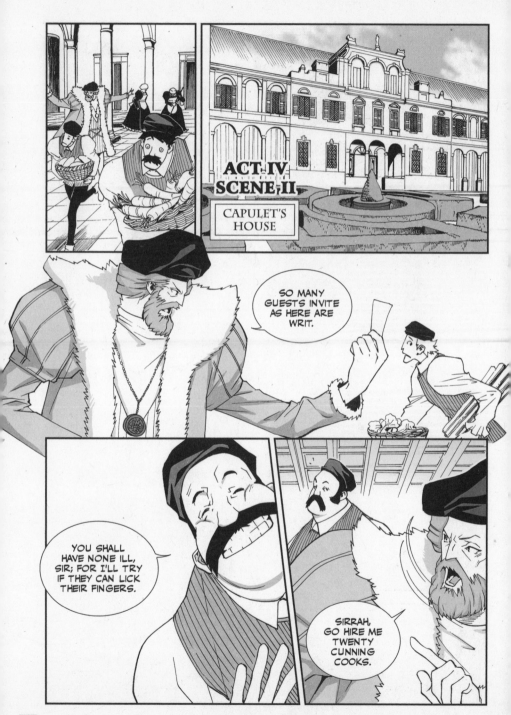

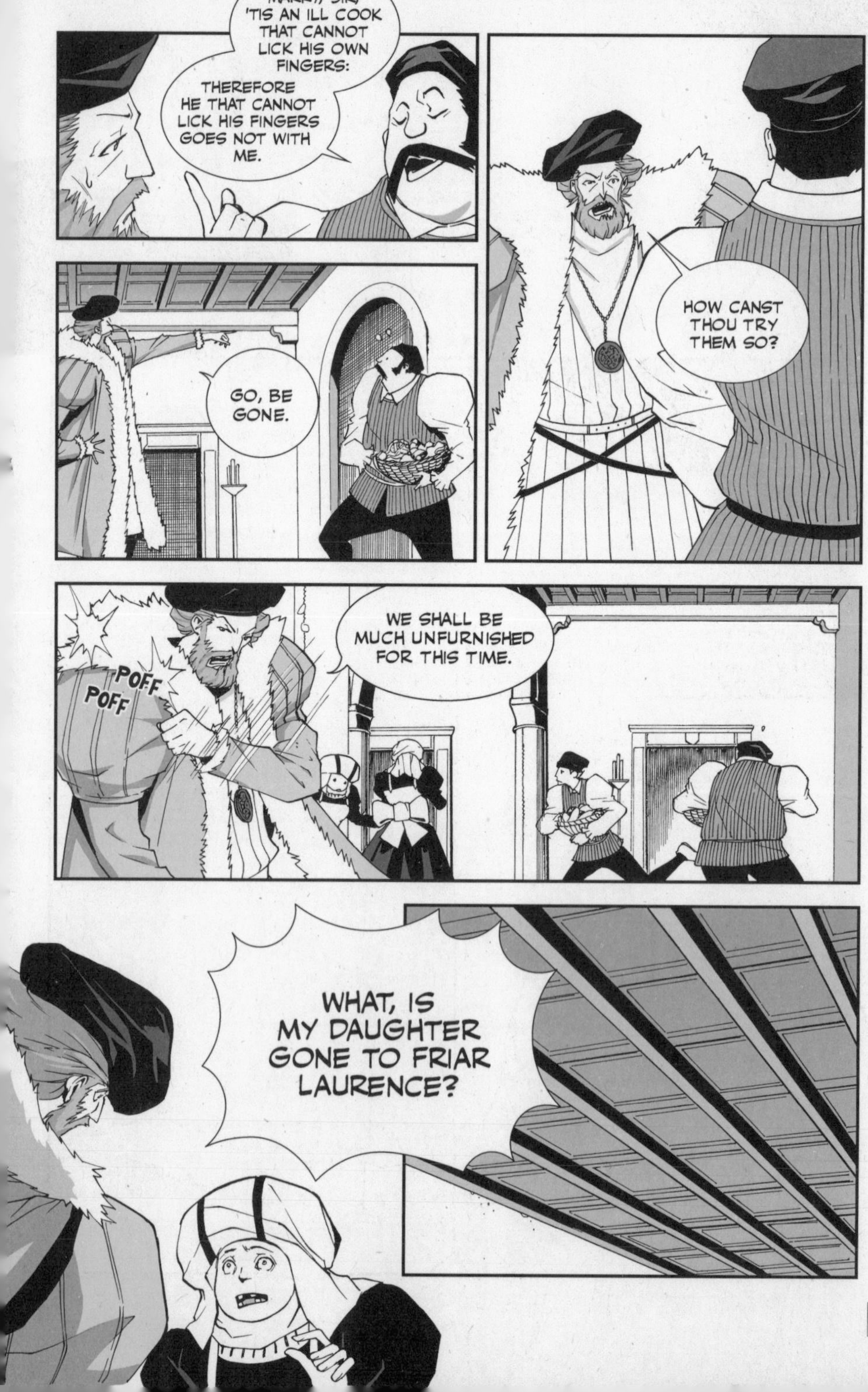
HOW CANST THOU TRY THEM SO?
MARRY, SIR, 'TIS AN ILL COOK THAT CANNOT LICK HIS OWN FINGERS:
THEREFORE HE THAT CANNOT LICK HIS FINGERS GOES NOT WITH ME.
GO, BE GONE.
WE SHALL BE MUCH UNFURNISHED FOR THIS TIME.
POFF POFF
WHAT, IS MY DAUGHTER GONE TO FRIAR LAURENCE?

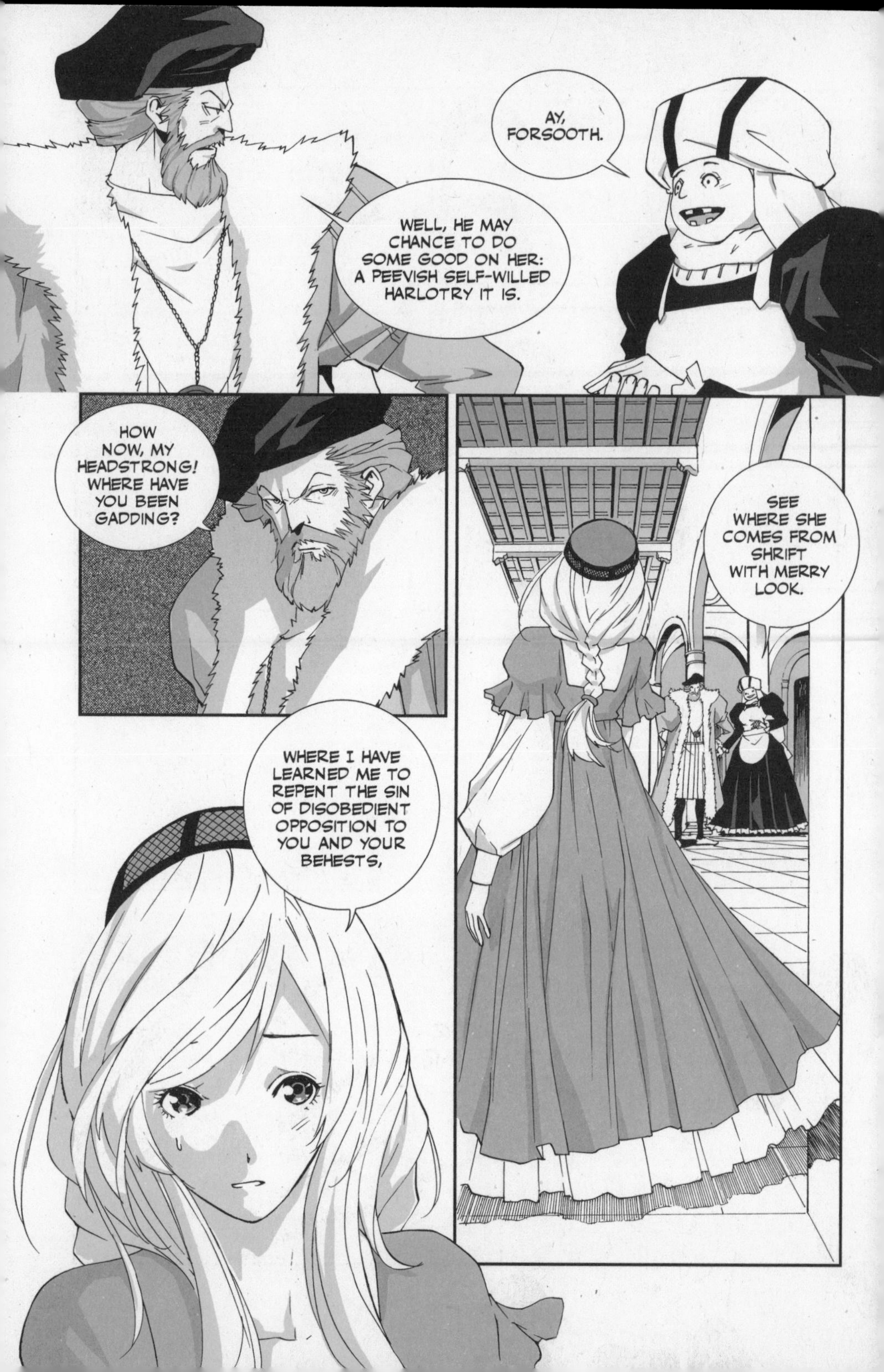
AY, FORSOOTH.
WELL, HE MAY CHANCE TO DO SOME GOOD ON HER: A PEEVISH SELF-WILLED HARLOTRY IT IS.
SEE WHERE SHE COMES FROM SHRIFT WITH MERRY LOOK.
HOW NOW, MY HEADSTRONG! WHERE HAVE YOU BEEN GADDING?
WHERE I HAVE LEARNED ME TO REPENT THE SIN OF DISOBEDIENT OPPOSITION TO YOU AND YOUR BEHESTS,

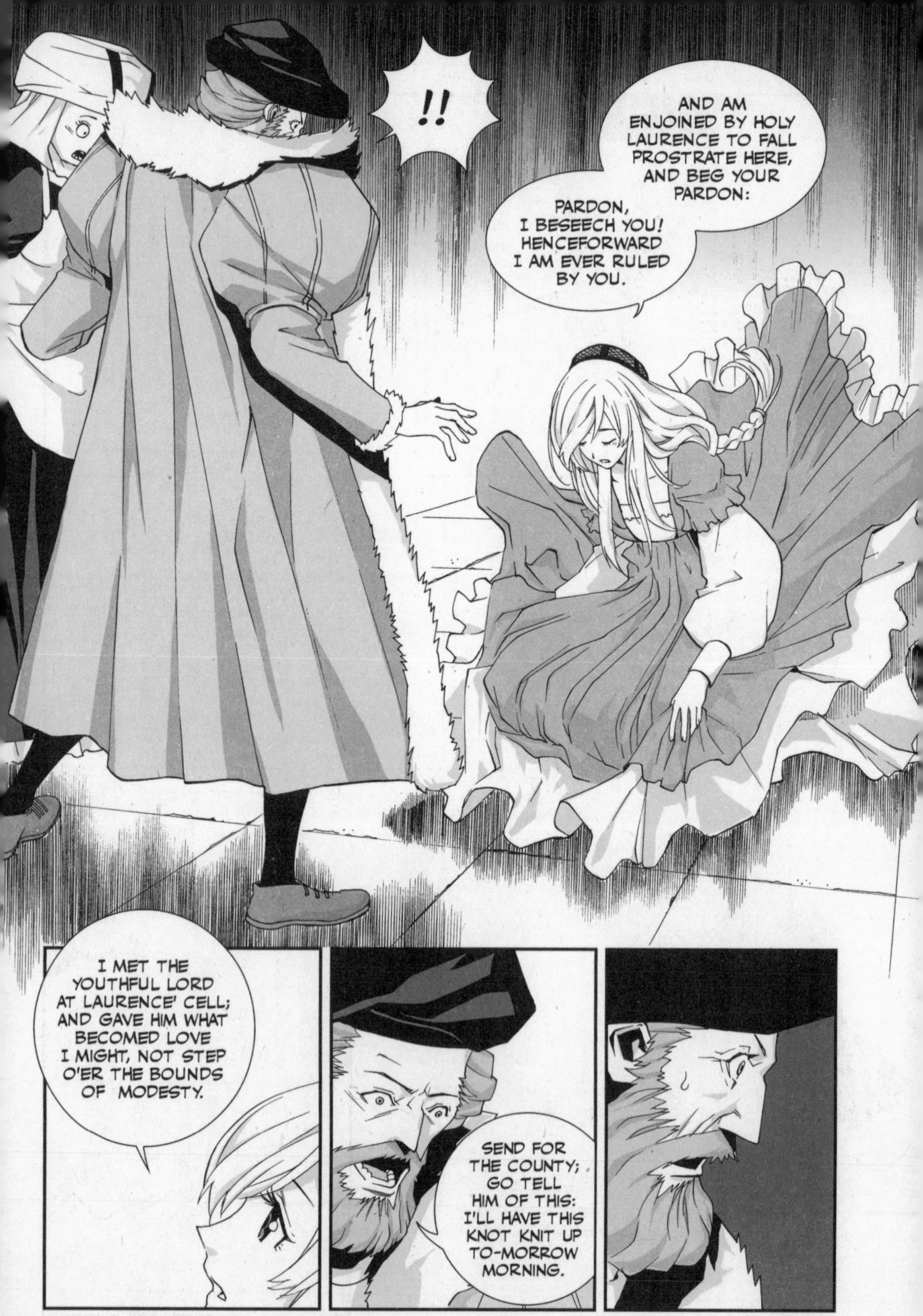
AND AM ENJOINED BY HOLY LAURENCE TO FALL PROSTRATE HERE, AND BEG YOUR PARDON:
PARDON, I BESEECH YOU! HENCEFORWARD I AM EVER RULED BY YOU.
!!
SEND FOR THE COUNTY; GO TELL HIM OF THIS: I'LL HAVE THIS KNOT KNIT UP TO-MORROW MORNING.
I MET THE YOUTHFUL LORD AT LAURENCE' CELL; AND GAVE HIM WHAT BECOMED LOVE I MIGHT, NOT STEP O'ER THE BOUNDS OF MODESTY.

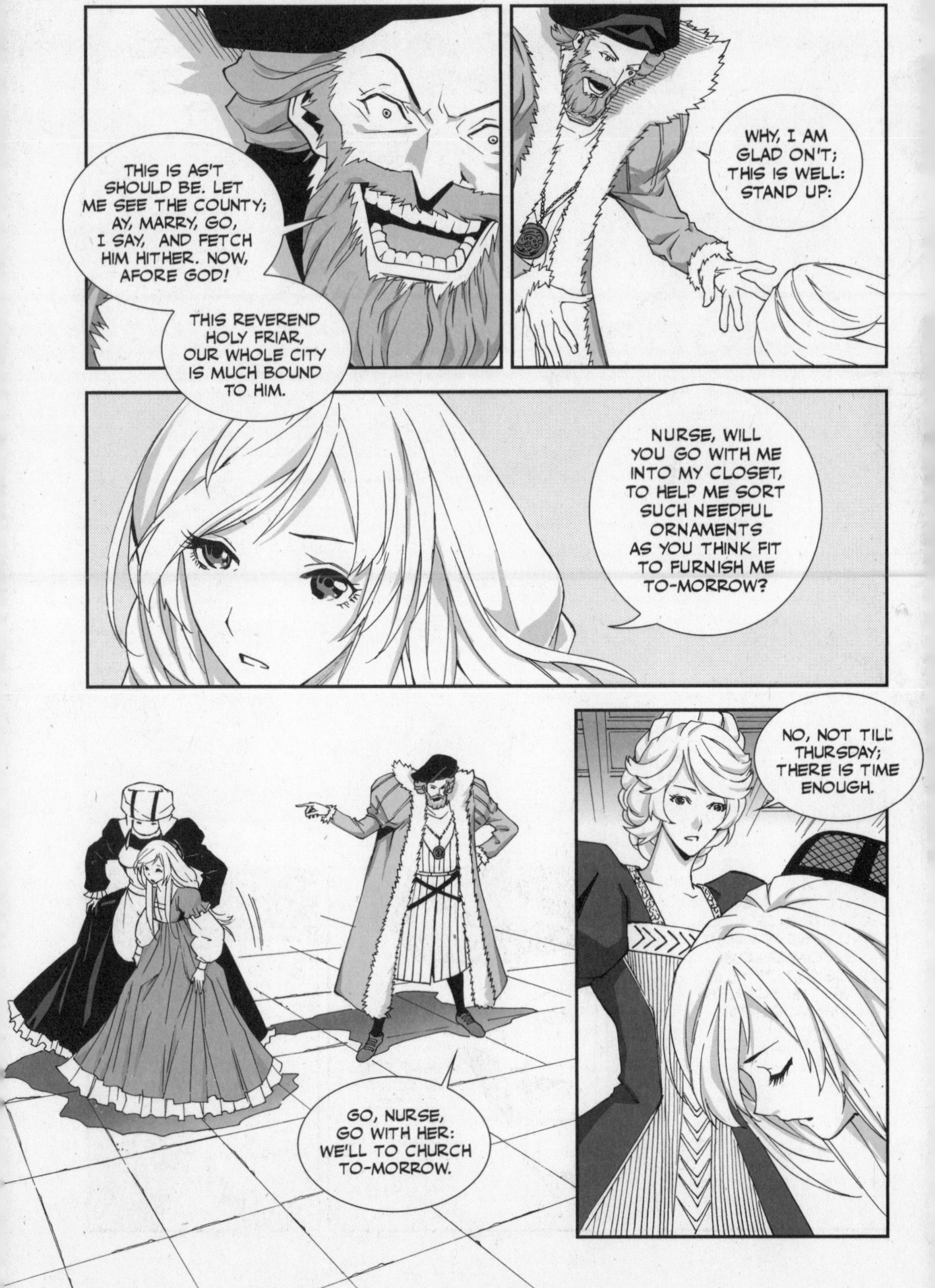
WHY, I AM GLAD ON'T; THIS IS WELL: STAND UP:
THIS IS AS'T SHOULD BE. LET ME SEE THE COUNTY; AY, MARRY, GO, I SAY, AND FETCH HIM HITHER. NOW, AFORE GOD!
THIS REVEREND HOLY FRIAR, OUR WHOLE CITY IS MUCH BOUND TO HIM.
NURSE, WILL YOU GO WITH ME INTO MY CLOSET, TO HELP ME SORT SUCH NEEDFUL ORNAMENTS AS YOU THINK FIT TO FURNISH ME TO-MORROW?
NO, NOT TILL THURSDAY; THERE IS TIME ENOUGH.
GO, NURSE, GO WITH HER: WE'LL TO CHURCH TO-MORROW.

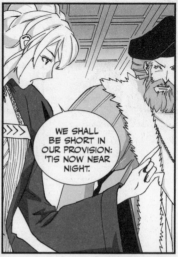

WE SHALL BE SHORT IN OUR PROVISION: 'TIS NOW NEAR NIGHT.
TUSH, I WILL STIR ABOUT,
AND ALL THINGS SHALL BE WELL, I WARRANT THEE, WIFE: GO THOU TO JULIET, HELP TO DECK UP HER;
I'LL NOT TO BED TO-NIGHT; LET ME ALONE; I'LL PLAY THE HOUSEWIFE FOR THIS ONCE.
WHAT, HO! THEY ARE ALL FORTH.

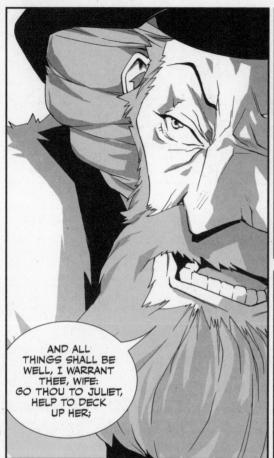

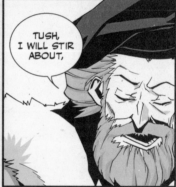

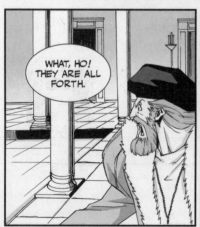

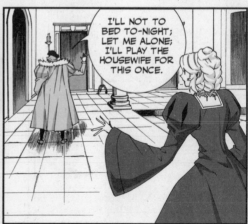

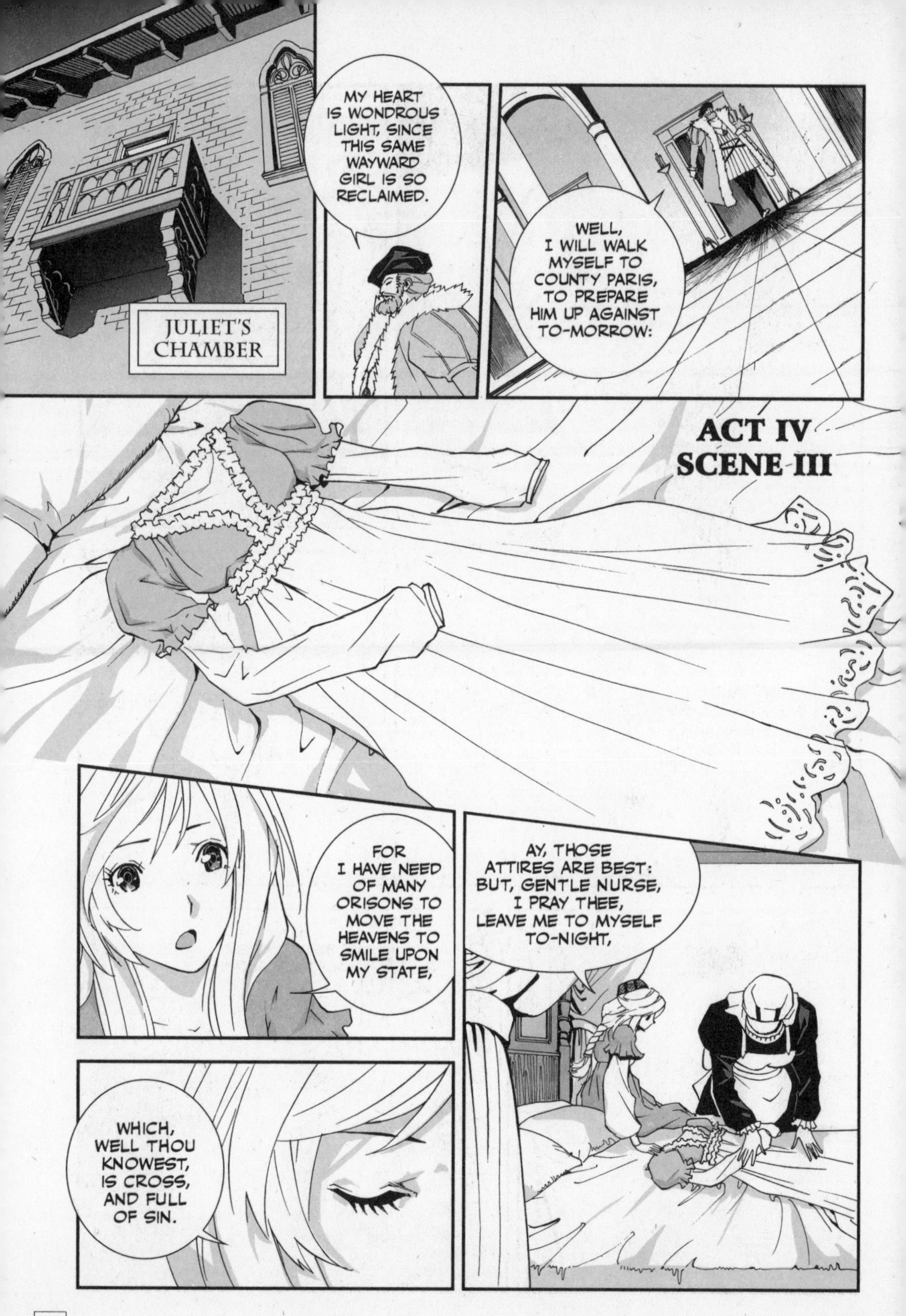

WELL, I WILL WALK MYSELF TO COUNTY PARIS, TO PREPARE HIM UP AGAINST TO-MORROW:
MY HEART IS WONDROUS LIGHT, SINCE THIS SAME WAYWARD GIRL IS SO RECLAIMED.
JULIET'S CHAMBER
ACT IV SCENE III
AY, THOSE ATTIRES ARE BEST: BUT, GENTLE NURSE, I PRAY THEE, LEAVE ME TO MYSELF TO-NIGHT,
FOR I HAVE NEED OF MANY ORISONS TO MOVE THE HEAVENS TO SMILE UPON MY STATE,
WHICH, WELL THOU KNOWEST, IS CROSS, AND FULL OF SIN.

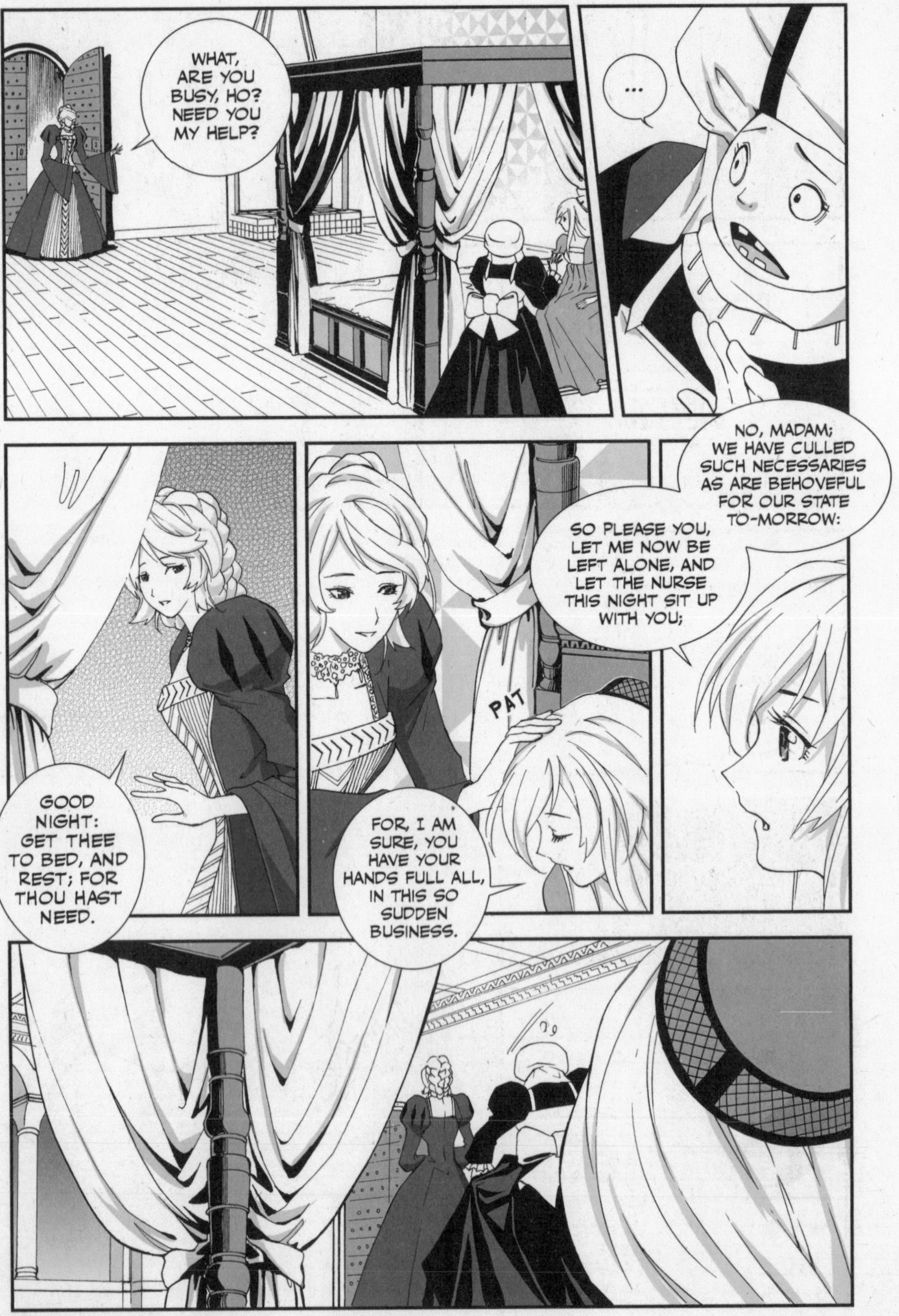
...
WHAT, ARE YOU BUSY, HO? NEED YOU MY HELP?
NO, MADAM; WE HAVE CULLED SUCH NECESSARIES AS ARE BEHOVEFUL FOR OUR STATE TO-MORROW:
SO PLEASE YOU, LET ME NOW BE LEFT ALONE, AND LET THE NURSE THIS NIGHT SIT UP WITH YOU;
PAT
FOR, I AM SURE, YOU HAVE YOUR HANDS FULL ALL, IN THIS SO SUDDEN BUSINESS.
GOOD NIGHT: GET THEE TO BED, AND REST; FOR THOU HAST NEED.

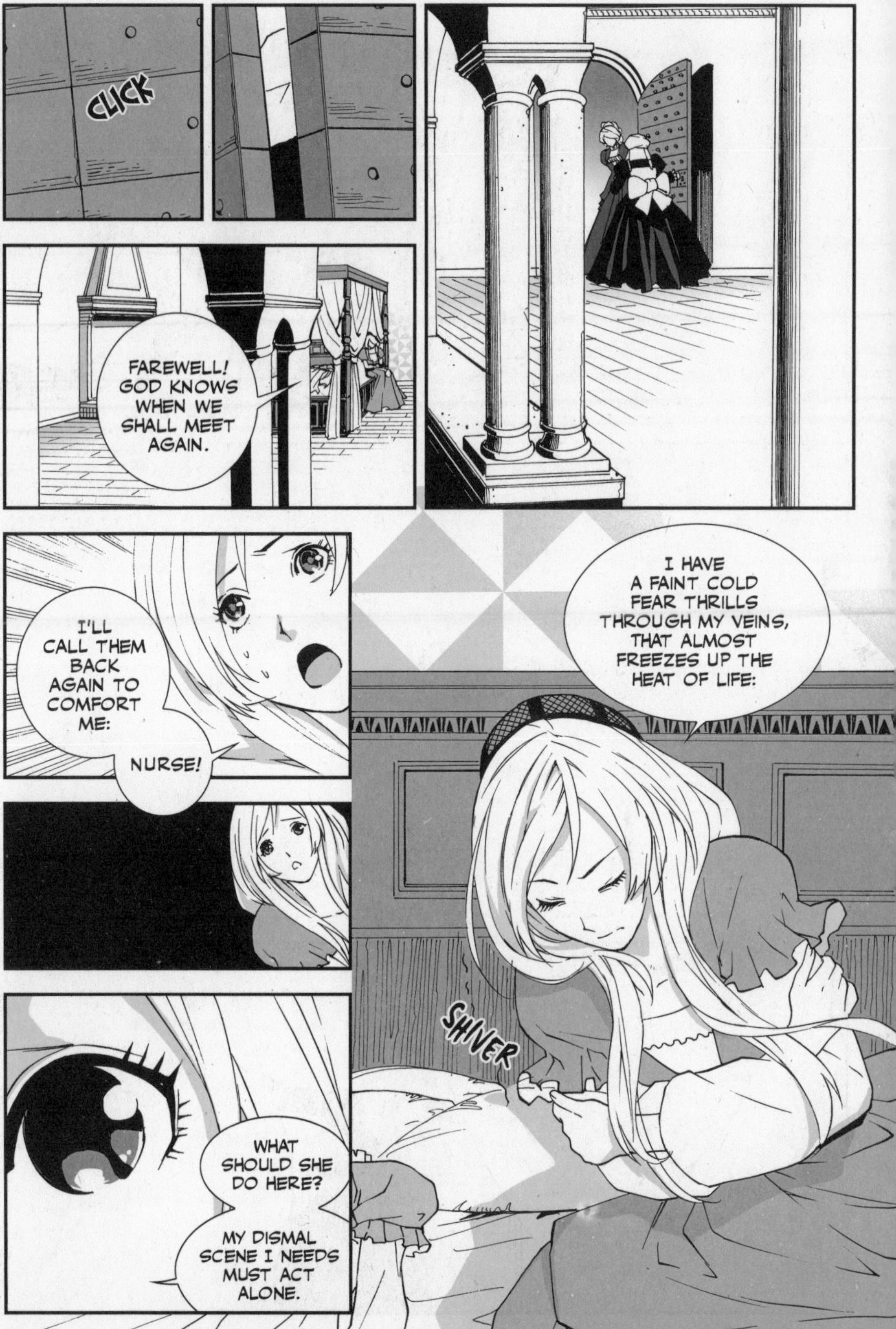
CLICK
FAREWELL! GOD KNOWS WHEN WE SHALL MEET AGAIN.
I HAVE A FAINT COLD FEAR THRILLS THROUGH MY VEINS, THAT ALMOST FREEZES UP THE HEAT OF LIFE:
SHIVER
I'LL CALL THEM BACK AGAIN TO COMFORT ME:
NURSE!
WHAT SHOULD SHE DO HERE?
MY DISMAL SCENE I NEEDS MUST ACT ALONE.

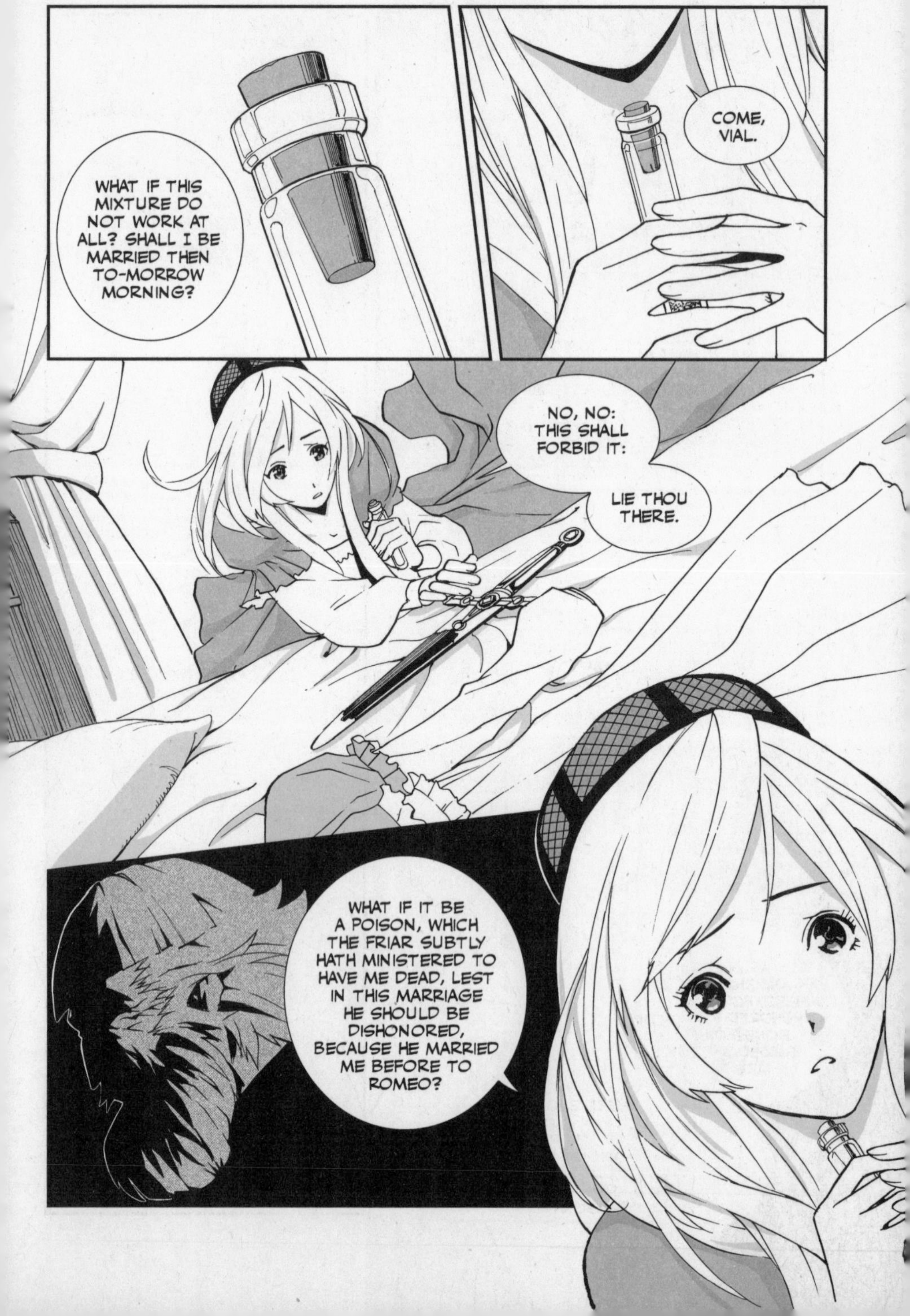
COME, VIAL.
WHAT IF THIS MIXTURE DO NOT WORK AT ALL? SHALL I BE MARRIED THEN TO-MORROW MORNING?
NO, NO: THIS SHALL FORBID IT:
LIE THOU THERE.
WHAT IF IT BE A POISON, WHICH THE FRIAR SUBTLY HATH MINISTERED TO HAVE ME DEAD, LEST IN THIS MARRIAGE HE SHOULD BE DISHONORED, BECAUSE HE MARRIED ME BEFORE TO ROMEO?

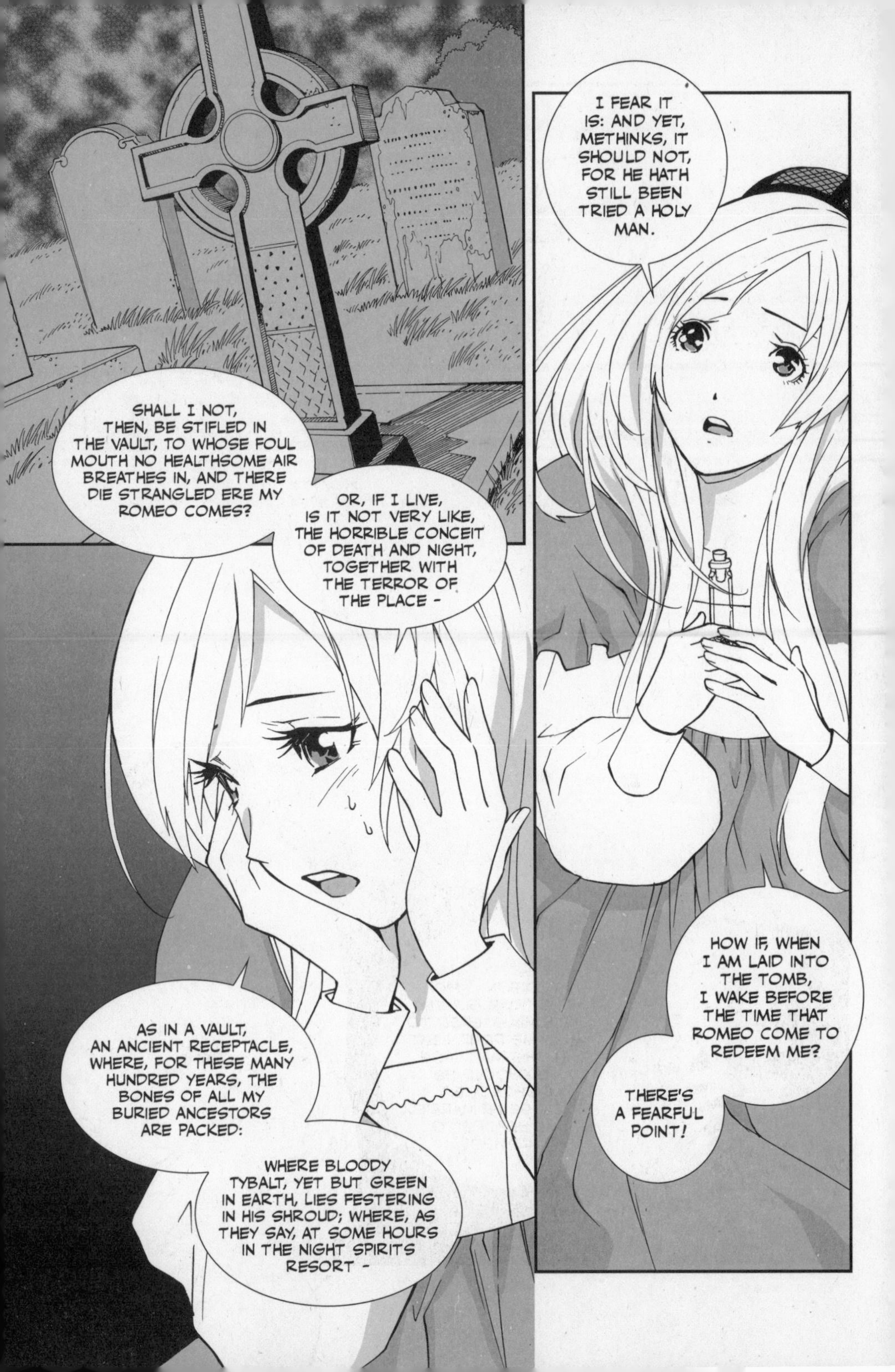

I FEAR IT IS: AND YET, METHINKS, IT SHOULD NOT, FOR HE HATH STILL BEEN TRIED A HOLY MAN.
HOW IF, WHEN I AM LAID INTO THE TOMB, I WAKE BEFORE THE TIME THAT ROMEO COME TO REDEEM ME?
THERE'S A FEARFUL POINT!
SHALL I NOT, THEN, BE STIFLED IN THE VAULT, TO WHOSE FOUL MOUTH NO HEALTHSOME AIR BREATHES IN, AND THERE DIE STRANGLED ERE MY ROMEO COMES?
OR, IF I LIVE, IS IT NOT VERY LIKE, THE HORRIBLE CONCEIT OF DEATH AND NIGHT, TOGETHER WITH THE TERROR OF THE PLACE -
AS IN A VAULT, AN ANCIENT RECEPTACLE, WHERE, FOR THESE MANY HUNDRED YEARS, THE BONES OF ALL MY BURIED ANCESTORS ARE PACKED:
WHERE BLOODY TYBALT, YET BUT GREEN IN EARTH, LIES FESTERING IN HIS SHROUD; WHERE, AS THEY SAY, AT SOME HOURS IN THE NIGHT SPIRITS RESORT -

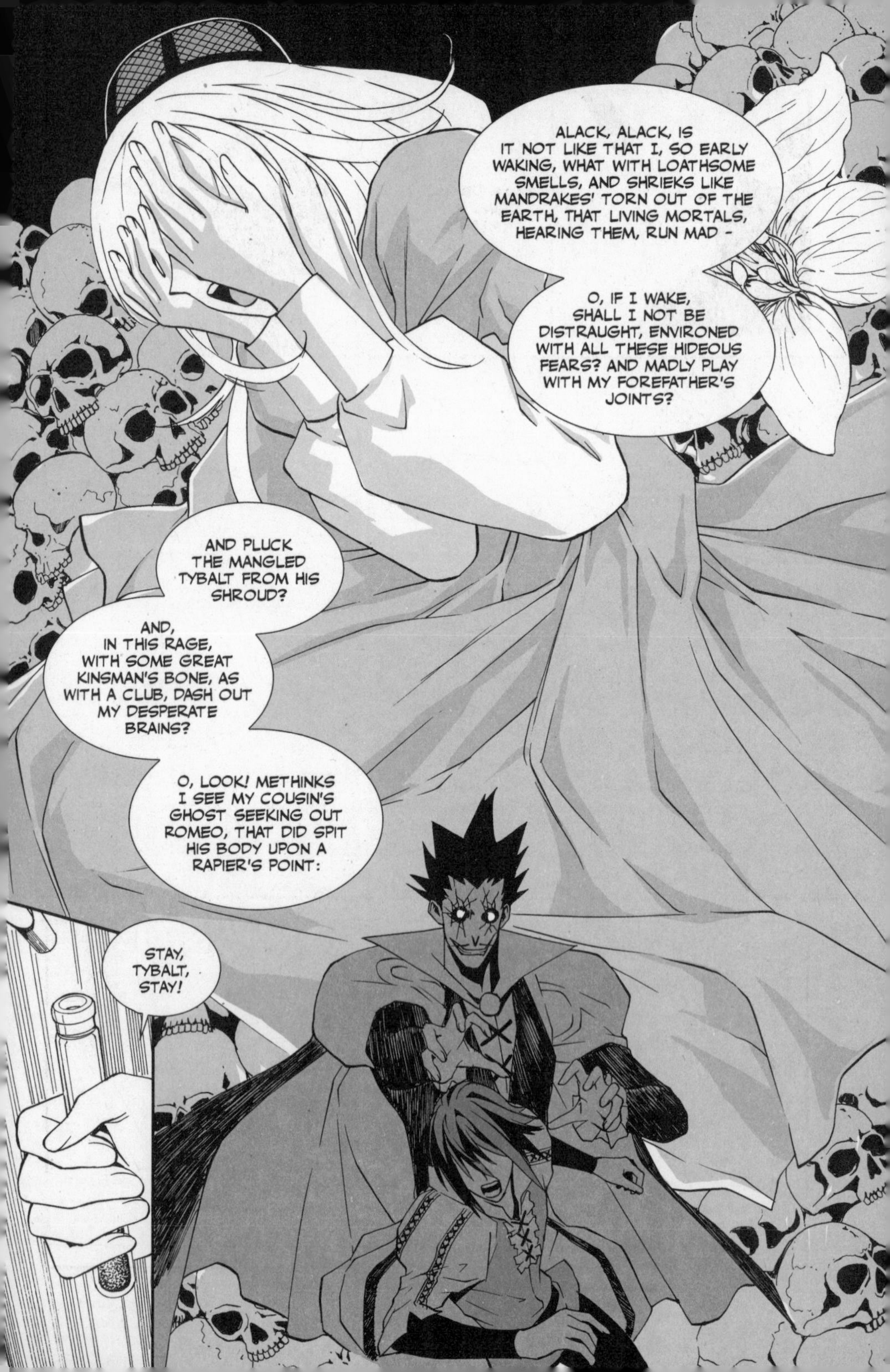
ALACK, ALACK, IS IT NOT LIKE THAT I, SO EARLY WAKING, WHAT WITH LOATHSOME SMELLS, AND SHRIEKS LIKE MANDRAKES' TORN OUT OF THE EARTH, THAT LIVING MORTALS, HEARING THEM, RUN MAD -
O, IF I WAKE, SHALL I NOT BE DISTRAUGHT, ENVIRONED WITH ALL THESE HIDEOUS FEARS? AND MADLY PLAY WITH MY FOREFATHER'S JOINTS?
AND PLUCK THE MANGLED TYBALT FROM HIS SHROUD?
AND, IN THIS RAGE, WITH SOME GREAT KINSMAN'S BONE, AS WITH A CLUB, DASH OUT MY DESPERATE BRAINS?
O, LOOK! METHINKS I SEE MY COUSIN'S GHOST SEEKING OUT ROMEO, THAT DID SPIT HIS BODY UPON A RAPIER'S POINT:
STAY, TYBALT, STAY!

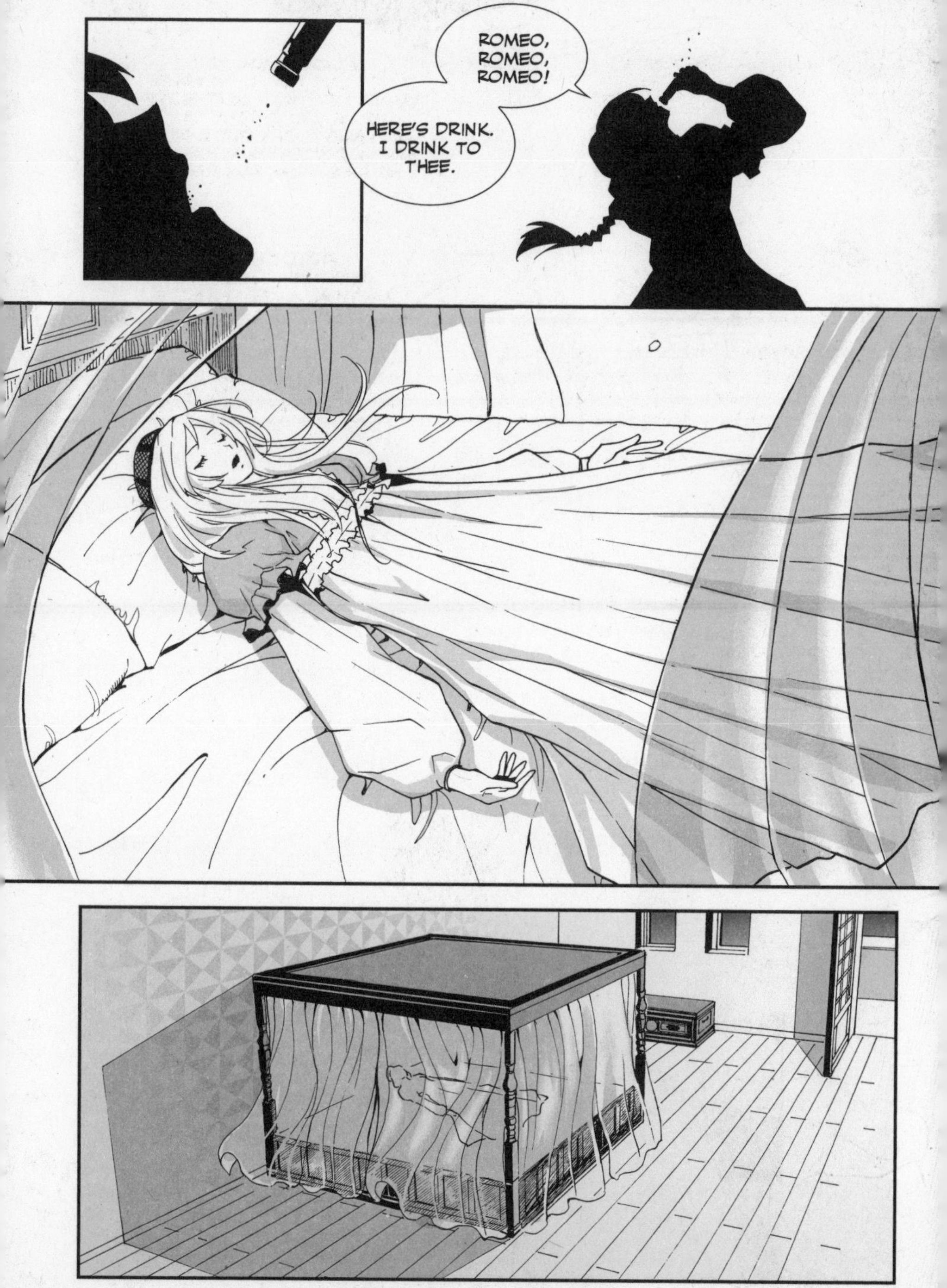
ROMEO, ROMEO, ROMEO!
HERE'S DRINK. I DRINK TO THEE.

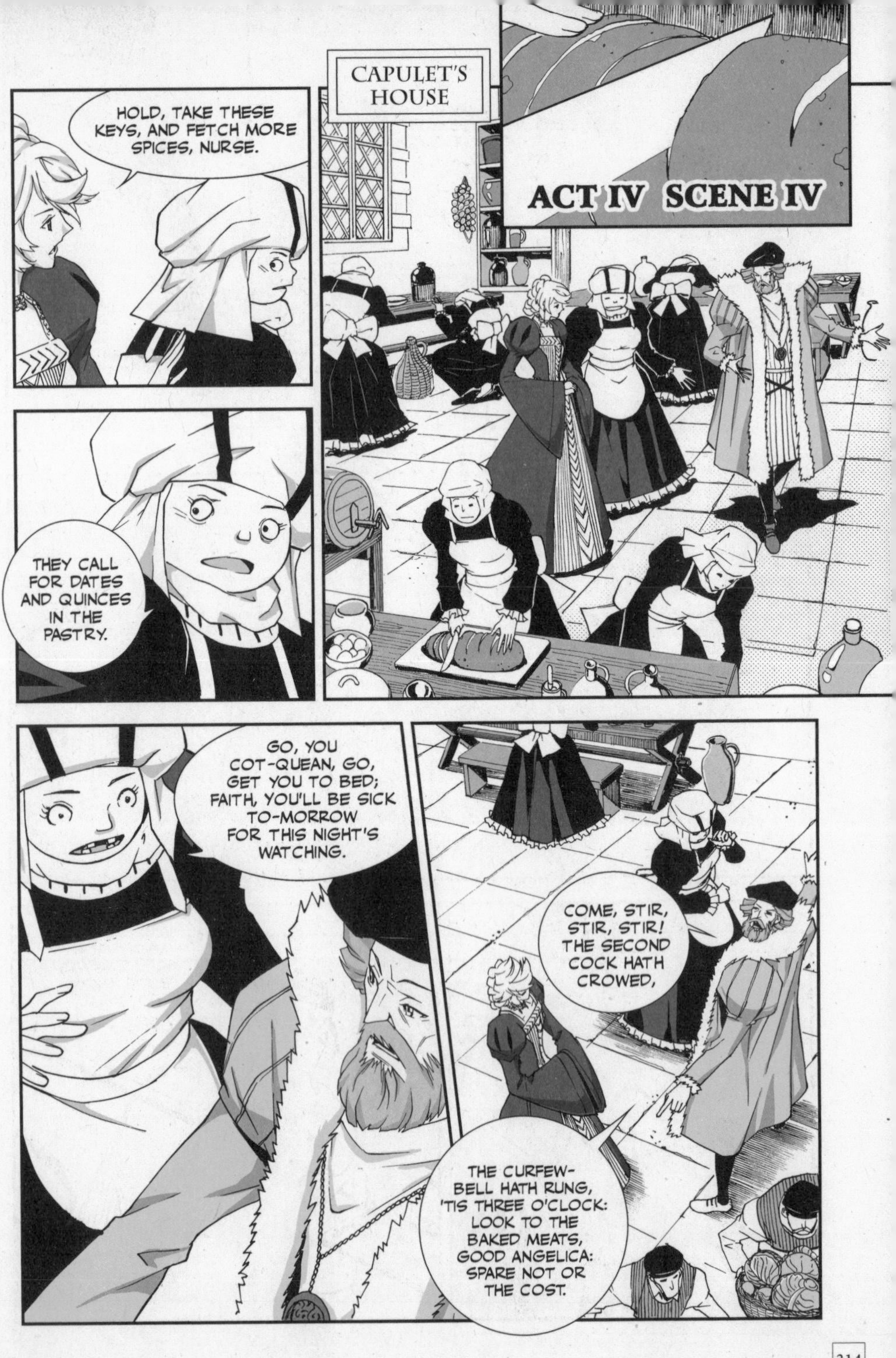
ACT IV SCENE IV
CAPULET'S HOUSE
HOLD, TAKE THESE KEYS, AND FETCH MORE SPICES, NURSE.
THEY CALL FOR DATES AND QUINCES IN THE PASTRY.
COME, STIR, STIR, STIR! THE SECOND COCK HATH CROWED,
THE CURFEW-BELL HATH RUNG, 'TIS THREE O'CLOCK: LOOK TO THE BAKED MEATS, GOOD ANGELICA: SPARE NOT OR THE COST.
GO, YOU COT-QUEAN, GO, GET YOU TO BED; FAITH, YOU'LL BE SICK TO-MORROW FOR THIS NIGHT'S WATCHING.

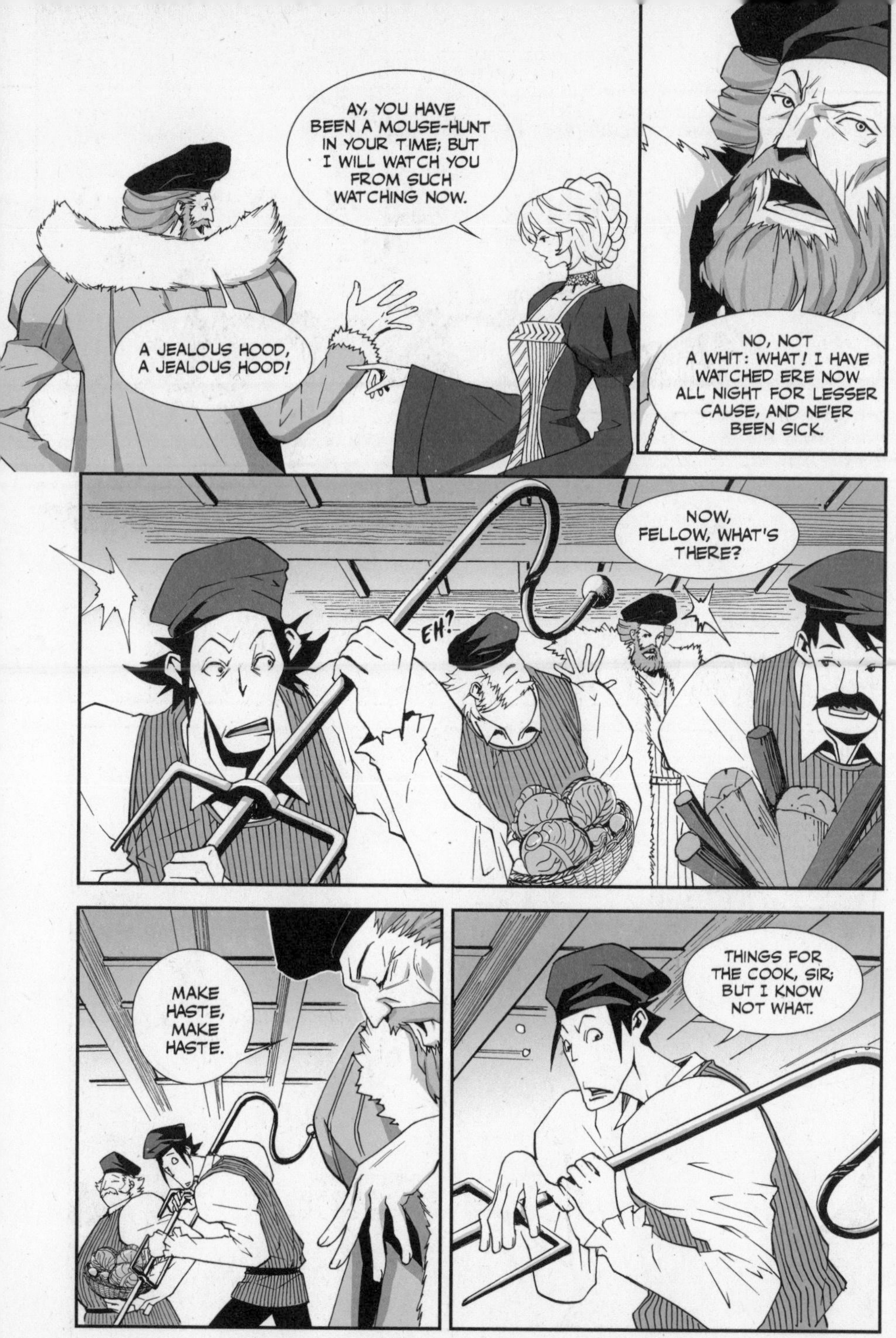
NO, NOT A WHIT: WHAT! I HAVE WATCHED ERE NOW ALL NIGHT FOR LESSER CAUSE, AND NE'ER BEEN SICK.
AY, YOU HAVE BEEN A MOUSE-HUNT IN YOUR TIME; BUT I WILL WATCH YOU FROM SUCH WATCHING NOW.
A JEALOUS HOOD, A JEALOUS HOOD!
NOW, FELLOW, WHAT'S THERE?
EH?
THINGS FOR THE COOK, SIR; BUT I KNOW NOT WHAT.
MAKE HASTE, MAKE HASTE.

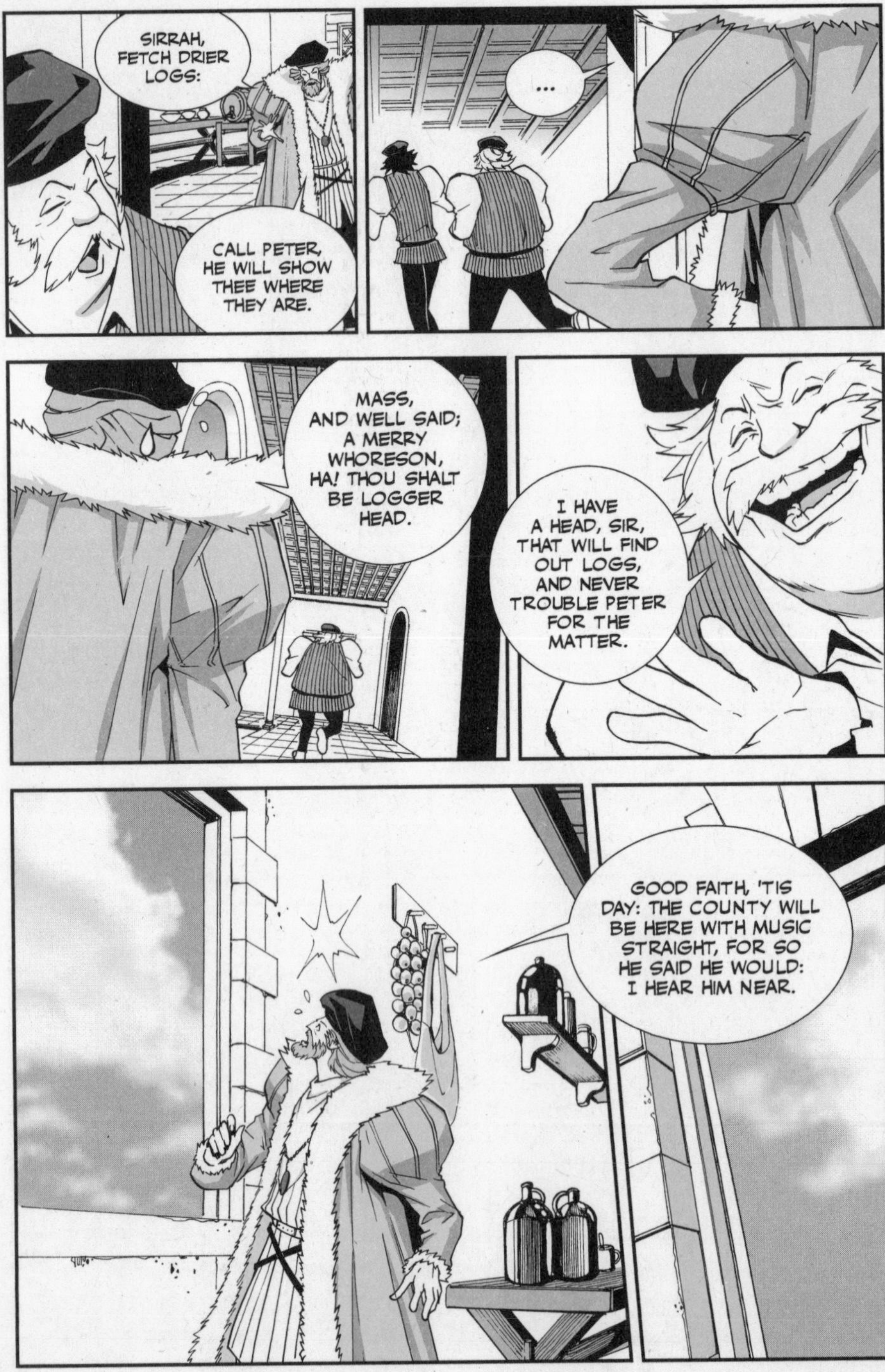
...
SIRRAH, FETCH DRIER LOGS:
CALL PETER, HE WILL SHOW THEE WHERE THEY ARE.
I HAVE A HEAD, SIR, THAT WILL FIND OUT LOGS, AND NEVER TROUBLE PETER FOR THE MATTER.
MASS, AND WELL SAID; A MERRY WHORESON, HA! THOU SHALT BE LOGGER HEAD.
GOOD FAITH, 'TIS DAY: THE COUNTY WILL BE HERE WITH MUSIC STRAIGHT, FOR SO HE SAID HE WOULD: I HEAR HIM NEAR.

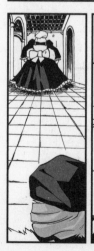

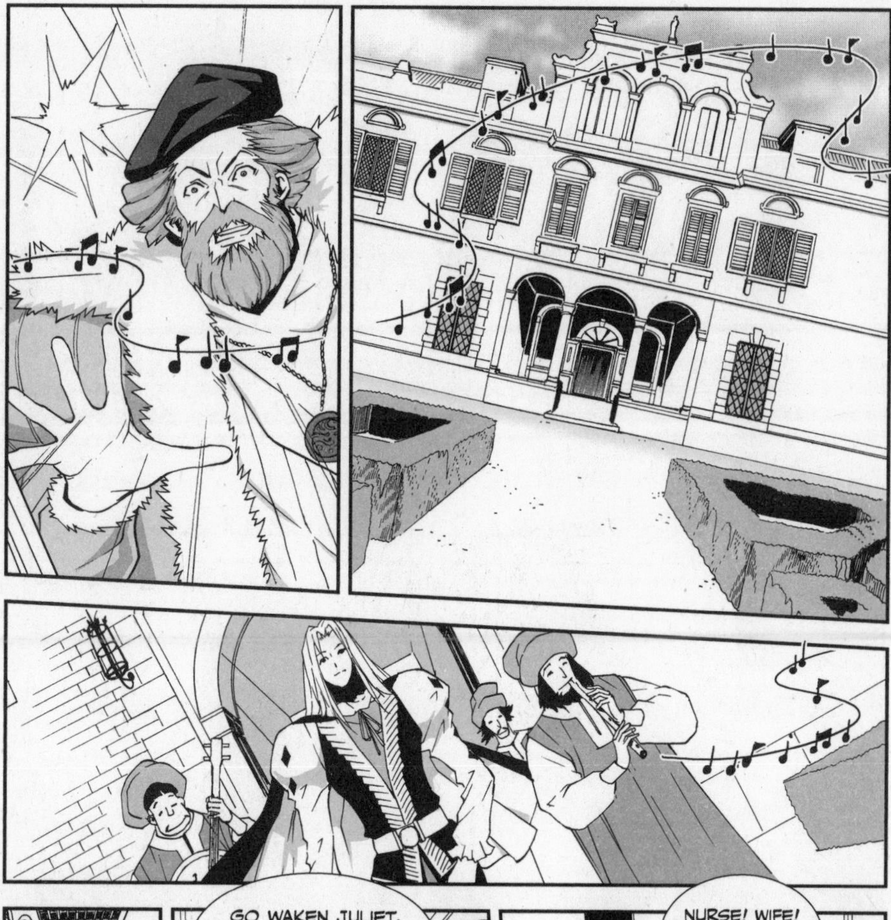
NURSE! WIFE! WHAT, HO! WHAT, NURSE, I SAY!
GO WAKEN JULIET, GO AND TRIM HER UP; I'LL GO AND CHAT WITH PARIS:
HIE, MAKE HASTE, MAKE HASTE; THE BRIDEGROOM HE IS COME ALREADY: MAKE HASTE, I SAY.

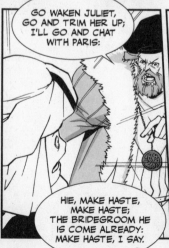

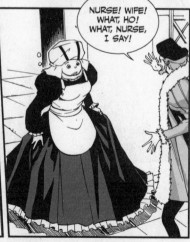

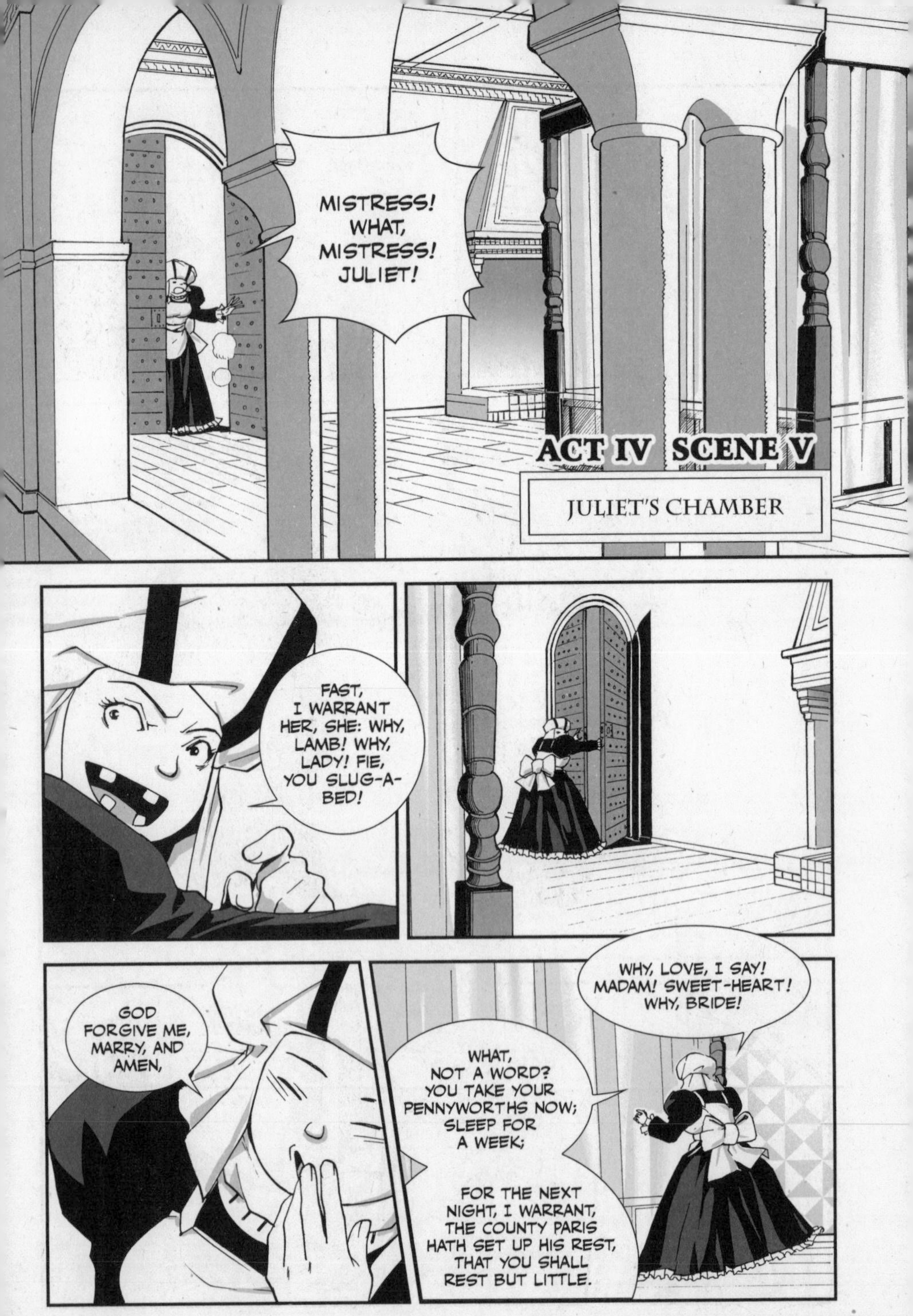
MISTRESS! WHAT, MISTRESS! JULIET!
ACT IV SCENE V
JULIET'S CHAMBER
FAST, I WARRANT HER, SHE: WHY, LAMB! WHY, LADY! FIE, YOU SLUG-A-BED!
WHY, LOVE, I SAY! MADAM! SWEET-HEART! WHY, BRIDE!
WHAT, NOT A WORD? YOU TAKE YOUR PENNYWORTHS NOW; SLEEP FOR A WEEK;
FOR THE NEXT NIGHT, I WARRANT, THE COUNTY PARIS HATH SET UP HIS REST, THAT YOU SHALL REST BUT LITTLE.
GOD FORGIVE ME, MARRY, AND AMEN,

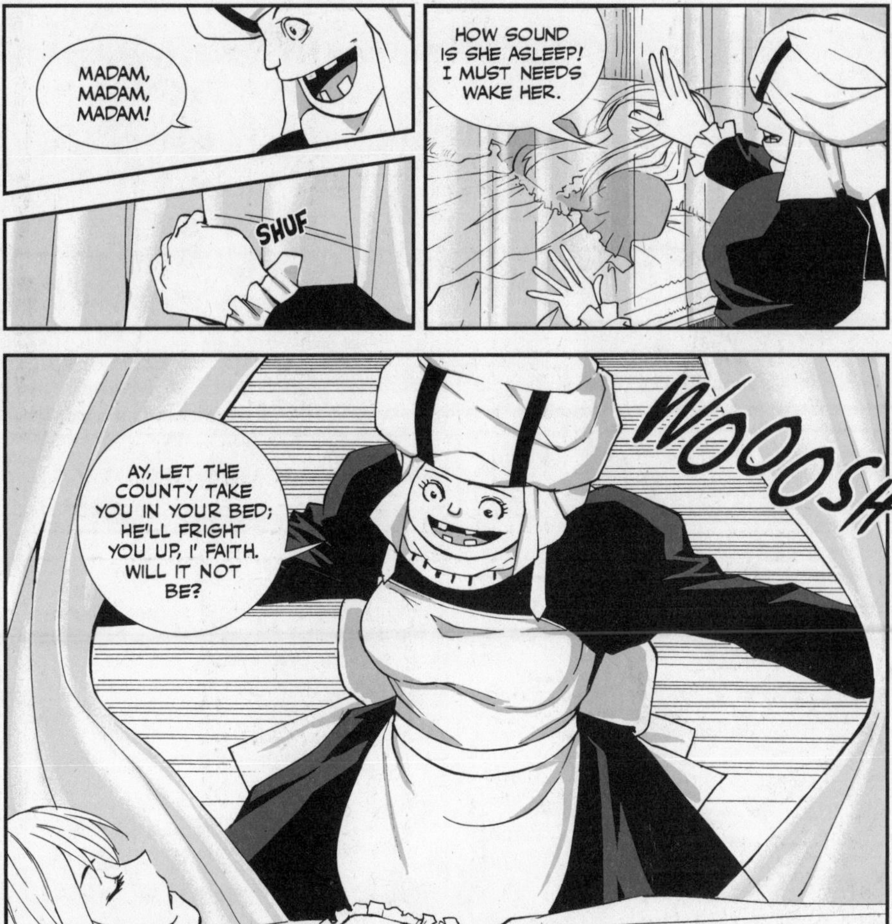
HOW SOUND IS SHE ASLEEP! I MUST NEEDS WAKE HER.
MADAM, MADAM, MADAM!
SHUF
WOOOSH
AY, LET THE COUNTY TAKE YOU IN YOUR BED; HE'LL FRIGHT YOU UP, I' FAITH. WILL IT NOT BE?
WHAT, DRESS'D! AND IN YOUR CLOTHES! AND DOWN AGAIN!
I MUST NEEDS WAKE YOU; LADY! LADY! LADY!
!!

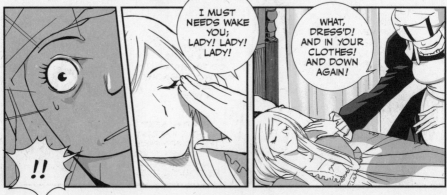

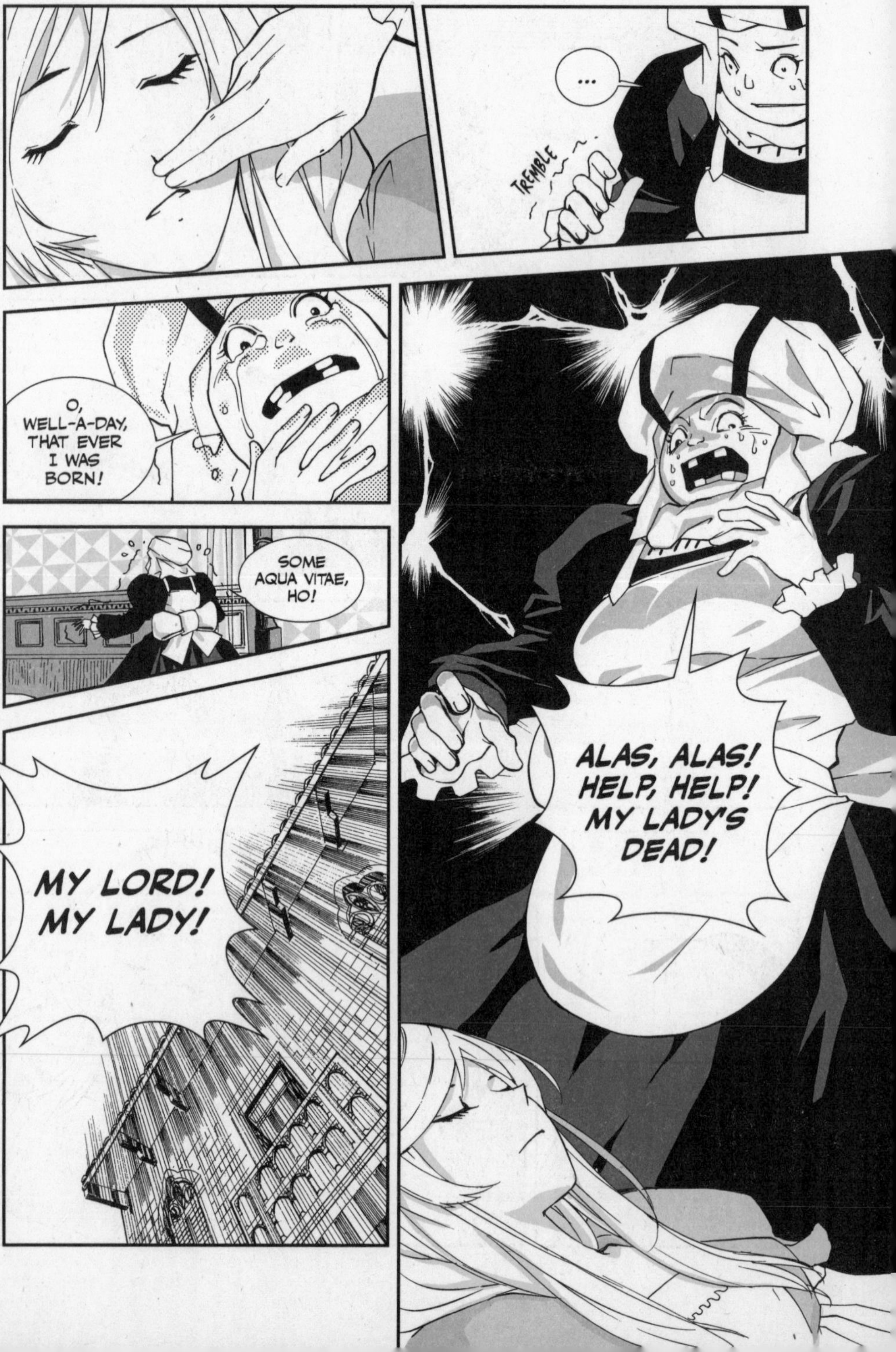
...
TREMBLE
ALAS, ALAS! HELP, HELP! MY LADY'S DEAD!
O, WELL-A-DAY, THAT EVER I WAS BORN!
SOME AQUA VITAE, HO!
MY LORD! MY LADY!

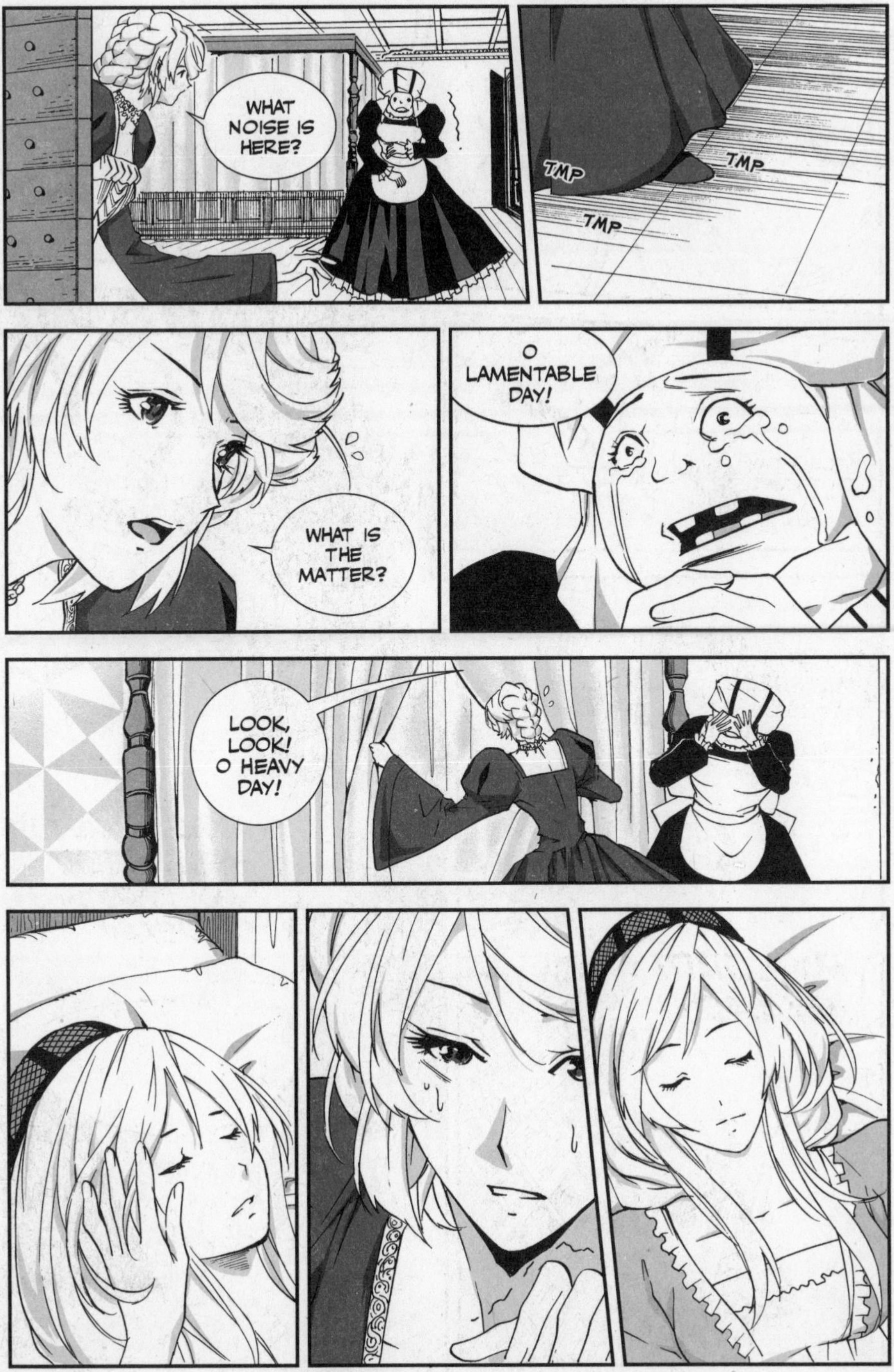
TMP
TMP
TMP
WHAT NOISE IS HERE?
O LAMENTABLE DAY!
WHAT IS THE MATTER?
LOOK, LOOK! O HEAVY DAY!

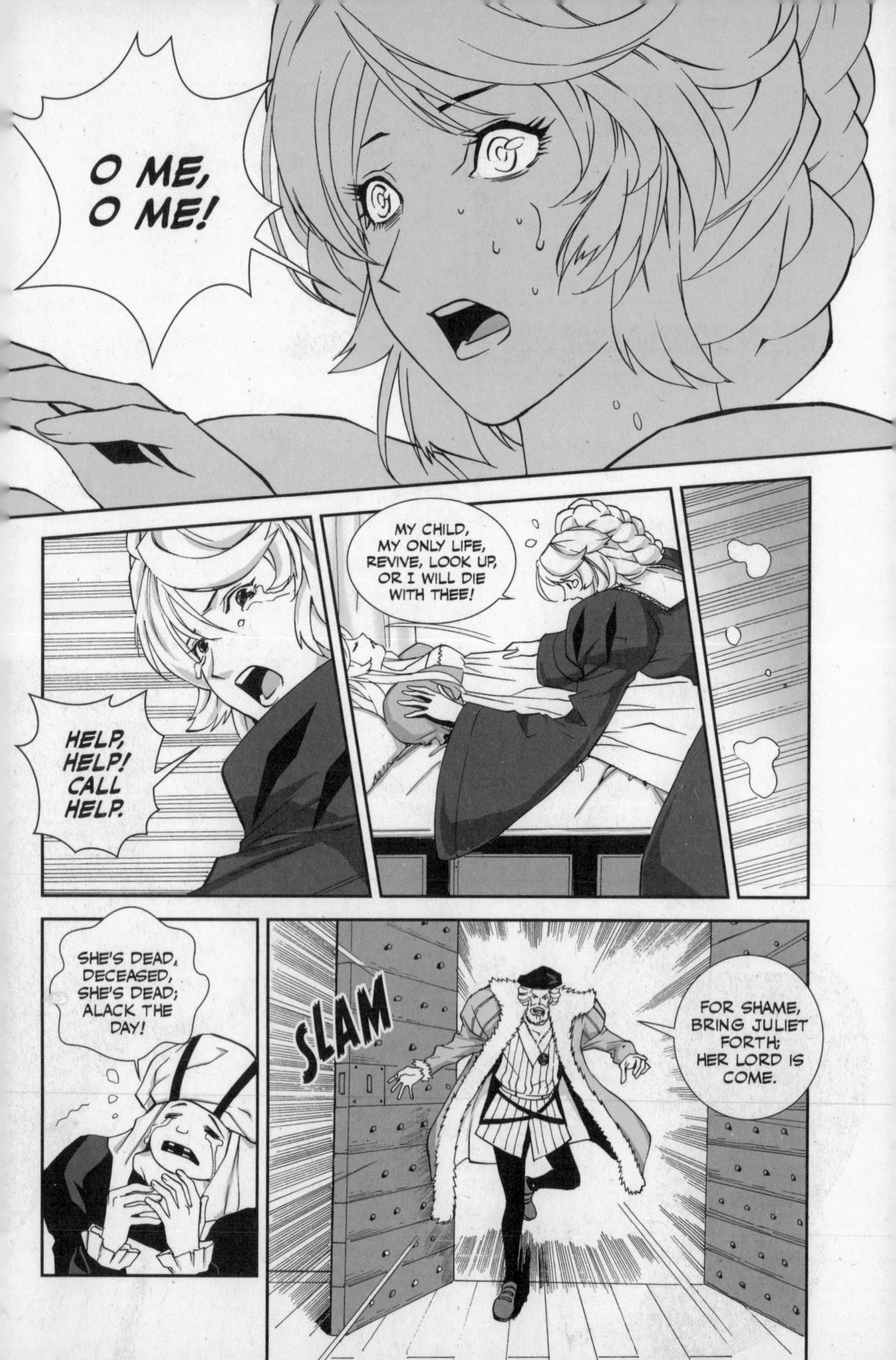
O ME, O ME!
MY CHILD, MY ONLY LIFE, REVIVE, LOOK UP, OR I WILL DIE WITH THEE!
HELP, HELP! CALL HELP.
FOR SHAME, BRING JULIET FORTH; HER LORD IS COME.
SLAM
SHE'S DEAD, DECEASED, SHE'S DEAD; ALACK THE DAY!

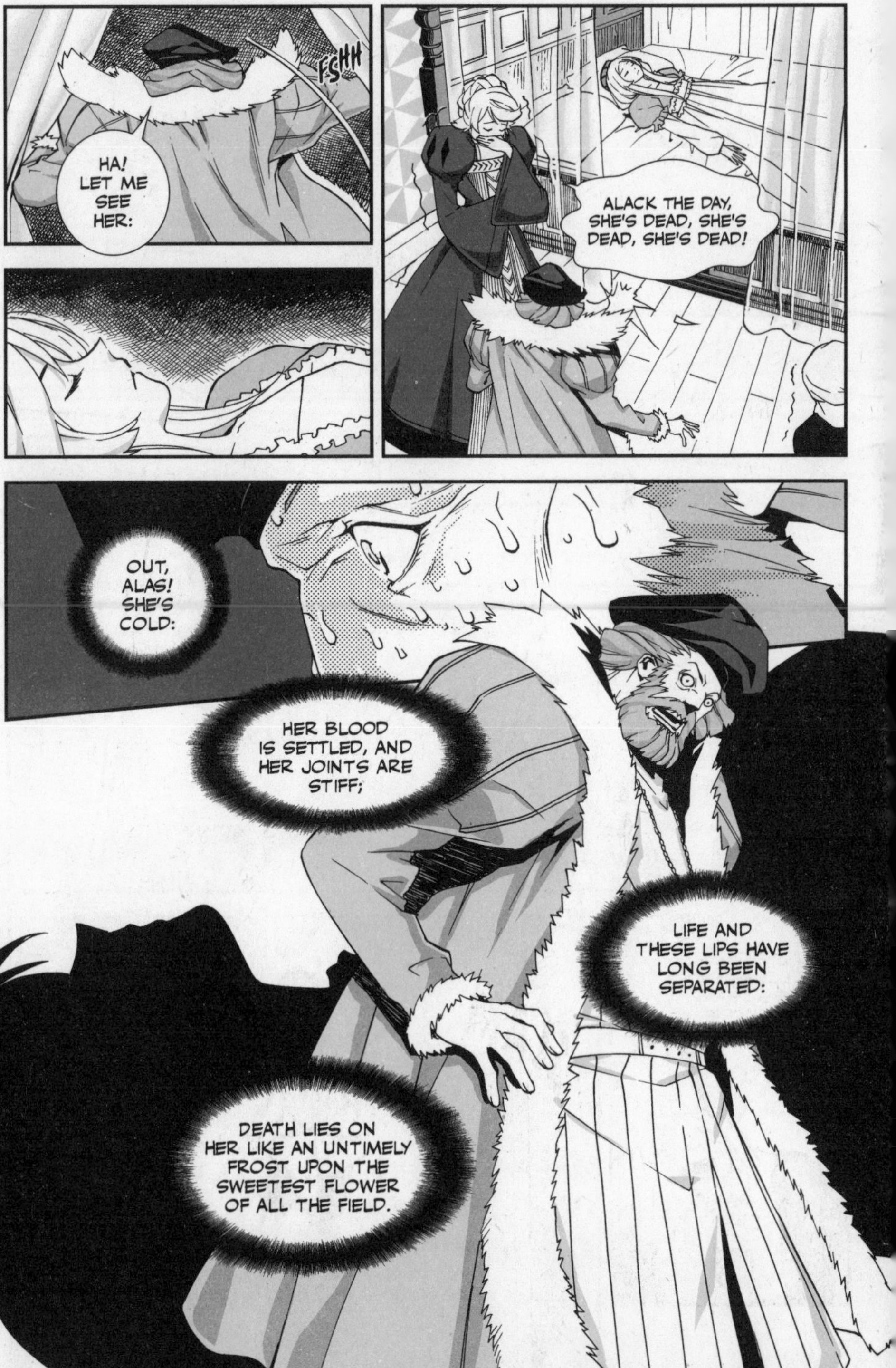
ALACK THE DAY, SHE'S DEAD, SHE'S DEAD, SHE'S DEAD!
FSHH
HA! LET ME SEE HER:
OUT, ALAS! SHE'S COLD:
HER BLOOD IS SETTLED, AND HER JOINTS ARE STIFF;
LIFE AND THESE LIPS HAVE LONG BEEN SEPARATED:
DEATH LIES ON HER LIKE AN UNTIMELY FROST UPON THE SWEETEST FLOWER OF ALL THE FIELD.

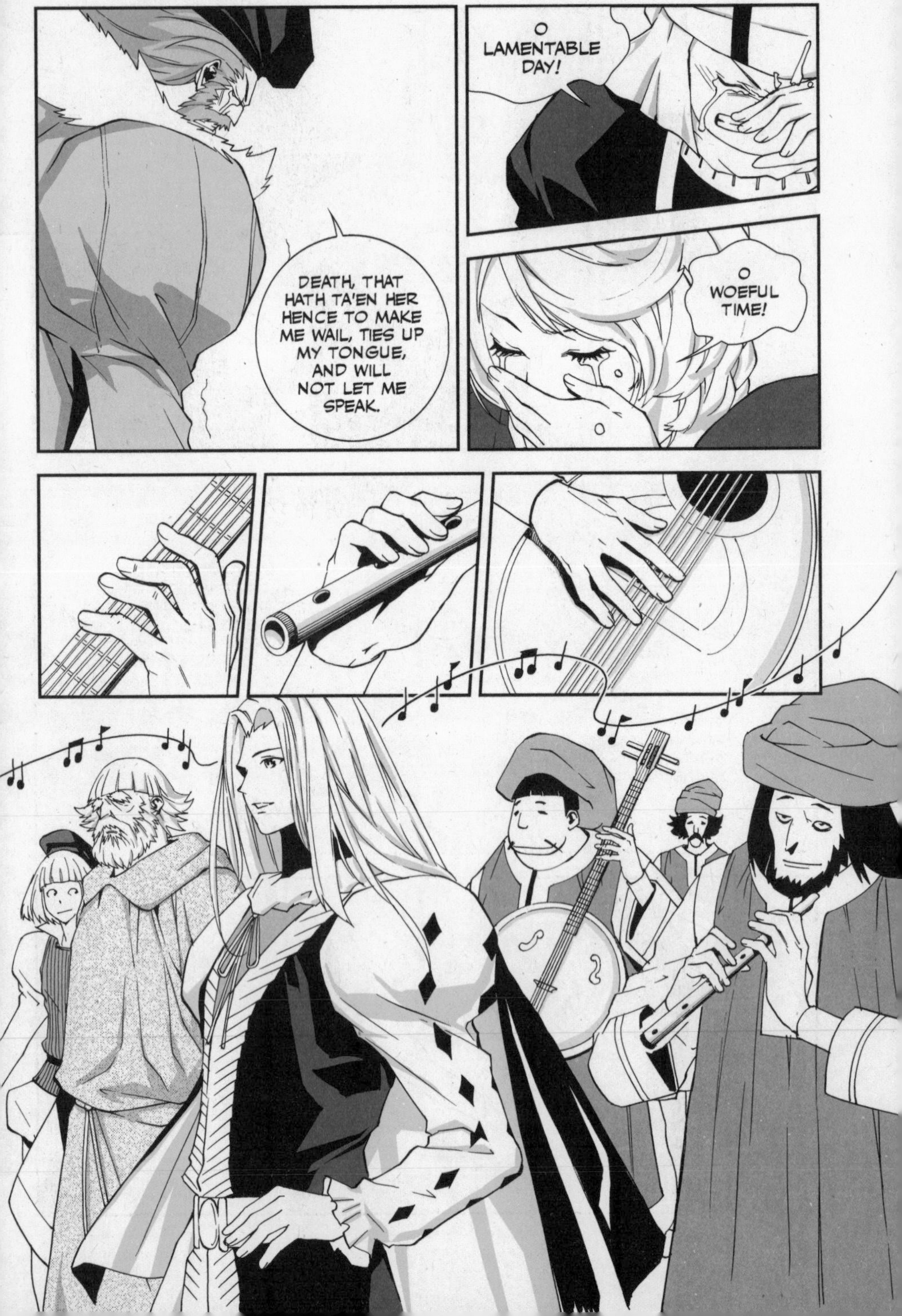
O LAMENTABLE DAY!
O WOEFUL TIME!
DEATH, THAT HATH TA'EN HER HENCE TO MAKE ME WAIL, TIES UP MY TONGUE, AND WILL NOT LET ME SPEAK.

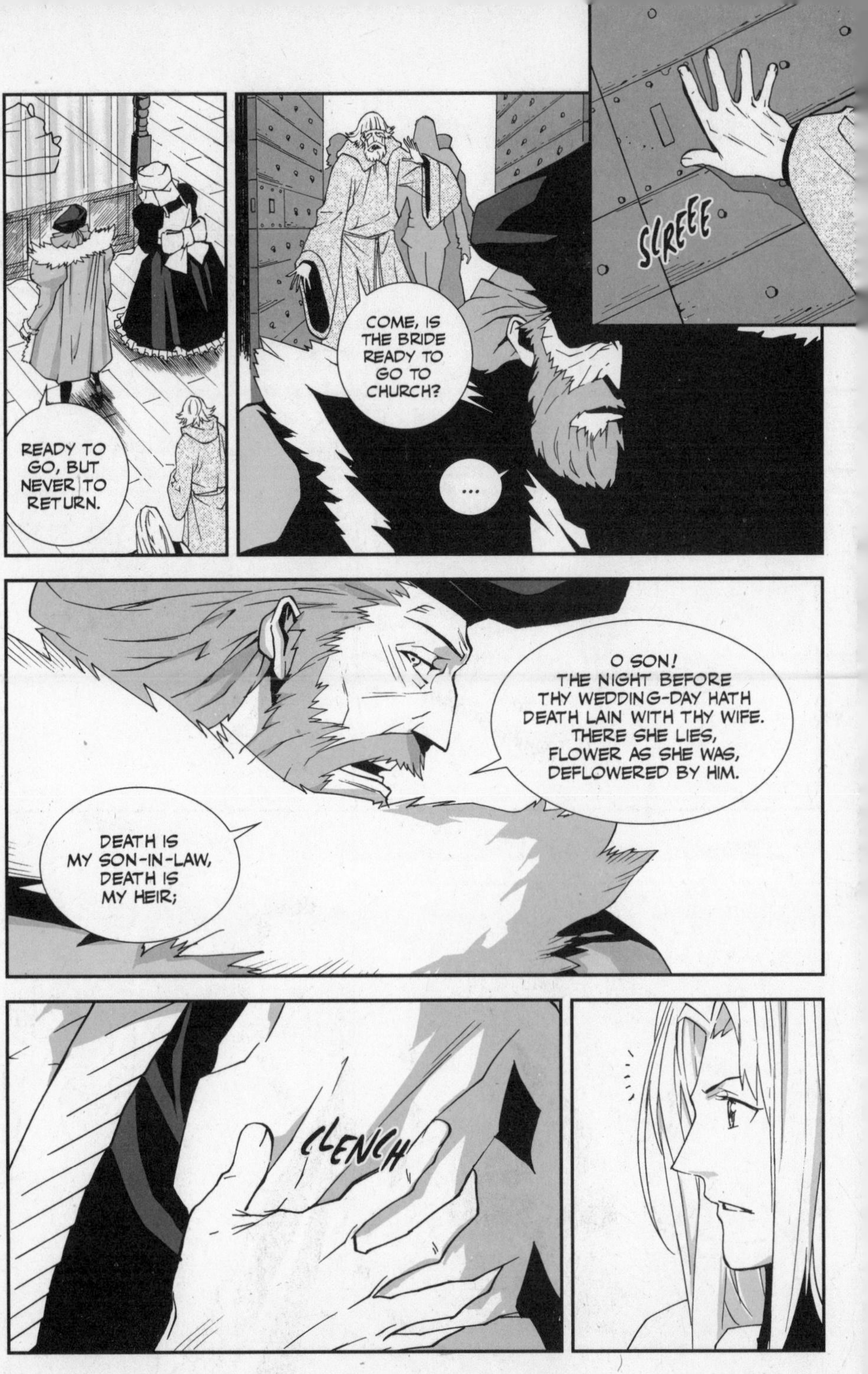
SCREEE
COME, IS THE BRIDE READY TO GO TO CHURCH?
...
READY TO GO, BUT NEVER TO RETURN.
O SON! THE NIGHT BEFORE THY WEDDING-DAY HATH DEATH LAIN WITH THY WIFE. THERE SHE LIES, FLOWER AS SHE WAS, DEFLOWERED BY HIM.
DEATH IS MY SON-IN-LAW, DEATH IS MY HEIR;
CLENCH

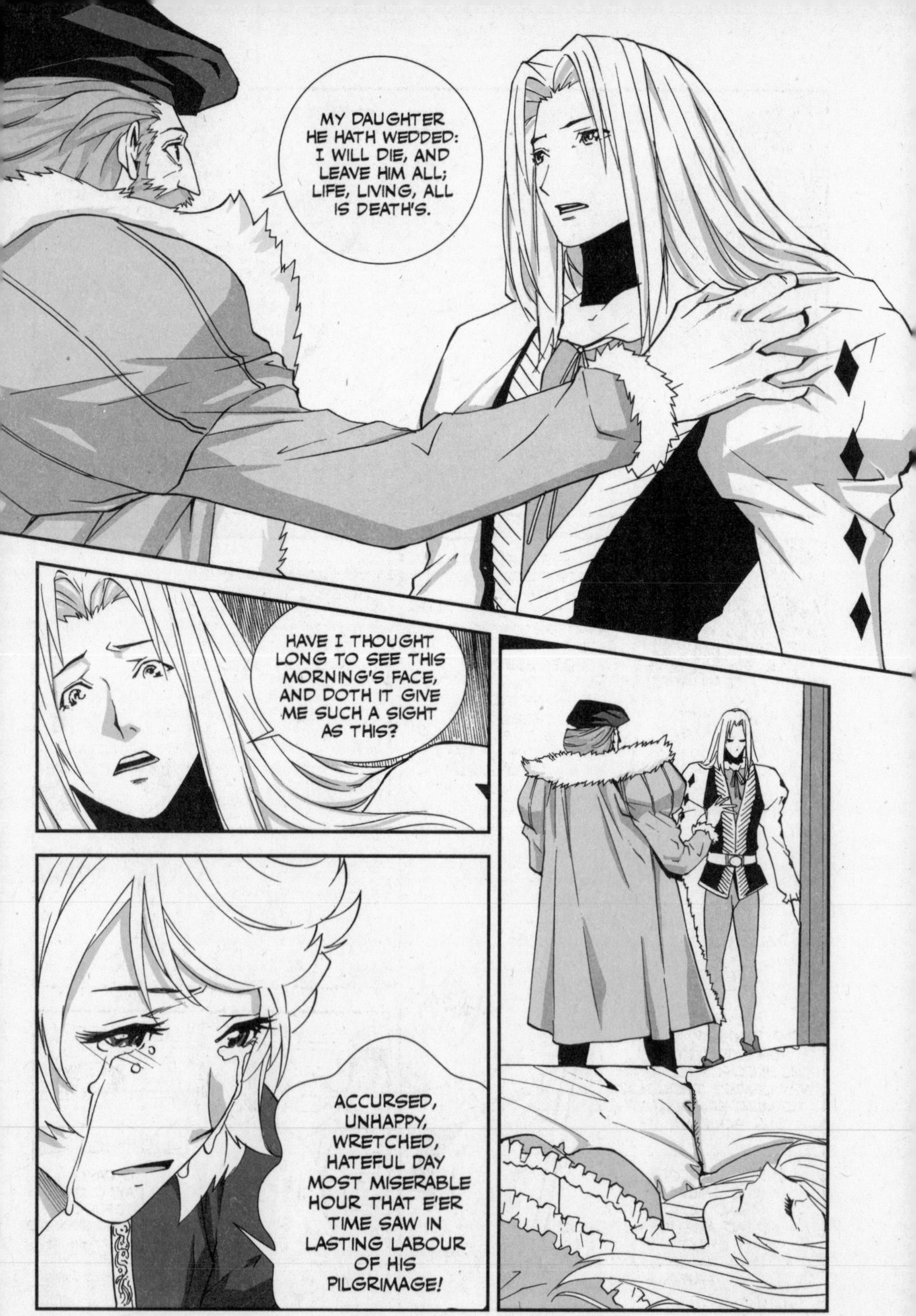
MY DAUGHTER HE HATH WEDDED: I WILL DIE, AND LEAVE HIM ALL; LIFE, LIVING, ALL IS DEATH'S.
HAVE I THOUGHT LONG TO SEE THIS MORNING'S FACE, AND DOTH IT GIVE ME SUCH A SIGHT AS THIS?
ACCURSED, UNHAPPY, WRETCHED, HATEFUL DAY MOST MISERABLE HOUR THAT E'ER TIME SAW IN LASTING LABOUR OF HIS PILGRIMAGE!

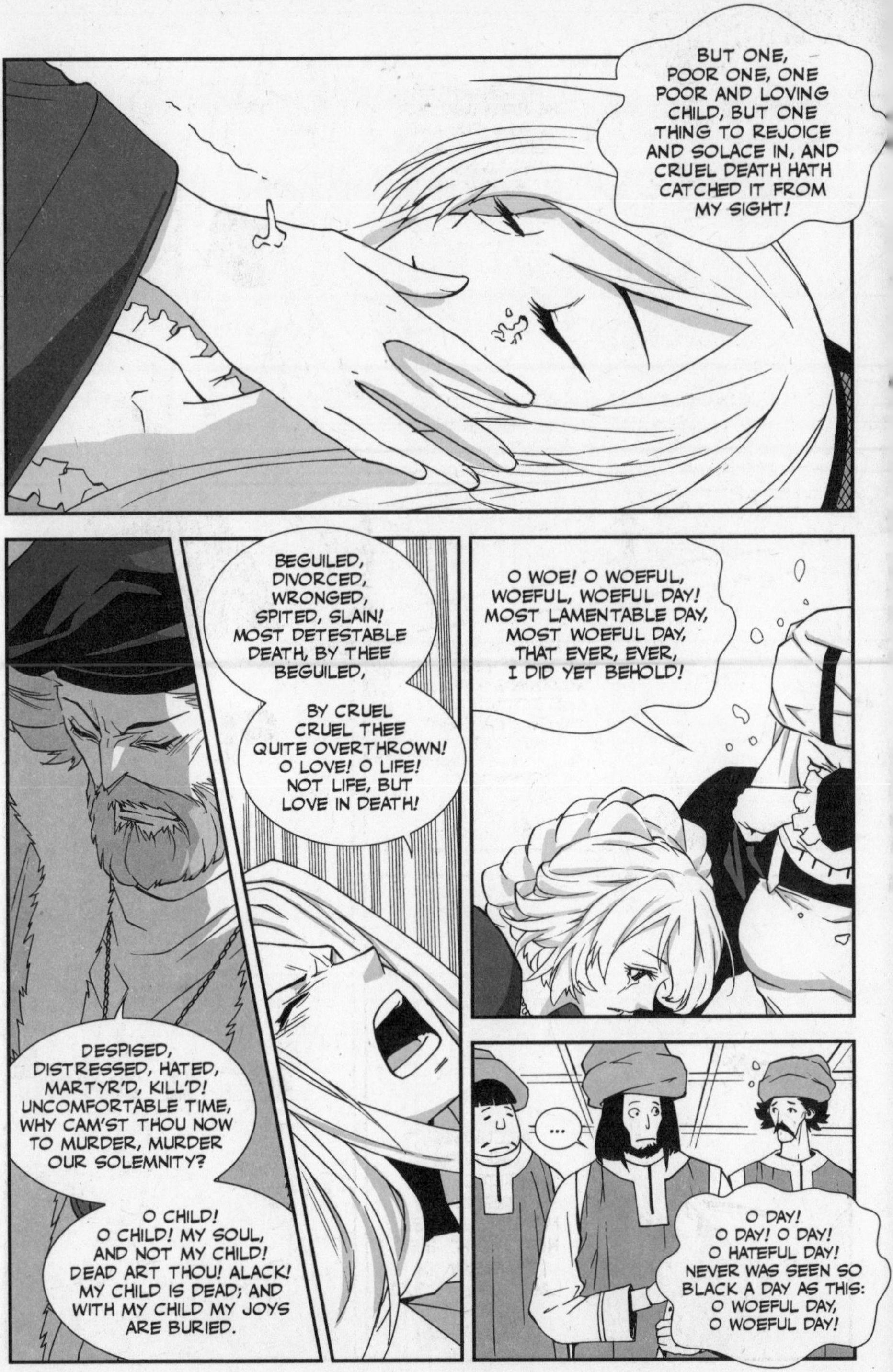
BUT ONE, POOR ONE, ONE POOR AND LOVING CHILD, BUT ONE THING TO REJOICE AND SOLACE IN, AND CRUEL DEATH HATH CATCHED IT FROM MY SIGHT!
O WOE! O WOEFUL, WOEFUL, WOEFUL DAY! MOST LAMENTABLE DAY, MOST WOEFUL DAY, THAT EVER, EVER, I DID YET BEHOLD!
...
O DAY! O DAY! O DAY! O HATEFUL DAY! NEVER WAS SEEN SO BLACK A DAY AS THIS: O WOEFUL DAY, O WOEFUL DAY!
BEGUILED, DIVORCED, WRONGED, SPITED, SLAIN! MOST DETESTABLE DEATH, BY THEE BEGUILED,
BY CRUEL CRUEL THEE QUITE OVERTHROWN! O LOVE! O LIFE! NOT LIFE, BUT LOVE IN DEATH!
DESPISED, DISTRESSED, HATED, MARTYR'D, KILL'D! UNCOMFORTABLE TIME, WHY CAM'ST THOU NOW TO MURDER, MURDER OUR SOLEMNITY?
O CHILD! O CHILD! MY SOUL, AND NOT MY CHILD! DEAD ART THOU! ALACK! MY CHILD IS DEAD; AND WITH MY CHILD MY JOYS ARE BURIED.

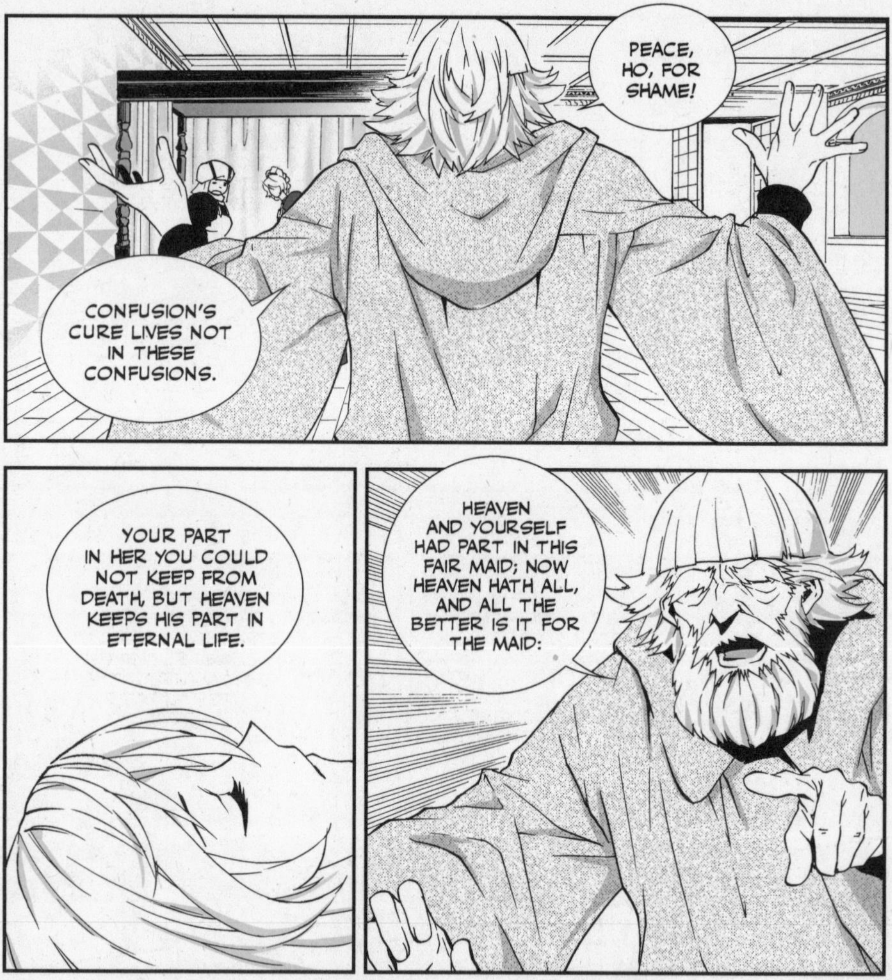
PEACE, HO, FOR SHAME!
CONFUSION'S CURE LIVES NOT IN THESE CONFUSIONS.
HEAVEN AND YOURSELF HAD PART IN THIS FAIR MAID; NOW HEAVEN HATH ALL, AND ALL THE BETTER IS IT FOR THE MAID:
YOUR PART IN HER YOU COULD NOT KEEP FROM DEATH, BUT HEAVEN KEEPS HIS PART IN ETERNAL LIFE.
THE MOST YOU SOUGHT WAS HER PROMOTION; FOR 'TWAS YOUR HEAVEN SHE SHOULD BE ADVANCED:

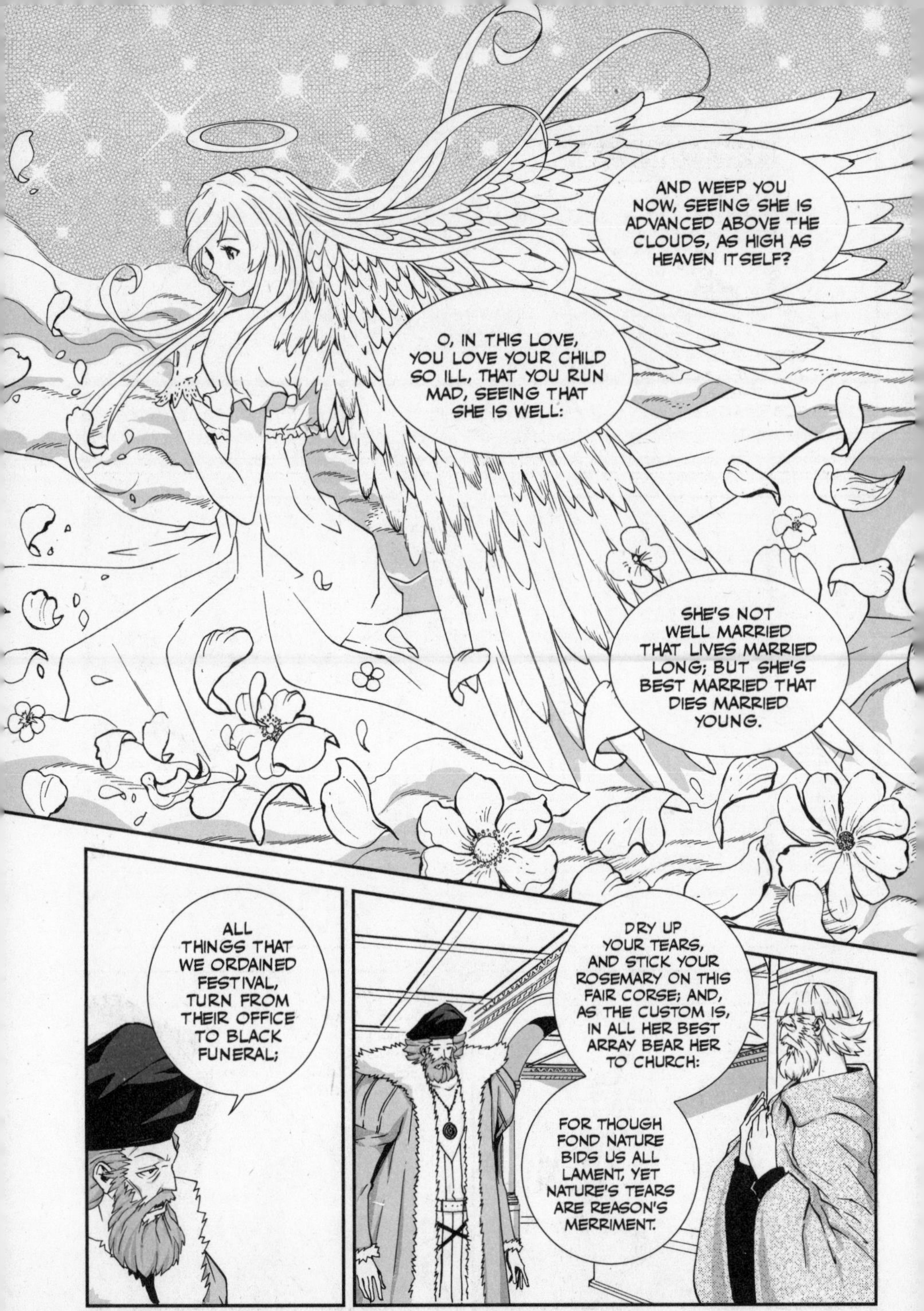
AND WEEP YOU NOW, SEEING SHE IS ADVANCED ABOVE THE CLOUDS, AS HIGH AS HEAVEN ITSELF?
O, IN THIS LOVE, YOU LOVE YOUR CHILD SO ILL, THAT YOU RUN MAD, SEEING THAT SHE IS WELL:
SHE'S NOT WELL MARRIED THAT LIVES MARRIED LONG; BUT SHE'S BEST MARRIED THAT DIES MARRIED YOUNG.
DRY UP YOUR TEARS, AND STICK YOUR ROSEMARY ON THIS FAIR CORSE; AND, AS THE CUSTOM IS, IN ALL HER BEST ARRAY BEAR HER TO CHURCH:
FOR THOUGH FOND NATURE BIDS US ALL LAMENT, YET NATURE'S TEARS ARE REASON'S MERRIMENT.
ALL THINGS THAT WE ORDAINED FESTIVAL, TURN FROM THEIR OFFICE TO BLACK FUNERAL;

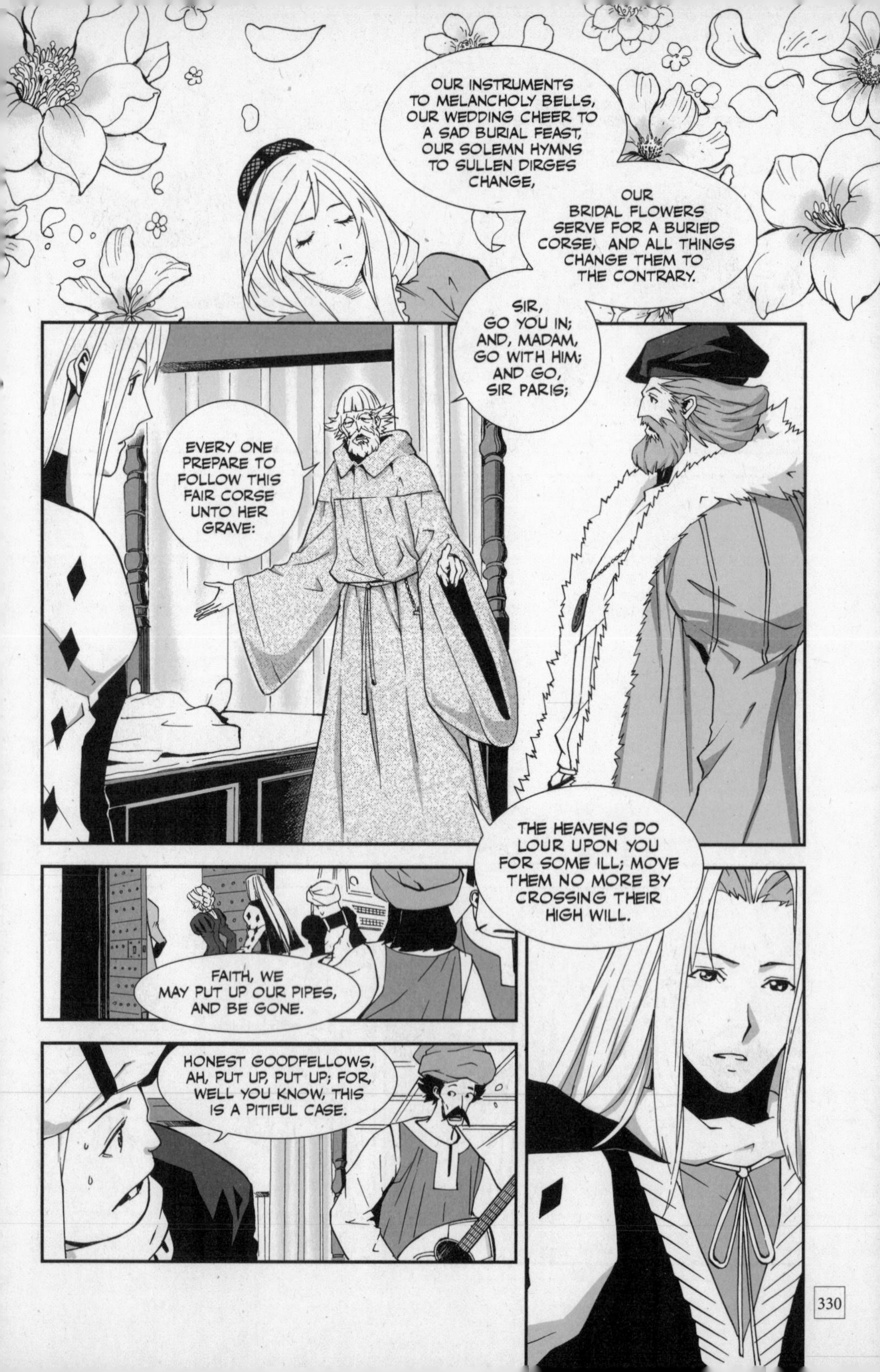
OUR INSTRUMENTS TO MELANCHOLY BELLS, OUR WEDDING CHEER TO A SAD BURIAL FEAST, OUR SOLEMN HYMNS TO SULLEN DIRGES CHANGE,
OUR BRIDAL FLOWERS SERVE FOR A BURIED CORSE, AND ALL THINGS CHANGE THEM TO THE CONTRARY.
SIR, GO YOU IN; AND, MADAM, GO WITH HIM; AND GO, SIR PARIS;
EVERY ONE PREPARE TO FOLLOW THIS FAIR CORSE UNTO HER GRAVE:
THE HEAVENS DO LOUR UPON YOU FOR SOME ILL; MOVE THEM NO MORE BY CROSSING THEIR HIGH WILL.
FAITH, WE MAY PUT UP OUR PIPES, AND BE GONE.
HONEST GOODFELLOWS, AH, PUT UP, PUT UP; FOR, WELL YOU KNOW, THIS IS A PITIFUL CASE.

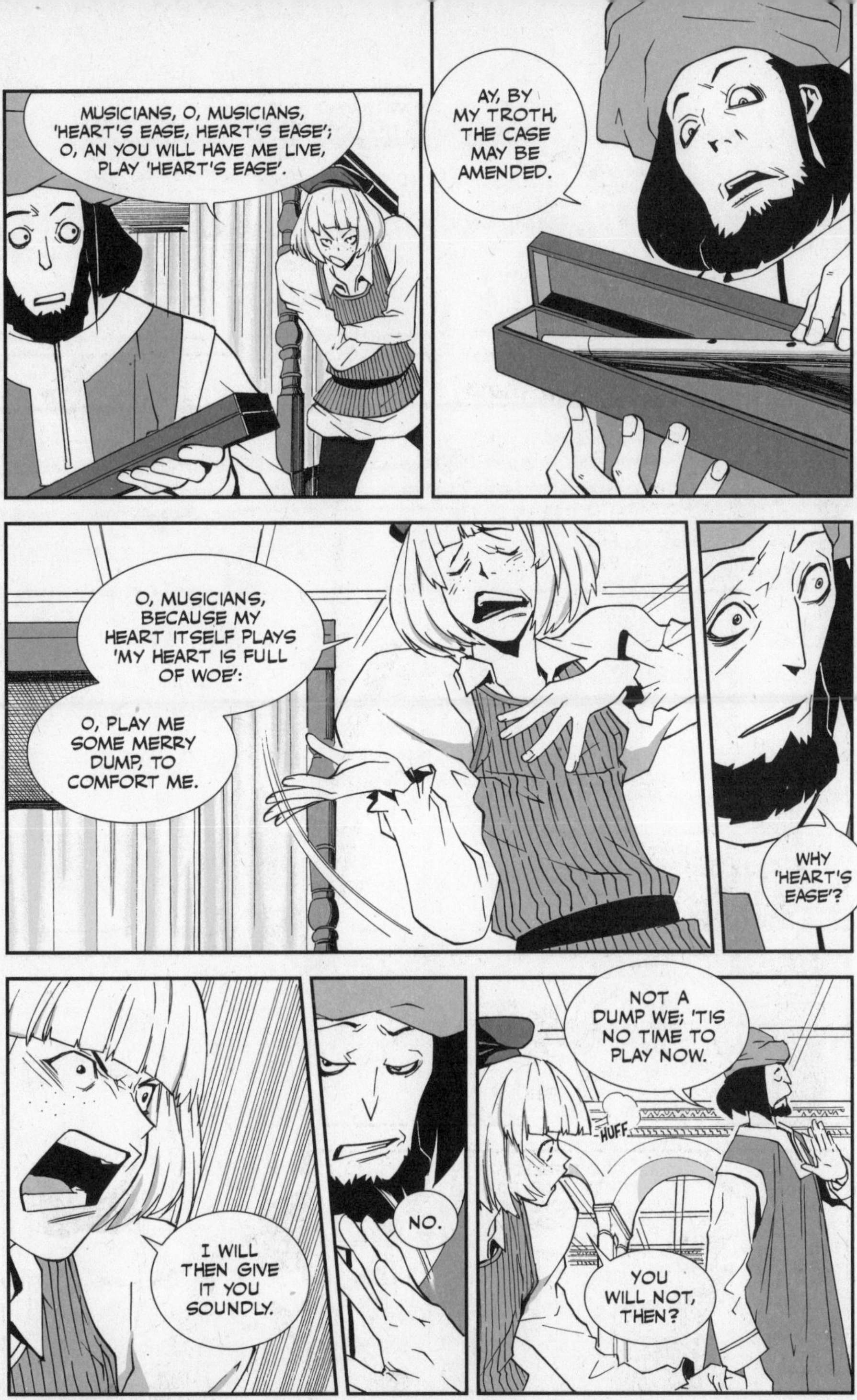
AY, BY MY TROTH, THE CASE MAY BE AMENDED.
MUSICIANS, O, MUSICIANS, 'HEART'S EASE, HEART'S EASE'; O, AN YOU WILL HAVE ME LIVE, PLAY 'HEART'S EASE'.
WHY 'HEART'S EASE'?
O, MUSICIANS, BECAUSE MY HEART ITSELF PLAYS 'MY HEART IS FULL OF WOE':
O, PLAY ME SOME MERRY DUMP, TO COMFORT ME.
NOT A DUMP WE; 'TIS NO TIME TO PLAY NOW.
HUFF
YOU WILL NOT, THEN?
NO.
I WILL THEN GIVE IT YOU SOUNDLY.

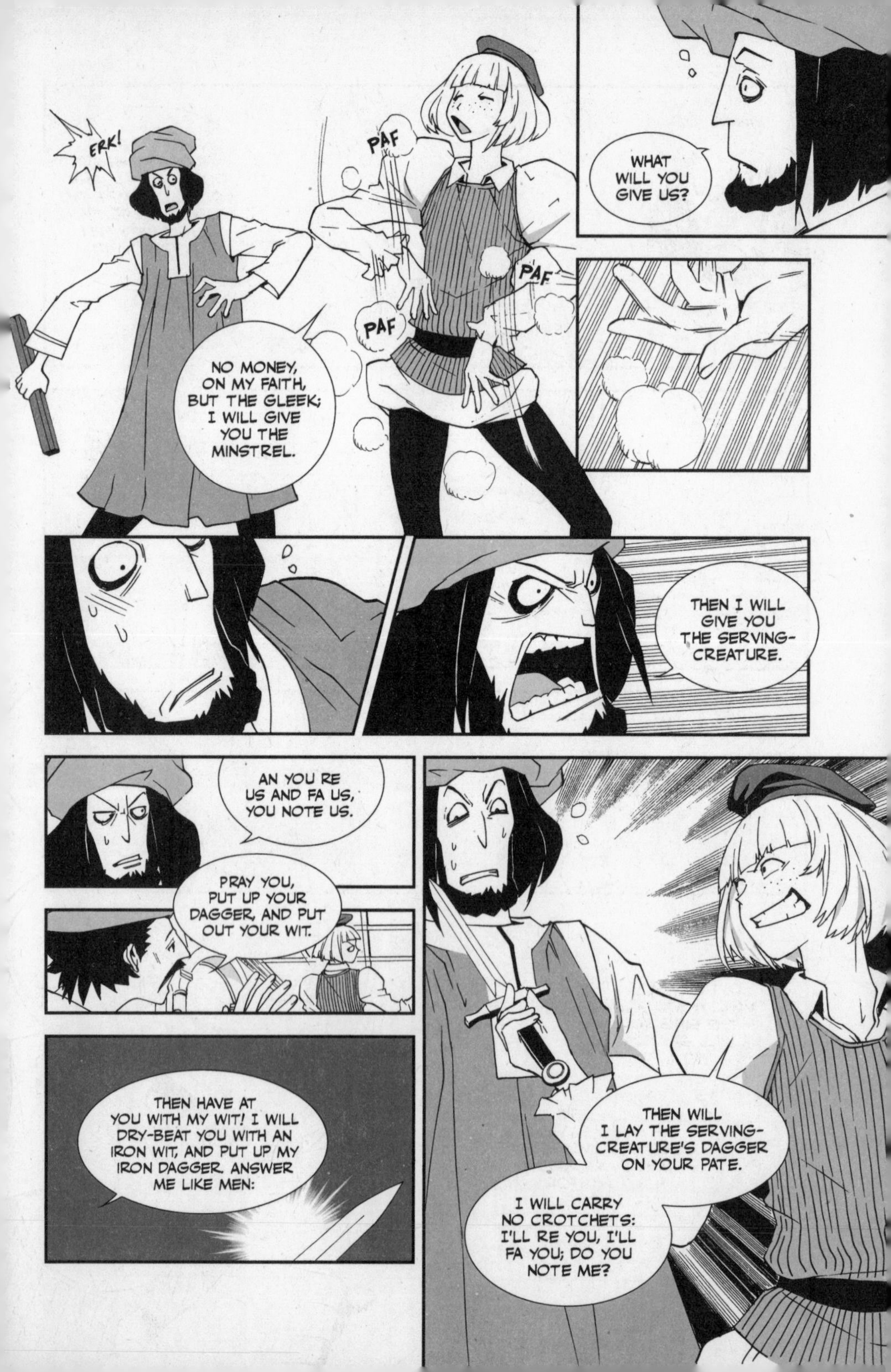
WHAT WILL YOU GIVE US?
PAF
ERK!
PAF
PAF
NO MONEY, ON MY FAITH, BUT THE GLEEK; I WILL GIVE YOU THE MINSTREL.
THEN I WILL GIVE YOU THE SERVING-CREATURE.
THEN WILL I LAY THE SERVING-CREATURE'S DAGGER ON YOUR PATE.
I WILL CARRY NO CROTCHETS: I'LL RE YOU, I'LL FA YOU; DO YOU NOTE ME?
AN YOU RE US AND FA US, YOU NOTE US.
PRAY YOU, PUT UP YOUR DAGGER, AND PUT OUT YOUR WIT.
THEN HAVE AT YOU WITH MY WIT! I WILL DRY-BEAT YOU WITH AN IRON WIT, AND PUT UP MY IRON DAGGER. ANSWER ME LIKE MEN:

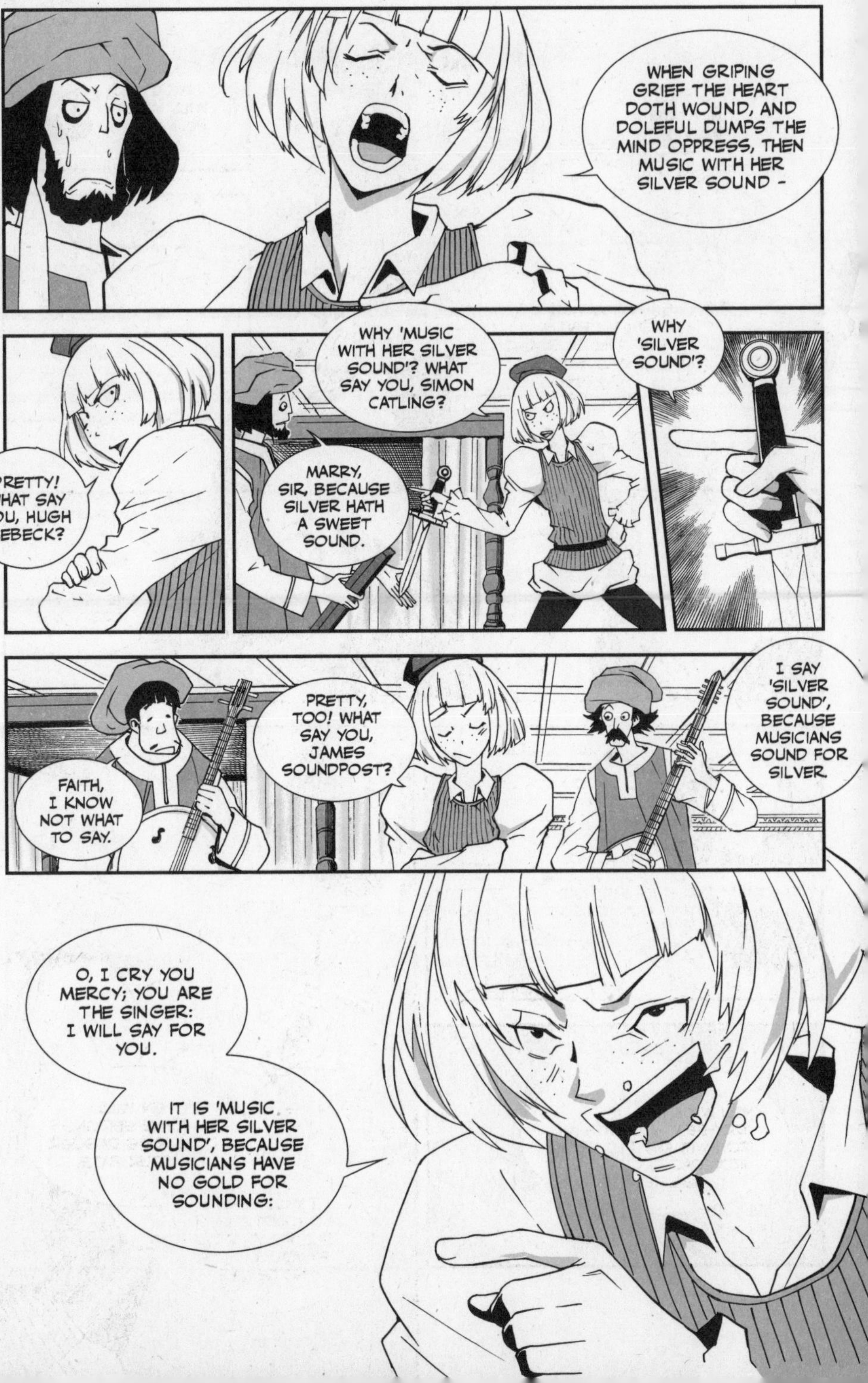

WHEN GRIPING GRIEF THE HEART DOTH WOUND, AND DOLEFUL DUMPS THE MIND OPPRESS, THEN MUSIC WITH HER SILVER SOUND -
WHY 'SILVER SOUND'?
WHY 'MUSIC WITH HER SILVER SOUND'? WHAT SAY YOU, SIMON CATLING?
MARRY, SIR, BECAUSE SILVER HATH A SWEET SOUND.
PRETTY! WHAT SAY YOU, HUGH REBECK?
I SAY 'SILVER SOUND', BECAUSE MUSICIANS SOUND FOR SILVER.
PRETTY, TOO! WHAT SAY YOU, JAMES SOUNDPOST?
FAITH, I KNOW NOT WHAT TO SAY.
O, I CRY YOU MERCY; YOU ARE THE SINGER: I WILL SAY FOR YOU.
IT IS 'MUSIC WITH HER SILVER SOUND', BECAUSE MUSICIANS HAVE NO GOLD FOR SOUNDING:

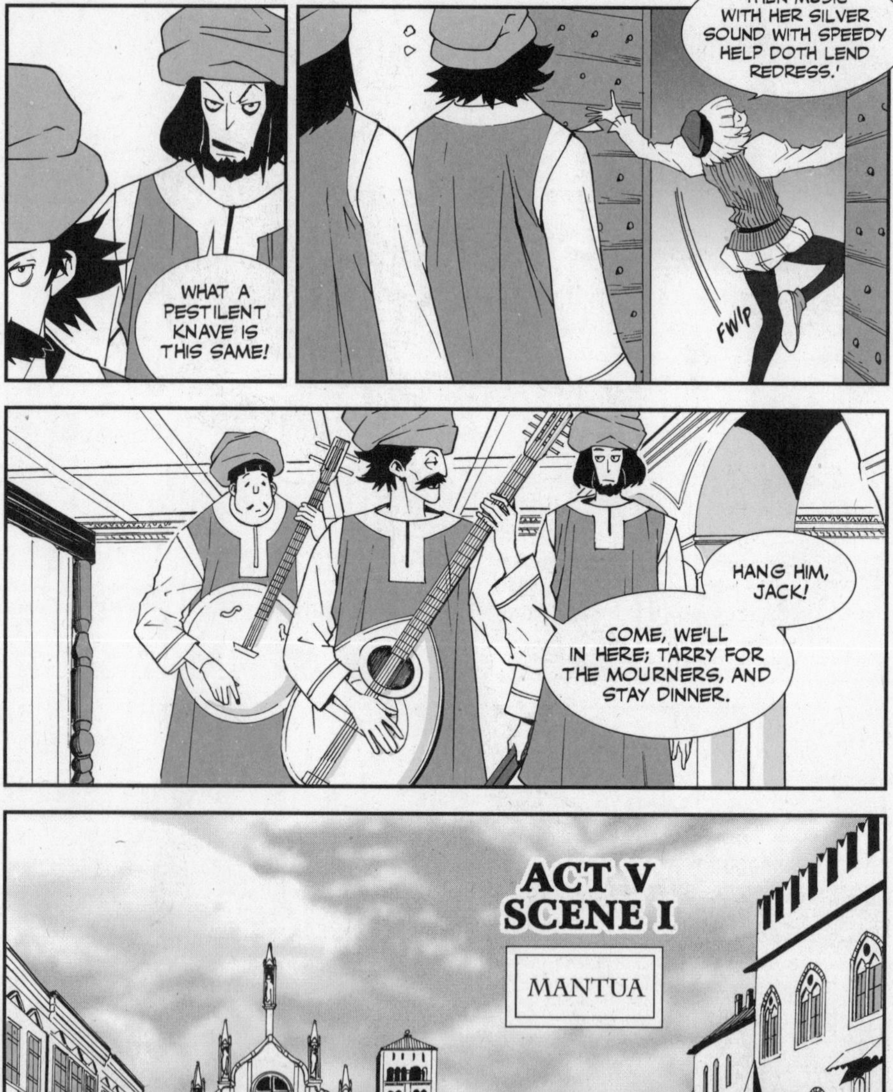
'THEN MUSIC WITH HER SILVER SOUND WITH SPEEDY HELP DOTH LEND REDRESS.'
FWIP
WHAT A PESTILENT KNAVE IS THIS SAME!
HANG HIM, JACK!
COME, WE'LL IN HERE; TARRY FOR THE MOURNERS, AND STAY DINNER.
ACT V
SCENE I
MANTUA

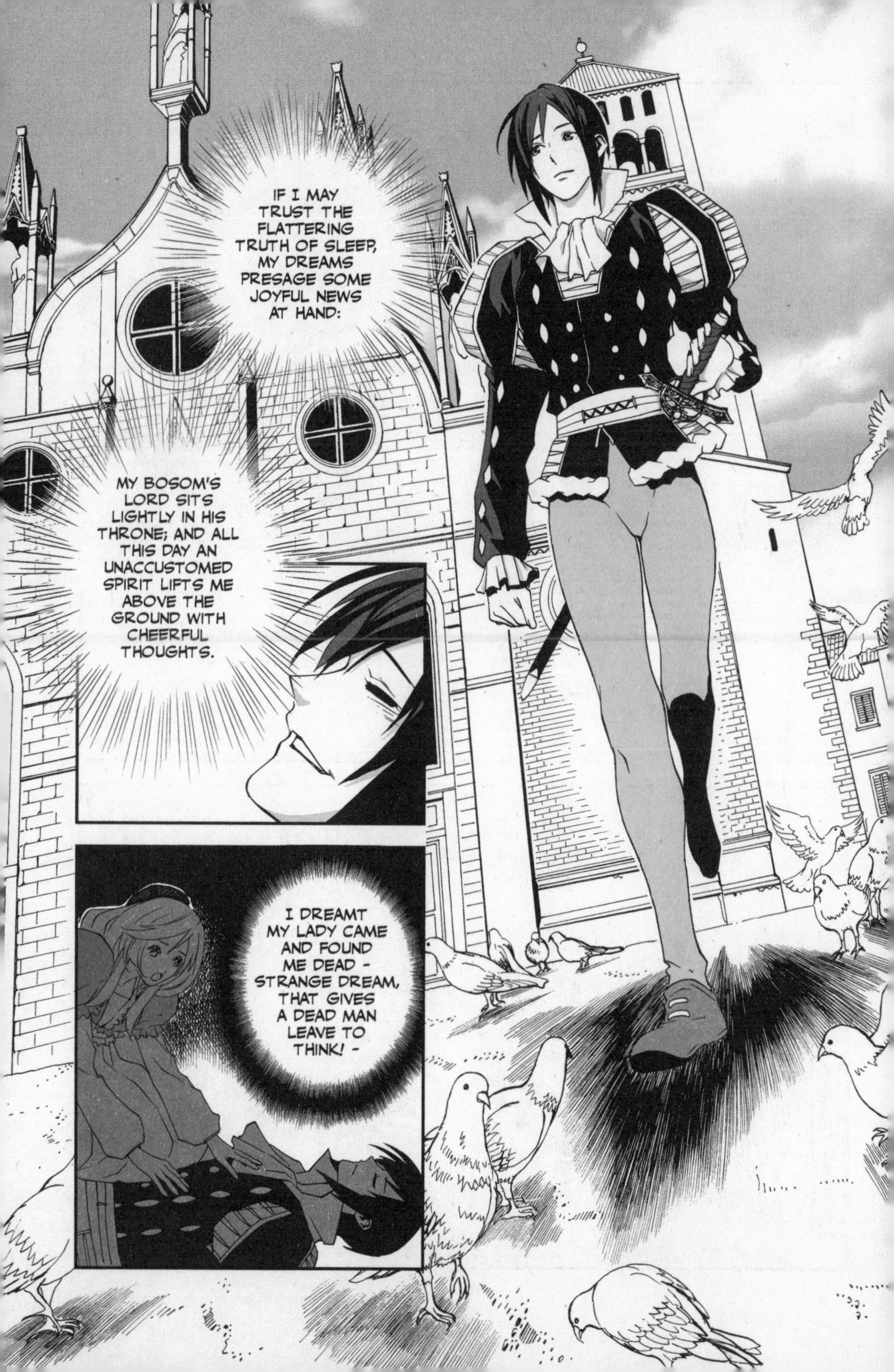
IF I MAY TRUST THE FLATTERING TRUTH OF SLEEP, MY DREAMS PRESAGE SOME JOYFUL NEWS AT HAND:
MY BOSOM'S LORD SITS LIGHTLY IN HIS THRONE; AND ALL THIS DAY AN UNACCUSTOMED SPIRIT LIFTS ME ABOVE THE GROUND WITH CHEERFUL THOUGHTS.
I DREAMT MY LADY CAME AND FOUND ME DEAD - STRANGE DREAM, THAT GIVES A DEAD MAN LEAVE TO THINK! -

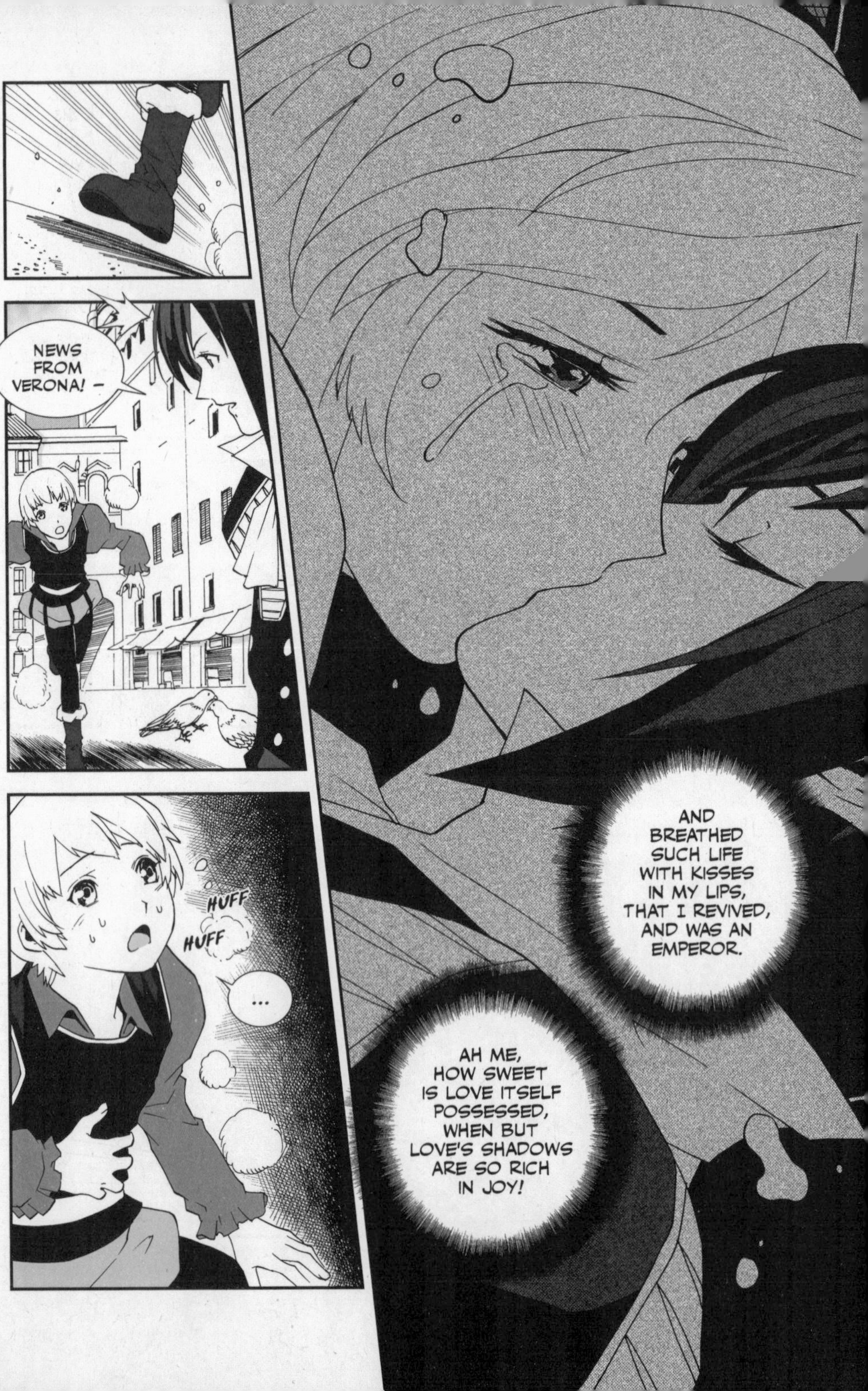
AND BREATHED SUCH LIFE WITH KISSES IN MY LIPS, THAT I REVIVED, AND WAS AN EMPEROR.
AH ME, HOW SWEET IS LOVE ITSELF POSSESSED, WHEN BUT LOVE'S SHADOWS ARE SO RICH IN JOY!
NEWS FROM VERONA! –
HUFF
HUFF
...

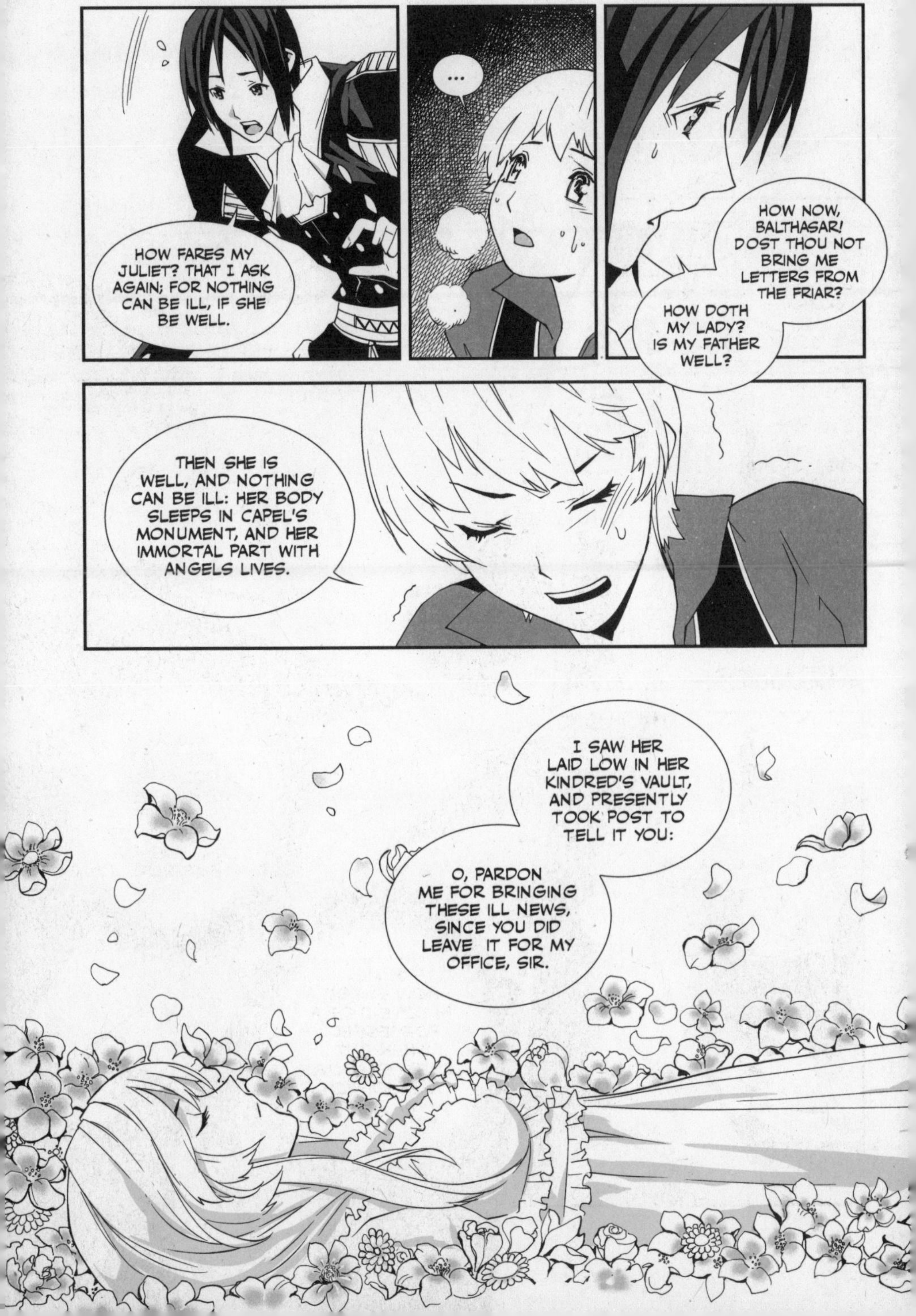

HOW NOW, BALTHASAR! DOST THOU NOT BRING ME LETTERS FROM THE FRIAR?
HOW DOTH MY LADY? IS MY FATHER WELL?
...
HOW FARES MY JULIET? THAT I ASK AGAIN; FOR NOTHING CAN BE ILL, IF SHE BE WELL.
THEN SHE IS WELL, AND NOTHING CAN BE ILL: HER BODY SLEEPS IN CAPEL'S MONUMENT, AND HER IMMORTAL PART WITH ANGELS LIVES.
I SAW HER LAID LOW IN HER KINDRED'S VAULT, AND PRESENTLY TOOK POST TO TELL IT YOU:
O, PARDON ME FOR BRINGING THESE ILL NEWS, SINCE YOU DID LEAVE IT FOR MY OFFICE, SIR.

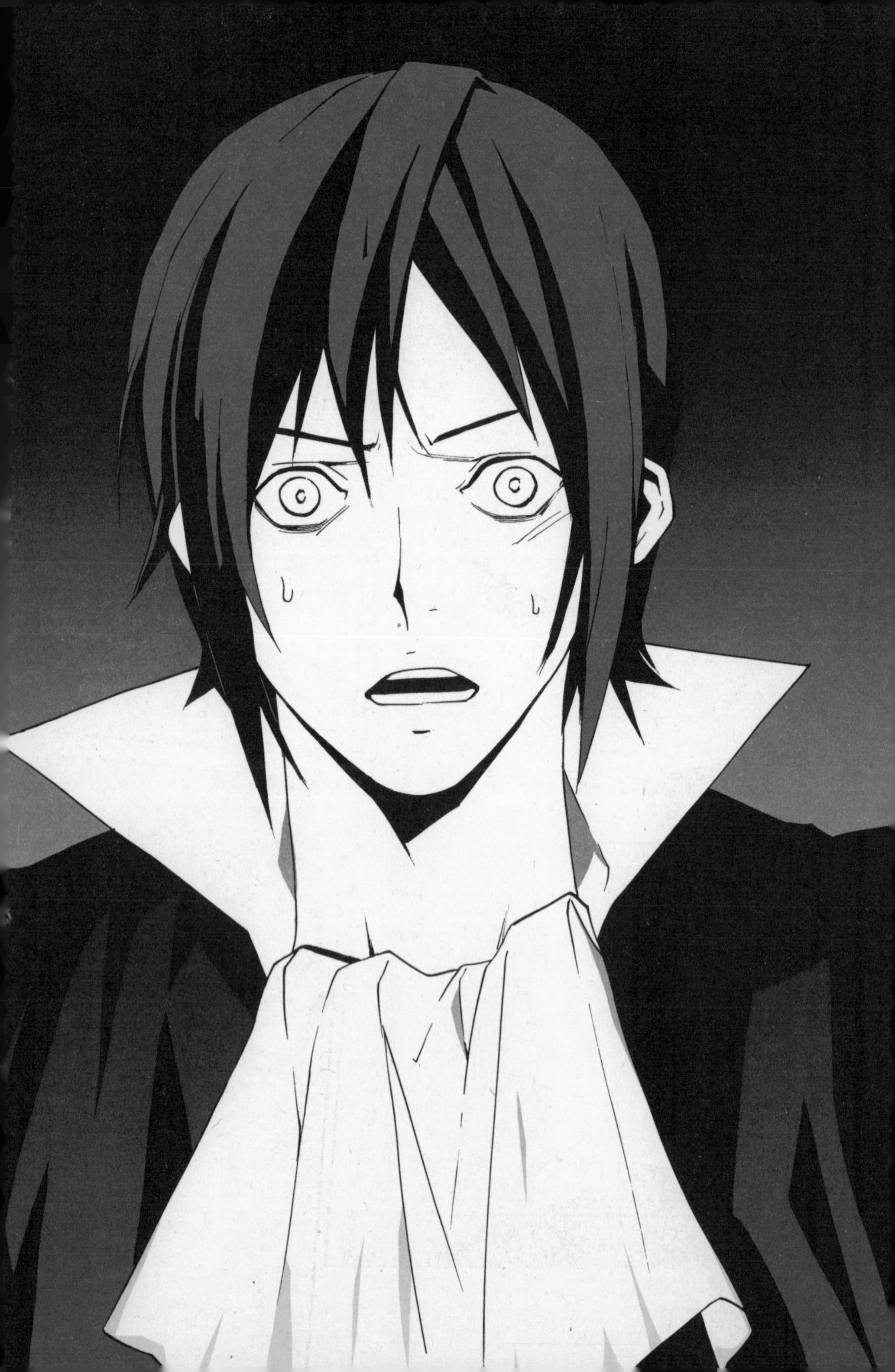

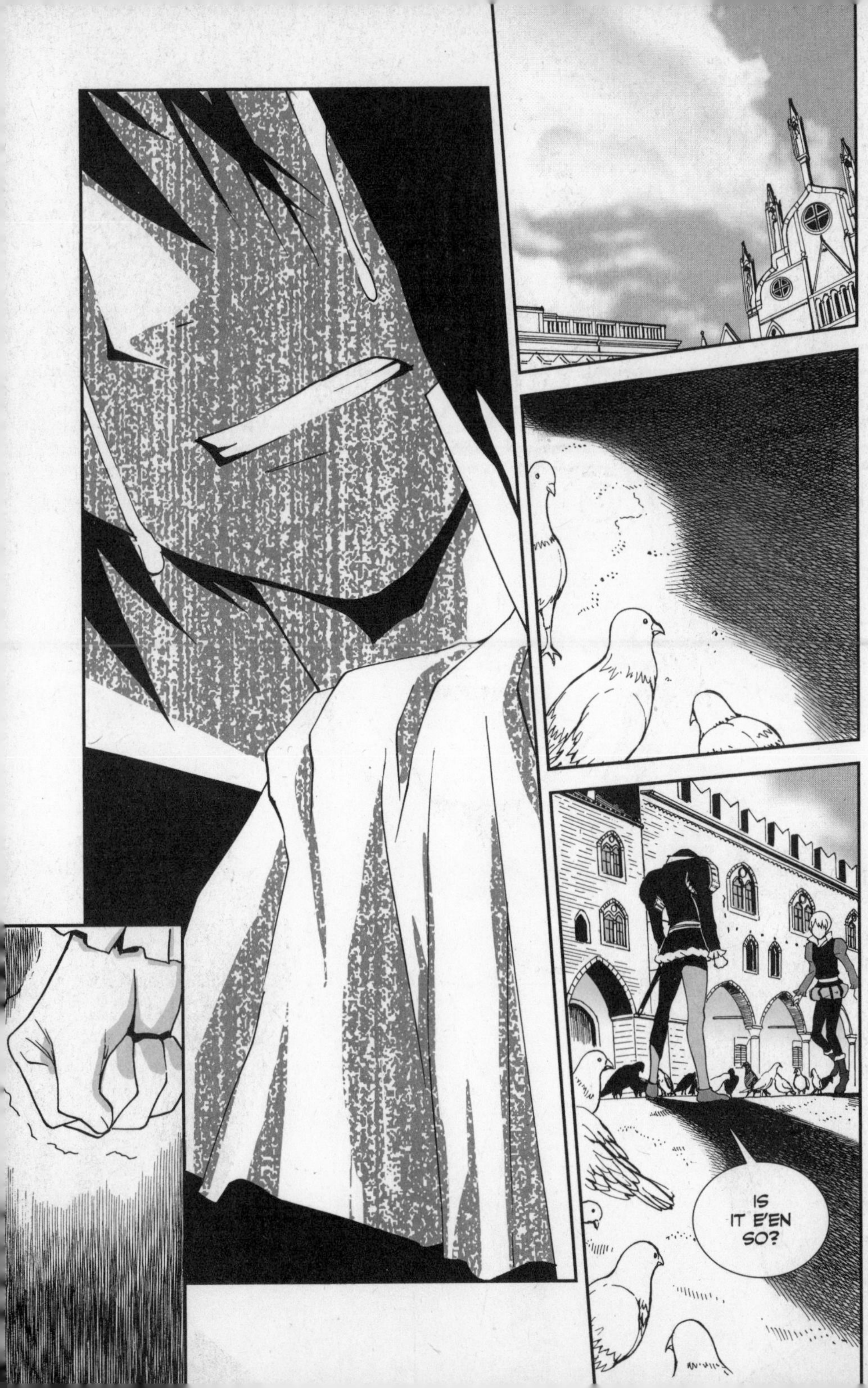
IS IT E'EN SO?

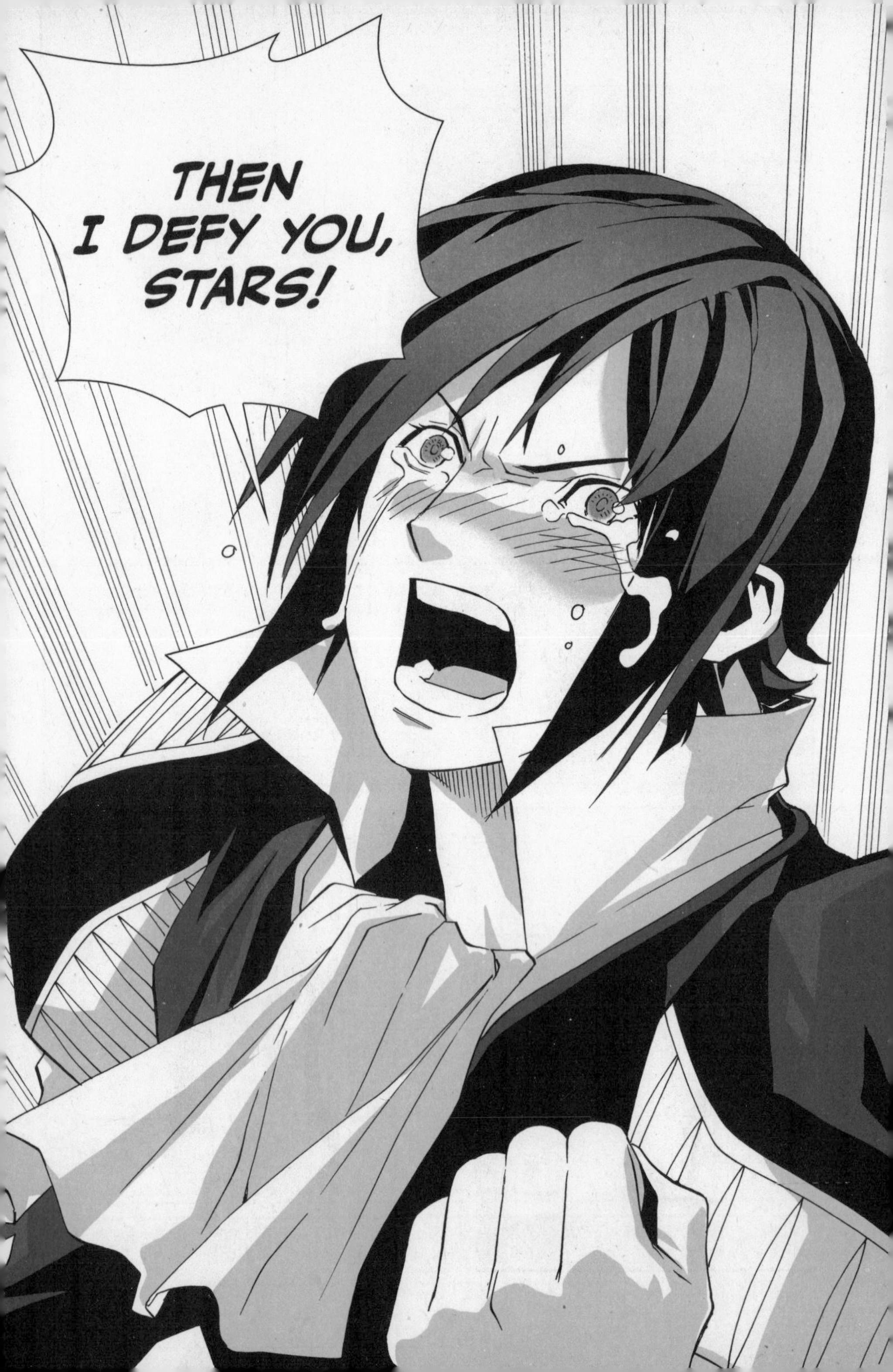
THEN I DEFY YOU, STARS!

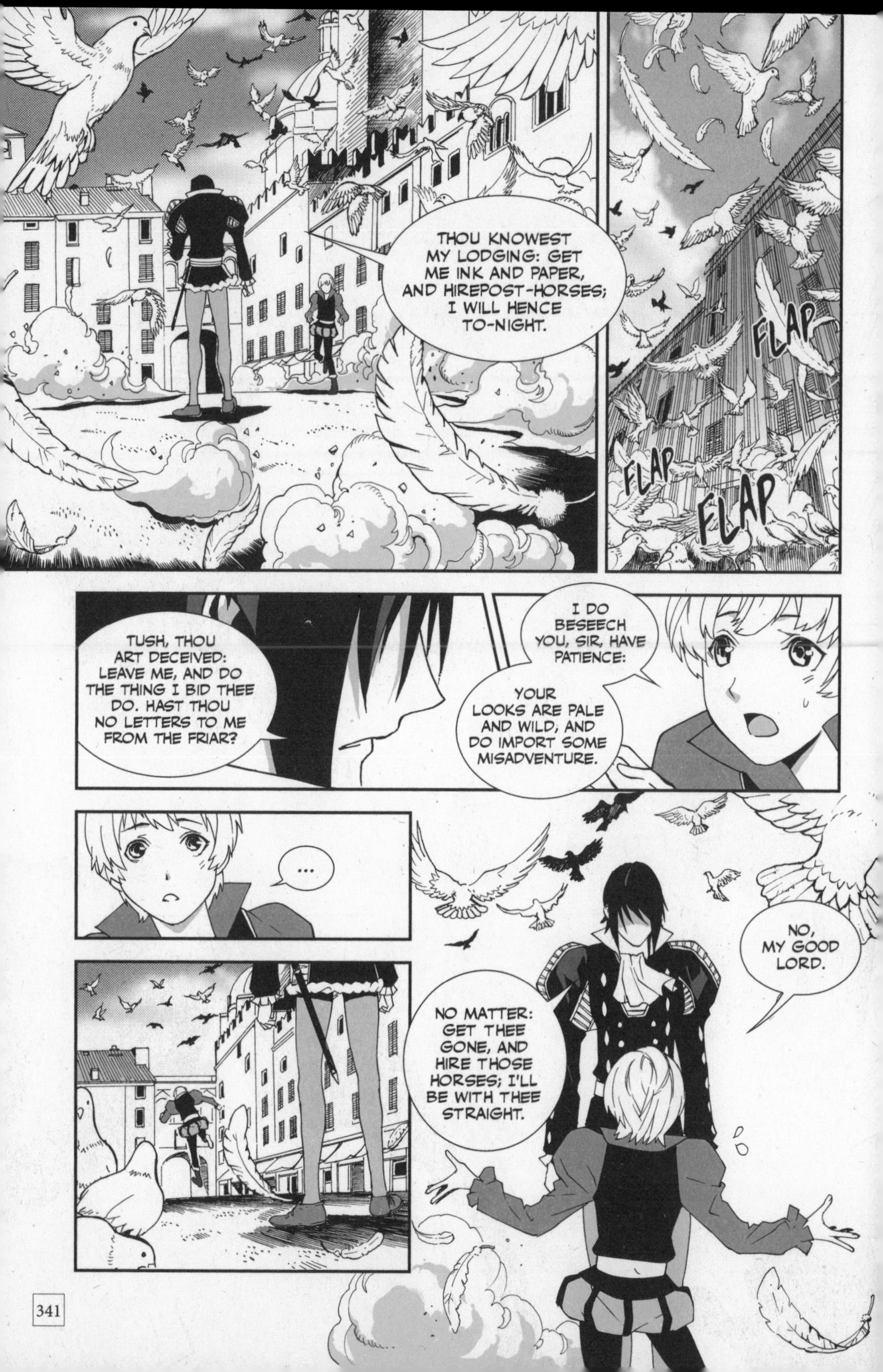
FLAP
FLAP
FLAP
THOU KNOWEST MY LODGING: GET ME INK AND PAPER, AND HIREPOST-HORSES; I WILL HENCE TO-NIGHT.
I DO BESEECH YOU, SIR, HAVE PATIENCE:
YOUR LOOKS ARE PALE AND WILD, AND DO IMPORT SOME MISADVENTURE.
TUSH, THOU ART DECEIVED: LEAVE ME, AND DO THE THING I BID THEE DO. HAST THOU NO LETTERS TO ME FROM THE FRIAR?
NO, MY GOOD LORD.
NO MATTER: GET THEE GONE, AND HIRE THOSE HORSES; I'LL BE WITH THEE STRAIGHT.
...

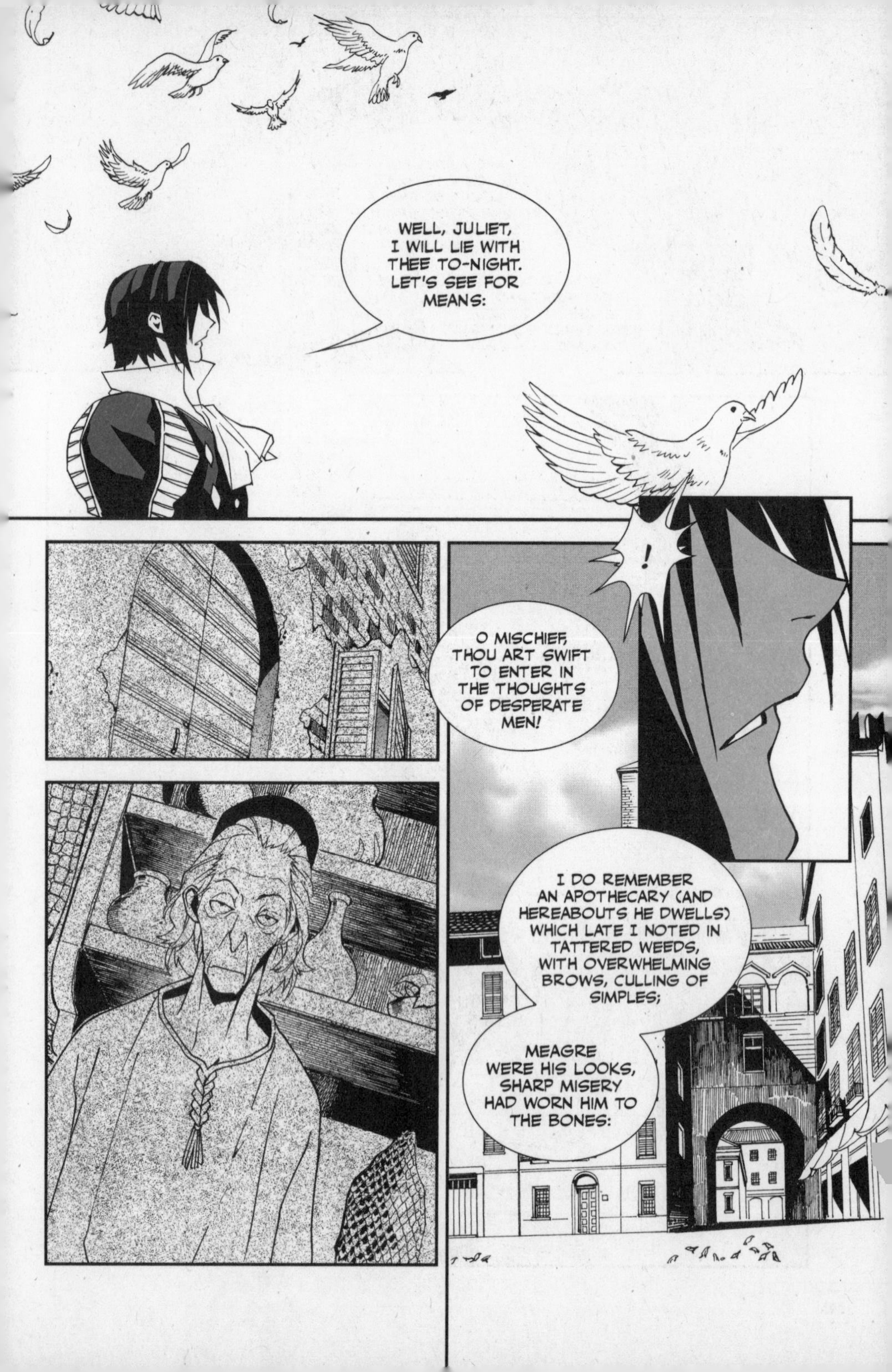
WELL, JULIET, I WILL LIE WITH THEE TO-NIGHT. LET'S SEE FOR MEANS:
!
O MISCHIEF, THOU ART SWIFT TO ENTER IN THE THOUGHTS OF DESPERATE MEN!
I DO REMEMBER AN APOTHECARY (AND HEREABOUTS HE DWELLS) WHICH LATE I NOTED IN TATTERED WEEDS, WITH OVERWHELMING BROWS, CULLING OF SIMPLES;
MEAGRE WERE HIS LOOKS, SHARP MISERY HAD WORN HIM TO THE BONES:

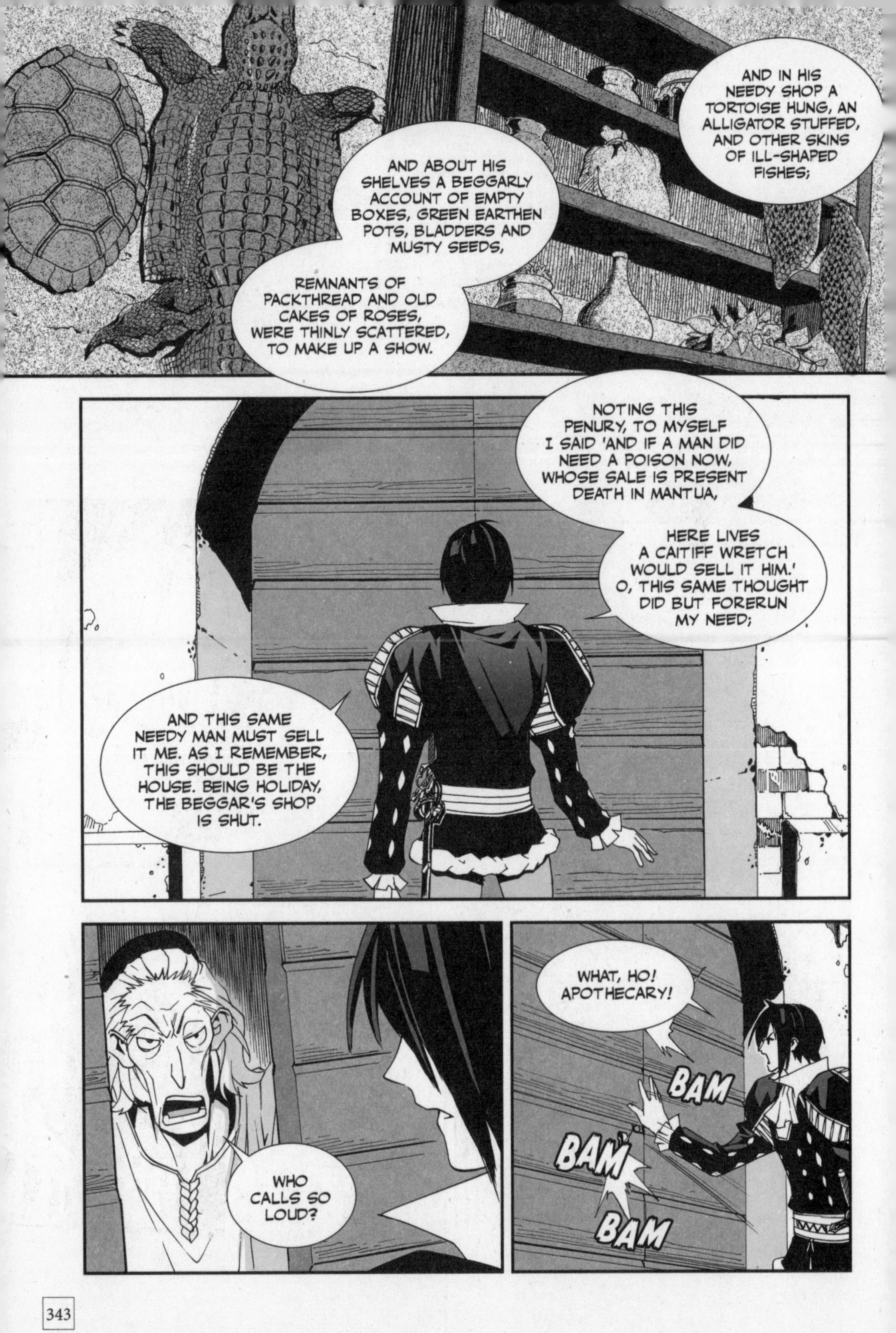
AND IN HIS NEEDY SHOP A TORTOISE HUNG, AN ALLIGATOR STUFFED, AND OTHER SKINS OF ILL-SHAPED FISHES;
AND ABOUT HIS SHELVES A BEGGARLY ACCOUNT OF EMPTY BOXES, GREEN EARTHEN POTS, BLADDERS AND MUSTY SEEDS,
REMNANTS OF PACKTHREAD AND OLD CAKES OF ROSES, WERE THINLY SCATTERED, TO MAKE UP A SHOW.
NOTING THIS PENURY, TO MYSELF I SAID 'AND IF A MAN DID NEED A POISON NOW, WHOSE SALE IS PRESENT DEATH IN MANTUA,
HERE LIVES A CAITIFF WRETCH WOULD SELL IT HIM.' O, THIS SAME THOUGHT DID BUT FORERUN MY NEED;
AND THIS SAME NEEDY MAN MUST SELL IT ME. AS I REMEMBER, THIS SHOULD BE THE HOUSE. BEING HOLIDAY, THE BEGGAR'S SHOP IS SHUT.
WHAT, HO! APOTHECARY!
BAM
BAM
BAM
WHO CALLS SO LOUD?

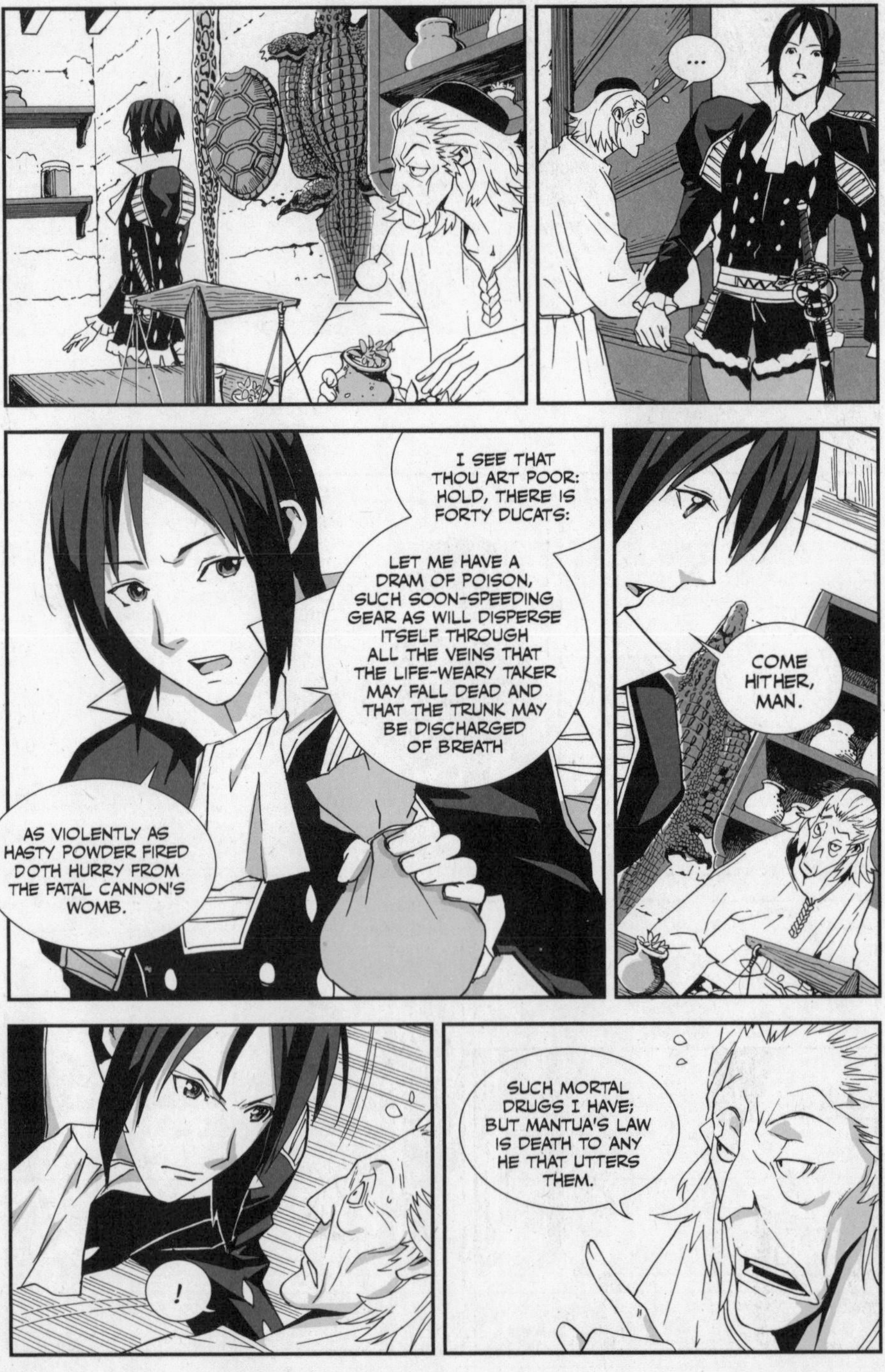
...
COME HITHER, MAN.
I SEE THAT THOU ART POOR: HOLD, THERE IS FORTY DUCATS:
LET ME HAVE A DRAM OF POISON, SUCH SOON-SPEEDING GEAR AS WILL DISPERSE ITSELF THROUGH ALL THE VEINS THAT THE LIFE-WEARY TAKER MAY FALL DEAD AND THAT THE TRUNK MAY BE DISCHARGED OF BREATH
AS VIOLENTLY AS HASTY POWDER FIRED DOTH HURRY FROM THE FATAL CANNON'S WOMB.
SUCH MORTAL DRUGS I HAVE; BUT MANTUA'S LAW IS DEATH TO ANY HE THAT UTTERS THEM.
!

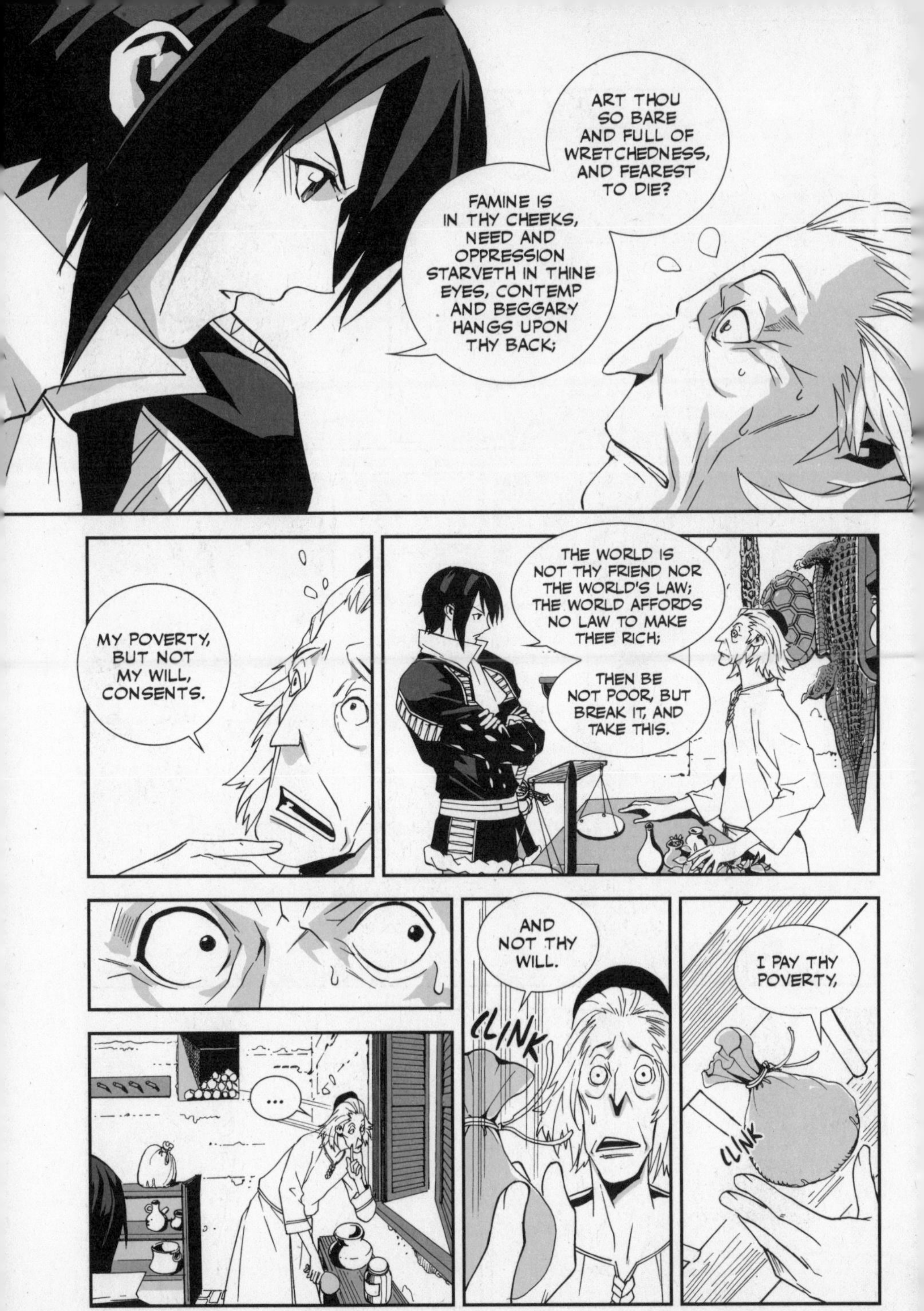
ART THOU SO BARE AND FULL OF WRETCHEDNESS, AND FEAREST TO DIE?
FAMINE IS IN THY CHEEKS, NEED AND OPPRESSION STARVETH IN THINE EYES, CONTEMP AND BEGGARY HANGS UPON THY BACK;
THE WORLD IS NOT THY FRIEND NOR THE WORLD'S LAW; THE WORLD AFFORDS NO LAW TO MAKE THEE RICH;
THEN BE NOT POOR, BUT BREAK IT, AND TAKE THIS.
MY POVERTY, BUT NOT MY WILL, CONSENTS.
I PAY THY POVERTY,
CLINK
AND NOT THY WILL.
CLINK
...

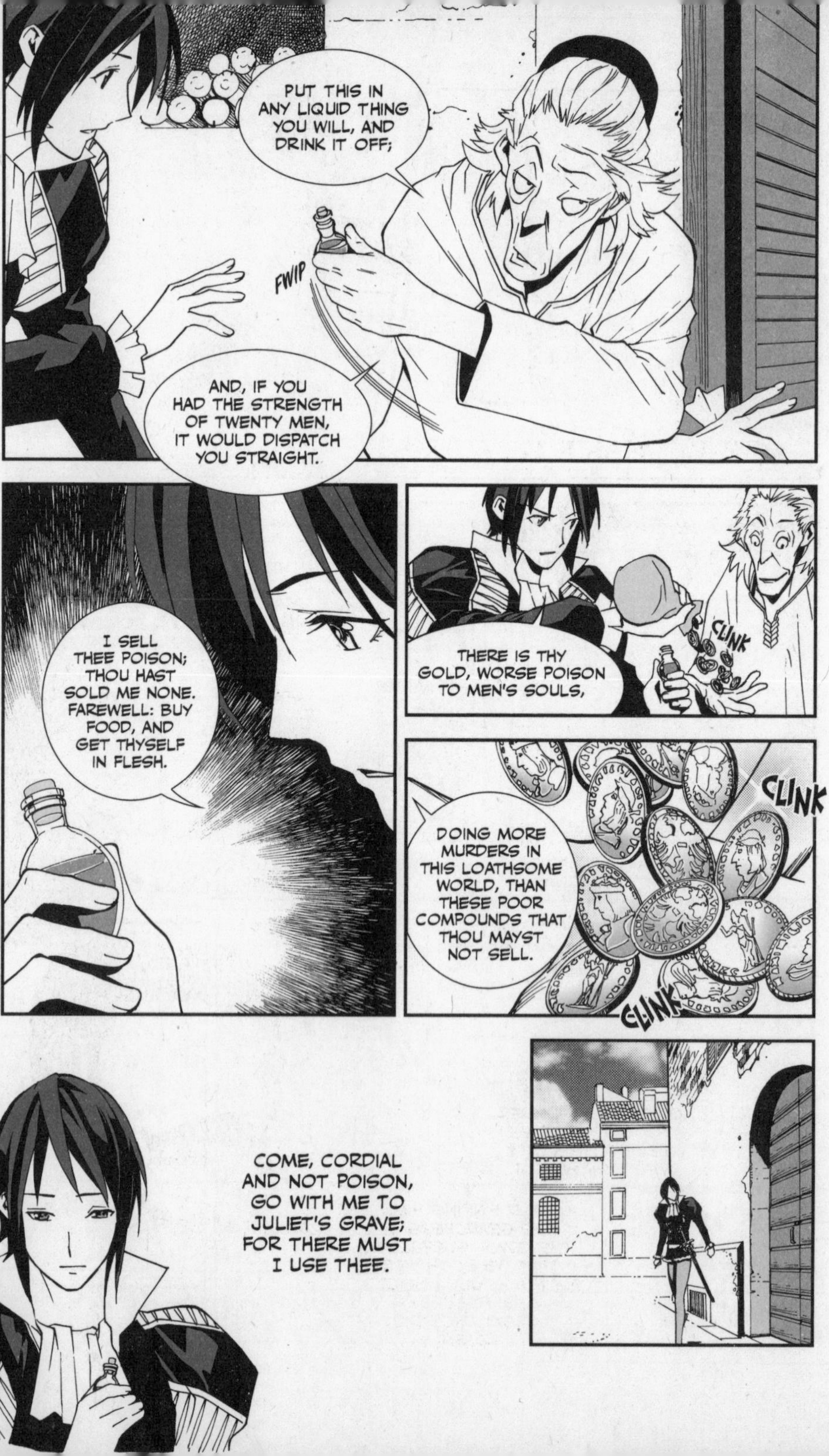
PUT THIS IN ANY LIQUID THING YOU WILL, AND DRINK IT OFF;
FWIP
AND, IF YOU HAD THE STRENGTH OF TWENTY MEN, IT WOULD DISPATCH YOU STRAIGHT.
THERE IS THY GOLD, WORSE POISON TO MEN'S SOULS,
CLINK
CLINK
DOING MORE MURDERS IN THIS LOATHSOME WORLD, THAN THESE POOR COMPOUNDS THAT THOU MAYST NOT SELL.
CLINK
I SELL THEE POISON; THOU HAST SOLD ME NONE. FAREWELL: BUY FOOD, AND GET THYSELF IN FLESH.
COME, CORDIAL AND NOT POISON, GO WITH ME TO JULIET'S GRAVE; FOR THERE MUST I USE THEE.

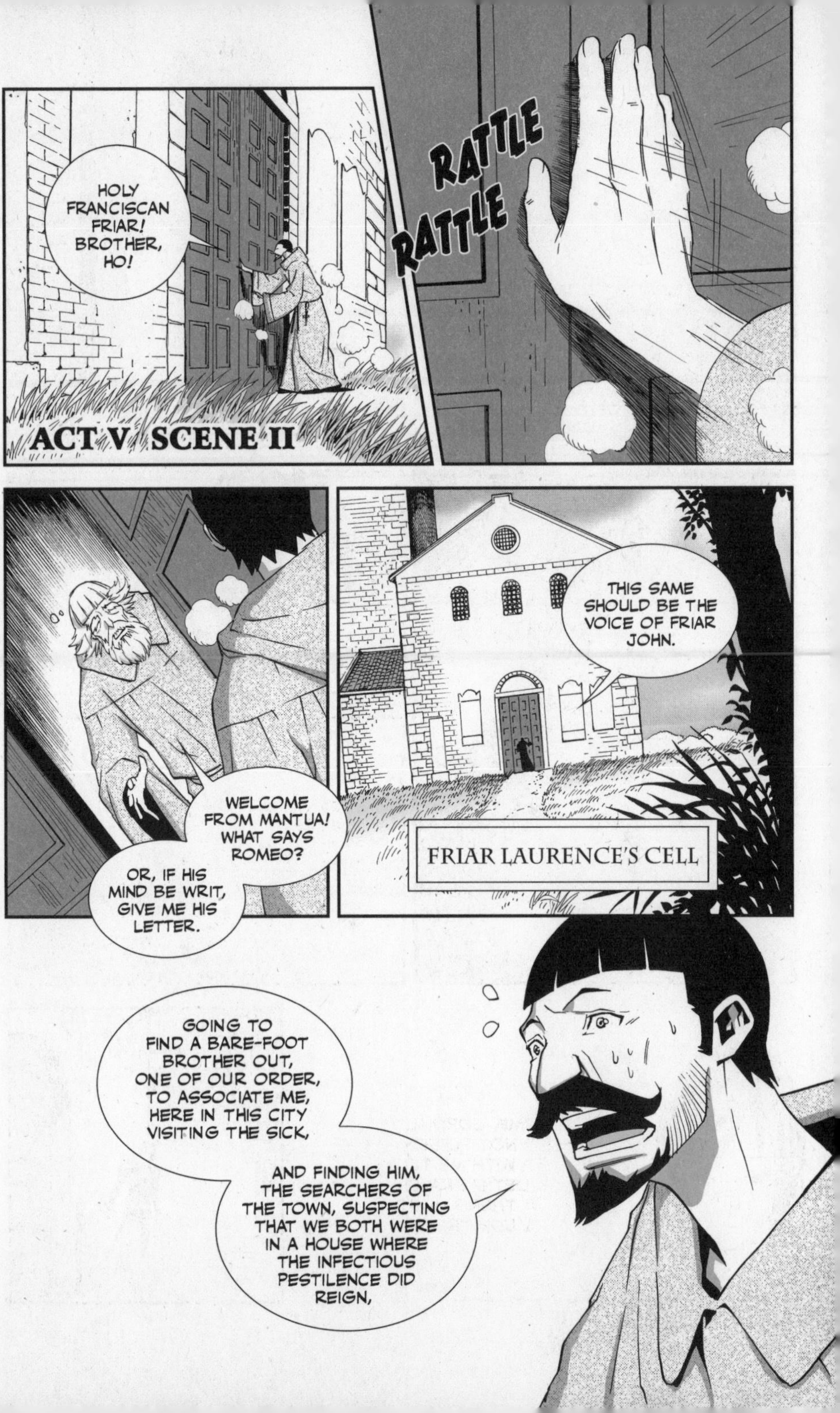
RATTLE RATTLE
HOLY FRANCISCAN FRIAR! BROTHER, HO!
ACT V SCENE II
THIS SAME SHOULD BE THE VOICE OF FRIAR JOHN.
FRIAR LAURENCE'S CELL
WELCOME FROM MANTUA! WHAT SAYS ROMEO?
OR, IF HIS MIND BE WRIT, GIVE ME HIS LETTER.
GOING TO FIND A BARE-FOOT BROTHER OUT, ONE OF OUR ORDER, TO ASSOCIATE ME, HERE IN THIS CITY VISITING THE SICK,
AND FINDING HIM, THE SEARCHERS OF THE TOWN, SUSPECTING THAT WE BOTH WERE IN A HOUSE WHERE THE INFECTIOUS PESTILENCE DID REIGN,

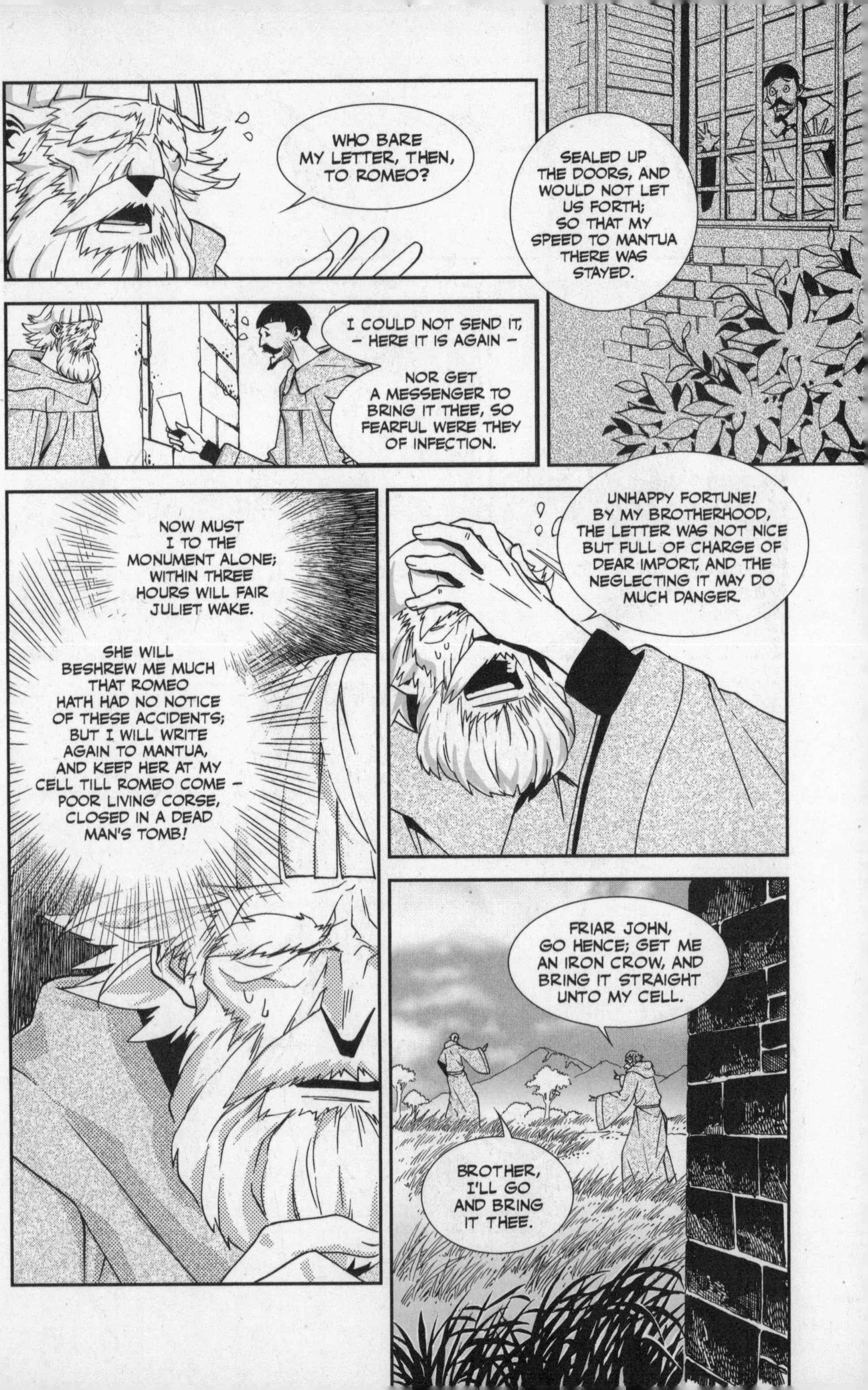
SEALED UP THE DOORS, AND WOULD NOT LET US FORTH; SO THAT MY SPEED TO MANTUA THERE WAS STAYED.
WHO BARE MY LETTER, THEN, TO ROMEO?
I COULD NOT SEND IT, – HERE IT IS AGAIN –
NOR GET A MESSENGER TO BRING IT THEE, SO FEARFUL WERE THEY OF INFECTION.
UNHAPPY FORTUNE! BY MY BROTHERHOOD, THE LETTER WAS NOT NICE BUT FULL OF CHARGE OF DEAR IMPORT, AND THE NEGLECTING IT MAY DO MUCH DANGER.
FRIAR JOHN, GO HENCE; GET ME AN IRON CROW, AND BRING IT STRAIGHT UNTO MY CELL.
BROTHER, I'LL GO AND BRING IT THEE.
NOW MUST I TO THE MONUMENT ALONE; WITHIN THREE HOURS WILL FAIR JULIET WAKE.
SHE WILL BESHREW ME MUCH THAT ROMEO HATH HAD NO NOTICE OF THESE ACCIDENTS; BUT I WILL WRITE AGAIN TO MANTUA, AND KEEP HER AT MY CELL TILL ROMEO COME – POOR LIVING CORSE, CLOSED IN A DEAD MAN'S TOMB!

CLOP

CLOP CLOP

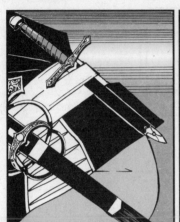

CLOP

CLOP

CLOP

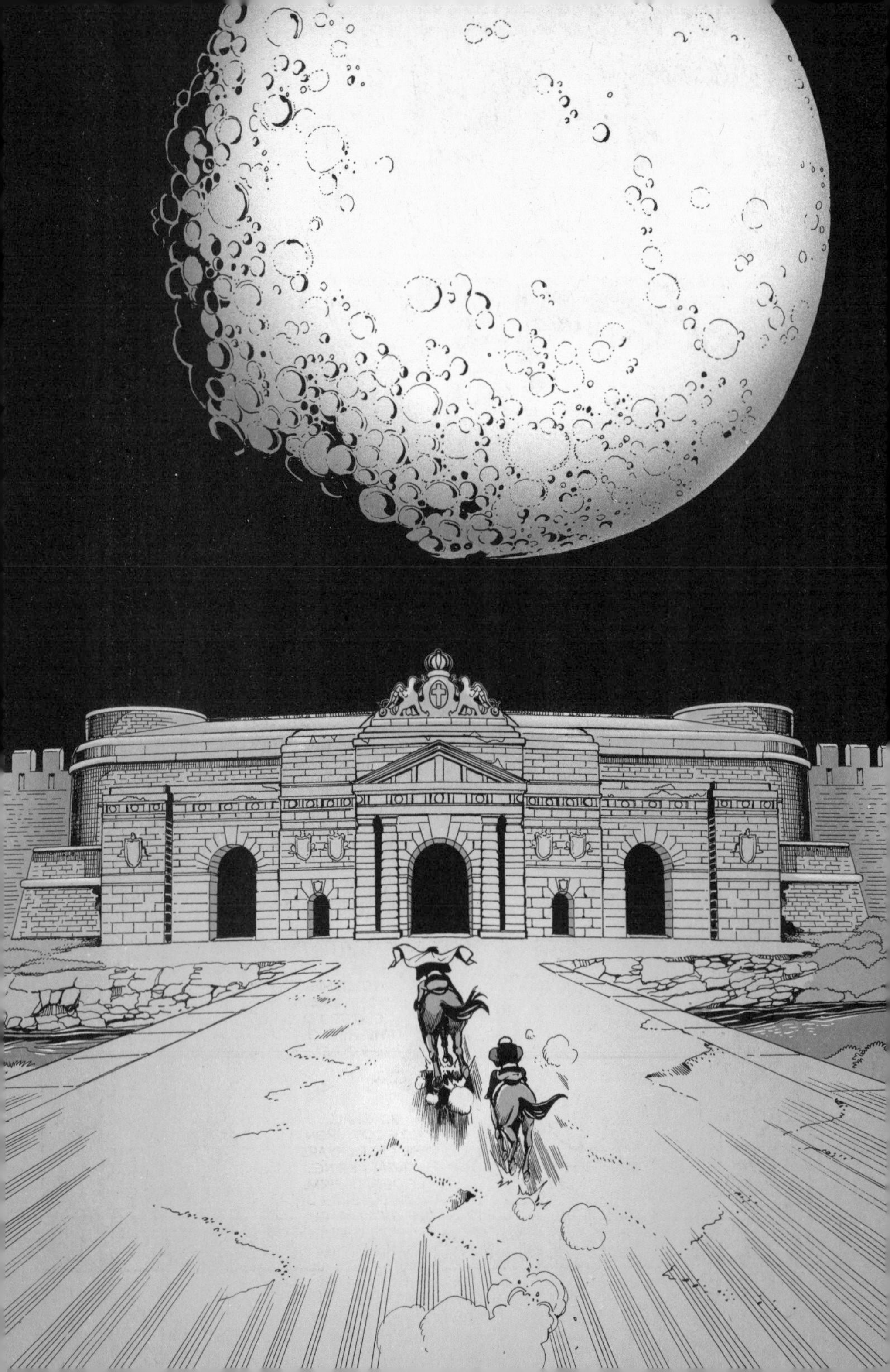

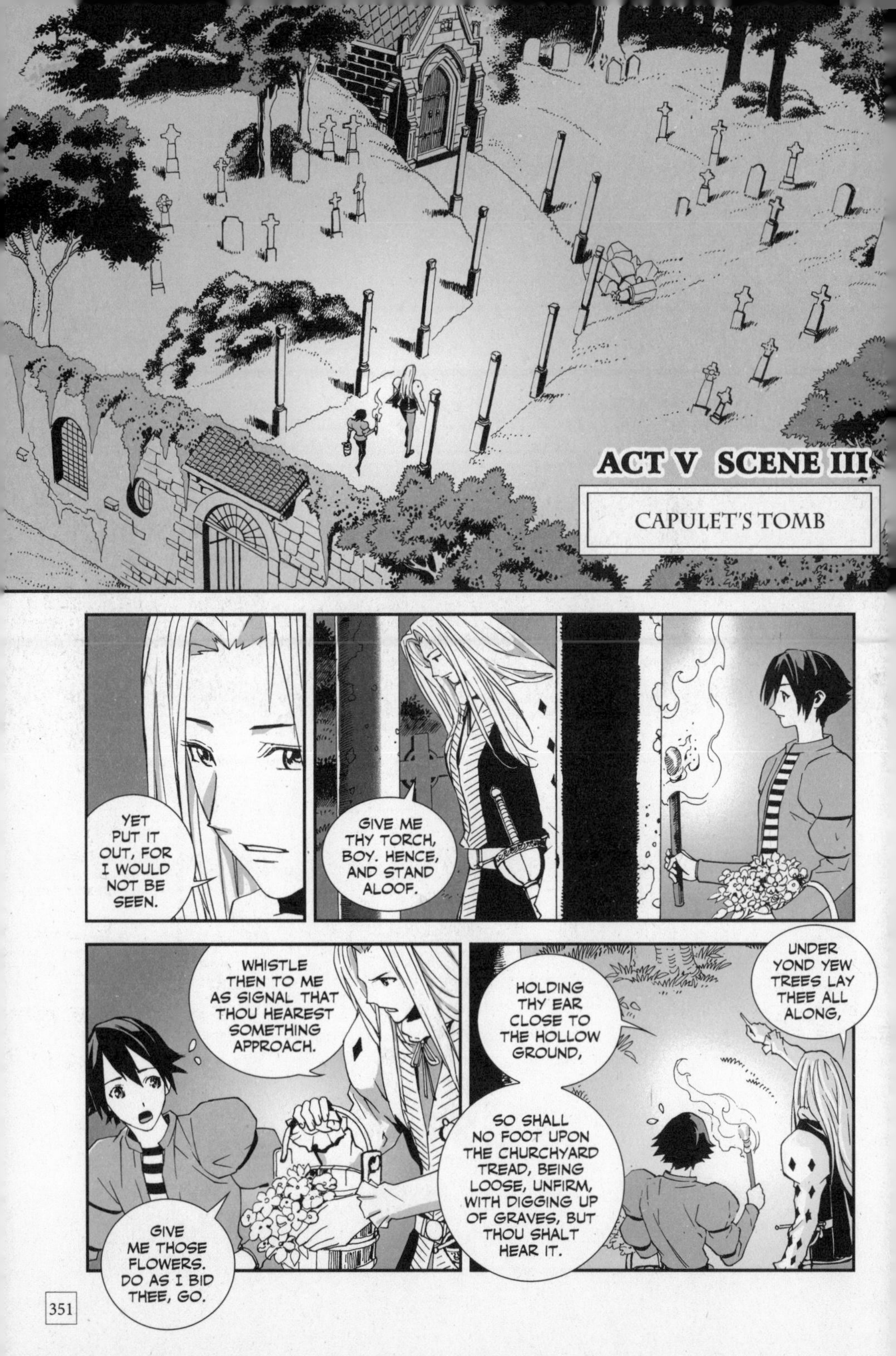
ACT V SCENE III
CAPULET'S TOMB
GIVE ME THY TORCH, BOY. HENCE, AND STAND ALOOF.
YET PUT IT OUT, FOR I WOULD NOT BE SEEN.
UNDER YOND YEW TREES LAY THEE ALL ALONG,
HOLDING THY EAR CLOSE TO THE HOLLOW GROUND,
SO SHALL NO FOOT UPON THE CHURCHYARD TREAD, BEING LOOSE, UNFIRM, WITH DIGGING UP OF GRAVES, BUT THOU SHALT HEAR IT.
WHISTLE THEN TO ME AS SIGNAL THAT THOU HEAREST SOMETHING APPROACH.
GIVE ME THOSE FLOWERS. DO AS I BID THEE, GO.

I AM ALMOST AFRAID TO STAND ALONE HERE IN THE CHURCHYARD, YET I WILL ADVENTURE.

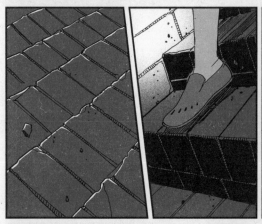

SWEET FLOWER, WITH FLOWERS THY BRIDAL BED I STREW –

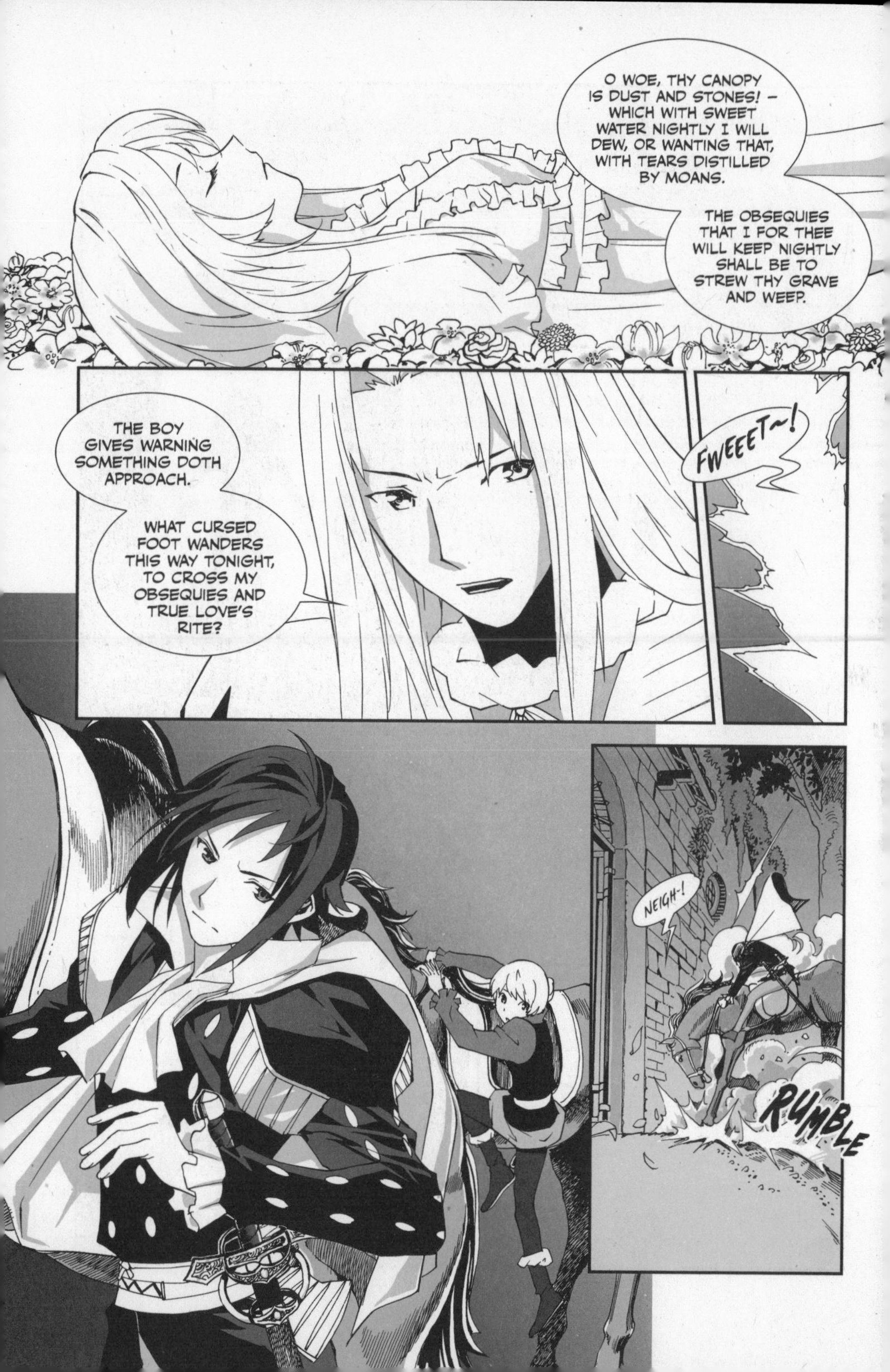
O WOE, THY CANOPY IS DUST AND STONES! – WHICH WITH SWEET WATER NIGHTLY I WILL DEW, OR WANTING THAT, WITH TEARS DISTILLED BY MOANS.
THE OBSEQUIES THAT I FOR THEE WILL KEEP NIGHTLY SHALL BE TO STREW THY GRAVE AND WEEP.
FWEEET~!
THE BOY GIVES WARNING SOMETHING DOTH APPROACH.
WHAT CURSED FOOT WANDERS THIS WAY TONIGHT, TO CROSS MY OBSEQUIES AND TRUE LOVE'S RITE?
NEIGH~!
RUMBLE

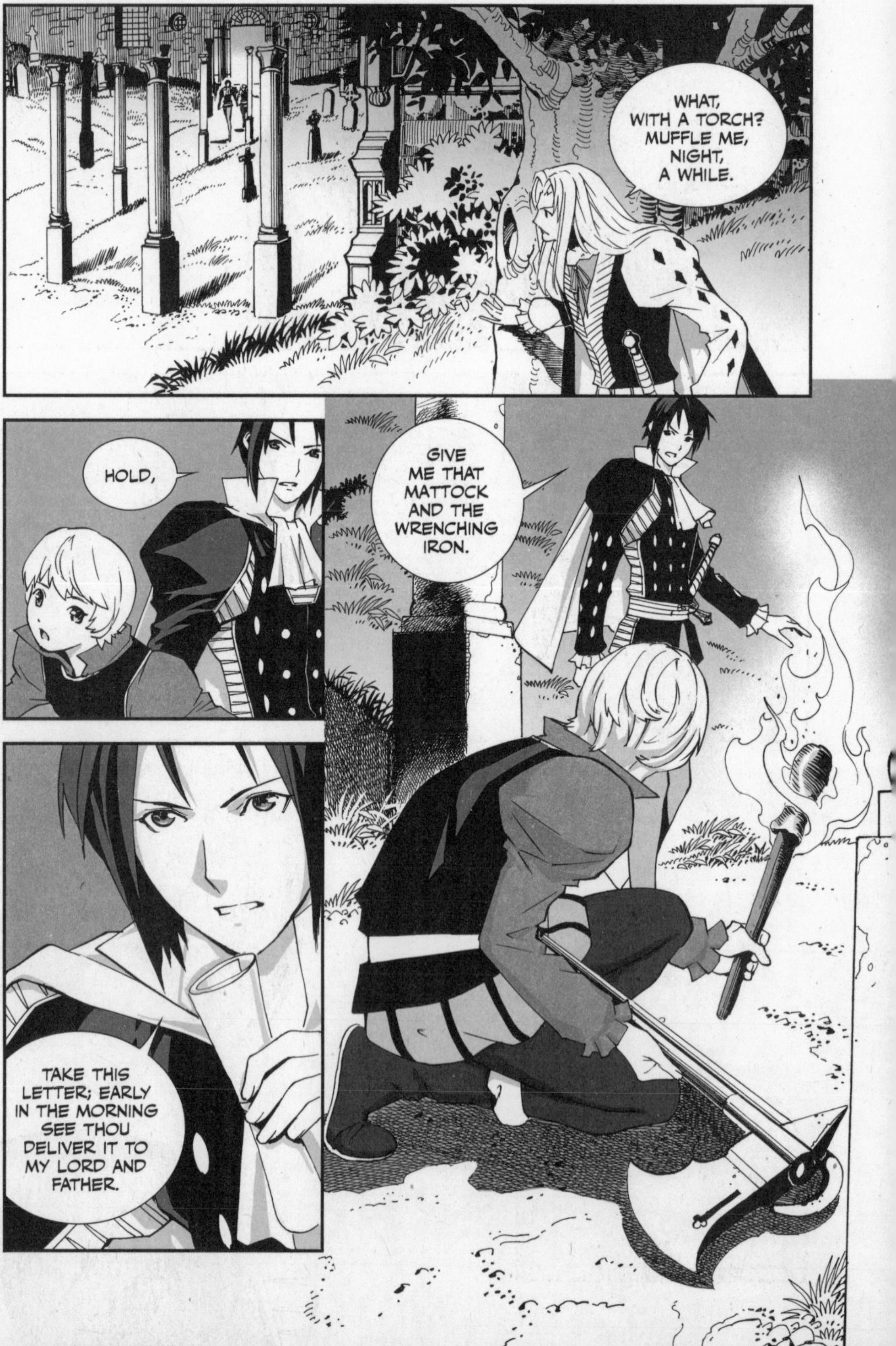
WHAT, WITH A TORCH? MUFFLE ME, NIGHT, A WHILE.
GIVE ME THAT MATTOCK AND THE WRENCHING IRON.
HOLD,
TAKE THIS LETTER; EARLY IN THE MORNING SEE THOU DELIVER IT TO MY LORD AND FATHER.

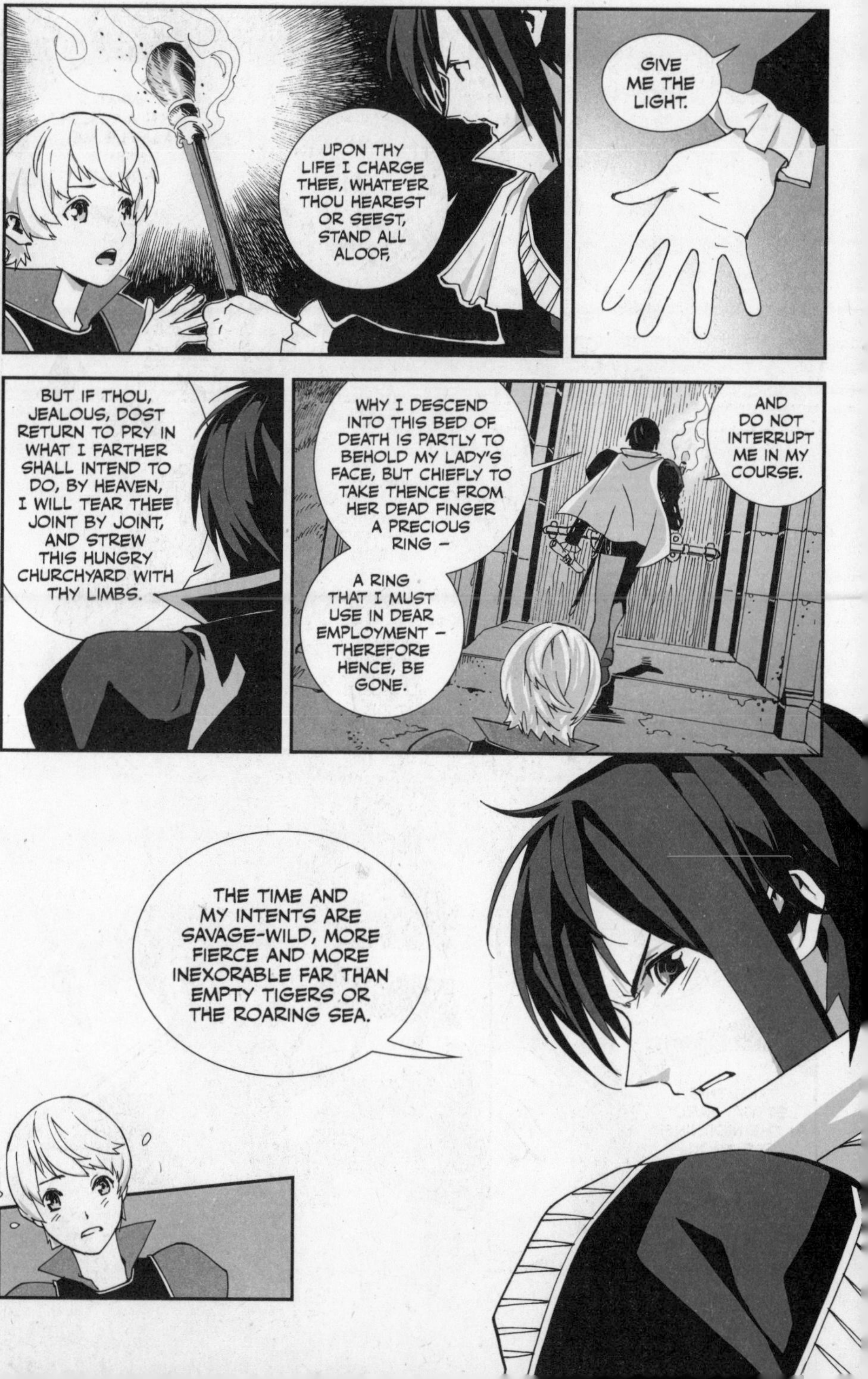
GIVE ME THE LIGHT.
UPON THY LIFE I CHARGE THEE, WHATE'ER THOU HEAREST OR SEEST, STAND ALL ALOOF,
AND DO NOT INTERRUPT ME IN MY COURSE.
WHY I DESCEND INTO THIS BED OF DEATH IS PARTLY TO BEHOLD MY LADY'S FACE, BUT CHIEFLY TO TAKE THENCE FROM HER DEAD FINGER A PRECIOUS RING –
A RING THAT I MUST USE IN DEAR EMPLOYMENT – THEREFORE HENCE, BE GONE.
BUT IF THOU, JEALOUS, DOST RETURN TO PRY IN WHAT I FARTHER SHALL INTEND TO DO, BY HEAVEN, I WILL TEAR THEE JOINT BY JOINT, AND STREW THIS HUNGRY CHURCHYARD WITH THY LIMBS.
THE TIME AND MY INTENTS ARE SAVAGE-WILD, MORE FIERCE AND MORE INEXORABLE FAR THAN EMPTY TIGERS OR THE ROARING SEA.

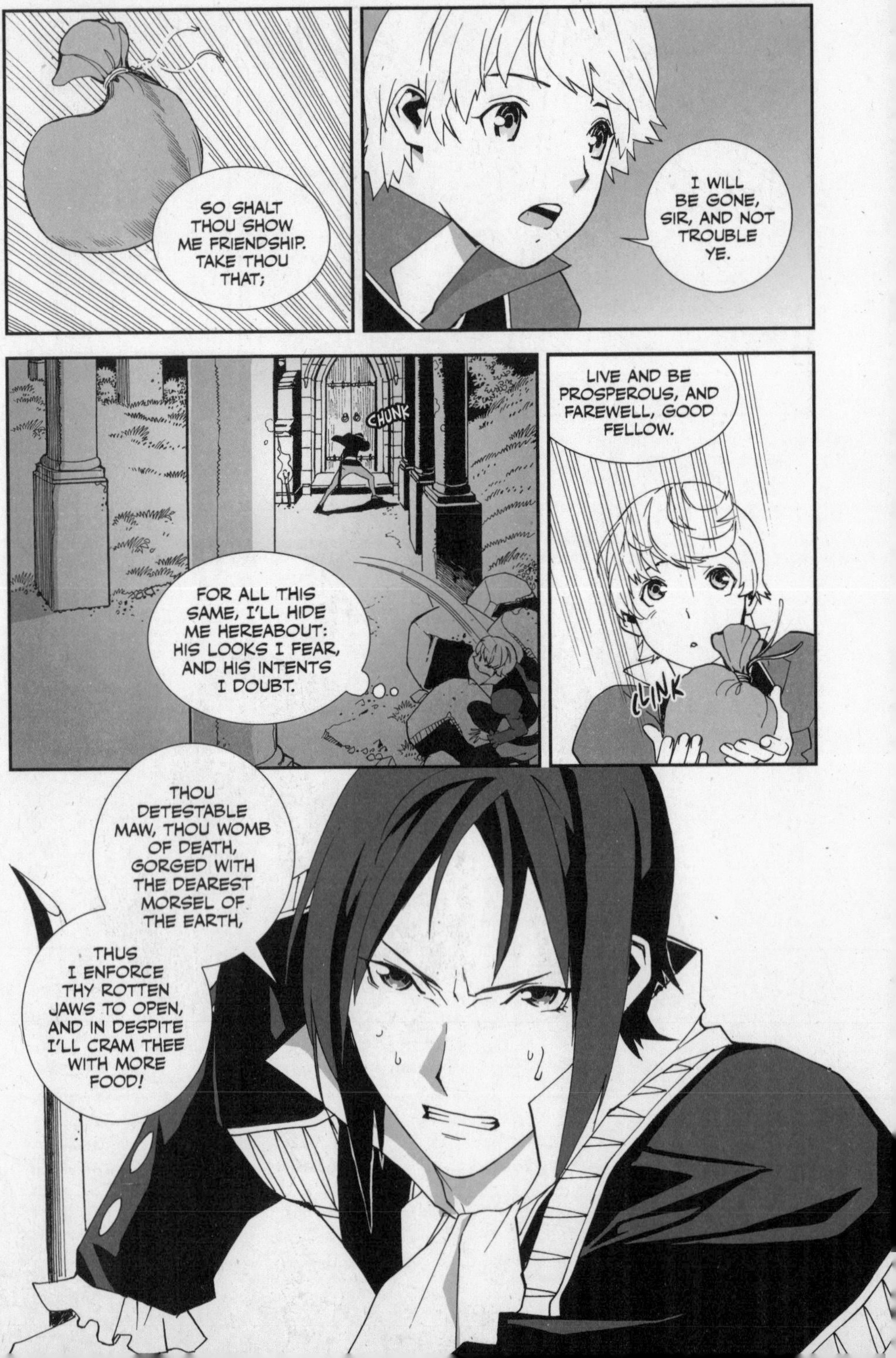
I WILL BE GONE, SIR, AND NOT TROUBLE YE.
SO SHALT THOU SHOW ME FRIENDSHIP. TAKE THOU THAT;
LIVE AND BE PROSPEROUS, AND FAREWELL, GOOD FELLOW.
CLINK
CHUNK
FOR ALL THIS SAME, I'LL HIDE ME HEREABOUT: HIS LOOKS I FEAR, AND HIS INTENTS I DOUBT.
THOU DETESTABLE MAW, THOU WOMB OF DEATH, GORGED WITH THE DEAREST MORSEL OF THE EARTH,
THUS I ENFORCE THY ROTTEN JAWS TO OPEN, AND IN DESPITE I'LL CRAM THEE WITH MORE FOOD!

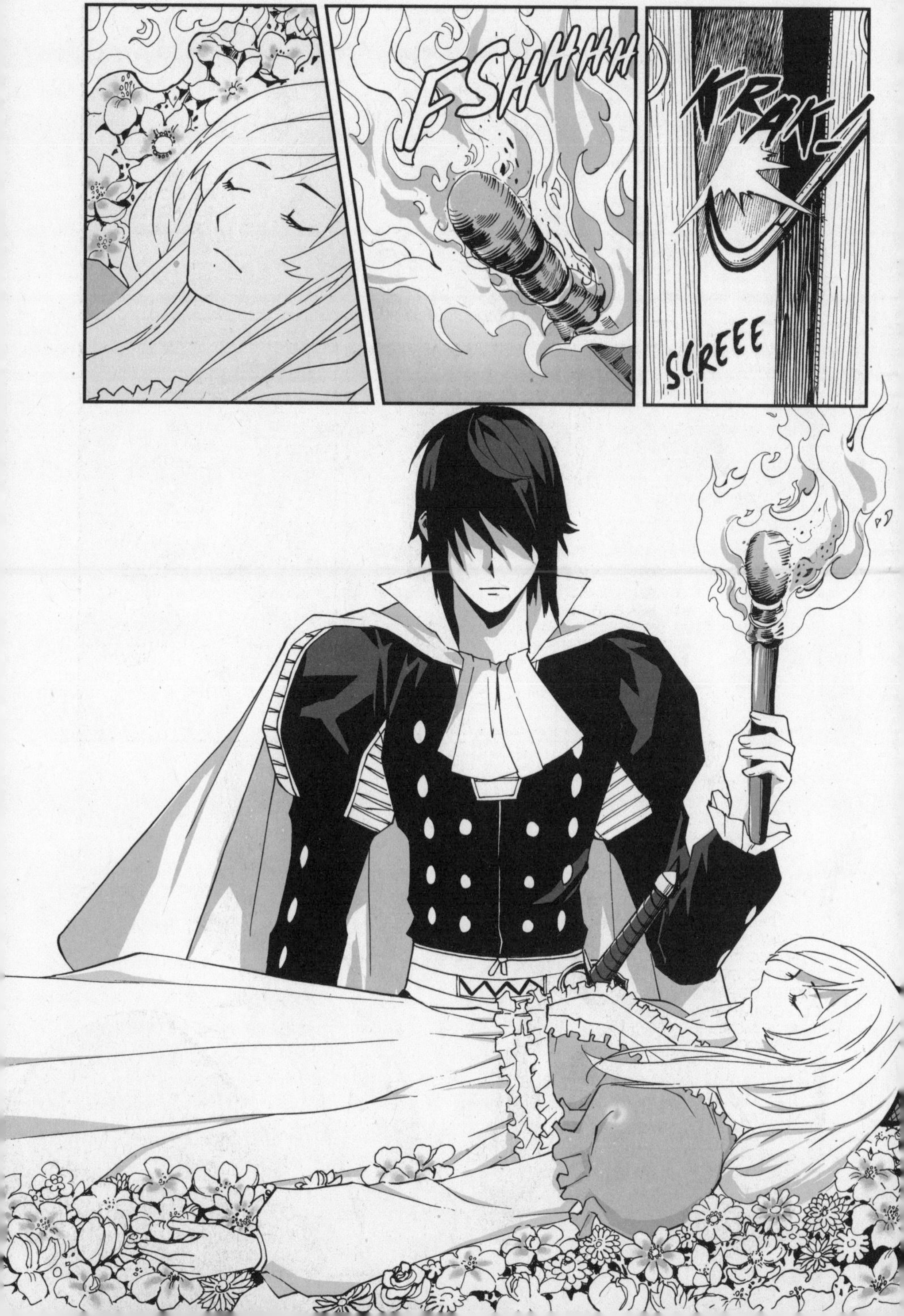
KRAK-!
SCREEE
FSHHHHH

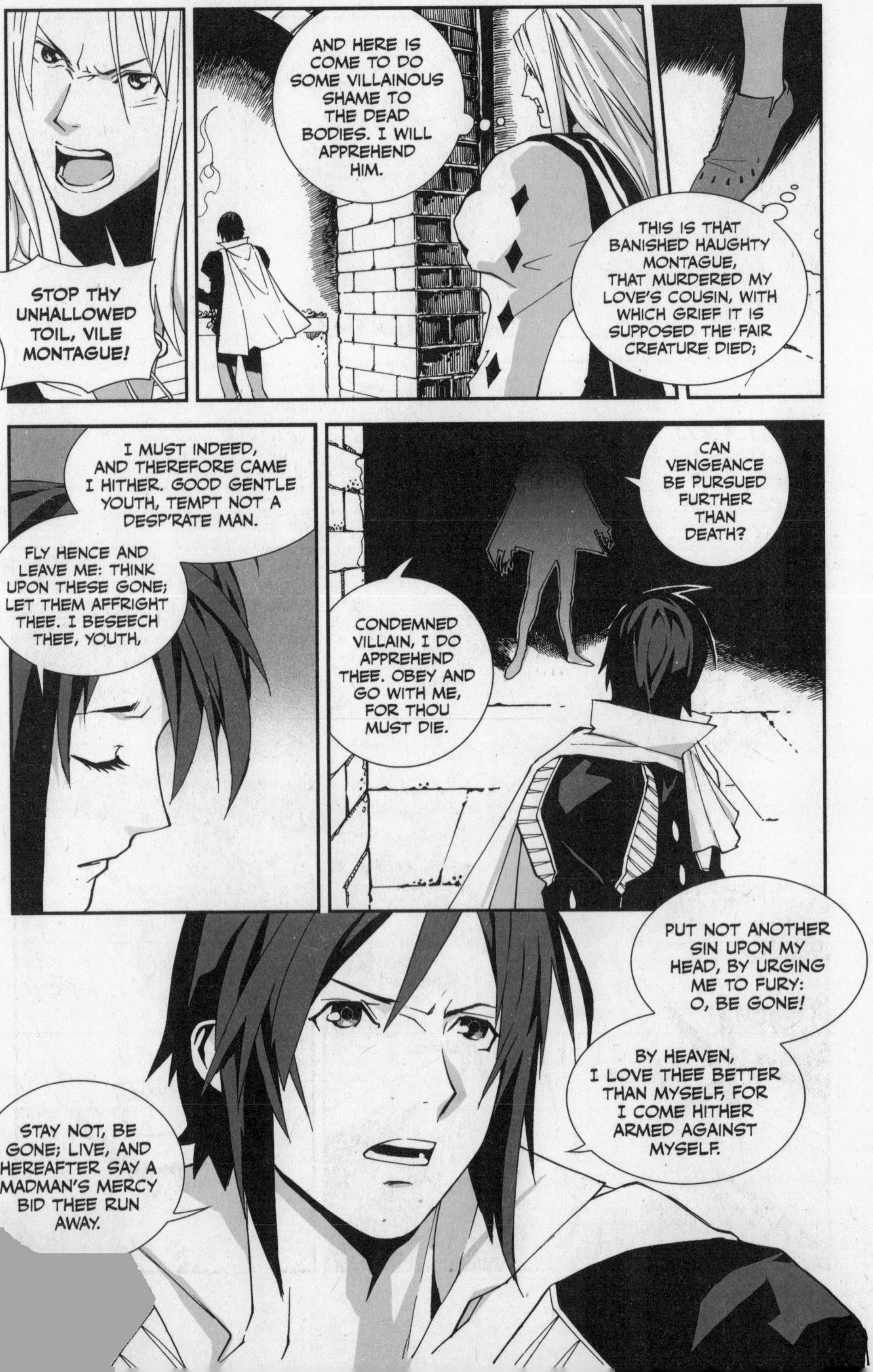

THIS IS THAT BANISHED HAUGHTY MONTAGUE, THAT MURDERED MY LOVE'S COUSIN, WITH WHICH GRIEF IT IS SUPPOSED THE FAIR CREATURE DIED;
AND HERE IS COME TO DO SOME VILLAINOUS SHAME TO THE DEAD BODIES. I WILL APPREHEND HIM.
STOP THY UNHALLOWED TOIL, VILE MONTAGUE!
CAN VENGEANCE BE PURSUED FURTHER THAN DEATH?
CONDEMNED VILLAIN, I DO APPREHEND THEE. OBEY AND GO WITH ME, FOR THOU MUST DIE.
I MUST INDEED, AND THEREFORE CAME I HITHER. GOOD GENTLE YOUTH, TEMPT NOT A DESP'RATE MAN.
FLY HENCE AND LEAVE ME: THINK UPON THESE GONE; LET THEM AFFRIGHT THEE. I BESEECH THEE, YOUTH,
PUT NOT ANOTHER SIN UPON MY HEAD, BY URGING ME TO FURY: O, BE GONE!
BY HEAVEN, I LOVE THEE BETTER THAN MYSELF, FOR I COME HITHER ARMED AGAINST MYSELF.
STAY NOT, BE GONE; LIVE, AND HEREAFTER SAY A MADMAN'S MERCY BID THEE RUN AWAY.

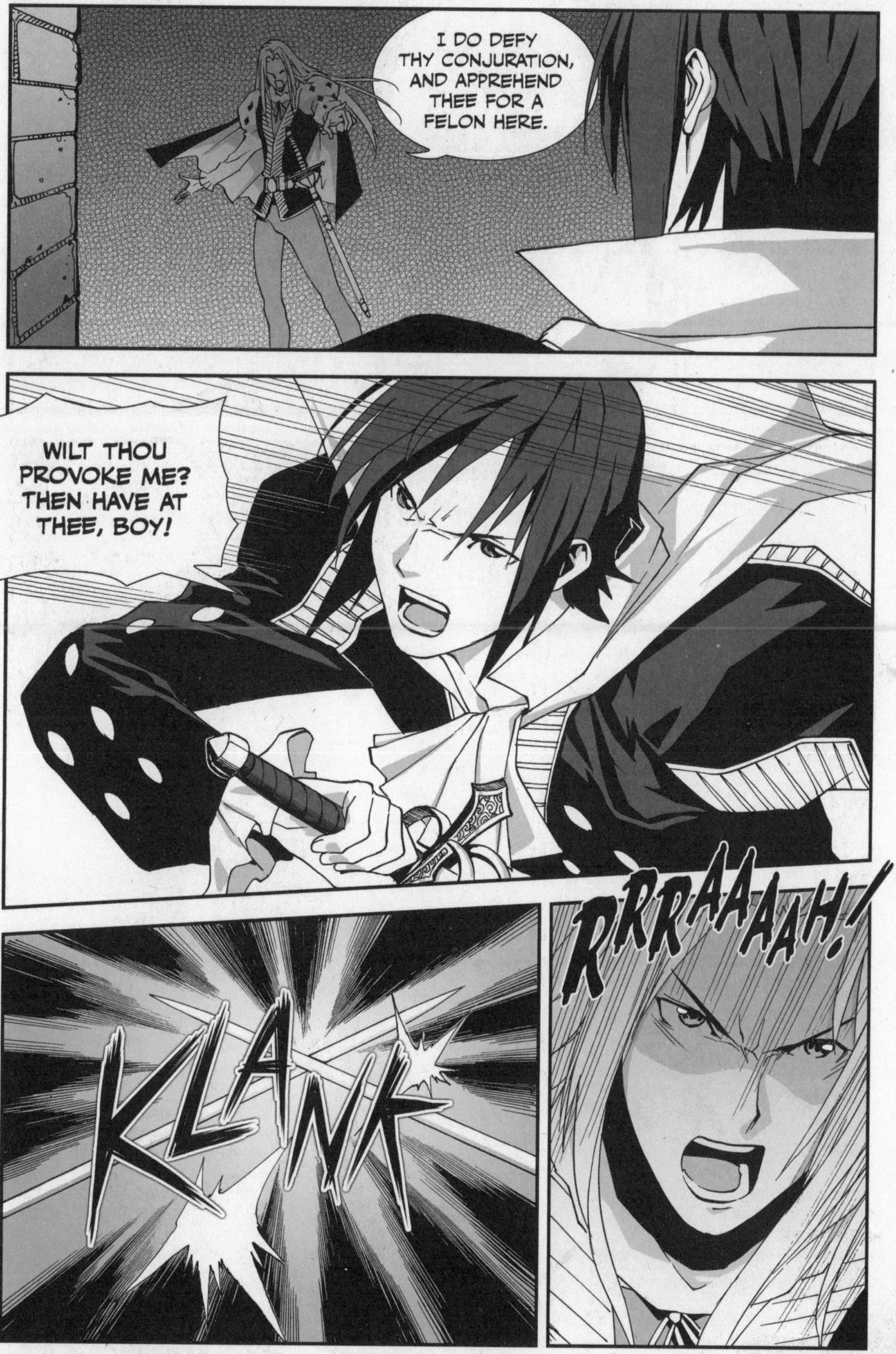
I DO DEFY THY CONJURATION, AND APPREHEND THEE FOR A FELON HERE.
WILT THOU PROVOKE ME? THEN HAVE AT THEE, BOY!
RRRAAAAAH!
KLANK

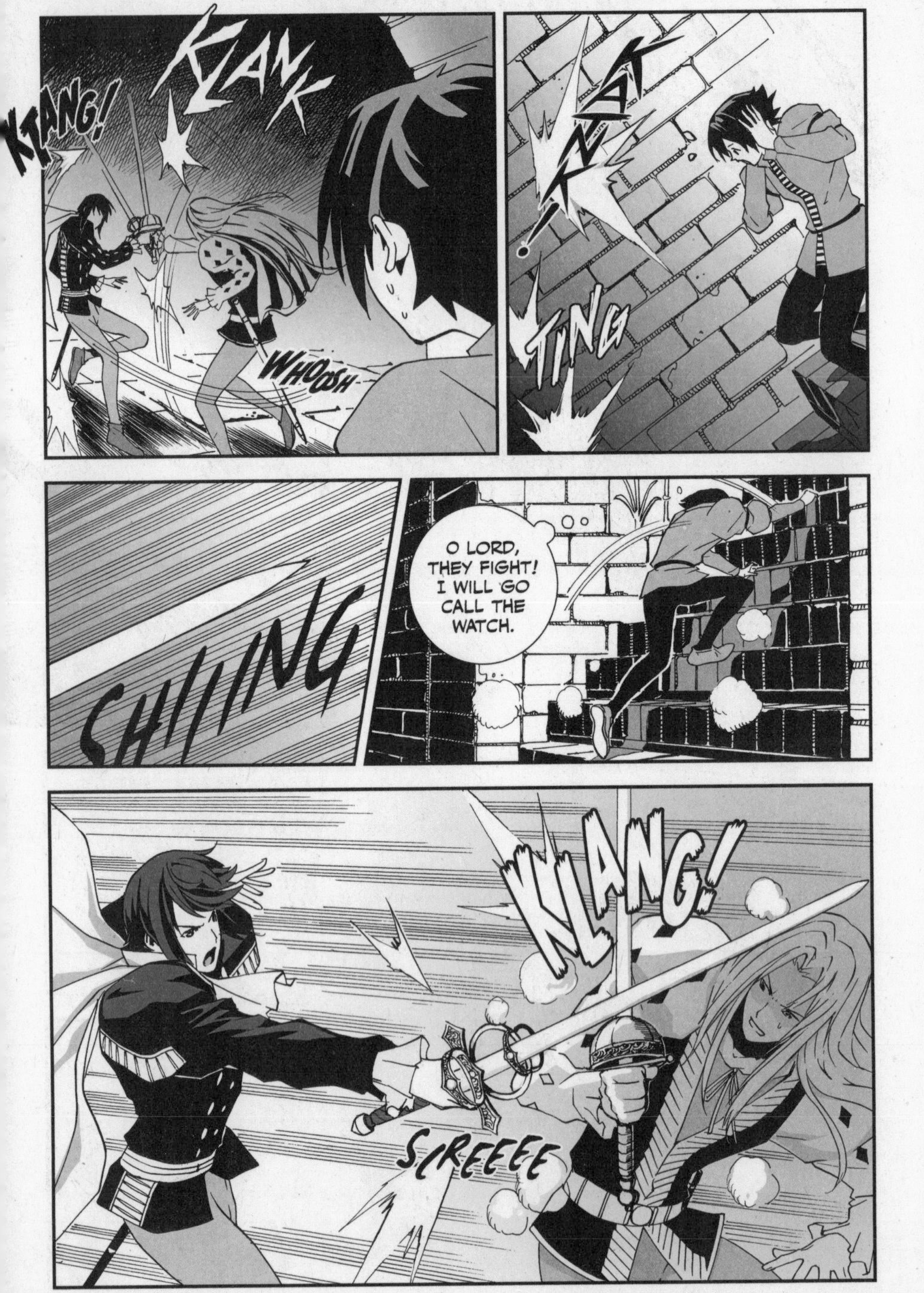
SNAK
TING
KLANK
KTANG!
WHOOSH
O LORD, THEY FIGHT! I WILL GO CALL THE WATCH.
SHIIIING
KLANG!
SCREEEE

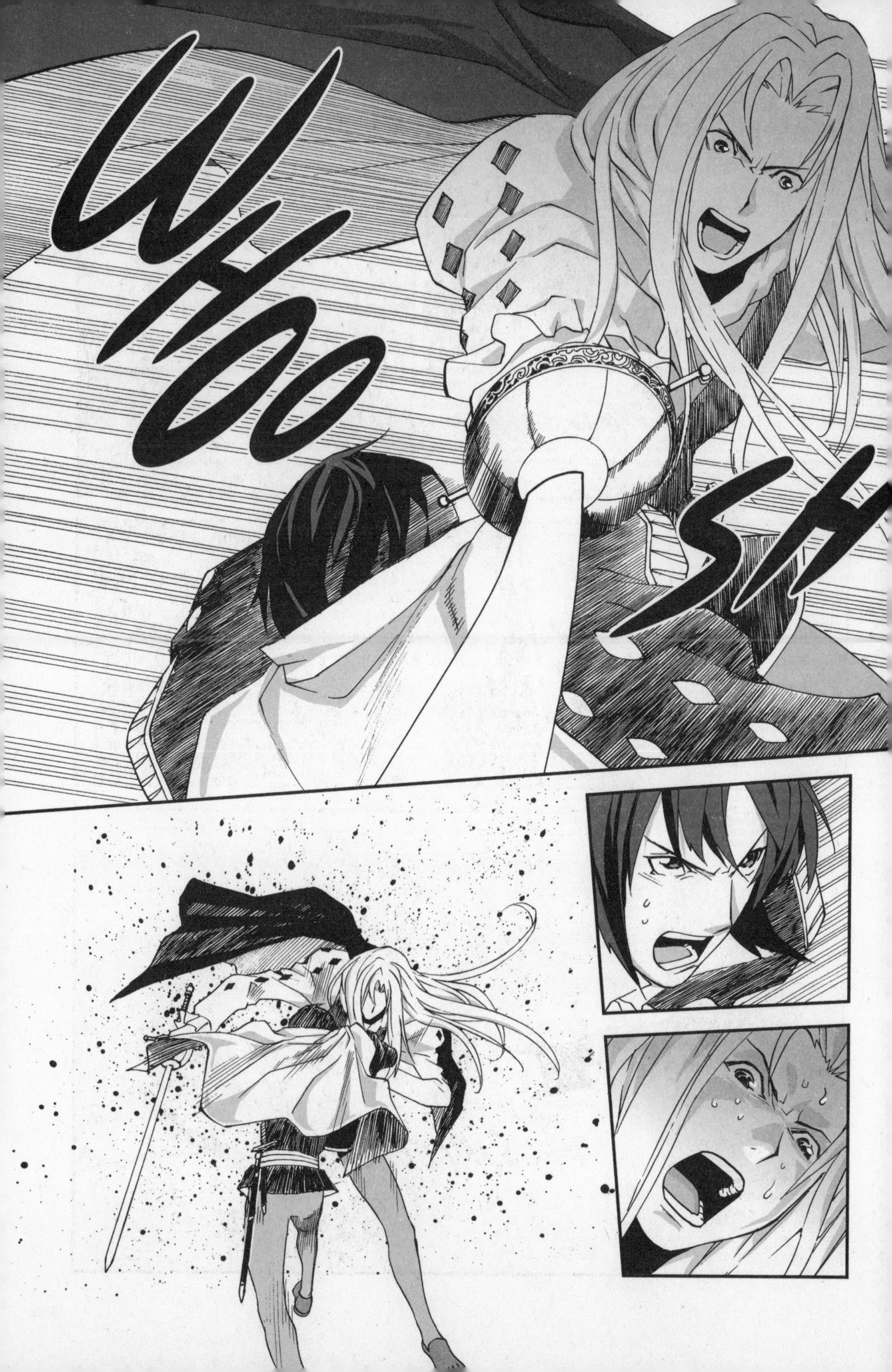
WHOOSH

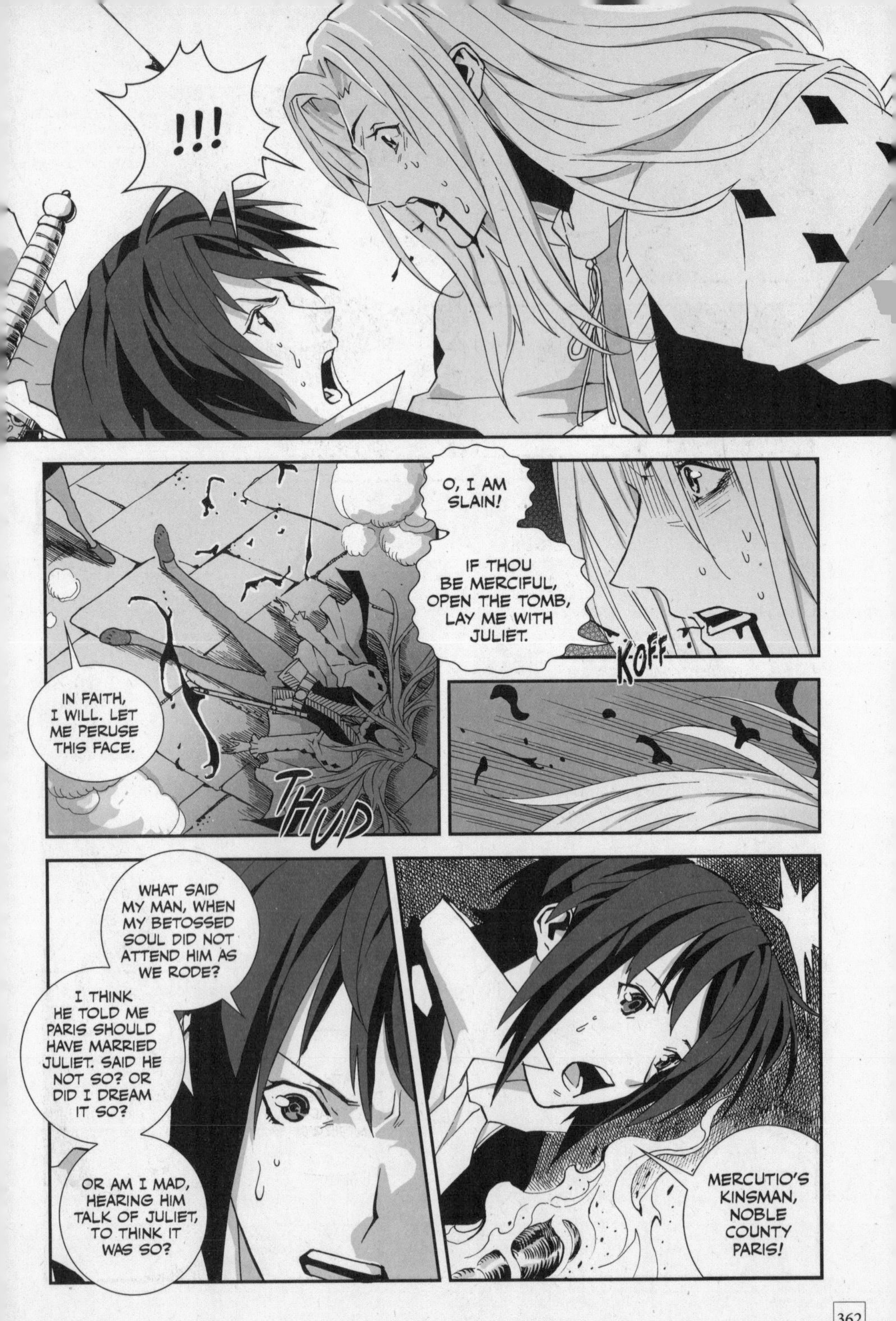
!!!
O, I AM SLAIN!
IF THOU BE MERCIFUL, OPEN THE TOMB, LAY ME WITH JULIET.
K-OFF
IN FAITH, I WILL. LET ME PERUSE THIS FACE.
THUD
MERCUTIO'S KINSMAN, NOBLE COUNTY PARIS!
WHAT SAID MY MAN, WHEN MY BETOSSED SOUL DID NOT ATTEND HIM AS WE RODE?
I THINK HE TOLD ME PARIS SHOULD HAVE MARRIED JULIET. SAID HE NOT SO? OR DID I DREAM IT SO?
OR AM I MAD, HEARING HIM TALK OF JULIET, TO THINK IT WAS SO?

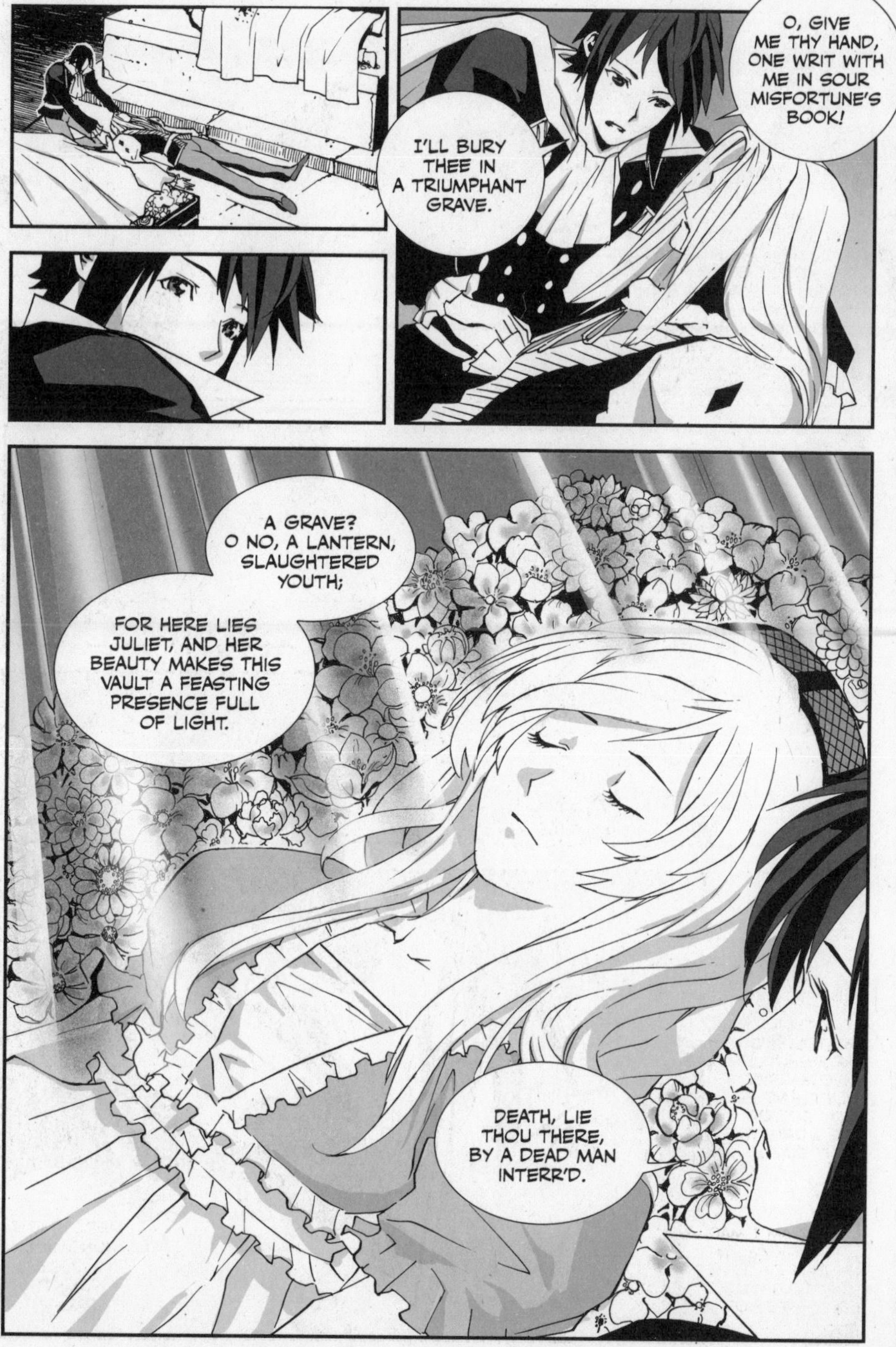
O, GIVE ME THY HAND, ONE WRIT WITH ME IN SOUR MISFORTUNE'S BOOK!
I'LL BURY THEE IN A TRIUMPHANT GRAVE.
A GRAVE? O NO, A LANTERN, SLAUGHTERED YOUTH;
FOR HERE LIES JULIET, AND HER BEAUTY MAKES THIS VAULT A FEASTING PRESENCE FULL OF LIGHT.
DEATH, LIE THOU THERE, BY A DEAD MAN INTERR'D.

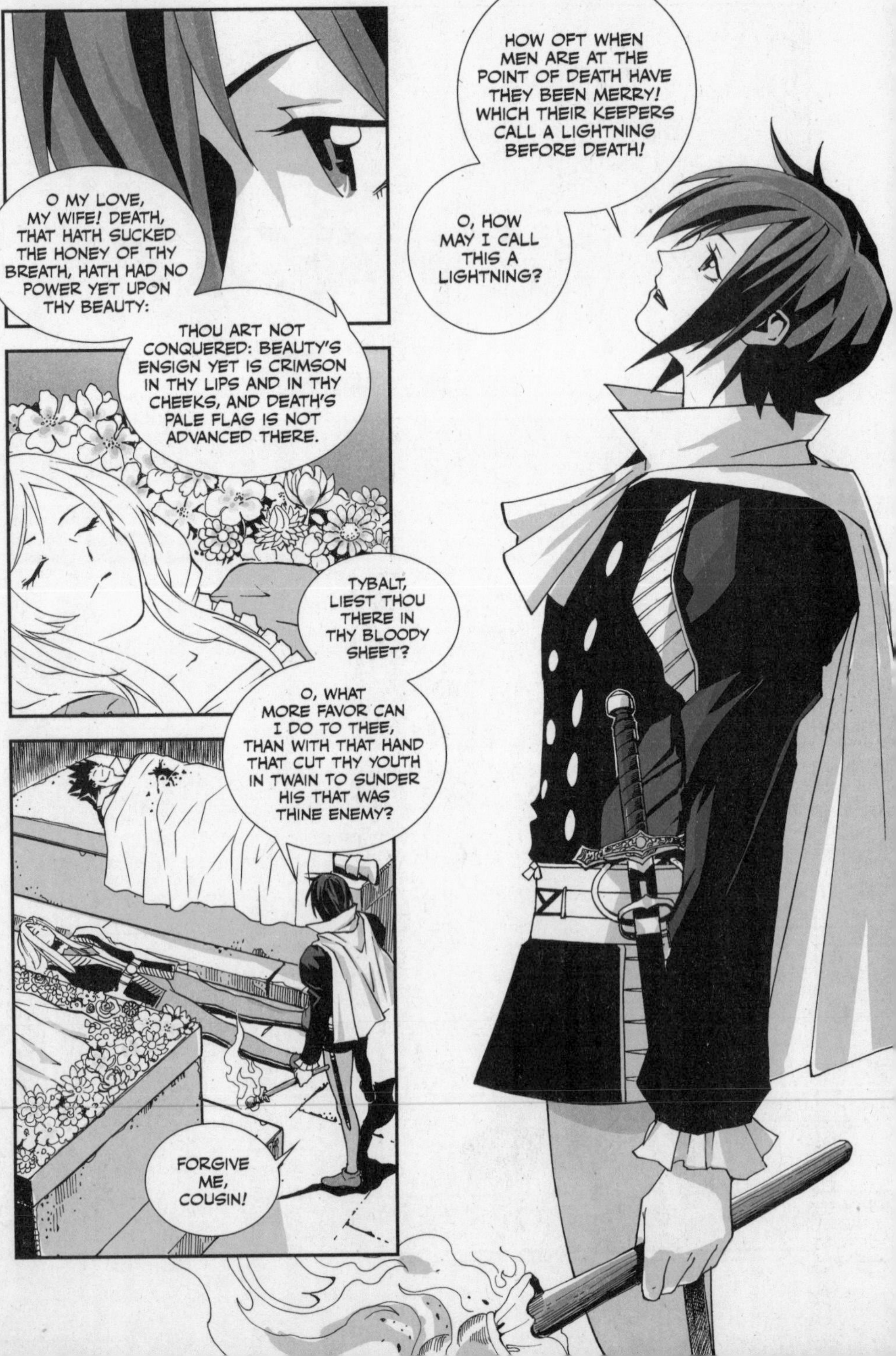
HOW OFT WHEN MEN ARE AT THE POINT OF DEATH HAVE THEY BEEN MERRY! WHICH THEIR KEEPERS CALL A LIGHTNING BEFORE DEATH!
O, HOW MAY I CALL THIS A LIGHTNING?
O MY LOVE, MY WIFE! DEATH, THAT HATH SUCKED THE HONEY OF THY BREATH, HATH HAD NO POWER YET UPON THY BEAUTY:
THOU ART NOT CONQUERED: BEAUTY'S ENSIGN YET IS CRIMSON IN THY LIPS AND IN THY CHEEKS, AND DEATH'S PALE FLAG IS NOT ADVANCED THERE.
TYBALT, LIEST THOU THERE IN THY BLOODY SHEET?
O, WHAT MORE FAVOR CAN I DO TO THEE, THAN WITH THAT HAND THAT CUT THY YOUTH IN TWAIN TO SUNDER HIS THAT WAS THINE ENEMY?
FORGIVE ME, COUSIN!

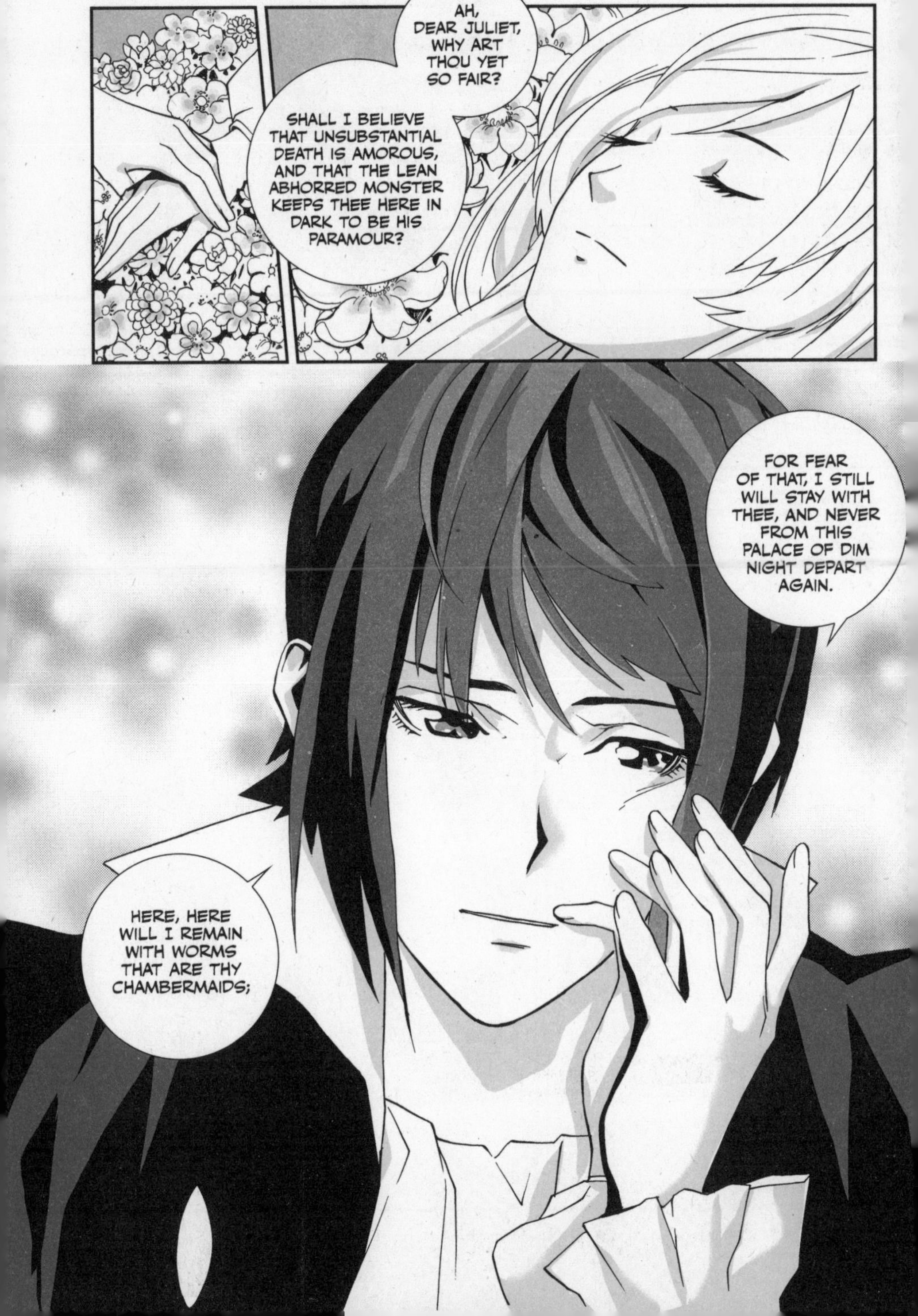
AH, DEAR JULIET, WHY ART THOU YET SO FAIR?
SHALL I BELIEVE THAT UNSUBSTANTIAL DEATH IS AMOROUS, AND THAT THE LEAN ABHORRED MONSTER KEEPS THEE HERE IN DARK TO BE HIS PARAMOUR?
FOR FEAR OF THAT, I STILL WILL STAY WITH THEE, AND NEVER FROM THIS PALACE OF DIM NIGHT DEPART AGAIN.
HERE, HERE WILL I REMAIN WITH WORMS THAT ARE THY CHAMBERMAIDS;

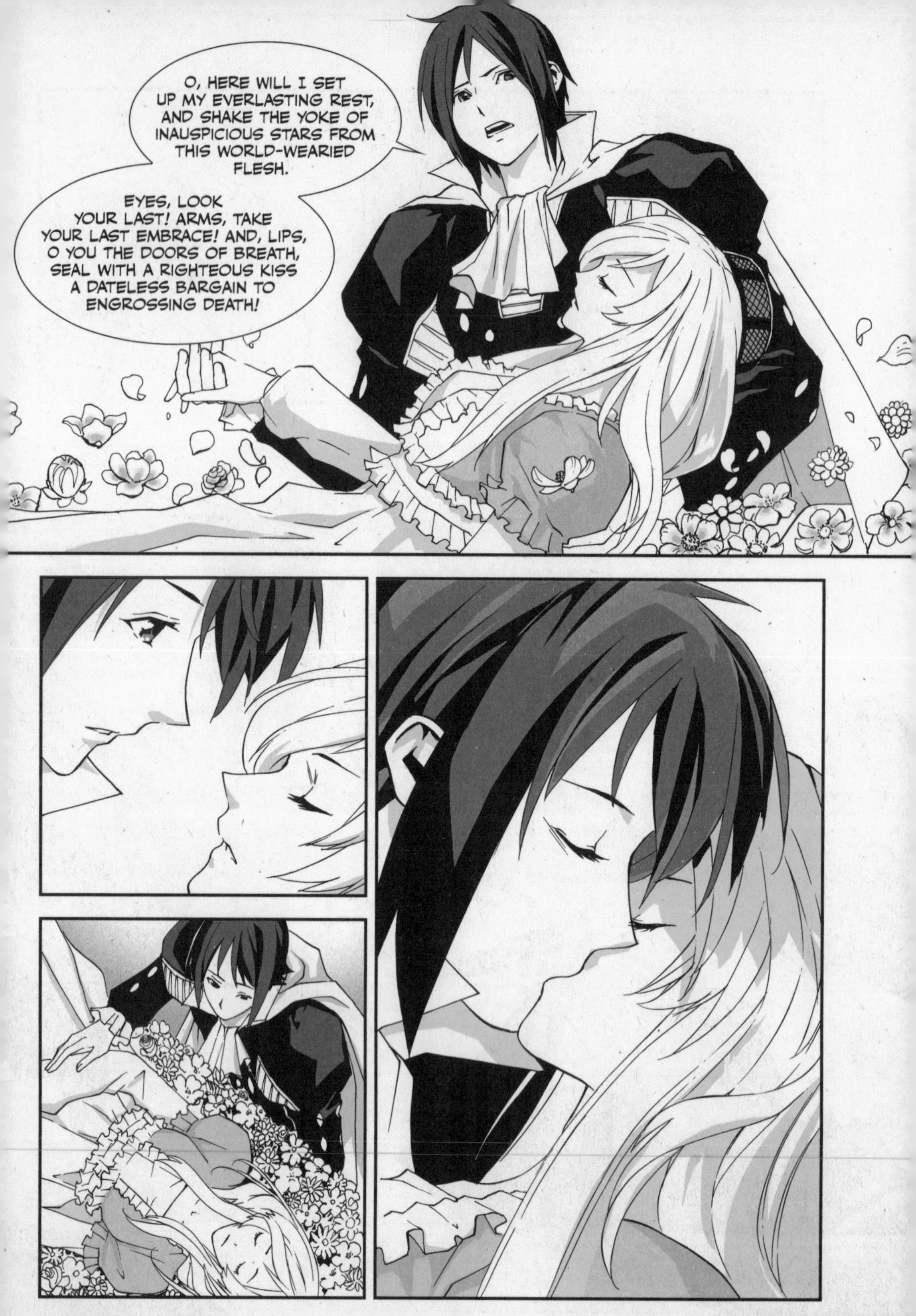
O, HERE WILL I SET UP MY EVERLASTING REST, AND SHAKE THE YOKE OF INAUSPICIOUS STARS FROM THIS WORLD-WEARIED FLESH.
EYES, LOOK YOUR LAST! ARMS, TAKE YOUR LAST EMBRACE! AND, LIPS, O YOU THE DOORS OF BREATH, SEAL WITH A RIGHTEOUS KISS A DATELESS BARGAIN TO ENGROSSING DEATH!

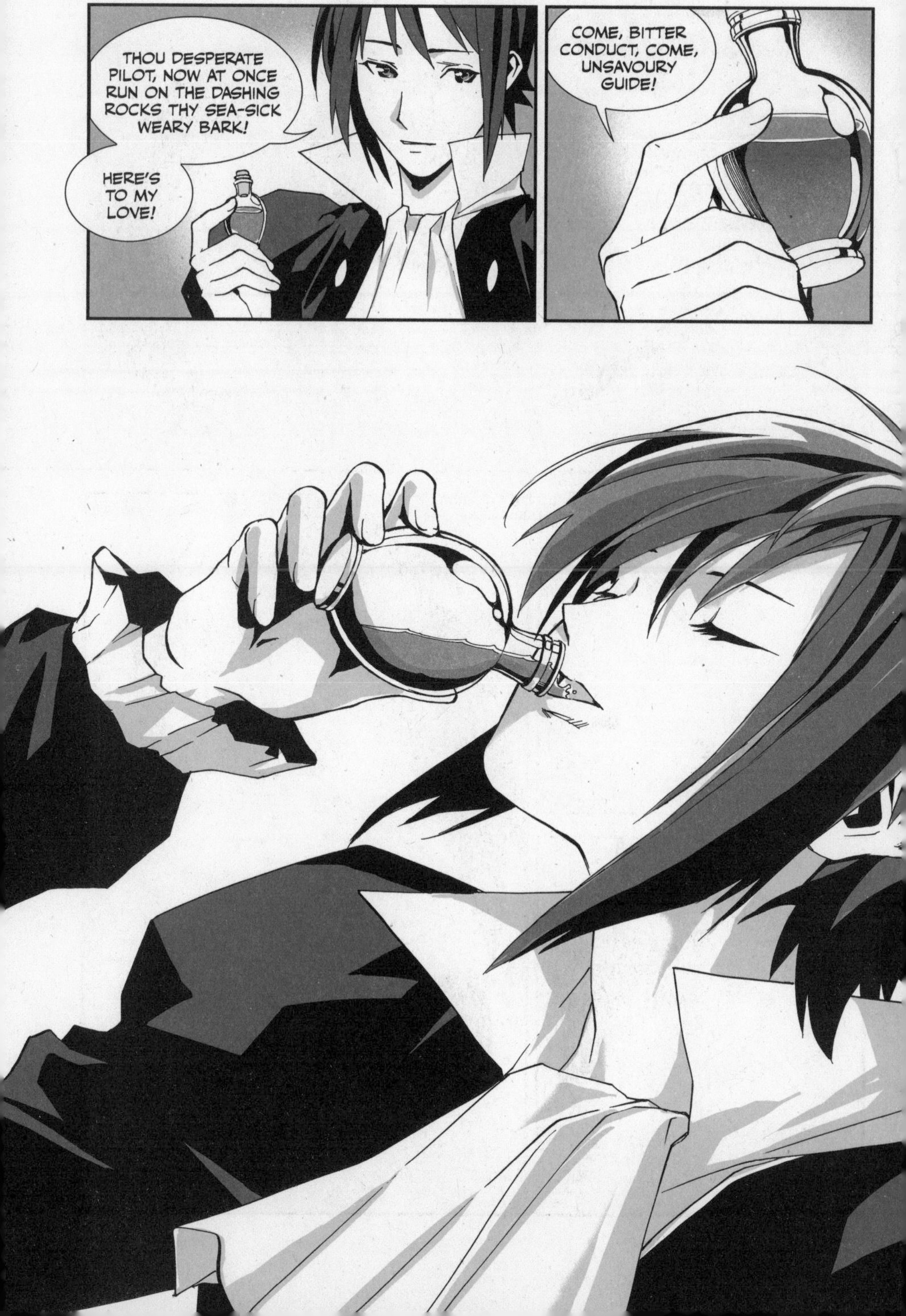
COME, BITTER CONDUCT, COME, UNSAVOURY GUIDE!
THOU DESPERATE PILOT, NOW AT ONCE RUN ON THE DASHING ROCKS THY SEA-SICK WEARY BARK!
HERE'S TO MY LOVE!

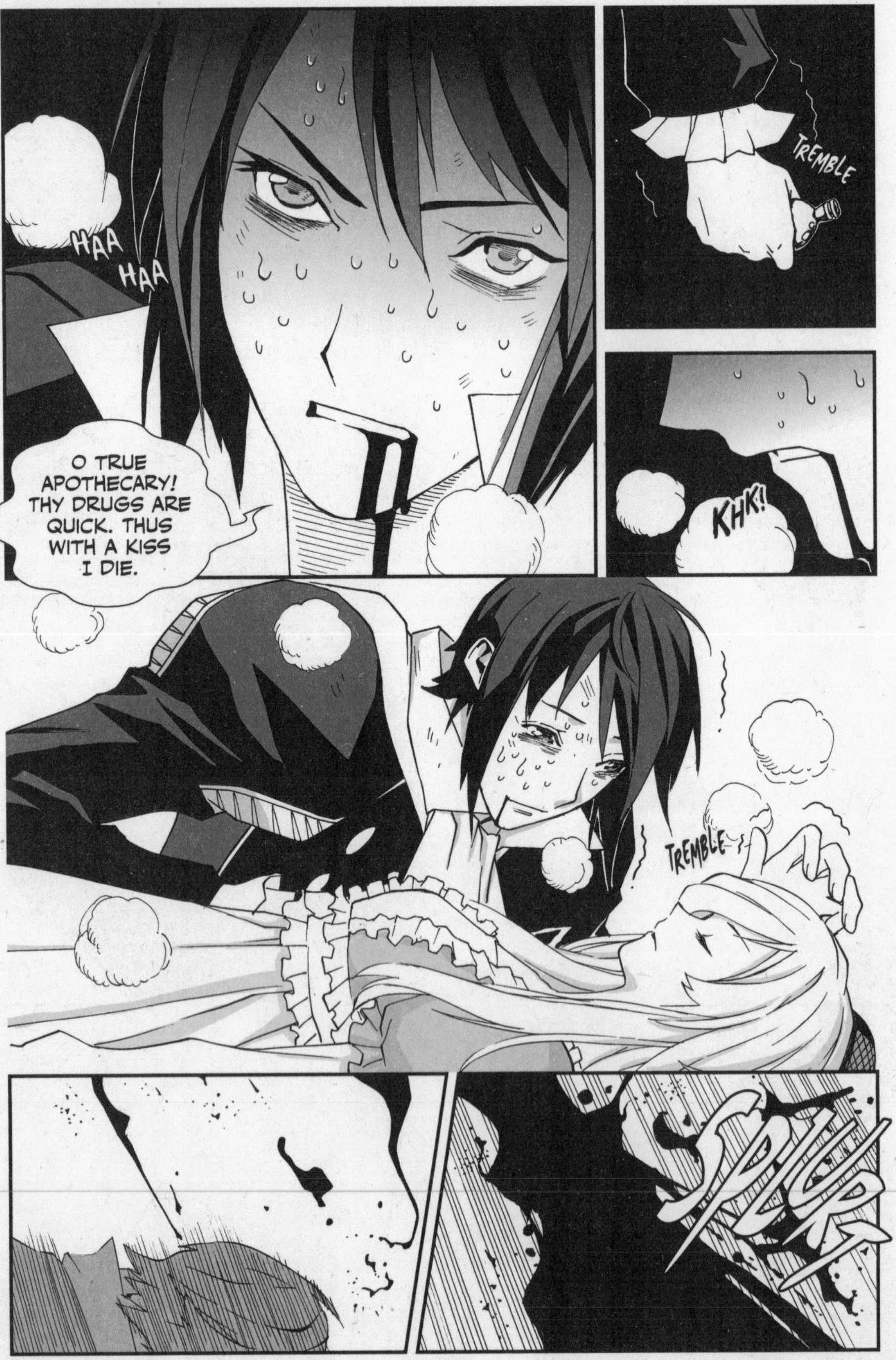
TREMBLE
KHK!
HAA HAA
O TRUE APOTHECARY! THY DRUGS ARE QUICK. THUS WITH A KISS I DIE.
TREMBLE
SPLURT

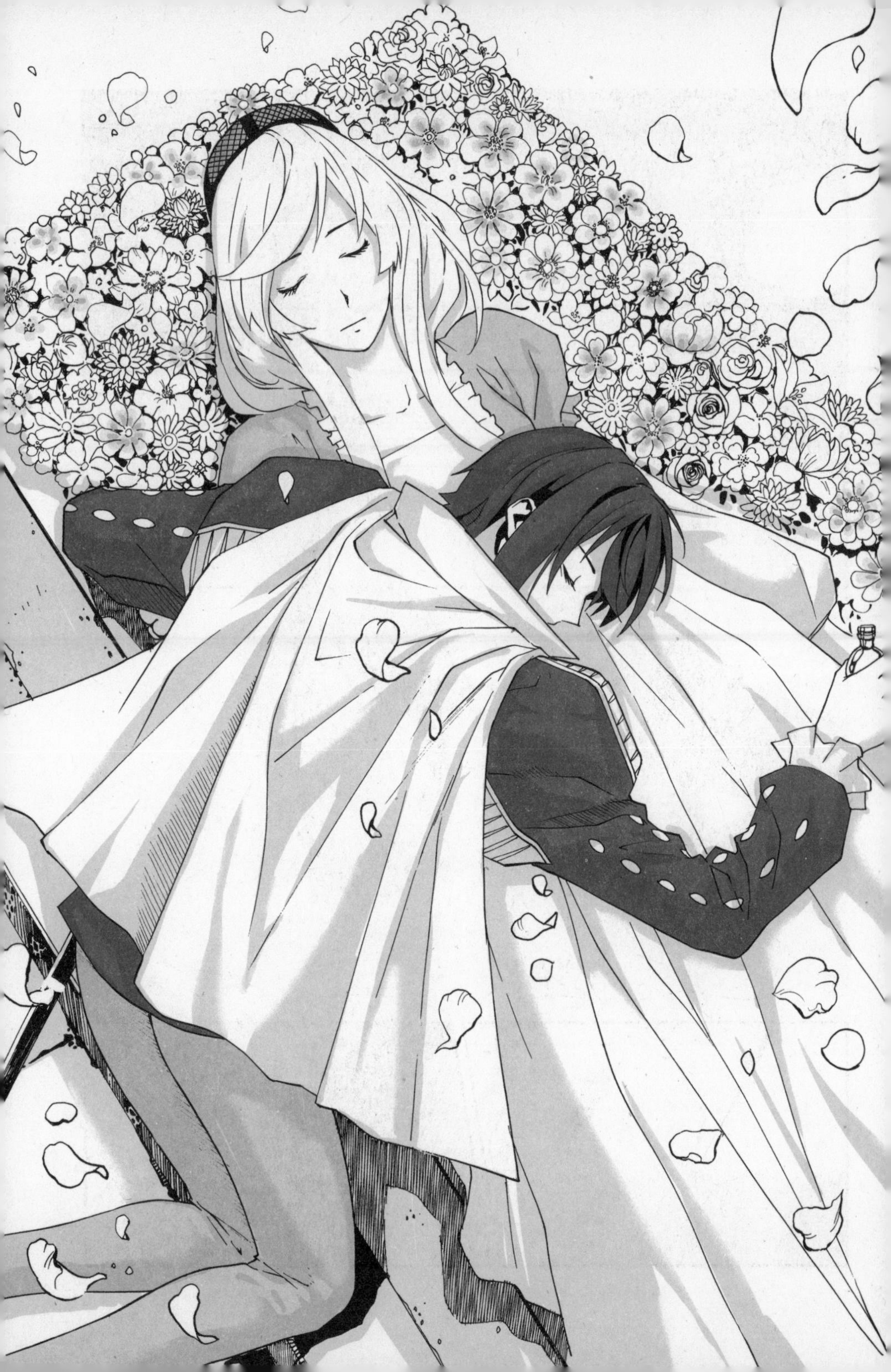

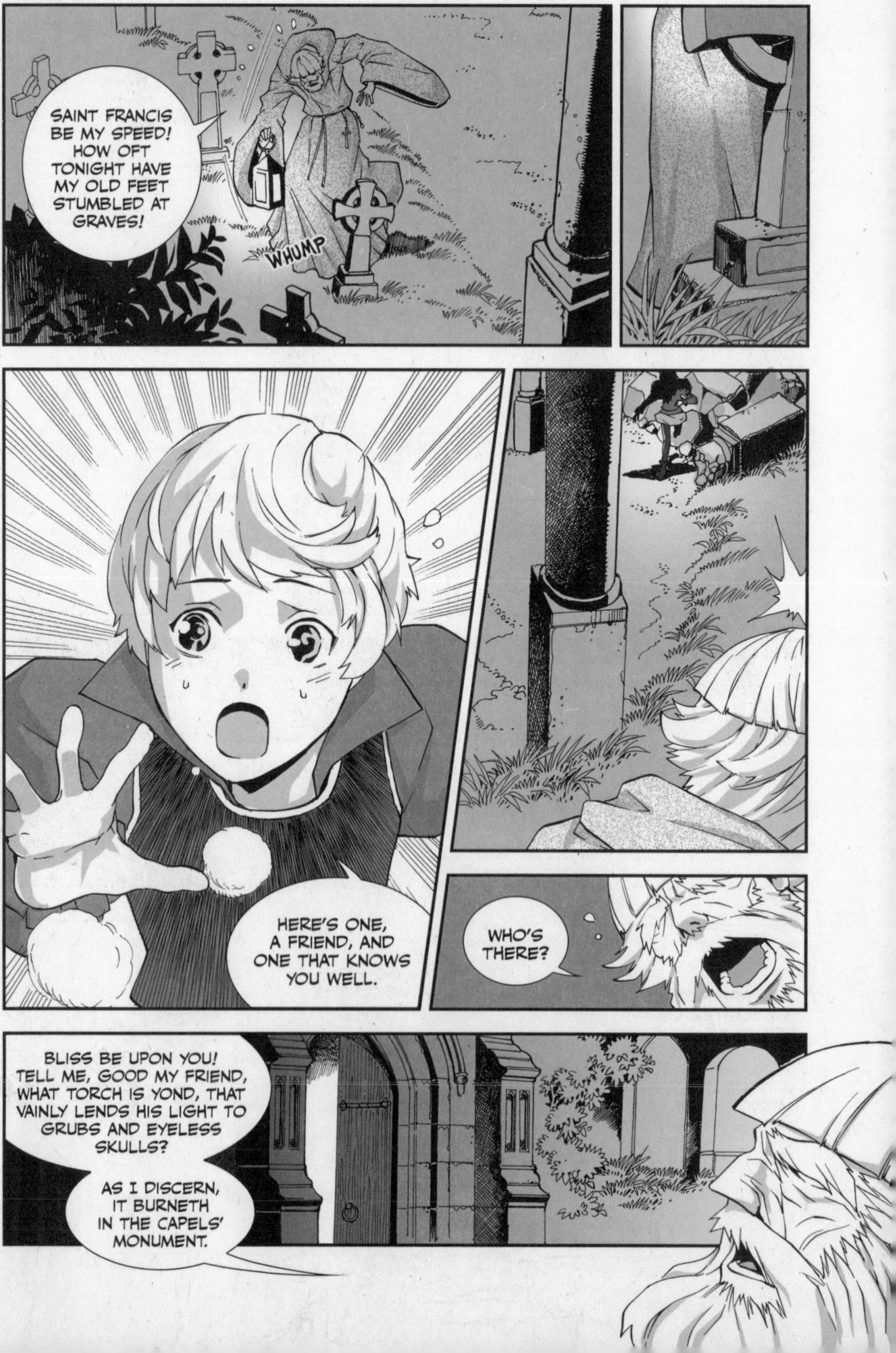
SAINT FRANCIS BE MY SPEED! HOW OFT TONIGHT HAVE MY OLD FEET STUMBLED AT GRAVES!
WHUMP
WHO'S THERE?
HERE'S ONE, A FRIEND, AND ONE THAT KNOWS YOU WELL.
BLISS BE UPON YOU! TELL ME, GOOD MY FRIEND, WHAT TORCH IS YOND, THAT VAINLY LENDS HIS LIGHT TO GRUBS AND EYELESS SKULLS?
AS I DISCERN, IT BURNETH IN THE CAPELS' MONUMENT.

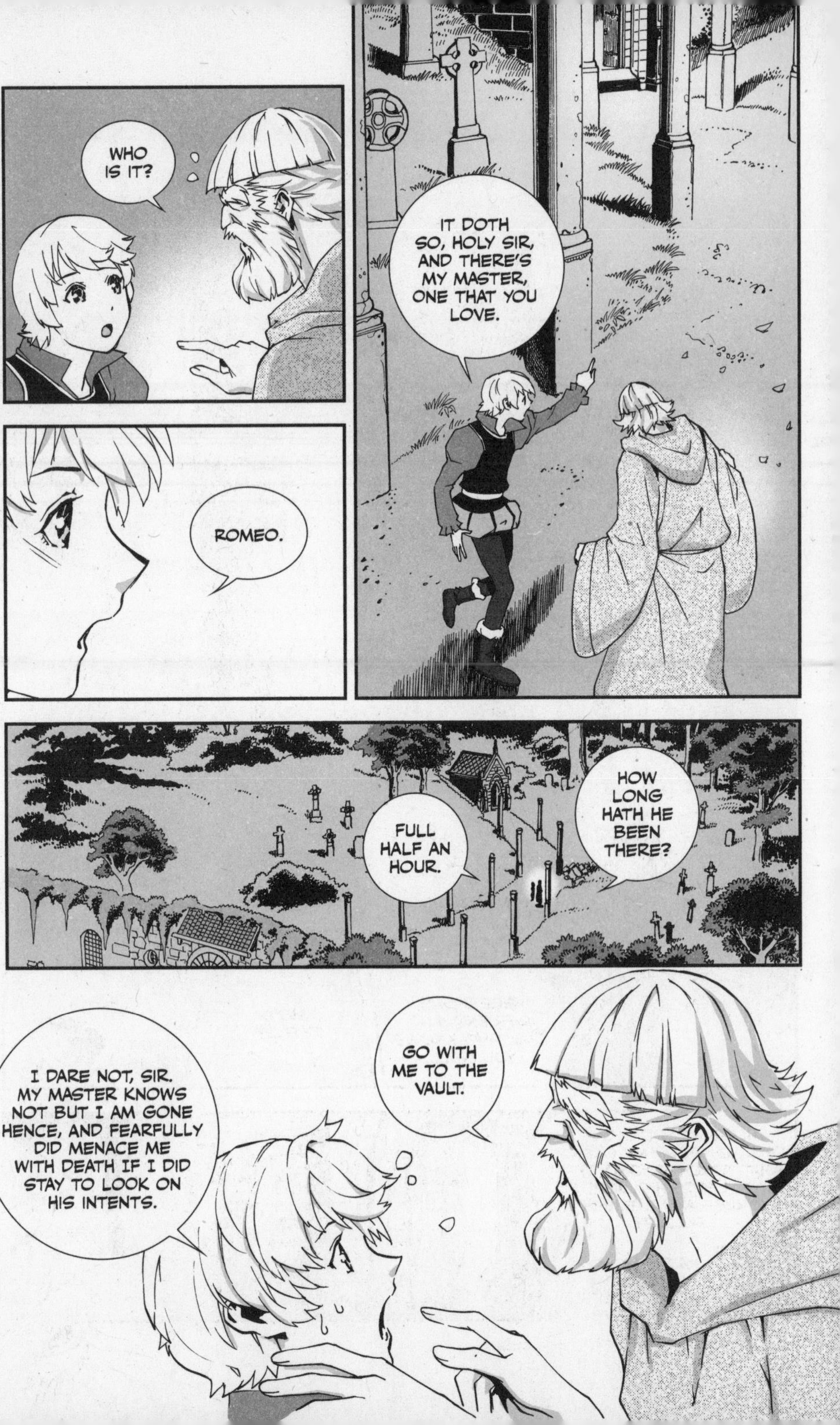

IT DOTH SO, HOLY SIR, AND THERE'S MY MASTER, ONE THAT YOU LOVE.
WHO IS IT?
ROMEO.
HOW LONG HATH HE BEEN THERE?
FULL HALF AN HOUR.
GO WITH ME TO THE VAULT.
I DARE NOT, SIR. MY MASTER KNOWS NOT BUT I AM GONE HENCE, AND FEARFULLY DID MENACE ME WITH DEATH IF I DID STAY TO LOOK ON HIS INTENTS.

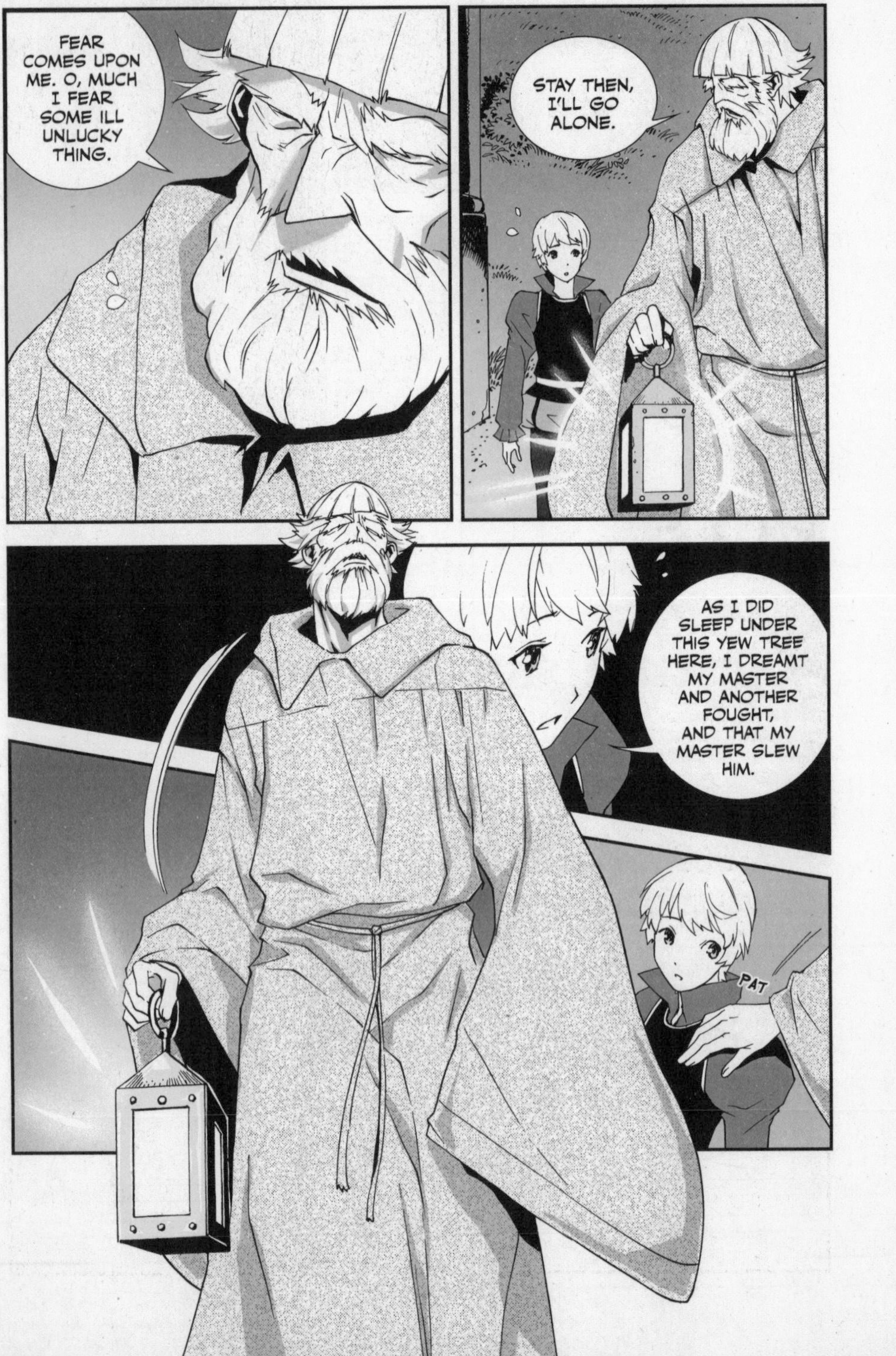
STAY THEN, I'LL GO ALONE.
FEAR COMES UPON ME. O, MUCH I FEAR SOME ILL UNLUCKY THING.
AS I DID SLEEP UNDER THIS YEW TREE HERE, I DREAMT MY MASTER AND ANOTHER FOUGHT, AND THAT MY MASTER SLEW HIM.
PAT

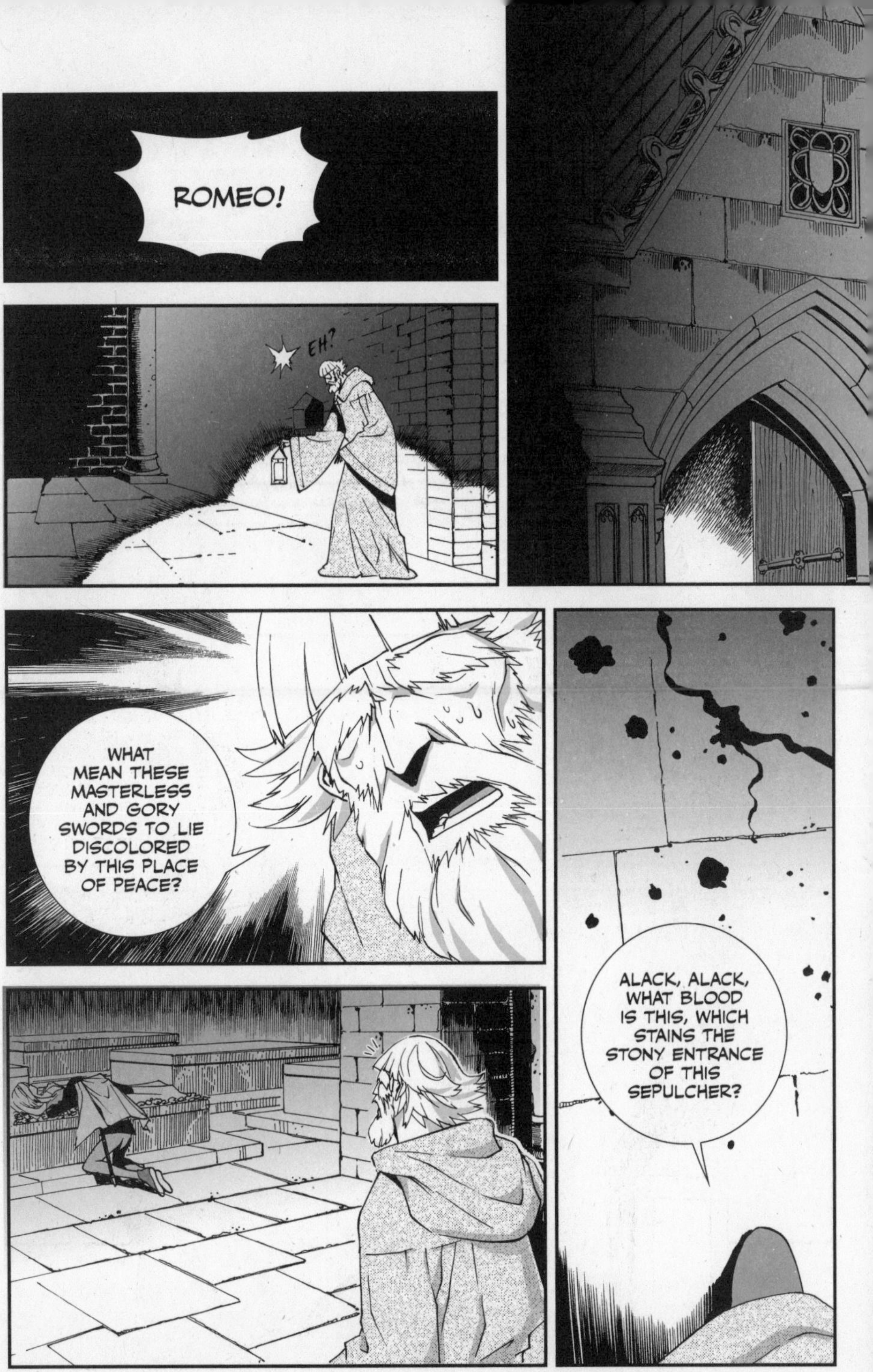

ROMEO!
EH?
ALACK, ALACK, WHAT BLOOD IS THIS, WHICH STAINS THE STONY ENTRANCE OF THIS SEPULCHER?
WHAT MEAN THESE MASTERLESS AND GORY SWORDS TO LIE DISCOLORED BY THIS PLACE OF PEACE?

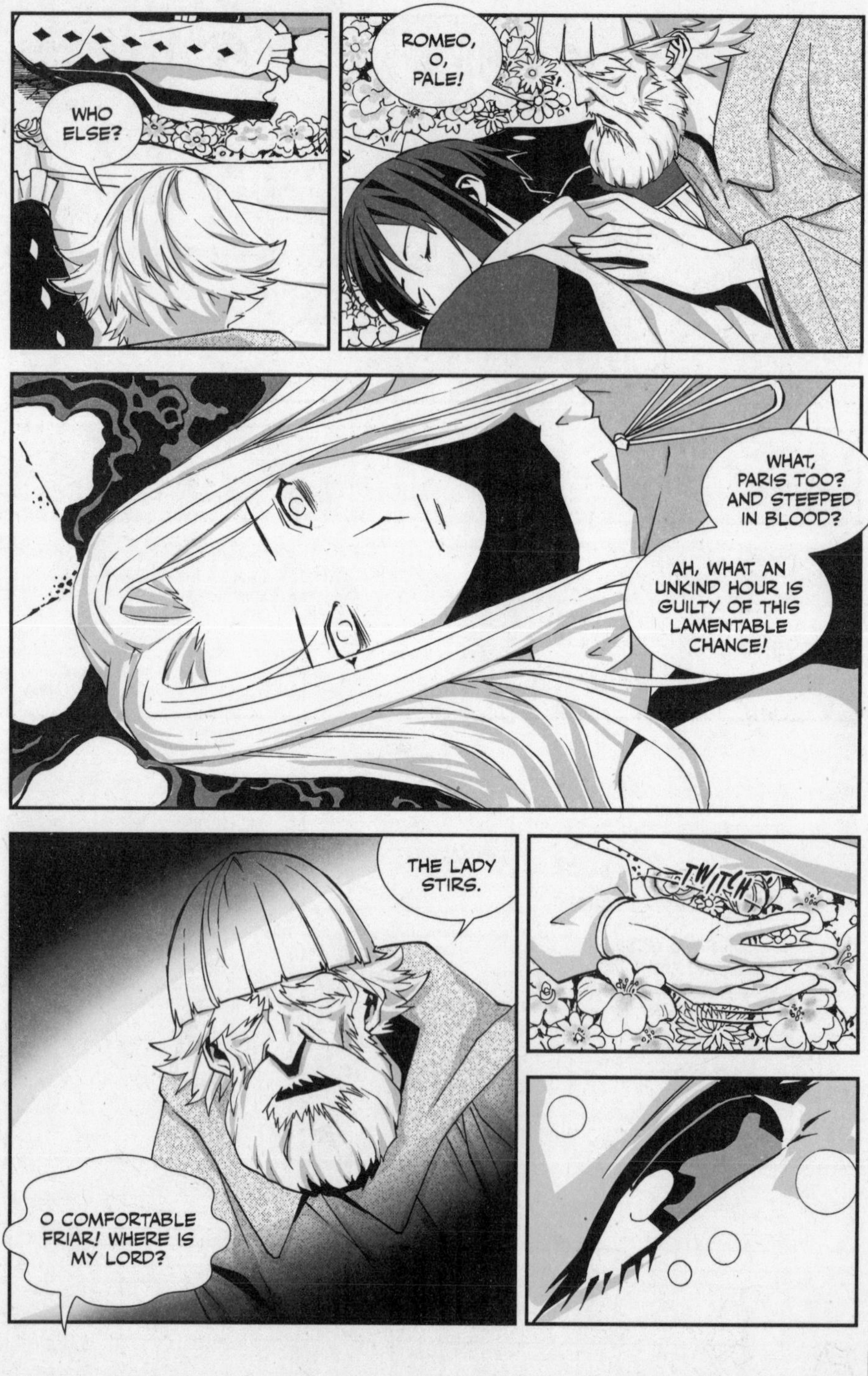
ROMEO, O, PALE!
WHO ELSE?
WHAT, PARIS TOO? AND STEEPED IN BLOOD?
AH, WHAT AN UNKIND HOUR IS GUILTY OF THIS LAMENTABLE CHANCE!
TWITCH
THE LADY STIRS.
O COMFORTABLE FRIAR! WHERE IS MY LORD?

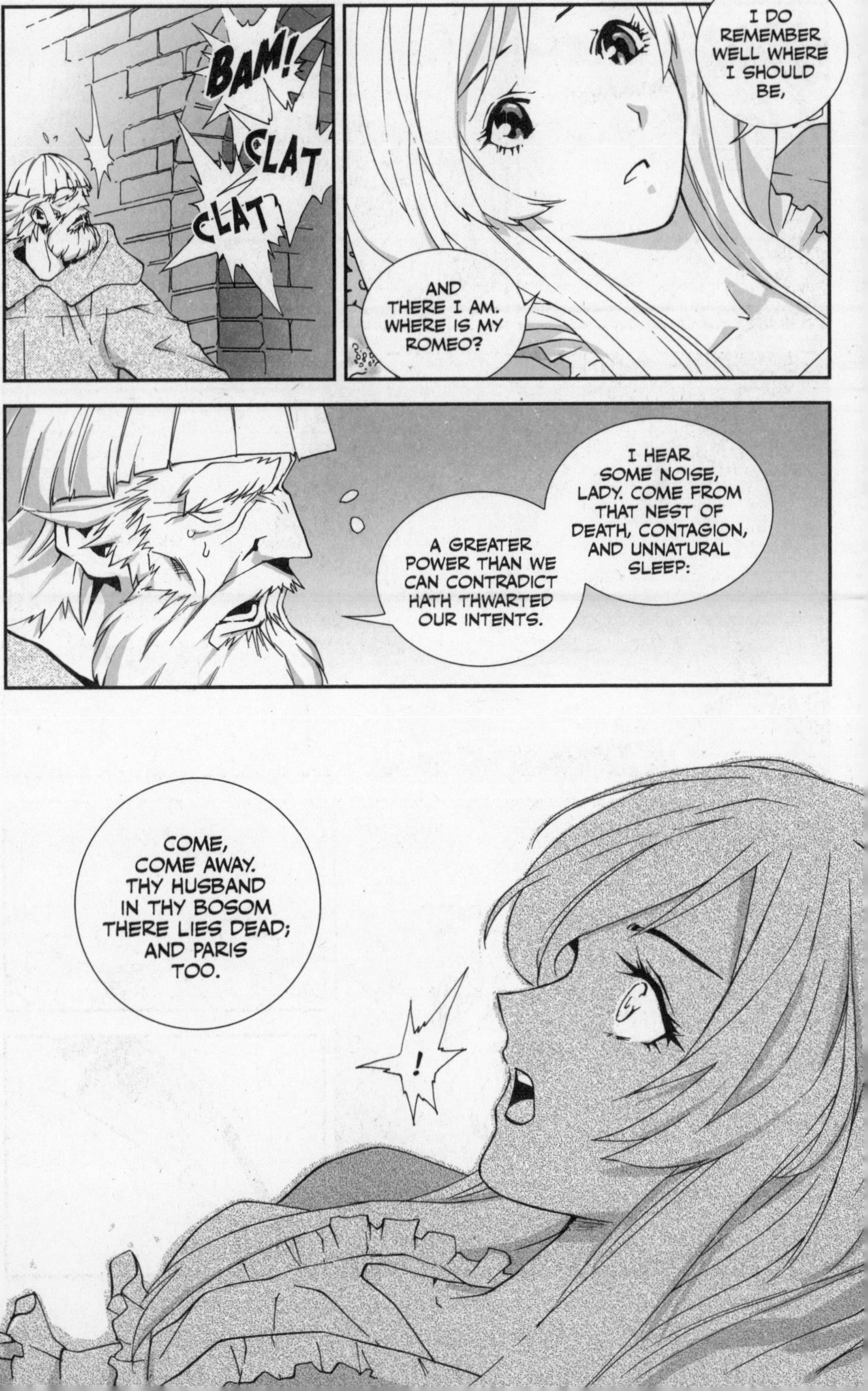
I DO REMEMBER WELL WHERE I SHOULD BE,
AND THERE I AM. WHERE IS MY ROMEO?
BAM!
CLAT
CLAT
I HEAR SOME NOISE, LADY. COME FROM THAT NEST OF DEATH, CONTAGION, AND UNNATURAL SLEEP:
A GREATER POWER THAN WE CAN CONTRADICT HATH THWARTED OUR INTENTS.
COME, COME AWAY. THY HUSBAND IN THY BOSOM THERE LIES DEAD; AND PARIS TOO.
!

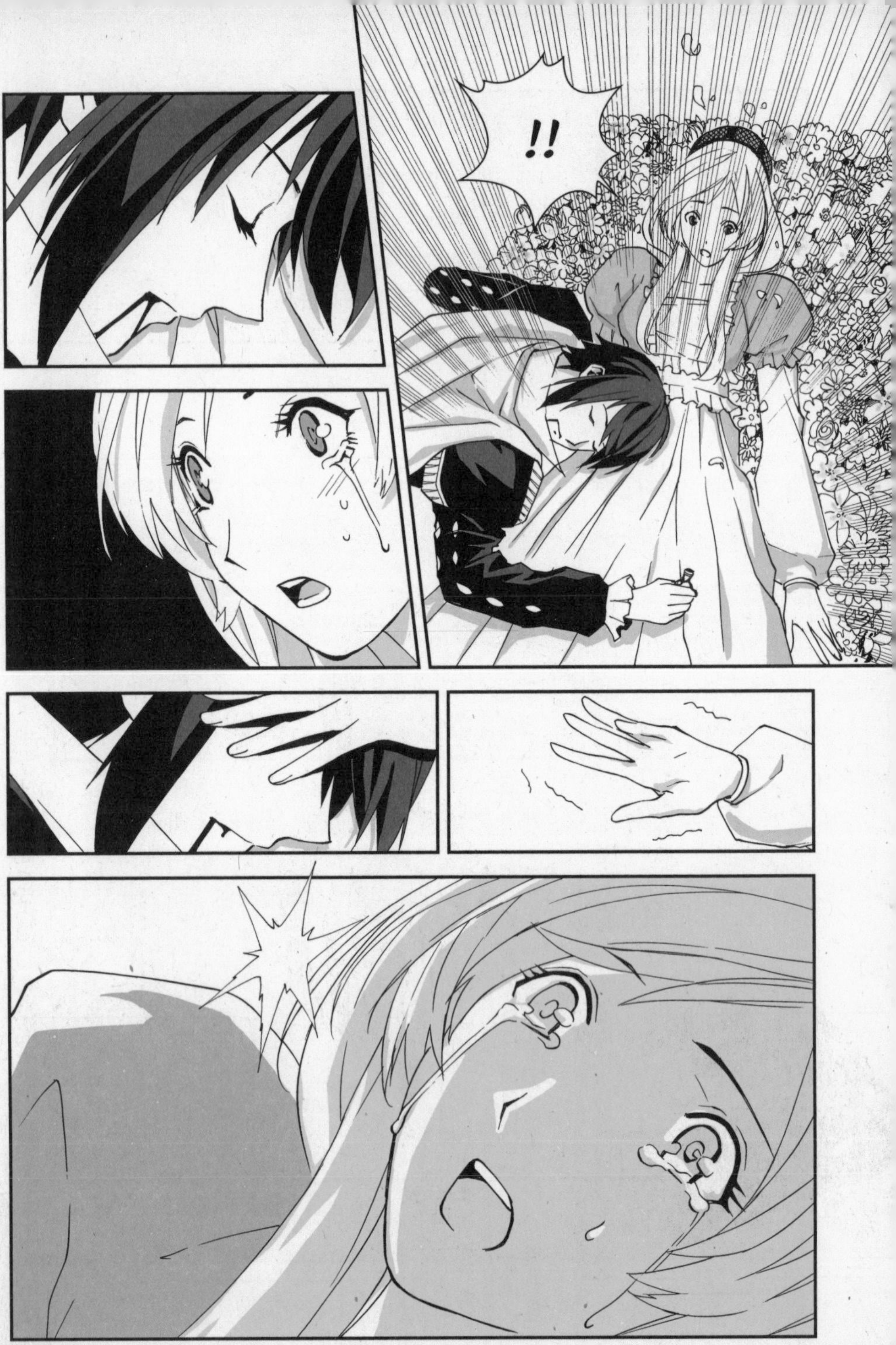
!!

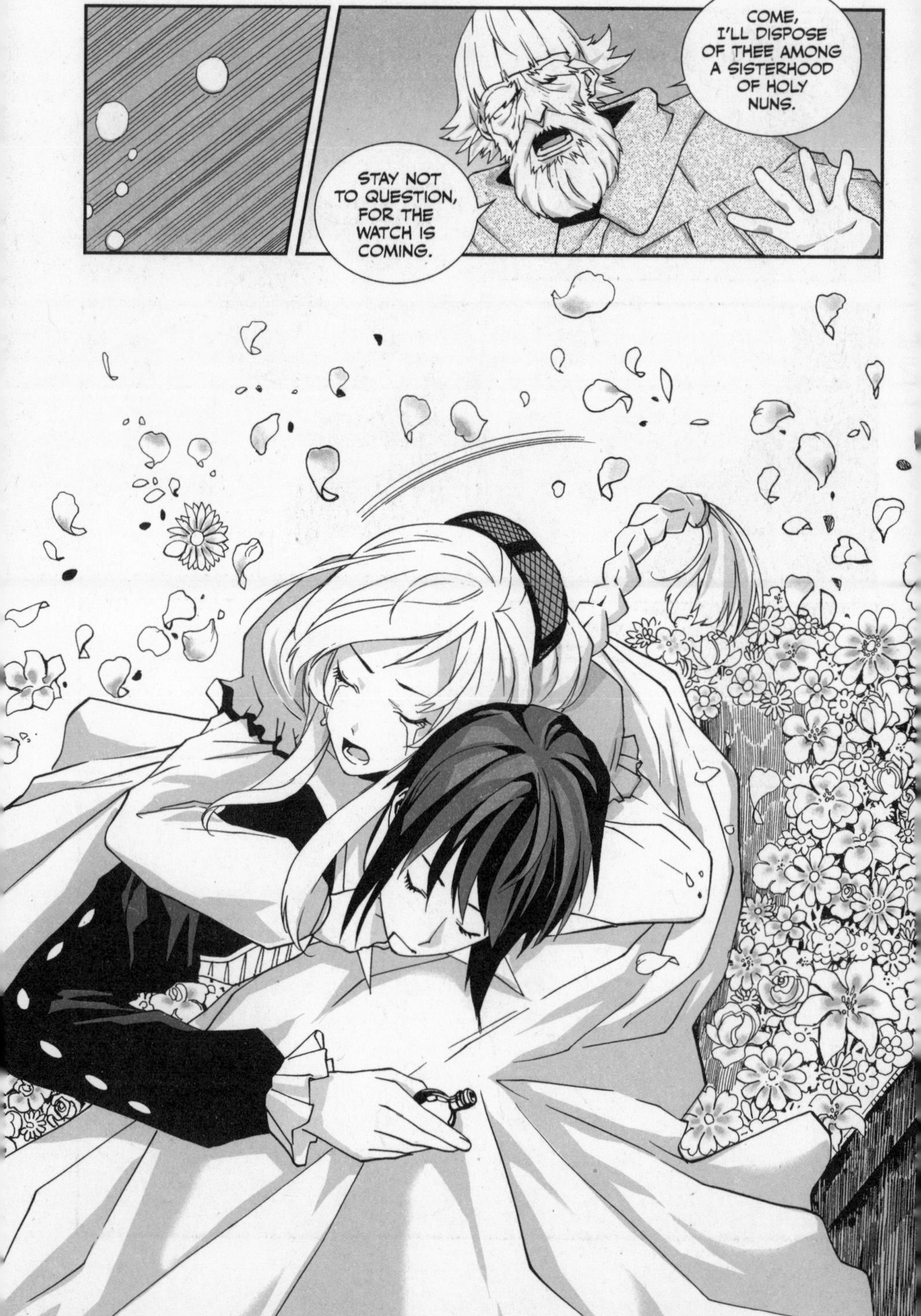
COME, I'LL DISPOSE OF THEE AMONG A SISTERHOOD OF HOLY NUNS.
STAY NOT TO QUESTION, FOR THE WATCH IS COMING.

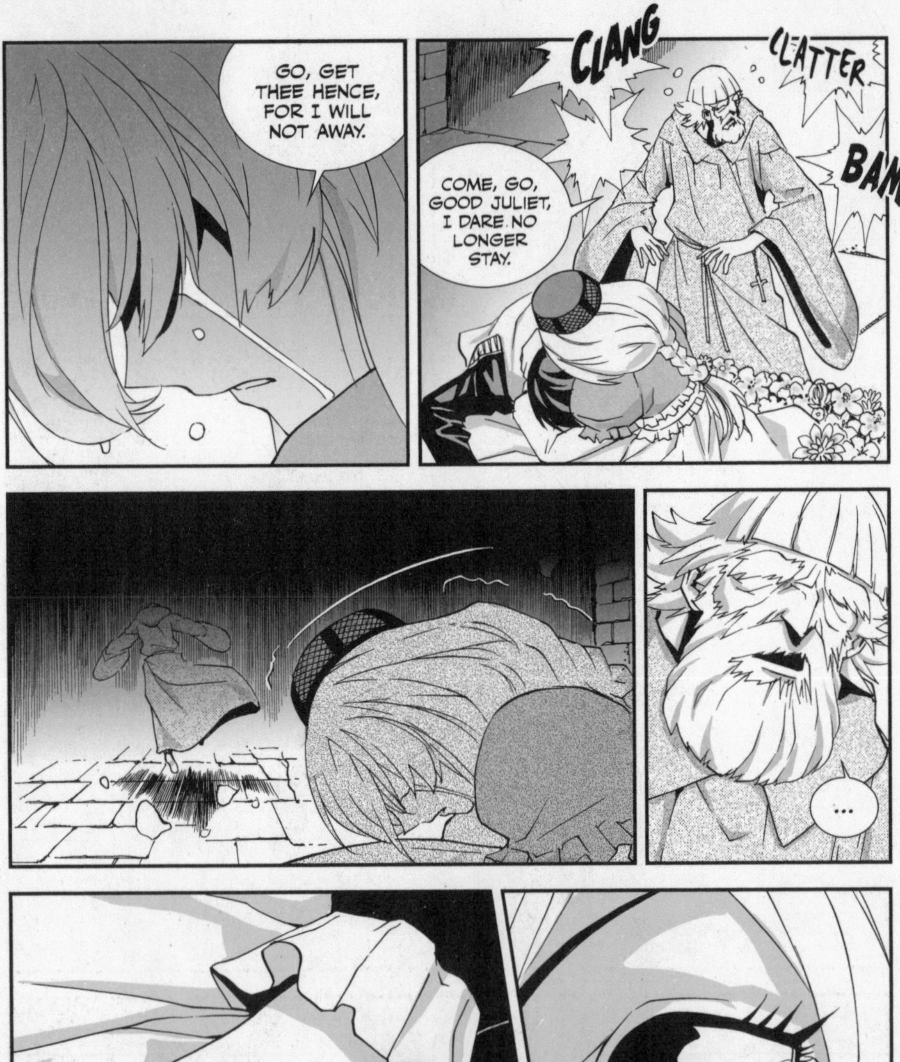
CLATTER
CLANG
BAM
COME, GO, GOOD JULIET, I DARE NO LONGER STAY.
GO, GET THEE HENCE, FOR I WILL NOT AWAY.
...

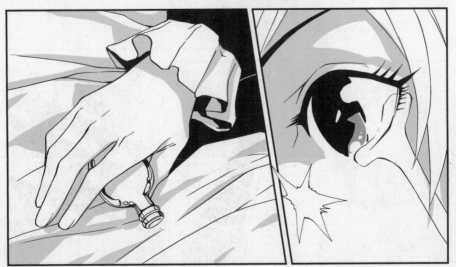

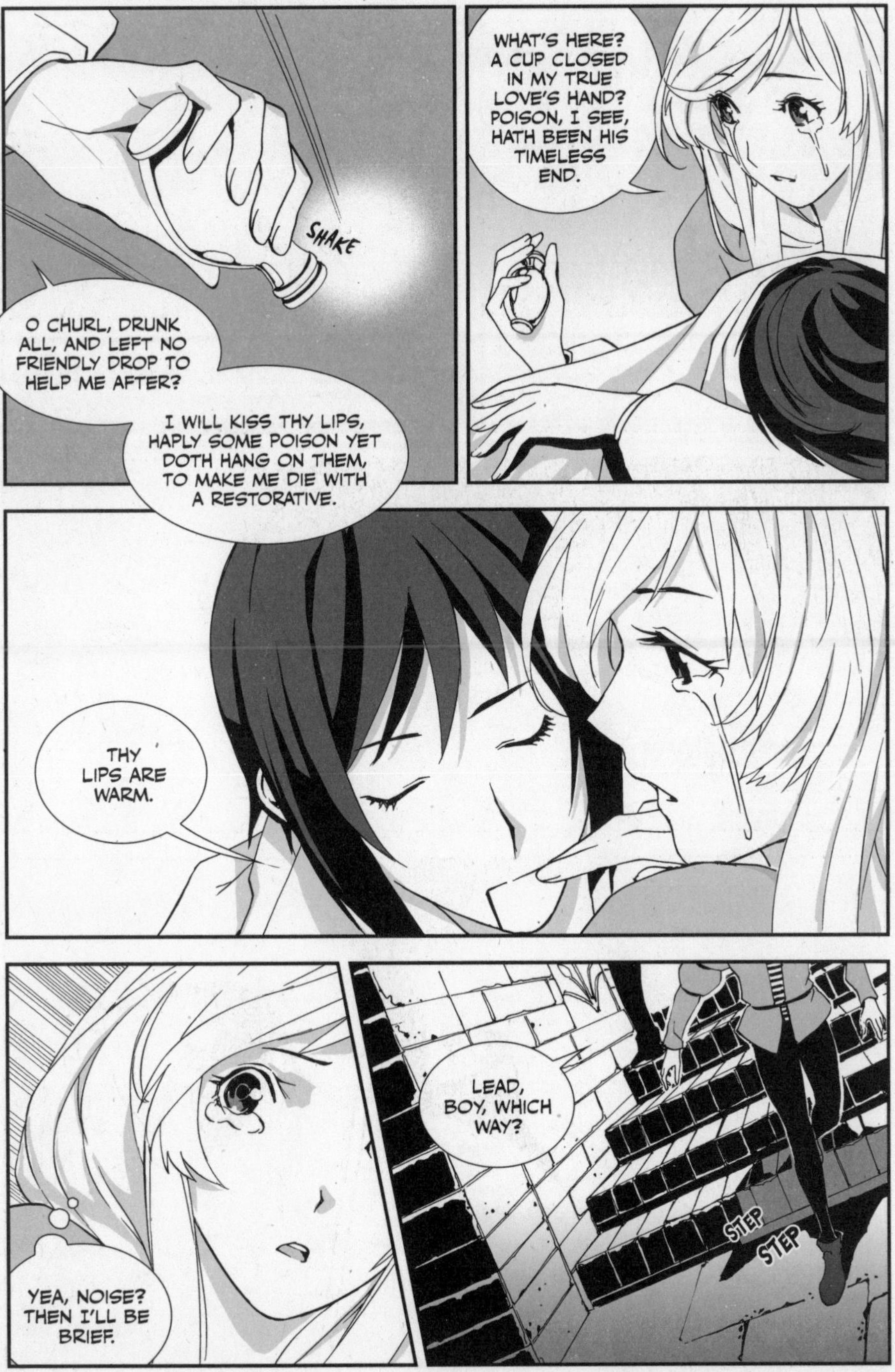
WHAT'S HERE? A CUP CLOSED IN MY TRUE LOVE'S HAND? POISON, I SEE, HATH BEEN HIS TIMELESS END.
SHAKE
O CHURL, DRUNK ALL, AND LEFT NO FRIENDLY DROP TO HELP ME AFTER?
I WILL KISS THY LIPS, HAPLY SOME POISON YET DOTH HANG ON THEM, TO MAKE ME DIE WITH A RESTORATIVE.
THY LIPS ARE WARM.
LEAD, BOY, WHICH WAY?
STEP
STEP
YEA, NOISE? THEN I'LL BE BRIEF.

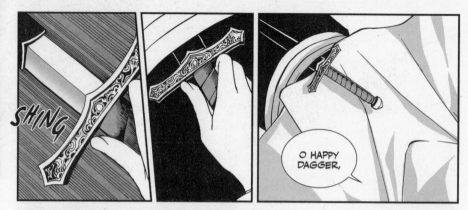

SHING

O HAPPY
DAGGER,

THIS IS
THY
SHEATH;

THERE
RUST,
AND LET
ME DIE.

TMP
TMP
TMP

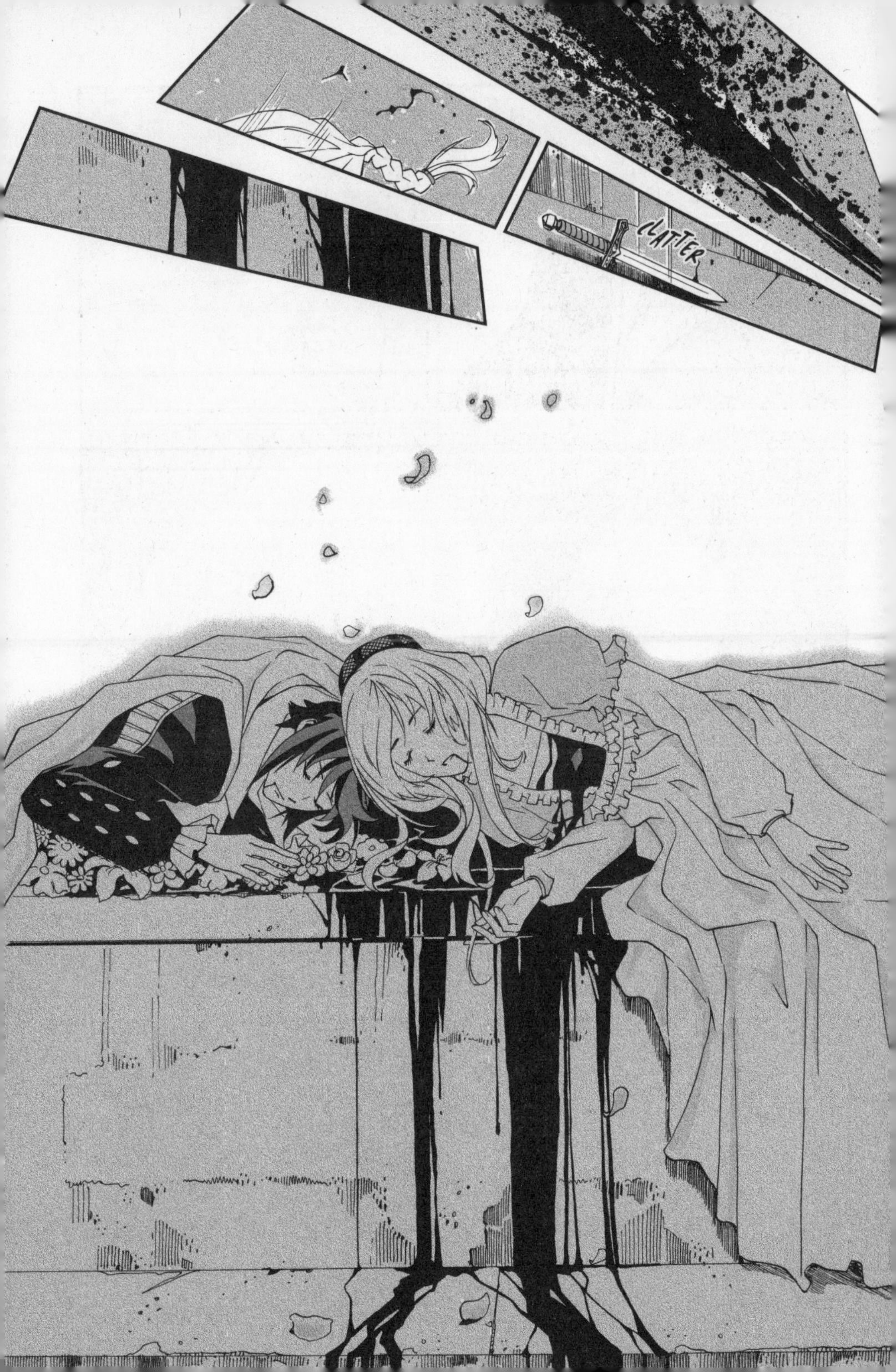
CLATTER

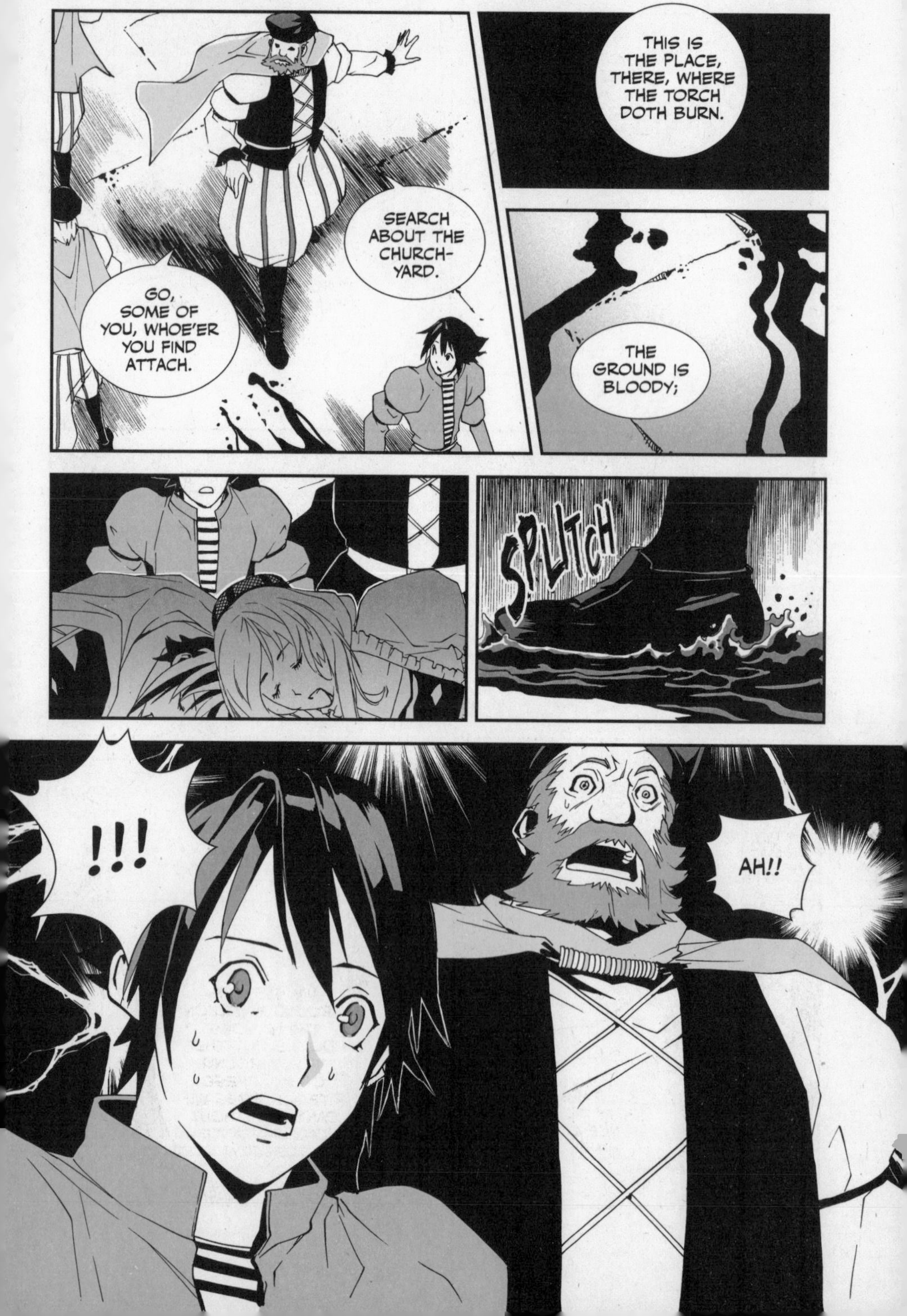
THIS IS THE PLACE, THERE, WHERE THE TORCH DOTH BURN.
THE GROUND IS BLOODY;
SEARCH ABOUT THE CHURCH-YARD.
GO, SOME OF YOU, WHOE'ER YOU FIND ATTACH.
SPLITCH
AH!!
!!!

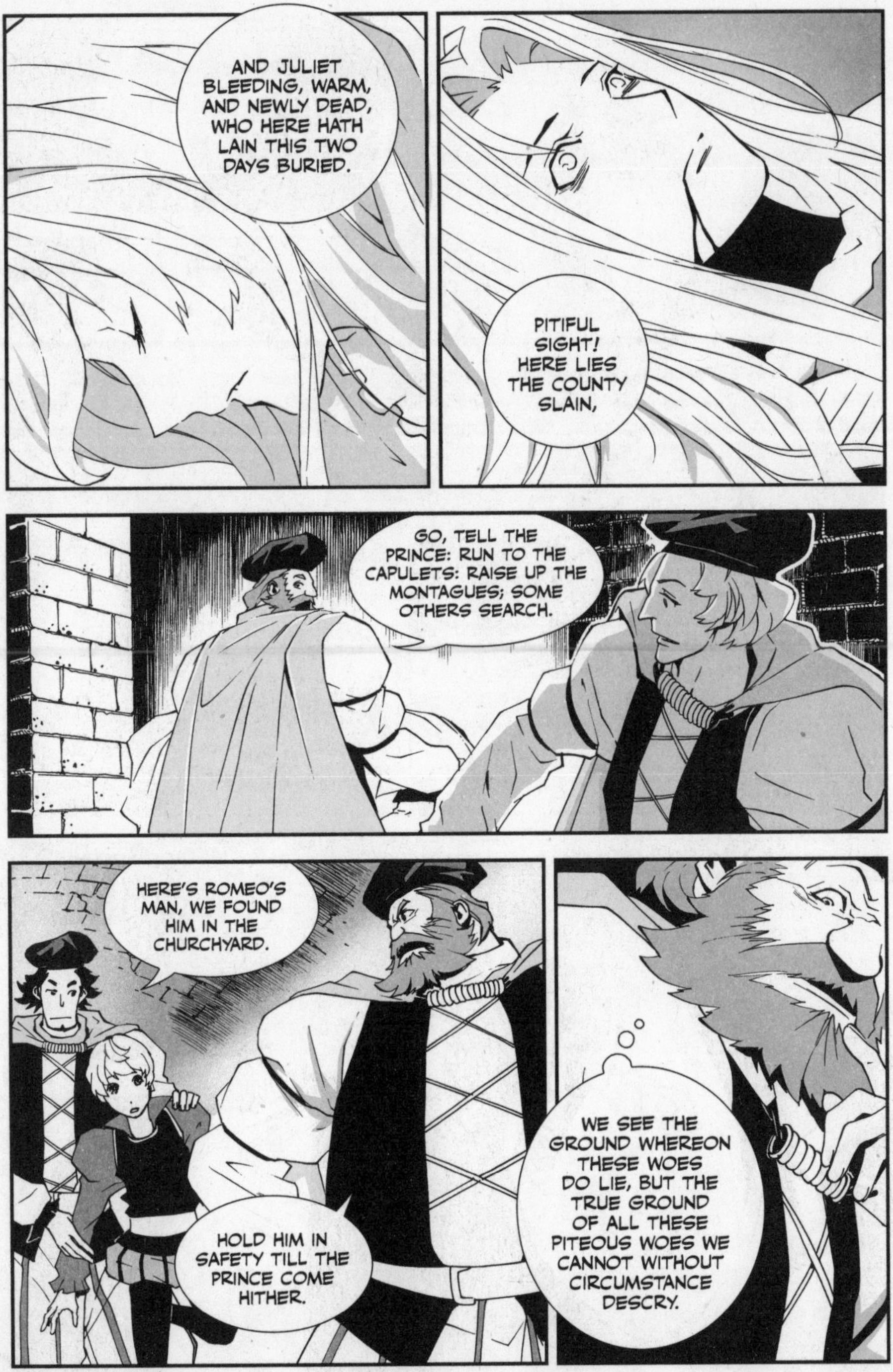
PITIFUL SIGHT! HERE LIES THE COUNTY SLAIN,
AND JULIET BLEEDING, WARM, AND NEWLY DEAD, WHO HERE HATH LAIN THIS TWO DAYS BURIED.
GO, TELL THE PRINCE: RUN TO THE CAPULETS: RAISE UP THE MONTAGUES; SOME OTHERS SEARCH.
WE SEE THE GROUND WHEREON THESE WOES DO LIE, BUT THE TRUE GROUND OF ALL THESE PITEOUS WOES WE CANNOT WITHOUT CIRCUMSTANCE DESCRY.
HERE'S ROMEO'S MAN, WE FOUND HIM IN THE CHURCHYARD.
HOLD HIM IN SAFETY TILL THE PRINCE COME HITHER.

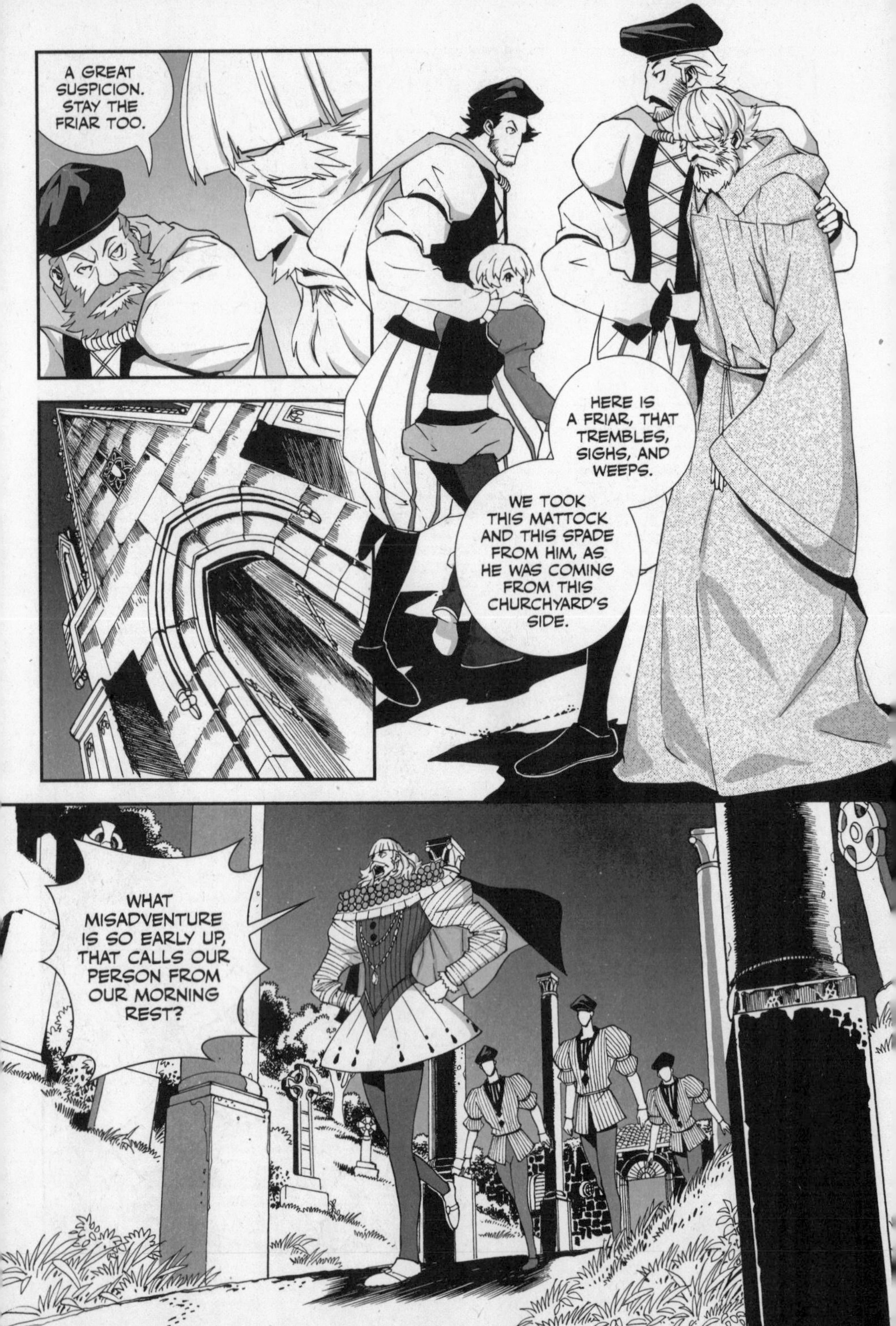
HERE IS A FRIAR, THAT TREMBLES, SIGHS, AND WEEPS.
WE TOOK THIS MATTOCK AND THIS SPADE FROM HIM, AS HE WAS COMING FROM THIS CHURCHYARD'S SIDE.
A GREAT SUSPICION. STAY THE FRIAR TOO.
WHAT MISADVENTURE IS SO EARLY UP, THAT CALLS OUR PERSON FROM OUR MORNING REST?

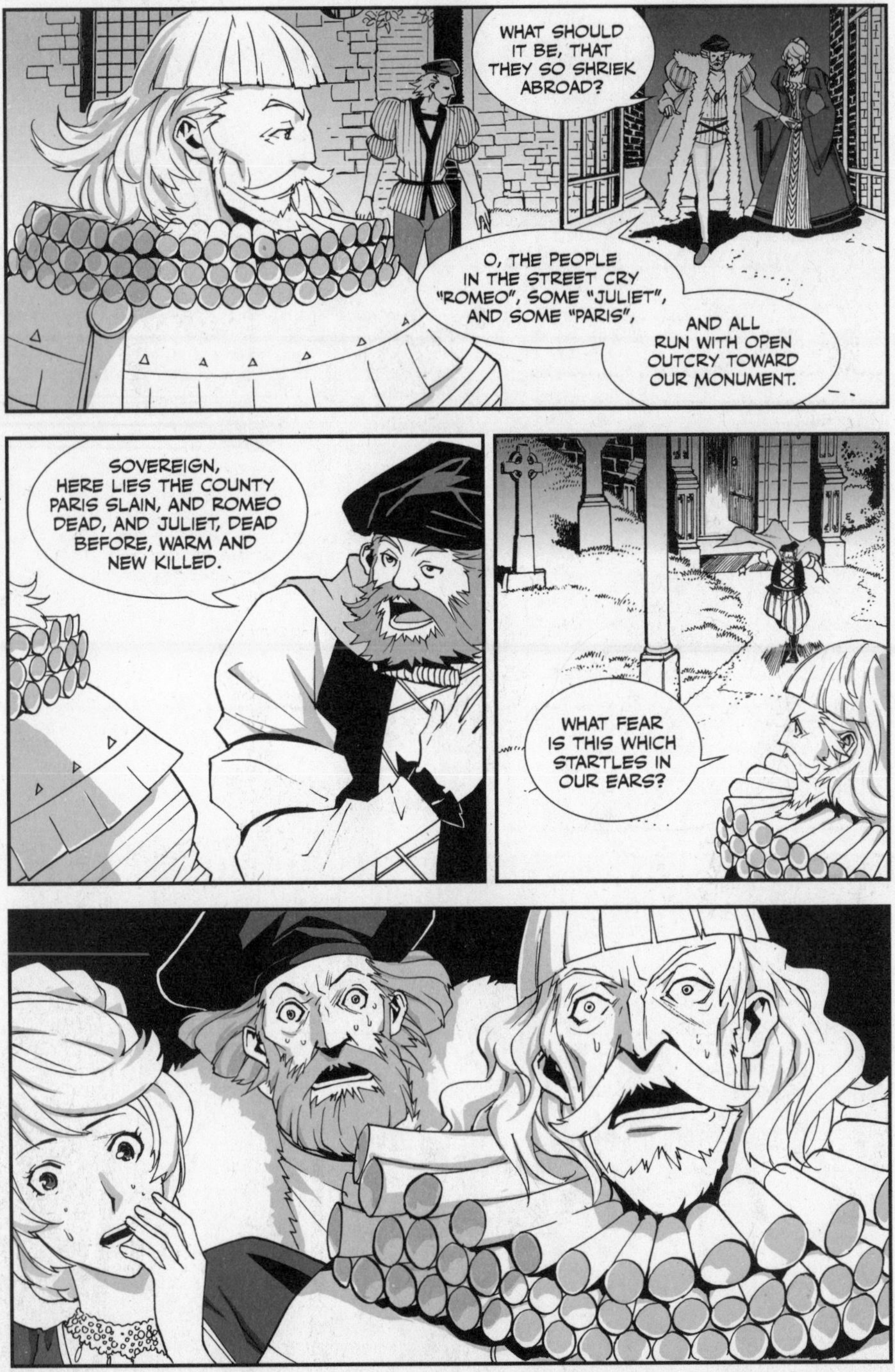
WHAT SHOULD IT BE, THAT THEY SO SHRIEK ABROAD?
O, THE PEOPLE IN THE STREET CRY "ROMEO", SOME "JULIET", AND SOME "PARIS",
AND ALL RUN WITH OPEN OUTCRY TOWARD OUR MONUMENT.
WHAT FEAR IS THIS WHICH STARTLES IN OUR EARS?
SOVEREIGN, HERE LIES THE COUNTY PARIS SLAIN, AND ROMEO DEAD, AND JULIET, DEAD BEFORE, WARM AND NEW KILLED.

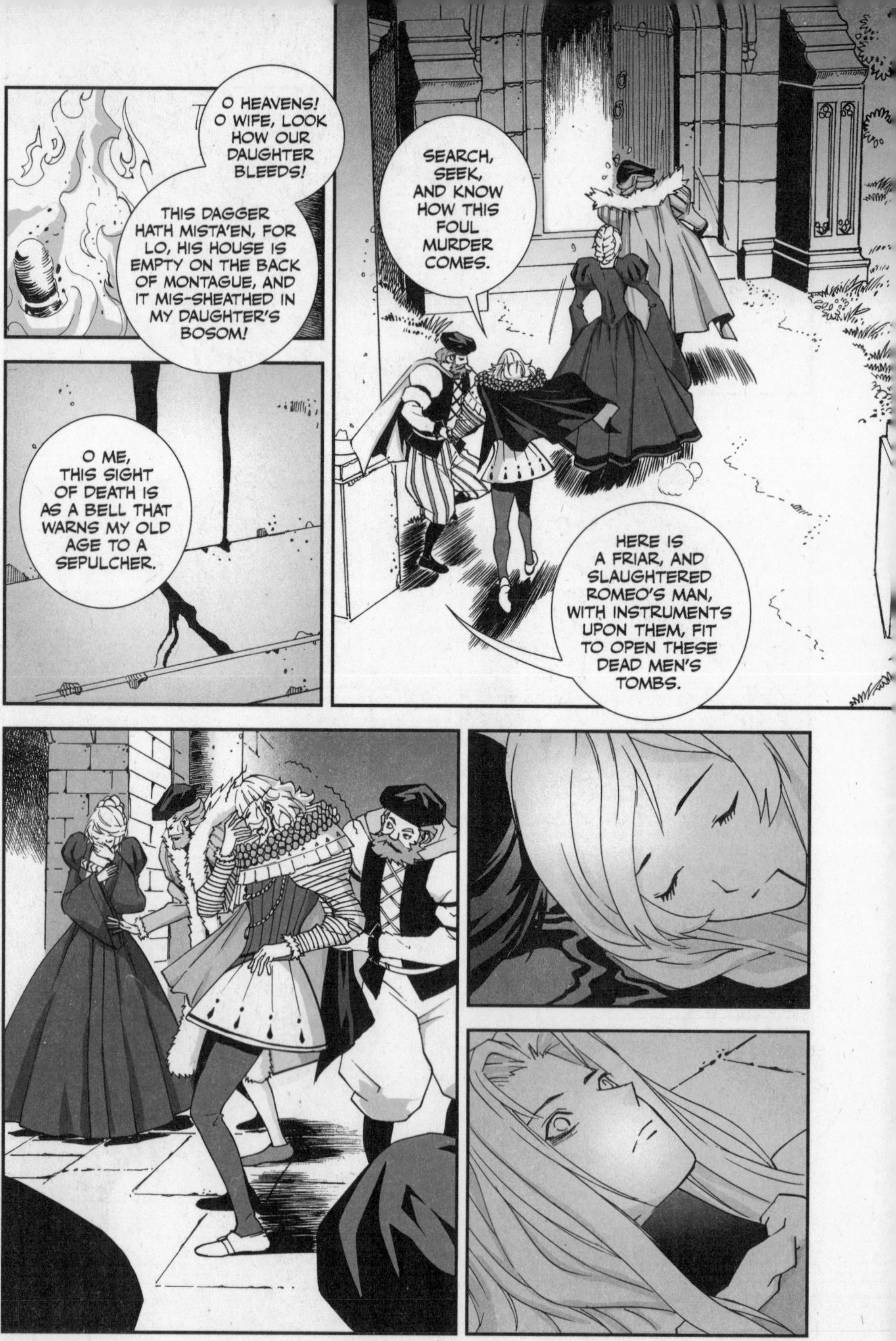
SEARCH, SEEK, AND KNOW HOW THIS FOUL MURDER COMES.
HERE IS A FRIAR, AND SLAUGHTERED ROMEO'S MAN, WITH INSTRUMENTS UPON THEM, FIT TO OPEN THESE DEAD MEN'S TOMBS.
O HEAVENS! O WIFE, LOOK HOW OUR DAUGHTER BLEEDS!
THIS DAGGER HATH MISTA'EN, FOR LO, HIS HOUSE IS EMPTY ON THE BACK OF MONTAGUE, AND IT MIS-SHEATHED IN MY DAUGHTER'S BOSOM!
O ME, THIS SIGHT OF DEATH IS AS A BELL THAT WARNS MY OLD AGE TO A SEPULCHER.

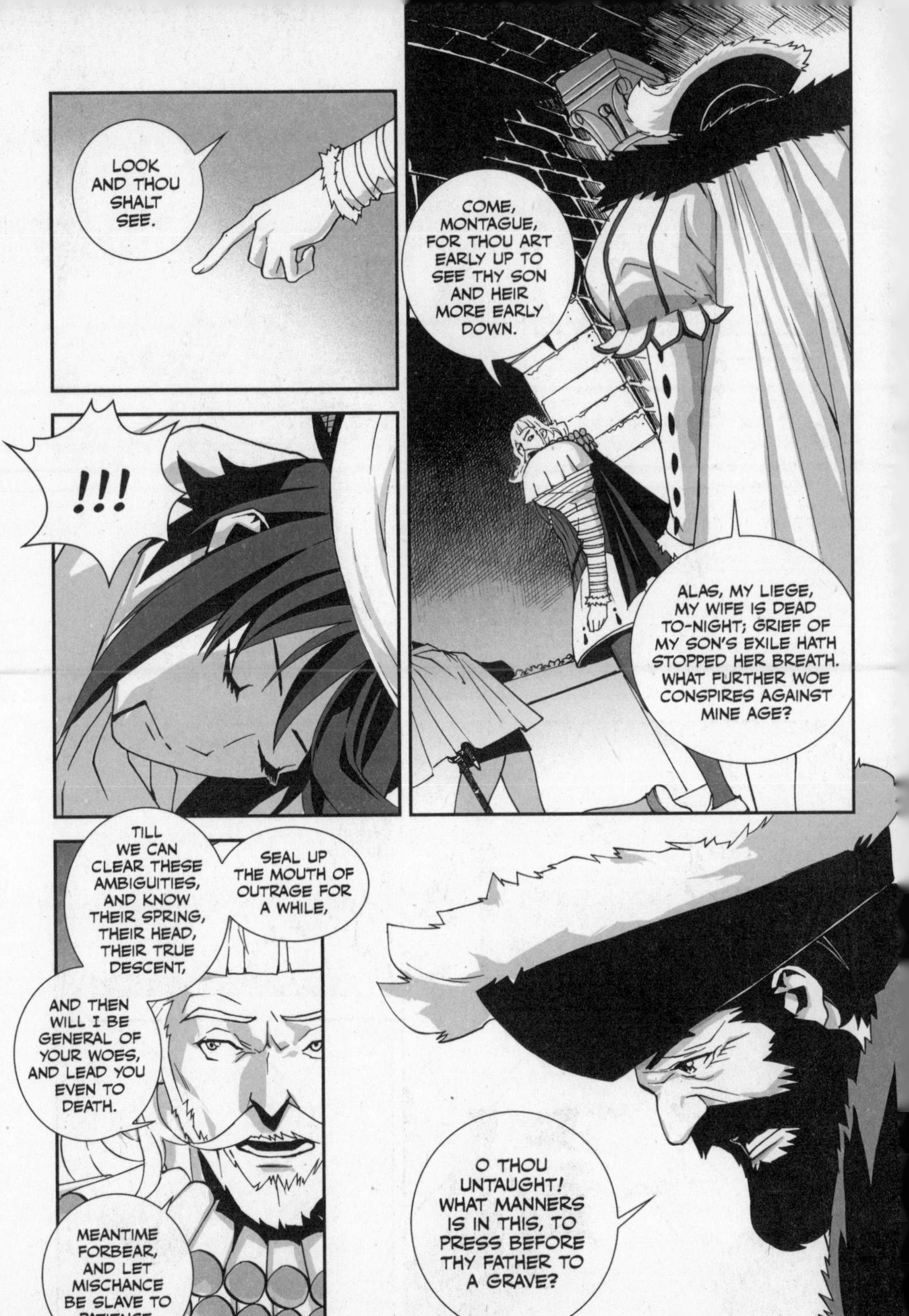
COME, MONTAGUE, FOR THOU ART EARLY UP TO SEE THY SON AND HEIR MORE EARLY DOWN.
ALAS, MY LIEGE, MY WIFE IS DEAD TO-NIGHT; GRIEF OF MY SON'S EXILE HATH STOPPED HER BREATH. WHAT FURTHER WOE CONSPIRES AGAINST MINE AGE?
LOOK AND THOU SHALT SEE.
!!!
O THOU UNTAUGHT! WHAT MANNERS IS IN THIS, TO PRESS BEFORE THY FATHER TO A GRAVE?
SEAL UP THE MOUTH OF OUTRAGE FOR A WHILE,
TILL WE CAN CLEAR THESE AMBIGUITIES, AND KNOW THEIR SPRING, THEIR HEAD, THEIR TRUE DESCENT,
AND THEN WILL I BE GENERAL OF YOUR WOES, AND LEAD YOU EVEN TO DEATH.
MEANTIME FORBEAR, AND LET MISCHANCE BE SLAVE TO PATIENCE.

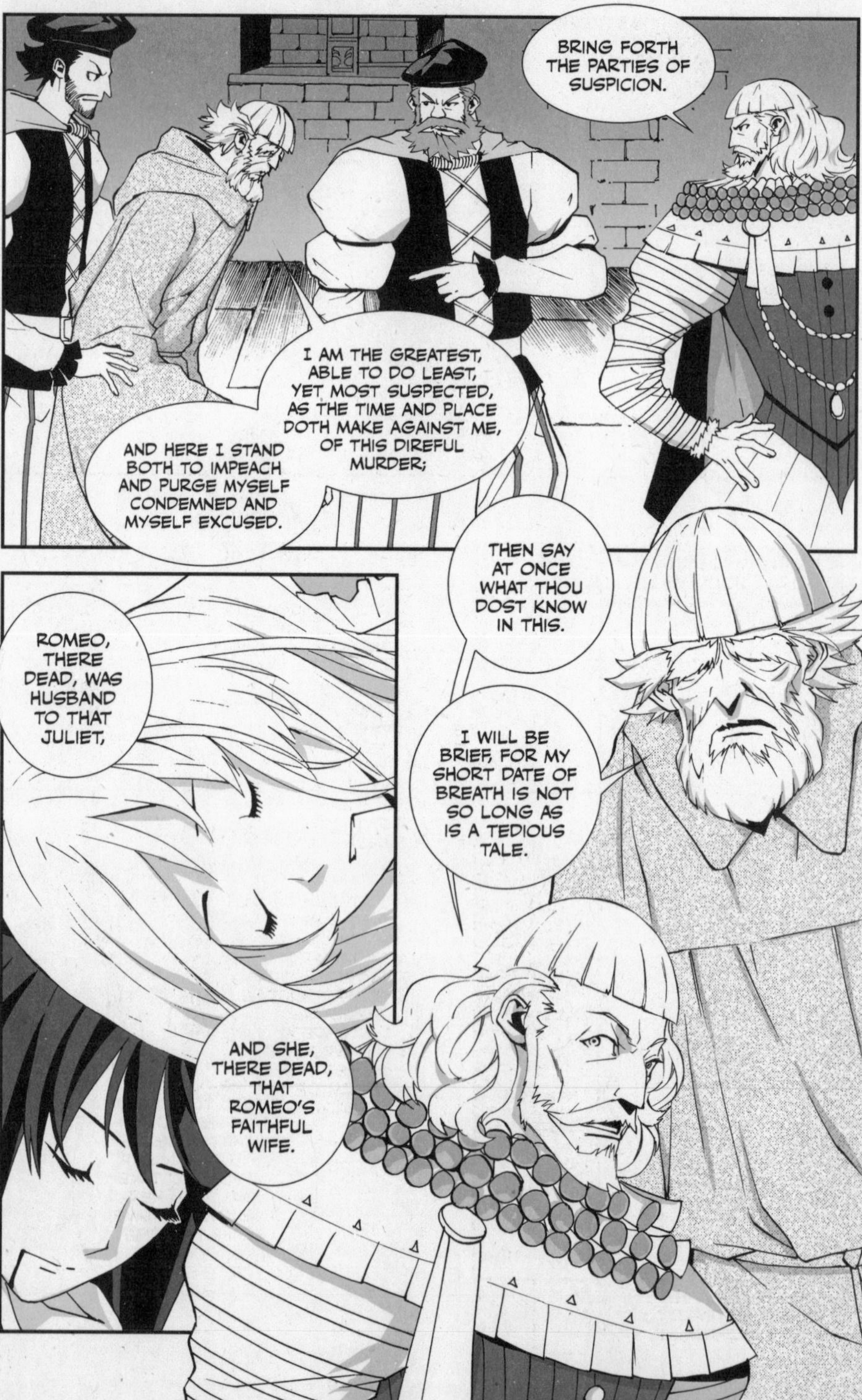
BRING FORTH THE PARTIES OF SUSPICION.
I AM THE GREATEST, ABLE TO DO LEAST, YET MOST SUSPECTED, AS THE TIME AND PLACE DOTH MAKE AGAINST ME, OF THIS DIREFUL MURDER;
AND HERE I STAND BOTH TO IMPEACH AND PURGE MYSELF CONDEMNED AND MYSELF EXCUSED.
THEN SAY AT ONCE WHAT THOU DOST KNOW IN THIS.
I WILL BE BRIEF, FOR MY SHORT DATE OF BREATH IS NOT SO LONG AS IS A TEDIOUS TALE.
ROMEO, THERE DEAD, WAS HUSBAND TO THAT JULIET,
AND SHE, THERE DEAD, THAT ROMEO'S FAITHFUL WIFE.

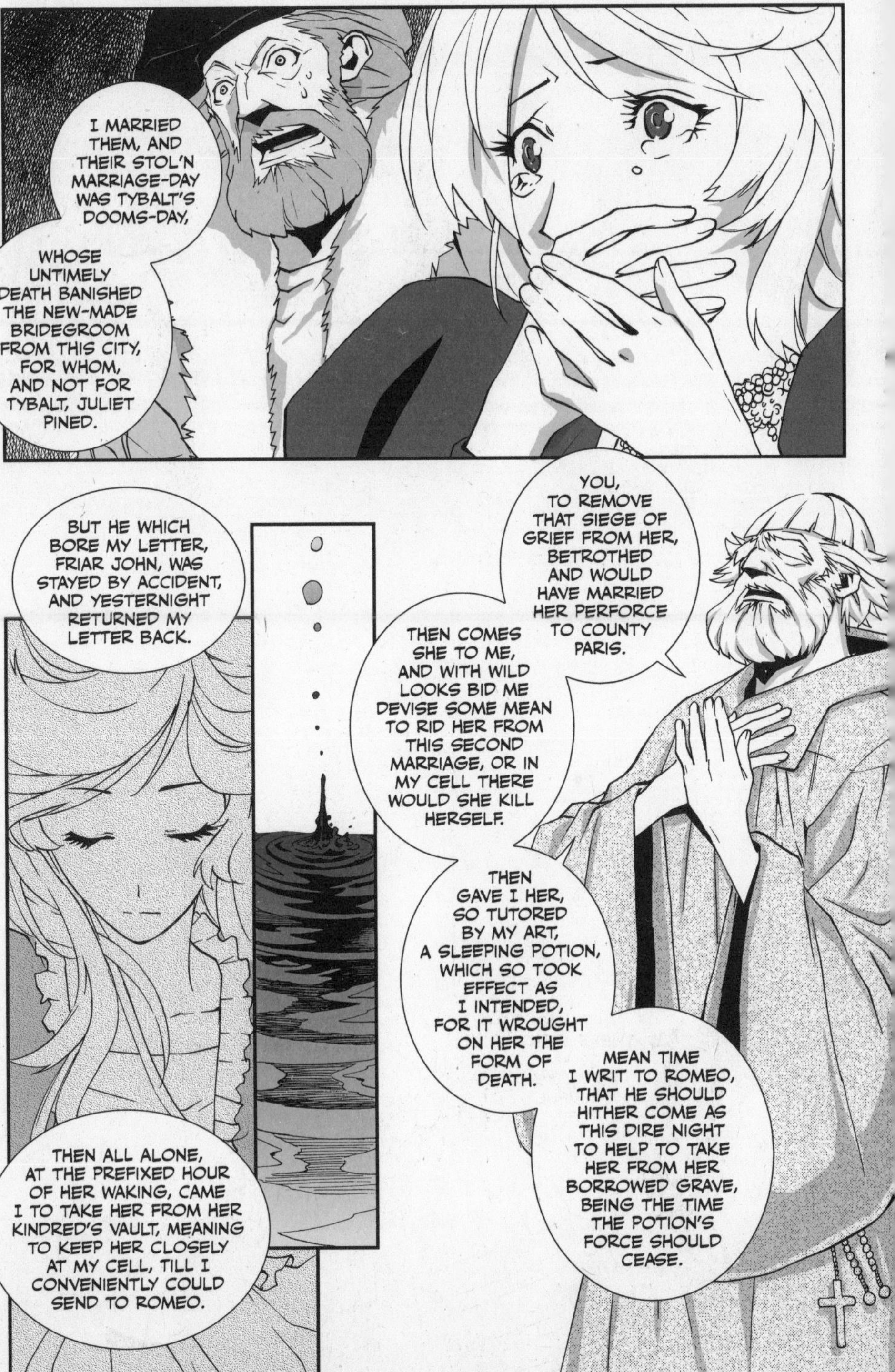
I MARRIED THEM, AND THEIR STOL'N MARRIAGE-DAY WAS TYBALT'S DOOMS-DAY,
WHOSE UNTIMELY DEATH BANISHED THE NEW-MADE BRIDEGROOM FROM THIS CITY, FOR WHOM, AND NOT FOR TYBALT, JULIET PINED.
YOU, TO REMOVE THAT SIEGE OF GRIEF FROM HER, BETROTHED AND WOULD HAVE MARRIED HER PERFORCE TO COUNTY PARIS.
THEN COMES SHE TO ME, AND WITH WILD LOOKS BID ME DEVISE SOME MEAN TO RID HER FROM THIS SECOND MARRIAGE, OR IN MY CELL THERE WOULD SHE KILL HERSELF.
THEN GAVE I HER, SO TUTORED BY MY ART, A SLEEPING POTION, WHICH SO TOOK EFFECT AS I INTENDED, FOR IT WROUGHT ON HER THE FORM OF DEATH.
MEAN TIME I WRIT TO ROMEO, THAT HE SHOULD HITHER COME AS THIS DIRE NIGHT TO HELP TO TAKE HER FROM HER BORROWED GRAVE, BEING THE TIME THE POTION'S FORCE SHOULD CEASE.
BUT HE WHICH BORE MY LETTER, FRIAR JOHN, WAS STAYED BY ACCIDENT, AND YESTERNIGHT RETURNED MY LETTER BACK.
THEN ALL ALONE, AT THE PREFIXED HOUR OF HER WAKING, CAME I TO TAKE HER FROM HER KINDRED'S VAULT, MEANING TO KEEP HER CLOSELY AT MY CELL, TILL I CONVENIENTLY COULD SEND TO ROMEO.

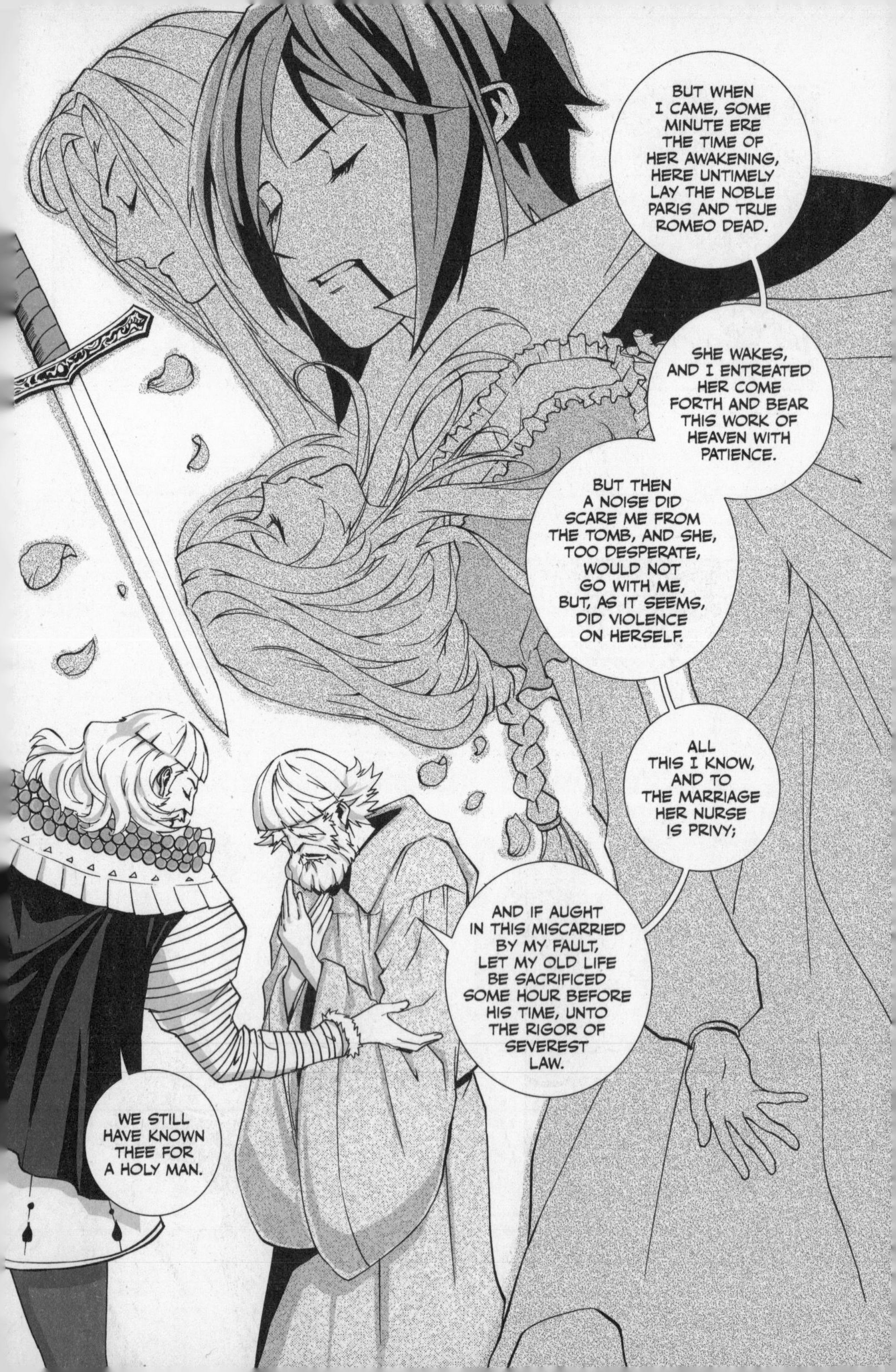
BUT WHEN I CAME, SOME MINUTE ERE THE TIME OF HER AWAKENING, HERE UNTIMELY LAY THE NOBLE PARIS AND TRUE ROMEO DEAD.
SHE WAKES, AND I ENTREATED HER COME FORTH AND BEAR THIS WORK OF HEAVEN WITH PATIENCE.
BUT THEN A NOISE DID SCARE ME FROM THE TOMB, AND SHE, TOO DESPERATE, WOULD NOT GO WITH ME, BUT, AS IT SEEMS, DID VIOLENCE ON HERSELF.
ALL THIS I KNOW, AND TO THE MARRIAGE HER NURSE IS PRIVY;
AND IF AUGHT IN THIS MISCARRIED BY MY FAULT, LET MY OLD LIFE BE SACRIFICED SOME HOUR BEFORE HIS TIME, UNTO THE RIGOR OF SEVEREST LAW.
WE STILL HAVE KNOWN THEE FOR A HOLY MAN.

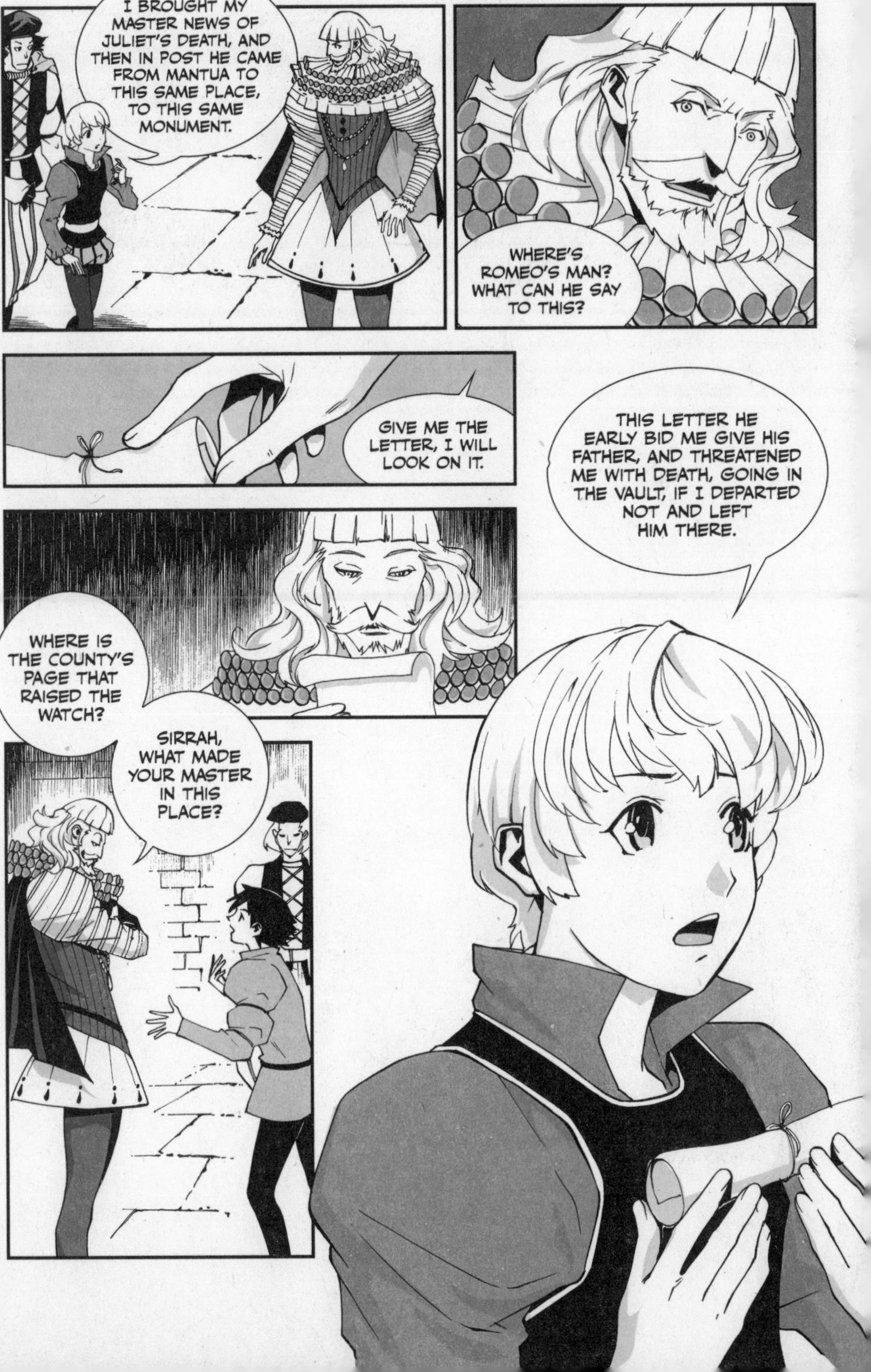
WHERE'S ROMEO'S MAN? WHAT CAN HE SAY TO THIS?
I BROUGHT MY MASTER NEWS OF JULIET'S DEATH, AND THEN IN POST HE CAME FROM MANTUA TO THIS SAME PLACE, TO THIS SAME MONUMENT.
THIS LETTER HE EARLY BID ME GIVE HIS FATHER, AND THREATENED ME WITH DEATH, GOING IN THE VAULT, IF I DEPARTED NOT AND LEFT HIM THERE.
GIVE ME THE LETTER, I WILL LOOK ON IT.
WHERE IS THE COUNTY'S PAGE THAT RAISED THE WATCH?
SIRRAH, WHAT MADE YOUR MASTER IN THIS PLACE?

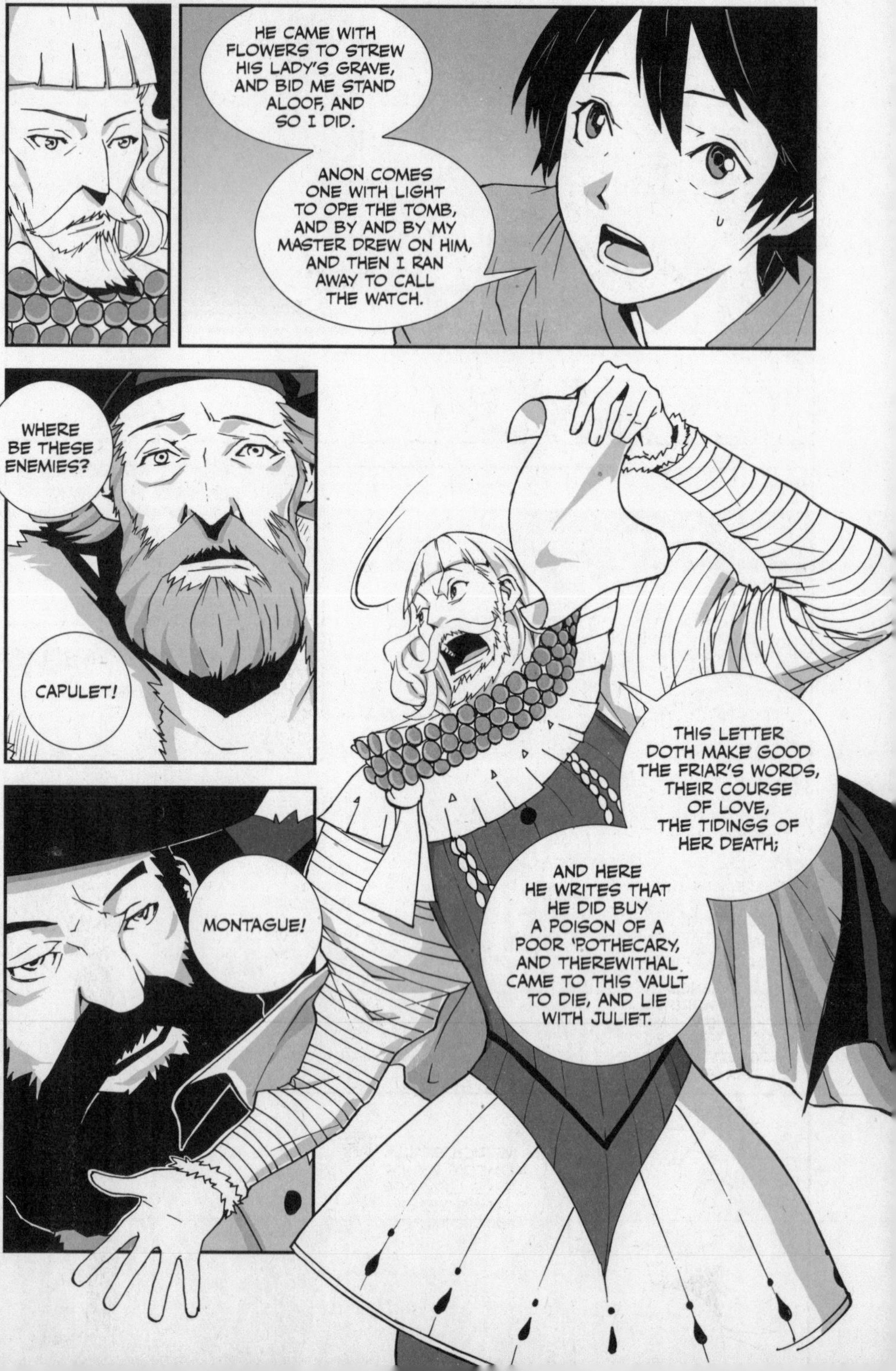
HE CAME WITH FLOWERS TO STREW HIS LADY'S GRAVE, AND BID ME STAND ALOOF, AND SO I DID.
ANON COMES ONE WITH LIGHT TO OPE THE TOMB, AND BY AND BY MY MASTER DREW ON HIM, AND THEN I RAN AWAY TO CALL THE WATCH.
THIS LETTER DOTH MAKE GOOD THE FRIAR'S WORDS, THEIR COURSE OF LOVE, THE TIDINGS OF HER DEATH;
AND HERE HE WRITES THAT HE DID BUY A POISON OF A POOR 'POTHECARY, AND THEREWITHAL CAME TO THIS VAULT TO DIE, AND LIE WITH JULIET.
WHERE BE THESE ENEMIES?
CAPULET!
MONTAGUE!

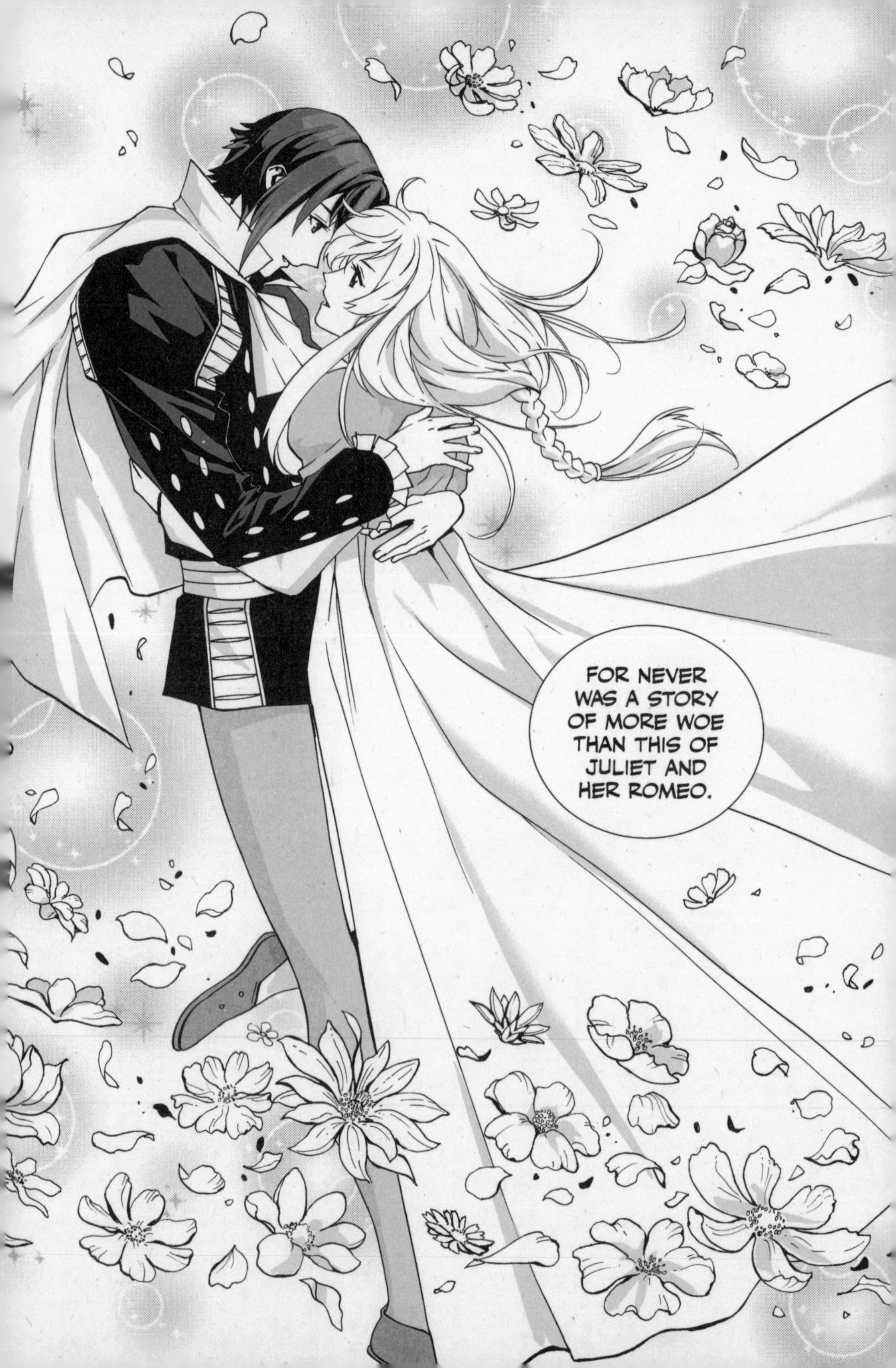
FOR NEVER WAS A STORY OF MORE WOE THAN THIS OF JULIET AND HER ROMEO.

~ *FINALE* ~

Romeo. Juliet is complaining that her nurse was no longer young and could not possibly hurry fast enough to suit her, so Juliet vents her anxiety by flicking little pebbles around. These little pebbles are also "*as swift in motion as a ball*", connecting the dialogue and the visual together.

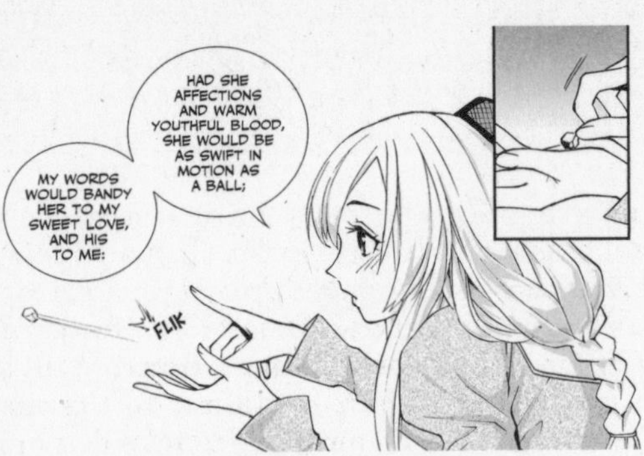
HAD SHE AFFECTIONS AND WARM YOUTHFUL BLOOD, SHE WOULD BE AS SWIFT IN MOTION AS A BALL;
MY WORDS WOULD BANDY HER TO MY SWEET LOVE, AND HIS TO ME:
FLIK

PROVIDING SPECIAL HINTS BASED ON THE PLOT:

In the original manuscript, not only dialogue but basic stage directions are provided to the actors. However, the size of a stage is limited, and in the manga world we can have a way broader environment for our characters to play out the story! Therefore, my adaptation work also includes expanding the locations and planning ahead on their actions to give the artist enough information to work with. For example: in ***Act 5, Scene 3***, Romeo meets Paris in the Capulet's tomb, argues with him, and eventually duels him. After the duel, however, Romeo is shocked: "*Let me peruse this face. Mercutio's kinsman, noble County Paris*!" Romeo did not recognize Paris until that very moment, when it was too late. I pointed this out in my script and suggested that the artist design the lighting and panel layout to make it clear that Romeo never sees Paris' face until the end - this allowed the artist to make informed decisions when storyboarding the manga. Thus, the readers won't find it strange that Romeo could not recognize Paris straight away, since they couldn't see his face either.

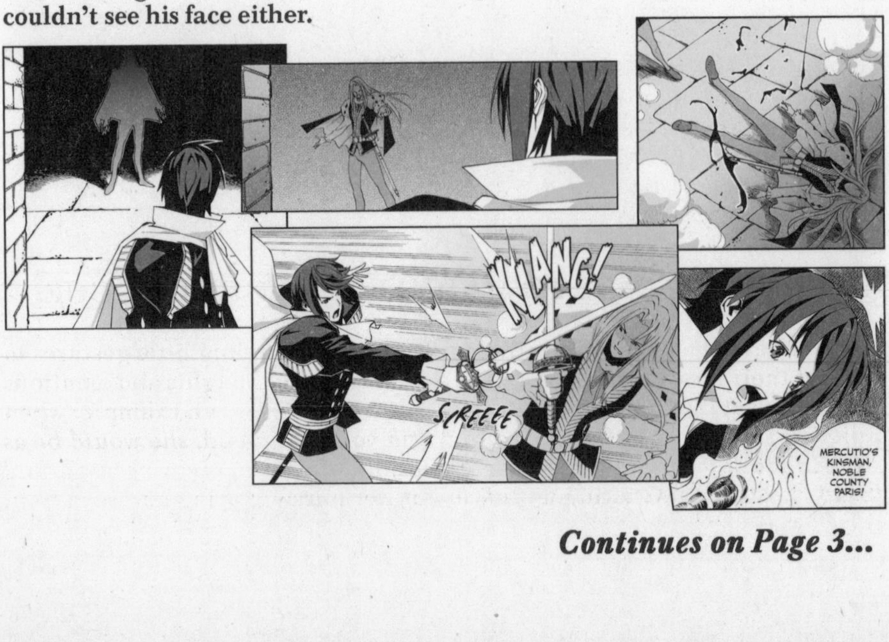
MERCUTIO'S KINSMAN, NOBLE COUNTY PARIS!
KLANG!
SCREEEE

Continues on Page 3...

CRYSTAL S. CHAN:
ADAPTING ROMEO & JULIET

I believe everyone must have heard of ***ROMEO AND JULIET***, the great stage play which exists in many different mediums. Our ***MANGA CLASSICS*** version takes the original script of the play and make sure that it is a word by word translation onto the pages. So you might ask, then, what am I here to talk about "adaptation"? Well, after all, stage plays and manga are two very different mediums, so the means of presenting the story is different as well. I would like to take this opportunity to tell you how much efforts our team has put in to bring this legendary masterpiece to life, using the characteristics of manga!

VISUALS ARE GREAT AIDS TO EXPRESSING METAPHORS:

Shakespeare's work is full of metaphor. When the show is staged with actors - as a stage play, a movie, a television show, or similar - it is only through the acting and the suggestion in dialogue that the metaphors can be presented to the audience. Manga has a lesser restriction on the visuals, so these metaphors can be drawn and presented more directly to the reader. For example: in ***Act 3***, ***Scene 2***, when Juliet says, "***Hood my unmanned blood, bating in my cheeks, with thy black mantle; till strange love, grown bold, think true love acted simple modesty,***" she is shy and blushing because she is looking forward to meeting her new husband on their wedding night. She imagines herself as a tamed eagle, with its head covered by a hood; she would need to be hooded so that no one could see her blushing. Therefore, I included a panel of the image in Juliet's imagination - did you notice that?

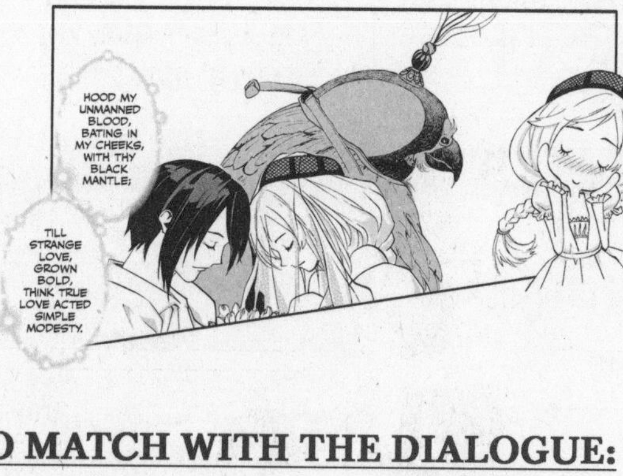
HOOD MY UNMANNED BLOOD, BATING IN MY CHEEKS, WITH THY BLACK MANTLE;
TILL STRANGE LOVE, GROWN BOLD, THINK TRUE LOVE ACTED SIMPLE MODESTY.

ADDING GESTURES TO MATCH WITH THE DIALOGUE:

I also believe that some of the dialogue calls for including little gestures to express their implications, as well as expressing the thoughts and emotions of the characters in the moment. Take ***Act 2***, ***Scene 5***, as an example: when Juliet says, "***Had she affections and warm youthful blood, she would be as swift in motion as a ball; my words would bandy her to my sweet love, and his to me,***" she was waiting anxiously for her nurse to bring her word from

VISITING THE LOCATION:

As the original manuscript clearly mentions that the story takes place in Verona, Italy, I decided to visit the place in person, much like I did when I was working on ***The Count Of Monte Cristo.*** Not only was I doing research, I was getting a feel for the atmosphere of the city – it was important to me to experience the same environment as the characters. Many literary analysts point out that Shakespeare may never have gone to Verona in person; however, since he chose this beautiful city as the stage for his story, I wanted to try my best to present the story to the readers as something that specifically happened in Verona.

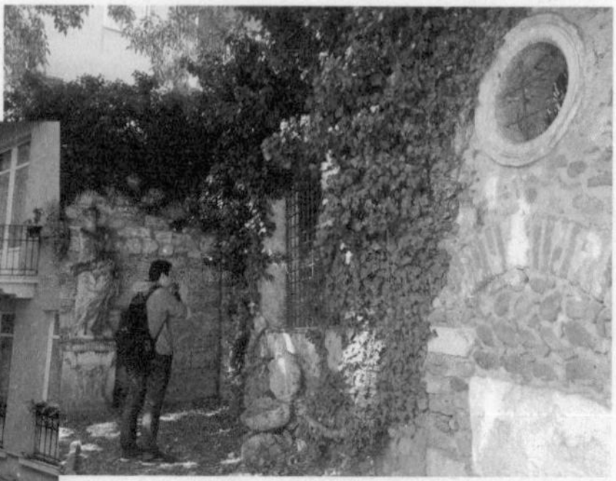

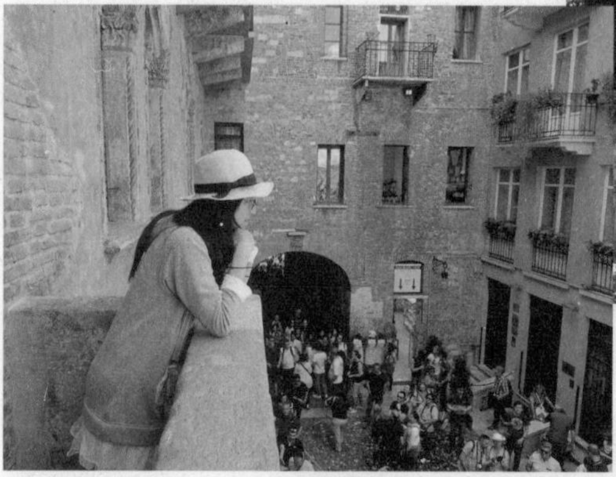

Juliet's house is a must-see for tourists, and I also went to the less-visited site of Juliet's tomb. The pillars in the photos were slightly redesigned and then used in the drawings of ***Act 5, Scene 3.***

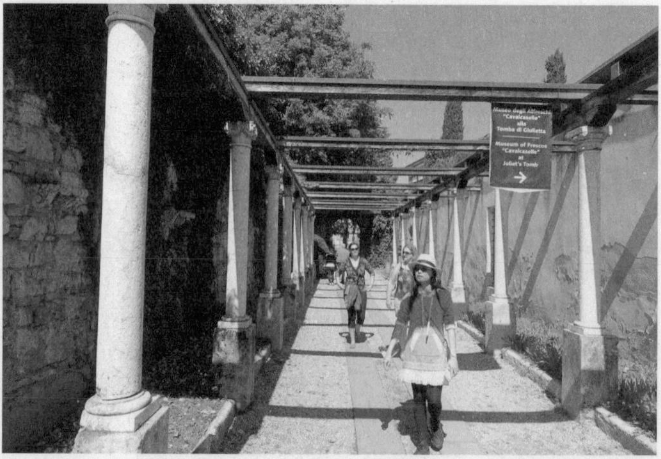
"Cavalcaselle"
alla
Tomba di Giulietta
"Cavalcaselle"
at
Juliet's Tomb

Continues on Page 5...

...continued from Page 2

Another important thing is the interchange between scenes. If it is not well done in the layouts, the readers can be confused. In a traditional play, change of scene is signified by the change of background panels and props; in the manga, such changes are signified through the language of the camera. In *Act 5, Scene 3*, everything takes place in various places outside the Capulet's tomb. The original manuscript only mentions when characters enter or exit the scene. That isn't enough for a manga artist to go on, so I divided the scene into six different 'areas' and drafted a floor plan for reference. This allows him to make informed decisions about where to set up the point of view for the readers, so that he can clearly present how the characters move among the different locations.

D
Stairs
Juliet's Tomb
Capulet's family graves
E
F
Romeo & Paris fight here
Tybalt's Tomb

CAPULET'S TOMB

C
B
A
Romeo and Balthasar get off horse here
Columns
Verona Graveyard Wall

D Stairs
F Juliet
E Romeo vs Paris
Columns
(Blue colour mark)

(Stone) Slabs

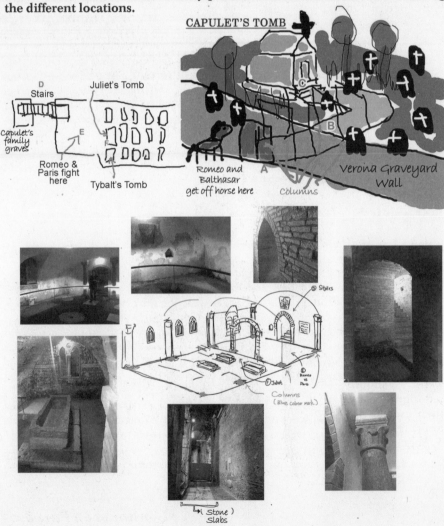

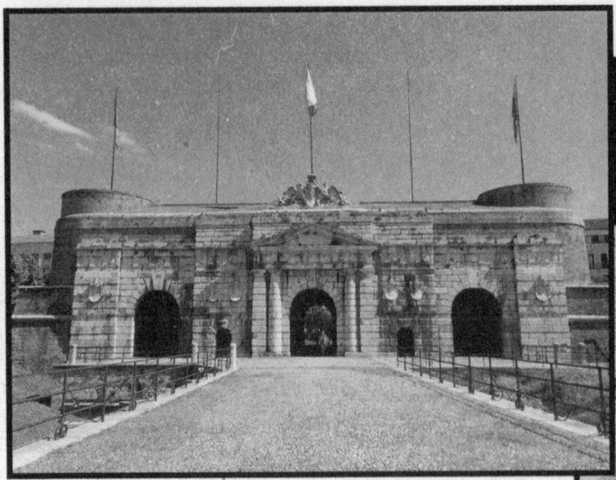

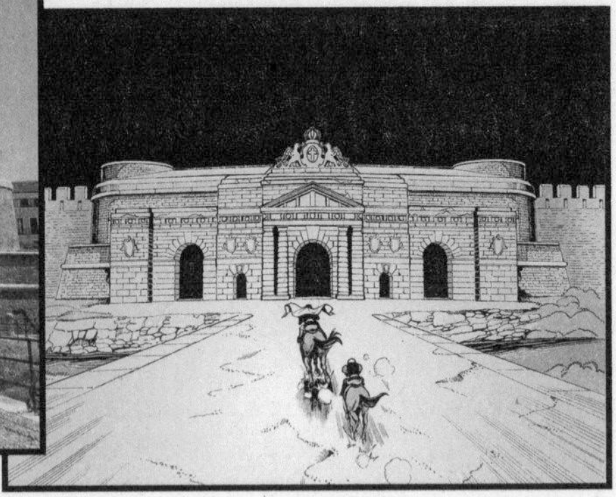

The above is *Porta Nuova.* It's not only some of the most famous architecture in the city, it was also built before ***Romeo and Juliet*** takes place - therefore, it's well suited to use in the manga, to strengthen the feeling of the characters being in Verona. I arranged for Romeo to pass by this building when he rushes back to Verona before ***Act 5.*** The photo here is not exactly the same as the drawing of the building in the manga; when I researched the city I discovered that *Porta Nuova* had been part of the city wall at the time of ***Romeo and Juliet.*** I suggested that the artist add the wall when drawing the background, to match the historical detail.

DESIGNING THE COVER:

Finally, I want to share a little secret with you: the cover layout was designed by me. When I read the phrase "*star-cross'd lovers*", I had this vision of ***Romeo and Juliet*** wanting to be together and being prevented by fate. After some thoughts I added other elements to represent this pair of tragic lovers that were not accepted by their world. As you can see, ***Romeo and Juliet*** are reaching towards each other, but the sword between them represents the fate which keeps them apart and prevents them from ever touching. I discussed this with the artist after finishing the draft, and he thought that it was well suited to the main theme. After he polished it up, the cover became the one you hold in your hands now.

I hope that my extensive adaptation work shows through the beautiful illustrations and smooth storyboards done by the artist. I truly believe this adaptation will help the readers achieve a better understanding of the story, expressing the thoughts and emotions of the original work in a way better suited for the manga medium. This is the goal I wanted to achieve through my hard work.

Crystal (Silvermoon) Chan

...continued from Page 4

This is one of the architectural landmarks of the city: the *Palazzo del Comune*. Today there is no cover over the stairs; however, inside the building (in the *Galleria d'Arte Moderna Achille Forte*) there is an old painting that shows the *Palazzo del Comune* complete with covered stairs. Therefore, I suggested that we add that cover to the manga version, to correspond with the classic appearance of the building.

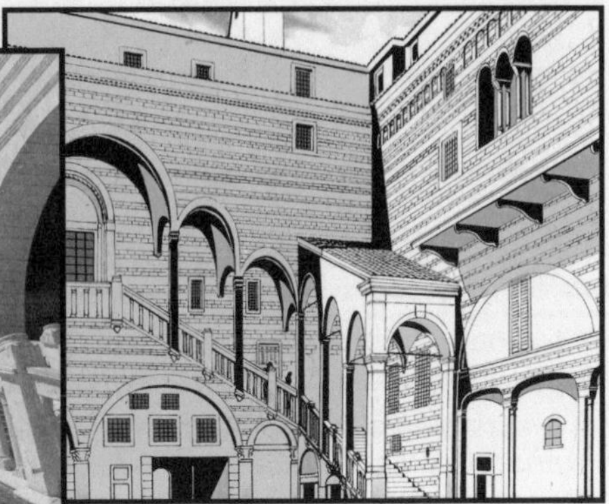

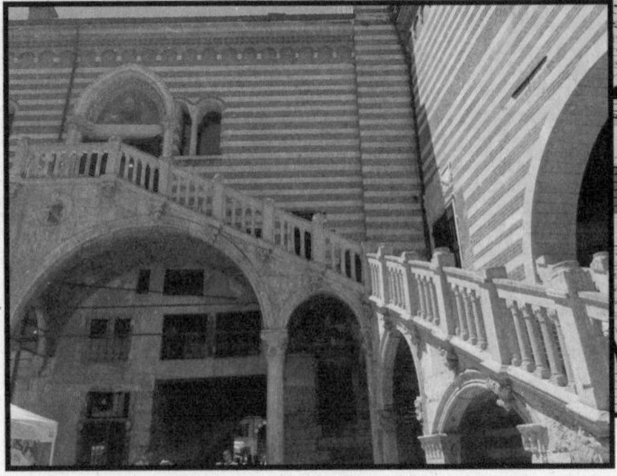

When I found suitable scenery during my visit to the city, I used it as the background to give the city atmosphere. Did you notice that there's a building similar to the Colosseum in one of the scenes in *Act 3*? This is actually another landmark of Verona: the *Arena di Verona*, which was built around the same time. Since it is a building associated with combat and competition, I suggested that we use it as part of that scene, to fit with Tybalt's killing of Mercutio and his own subsequent death at Romeo's hands.

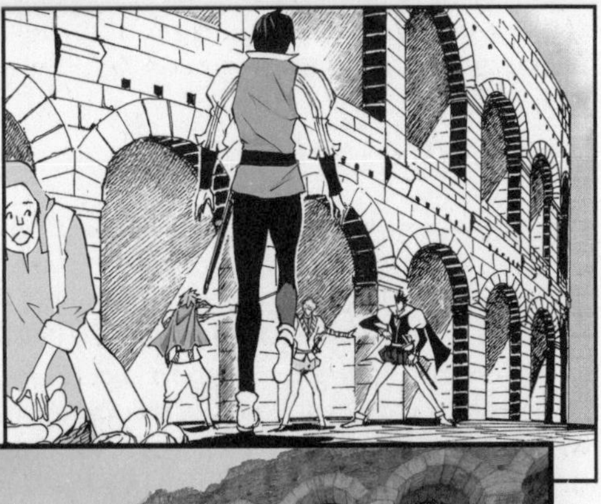

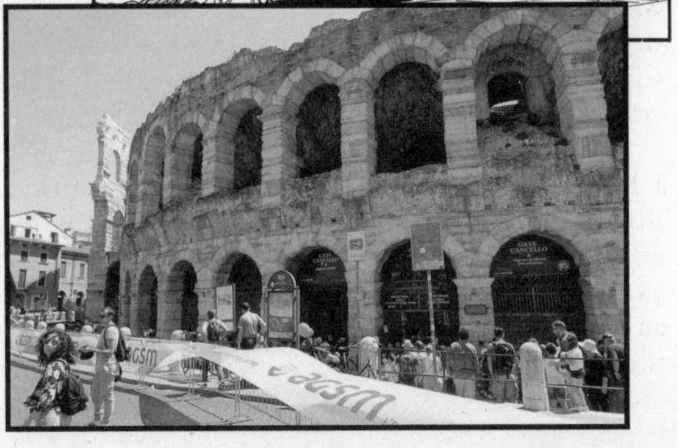

Shakespeare is one of the world's pre-eminent writers, and his works are the world's heritage.

It was really exciting for me to draw his work as a manga, but it also made me nervous. Especially since it was **ROMEO AND JULIET**, the classic story that is so well known. Ever since I was small, I have read and watched many versions of the story.

I am over the moon to have been the artist of this book. I feel so fortunate — this is the most overwhelming experience I have ever had in my years in the comic industry.

Thank you, **MANGA CLASSICS**, for publishing graphic novels based on classic literature, and for establishing such great creative opportunities. The production principle is to present a touching story as faithful as possible to the original work, and I unleashed all my creativity according to this principle. Therefore, no matter whether it was adaptation or illustration, I had to try my very best to master the actual era of the story.

Every stage of the manga production is carefully done; everyone was meticulous, from the producer to the scriptwriter to the artist and the assistants. We did not take it lightly — we did endless research to present a comprehensive version of the story. I have never before in my career felt so nervous about a title. Fortunately, I had a lot of help from the producer, Mr. Tai, and the scriptwriter, Crystal, who always fixed the mistakes I made; whenever I put dialogue in the wrong panel or duplicated dialogue by mistake or drew the wrong costume detail, they would make sure it was corrected. I will never forget these tidbits.

The whole team poured our hearts in every single panel of this classic piece. We all worked together to amend every panel over and over in order to take care of readers of all levels; we strived to do our best to bring our readers a masterpiece that would provide enjoyment and pleasure.

I hope this book will bring you satisfaction. We are all very proud of it!

Thank you for supporting us!

Julien Choy

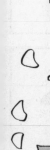

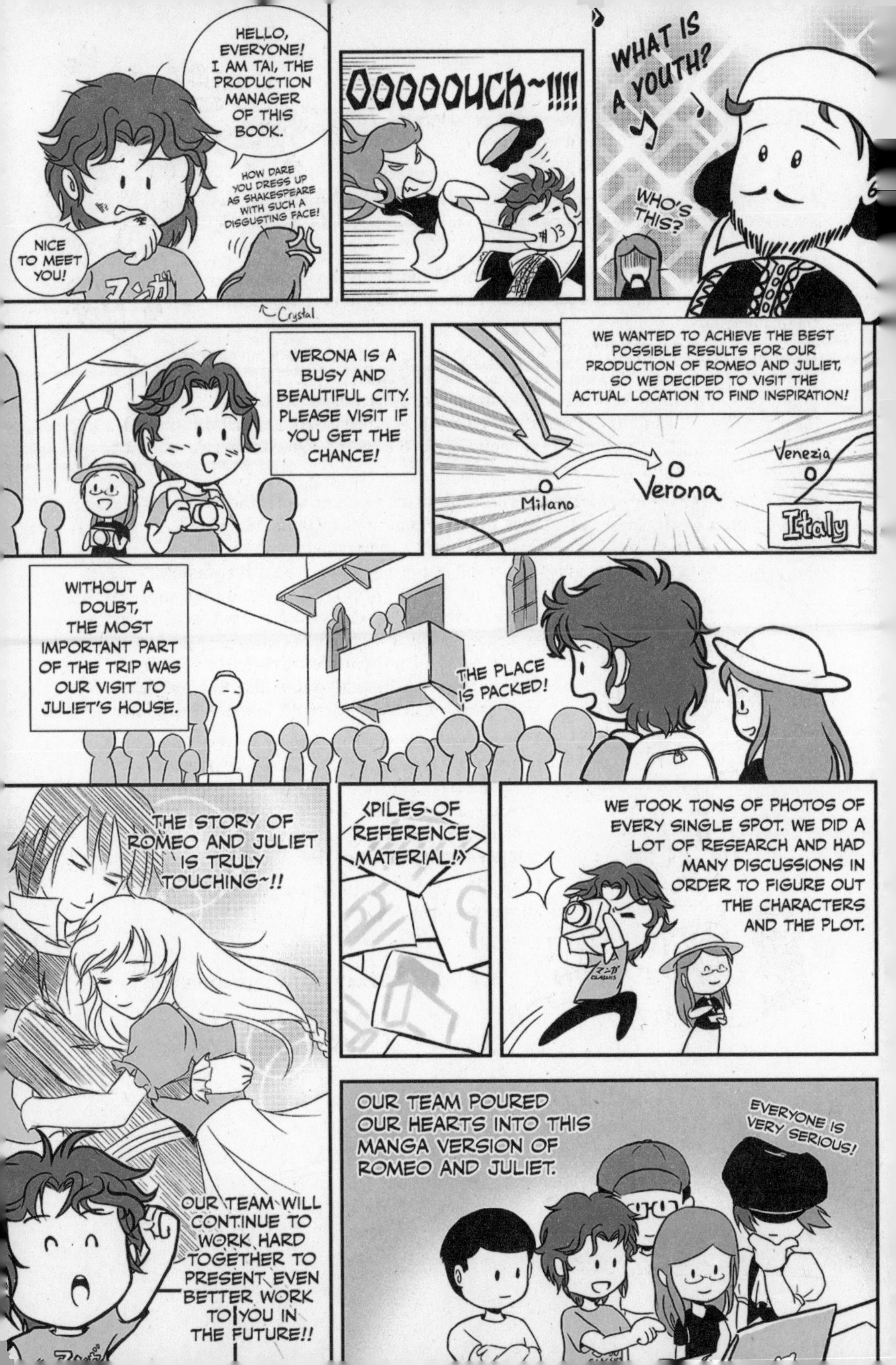
WHAT IS A YOUTH?
WHO'S THIS?
Oooooouch~!!!!
HELLO, EVERYONE! I AM TAI, THE PRODUCTION MANAGER OF THIS BOOK.
HOW DARE YOU DRESS UP AS SHAKESPEARE WITH SUCH A DISGUSTING FACE!
NICE TO MEET YOU!
Crystal
WE WANTED TO ACHIEVE THE BEST POSSIBLE RESULTS FOR OUR PRODUCTION OF ROMEO AND JULIET, SO WE DECIDED TO VISIT THE ACTUAL LOCATION TO FIND INSPIRATION!
Venezia
Verona
Milano
Italy
VERONA IS A BUSY AND BEAUTIFUL CITY. PLEASE VISIT IF YOU GET THE CHANCE!
WITHOUT A DOUBT, THE MOST IMPORTANT PART OF THE TRIP WAS OUR VISIT TO JULIET'S HOUSE.
THE PLACE IS PACKED!
WE TOOK TONS OF PHOTOS OF EVERY SINGLE SPOT. WE DID A LOT OF RESEARCH AND HAD MANY DISCUSSIONS IN ORDER TO FIGURE OUT THE CHARACTERS AND THE PLOT.
⟨PILES OF REFERENCE MATERIAL!⟩
OUR TEAM POURED OUR HEARTS INTO THIS MANGA VERSION OF ROMEO AND JULIET.
EVERYONE IS VERY SERIOUS!
THE STORY OF ROMEO AND JULIET IS TRULY TOUCHING~!!
OUR TEAM WILL CONTINUE TO WORK HARD TOGETHER TO PRESENT EVEN BETTER WORK TO YOU IN THE FUTURE!!

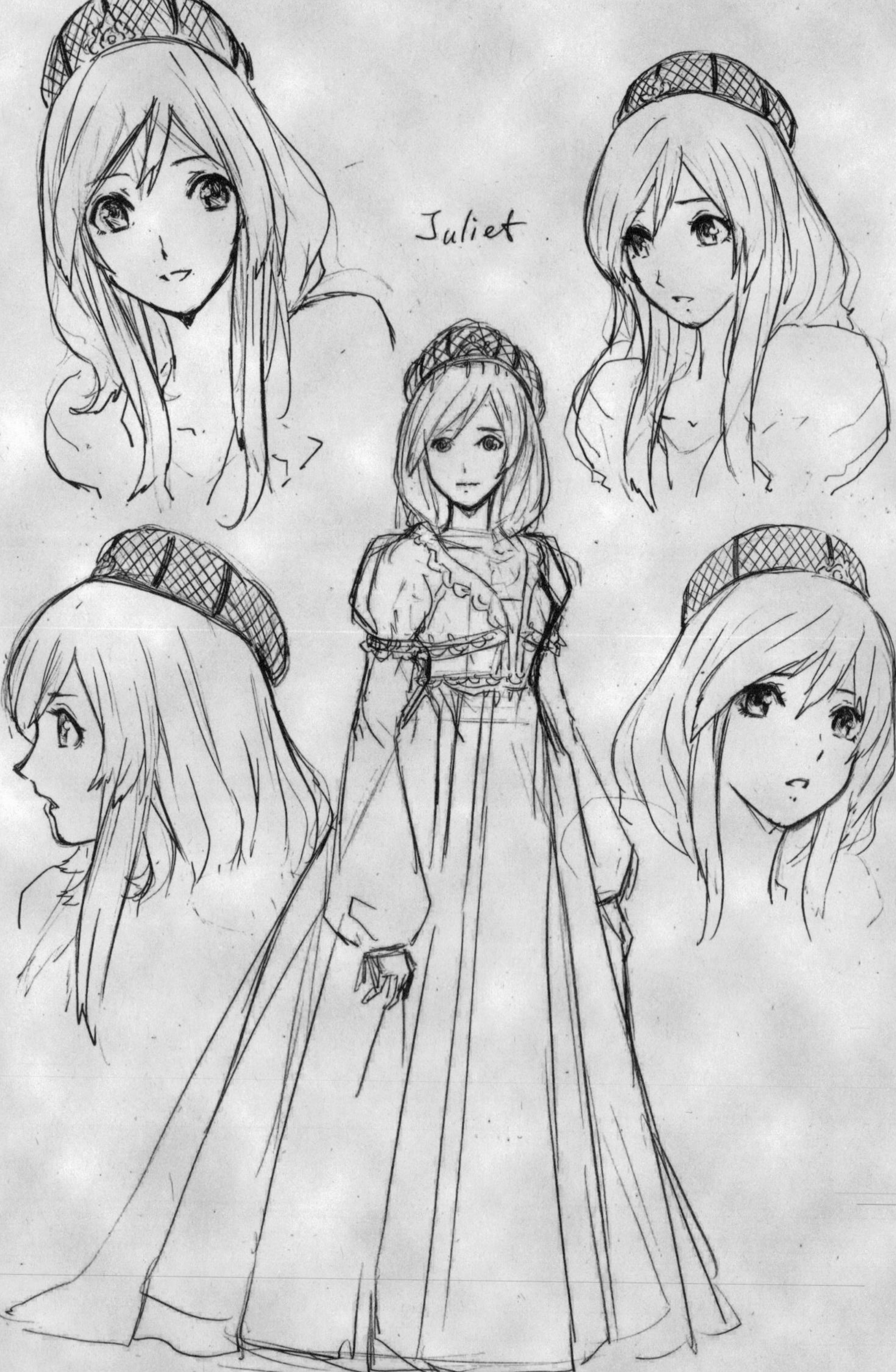
Juliet

CHARACTER DESIGN SKETCHBOOK

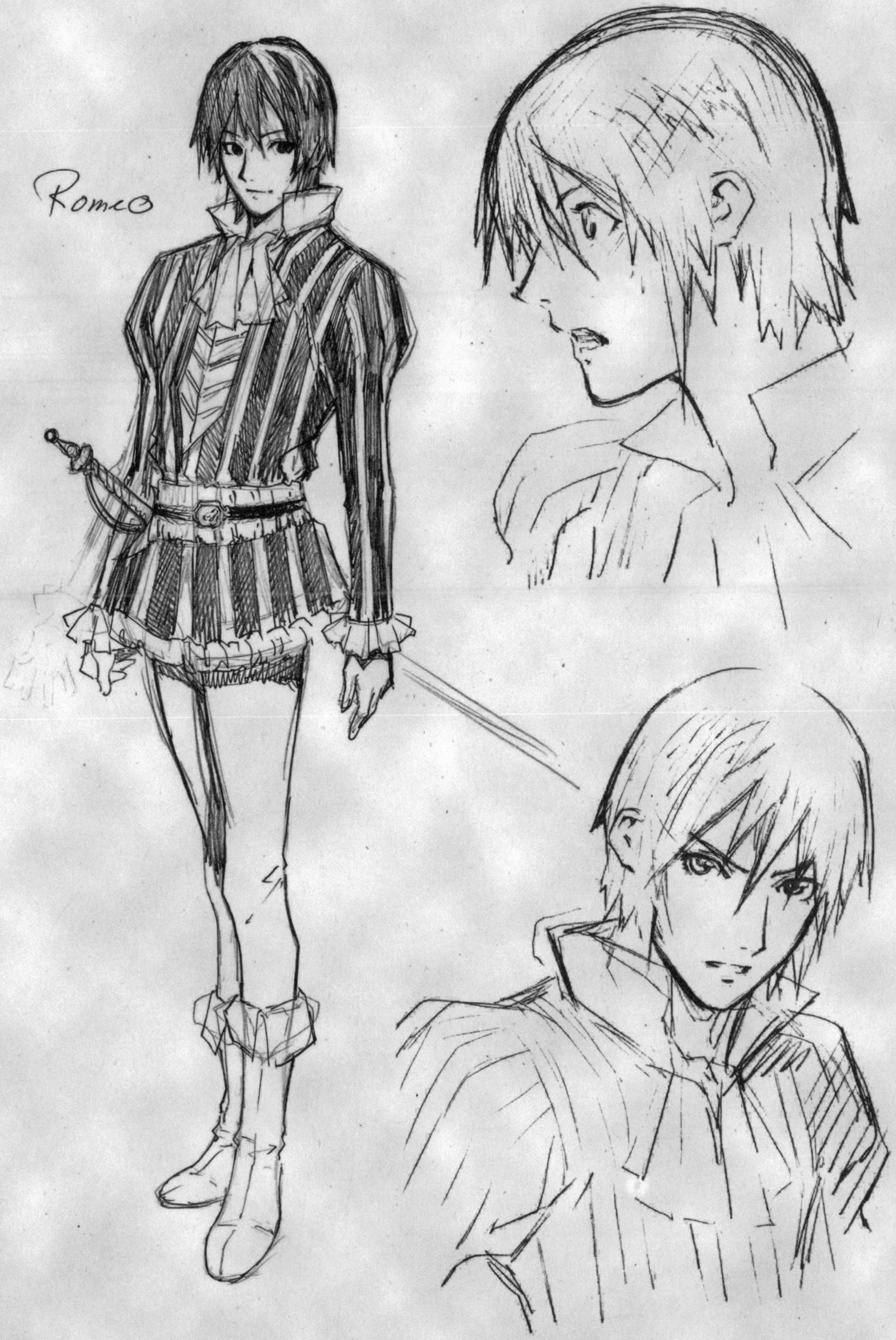
Romeo

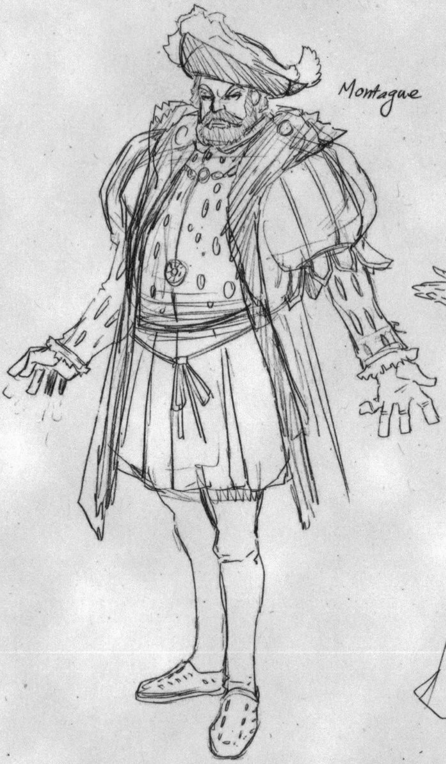

Montague

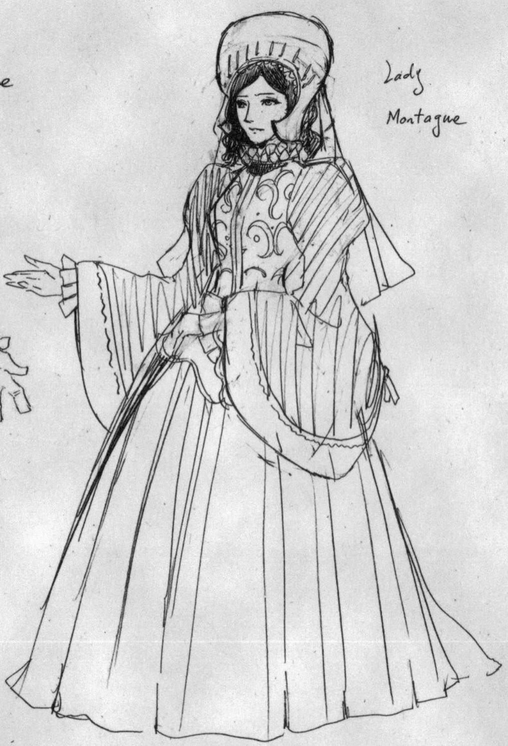

Lady Montague

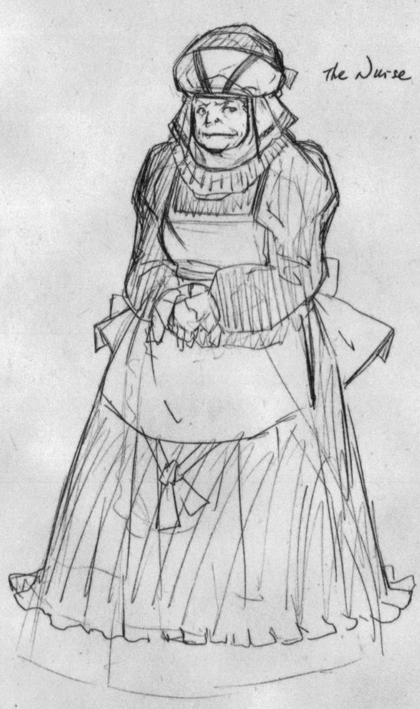

The Nurse

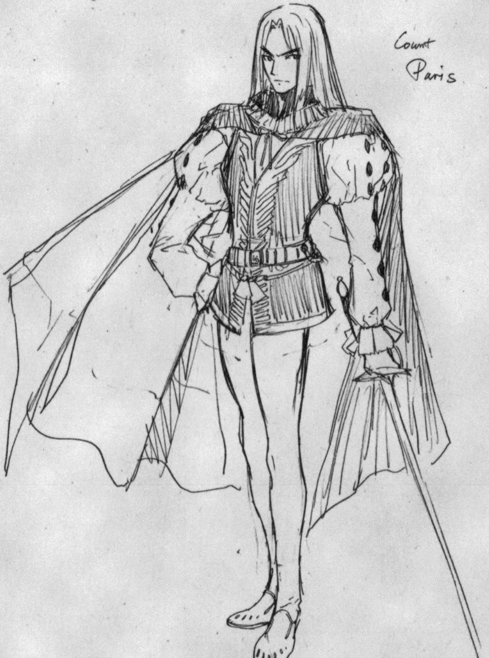

Count Paris

CHARACTER DESIGN SKETCHBOOK

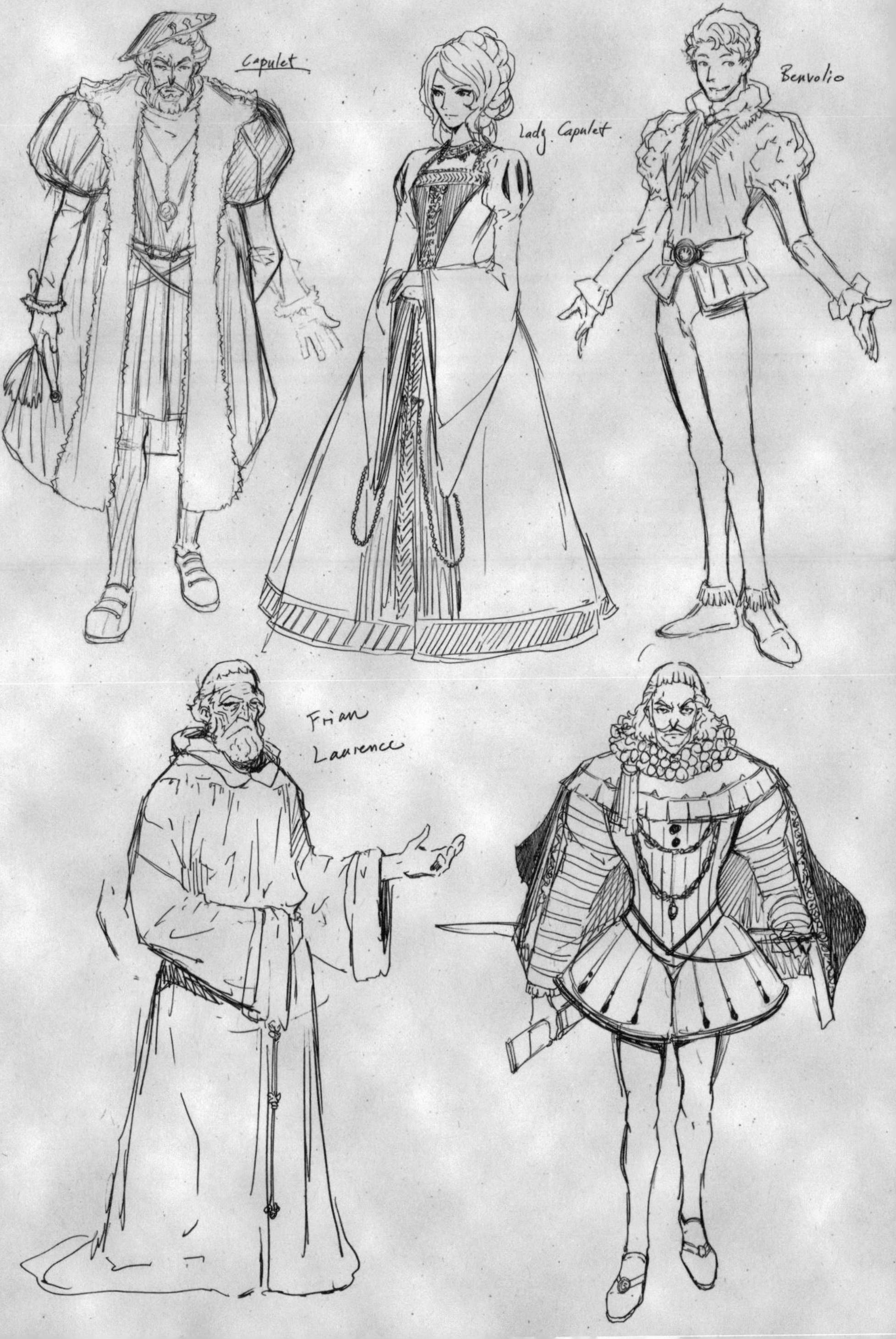
Capulet
Lady Capulet
Benvolio
Friar Laurence

Swordfights play a key role throughout **Romeo and Juliet**. From Sampson, Gregory, Abram, and Benvolio introducing the conflict between the two families at the beginning, to the unfortunate deaths of Mercutio and Tybalt, to the inevitable duel between Romeo and Paris near the end, the characters clash again and again - and all of them wield their own personalized weapons in battle.

Since the props in a play are very important elements, we paid a lot of attention to the characters' weapons when we were designing them. We decided that, since all these men are wealthy or work for wealthy families, they would all have had their swords customized to their liking. Thus, we made sure that everyone's blade was different.

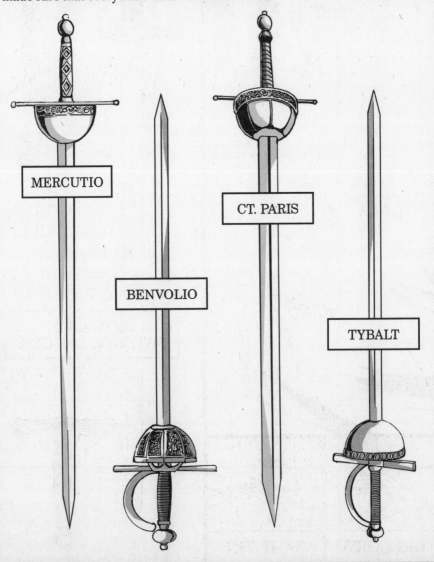

MERCUTIO

CT. PARIS

BENVOLIO

TYBALT

THE SWORDS IN ROMEO AND JULIET

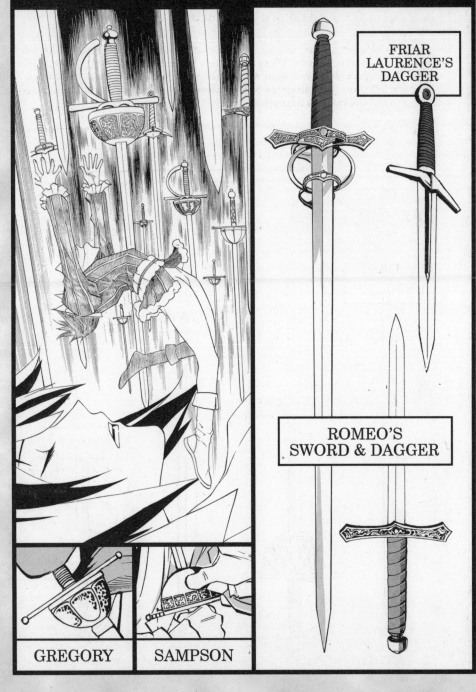

FRIAR LAURENCE'S DAGGER

ROMEO'S SWORD & DAGGER

GREGORY

SAMPSON

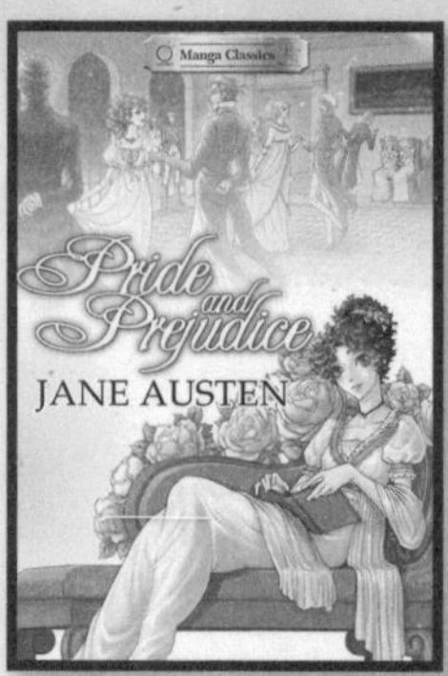
Manga Classics
Pride and Prejudice
JANE AUSTEN

Manga Classics:
Pride and Prejudice
Hard Cover $24.99
ISBN #978-1-927925-17-1
Soft Cover $17.99
ISBN #978-1-927-925-18-8

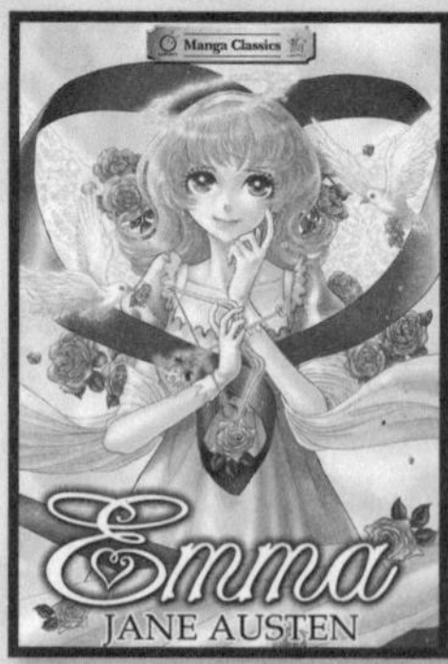
Manga Classics
Emma
JANE AUSTEN

Manga Classics:
Emma
Hard Cover $24.99
ISBN #978-1-927925-36-2
Soft Cover $17.99
ISBN #978-1-927-925-35-5

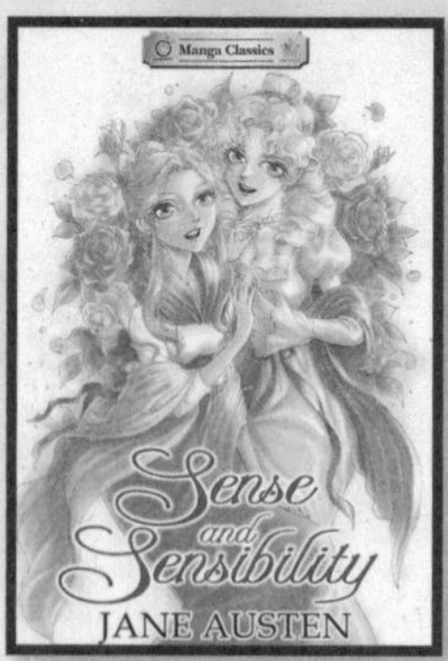
Manga Classics
Sense and Sensibility
JANE AUSTEN

Manga Classics:
Sense and Sensibility
Hard Cover $24.99
ISBN #978-1-927925-62-1
Soft Cover $17.99
ISBN #978-1-927925-63-8

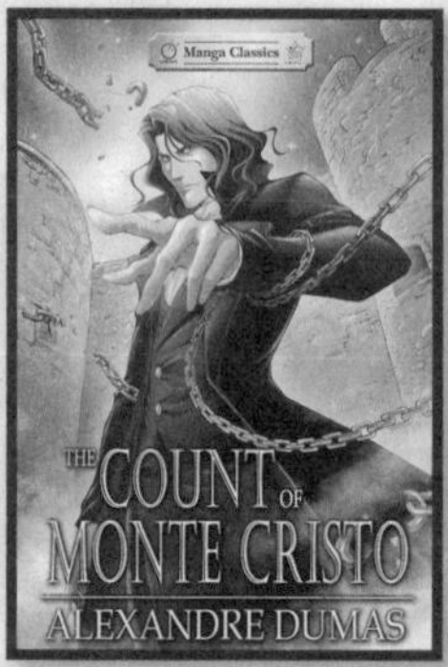
Manga Classics
THE COUNT OF MONTE CRISTO
ALEXANDRE DUMAS

Manga Classics:
The Count of Monte Cristo
Hard Cover $24.99
ISBN #978-1-927925-60-7
Soft Cover $17.99
ISBN #978-1-927925-61-4

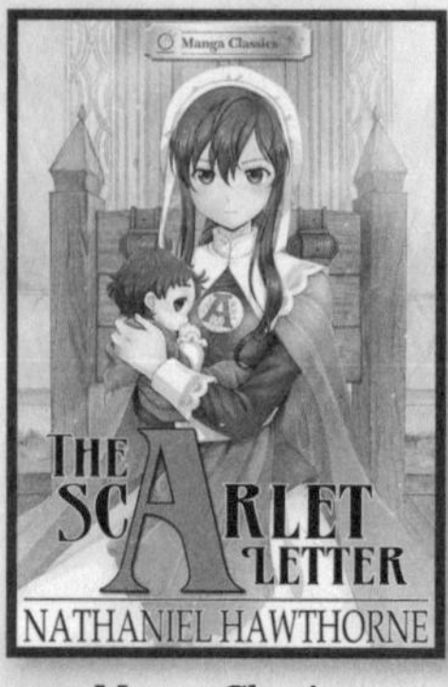
Manga Classics
THE SCARLET LETTER
NATHANIEL HAWTHORNE

Manga Classics:
The Scarlet Letter
Hard Cover $24.99
ISBN #978-1-927925-34-8
Soft Cover $17.99
ISBN #978-1-927925-33-1

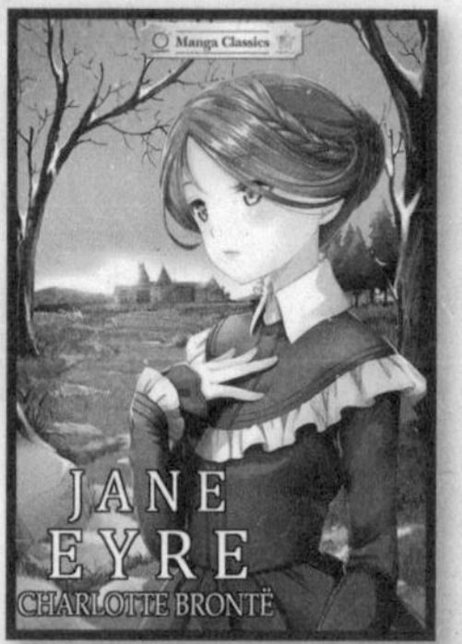
Manga Classics
JANE EYRE
CHARLOTTE BRONTË

Manga Classics:
Jane Eyre
Hard Cover $24.99
ISBN #978-1-927925-64-5
Soft Cover $17.99
ISBN #978-1-927925-65-2

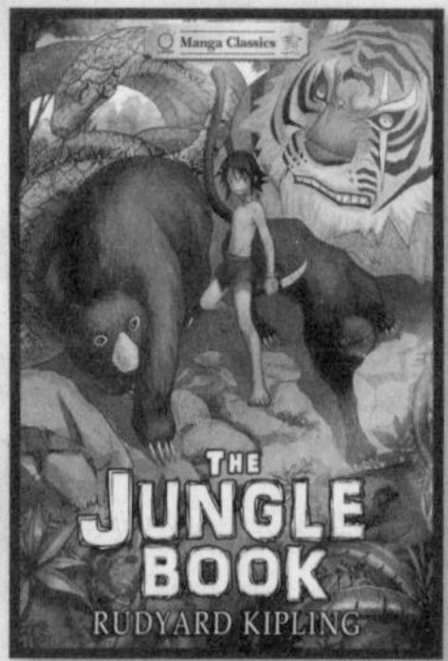
Manga Classics
THE JUNGLE BOOK
RUDYARD KIPLING

Manga Classics:
The Jungle Book
Hard Cover $24.99
ISBN #978-1-772940-18-3
Soft Cover $17.99
ISBN #978-1-772940-19-0

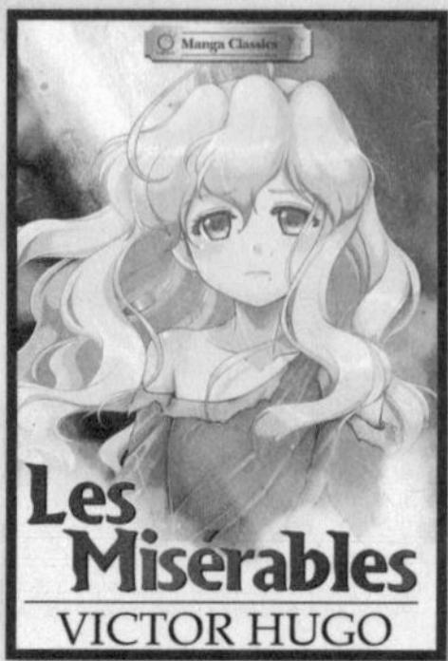
Manga Classics
Les Misérables
VICTOR HUGO

Manga Classics:
Les Miserables
Hard Cover $24.99
ISBN #978-1-927925-15-7
Soft Cover $17.99
ISBN #978-1-927925-16-4

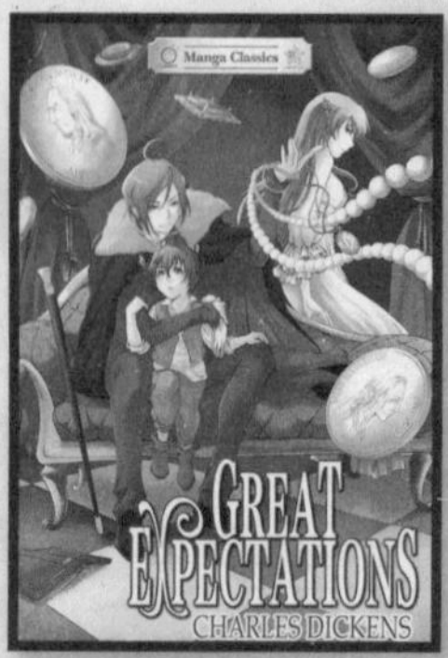
Manga Classics
GREAT EXPECTATIONS
CHARLES DICKENS

Manga Classics:
Great Expectations
Hard Cover $24.99
ISBN #978-1-927925-32-4
Soft Cover $17.99
ISBN #978-1-927925-31-7